Human Development

MULTIDISCIPLINARY CONSULTANTS
AND CONTRIBUTORS

E. ROBERT ACKERMAN, M.A.
Elementary School Teacher and Orthoptist
Warner Springs, California

STEWART COHEN, Ph.D.
Professor of Psychology
Child Development and Family Planning
University of Rhode Island

MARGARET FRANKS, R.N.
Nursing Division
Cypress College
Cypress, California

JOY GRAVES, R.N.
Nursing Division
Cypress College
Cypress, California

WILLIAM O. HECKMAN, M.A.
Humanities Division and Reading Skills Center
Fullerton College
Fullerton, California

WILLIAM L. KIMBALL, Ph.D.
Research Sociologist and Anthropologist
Welfare Planning Council
Los Angeles, California

DOUGLAS KIMMEL, Ph.D.
Professor of Psychology
City University of New York

ROBERT B. McLAREN, Ph.D.
Professor of Philosophy
California State University at Fullerton

HENRY J. PARIS, M.S.W.
Psychiatric Social Worker
North Orange County Child Guidance Clinic
Fullerton, California

Human Development

A Multidisciplinary Approach to the Psychology of Individual Growth

James O. Lugo & Gerald L. Hershey

Department of Psychology, Fullerton College, Fullerton, California

Photographic Design by Gerry Owen

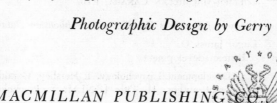

MACMILLAN PUBLISHING CO., INC.
New York

COLLIER MACMILLAN PUBLISHERS
London

Chapter 1 logo: Gerry Owen. Chapter 2 logo: courtesy Von Hershey. Fig. 2-1(a) courtesy Historical Pictures Service, Chicago, and (b) Gerry Owen. Fig. 2-2 courtesy Nicolas Bouvier, Geneva. Fig. 2-3 courtesy Historical Picture Service, Chicago. Chapter 3 logo: Gerry Owen. Chapter 4 logo: courtesy Historical Pictures Service, Chicago. Fig. 4-1 Gerry Owen. Chapter 5 logo: Gerry Owen. Fig. 5-1 courtesy *Los Angeles Times.* Fig. 5-2 Gerry Owen. Chapter 6 logo: Gerry Owen. Chapter 7 logo: Gerry Owen. Chapter 8 logo: Gerry Owen. Fig. 8-2 Gerry Owen. Fig. 8-8 Gerry Owen. Fig. 8-9 Gerry Owen. Chapter 9 logo: Gerry Owen. Fig. 9-3 courtesy VISTA. Fig. 9-4 Gerry Owen. Chapter 10 logo: E. J. Korba, courtesy Tom Stack and Associates, Lindenhurst, Ill. Fig. 10-2 Gerry Owen. Fig. 10-3 Gerry Owen. Fig. 10-4 Gerry Owen. Chapter 11 logo: Bob Mader, courtesy Tom Stack and Associates, Lindenhurst, Ill. Fig. 11-2 Gerry Owen. Fig. 11-3 courtesy the Peace Corps. Fig. 11-5 Gerry Owen. Fig. 11-7 Gerry Owen. Chapter 12 logo: Gerry Owen. Fig. 12-2 Gerry Owen. Fig. 12-3 Gerry Owen. Fig. 12-4 Gerry Owen. Chapter 13 logo: Gerry Owen. Figs. 13-1, 2, 3 courtesy The National Foundation—March of Dimes. Chapter 14 logo: Gerry Owen. Fig. 14-4 Gerry Owen. Fig. 14-8 Gerry Owen. Fig. 14-10 Gerry Owen. Chapter 15 logo: Tom Stack, courtesy Tom Stack and Associates, Lindenhurst, Ill. Fig. 15-1 Gerry Owen. Fig. 15-3 Gerry Owen. Fig. 15-5 Gerry Owen. Fig. 15-6 Gerry Owen. Fig. 15-8 Gerry Owen. Fig. 15-9 Gerry Owen. Fig. 15-10 Gerry Owen. Fig. 15-11 Gerry Owen. Fig. 15-12 Gerry Owen. Chapter 16 logo: Gerry Owen. 16-2 courtesy ACTION/VISTA. Fig. 16-6 Gerry Owen. Fig. 16-7 Gerry Owen. Fig. 16-8 Gerry Owen. Fig. 16-9 Gerry Owen. Fig. 16-10 Gerry Owen. Fig. 16-11 Gerry Owen. Fig. 16-12 Gerry Owen. Fig. 16-13 Gerry Owen. Fig. 16-14 Gerry Owen. Fig. 16-15 Gerry Owen. Fig. 16-16 (a) Bob Perkins—Photo Trend; (b) (c) Gerry Owen. Chapter 17 logo: Gerry Owen. Fig. 17-1 Gerry Owen, with the cooperation of Children's Hospital of Los Angeles. Fig. 17-2 Gerry Owen. Fig. 17-3 Gerry Owen. Chapter 18 logo: Stephen Santangelo. Fig. 18-4 Gerry Owen. Chapter 19 logo: Gerry Owen. Fig. 19-4 courtesy ACTION/Peace Corps. Fig. 19-5 Gerry Owen. Chapter 20 logo: Gerry Owen. Fig. 20-1 Gerry Owen. Chapter 21 logo: Gerry Owen.

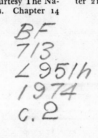

MACMILLAN PUBLISHING CO., INC.
866 Third Avenue, New York, New York 10022

COLLIER-MACMILLAN CANADA, LTD.

Library of Congress Cataloging in Publication Data

Lugo, James O.
  Human development.

    1. Developmental psychology. I. Hershey, Gerald L., 1931–
        joint author. II. Title [DNLM: 1. Psychology. BF701
L951h 1974]
BF713.L83   155   73-11693
ISBN 0-02-372300-9

Printing: 3 4 5 6 7 8   Year: 4 5 6 7 8 9 0

We dedicate this book to our students
with the hope that they will
try to make this a better world for all people,
regardless of age

A N D

To the memory of Clementine Hershey
A Model of "Motherly Love"

A N D

Para mis madres queridas, Yiya y Nana,
que me enseñaron amar

Preface

THE primary intent of this book is to provide a broad, comprehensive background in the study of human development. The three major components of the study are (1) a multidisciplinary survey, emphasizing the chief conceptual and methodological tools of the various disciplines and their application to the field of human development; (2) a delineation of the four major domains of the human condition—the biologic, the cognitive, the affective, and the social—and an attempt to establish worthwhile developmental goals within these domains; and (3) a chronological survey of the individual's development from conception to death, emphasizing the interaction of the four domains.

A major underlying theme is what can be done to facilitate the development of more fully functioning individuals at each particular stage of life. The authors hope this approach will encourage students to read more widely and to engage in research.

A further distinguishing feature is the attempt to satisfy diverse preprofessional and personal needs of the biologically orientated medical and nursing students, the cognitively orientated education students, the affectively orientated psychology students, and the socially orientated human service students.

The authors, who are basically teachers, are unequivocally indebted to researchers who provided a continuous flow of information and hypotheses. We are also indebted to our former professors who exposed us to their humanity and provided us with insights into human behavior, among them James C. Coleman, Waldo Ferguson, John Krumboltz, Eric Fromm, Robert A. Naslund, Newton S. Metfessel, and William B. Michael. We are grateful to our consultants: E. Robert Ackerman, teacher and orthoptist; William Heckman, humanist; William L. Kimball, sociologist; and Robert B. McLaren, philosopher. Warm thanks are extended to our contributors, Douglas Kimmel, professor of psychology from the City University of New York; Margaret Franks and Joy Graves, nursing instructors from Cypress College; Henry J. Paris, psychiatric social worker from the North Orange County Child Guidance Clinic; and Stewart Cohen, Child Development Center at the University of Rhode Island. We also thank Gerald Owen for his artistic photographic views of human development and are grateful for our typists, Maria E. Lugo and Lillian Johnson. We also express our appreciation to our wives and children for their encouragement and understanding.

J. O. L.
G. L. H.

Contents

PART I   *PROLOGUE*   1

CHAPTER 1   The Study of Developmental Psychology   3

PART II   *MULTIDISCIPLINARY PERSPECTIVES*   17

CHAPTER 2   Historical Perspectives   19

CHAPTER 3   Philosophical Perspectives   32

CHAPTER 4   Anthropological Perspectives   51

CHAPTER 5   Sociological Perspectives   69

CHAPTER 6   Biological Perspectives   83

CHAPTER 7   Psychological Perspectives   94

PART III   *LIFE GOALS*   109

CHAPTER 8   The Biological Domain   112

CHAPTER 9   The Cognitive Domain   130

CHAPTER 10   The Affective Domain   147

CHAPTER 11   The Social Domain   165

CHAPTER 12   The More Fully Human Person: Some
Models and Processes   180

PART IV   *THE LIFE CYCLE*   213

CHAPTER 13   The Preconception Stage   215

CHAPTER 14   The Prenatal and Neonatal Stages   241

CHAPTER 15   Infancy   270

CHAPTER 16   Early Childhood   348

CHAPTER 17   Later Childhood   422

CHAPTER 18   Adolescence   488

CHAPTER 19   Early and Middle Adulthood   512

CHAPTER 20   Old Age and Death   536

CHAPTER 21   Reducing Barriers to Becoming a More
Fully Human Person   552

EPILOGUE   569

INDEX   571

PART I
Prologue

ALTHOUGH *this section is brief, it sets forth the basics of the entire text. In this section, the authors share with the readers their orientation, assumptions, and attitudes toward human development and life. In addition, the structure of the text is carefully explained and its purposes made clear.*

In so doing, the authors hope that they will provide the readers with a useful guide for better understanding the what and the why of the complete book.

The Study of
Developmental Psychology

Prelude
  Personal Memories
  Research Findings
  Applications
Basic Theory and Research
  Assumptions and Values
  Design and Structure of the Text
Implications
  Understanding Yourself and
    Others
  Living and Working with Chil-
    dren, Adolescents, and Adults
  Conclusions

PRELUDE

THIS chapter is unusual because its major purpose is to introduce you to the assumptions that underlie the organization of this text. We feel that a superior comprehension of human development will follow as a result of your knowing beforehand the goals of the authors and how they intend to achieve them.

We believe that for a more effective study of human development, priority must be given first to the subjective side (that is, to personal experiences and feelings) and then to the objective side (that is, information based essentially on research findings). For example, we believe that the successful study of children and adolescents and the implementation of this knowledge are highly personal processes. Certainly the drama of human birth or of early language acquisition is more personal than are the study of the imperative mood, the Pythagorean theorem, or the acceleration of falling bodies. Therefore, whenever possible, the authors emphasize the subjective side first and the objective second.

This sense of personal involvement with the subject matter of human development is supported by the following excerpts from Arthur T. Jersild's (1965) presidential address given before the Division on Childhood and Adolescence of the American Psychological Association several years ago:

> Historically the psychology of childhood and adolescence has been a science which some psychologists try to teach to other psychologists and to college students. My theme today is that we have held too restricted a conception of what child psychology is and what it might be. The proper study for all human beings from the earliest possible age is the human being himself.
>
> Every child is actually or potentially a child psychologist. From an early age, without being deliberate about it, he acquires ideas and attitudes about himself and others. These are woven into the pattern of his life. They may be true or false, healthy or morbid.
>
> It is a curious thing that the subject of self-understanding has been so neglected when we consider how eager we are to teach other things. Children learn to bound the states of the Union and they memorize the names and dates of bygone wars; they study the habits of beavers, learn about the distant stars, and the antics of Mother Goose. But the subject of human behavior, human motives, and the inner life of man has been pretty much ignored.

PERSONAL MEMORIES

To view learning primarily as an involvement with and a commitment to life, let us listen to some voices from childhood. As you listen try to recall your own childhood experiences.

Childhood Memories

I always felt insecure and in the way (she once said), but most of all I felt scared—I guess I wanted love more than anything in the world. (Interview with Marilyn Monroe, by Clare Booth Luce)

The earliest childhood experience that I can remember is when I discovered flowers. My first word was flower, at least that is what my folks tell me. My dad had the whole back yard growing in flowers. I can remember my dad explaining to me what makes them grow and how he planted them. (Anonymous student)

The earliest thing I can remember was the wonderful times I had at my grandparents' house. I spent a good deal of my early childhood with my mother's parents and I can remember the shopping trips, bedtime stories, being everyone's little girl, and "helping" grandma cook or bake. I remember the baths in the kitchen sink and the treat of ice cream which grandpa brought home if I was good. (Anonymous student)

Parent's Memories of Their Children

She dominates the home too much . . . this dependency on me depresses me. I don't like it . . . she has cost me a tremendous amount of vitality to break away from her hold on adults. She has drained everything out of me some days. . . . I have been unbearably tired because of Mary. . . . She has no elasticity, she is very set in her ways. . . . The other day I started to dress her at 4:45 and finished at 6:30 and I was a wreck. She insisted on wearing a petticoat too long for her dress and too large shoes and panties with yellow ribbons that everyone must and did see. . . . (Mother of nursery school child)

We thought of her as a little angel from the first. . . . She adjusted well with people. . . . They enjoy having her—she's just happy. . . . (At home) she was very affectionate. She liked her father and he was responsive to her—would carry her a great deal—very strong affection for her father. . . . He was a very good father—unusually good with a little child, teaching them to observe—he liked to go walking and see them observe nature. (The mother continues, she was a) happy child—didn't bring any great problems—just joy having Ann. (Mother of nursery school child)

Anonymous Twelve-Year-Olds

When I was ten months old, my mother went away. She left me with her mother and father on their farm where I was raised.

I never saw my mother again till I was five years old.

It was not till I was nine years old I learned I had another father and that my sister and brother were my step-sister and brother. I was sick. And from then on my life was worthless. I also have hated my life. . . . I have only one dislike and that is that I am living, Why? Because it has made me very unhappy . . . .

In all my twelve years in this confusing world, I have found myself to be an interesting person. I have finished a diagnosis and concluded myself very different from others, though very nice and smart (uck, uck!). I have special ideas, beliefs, restraints, hopes, and a different world in which all these are my life.

The Study of
Developmental
Psychology

Anonymous Letters to Dad

Dad:

I've always wanted to hug you, I never could. I'm afraid of you.

You've got your problems, just as I've got mine. I just wish that our problems wouldn't keep us apart. It angers me the way you treat me, and our family, sometimes I wished you were damned.

I look into your eyes and think of all the times we didn't have, all of the petty arguments. I wish we could bring something back.

You're getting old now, and look at me with jealousy. Some day soon you'll die: I wish that once, before we leave, we could put down our defenses and hug each other with all our might, just once—

Through our hates and jealousies
I Love You Dad

P.S. But I won't kiss your "feet."

Dear Dad:

I think you're the greatest father in the world. I'm always asking you for help and advice, which you find an answer everytime. Seems like you're always busy, never idle and you stop what you're doing to give me help. I know a lot of my friends' fathers and none of them can hold a candle to you. You have brought me up so good. I can't think of anything you did wrong through the years.

I'd like to thank you for doing such a good job as a dad, and only hope to be half as great to my children. I really do appreciate it, but it's hard for me to show affection.

Love, your son

Dear Father:

It's strange how often times people in the same family can live together for many years and not understand each other. It's taken me twenty years to just begin to know what makes you tick. The old saying "The 20-year-old's realizing how smart his dad really is," is so true.

You haven't changed, it's I who have grown up. You understand me so well, and yet, I don't understand myself. Being able to understand you has made living at home so much nicer. Something I don't think the young adults take any time to learn about is parents. I now realize that you are human, with faults and frailties and not a super human, as I pictured you for so many years.

Knowing these things doesn't make me love you less, it actually brings me closer to you. I have a great amount of respect for you and I know you care for me a great deal. I want to thank you for the care and love you have given me during my life.

With Love

You can see, from the preceding quotations, that the starting point in the study of human development is the same for all of us—the contents of our lives. We all bring to the study of children our experiences and feelings, whether joyful or bitter, and that into such diverse backgrounds we incorporate each new finding about human development.

Our personal experiences should influence what we learn about children beyond what we now observe or read. We may call this phenomenon "observer or participant involvement," and it should lead us to approach the

Prologue

formal study of developmental psychology in the same refreshing way that children approach us; that is, with curiosity and receptivity. While living, learning, and working with children, we should try to be our true selves. In the presence of children, there is no need for the facades, pretenses, and role-playing that are so typical in the adult community where we are often being judged and criticized. An example of this unpretentious approach to children is that of a mother playing with her infant. The mother can giggle, be silly and even preposterous, but her baby will look at her with unquestioning acceptance and loving eyes.

RESEARCH FINDINGS

The second major section of each chapter is entitled "Basic Theory and Research." In this section, we summarize relevant scientific findings. If we can conceive of the subjective and personal "Prelude" as the "heart" of each chapter, we can then conceive of the "Basic Theory and Research" section as the "brain."

Actually, we see no need to form a polarity between scientific descriptions and hypotheses and the private world of experience and intuition. Scientific hypotheses often stem from hunches, and in turn, the results of scientific investigations often change ideas and feelings about children that were originally derived from personal experiences. We visualize in this interplay of the subjective and the objective a mutually enhancing dynamic relationship.

APPLICATIONS

The third major section of each chapter is entitled "Implications." It includes the sections "Living with Yourself and Others," "Living and Working with Children, Adolescents, and Adults," and "Developing Positive Models." The purpose of this last section is to attempt to answer the questions often posed by students after reading a chapter or a book: "So what? What's the point? What good will all this do for me and my children?"

To help find answers to these questions, you are asked to become active participants in the learning process, since the possible implications for everyday living and future research are many and varied. Much excitement can be generated because imagination, intuition, feeling, and intellectual know-how can be combined into a creative, free-wheeling force. Better answers to our questions regarding human development are produced.

As we apply what we have learned, we will, of course, often feel indebtedness to the researchers, academicians, and practitioners for sharing their knowledge and wisdom with us. As often, however, we will despair at the lack of information concerning so many vital areas of human development. We will ask "Why, in God's name, does a nation as rich as ours know so little about its most precious resource—our children?" The present state of affairs regarding our knowledge of human development will probably remain unchanged until the welfare of children becomes a major national goal. The words of Urie Bronfenbrenner (1971) in his recent address to the National Association for the Education of Young Children seem appropriate:

We like to think of America as a child-centered society, but our actions belie our words. A hard look at our institutions and ways of life reveals that our national priorities lie elsewhere. The pursuit of affluence, the worship of material things, the hard and the soft; the willingness to accept technology as a substitute for human relationships; the imposition of responsibility upon families without support, and the readiness to blame the victims of evil for the evil itself, have brought us to the point where a broken television set or a broken computer provokes more indignation and more action than a broken family or a broken child. (pp. 157–158).

BASIC THEORY AND RESEARCH

Just as our activities, attitudes, and feelings are often guided or determined by our personal philosophy of life, so researchers, academicians, and practitioners are guided by their values and assumptions about human nature in their research and application of knowledge about human development. The problem is that the guidelines derived from their theoretical orientations are frequently implicit and therefore difficult to communicate clearly. Nevertheless, we owe it to you to try to clarify for ourselves and others the whys that underlie this book. Here then, are the authors' assumptions and values concerning the study of human development. They are given without self-righteousness and as encouragement to readers to examine their own assumptions and values.

Assumptions and Values

We believe that through the study of the child and the adolescent one can gain a depth of insight into his own developmental history as well as into that of his fellow man. As Jersild (1970) says:

the child each of us once was still resides in us. Even if we try to abandon him by turning our minds to other things he will never abandon us. He is an essential part of *my* existence as I write, and of *your* existence as you read. And nothing comes closer to the essence of life than our own existence. For this reason it is a rewarding task to endeavor to understand children we know in the light of the children we once were. (p. 4)

Parent's Contribution. We believe that all parents, potential parents, and individuals acting in the role of parent substitute have the responsibility to attempt to rear children who will become creative, alive, and growing citizens.

We believe that the seeds of joy, creativity, and human love are planted in childhood by most parents. However, with further study and awareness, parents may increase their harvest of these precious human qualities by recognizing that the best gift they can give their child is love, understanding, and the example of an acceptable pattern of living . . . all of which are priceless commodities.

Children's Contribution. We believe that given the opportunities in childhood, children can grow and develop far more of their potential . . . more than so many others think possible. It is a basic principle of human nature as well as democracy that free men can find their own best ways. We are told by modern psychology that there is a normally inherent, deep, and never-ending drive to become the very best person we can.

Study of the Whole Child. We believe that only through an interdisciplinary approach (e.g., a study of all areas of research that have implications for a better understanding of children and adolescents—nursing, social work, and the like) can one fully grasp the significance of the childhood and adolescent periods. We believe that by studying theories and research findings in the broad areas of psychology, biology, and sociology one can better appreciate the importance of these developments during the entire human life cycle. A recent monograph of the Society for Research in Child Development further confirms our premise (Yarrow et al., 1970):

> Adjustive behavior can be viewed in terms of biological, psychological, and sociological levels of defense and action. Thus we have cellular or immunological defenses against disease: we have psychological resources, including defensive mechanisms for coping with stress and protecting the self from devaluation; and on a sociological level we have interpersonal and group resources, such as family, friends, labor unions, and police forces. . . . Thus again we see the integrated and holistic functioning of the human organism in its complex and continuing transaction with its environment.

Developing Potentialities. We believe that the recent research in the areas of human potentialities and self-actualization have profound implications for parents, children, and adolescents. We believe that there are many exciting and valuable ongoing pilot projects in research centers and schools for children and adolescents whose findings, however tentative, have important implications for parents, potential parents, and those working with children and adolescents. Through these projects, the potential of the human mind has been found to be virtually unlimited in its ability to acquire vast stores of knowledge. Anthropological, psychological, and physiological findings indicate that our brain operating at only half its capacity can learn numerous languages, memorize volumes of texts, and complete the curricula of dozens of colleges.

World Viewpoint. We believe that through the inter- and intracultural study of childhood and adolescence, people will learn to appreciate the differences between and among the peoples of not only our own country but the world, hopefully reducing some of the misunderstandings and tensions that now exist.

We also believe that many of the seeds of hatred, fear, and prejudice are planted during childhood, and that with understanding and study many parents and potential parents may be able to avoid planting such seeds that will develop into weeds with thorns and poisonous berries that hinder human growth.

As children, we believed that the world centered around us and that everyone saw, felt, and heard exactly what we did. Experience removed the blinds of our childhood. International education will remove our adult blinds of ethnocentrism so that we may appreciate or commiserate with our brothers wherever they may be on earth.

Child Rearing for the Future. We believe that the technological advances of the next fifty years will require parents to consider more the necessity for rearing children to live in a future world that is very different from that in which they themselves were reared. For instance, the giant informational and technological explosion surrounding us could lead to dramatic events

The Study of
Developmental
Psychology

that promise to radically improve our ways of living. The greatest and most significant unexplored frontier today is man himself. We cannot and should not ignore the greatest treasures of all: man and his children.

Moral Development. We believe that the development of moral values is essential to happiness, welfare, and possibly the survival of the human race. Sane people everywhere seem to desire, *in other people* at the very least, the ethical principles described for the Rational-Altruist. Few of us would say that we prefer to live with people who cannot be reasoned with or who are hostile or coldly indifferent rather than friendly. Not many of us would choose to live with people who are undependably erratic and unpredictably unstable, or with unscrupulous, untrustworthy people on whom we dare not turn our backs. No one in his right mind would seriously choose this kind of life.

Research. We believe that the area of child and adolescent psychology is a continually developing discipline that is still in need of a more systematic organization; that there are presently large gaps in the research and theoretical development of this field. Among the many differing theoretical approaches we believe that there are some which have greater relevance and implications for students, parents, and those who work with children and adolescents. B. L. White, (1971) in his book on human infants, says:

> In spite of the recent upsurge in the field of research in human infancy, one does not have to look far to find signs of serious trouble. Whether one is dealing with the practical problem of society or the more esoteric concerns of the student or research worker, one finds the field consistently wanting. At the practical level, parents and educators need to know how to structure the environment of each child so as to make likely optimal development of intellectual, linguistic, emotional, social, and motor capacities. . . .

DESIGN AND STRUCTURE OF THE TEXT

In this section, the overall structure of the text, the chapter organization, the major goals, and the models and processes employed to define and to develop the goals of the text are explained.

The Use of a Modified Systems Approach

A recent approach to the solving of human problems has been the development of a method called systems analysis (Corrigan and Kaufman, 1962; Meals, 1967; De Cecco, 1968). Essentially, this involves a relatively complex process of studying all aspects of a certain problem and carefully setting up a structured approach for solving the problem along with the means for evaluating how effective the problem-solving methods were. One authority, De Cecco, (1968) explains some of its applications as follows:

> When you increase the number of objectives you try to reach, the amount of material and the array of media you utilize, and the number of students and teachers involved in a total operation, you usually need comprehensive and detailed planning. Getting the best equipment in the best place for the best people at the best time and at the best price becomes a rather monumental problem. With its emphasis on efficiency and productivity in the competitive market, industry has probably given

Prologue

more serious consideration than any other group has to the systematic planning of complex operations which involve people, machines, materials, and ultimate delivery of a product of precise specifications. The armed services, as well, are often faced with a situation in men who must be trained for the performance of complex tasks in very short periods of time, especially during national emergencies. Here also the systematic planning of instruction is a more critical issue than it is in our schools. In our schools and colleges, however, there is increasing competition for the students' time as we try to crowd the acquisition of increased knowledge and skill into the traditional time limits set on education and as the schools compete for their share of the tax dollar. Because of this additional pressure, we must improve the effectiveness and efficiency of instruction. (p. 530).

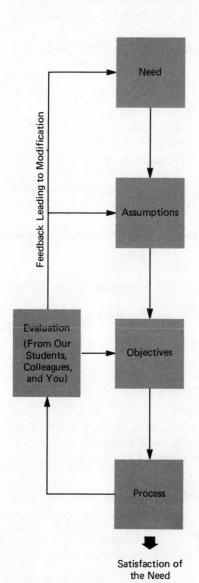

Need

To write a meaningful human development text.

Assumptions

1. Through the study of childhood and adolescence we learn more about ourselves.
2. Those responsible for rearing children have obligations not only to the individual child, but to the society in which the child will eventually live.
3. An individual has the responsibility to strive to become all that he is capable of becoming.
4. In most people there is a vast human potential waiting to be developed.
5. The most meaningful contributions to the individual and to society come about through systematic study and application of the findings.

Objectives

1. To understand yourself better.
2. To understand your parents better.
3. To understand your own children better.
4. To present basic information on human development.
5. To show research methods, concepts, and results.
6. To demonstrate the relevance of some research and theory to your lives.
7. To present some contributions of other disciplines to the study of human development.
8. To help you consider the implications of developmental psychology in the conduct of your daily lives.
9. To encourage you to engage in further study.
10. To encourage you to consider a career in human service.

Process

1. Present multidisciplinary contributions to the study of human development.
2. Present guidelines for establishing life goals in behavioral development.
3. Present basic research findings and applications for each stage in the human life cycle.

FIG. 1–1.
Flowchart of the modified systems approach used in developing this text.

For us, the writing of a meaningful text in developmental psychology was the major problem, or need. To meet this need, we began by stating the assumptions to which you have just been introduced. On the basis of these assumptions, we developed certain goals and objectives from which we carried out the tasks of designing and writing this text. In addition, we provided for evaluation, or feedback, to determine if we had met our original goals or objectives. Figure 1–1 presents a visual flow chart of this process.

Objectives of the Text

Now that you have a general idea about some of our needs, feelings, and basic assumptions, we would like to elaborate on the various phases of the modified systems analysis process illustrated in the flow chart.

We decided that there were essentially four basic frameworks, or models, that we were planning to follow in presenting our objectives: motivation, information, thinking, and stimulation. Table 1–1 presents a summary of these models.

In order to carry out our goals, we designed the text in a way we believe

TABLE 1–1
BASIC MODELS USED IN DEFINING GOALS OF TEXT

Motivation Model Goals

1. To understand yourself better through the understanding of the development of your own childhood and adolescence.
2. To understand your parents better through the understanding of their childhood and adolescence.
3. To understand your own children better.
4. To show you the relevance of some of the research and theory for understanding yourself and others better.

Information Model Goals

1. To introduce you to some of the basic theoretical orientations in the various areas of research.
2. To present the research findings in the various areas of research in child, adolescent, adult, and old-age psychology.
3. To present basic developmental aspects of the four major areas of human behavior (affective, cognitive, biological, and social).
4. To integrate the interdisciplinary aspects of developmental psychology with other disciplines: sociology, anthropology, biology, philosophy, and history.

Thinking Model Goals

1. To help you think more clearly about the implications of the theory and research for you as a student, parent, and/or child and adolescent worker (e.g. nurse, home economist, teacher, child psychologist, social worker).

Stimulation Model Goals

1. To encourage you to do further reading about developmental psychology even after the course is completed.
2. To stimulate you to consider orienting your life goals around one of the "helping professions," that is, working with children and adolescents in teaching, nursing, medicine, psychology, social work, home economics, or other human service careers.

Prologue

to be logical and interesting, a way that conveys continuity. The four major parts to the text are summarized in Table 1–2.

TABLE 1–2
ORGANIZATION OF PARTS

Part I	Prologue (Overview of the subject matter, and the text.)
Part II	Multidisciplinary Perspectives (Contributions and background from other areas of study.)
Part III	Life Goals (The four domains of human behavior and their potential for change.)
Part IV	The Life Cycle (The chronological development of the individual from preconception to old age.)

Parts I, II, and III are composed of a series of "minichapters," short chapters that focus on a highly specific area of knowledge. Part IV contains the major body of the text.

Figure 1-2 contains a three-dimensional view of this organizational pattern.

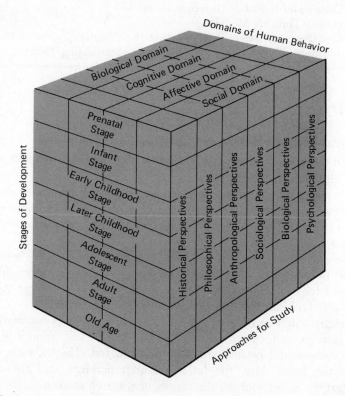

FIG. 1–2.
Three-dimensional model for this text.

We hope you can now see how we plan to approach the study of developmental behavior in line with this three-dimensional model. The first dimension is a developmental stage point of view going from the prenatal through old age. The second dimension consists of the four major domains of human behavior: (1) the cognitive, which includes such processes as thinking and learning; (2) the affective, which includes the area of human feeling and

The Study of Developmental Psychology

emotions; (3) the biological, which includes such areas as genetics, heredity, and basic physiological processes; and (4) the social, which includes such variables as society, institutions, group processes, and socioeconomic level. The third dimension of our model includes the major perspectives for the study of human development. It should be noted that we are using a "taxonomy" model originally developed by Bloom et al. (1956) for use in developing educational objectives. We are indebted to them for their original work in delineating these four domains. We have adapted them, however, for a different purpose and with a slightly different meaning.

Within-Chapter Structure

Every chapter in this book is organized in the same way and around the same four basic models. Table 1–3 illustrates the four basic sections of each chapter along with the particular objective or model it was designed to support.

TABLE 1–3
WITHIN-CHAPTER OUTLINE

   I. Prelude (Motivation Model)
  II. Basic Theory and Research (Information Model)
 III. Implications (Thinking Model)
 IV. Specialized Features Included Throughout the Chapters including bibliographies, illustrations, and research descriptions (Stimulation Model)

IMPLICATIONS

UNDERSTANDING YOURSELF AND OTHERS

You need to understand the rationale in our having this kind of section at the end of all succeeding chapters.

We have already introduced the idea of the need for the development of a more personal understanding of a subject area so that you will see the meaning in studying that material. We have called this our motivation model (see Tables 1–1 and 1–3).

You have just read about some theories and research upon which the design and development of this text was based. This section provides the core material for our Information Model (see Tables 1–1 and 1–3). Again, a section of this type appears in each of the following chapters.

The basic research and theory sections in future chapters summarize the research findings and various theoretical points of view upon which the field of developmental psychology is currently based. That is, each section gives you the latest data, the latest research findings, and the current theories that try to account for the results of research studies.

We believe that to study facts and figures purely for their own sake is an interesting pastime. To delve into an area of human knowledge and explore the many facets of its structure, its theories and principles, and its basic research findings is a part of a "general education." However, just to go that far, we believe, is not enough for living in and contributing to the dynamic world of today. So many of our students have thought this way that

Prologue

we have come to believe that this is what most young people today mean when they talk about relevancy in education. They want to make their education a more human, personally meaningful kind of experience. Jerome Bruner, in his recent book *The Relevance of Education* (1971) puts it in a slightly different form:

> Knowledge has a structure, a hierarchy, in which some of what is known is more significant than the rest of what is known about some aspect of life or nature. It is more significant because armed with the significant knowledge and armed with a theory and operations for putting the significant knowledge together and for going beyond it, one can reconstruct with reasonable approximation the less significant knowledge and the multiple of stray items that constitute the whole body of knowledge. The task of the curriculum maker and of teachers is to give to the student a grasp of this underlying structure along with a highly discriminating sense of its importance so that he may be saved from that most common blight on human thinking: clutter. (p. 123).

Thus, in the third major section of each chapter, we attempt to point out what we believe are the relevant implications of theories and basic research findings. We go beyond the raw data, the basic facts if you will. We point out how you might use these facts and theories in your own life and in living and working with children and adolescents. This is risky, we admit. The observations are from our own frame of reference. Hopefully, as you become more familiar with what we are doing in the Implications Sections you will be able to write your own "implications section" for this book as well as for the course you are taking.

LIVING AND WORKING WITH CHILDREN, ADOLESCENTS, AND ADULTS

Taking our departure a bit further, we wish to point out that the real "payoff" of this text for any context or course of study is whether it makes a difference; that is, whether it changes your behavior. We are using the term *behavior* in a broad manner to include such things as feelings, attitudes, and patterns of thinking as well as ways of behaving in general.

Therefore, we have included two other sections under the implications to take into account and to offer ideas for behavioral consequences. One of these sections is called "Implications for Living and Working with Children, Adolescents and Adults" and the other is called "Developing Positive Models." After you become familiar with what and how we apply the research and theories to living and working with children and adolescents, we believe that you can write these sections for yourself because you will be looking from your personal frame of reference, from your own childhood and adolescent experiences, and not just from the perspective of a potential parent, nurse, teacher, psychologist, or home economist.

CONCLUSIONS

We hope that this discussion has helped you understand some of the thoughts and feelings we have had in relation to our "developmental task"— the inception and rearing of a "newborn text."

If this book achieves some of the goals we have set for it and if it is effec-

The Study of
Developmental
Psychology

tive in relating to you, the reader, then it should lose its reason for being: you no longer need it. Erich Fromm said the same thing in a slightly different fashion: "The sign of an effective teacher is when the teacher has lost his justification for existence with his students—they are now as competent and effective as he is!"

CHAPTER REFERENCES

BLOOM, B. S., M. D. ENGELHART, E. J. FURST, W. H. HILL and D. R. KRATH-WHOHL. *Taxonomy of educational objectives, handbooks 1 and 2: cognitive and affective domain.* New York: McKay, 1956.

BRONFENBRENNER, U. "Who cares for America's children?" *Young Children,* January 1971, 157–163.

BRUNER, J. S. *The relevance of education.* New York: Norton, 1971.

CORRIGAN, R. E., and R. A. KAUFMAN. *Why system engineering?* Palo Alto, Calif.: Fearon, 1962.

DE CECCO, J. P. *The psychology of learning and instruction.* Englewood Cliffs, N. J.: Prentice-Hall, 1968.

JERSILD, A. T. *Child psychology,* 6th ed. Englewood Cliffs, N. J.: Prentice-Hall, 1970.

———. Self-understanding in childhood and adolescence. In D. E. Hamacheck (ed.), *The self in growth, teaching, and learning.* Englewood Cliffs, N. J.: Prentice-Hall, 1965.

MEALS, D. W. Heuristic models for systems planning. *Phi Delta Kappan,* 1967, **48**:199–203.

WHITE, B. L. *Human infants.* Englewood Cliffs, N. J.: Prentice-Hall, 1971.

YARROW, M. R. et al. Recollections of childhood: a study of the retrospective method. *Monographs of the Society for Research in Child Development,* 1970, **35**:5.

Prologue

PART II
Multidisciplinary
Perspectives

IN this section the major emphasis is on a multidisciplinary approach to the study of developmental psychology. The authors believe that other fields can make major contributions toward a better understanding of the behavior and development of human beings.

In a single book, of course, only a brief overview of other disciplines can be presented. These subjects are surveyed in the form of minichapters with a frank admission that this procedure results in grave injustices to the many great contributions and contributors to these complex fields. We believe that the ends justify the means; we want you to understand infants, children, adolescents, and adults more fully, and you can do so much better by realizing the essential contributions from related fields. We hope you will want to fill in the details of our sketches by further reading and thinking after you have completed this book.

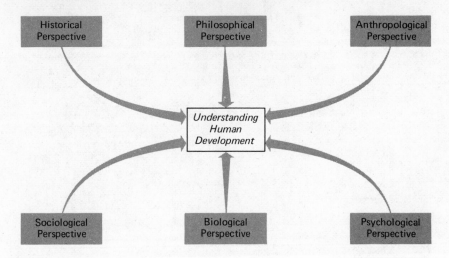

A multidisciplinary approach will enable us to better understand human development.

Historical Perspectives

Prelude
Basic Theory and Research
  The Concept of Children and
    Adolescents
  The Growth of the Modern Con-
    cept of Childhood
  Trends in Education in the
    United States
Implications
  Understanding Yourself and
    Others
  Living and Working with Chil-
    dren, Adolescents, and Adults
  Developing Positive Models

PRELUDE

ACH day we are confronted with the simple truth that our present lives are being continuously influenced by the total history of man. A brief introduction to the history of childhood may provide us with important insights into our own behavior as well as our attitudes toward children and youth.

In a true sense, all of us, as students of human development, are about to enter a new and different world because few of us have clear memories of our own developmental experiences prior to age four (Lugo and Canon, 1964). It is well to remember to enter this new world cautiously; as strangers we are apt to lose our ways readily and to make numerous mistakes. Perhaps the following historical accounts may provide us with some preliminary guidelines for entering the realm of childhood.

This historical description is limited to two major areas of life. The first area covers various aspects of children's lives such as dress, discipline, and work. The second presents the development of formal education in the United States.

BASIC THEORY AND RESEARCH

THE CONCEPT OF CHILDREN AND ADOLESCENTS

For centuries, most children and adolescents were looked upon as immature adults, who only needed to grow up physically and psychologically. A baby and an adult were considered to be only quantitatively different. The clothing worn by children was often small replicas of those worn by adults. Children in early paintings were portrayed as miniature adults. Toys were first the playthings of adults and, only later, were they passed on to children. Even books for children were not produced until the nineteenth century.

Children As Adults

You may gain some insights into the past treatment of children from the following quotes from Aries (1962):

> In 1600 the specialization of games and pastimes did not extend beyond the age of three or four. From then on the child played the same games as the adult. . . . (p. 71)

> When he was three, Louis XIII was dancing the galliard, the saraband and the old bourrée, and taking part in the court ballets. At five, he was watching farces, and at seven, comedies. He sang, and played the violin and lute . . . . (p. 97)

> In the society of the same period (1500), a boy aged between thirteen and fifteen was already a full-grown man and shared the life of his elders. . . . (p. 194)

> At the end of Louis XIV's reign there were fourteen-year-old lieutenants in the army. Chevert joined the army at the age of eleven . . . common to both officers and men in the seventeenth century, this precocity would continue for a long time in the rank and file; it disappeared in the eighteenth century among the officers . . . . (p. 67)

Multi-
disciplinary
Perspectives

Even during early Colonial times in the United States, children were scarcely considered worthy of recognition, although Kiefer (1948) describes the gradual realization that children are unique and not small imitations of adults. Kiefer believed that the era following the American Revolution marked not only the beginning of political freedom for the American people but also the emerging emancipation of American children.

The realization that children have special needs was a gradual process, however, and it advanced with the growth of the country toward a democratic ideal. Thus, by 1835, the foundations for freedom and self-expression

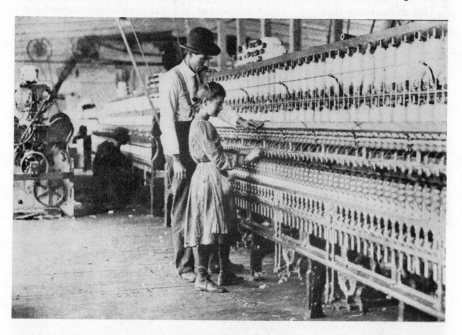

FIG. 2–1.
Compare the life styles of a child in 1909 and today.

21

that characterize both the American government and American child today had been established; the pursuit of life, liberty, and happiness had become the right of children as well as adults. By means of child labor laws and other social reforms, children were accepted as immature human beings with a unique legal status. Gradually, most adults became convinced that children should not be expected to play the roles of "little men and women" without the interlude of childhood.

Children and Etiquette

The attitude of the early Colonial parent toward children seems to have been that they were "to be seen not heard." The following is an excerpt from an etiquette book apparently widely read in Colonial days (Calhoun, 1945):

Never sit down at the table till asked, and after the blessing. Ask for nothing; tarry till it to be offered thee. Speak not. Bite not thy bread but break it. Take salt only with a clean knife. Dip not the meat in the same. Hold not thy knife upright but sloping, and lay it down at right hand of plate with blade on plate. Look not earnestly at any other that is eating. When moderately satisfied leave the table. Sing not, hum not, wiggle not. Spit nowhere in the room but in the corner. . . . When any speak to thee, stand up. Say not I have heard it before. Never endeavor to help him out if he tell it not right. Snigger not; never question the truth of it. (pp. 112–113)

Children and Discipline

For disobedience or impertinence, some colonists prescribed the death penalty for children although it was rarely, if ever, enforced. A Connecticut statute read as follows (Calhoun, 1945):

If any child or children above 16 years old of competent understanding, shall curse or smite their natural father or mother, he or they shall be put to death unless it can be sufficiently testified that the parents have been very unchristianly negligent of the education of such children. . . . If any man have rebellious stubborne son of sufficient years and understanding, viz. 16 years of age or upwards, which shall not obey the voice of his father or the voice of his mother, yet when they have chastened him will not hearken unto them . . . such son shall be put to death, or otherwise severely punished. (p. 121)

Children and Work

The lack of sensitivity to the special needs of childhood also extended into the area of work as children were often laborers (Hersch, 1969). In England, children of both sexes were expected to work in coal mines alongside seasoned bondsmen. The children were clad in male attire, naked to the waist in canvas trousers, with an iron chain fastened to a belt of leather between their legs. Children hauled tubs of coal up subterranean roads for twelve to sixteen hours a day. It was not unusual to find children of four or five years of age working in these conditions—conditions so terrible that criminals today would certainly choose the death penalty rather than be forced to endure them.

Fig. 2–2.
A child at work in
the galleries of a
coal mine, 1860.

Children and Literature

It wasn't until the latter part of the nineteenth century that a deliberate effort was made to produce literature for children. A survey of children's books in England and the United States from earliest times to the present is documented in *A Critical History of Children's Literature* (Miegs et al., 1969).

This book shows clearly how the Victorian era witnessed the beginnings of literature that was written especially for children not simply to edify them but to entertain them as well. France offered the magic stories of Perrault and the fantastic world of Jules Verne; Italy submitted *Pinocchio*; Switzerland produced the tales of Spyri and Malot. From Germany came the folk tales of the brothers Grimm; from Norway, the fairy tales of Asbjørnsen and Moe; from Sweden the imaginative stories of Selma Lagerlog; and finally, the tales of Hans Christian Andersen from Denmark completed the collection. America inherited and enlarged this tradition through the works of such writers as James Fenimore Cooper (The Leatherstocking Tales), Mark Twain (*Huckleberry Finn* and *Tom Sawyer*) and Louisa May Alcott (*Little Women* and *Little Men*). Even Nathaniel Hawthorne, who is not normally known as a children's author, contributed his *The Wonder Book* and *Tanglewood Tales* to children's literature.

Children and Dress

Children's clothing during Colonial times was simply an imitation of adult fashion; "a minature adult." Babies were dressed in shapeless sacques that were gathered at the neck with narrow cotton ferret, or in straight waisted "gowns of state." All clothing was exquisitely handmade, usually of fine material, although frequently it was homespun. A story is told of a baby in a pioneer settlement whose city-bred grandmother "cried bitter tears at seeing the infant dressed in a gray woolen homespun slip complete with apron, after the fashion of her mother." (Calhoun, 1945)

THE GROWTH OF THE MODERN CONCEPT OF CHILDHOOD

The gradual emergence of the modern concept of childhood can be fully understood only within the broader context of the modern family. In turn, the emergence of the modern family can be fully understood only within the

Historical
Perspectives

still broader context of the impacts of many historical influences including the religious reformationists, the great philosophers, the kings and secular leaders who took over political power during the emergence of modern civilization, the Industrial Revolution, and the appearance of public laws defining the rights and obligations of husband and wife, parent and child, and state and child.

It is informative to speculate on the attitudes of the early colonists based on their treatment of children as noted in the following passages (Calhoun, 1945):

> Those that survived infancy, tho probably as dearly loved as are children today, were denied all the normal sources of joy and happiness. Childish manners were formal and meek. Parents were addressed as "esteemed parent" or "honored sir and madam." A pert child was generally thought to be delirious or bewitched. One son of a stern Puritan said that "he never ventured to make a boy's simple request of his father, to offer so much as a petition for a knife or a ball without putting it into writing in due form." Children were now and then favored with a visit to some sainted person who would bless them or warn them to flee from the wrath to come. Everybody went to funerals. There was a dire scarcity of anything worthy to be called children's literature. The children of today would hardly be attracted by such advertisements as these: "Small book in easy verse Very Suitable for Children, entitled the Prodigal Daughter or Disobedient Lady Reclaimed: adorned with curious cuts, Price 6d." "A token for Children. Being the exact account of the Conversation and Holy and Exemplary Lives of several Young children." How glad the children, after the first quarter of the eighteenth century, must have been to get Mother Goose! Of course to the stern Puritan, inexorably utilitarian, what afforded amusement seemed sinful. Child nature being depraved and wicked must be dampened. Play instincts were inexcusable. (pp. 106–112)

The development of the idea and the reality of treating children as unique human beings with special needs were gradual and profound. Table 2–1

TABLE 2–1
SOME HISTORICAL TRENDS TOWARD MODERN CHILDHOOD IN THE FAMILY

Dates	Historical Behaviors	Modern Behaviors
1700	Child entrusted to strangers: boarding schools, tutors, and apprenticeships	Child takes a central place in the family: local day schools
1800	Oldest son was high privileged: sole heir to family fortune	Equality among all children: love, wealth, and education
1800	Focus of family life and activities was the community-at-large	Focus of life is the family unit with emphasis on welfare of children
1800–1900	Formal education for girls was rare	Formal education for girls is common

(Adapted from Aries, 1962)

lists some of the important historical antecedents of the modern concept of childhood. Prior to the seventeenth century, children had to mingle with adults to ensure proper preparation for their future. Everyday life constantly brought children and adults together in trade, crafts, and social life. In the light of the reality of that time, children were truly miniature adults.

Because children were deposited so early and for so long a period of time into the midst of the community, there remained little time for the parents and the child to develop a truly warm family relationship. The seeds of life existed, but for the seed to grow it had to be nourished, and proper nourishment takes time. Along this line, the advent of local day schools as the normal instrument for the progression from childhood to manhood allowed the family to center itself more on the child.

Even with the introduction of local schools, the major thrust of family life remained directed toward the community. Life centered much more on public rather than family affairs. Even the homes tended to be extensions of the collective society much like a public recreation center of today. Starting in the eighteenth century, the home became "the castle" and the principal audience was "one's family."

Twentieth-Century Childhood

A child apart, a youth apart, an adult apart—they are so near yet so far. Kept apart, for hundreds of years, from full participation in the mainstream of life, youth has had to gradually create its separate subculture with its own variety of language, music, dress, values, literature, and recreation. In our time the gulf between young and old has widened so perceptively that both parties have agreed on a label—the generation gap.

From a historical viewpoint, the generation gap can be understood as an end product of centuries of upheavals in economic requirements for earning a living, religious values, education, division of labor, and population shifts from rural to urban. From a psychological perspective, however, the price has been too heavy—separation, misunderstanding, anxiety, and alienation. It is up to the adult society to seek unity since it produced the division. There are signs that the adult society is moving in the direction of reunification with its youth—lowering of the legal voting age, equality of the sexes, election of young people to public office, and an increasing attention by adults to the cries of the young for social justice and brotherhood. If adults listen and accept, they will have gone full circle by taking youth back into their bosoms after a period of almost four hundred years.

TRENDS IN EDUCATION IN THE UNITED STATES

It is understandable that the vast majority of early colonists were only able to give little time or thought to formal education since they were so busy clearing the wilderness and extending the frontier. Furthermore, they were immigrants from Europe, where the reality of public education was just dawning. Schools were constructed and maintained in towns where a sufficient number of families and scholars resided. However, the conditions for learning in these schools were in sharp contrast to modern education, as described by Earle (1943).

Full descriptions exist of the first country school-houses in Pennsylvania and New York. They were universally made of logs. Some had rough puncheon floors, others a dirt floor which readily ground into dust two or three inches thick that unruly pupils would stir up in clouds to annoy the masters and disturb the school. The bark roof was a little higher at one side that the rain might drain off. Usually, the teacher sat in the middle of the room; pegs were thrust between the logs around the walls, three or four feet from the ground; boards were laid on these pegs; at these crude desks sat the older scholars with their backs to the teacher. Younger students sat on blocks or benches of logs.

While the education of the sons of the planters in all the colonies was bravely provided and supported, the daughters fared but poorly. The education of a girl in booklearning was deemed vastly less important than her instruction in household duties. But small arrangement was made in any school for her presence, nor was it thought desirable that she should have any great variety of knowledge. That she should read and write was certainly satisfactory, and cipher a little; but many girls got on very well with the ciphering, and many, alas! without the reading and writing." (pp. 63–91)

It should be noted that the primary purpose of education in the New England colonies was religious. In these schools, the earliest permanent beginnings of education in the United States, there was a definite commitment to moral development that had as its source the religious ideals held by the early colonists.

Education from 1630 to 1750

A milestone in the history of education in the United States was the Massachusetts Act of 1642, the first example of compulsory education. By 1671, all New England colonies except Rhode Island had enacted similar laws although it was up to the local community to determine whether or not the requirements of the law had been met. Although the intent of the state legislature was serious, many children never enjoyed any of the educational opportunities prescribed by law (Power, 1970).

In 1647, Massachusetts passed the famous "Old Deluder Satan Law" that required every community having at least fifty homes to provide elementary instruction for every boy and girl. The primary purpose of this law was again a religious one. It ensured that every citizen would be able to read the Bible and thereby frustrate the evil intentions of Satan. Again, it should not be assumed that all school-age children benefited from the laws of 1642 and 1647. For many years the schools required that the child be able to read prior to admission. For this purpose dame schools, which were located in the home of a woman who had the time and the ability to teach reading to children, were founded. The woman in charge of the school charged fees for her teaching. Little is known however, about these dame schools since they were outside the domain of public responsibility.

Education in the Middle Colonies—New York, New Jersey, and Pennsylvania—also reflected the values and customs of its people. In this region the church was not as strong as it was in New England; therefore, education was left up to the individual communities or to various religious denominations.

Education in the South consisted mostly of private tutors for wealthy

Multi-
disciplinary
Perspectives

26

Fig. 2–3.
*Colonial Dame
School about 1699.*

children, and workhouses and apprentice schools for the poor and the orphaned. An important reason for the lack of town schools in the South was that its population lived in widely scattered, large plantations. It was not until about 1850 that most of the Southern states adopted measures of compulsory schooling.

Education from 1750 to 1850

After the American Revolution, progress was made in education as a result of economic and philosophical changes. We were now an independent nation and could turn our attention more toward internal affairs and growth. The frontier opened new horizons that held enormous promise for self-fulfillment. Furthermore, from Europe came the spirit of humanitarianism, an idea and hope that all men could improve their lives. Consequently, we became enamored with education as a hope for a better future. Power (1970) describes this new outlook as follows:

> Man was able, according to this view, to control the world and other men in such a way that progress would be inevitable and possibly even infinite. The key to the whole program of human progress was knowledge. And who could speak of knowledge without thinking at once of schools and the means for education? With such a deep and sincere faith, a faith not to be despised or scorned, education came to be a kind of religion. Men could become excited about it, and they could defend its virtues with infectious arguments and seductive devices. Of course it would be unreasonable to suppose that this new humanitarianism was not challenged by the old order. If society's stamina is to be found in knowledge, and if knowledge is available and waiting to be found and is not an exclusive prerogative of an aristocracy, the aristocracy loses its position of influence. . . .

The philosophical idea was expressed, and more often than not in clear and precise language: Men are equal before the law and they should have

Historical
Perspectives

27

almost limitless opportunities for political and social equality. The testing ground for this theory of social equality and social mobility, as well as for freedom and self-reliance, was the vast frontier waiting exploration and settlement, and on this frontier democratic ideals were further incubated. (pp. 556–557)

History, however, reminds us that there is typically a time gap between the emergence of ideals and their translations into reality. In fact, we are still trying today to fulfill this dream for all of our children. An important event in the growth of our educational system was the private school, called the academy, which became prominent after the Revolutionary War. Eventually this was to become the foundation of American secondary education. The model for all academies was set up by Benjamin Franklin in his Academy of Philadelphia. Franklin wished to teach youngsters those things that were likely to be the most useful for everyday living. From about fifty schools in 1800, the academies grew in number to about six thousand by 1850. However, since the academies charged tuition they were therefore not available for many children.

It was not until 1821 that the first free, public, nonsectarian high school appeared in Boston. The impetus for the public school came from the rise of industrialism, which required better education, and the spirit of humanitarianism, which desired the social condition of all men to be improved. In order to encourage free public education, in 1787 Congress passed the Northwest Ordinance that provided for free federal land to be given to towns for the support of schools. By 1849 free schools were available for all the people, but there was no compulsory attendance.

Education from 1850 to 1950

No central government agency controlled education in the United States. No mention of education is made in the Constitution, so that the major responsibility for education resided in the individual states, which in turn passed on the responsibility to local school districts. All this accounted for the wide diversity of educational opportunities that existed within the states and within local systems of education. In 1852, Massachusetts passed the first law compelling school attendance for every child between the ages of eight and fourteen. By the beginning of the nineteenth century practically every state had legislation requiring compulsory school attendance. In 1874 the Supreme Court decided that school districts could collect taxes for the support of secondary education. This decision provided for the phenomenal growth of public schools. Yet all was not well, as pointed out by Meyer (1965):

So vast had become the patronage of the public school that the number of available teachers proved utterly inadequate, and their pedagogic capacity, hence, was seriously disabled.

To attend and instruct its gigantic flock, the emerging public school pinned its hopes on regimentation. Its offerings it arranged as graded subjects, teaching them by a rigorous timetable, and assigning certain years for coming to terms with certain facts and operations. The effect was that, for all the massed wisdom of the world's foremost pedagogical minds, teaching in the public school was reduced to drumming knowledge into pupils, belaboring them stiffly with homework and examinations, goading the slow, and exacting penalty from the loafers and skylarkers. What the learner did was translated into the record as marks, of which the most meritorious went not necessarily to the brightest, but more likely to the ones who could summon forth the most numerous facts from their files of memory. It was, of course, education of a dreary order, a hollow artificiality, but until someone came along to do it in, it was to be the rule. (p. 468)

College Education

The first universities in the New World were established in Mexico, Peru, and the Dominican Republic, a century before Harvard College was founded in 1636. The second American college was the College of William and Mary, founded in 1695. The primary purpose of the early colleges in America was religious education. As in the cases of elementary and secondary education, the shift to practical studies in the colleges such as science and mathematics, was a gradual one. The Land Grant Colleges Act signed by President Lincoln in 1862 provided the major impetus toward public colleges. This act provided a land grant of thirty thousand acres for each congressman of every state for the support of public colleges, and laid the foundation for the creation of almost seventy colleges. An important note is that women were first permitted to higher education in 1833 at Oberlin College.

Today, the opportunity for free, public, and continuing education for all Americans seems to be a birthright. An immediate goal is that every young person completing high school will be ready to enter higher education or to enter useful and rewarding employment.

IMPLICATIONS

UNDERSTANDING YOURSELF AND OTHERS

This self of ours, which we should understand, is partly illuminated by the study of the history of man. Actually, before conception, two important determinants of personality have already begun—our biological and social inheritances. Our social inheritance may include the kind of dwellings we live in, our style of dress, religious preference, social standards, and neighborhood atmosphere, all of which will help to form our earliest attitudes toward the world and, in turn, how others will react to our particular life styles.

More important was the attitude of parents about their children. Were children to be "seen and not heard" and, preferably, not to be seen too much, either? Did parents believe that the major goal of child rearing was to make their children into living replicas of themselves? Or did they believe that children had birthrights of their own and were, therefore, entitled to be treated as unique human beings, free to fulfill their own needs and potentials?

The answers to such questions may be found in how our parents were treated when they were children. The origin of these attitudes probably lies somewhere in the history of childhood.

LIVING AND WORKING WITH CHILDREN, ADOLESCENTS, AND ADULTS

History has demonstrated that children are quite capable of living and working in the adult world, even with a concurrent danger of abuse and overextension of their abilities and sensitivities. Today, a somewhat similar situation may be arising because of the trend toward earlier physical maturity. For example, when we associate with a physically mature fourteen-year-old, we may tend to assume that his social and emotional maturities are equal to his physical development. In other words, we are in danger of confusing size with age. However, we must be prepared to face the fact that late teen-agers are truly more mature socially, psychologically, and biologically than ever before and that the world they face is much more complex. In 1971, the United States Congress proposed and the states ratified the Twenty-Sixth Amendment to the Constitution that lowered the voting age to eighteen.

The possibility of future generations of even more mature teen-agers gives rise to some interesting and complex questions. Is it possible that infants and children are also maturing at a faster rate? Will this process increase or decrease the so-called generation gap? Can we continue to use the same school curriculums and disciplinary methods? Finally, is the time lapse between physical, social, and psychological maturity and the ever-increasing time required for proper education in a highly technological society becoming too lengthy?

DEVELOPING POSITIVE MODELS

Our brief history of childhood may provide us with some insights for developing more positive models for present and future childhoods. We have seen some historical models of childhood: the downgrading of females, favoritism toward the oldest male child, and the almost incredible lack of sensitivity toward the special needs of the growing child. However, we have also seen that these historical concepts have been modified and often replaced by more democratic and humanitarian ideals. Apparently, it takes time for the voices of concern for better treatment of children to be heard. Today, there are continuing voices of concern in the "air." Perhaps as more voices join in, the volume will be high enough so that the majority of adults will become "tuned in" to the need for further improvements. In other words, what the future holds in store for our children and their children lies partly in our ability and willingness to make the welfare of children our number one national and personal priority.

CHAPTER REFERENCES

ARIES, P. *Centuries of childhood.* New York: Vintage, 1962.

CALHOUN, A. W. *The social history of the American family,* vol. 1. New York: Barnes & Noble, 1945.

EARLE, A. *Child life in colonial times.* New York: Macmillan, 1943.

HERSCH, J. *Birthright of man.* New York: UNIPUB, 1969.

KIEFER, M. *American children through their books 1700–1835.* Philadelphia: U. of Pennsylvania Press, 1948.

LUGO, J. O., and R. CANON. *A survey of the earliest childhood memories of Fullerton College students.* Fullerton, Calif.: The College, 1964.

Multi-
disciplinary
Perspectives

MEYER, A. *An educational history of the Western world.* New York: McGraw-Hill, 1965.

MIEGS, C., A. T. EATON, E. NESBITT, and R. H. VIGUERS. *A critical history of children's literature.* London: Macmillan, 1969.

POWER, E. *Main currents in the history of education.* New York: McGraw-Hill, 1970.

RECOMMENDED FURTHER READING

ANDERSON, J. E. Child development: a historical perspective. *Child Development,* 1956, **27**:181–196.

AULETA, M. A. *Foundations of early childhood education: readings.* New York: Random, 1969.

BUTTS, R. F. *A cultural history of Western education.* New York: Holt, 1956.

CALHOUN, A. W. *A social history of the American family,* vols. 2 and 3. New York: Barnes & Noble, 1945.

DENNIS, W. Historical beginnings of child psychology. *Psychological Bulletin,* 1949, **46**:224–235.

MORT, P. R., and W. S. VINCENT. *Introduction to American education.* New York: McGraw-Hill, 1954.

ZIMMERMAN, C. C. *Family and civilization.* New York: Harper, 1947.

Historical
Perspectives

Philosophy, like the framework of a house, provides the structural supports for our exterior society, culture, and behavior.

Philosophical Perspectives

Prelude
Basic Theory and Research
   Some Areas of Study Within
      Philosophy
   Idealism
   Realism
   Religion
   Pragmatism
   Existentialism
   A Summary and Comparison of
      the Different Philosophies
Implications
   Understanding Yourself and
      Others
   Living and Working with Children, Adolescents, and Adults
   Developing Positive Models

PRELUDE

ROM reading the last chapter, you understand some historical aspects of childhood and adolescence. You saw how the historical period had a profound effect on how children were viewed and reared. You are now able to understand some of the values of studying history in order to gain additional perspectives on children. In this chapter we provide you similar insights in the area of philosophy and show how the dominant philosophy of a period influenced the views and rearing of children and adolescents. Furthermore, these philosophies are related to some present-day trends and issues of children and adolescents.

In psychology, there is a general principle that states that your behavior is affected by how you characteristically view the world. For example, if your view of people in general is a positive one (people are "good" and "loving" or "humans are not really just animals" or "man is not a machine to be programmed") then the way you relate to others will often reflect this basic position. In a sense, you might say that your "personal philosophy of life" (often hidden and rarely spoken of directly) is significantly related to this perceptual principle.

One of the more important reasons for studying some philosophy is to help you become more aware of your own latent or potential philosophical perspectives. We hope that you will develop from this chapter an appreciation for your parents' philosophical perspectives and a better understanding of how their philosophy of child rearing affected and still affects you. Another "fringe benefit" from this type of approach will be to develop an appreciation for the many contributions that the discipline of philosophy has made and can make toward our understanding of the nature of man.

One caution should be observed: this chapter merely attempts to give you an abbreviated overview and, hence, an appreciation for a very highly complex field of knowledge. In addition, we hope it accomplishes the following objectives: (1) lends dimension and/or perspective to the rest of the book; (2) stimulates you to look into some of these philosophies more thoroughly; (3) develops within you a respect and appreciation for this discipline; (4) develops some feeling of how this field complements our understanding of human development; (5) stimulates you to examine your own philosophical predispositions and those of your parents; and (6) hopefully, helps you become more understanding of and compassionate toward people of other societies who often have, and are entitled to, different philosophical views about their place in nature.

Another element of our approach should be noted before proceeding: philosophies do not originate in limbo; they develop as a result of interacting factors. The complex interplay among the cultural, social, institutional, and time variables is left to you to pursue through further reading and study to develop a broader perspective. Although we discuss such great men as Plato, Rousseau, and Dewey, we do so only in relation to some of their ideas about children. We do not delve fully into the beauty and intellect of these men as they lived and wrote during their lives; this rewarding task we leave to you.

Philosophical
Perspectives

BASIC THEORY AND RESEARCH

Philosophy is an area of human knowledge that collects, selects, develops, and critically analyzes all forms of communication—writings, words, theories, as well as ideas or concepts surrounding the very basic questions pertaining to man and life. Although there is no single definition to encompass all of the functions and roles of philosophy, a few definitions by some well-known authorities cover much territory.

Titus (1970) defines philosophy from five different points of view:

1. Philosophy is a personal attitude toward life and the universe.
2. Philosophy is a method of reflective thinking and reasoned inquiry.
3. Philosophy is an attempt to gain a view of the whole.
4. Philosophy is the logical analysis of language and the clarification of the meaning of words and concepts.
5. Philosophy is a group of problems as well as theories about the solution of these problems.

Another philosopher, Tomlin (1968), perceives philosophy more prophetically:

> The Great Philosophers are merely those for whom the impulse to inquire into the nature of things has become a passion. Thought is the profession from which they never retire. Almost all such men have been distinguished by the nobility of their lives, and particularly by that form of courage which is needed to plough a lonely furrow, to voyage through "strange seas of thought alone." For philosophy is essentially the flower of solitude; it is the unstill and unstillable small voice in each of us which we can ignore at our peril. It is conscience, resurgent, exchanging the role of plaintiff for that of judge.

Certain philosophers specialize in studying and then raising questions about specific areas of life. Thus we have philosophy of science, philosophy of art, philosophy of education, philosophy of literature, and philosophy of religion.

Educational philosophers believe that the individual human being who shows up for instruction is of as much interest as what he is there for. They question what "man" is as well as what he can become; what the nature of human nature is—the basis, in effect, on which all education eventually works. The educational philosopher is interested in society and the world, and he analyzes them to determine what possibilities and prospects education provides for man. In short, the educational philosopher questions the meaning of life and whether this meaning can find expression in our school program.

SOME AREAS OF STUDY WITHIN PHILOSOPHY

Another way to understand philosophy is to look at the way the field is organized in terms of certain questions that are studied. Table 3–1 shows a breakdown of the major subfields of modern-day philosophy according to certain problems or questions.

Philosophers thus attempt through their teaching and writing to encourage

Multi-
disciplinary
Perspectives

TABLE 3–1

MAJOR FIELDS OF PHILOSOPHICAL STUDY

Problem or Question	Area of Philosophical Study
What is correct moral behavior?	Ethics
What is beauty?	Aesthetics
What is of value?	Axiology
What is true and valid and how is it known?	Epistemology
What is real?	Metaphysics
What is ultimate reality?	Ontology (a branch of metaphysics)
How did the universe develop?	Cosmology (a branch of metaphysics)

the individual to stop for a moment and think about some of the basic human questions of existence that man has raised since he developed his ability to reason and think such as: What purpose does philosophy serve? What is its role in the modern world?

One of the serious problems of many of the students that we as teachers interact with (in and out of class) is a lack of purpose and a searching for meaning in life. Who am I? Where am I going? Who or what put us here on earth and for what purpose? What is right and what is wrong? What is good and what is bad? What is moral? What is beautiful and what is ugly? We remember raising such questions as these ourselves during our youth, and we still find ourselves contemplating these important matters.

In psychological jargon, we call this an identity crisis. This combination of feelings of alienation, anomie, and meaninglessness of life seems to be more prevalent today perhaps because of the many factors and trends of the modern world: rapid technological changes; a high degree of mobility of families moving around the country and world as one job is replaced by a computer and the father is being trained for another; the knowledge explosion wherein cherished and often highly valued ideas about the world and its people are shattered overnight; the "shrinking world" where separate countries have to become concerned with living with each other; the development of nuclear weapons that have the capability of destroying an entire civilization; the demands of the poor and oppressed minorities of the world, who will no longer wait for their need for a better life to be met; and the demands of the young who want a more "human" life for all.

What then, does philosophy have to offer the person in the present day and age as he tries to "stay alive" and function in the modern world?

We believe that through a study of some of the basic philosophical positions that have been postulated over the centuries, one may begin to locate himself and his own philosophy of life in relation to other people and the world in general. That is, we all have a philosophy of life that is already developed as we grow into adulthood. However, very often as we examine our philosophy more closely, we find that it is more our parents' philosophy than it is our own.

A study of philosophy may help you uncover your true philosophical leanings and predispositions so that as you interact with your friends, family, and fellows, you will have some basis upon which to make decisions.

Philosophical
Perspectives

Let us now examine some of the better known philosophies of life that have influenced mankind through the ages. Which, you should ask, sounds and feels the most valid and "right" for you?

In order to make a comparison among the different philosophies presented in this section, we discuss each one under the three basic philosophical questions to which all philosophical positions address themselves: What is true? What is real? and What is good?

IDEALISM

One of the earliest global views regarding the relationship between man and the world around him was called idealism. Although this philosophy has taken different forms since its earliest beginnings in the writings of Plato, certain basic ideas are found in all versions.

1. What is true? (The epistemology of the idealist)

Truth lies in a world beyond sense experience, the world of ideals. The human body is like a prison that prevents man from completely knowing these ideals. However, with much introspection and logic and mental discipline, these ideals, or universal truths, can be known.

2. What is real? (The ontology of the idealist)

Reality consists of two realms; the apparent and the real. The apparent world consists of our daily interactions with the world, and the real world consists of the mind and the world of "eternal truths" and ideas. Morris (1961) perceives these two realms in much the same fashion. In elaborating on our daily experience—the apparent world—he speaks of the region of change, of coming and going, of being born, growing, aging, and dying. The apparent world is the realm of imperfection, irregularity, trouble, suffering, evil, and sin. The real world, on the other hand, is not so bleak; it is the home of the mind, the realm of ideas and eternal qualities. The real world has permanence, regularity, order, and absolute truth and value.

3. What is good? (The axiology of the idealist)

The major goal in life is in the development of this "mind" or absolute self to contemplate and understand the basic "ideas" or concepts of life and the universe.

To the idealist then, the highest virtue is to develop one's ability to see through the apparent features of daily living to the more lasting universal ideals of life. Plato, as we see, developed his entire Republic from the basic idea that true happiness could be achieved only by "philosopher-kings" who developed this ability to appreciate the true meaning in life.

Plato's views on children and youth are found in various parts of his writings. Underlying many of the references to child rearing is his theory on the layer structure of the soul. That is, Plato postulated that the soul has three layers: in the first are the basic appetites and desires; the second includes such feelings as endurance and courage; and the third layer is concerned with human reason and contains the "essence" of the universe. Layer one and two are more related to the animal world, whereas layer three is the real soul and temporarily resides in our bodies while we are alive.

Plato suggests that children develop these layers as they grow older: that is, layer one develops early in a child's life. As the child grows older, layer two develops as he asserts his courage. The third layer develops as the person becomes more mature and intelligent; however, not all persons reach this third level of development.

To Plato, the role of parents and the state is to rear and educate the child to the best of his potential as defined by the quality of soul he is born with. Since not all people develop the three layers of the soul, part of the function of education is to find out into which role the child will fit for the good of the ideal state. For example, workers (primarily controlled by their emotions), soldiers (primarily controlled by spirit), and philosophers (controlled more by their reason). In the good state, family and individual reason must dominate spirit and passions.

Titus (1970) summarizes the idealist's view as follows:

> Idealists in general tend to have considerable respect for culture and tradition. They think of the values of life as grounded in a realm beyond the individual and the social groups. . . .
>
> In contrast to Platonic and Hegelian types of idealism, many modern idealists, from Descartes and Leibnitz to the contemporary personalities, have emphasized the person or the consciousness of the individual. Men are viewed as free moral agents capable of discovering values. Idealism, thus, gives an objective basis for moral values and obligations, as opposed to relativistic views, which stress customs and opinion. Self-realization, or the development of selfhood, is the supreme value to which all other values are subordinate. (pp. 233–234)

REALISM

Another global theory that was originally developed by Aristotle is called realism. Although some of the ideas of realism are similar to the idealist philosophy, its basic position is different. Let us again look at the philosophy of realism in terms of the three basic questions.

1. What is true? (epistemology of the realist)

To the realist the truth lies in patterns within the real sensory world, not in the realm of thought and ideas as Plato had suggested. Thus, the emphasis is on the universal patterns found in the environment.

2. What is real? (the ontology of the realist)

For the realist, objects and things do exist in the real world, independent of man. It is the task of man to come to grips with "objective reality" as best he can without messing it up with his own thoughts and ideas.

3. What is good? (the axiology of the realist)

To the realist, "good" or the "good life" comes from examining and studying nature and our environment and finding the basic laws or truths found in the world around us. It is from these basic laws that we can learn about living a good or valuable life. Thus, the realist emphasizes the use of logic and rational thought in making observations about reality.

The position of the realist can be summarized as follows: (1) there is a world of real existence that is not man-made; (2) this real existence can be known by the human mind by the use of reason; and (3) knowledge of the real existence so determined through reason is the only reliable guide to human conduct.

In this sense, realists are very practical people. Since realism depends on reason rather than sentiment, the realist is prepared to find that the world is quite different from what man may wish it to be. It is upon this realist perspective that modern science and scientific method is based.

Philosophical
Perspectives

RELIGION

One of the most prevalent views of man that has influenced much of our history is the religious view. Although there have been many variations of this point of view during different periods of time and in different parts of the world (e.g. Western and non-Western religions), we focus on the Judaeo-Christian interpretation of man since it has played a role in most of our lives.

1. What is true? (Epistemology of the religious view)

In the Judaeo-Christian religion, the truth is revealed through the word of God (the Bible), through direct revelation (in prayer, miracles, and communion) and in historical events as reflected in the laws of Moses and later prophetic writings, and in the life and teachings of Jesus as expressed in the New Testament. Thus, the word of God is found in these sources and has often been open to wide interpretation, depending on the particular interpreter.

2. What is real? (The ontology of the religious view)

Life is meaningful and purposeful. Since it is part of a grand scheme or plan, everything in life has value and intrinsic worth. Our experiences with other humans, our feelings of love and hate, our passions, our selfishness, and our compassion are all part of being a "child of God" and are, therefore, real.

Man's basic depravity and sinfulness is an emphasis in the Christian view although less so in the Jewish view. For the Christian, it is through union with God that one may overcome these tendencies, whereas Judaism emphasizes obedience to God's laws. The forgiveness of God and the fact that one can earn forgiveness for sinful acts is an important part of religious reality.

3. What is good? (The axiology of the religious view)

Man himself is of basic worth and value (since he is created in the image of God). Thus, any society that provides for the development of man is good. Love and social usefulness are also important virtues.

In reading these brief descriptions of the religious view, you must keep in mind that religion is diverse in scope, personal in its usefulness, and fundamental in its importance to most cultures and society. For many people, religion is the rock upon which they build their lives, their beliefs, and their course of action. Any study or discussion of an enterprise so human as human development would be remiss indeed if it failed to note the significance of religion to the process of becoming a more fully human individual.

PRAGMATISM

A recent and particularly American philosophical development that emerged partly as a protest against the more classical and religious philosophies is called pragmatism (it is also often referred to as experimentalism). This movement, led by such men as John Dewey (1859–1952) and William James (1842–1910), flourished in the developing technological and highly functional American society.

1. What is true? (The epistemology of pragmatism)

To the pragmatist, truth is defined merely as that which works or functions well. Thus, the pragmatist's final payoff is to test out an idea or to solve a problem and let the results or consequences of that idea or the solution of the problem be the test of its validity. If the idea works to a certain degree, then it is valid. Thus, truth is more a matter of degree rather than an all or none proposition.

2. What is real? (The ontology of the pragmatist)

The pragmatist views reality as more of a process than a thing. Reality thus becomes the results of our experiences in relating to the world through our various senses (seeing, hearing, touching). Thus, reality is closely related to the activities of knowing, searching, and problem-solving activities. Specifically, it is related to the result of scientific finding that is a result of the use of the experimental method.

3. What is good? (The axiology of the pragmatist)

This question is answered by the pragmatist in a similar vein. What is good is what works. Thus an act is judged by its outcome. For example, if an act brings about better living conditions for more people, it is good; if it creates still more problems, it is not.

One of the most influential philosophers to develop the theory of pragmatism was John Dewey (1969). Many of his writings apply to education and children as well as to other areas of life. Daley (1966) summarizes some of these as follows:

1. Dewey was influenced by the theory of evolution. He affirmed that the mind as well as the body evolved. Ideas arise from experience and are nothing more than plans of action by which the organism adjusts satisfactorily to his environment.

2. The truths of philosophy are not privileged. If the scientist must subject his hypothesis to the careful scrutiny of controlled observations and verification, so must the philosopher. Through inquiry, collecting facts, experimentation and verification will the philosopher provide new truths.

3. The best form of government is democratic government. The cornerstone of Dewey's thought is growth. What contributes to individual and social growth is good.

4. The school is a miniature community. It provides for social and individual growth. He rejected the teaching of subjects for their own sake. Any subject is merely a means and not an end in itself. It is the means by which the individual reconstructs his experience, extracts its meaning and thereby prepares himself for the future.

5. Discipline is internal and positive. A pupil must be trained to consider his actions so that he will undertake them with deliberation.

6. Children must never be treated exactly alike. Each child has needs and experiences which are uniquely his own. The child should be interested in and disciplined toward the development and maintenance of intelligence on an individual basis. Since society changes, the individual pupil must learn how to think in order to cope with a changing environment. (p. 107)

Pragmatism has permeated every fiber of our society. It has shaped a liberal tradition in politics, education, and technology. The pragmatic philosophy is directed toward using man's creative processes to make things work for man's eventual betterment. The pragmatist organizes the resources of his society in an effort to improve human life and its environment.

Philosophical
Perspectives

39

EXISTENTIALISM

Another recent philosophy to develop, as a reaction against some of the classical philosophies, is existentialism. The development of this point of view can be traced from writings in religion and literature as well as philosophy and psychology. Let us look at how this world view answers the three basic questions.

1. What is true? (The epistemology of existentialism)

The existentialist places all his eggs in the "basket called man." That is, truth is based purely on the feelings and decisions of the unique, free, individual being. In a sense, we all must come to grips with our own intuitions and inner voices and relate these to the world around us in order to find our own personal truths.

In this view, truth does not rest so much upon some ideal concepts of what *should* be nor does it rest upon some external force or on the basis of a certain set of "operations for finding truth." Truth rests upon the shoulders of each one of us since each of us is unique, an individual existing and growing into our own selfhood.

2. What is real? (The ontology of existentialism)

Man by the nature of his existence has the freedom and choice to determine what to do with his life. The first task is to determine who he is as a living, existing being. Once he has examined and accepted his existence, he then can *himself* decide what reality is for him. Thus, experience is a highly personal and subjective thing. It is our interpretation of our experiences that makes our reality.

3. What is good? (The axiology of the existentialist)

What is good is a function of the existence of the individual at that moment. What is good is a result of the freedom of choice that each of us exercises at any moment in time.

Thus, what is good is realizing that one has this freedom of choice or freedom of existence. Along with this freedom comes the responsibility for making the decisions and choices that you have made, for living the life that you live.

As we mentioned earlier, existentialism has had an impact not only on the development of philosophy but in other areas such as religion, literature, and the social sciences, particularly psychology. In fact, existentialism has been indirectly responsible for a new movement in psychology called variously The Third Force, Existential Psychology, and Humanistic Psychology. Rollo May (1961) discusses its development in the United States as follows:

> It is a curious paradox, we note at the outset, that whereas there is a great deal of hostility and outright anger in this country toward existential psychology, there is at the same time a deep underlying affinity between this approach and our American character and thought in psychology as well as in other areas. The existential approach, for example, is very close to the thought of William James. Take, for example, his emphasis on the immediacy of experience and the union of thought and action, emphasis which became passionate in James as it had been in Kierkegaard. Indeed, when Kierkegaard proclaims, "Truth exists for the individual only as he himself produces it in action," the words have a familiar echo to those of us raised in the American pragmatic tradition. Another aspect in

William James that expresses the same approach to reality as existential psychology is the importance of decision and commitment—his argument that you cannot know truth by sitting in a detached armchair, but that willing and decision are themselves prerequisites to the discovery of truth. Furthermore, his humaneness and his great breadth as a human being enabled him to bring art and religion into this thought without sacrificing his scientific integrity, another parallel to the existential psychologists. (p. 12)

The humanistic psychologist's basic positions are summarized as follows:
1. Human behavior cannot adequately be described by analogy to sub-human species.
2. Meaningful human experiences should be topics for study by humanistic psychologists. We should design and conduct studies based on their relevance to meaningful experience rather than on the methods that are currently available to us.
3. Man's subjective experience is the quality that makes him human, not just his actions.
4. There is no pure science without application. To try to separate them is artificial.
5. Humanistic psychology should be concerned with the individual and the exceptional circumstance, rather than trying to fit all humans into conformitive and predictable behavior patterns.
6. Humanistic psychology should seek to enrich man's experience and capabilities.

The implications of existentialism as translated through humanistic psychology are explored in later sections of the text. One of the most significant implications of this position insofar as children and adolescents are concerned is pointed out in the premise that, in man, essence precedes existence. We *are* first; then we begin to look for a definition for the "we." We have all experienced that dawning of realization, that existential moment, when we recognize our own existence. It doesn't matter how you got here, or why. You are here—now—a person. You are no longer an essence; you are now committed to existence.

A Summary and Comparison of the Different Philosophies

Now that we have surveyed five of the most influential philosophies of man, let us briefly summarize these in a table format so that you may see some of the basic similarities and differences of these philosophies. Table 3-2 presents a brief overview of these philosophies, along with their approach to the three basic philosophical questions.

We have also identified some men who were originally associated with these movements. It should be noted that many other philosophers contributed to these points of view as the years progressed. The later contributors and the changes they brought about to the movements are discussed more fully in the references listed. These references are all from secondary sources since we believe that from these the reader will get a better overall perspective of the particular philosophical position. The reader is, however, encouraged to seek original sources whenever his time and interest permits.

Philosophical Perspectives

TABLE 3–2
AN OUTLINE OF FIVE BASIC PHILOSOPHIC POSITIONS

Name of Philosophy	Philosophers	When?	What Is True?	What Is Real?	What Is Good?	Some Basic References
Idealism	Plato	427–347 B.C.	Ideas as conceived by the mind.	The mind as it reflects upon the "real" world.	Development of mind in order to determine external truth and ideas.	Ewing (1957) Tomlin (1968) Radhakrishnan (1951)
Realism	Aristotle	384–322 B.C.	Reality as it is found in the environment.	Objects and things in the real world.	That which is discovered through study and contemplation of nature.	Sahakian (1968) Watson (1963)
Religious View	Jesus Christ St. Augustine	354–430	The word of God as revealed in the Bible, revelation, and the teachings of Jesus.	Man, being a "child" of God, is a part of the universe and his behavior is a reflection of the reality of life.	Man himself is of value since he is created in the image of God.	Titus (1970) Butler (1957)
Pragmatism	John Dewey William James	1859–1952 1842–1910	That which works or functions well.	The results of our experiences through such processes as problem solving and searching.	The consequences for the community are the basic criteria of "goodness."	Nakosteen (1965) Power (1970)
Existentialism	Kierkegaard Jaspers Buber Sartre	1813–1855 1883–1969 1878–1965 1905–	That which man arrives at through decision and choice.	Man's existence as a unique being with free will is the prime reality.	What is "good" is man's facing up to his freedom of being and accepting this freedom with all its frustration.	May (1961) Bugental (1967)

Although the five basic views discussed earlier have had the greatest impact on thoughts about children and adolescents (as seen in the next section), there have been a number of other contributions from men who are not necessarily associated with one of these five basic positions. In order to include some of these important influences upon modern-day views of children and adolescents, we have summarized them in Table 3–3. Again, the reader is encouraged to do further study on his own using the cited references.

Multi-disciplinary Perspectives

42

TABLE 3–3

ADDITIONAL CONTRIBUTORS TO A PHILOSOPHY OF CHILDHOOD AND ADOLESCENCE

Name	Philosophical Category	Dates	Basic Contributions	References
Jan Amos Comenius	Educational Philosopher and Realist	1592–1670	—Developmental stages related to types of learning. —Importance of learning through senses. —Importance of preschool learning at home.	Boyd (1965) Daley (1966)
John Locke	Philosopher and Empiricist	1623–1704	—Child's mind at birth a "blank slate." —All ideas come from experience. —All differences among children are due to environment. —A newborn child is not a "miniature adult."	Tomlin (1968)
Jean Jacques Rousseau	Romantic Naturalism	1712–1778	—Children born essentially "good." —Evils of society corrupt children. —Importance of natural development of children reared in nature.	Good and Teller (1960) Stott (1967) Rousseau (1902)
Charles Darwin	Scientist	1809–1882	—Man a part of nature (not a divine creature). —Evolutionary principles applied to all organisms. —Survival of fittest principle.	Stott (1967)

IMPLICATIONS

Now that you have some ideas about five of the most influential philosophical positions, you might be asking such questions as: So what? What difference does a philosophy make with respect to children and adolescents? How is philosophy related to the other disciplines: history, sociology, anthropology, biology, and psychology? How do philosophical positions affect society in general? How do they affect the various institutions such as the family, education, government, and business? And finally, what are the implications of philosophy for me, for the individual in his own sphere of existence?

UNDERSTANDING YOURSELF AND OTHERS

What relevance do these philosophies have for you in your personal life? In a sense we feel that our discussion of different views of man may help you examine the makeup of your own "world view." In order to show you the relevance of these philosophies in your own life, how they developed, and how they relate to other areas of study and behavior, we will use the analogy of "building a house." We are aware of the limitations in using and

Philosophical Perspectives

stretching such an analogy too far, yet, we believe that it will be worthwhile to visually depict the very complex process of "philosophy building" that occurs right under the noses of the almost totally unaware architects—our parents. Let us begin with the starting point in building a house, the foundation.

Building the Philosophical Foundation. As we have seen, over the span of centuries a number of ideas of man, his nature, and his relationship to the world developed. Of these, in the Western world at least, five appear to be "world views" that have influenced and continue to influence many of the underlying principles of Western thought. These five views, then, might be thought of as the foundation upon which much of our life is based. These views, as the foundation of most houses, are hidden from view; yet they not only support the structure of the house but have a lot to do with the design, how temporary or permanent the house will be, and how much stress or strain it will take from storms or earthquakes.

Constructing the Supports. What is it that gives a house its basic character, its strength, and holds it together over time, helping to preserve its basic structure and appearance? The supports and walls upon which the roof rests, of course. In our analogy, the supports symbolize the basic structures through which the individual learns such things as who he is, what is of value, how much worth he has, what opportunities he has in life, or whether he wants to succeed in certain areas of life. In a sense then, the pillars represent the various processes through which all children and adolescents go to become unique individuals.

These structures include such things as the various institutions through which the socialization process occurs: family, education, government, and religion. You can see how these basic, underlying foundation philosophies are translated (sometimes in very outward or overt ways and sometimes in very covert or subtle ways) into everyday behavior that affects the developing personality of the child and adolescent.

Development of the "Shingled Self." As you will see later in the text, the child as he develops under the influences of the major institutions (especially family and education) is a product of forces at work in four areas that affect behavior; the cognitive, affective, biological, and social. The composition of the roof (the emerging personality of the individual) is thus composed of shingles that are related to what you learned in the family, education, government, and religion.

As can be seen in Figure 3-1, the shingles are attached to the four behavioral domains of an individual and are related to certain variables under each category. Such variables as how a person thinks and feels about himself and others (cognitive and affective domain), how a person views society (social domain), and how healthy he may be (biological domain) are all largely a function of the institutions (supports) upon which his personality (the roof) rests.

Figure 3-1 visually illustrates this "house that philosophy built." In it you may be able to better appreciate the relationship between philosophy (a study of the basic "world views"), sociology (a study of the major institutions of society through which these philosophical views are most frequently translated), and psychology (a study of the developing person as he grows in the four major areas of his behavior—cognitive, affective, social, and biological).

Multi-
disciplinary
Perspectives

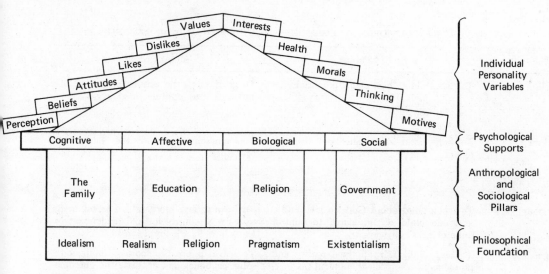

FIG. 3–1. *The relationship between philosophy, sociology, psychology, and individual behavior.*

Looking at Your Parents' Philosophy. Most of your attitudes about the world came from some very important people in your life, your parents. We now know that most of the attitudes, beliefs, and feelings that people have about themselves and others originate to a large degree from the kinds of interactions they have had with their parents. The kinds of interactions that parents have with their children result to a large extent from their parents' basic philosophy about man in general. That is, if a parent's view tends to be more toward the notion of man's basically evil nature, he will probably rear his children differently than a parent who believes in man's basic goodness and the encouragement and nurturing of this beauty and goodness.

What we are saying is that it may help you to understand how some of your basic underlying philosophical leanings developed by looking at and discussing some of these leanings with your parents.

LIVING AND WORKING WITH CHILDREN, ADOLESCENTS, AND ADULTS

We have summarized some specific implications of these five philosophical positions, in Table 3–4, according to some of the applications to certain areas of developmental psychology. From these applications, you can see how different theories may be translated into actual role prescriptions. Try to see some of your own roles. Think about which ones your parents leaned toward. Consider which ones you agree or disagree with.

To give some examples of the behavioral consequences of parents with different philosophical positions, let us look at some hypothetical situations. In doing so, we should note that family philosophical styles are rarely of one type; that is, you will find strands of different philosophies guiding family interactions.

The Traditional and/or Classical Philosophical Family Style. Families in which the parents tend to believe in some of the more traditional approaches such as idealism or realism probably value highly such ideas as reason (or rationalism), beauty, form, the sacredness of honesty, logic, and clear think-

Philosophical
Perspectives

45

TABLE 3–4
IMPLICATIONS OF VARIOUS PHILOSOPHICAL POSITIONS FOR CHILDREN AND ADOLESCENTS

Philosophy	Role of Parent	Role of Child
Idealism	To rear child to best of his potential.	To go through the various periods of life and find your position in society.
Realism	To help child appreciate and discover reality.	To train senses to study the "basic laws of nature."
Religious View	To teach child about God; to love child; to guide child as he learns to control some of his "evil ways."	To learn to love God and his fellow men; to learn to control his evil tendencies; to learn how to ask forgiveness.
Pragmatism	To help child learn to face reality and problems in a logical, thoughtful manner.	To learn to use the tools of intellect to solve problems and evaluate the outcome in human terms.
Existentialism	Give child freedom to be and become.	Child assumes freedom with responsibility to make his own choices.

ing. This family would have many "ideals" the children would have to live up to. There would be a tendency in this family to highly value education, learning, and the development of the self. Art, poetry, and music would be encouraged at an early age, and an emphasis on social service to the government and others would be fostered.

Since reason is considered by this family as one of the highest virtues, control over one's emotions and basic urges is to be encouraged. To be carried away at times or to lose control is considered a weakness. Guilt would probably play an important role in such families, since the child would always have a higher and more virtuous goal to achieve in learning, thinking, and reasoning.

Such families are probably rare in today's world—since children are influenced so much by other institutions in our culture such as education, business and industry, religion, and the mass media.

The Religious Family Style. This family would probably emphasize the traditional religious views that underlie many modern-day religions. The innate depravity of the child is an important concept in many of these families. Training the child to do the right thing is most important—even if it means physical punishment of the child. Living up to the Ten Commandments is considered a basic rule. Guilt plays a role in these types of families, and confession is used by many religious groups to handle these feelings.

The significance of life and the nurturance of life is also considered important as is the love of children. The child's relationship to a divine God is stressed. The child, all too often, goes against this "God," and a sin takes place. Yet, this "Being" is a very loving and tender person, and forgiveness may be achieved if it is asked for.

The basic dignity of life and man is stressed in this home. Helping others

Multi-
disciplinary
Perspectives

46

Role of Family	Goals of Child Rearing	Goals of Education
To train child to take his part in the "ideal state."	To help child find his place in life.	To train his mind to study and reflect the "ideal" essences of the world (study of literature, history, etc.).
To prepare child to relate to "real world."	To develop the ability to reason and use logic in examining reality.	To train senses to observe reality as is (study of physical world through the "exact sciences" such as mathematics, physical sciences, etc.).
To rear children to believe in God and dignity of life; especially life hereafter.	To prepare child for life after death by training him to live a "good" life without sin.	To encourage moral values as expressed in life of Jesus. To teach about dignity of life.
To help child learn to work for common good of community and others.	To train child to think clearly and to work for good of community.	To help child to learn through experiences found through living in and solving problems of real world.
Provide atmosphere where basic "existence" and being of family members is allowed.	To allow the child to have the courage to be. To rear child to realize the freedom, choice, and responsibility in being alive and human.	To experientially relate to the "being" and existence of all life as a part of growth and education.

and doing well toward his fellow man are encouraged. In many of these families, religion provides a kind of saving up for "the next life," the idea that what good you do here on earth will all "pay off" later on. So the emphasis is placed on hard work and doing good to others. Many of you know families where such religious philosophy plays a major role.

The Pragmatic Philosophical Family Style. A family whose philosophical position is based mainly on an objective, scientific and/or a practical view of man would emphasize some of the basic problem-solving methods that are used in interactions with the world. The assessment and careful analysis of problems as they arise before one acts would be stressed.

The use of logic and strategies for attacking problems would be fostered at an early age in these families and emotional outbursts and emotional solutions to problems would not be encouraged. These families would be very task oriented toward achieving a goal and would make a careful analysis and evaluation before setting out on another project. This family would encourage very pragmatic type interactions with the world. For example, "Is it useful?" and "Is it functional?" would be the main questions asked and answered before this family decided to buy something.

A child in such a family might tend to look upon others as to how useful they would be to his ultimate purposes. That is, he may tend to use people as means to his own ends.

The parents would foster early independence of the child and allow him to "work out" his own solutions. If the child makes mistakes, all the better; he can then analyze where he made them and learn not to repeat them.

These families would also be concerned with social problems and improving the society in which they live. They would encourage their children to be active problem solvers in community and school projects.

Perspectives
Philosophical

This pattern of family life is also probably familiar to many of you, for it and the religious orientation are the two dominant patterns of much of middle-class America. Such families would tend to produce a person who fits into our educational and business institutions very well. These types of individuals often tend to make very efficient scientists and professional and business workers.

The Existential or Humanistic Philosophical Family Style. Freedom and choice would be the guiding themes in an existential family pattern. The child would be allowed to grow into whatever he or she chose. There would be very little in the way of rules and regulations in such a family. Guilt would play a minimal role. A high degree of freedom to feel would be encouraged. There would be little or no disciplining of children.

Role conflicts would not arise among family members since there would essentially be no roles. (That is, mother, father, son, and daughter would all be free to be their own—"mother-father.") There would be little or no expectation of what role each family member should play. The emphasis in this family would be the freedom to grow—to become. Hence, no two days would be the same.

There is a very real danger that children in such families will not be able to fit into the educational system with its highly structured roles and games. These children may also find it hard to adapt to the world of work.

Since competition and working hard and long for an end goal may be foreign to such families, financial problems may occur frequently. These families would tend to encourage personal expression of feelings through the arts, such as writing and painting.

As you might imagine, a person reared in a family with an existential foundation would have some problems adjusting to many of the demands in the Western world. He may have problems conforming to some of the expectations of education and later of the business world. We find that many of our students tend to be leaning more toward this position. Many young people today are trying experiments in existential communal living. The results of these experiments are too new to permit us to make a complete evaluation, but they seem to offer a way to allow for some of the freedom of self to be expressed and experienced in a "subculture" of our society.

DEVELOPING POSITIVE MODELS

What can we conclude from our venture into some of the philosophical foundations of the Western world? We can see how the acceptance of certain views of man do, in fact, have profound implications for our psychology of human development.

In a sense, you might look upon these philosophical views and their development as fundamental to an understanding of the nature of mankind in general and a newborn infant in particular. Such questions as:

Is man basically evil?

Is man basically good?

Is man born with a predestined personality?

Is man born with a "blank slate" upon which parents and society inscribe his life pattern?

At another level, all philosophies may be looked upon as raising the basic question of how "free" is the newborn child? How many "degrees of freedom" does a newborn have to become whatever he will become? How much

Multi-disciplinary Perspectives

48

of a child's personality is related to his parents, society, his biology, and his basic intelligence? Does the newborn child have any freedom?

Do parents have much freedom to help the child become something they wish him to become? Or, do parents have little or no influence on what the child may become since the child is already programmed by a "master plan" written in the genes?

We certainly must be aware of the effects of man's biology, society, and intellect on his growth; all these influences are discussed in the remainder of the book. But we are equally convinced of the fact that man has far more freedom than he realizes. The newborn child would have a large amount of "wiggle room" for growth and actualization if parents were only more aware of this. We are furthermore convinced of the fact that man can actualize far more of his potential than was ever thought possible.

CHAPTER REFERENCES

BOYD, W. *The history of Western education*. New York: Barnes & Noble, 1965.

BUGENTAL, J. F. T. (ed.). *Challenge of humanistic psychology*. New York: McGraw-Hill, 1967.

BUTLER, J. D. *Four philosophies and their practice in education and religion*. New York: Harper, 1957.

DALEY, L. C. *The history of education*. New York: Monarch, 1966.

DEWEY, J. The new era in home and school. In Margaret Gillet (ed.), *Readings in the history of education*. Toronto, Ont.: McGraw-Hill, Canada, 1969.

EWING, A. C. (ed.). *The idealist tradition: from Berkeley to Blanshard*. New York: Free Press, 1957.

GOOD, H. G., and J. D. TELLER. *A history of Western education*. New York: Macmillan, 1960.

MAY, R. *Existential psychology*. New York: Random, 1961.

MORRIS, V. C. *Philosophy and the American school*. Boston: Houghton, 1961.

NAKOSTEEN, N. *The history and philosophy of education*. New York: Ronald, 1965.

POWER, E. J. *Main currents in the history of education*. New York: McGraw-Hill, 1970.

RADHAKRISHNAN, S. *An idealist view of life*. London: Allen & Unwin, 1951.

ROUSSEAU, J. J. Infancy and general principles. In William H. Payne (tr.), *Emile*. London: E. Arnold, 1902.

SAHAKIAN, W. S. *History of philosophy*. New York: Barnes & Noble, 1968.

STOTT, L. H. *Child development*. New York: Holt, 1967.

TITUS, H. H. *Living issues in philosophy*. New York: Van Nostrand, 1970.

TOMLIN, E. W. F. *The Western philosophers: an introduction*. London: Hutchinson, 1968.

WATSON, R. I. *The great psychologists from Aristotle to Freud*. Philadelphia: Lippincott, 1963.

RECOMMENDED FURTHER READING

ADLER, M. *The conditions of philosophy*. New York: Dell, 1967.

ADLER, M. J. *The difference of man and the difference it makes*. New York: Holt, 1967.

AUNE, B. *Knowledge, mind, and nature*. New York: Random, 1967.

BURTT, E. A. *In search of philosophical understanding*. New York: New Am. Lib., 1965.

Philosophical Perspectives

Downs, R. B. *Molders of the modern mind: books that shaped Western civilization.* New York: Barnes & Noble, 1961.

Edwards, P. (ed.). *The encyclopedia of philosophy,* 8 vols. New York: Macmillan, and Free Press, 1967.

Heinemann, F. H. *Existentialism and the modern predicament.* New York: Harper, 1958.

Hook, S. (ed.). *Determinism and freedom.* New York: Collier Books, 1961.

Maslow, A. H. (ed.). *New knowledge in human values.* New York: Harper, 1959.

Rorty, A. (ed.). *Pragmatic philosophy: an anthology.* Garden City, N. Y.: Doubleday, 1966.

Titus, H. H., and M. H. Hepp (eds.). *The range of philosophy: introductory readings,* 2nd ed. New York: Van Nostrand, 1970.

Anthropological Perspectives

Prelude
Basic Theory and Research
  The Pluralistic Nature of Our
    Society
  The Polish
  The French
  The Italians
  The German
  The Spanish-Speaking
  Cross-National Child-Rearing
    Practices
  The United States and
    Germany
  The United States and
    England
  The United States and the
    Soviet Union
  Tapping Our Rich Cultural
    Resources

Implications
  Understanding Yourself and
    Others
  Living and Working with Chil-
    dren, Adolescents, and Adults
  Developing Positive Models

PRELUDE

THE SCIENCE of anthropology provides us with another important means for acquiring a better understanding of ourselves as well as of children and adolescents. Anthropology is selective in its approach to the study of man. Anthropology is partly biological because it deals with the origins of man and variations in the human species, and it is partly a social science because it deals with a comparative analysis of different cultures both preliterate and literate. It is also part of the humanities because it is concerned with the history, mythology, and literature of man and his cultures.

This chapter highlights selected aspects of cultural anthropology in order to increase our insights into the society of all mankind, our pluralistic society, and the highly personal world within. All this will add to our perspectives on human development.

The basic assumption underlying many cross-cultural studies of child-rearing practices is that the early years of life form the foundation for later personality; hence, similar childhoods will produce similar adult personalities. Since a culture determines the what, how, and why of learning, a given culture should produce fairly distinctive personality types. Future parents, in turn, tend to perpetuate the distinctive personality types by rearing their children mainly in the manner of their own upbringing.

You should be aware of certain limitations that characterize this approach: (1) the heredity of the individual plays a significant, although as yet unspecified, role in personality development; (2) the different cultures tolerate varying amounts of variation in individual behaviors; (3) the time gap between childhood and adulthood, especially long in the United States, can produce some significant variations in mature personalities; and (4) even when the cultural heritage is relatively simple and unchanging for all members of the society, its effects would not be the same because of different interpretations of the same regulations, customs, and attitudes. Thus, we should avoid stereotyping human beings, fitting them into neat classifications of personality types based solely on their national origin or descent.

The major emphasis in this chapter is on demographic information about five ethnic minorities (the Polish, the French, the Italian, the German, and the Spanish-speaking), and on cross-cultural comparisons of child-rearing practices in the United States with those in England, Germany, and the Soviet Union.

BASIC THEORY AND RESEARCH

According to Astronaut Frank Borman (1969) "We are one hunk of ground, water, air, clouds, floating around in space. From out there it really is one world." Certainly the view of the world from lunar orbit is distinctly different from the disjointed picture put together by the millions of observers located around the earth. The 3.5 billion riders on the earth, seated on their 130 or so pieces of real estate while cruising through endless tracks of cold nothingness, tend to forget that they are all passengers sharing the same little fragile ship on an eternal voyage.

Multi-disciplinary Perspectives

Although we are widely separated geographically, as well as by different cultures, languages, attitudes, and political and religious loyalties, we can

TABLE 4-1

IMMIGRANTS ADMITTED, BY COUNTRY OR REGION OF BIRTH: YEARS ENDED
JUNE 30, 1958–1967

Country or Region of Birth	1958–1967	Country or Region of Birth	1958–1967
All countries	2,914,673	North America	1,092,102
Europe	1,312,623	Canada	310,746
		Mexico	393,103
Austria	17,090	Cuba	154,257
Belgium	10,187	Barbados	4,543
Czechoslovakia	19,303	Dominican Republic	66,186
Denmark	13,664	Haiti	19,497
Finland	6,652	Jamaica	25,938
France	39,237	Trinidad & Tobago	6,132
Germany	260,422	St. Christopher	2,461
Greece	54,383	Other West Indies	16,963
Hungary	50,593	British Honduras	2,919
Ireland	61,281	Costa Rica	14,552
Italy	190,130	El Salvador	12,430
Netherlands	35,617	Guatemala	10,712
Norway	21,338	Honduras	13,852
Poland	82,511	Nicaragua	12,151
Portugal	48,684	Panama	18,147
Rumania	13,024	Other North America	7,513
Spain	21,792		
Sweden	20,220		
Switzerland	18,047	South America	194,277
Turkey (Europe and Asia)	11,577	Argentina	38,820
United Kingdom	245,904	Bolivia	6,044
U.S.S.R. (Europe and		Brazil	18,273
Asia)	20,182	Chile	11,136
Yugoslavia	31,280	Colombia	57,478
Other Europe	19,505	Ecuador	27,769
Asia	274,108	Peru	18,365
		Venezuela	8,712
China (includes Taiwan)	67,047	Other South America	7,740
Hong Kong	14,228	Africa	27,183
India	11,865		
Indonesia	15,712	Cape Verde Island	580
Iran	7,105	Morocco	3,120
Iraq	4,141	South Africa	3,784
Israel	13,358	United Arab Republic	
Japan	44,331	(Egypt)	9,266
Jordan	8,209	Other Africa	10,433
Korea	21,458		
Lebanon	4,794	Oceania	14,248
Pakistan	2,317		
Philippines	40,710	Australia	7,427
Ryukyu Islands	3,942	Fiji	992
Syrian Arab Republic	2,699	New Zealand	2,844
Vietnam	1,690	Other Oceania	2,985
Other Asia	10,502	Other countries	132

From Department of Justice, Immigration and Naturalization Service. *Annual Report 1967.*
p. 61. (Andersson and Boyer, 1970)

Anthropological Perspectives

become more united, and add immeasurably to our wisdom of childhood, by studying other cultures as well as our own. Cultural anthropological studies are of particular importance to us because the United States since its earliest days has had immigrants from a wide variety of different cultures, as noted in Table 4–1. In this respect, the United States may be considered the best single representative of a world society.

The Pluralistic Nature of Our Society

The United States is often referred to as "a nation of immigrants" or "the great melting pot." Table 4–2 gives some indication of annual immigration to the United States. As a young people we do not have direct ethnic roots in the past as do many other people whose cultures date back thousands of years. Americans had to establish their unique national characteristics relatively quickly. Americanization of the new immigrants was achieved essentially through education. The process has been quite successful partly because many new arrivals came with "Old World wariness" and a desire for a new life style. Fortunately, assimilation of the newly arrived was not total. The openness of the American social system has permitted some accommodations to new values and traditions. In fact, some ethnic groups still maintain cultural and language loyalties to their old countries even into the third generation. It is, we believe, both the understanding and assimilation of different cultures that has created the ever-changing and dynamic culture in which we live. All Americans should understand and take pride in the many voices, the many cultures, and the many languages that have added strength, beauty, and diversification to our culture.

TABLE 4–2
ANNUAL IMMIGRATION IN SELECTED
YEARS, 1820–1960

1820	8,385
1830	23,322
1840	84,066
1850	369,980
1860	153,640
1870	387,203
1880	457,257
1890	455,302
1900	448,572
1910	1,041,570
1920	430,001
1930	241,700
1940	70,756
1950	249,187
1960	265,398

From U.S. Bureau of the Census. *Historical Statistics.* pp. 56–57. (Andersson and Boyer, 1970)

Multi-
disciplinary
Perspectives

The Polish

Polish is the fourth most common foreign language spoken in the United States. According to the New Catholic Encyclopedia of 1967, this country has approximately 6.5 million citizens of Polish descent, the largest Polish population in any country outside of Poland itself. In 1960, Chicago claimed 700,000 residents of Polish descent, making it the American city with the largest Polish community and the second largest Polish city, after Warsaw, in the world. Although many Polish Americans have been able to maintain a high degree of loyalty to their mother culture and language, there has been a gradual disappearance of many of their distinctive ethnic characteristics.

The French

Well over a million people in the United States speak French, making it the fifth most common foreign language. It is preceded only by Italian, Spanish, German, and Polish, and followed by Hebrew. The largest concentration of French-speaking Americans are of Canadian origin and reside in New England and another half million live in Louisiana. Compared with most other groups of immigrants the Franco-American culture has survived with surprising vigor since Colonial times.

Fewer and fewer Americans today claim French as their mother tongue. Table 4–3 indicates the number of foreign-born French speakers in those states in which they are most populous.

TABLE 4–3
FOREIGN-BORN FRENCH BY STATES

Rank	State	French-Mother-Tongue Foreign-Born Residents of State
1	Massachusetts	59,032
2	New York	56,412
3	California	34,765
4	Connecticut	23,295
5	Maine	21,091
6	New Hampshire	17,640
7	Michigan	15,951
8	Rhode Island	14,542
9	New Jersey	10,898
10	Vermont	9,129
11	Florida	9,048
12	Illinois	8,585
13	Pennsylvania	7,039
14	Ohio	5,233
15	Texas	3,223

From U.S. Bureau of the Census, 1960. (Andersson and Boyer, 1970)

The Italians

Italians in the United States constitute the second largest ethnic minority group. Even as late as 1960 the number of Italian-speaking (foreign born) residents of the United States was more than 3.5 million. (See Table 4–4.) Despite their large number and relatively recent arrival in this country, the

Anthropological Perspectives

majority of Italian immigrants have been readily "Americanized" in their language and culture.

The reasons for this changeover have been attributed to the lack of awareness, on their part, of the great cultural heritage associated with the Italian language. Many of the immigrants were from rural areas of Italy and did not bring with them the sense of cultural pride that belonged to their more urban counterparts in Italy.

TABLE 4–4
FOREIGN BORN ITALIANS BY STATES

Rank	State	Number of Italian-Mother-Tongue Foreign-Born
1	New York	445,908
2	New Jersey	139,696
3	Pennsylvania	132,780
4	California	106,823
5	Massachusetts	87,672
6	Illinois	73,360
7	Connecticut	65,889
8	Ohio	50,827
9	Michigan	38,111
10	Rhode Island	18,634
11	Florida	16,559
12	Maryland	10,530
13	Missouri	9,233
14	Wisconsin	8,709
15	Washington	6,218

From U.S. Bureau of the Census, 1960. (Andersson and Boyer, 1970)

The Germans

Speakers of German comprise the third largest ethnic minority; however, if we sum up the total number of German-speaking immigrants since 1700 they would constitute the largest subgroup in the United States. The following is an analysis of the most recent data on German-speaking Americans (Andersson and Boyer, 1970):

The 1960 census placed the number of foreign-born whose mother tongue was German at 1,278,000. On the other hand, 4,320,100 individuals of foreign stock (i.e., foreign born and children of foreign-born) named Germany as their country of origin. Since in recent years we can only (at best) expect the children of German immigrants, but never their grandchildren, to consider German as their native tongue, the number of American residents whose mother tongue was German was unlikely to have been much above the 4 million mark in 1960. It is also important to realize that a great many "German speakers" came to the United States from countries other than Germany. In the 18th century and until the 1870's, these came mainly from Switzerland, Alsace-Lorraine, and Lux-

Multi-disciplinary Perspectives

56

embourg. After 1880 many also came from eastern Europe. In 1910, 1,100,000 persons of "foreign white stock" who claimed German as their mother tongue claimed a country of origin other than Germany. A majority came from Austria-Hungary (374,000), Russia (former boundaries, 245,000), and Switzerland (263,000). No other single country of origin was reported by more than 40,000 claimants of German mother tongue.

Prior to World War I, most German-Americans maintained strong ties with the mother culture. They established a number of private, parochial, and public schools where subjects were taught in both English and German. After World Wars I and II, there were sharp declines in the use of the German language partly as a result of intense anti-German sentiment.

The Spanish-Speaking

The Spanish-speaking communities in the United States constitute, numerically and culturally, the most important ethnic minority group. Approximately 80 per cent of the 5 million Americans of Mexican ancestry live in California, Arizona, New Mexico, Texas, and Colorado (Forbes, 1970). The tenacious preservation by the Mexican-American of his language and culture is little understood by most other Americans. The Mexican-American, like many immigrant Jews to this country, often seeks to obtain what is good and of benefit to him and his family in American society without losing the ethnic identity or the customs and traditions of the old country. Many, but not all, Mexican-Americans preserve their contacts with the people and institutions of old Mexico and take great pride in the history and culture of their ancestors. In recent years, there has been a great deal of interest among young Mexican-American intellectuals in promoting this sense of identity and pride among Mexican-Americans. The term *la raza*, for example, means race, but it evokes far more in feelings of brotherhood and comradeship.

It is informative to note that the cultural heritage of most Mexican-Americans can be traced back to the Indian builders of the magnificent cities of Teotihuacán, Monte Albán, and Chichén Itzá. Many Mexican-Americans are thus a racial as well as a cultural minority.

Puerto Ricans living in this country number about 1.5 million and are ranked second to the Mexican-Americans among Spanish-speaking citizens. They are concentrated in New York, New Jersey, Illinois, California, Pennsylvania, Florida, and Connecticut. In general, Puerto Ricans are more fully assimilated into the American culture than Mexican-Americans partly because English is compulsory in the school system of Puerto Rico. The study of English is valued by Puerto Ricans prior to their migration and urban orientation.

We have limited this brief description of ethnic minority groups to these five to illustrate the pluralistic nature of our society. Although about 90 per cent of our population are native speakers of English and have already contributed much of their cultural and linguistic treasures to the "national melting pot," millions remain waiting to share their cultural riches with us. Therefore, we should continue to study these cultures and others not only in order to understand our neighbors better but also to improve the national lifestyle. For example, it is not difficult to realize that many Americans with their plumbing, television, and mass transportation are no nearer the limits of human potential than are many speakers of Spanish with their stable

Anthropological Perspectives

and effective family structure, and their tradition of racial and ethnic tolerance.

CROSS-NATIONAL CHILD-REARING PRACTICES

We believe that additional insights into childhood can be achieved by comparing our child-rearing practices with those of other nations. In so doing, caution is required because child-rearing practices can vary dramatically within the same nation, practices change with time, the data is usually gathered from small and limited samples, and there is a lack of sufficient studies needed for in-depth understanding.

Before sampling cross-national studies, let us briefly survey American child-rearing practices in order to develop a better perspective for understanding those in other countries.

Bronfenbrenner (1961) has reviewed the extensive literature on patterns of child rearing in the United States during a twenty-five-year period, up to 1966. He reports the following major trends:

1. Greater permissiveness toward the child's spontaneous desires.
2. Freer expression of affection.
3. Increased reliance on indirect "psychological" techniques of discipline (such as reasoning or appeals to guilt) versus direct methods (such as physical punishment, scolding, or threats).
4. In consequence of these shifts in the direction of what are predominantly middle-class values and techniques, a narrowing of the gap between social classes in their patterns of child rearing.
5. In succeeding generations the relative position of the father vis-à-vis the mother is shifting with the former becoming increasingly more affectionate and less authoritarian, and the latter becoming relatively more important as the agent of discipline, especially for boys.

Additional trends in child-rearing practices are the tendency to treat boys and girls more nearly alike and the trend toward a more democratic family life. The significance of all these trends will become clearer when they are compared with those from other countries.

The United States and Germany

Devereux, Bronfenbrenner, and Suci (1962) studied some patterns of parent behavior in the United States and the Federal Republic of Germany, as reported by limited samples of sixth-grade children. The researchers did not consider these samples as truly representative of the cultures from which they were drawn. Nevertheless, the data does provide the student of comparative childhood with some tentative insights into the child-rearing practice of both cultures.

In general, German youngsters gave their parents higher ratings in affection, companionship, and discipline. The American parents received higher ratings on rejection, deprivation of privileges, and, somewhat, on pressure for achievement. The role of the American mother was perceived as much more prominent, whereas in the German group, the ratings for the father not only approach those of the mother but in three parental practices— nurturance, principled discipline, and power—surpassed them. Some examples of these three parental practices are classified in Table 4–5. In summary, the German father exceeds his wife and his American counterpart in prescribing responsibilities, exerting discipline, and expressing warmth

Multi-
disciplinary
Perspectives

to his children, whereas the American mother is the major source of disapproval and the pressure to excel.

TABLE 4–5
SOME CHILD-REARING PRACTICES OF GERMAN FATHERS AND SAMPLE ITEMS

Child-Rearing Factors	Items
1. Nurturance	I can talk with him about everything. He comforts me and helps me when I have troubles. He is there for me when I need him.
2. Principled discipline	When I must do something, he explains why. When punishing me, he explains why.
3. Power	He insists that I get permission first before I go to a cinema, carnival, or some other entertainment. He wants to know exactly how I spend my money when I want to buy some little things for myself.

Compiled from Devereux, Bronfenbrenner, and Suci (1962)

Cultural differences in the parental treatment of boys and girls suggest relatively little variation except for German boys in the area of discipline especially with regard to the deprivation of privileges. American girls, as compared to the German girls, are assigned more responsibilities than the American boys. In both cultures, each parent tends to interact more with the child of the same sex than with the child of the opposite sex, although this tendency is more marked among the American families.

Regarding the effects of differential parent practices on later personality, Devereux, Bronfenbrenner, and Suci suggest in the same study that the greater affection and control by the German family have the effect, at least on males, of reducing independency, self-directed motivation for achievement, and association with peers. On the other hand, the German youngster is more submissive to adult standards and less influenced by peer-group pressures, which may ultimately result in a more integrated and autonomous individual. These conclusions are supported by cross-cultural studies by Rapp (1961) and McClelland (1961).

The United States and England

Devereux, Bronfenbrenner, and Rodger's study (1969) of child-rearing practices in the United States and England was similar in procedure to the one just described involving German and American children. All the subjects in this study were schoolchildren in the sixth school year who responded on a group-administered questionnaire about their parents' child-rearing practices. Although the English and American samples were both selected to cover a wide range of socioeconomic status and communities, the researchers make no claim that their findings are typical of American or English studies.

Children in both cultures saw their parents as being more supporting and helpful than controlling and punishing. However, American children tended

Anthropo-
logical
Perspectives

59

to see their parents as more supporting, demanding, and controlling than did the English children. In the area of control, the American parents relied more on psychologically oriented punishment techniques such as withdrawing affection, showing disappointment, revoking privileges, or attempting to make the child feel guilty about his behavior. In contrast, the English parents were seen as employing more direct forms of punishment such as spanking and scolding. The English parents were also seen as more inconsistent and indulgent to their children. From this, it would seem that there may be more emotional involvement and psychological pressures between American parents and children than between their English counterparts.

Child-rearing in America and England is seen, primarily, as women's work. Children in both cultures report receiving more of practically every type of treatment from their mother. Only with respect to the encouragement of autonomy and initiative did the father receive slightly higher scores than the mother. Nevertheless, the researchers believe that the fathers' roles as a regulator and moderator was crucial to family well-being.

In both cultures, boys are handled differently from girls. Boys perceive themselves as recipients of more achievement demands and punishments of all kinds, whereas girls see themselves as given more household responsibilities and treated more protectively. In America, the treatment of both sexes was found to be more similar than in England. English girls experienced significantly more nurturance, companionship, and indulgence than English boys, who received far more spankings and scoldings than American boys.

Different parental treatments according to the sex of the parent and the child were reported for both cultures. For example, in areas of control, discipline, and companionship fathers were more concerned with sons, whereas mothers were more concerned with daughters. It is informative to note that parents in both cultures were somewhat more lenient and indulgent with children of the opposite sex.

In summary, although child-rearing practices are rather similar in both American and English cultures, American parents are seen by their children as not only more demanding and controlling but also as more loving and supporting. English parents are described as less affectionate and supportive, as less demanding, but as more punitive. Thus, it would seem, parent-child relationships in America may be richer, stronger, and more binding than in England.

The United States and the Soviet Union

Bronfenbrenner (1970) offers us a cross-cultural view of childhood in the two most powerful nations of our time. The researcher made numerous visits to the Soviet Union extending over a five-year period, during which he developed and carried out field observations, interviews, and experiments.

All human beings possess the same basic needs. We cannot assume that any particular national group has sole possession of a given need. The differences among groups or individuals are found in the degrees to which their needs are met or stressed. The dominant characteristics of Soviet child-rearing practices, which are reflected in the adult population, are affiliation, group dependency, and altruism. In the United States, the corresponding dominant characteristics seem to be the needs of achievement, social approval, and autonomy.

By affiliation we mean the need for intensive, direct, and warm relation-

FIGS. 4-1.
U.S. and Soviet
children engaged
in games of chess.

ships with many people. The beginnings of these traits are implanted in the Russian child by the diffusion of maternal responsibility, not only by the child's relatives but even by complete strangers. Delegation of child care is standard practice in the Soviet Union, primarily because almost 50 per cent

Anthropo-
logical
Perspectives

of all age-eligible women are in the labor force. Public nurseries and pre-school institutions offer continuous reinforcement of affiliative needs for many infants and children.

Dependence on the group for the satisfaction of basic psychological needs is heavily stressed in Russian schools. Each child is evaluated weekly by his peers and teachers. His status depends also on the standing of his group within the class. If a child fails to live up to group expectations, public criticism and group sanctions follow. In other words, the group or collective is the major source of reward and punishment.

Apparently the mutual dependence of the individual on the group, and vice-versa, has caused Soviet education to stress altruistic behavior. By altruism we mean concern for the welfare of others. Children in each group are taught to help each other. In turn, each class "adopts" a lower grade class and acts as older brothers and sisters by escorting the younger ones to school, teaching them new games, reading to them, and helping them with their schoolwork. The system of "adoption" also includes adult collectives so that each school may also be a "ward" of a factory, business, or govern-ment agency. The adults devote their time to helping their adopted class. This social intimacy seems somewhat contrary to American attitudes. Adult Americans often seem to fear close associations, because they are seen as potentially restrictive of individual freedom. At the same time, Americans experience a strong desire for group approval and acceptance.

Perhaps the ethos of Soviet family life is captured in the following state-ments from an influential Soviet publication, as quoted by Bronfenbrenner (1970):

> Our family is not a closed-in collective body, like the bourgeois family. It is an organic part of Soviet society, and every attempt it makes to build up its own experience independently of the moral demands of society is bound to result in a disproportion, discordant as an alarm bell.

> Our parents are not without authority either, but this authority is only the reflection of social authority. In our country the duty of a father toward his children is a particular form of his duty toward society. It is as if our society says to parents:

> You have joined together in goodwill and love, rejoice in your children, and expect to go on rejoicing in them. That is your own personal affair and concerns your own personal happiness. But in this happy process you have given birth to new people. A time will come when these people will cease to be only a joy to you and become independent members of society. It is not at all a matter of indifference to society what kind of people they will be. In handing over to you a certain measure of social authority, the Soviet state demands from you correct upbringing of future citizens. Particularly it relies on a certain circumstance arising naturally out of your union—on your parental love.

> If you wish to give birth to a citizen and do without parental love, then be so kind as to warn society that you wish to play such an underhanded trick. People brought up without parental love are often deformed people. . . . (p. 3).

Table 4–6 presents some comparisons of child-rearing practices in this country and Russia. In a sense, the Soviet child is brought up in the group, by the group, and for the group. Nonetheless, we must be aware that, just as child-rearing patterns are changing in the United States, conditions are also changing in the Soviet Union.

TABLE 4–6
SOME COMPARISONS OF CHILD-REARING PRACTICES BETWEEN THE
UNITED STATES AND THE SOVIET UNION

Major Areas of Child-Rearing	United States	Soviet Union
Primary responsibility	The immediate family	Society as represented by the children's collective.
Infant care	Less physical handling and affection but more physical freedom	More hugging, kissing, and cuddling, but less physical freedom.
Child care	Strive for early independence	Less mobility and initiative because more protected against discomfort, illness, and injury.
Interpersonal relationships	Primarily with the immediate family and friends	Much more contact with adults and older children; strangers often step into parental roles spontaneously; older children of both sexes take more responsibility for the very young.
School objectives	Subject matter	Subject matter and character development.
Autonomy	Emphasis on individuality	The child is taught to set the judgment of the group above his own and to subordinate his interest to those of the collective.
Motivation	Individual excellence	Membership in an excellent social unit.
Rewards and punishment	Parents and teachers	Parents, teachers, and peers (emphasis on group pressure and criticism).
Altruism	No particular emphasis	Great emphasis; children are to help members of own group; older groups "adopt" younger groups; schools are "adopted" by local adult organizations.

Compiled from Bronfenbrenner (1970).

TAPPING OUR RICH CULTURAL RESOURCES

Further insights into American child-rearing practices can be developed by the study of the diversified ethnic, racial, and religious groups that together make up the mainstream of our society and culture. Of particular

Anthropological Perspectives

63

importance is the need to tap some of the as yet unassimilated cultural riches of our minority groups. We turn our full attention to this topic later in the text when we discuss multilingual and multicultural education. For now, consider the following: black people comprise the single largest racial minority group in the United States; in 1967, according to the United States Bureau of the Census, there were approximately 22 million blacks living in all fifty states; in 1961 the American Indian population exceeded 600,000. Recently each of these groups, as well as others, has been expressing increased pride in their heritage and contributions to the American national character.

TABLE 4–7
CHILD-REARING PRACTICES IN CERTAIN EUROPEAN COUNTRIES

Geographic Location	Child Practices	Underlying Assumptions
Central and Eastern	Swaddling the baby.	Custom, physical safety, prevent genital play.
Russia	Very tight swaddling for a long period.	Infant is violent and needs physical restraints but not emotional, assures greater personal inviolability.
	Wet nurses and use of older women for infant care.	Assures increased contacts with society.
	Warm and permissive during nursing, toilet training; gradual weaning.	Feelings have positive value.
Poland	Swaddling the baby; crying without attention, sudden weaning; physical restraints even when unswaddled, diapering.	Infants are very fragile; first steps in the long process of hardening the child; separate "clean" from "dirty" parts of the body.
Poland and Russia (Jewish families)	Very loose swaddling, special stress on warmth and comfort, diapering.	Introduction to close physical intimacy with mother so that love imparted to child will be given to babies in the future.

Compiled from Benedict (1960).

Because we have presented only a very small segment of cross-national comparisons of child-rearing practices, we hope that the readers will continue to study this aspect of cultural anthropology. Table 4–7, for example, provides some insights into the child-rearing practices of some European countries and some assumptions that may help to account for the behavior of children in these countries. The study of world childhood should also include the primitive cultures that often abound with mysterious beauties and, at times, with seemingly incomprehensible cruelties. Such a study of primitive people may provide us with insights into our own "cruelties" that are equally incomprehensible to them such as the tremendous poverty, the killing of animals, and the apparent acceptance of the high rate of automobile deaths (the major cause of death among children).

Multi-
disciplinary
Perspectives

IMPLICATIONS

UNDERSTANDING YOURSELF AND OTHERS

Perhaps one of the major values in studying worldwide childhood is a highly personal one. We want to know more about the whats and whys of our own early upbringing, because all of us are irrevocably tied, although in varying degrees, to our own childhood experiences—whether at the conscious or unconscious level. In this sense, the "apron strings" are never really cut but merely stretched out. Why our parents reared us in the way that they did can often be traced back to the cultural heritage of our ancestors. To ignore this long past is to deny ourselves an important source for understanding ourselves better. The importance of this area for greater self-understanding was brought to the attention of one of the authors during an informal discussion after a major conference on the educational problems of minority students. An observer at the conference, who was not himself a social scientist or an educator, believed that the experts had ignored an important consideration for understanding these students. The story he told was more or less as follows:

> By society's standards I am a very successful person. I own a large successful business, a beautiful home, my children are in college, and I have an Anglo surname (he had his name legally changed). If I had my life to live over again, I would have stayed in the ghetto. Right now I would gladly give up all my material gains, if I could just be my real self again. I gave up everything that was dear to me, everything that I really loved, so that I could appear to be and act like a typical middle-class white American. The price I paid was far too high!

The gist of his argument is that an individual's sense of dignity and identity is also rooted in his childhood experiences. To ignore the values of these natural ties is also to ignore the value of one important component of one's self. Research support for this argument comes from a study of French-Canadian college students (Lambert, 1955). It was found, within the limits of the sample taken, that students with the highest grades were those scoring highest on anomie (feelings of uncertainty and insecurity, usually in regard to social relations). Apparently the French-Canadian students who identified most with the English culture and least with their mother culture did better academically but suffered psychological maladjustments. In summary, it seems that all of us would benefit psychologically and socially through awareness, study, and appreciation of those aspects of our early childhood experiences that were brought from the "old countries." Acknowledgement and respect for one's heritage is one of the fundamental tasks for acquiring a healthy self-concept. Otherwise one's self-concept can become vague and chameleonlike, shifting erratically depending with whom or where one is.

Getting along well with others is an essential requirement for effective living in a mobile, pluralistic society. The excitement of living in such a society is partly a result of the enormous diversity of attitudes and behaviors. However, both getting along well with others and the excitement of diversity are predicated on the understanding and appreciation of behaviors that are different. For example, many Americans frown on the manner in

Anthropological Perspectives

which Frenchmen embrace and kiss their male friends and are prone to giggle when a Latin kisses the extended hand of a woman. Such behaviors may be understood and appreciated when some argument for greater tactile affection is presented. Here are a few: (1) the skin is the largest sensory organ and should be stimulated more because it may well be our single greatest source of continuous pleasure; (2) tactile stimulation may have therapeutic benefits, as noted by the relaxing feelings that follow a physical massage or when the cool night air gently caresses our faces; (3) embraces and kisses make us feel more alive and human in the presence of others; and (4) when we embrace and kiss we are engaging in a symbolic communion with all mankind. The recent growth of sensory-awareness centers in the United States provides additional support for the hypothesis that we have a need for greater tactile stimulation and affection. The overt demonstration of affection is probably healthier psychologically than covert feelings which are rarely translated into action.

Living and Working with Children, Adolescents, and Adults

Information from cross-cultural studies would be of little practical value in isolated, stable, and homogeneous communities that have no members of recent immigrant or minority groups. However, in the presence of substantial subcultures such as we have with our linguistic and racial minorities, direct and conscious attention must be focused on the impact of culture on everyday contacts by teachers, nurses, counselors, and the community-at-large. As an example, let us consider the expected behaviors of a traditional Pueblo Indian child with that of a middle-class white teacher as summarized in Table 4–8.

TABLE 4–8

A Comparison of Expected Behaviors of Pueblo Indian Children and Those Expected by Middle-Class White Teachers

The Pueblo Indian child is likely to be taught at home to value:	The white teacher is almost sure to place the highest value on:
1. Harmony with nature.	Mastery over nature.
2. Mythology. (The supernatural is feared, and sorcerers and witches are thought to cause unexplained behavior.)	Scientific explanations for everything. (Nothing happens contrary to natural law.)
3. Present-time orientation.	Future-time orientation.
4. Time as infinite.	Efficient use of time. (Time can never be regained.)
5. Working to satisfy present need.	Working to get ahead.
6. Following the ways of the old people.	Climbing the ladder of success.
7. Cooperation.	Competition.
8. Anonymity.	Individuality.
9. Submissiveness.	Aggression (socially acceptable).
10. Humility.	Striving to win.
11. Sharing.	Saving for the future.

Compiled from Zintz (1970).

Multi-disciplinary Perspectives

As can be noted, the behavioral value systems of the Pueblo Indian child is in most respects a mirror image of his teacher's and is incongruent with the attitudes and behaviors needed for academic and social success in the United States. Again, we must be aware of the danger of stereotyping members of any cultural or racial group. Nevertheless, an awareness of the child's cultural background may enhance immeasurably the child worker's chances of successfully coping with the child's behavior.

DEVELOPING POSITIVE MODELS

It is logical to suppose that we can improve ourselves not so much by focusing on ourselves as on the treasurehouse offered to us through the study of worldwide child-rearing practices. Other cultures provide "mirrors" we can use to judge ourselves better. Without the benefit of comparisons, it would be difficult to evaluate our child-rearing practice. We would have fewer observable models to judge by.

Increased human understanding may be achieved when we step outside of our culture. Seeing our child-rearing practices in the broad context of worldwide practices permits us to consider attractive alternatives and weakens the belief that our culture is superior to others. Belief in the superiority of one's culture is known as ethnocentrism and it is a highly questionable assumption, in light of anthropological studies, that any culture in our world is superior to any other.

CHAPTER REFERENCES

ANDERSSON, T., and M. BOYER. *Bilingual schooling in the United States,* vol. II. Austin, Tex.: Southwest Educational Development Laboratory, 1970.

BENEDICT, R. Child rearing in certain European countries. *American Journal of Orthopsychiatry,* April 1969, 342–350.

BORMAN, F. International education. *American Education,* May 1969.

BRONFENBRENNER, U. The changing American child—a speculative analysis. *The Journal of Social Issues,* 1961, 17:6–18.

————. *Two worlds of childhood: U.S. and U.S.S.R.* New York: Russell Sage, 1970.

DEVEREUX, E. C., JR., U. BRONFENBRENNER, and R. R. RODGERS. Child-rearing in England and the United States: a cross-national comparison. *Journal of Marriage and the Family,* 1969, 257–270.

————, U. BRONFENBRENNER, and G. J. SUCI. Patterns of parent behavior in the United States of America and the Federal Republic of Germany: a cross-national comparison. *International Social Science Journal,* 1962, 14:488–506.

FORBES, J. *Mexican-Americans: a handbook for educators.* Berkeley, Calif.: Far West Laboratory for Educational Research and Development, 1970.

LAMBERT, W. E. Measurement of the linguistic dominance of bilinguistic dominance of bilinguals. *Journal of Abnormal Social Psychology,* 1955, 50: 197–200.

McCLELLAND, D. C. *The achieving society.* New York: Van Nostrand, 1961.

New Catholic Encyclopedia. New York: McGraw-Hill, 1967.

RAPP, D. W. Child-rearing attitudes of mothers in Germany and the United States. *Child Development,* 1961, 32:669–678.

ZINTZ, M. American Indian. In T. D. Horn (ed.), *Reading for the disadvantaged.* New York: Harcourt, 1970.

Anthropological Perspectives

AL-ISSA, I. and W. DENNIS. *Cross-cultural studies of behavior*. New York: Holt, 1970.

FISHMAN, J. et al. *Language loyalty in the United States*. London: Moulton, 1966.

HUNT, R. (ed.). *Personalities and cultures*. Garden City, N. Y.: Natural History P., 1967.

HSU, F. L. K. (ed.). *Aspects of culture and personality*. New York: Abelard-Schuman, 1954.

KAPLAN, B. (ed.). *Studying personality cross-culturally*. New York: Harper, 1961.

KLUCKHOHN, C., H. A. MURRAY, and D. M. SCHNEIDER. *Personality in nature, society and culture*. New York: Knopf, 1954.

KLUCKHOHN, R. (ed.). *Culture and behavior*. New York: Free Press, 1962.

KNELLER, G. F. *Educational anthropology*. New York: Wiley, 1965.

LAMBERT, W. E. and O. KLINEBERG. *Children's views of foreign peoples*. New York: Appleton, 1967.

LANDY, D. *Tropical childhood: cultural transmission and learning in a rural Puerto Rican village*. New York: Harper, 1959.

LEWIS, O. *Five families*. New York: Science Editions, 1962.

———. *The children of Sanchez*. New York: Vintage, 1961.

MACARDLE, D. *Children of Europe: a study of children of liberated countries (World War II)*. Boston: Beacon, 1951.

MEAD, M. *Coming of age in Samoa*. New York: Dell, 1961.

———. *Growing up in New Guinea*. New York: Dell, 1968.

———. *Male and female: a study of the sexes in a changing world*. New York: Dell, 1949.

———, and M. WOLFENSTEIN (eds.). *Childhood in contemporary cultures*. Chicago: U. of Chicago, 1955.

MIDDLETON, J. (ed.). *From child to adult: studies in the anthropology of education*. Garden City, N. Y.: Natural History P., 1970.

MINTURN, L. and W. W. LAMBERT. *Mothers of six cultures*. New York: Wiley, 1964.

PARK, R. E. *Race and culture*. New York: Free Press, 1950.

QUEEN, S. A., R. W. HABENSTEIN, and J. B. ADAMS. *The family in various cultures*. Philadelphia: Lippincott, 1961.

TAYLOR, R. B. *Cultural ways: a compact introduction to cultural anthropology*. Boston: Allyn, 1969.

WERNER, E. E., J. M. BIERMAN, and F. E. FRENCH. *The children of Kwai*. Honolulu: U. of Hawaii, 1971.

Multi-
disciplinary
Perspectives

Sociological Perspectives

Prelude
Basic Theory and Research
  The Prenatal Stage
  Infancy and Early Childhood
    Stages
  Later Childhood and Adolescent
    Stages
  Adulthood and Old Age Stages
  What Sociologists Actually Do
Implications
  Understanding Yourself and
    Others
  Living and Working with Chil-
    dren, Adolescents, and Adults
  Developing Positive Models

PRELUDE

BY NOW, you should have a feeling for three areas of knowledge that contribute to a broader view of human development. Sociology is a field that incorporates and integrates knowledge from history, philosophy, and anthropology in a most informative way. Sociology, as one of the social sciences, attempts to describe the "social fabric"—the kinds of cloth society is made of and how the threads are woven together—as well as what makes it weaken and rip open and what is needed to reweave it and make it stronger.

In this chapter we explore the ordinary substance of our beliefs, our loyalties, associations, and institutions. We also look into the extraordinary; the myths, prejudices, and easy explanations that underlie the most dramatic aspects of contemporary American life. We glimpse the frustration of poverty and self-denial as well as the gluttony of political power.

Sociology can be, for many people, an eye-opening experience; a shedding of old beliefs, a seeing with new eyes.

Before we begin our exploration, we must remind you that although sociology is a fascinating complex of research methods and theories we focus on only those areas that have direct relevance for gaining an understanding of human development. We hope those of you who find these ideas, methods, theories, and research findings exciting will do further reading in this field (see bibliography at end of chapter).

Things certainly were easier to understand in earlier days and in other societies. For example, in small rural farm economies, the social forces on parents and children were readily discernible. When there was a loss of income, for example, it could readily be traced to a drought, or to locusts, or to a hailstorm. Even the family of the businessman who owned the country store knew why it wasn't selling as much during the harvest days— the farmers' crops had failed, so the farmers had less money to spend. If there was tension in the local church, it could readily be pinned down (often through the "gossip grapevine") to a fight between two prominent families in town.

People knew their places in those days. The banker's daughter had a ready-made role with certain privileges; people knew who she was when she walked downtown, went to school, or sat in church. The son of the town "drunk" found that lack of status and prestige followed him everywhere.

When family problems arose, there were a host of relatives, friends, and the minister to whom the family could turn.

Children, too, knew their roles in the family. They knew a lot about their family history from sitting on the porch and listening to grandpa and grandma during those hot summer evenings. They knew, as they grew older, that they had to take on more responsibility on the farm. They looked forward to their eighteenth birthday when they could smoke or drink with the family at dinner.

Children also shared in the joys of living, such as the arrival of a new baby, family reunions, birthdays, anniversaries, and town and church picnics. And they shared in life's sadness and despair—the death of a pet animal or grandpa's "passing away" in his bedroom next to that of his grandchild. They sensed the seriousness of pneumonia when dad lay upstairs waiting for the family doctor to arrive on horseback.

Multi-
disciplinary
Perspectives

70

One could say that people in those days were much more deeply involved with the drama of life, that they had a greater part in writing the scenario, even building the stage upon which it was to be played. They knew that they were actors. They had to go ahead with the production because "the show had to go on!" That is, they were caught in a part and had to assume responsibility for opening and closing the scene even though a calamity was going on backstage. The result was that they grew in their roles as they got more deeply involved in the drama of life.

Contrast that picture with family life today. When something serious happens, such as unemployment, or a housing problem it is often the result of complicated political, economic, and social forces of which family has little or no understanding and even less control. A specialist may be necessary to help the family find a solution to the problem.

If there is tension in the community, it may be the result of several interrelated deep-seated pressures of a political, racial, economic, and religious nature.

Many families today who live in large urban areas are hardly noticed by their nextdoor neighbors. The children of these families have little sense of status or identity in the community. (It can be said that sometimes there really is no community to identify with.)

The so-called immediate family of today is very often "spread out over the country." When troubles arise, the family does not dare go to the neighbors to ask their advice, but may instead go to a "clinic" to seek the advice of an expert.

Children know they are growing up today by their grade level in school and by such a milestone as getting their driver's license. Participation in sickness and death has been removed from the experience of most children by the modern hospital and the mortuary.

Television viewing has replaced the family's evening of singing and dancing, and both father and mother often hold down jobs to keep food on the table or two cars in the family garage.

The children of today very seldom feel like actors in the drama of life. They often feel manipulated like puppets and they become alienated because of vast worldwide, social, political, and economic revolutions. The rapidity of change is overwhelming.

We are not arguing the case for returning to the "good old days"—for we admit that there were many negative features, especially much needless human suffering. What we are saying is that developing a sociological perspective about children and adolescents can help us become more perceptive about our own family's "sociological drama" in the world of yesterday and today. It can give us insight for writing the "scenario" for our own family drama as it grows and develops in the world of tomorrow.

Consider with us Berger's (1963) analogy of life as a "puppet show":

We see the puppets dancing on their miniature stage, moving up and down as the strings pull them around, following the prescribed course of their various little parts. We learn to understand the logic of this theater and we find ourselves in its motions. We locate ourselves in society and thus recognize our own position as we hang from its subtle strings. For a moment we see ourselves as puppets indeed. But then we grasp a decisive difference between the puppet theater and our own drama. Unlike the

Sociological Perspectives

puppets, we have the possibility of stopping in our movements, looking up and perceiving the machinery by which we have been moved. In this act lies the first step towards freedom. And in this same act we find the conclusive justification of sociology as a humanistic discipline. (p. 176.)

Developing a sociological perspective regarding children and adolescents can thus help us become more aware of the importance of the social influences that have shaped our lives and will affect our children's lives in the future.

Sociology, a young science, has developed some theories about these social influences. Using certain research methods to study these processes, sociology has accumulated quite a few general, yet tentative, research findings.

BASIC THEORY AND RESEARCH

In order to gain some insight into sociology as a field of study, we now describe some of the phenomena that sociologists find important in the lives of children and adolescents.

PRENATAL STAGE

Considering the moment of conception, one thinks mainly of the genetic and physiological variables related to the development of the fetus. Yet, there exists at that moment and beyond, a whole host of variables that play an almost equally important role. Some of these sociological variables may not manifest themselves until much later in the development of this new human, but they are continually working in the background.

Within the mother and father are a number of historical sociological variables related to their upbringing: their parents' socioeconomic status, their racial backgrounds, their educational levels, and their parents' occupations, for example.

Outside the mother and father's personal domain, there are also many social factors helping to set the stage for the new arrival: the job of the father, the number of children already in the family, the family's friends and relatives, the relation of this family unit to the other institutions in the community, the church, government, economics, and education.

Beyond the family unit in a particular society, a large number of social forces also have an effect on the family. They include economic and political conditions in the country, whether a war is in progress, in what country this family resides, the technological changes that are taking place at the time, and the content of the mass media.

A sociologist is interested in various social phenomena as they manifest themselves within *and* without the person. Sociologists study social relationships of the family unit (husband-wife-child interactions); they study how the family unit interacts with other family units (relatives, friends); they study how the institution of the family interacts with other institutions in this society (education, religion, economic institutions, and government); they study the impact of the mass media on the family; they study how the cultural mores and customs affect families and children; they study how a society exerts social controls on its newly arrived members; and they study how some members of the society may deviate from these social controls.

Multi-
disciplinary
Perspectives

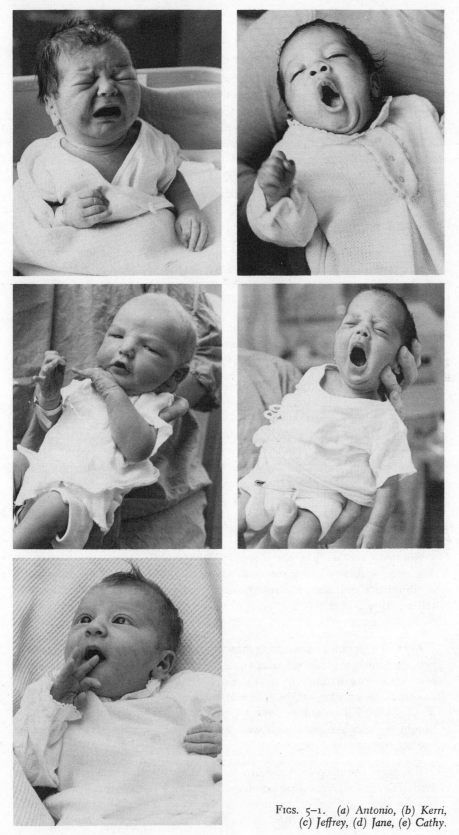

FIGS. 5–1. (a) Antonio, (b) Kerri,
(c) Jeffrey, (d) Jane, (e) Cathy.

Sociological
Perspectives

73

Let us look at some of these areas as the child is born and matures throughout the life cycle.

INFANCY AND EARLY CHILDHOOD STAGES

The birth of a child marks the beginning of a series of social encounters that are of prime importance in shaping the personality and life of a child. Figure 5–1 shows the photographs of six newborn children, all with different potentials, largely a result of their status at birth. Evelyn de Wolfe explains the birth of these six babies as follows:

A THRESHOLD OF HOPE FOR THE NEWBORN

For a short while we joined the baby watchers in the hospital's maternity ward. Standing on the outside looking in forbidden to touch, to contaminate.

For a few days, these babies will live a sameness with their contemporaries, until they are slipped into their respective social slots, with different opportunities, different homes, different neighborhoods and different ideologies shaping their futures and personalities.

Picked at random, five babies who look so alike in their cribs today will have different lives in years to come. What can they look forward to as they begin to sense reality?

Cathy will never know her natural parents but chances are she will find a good home before she is 2 months old. More than 50% of adoptive fathers eligible to choose her for their own will be college graduates. The majority will be in their early 30s, the mothers in their late 20s. Approximately 34% of these prospective parents will be in a $10,000 to $14,000 income bracket, 14% will be above that figure. Cathy's chances of being adopted are better than the average child born out of wedlock. Our society classifies her as "ideally adoptable." Why? Her parents and both sets of grandparents are college educated. In addition, she's charming, she's a WASP—White, Anglo-Saxon, Protestant.

Antonio's mother left her home in Guatemala a year ago, married an American and bore him a son in this country. Antonio can look forward to a bilingual childhood. His mother cannot speak English. Only time will tell whether Antonio will choose to dismiss his Spanish heritage or draw on it as an asset.

Kerri is the child of working parents involved in education and youth projects. Both are college educated, both are anxious to give their first-born every opportunity to develop a healthy mind and body. Kerri can anticipate good care, a good education and above all a realistic outlook on life. She will be shown how to cope with her limitations. She will be taught to hold her head high with good reason—because she'll be proud she is a Negro.

Jeffrey is the second boy born to an attractive housewife in Baldwin Park. His father is a stockroom clerk. The family lives in an average home, has the average kind of problems. Jeffrey can anticipate an average education, a life free of hangups except for those he can create himself. He is healthy, good-looking Caucasian whose parents believe in the fundamental right to equal opportunity for all.

Little *Jane* is 25 days old. At birth she was tossed into a trash can in an alley behind a market. Miraculously, she survived suffocation in her garbage crib.

These are just a few of the thousands of infants who, newborn, will be finishing their first year and beginning another. Never again will they share total ignorance of what it means to have or not, to hurt or be hurt, to be accepted or rejected.

And, like their parents, they're unaware as to what the future will hold.

Evelyn de Wolfe, 1969

* Courtesy, *Los Angeles Times*

FIGS. 5–2. *Socialization takes place through contact with your family, friends, and schoolmates.*

One of the most important things that happens to a child during early childhood is the process of interaction that takes place between the child and different social institutions. This process is called socialization and involves the gradual exposure of the child to the various cultural components of his society. Children are slowly brought into contact with other human groups and are expected to acquire the necessary knowledge, traits, and characteristics to eventually fit into the whole social structure.

This process of socialization never really ends. For most people, gaining knowledge of other groups and acquiring a functional ability within these groups is a lifelong process.

We can thus see that the socialization process is of prime importance in any society in order to keep it functioning and in order to develop appropriate values and roles in the new arrivals.

During infancy and early childhood, the family plays the major role as a socializing institution. The parents may not be aware of the role or responsibilities of the family in this process of childhood socialization. However, within a matter of weeks the parents unconsciously begin to develop a set of expectations for the child. These expectations, or tasks for the child to perform, are the first steps on the road to socialization and the eventual achievement of an established adult level of social performance consistent with the requirements of our complex society. Clausen (1968) summarizes these tasks of early childhood in the family setting in Table 5–1.

TABLE 5–1
TYPES OF TASKS OF EARLY CHILDHOOD SOCIALIZATION IN THE FAMILY

Parental Aim or Activity	Child's Task or Achievement
1. Provision of nurturance and physical care.	Acceptance of nurturance (development of trust).
2. Training and channeling of physiological needs in toilet training, weaning, provision of solid foods, etc.	Control of the expression of biological impulses; learning acceptable channels and times of gratification.
3. Teaching and skill-training in language, perceptual skills, physical skills, self-care skills in order to facilitate care, insure safety, etc.	Learning to recognize objects and cues; language learning; learning to walk, negotiate obstacles, dress, feed self, etc.
4. Orienting the child to his immediate world of kin, neighborhood, community, and society, and to his own feelings.	Developing a cognitive map of one's social world; learning to fit behavior to situational demands.
5. Transmitting cultural and subcultural goals and values and motivating the child to accept them for his own.	Developing a sense of right and wrong; developing goals and criteria for choices, investment of effort for the common good.
6. Promoting interpersonal skills, motives, and modes of feeling and behaving in relation to others.	Learning to take the perspective of another person; responding selectively to the expectations of others.
7. Guiding, correcting, helping the child to formulate his own goals, plan his own activities.	Achieving a measure of self-regulation and criteria for evaluating own performance.

Adapted from John A. Clausen, *Socialization and Society*, p. 141. Copyright © Little, Brown and Company, Inc., Boston, 1968. Reprinted by permission.

Through the process of socialization the helpless infant learns certain tasks, "rules of the game," ways of thinking, feeling, and valuing. As he becomes older, another institution, the school, plays a more dominant role in the child's socialization process.

LATER CHILDHOOD AND ADOLESCENT STAGES

Socialization, as a process, does not end in early childhood but rather continues as the child develops into an adolescent and then into an adult. The basic trend of the child relating to more dimensions of society continues. The emphasis for a number of years is on education as a social institution. Sociologists are thus interested in the kinds of interactions the child has in a school setting. The sociology of education is one of the major areas of research in sociology today.

Schools play a much larger role in our society than just a place where a child goes to learn (Havighurst and Neugarten, 1967). If the socialization process is effective, the school becomes a means for social mobility. That is, in the United States, with its rather flexible social class system, people can change their social and economic levels through education.

Another important role of the schooling process is that of affecting change in the individual and eventually in the society it serves. As a child is subject to the enlarged realm of experience that schooling offers, he tends to filter this experience, to modify and interpret it in light of his family's beliefs and values. As the child grows older and acquires additional information and exposure to other values, he very often modifies his individual attitudes from those held by his parents. Through the successive generations, substantial changes in basic beliefs may occur.

The years of preadolescence and adolescence are of special significance to the sociologist, since it is then that the young gradually become adults. This period is often a painful process for the young and an equally painful process for their parents. Thomas Cottle (1971) describes the moment when a parent realizes that his children are no longer children. "Parents discover that children who depart take a chunk of time with them, an irretrievable chunk which makes us feel that we may never again get close to young people or, even worse, to the remnants of our own childhood."

Sociologists also look at the different periods of growth as having certain primary developmental tasks to be completed. As examples, the small child must master walking, talking, and controlling his excretory functions. The middle child must learn to play games, read, and cooperate or collaborate. For the adolescent, these tasks are more complex, but just as vital to his development. Havighurst (1953) lists the developmental tasks for adolescents as follows:

1. Achieve new and more mature relations with individuals of the same age group . . . of both sexes.
2. Achieve a masculine or feminine social role.
3. Accept your own body.
4. Achieve emotional independence from your parents or other adults.
5. Start taking steps to achieving economic independence by preparing and planning for an occupation.
6. Start preparing for marriage and family life.
7. Develop intellectual skills and concepts necessary for civic competence.

Sociological Perspectives

8. Acquire social responsibility.
9. Acquire a set of values as a guide to behavior.

ADULTHOOD AND OLD AGE STAGES

Sociologists are becoming increasingly interested in adulthood and old age as major areas of research. The rapid changes in family living styles for example have revolutionized research in the sociology of the family. Such things as the large number of one-parent families caused by higher separation and divorce rates, the increasing number of women working, the high mobility of the family along with a shift from a large, extended family to a small, nuclear family have created a need for research on its impact on the family unit.

With the high degree of technological and social change, many men and women are being forced to change careers more than once during their lifetime. What impact does this have on the middle aged man or woman? What implications does this have on selecting a career? Whose responsibility is the retraining—government or education? These questions are being researched in the fascinating area of the sociology of work and occupations.

The sociology of old age too is an expanding field of study, since our elderly population is expanding. Some sociologists study how the various social institutions can help meet the many needs of the elderly. Government programs like Vista and the Peace Corps are using the talents of the elderly to help others. Churches and some businesses offer special social and educational programs for the elderly.

Some sociologists work with city planners on the sociological effects on the aged in urban renewal programs. What are the social and psychological effects of relocation on the elderly?

We hope this section has given you a feel for the variety of contributions this exciting field has to make in our understanding of all stages of human development.

WHAT SOCIOLOGISTS ACTUALLY DO

You have just read that sociologists are interested in certain variables during the various stages of human growth and development. Yet, you still may be wondering just what a sociologist does to help us understand the factors influencing human development. In this section we try to answer these questions by giving you some concrete examples of some sociological activities and contributions.

1. *Sociologists Study Social Phenomena.* Part of the training of a sociologist involves him in the development of skills in making observations about human social interaction. These observations can vary from quite subjective (personal) impressions of an event to very highly structured objective-impersonal impressions. Some sociologists do most of their research in the "field," where the actual social interactions are taking place. Sociologists, for example, have studied street gangs by going into urban neighborhoods and actually joining such gangs, functioning as both participants and observers (Cohen, 1955).

Other sociologists conduct highly structured laboratory experiments where they test out certain hypotheses under controlled conditions. Many studies

Multi-
disciplinary
Perspectives

78

in the area of group dynamics and group leadership have been conducted in this manner.

A sociologist can study social interactions, social institutions, and family group interactions using a variety of research tools provided him during his training. Such research methods as the interview, the survey or questionnaire, the experiment, and observation techniques are used depending on the type of social phenomena being studied.*

2. *Sociologists Develop Theories to Explain Social Interactions.* Sociologists gather research findings and then try to interpret them. They develop theories, which are tentative explanations of social phenomena and interactions. Each theory is then used to make predictions or hypotheses about the outcome of future studies. If the results turn out as predicted and the same pattern emerges in repeated studies, the sociologist then feels more certain that his theory has validity.

Some theories are designed to provide insight about small social events (e.g., the social interactions among a small play group of children in a classroom), whereas others try to explain and predict larger social phenomena (e.g., the reasons for major social unrest, such as a riot or racial prejudice against a minority group). Examples of such sociological theories are discussed in later chapters under developments in the social domain of children and adolescents.

3. *Sociologists Make Recommendations for Solving Serious Social Problems.* Within the past ten years, sociologists have been called upon more frequently to participate in the development of programs to help solve some of our major social problems (Duhl, 1969; Finney, 1970). Problems of the poor, the aged, and the minorities have come under study by sociologists.

Some important social legislation has been enacted into law as a result of sociological research and recommendations. For example, the Supreme Court decision on school segregation was preceded by years of research conducted by social scientists which indicated that the social and psychological effects of school segregation on children were harmful to both the minority group children and the majority group children.

As the minority group child observes the fact that his group is always segregated from the majority, and it is the majority group that is treated with more respect by society, as a whole, the minority group child may develop feelings of inferiority and doubts about his personal worth. These doubts often lead to hostility and perhaps aggressive behavior toward the majority and sometimes his own group.

Of course, not every minority child reacts in this same way. A great deal depends on the individual, his family background, the culture and tradition of his minority group, and his own ability to cope with the situation. However, many minority group children of all classes tend to be hypersensitive and anxious about their relations with society in general, and often develop the trait of seeing hostility and rejection even in those areas where none exists.

In producing such effects, segregated schools impair the ability of the child to profit from the educational opportunities and the socialization opportunities that should be provided him by the schools.

* For further insight, the reader is encouraged to examine some introductory texts in sociology. Examples are: Dressler (1969); DeFleur (1971); and Hodges (1971).

Sociological
Perspectives

IMPLICATIONS

UNDERSTANDING YOURSELF AND OTHERS

You should now have a better idea of how these sociological variables affected your development from early infancy through adolescence. Hopefully, as you have been reading, you have related some of these concepts to your own life. What sociological variables were present in your family as you were born? How did your father's occupation influence where you lived and the manner in which you lived? How did your family relate with community institutions? From this analysis you may understand why your values have developed in a certain direction.

Another "fringe benefit" from this section may be a greater awareness of your parents' sociological history and how their parents' social position affected some of their present attitudes, values, and behaviors.

LIVING AND WORKING WITH CHILDREN, ADOLESCENTS, AND ADULTS

Sociological perspective is a necessity for anyone interested in children. To comprehend the sociological influences on children and adolescents is certainly a prerequisite to engaging in emphatic and meaningful communication with them. Teachers who work in large urban schools with children from mixed racial backgrounds must integrate the sociological perspective into their daily contacts with students. To understand what students are really saying, what they really mean, is to be able to respond to the often hidden message that students communicate.

Grasping even a portion of the significance of the vast changes taking place in the community, the nation, and the world means that you will work with children, adolescents, and their families in a different way—on a level of understanding, sensitivity, and compassion for their troubles. You will recognize that people are often the victims of vast social forces.

Knowing the major sociological theories and concepts helps one offer ideas to children and adolescents to help them develop into more fully functioning citizens. Just realizing that this is an interdisciplinary approach to solving some serious human problems can result in your thinking of a diversity of ways to solve problems.

We believe that a sociological perspective can help develop the kinds of human sensitivity and compassion that is needed far more today than ever before. All of us want to live more productive lives in this "shrinking world" that we share. We quote from Mills (1959), who focuses on the human benefits in the study of sociology:

> The sociological imagination enables its possessor to understand the larger historical scene in terms of its meaning for the inner life and the external career of a variety of individuals. It enables him to take into account how individuals, in the welter of their daily experience, often become falsely conscious of their social positions. Within that welter, the framework of modern society is sought, and within that framework the psychologies of a variety of men and women are formulated. By such means the personal uneasiness of individuals is transformed into involvement with public issues.

Multi-
disciplinary
Perspectives

80

The first fruit of this imagination—and the first lesson of the social science that embodies it—is the idea that the individual can understand his own experience and gauge his own fate only by locating himself within his period, that he can know his own chances in life only by becoming aware of those of all individuals in his circumstances. In many ways it is a terrible lesson; in many ways a magnificent one. We do not know the limits of man's capacities for supreme effort or willing degradation, for agony or glee, for pleasurable brutality or the sweetness of reason. But in our time we have come to know that every individual lives, from one generation to the next, in some society; that he lives out a biography, and that he lives it out within some historical sequence. By the fact of his living he contributes, however minutely, to the shaping of this society and to the course of its history, even as he is made by society and by its historical push and shove. (pp. 5–6.)

DEVELOPING POSITIVE MODELS

Most of us are culture bound in a sense by our socializing experiences which are often limiting. Yet, the child who is reared by a parent with some sense of importance for the sociological perspective for development of a more humanly fulfilling world has a much greater chance of becoming a compassionate and altruistic individual, who has developed an ability to express "brotherly love" for his fellow man.

It is in these models, in which altruism, compassion, and brotherly love play such key parts, that much of the human suffering in the world of today will be alleviated in the world of tomorrow. With the magnitude of social change going on around us, we will need to rear millions of children who are concerned not only about themselves, their families, and their country but who are concerned with all of humanity.

Erich Fromm (1960) in his book *Revolution of Hope* (1968) speaks of some of the individual changes that will be needed:

Man's development requires his capacity to transcend the narrow prison of his ego, his greed, his selfishness, his separation from his fellow man, and hence, his basic loneliness. This transcendence is the condition for being open and related to the world, vulnerable, and yet with an experience of identity and integrity; of man's capacity to enjoy all that is alive, to pour out his faculties into the world around him, to be "interested"; in brief, to *be* rather than to *have* and to *use* are consequences of the step to overcome greed and egomania. (pp. 141–142.)

CHAPTER REFERENCES

BERGER, P. L. *Invitation to sociology: a humanistic perspective*. Garden City, N. Y.: Doubleday, 1963.

CLAUSEN, J. A. (ed.). *Socialization and society*. Boston: Little, Brown, 1968.

COHEN, A. K. *Delinquent boys: the culture of the gang*. New York: Free Press, 1955.

COTTLE, T. J. *Times children: impressions of youth*. Boston: Little, Brown, 1971.

DE FLEUR, M. L., W. D. D'ANTONIO, and L. B. DE FLEUR. *Sociology: man in society*. Glenview, Ill.: Scott, Foresman, 1971.

Sociological
Perspectives

DE WOLFE, E. *A threshold of hope for newborn.* Los Angeles *Times*, January 1, 1969.

DRESSLER, D. *Sociology: the study of human interaction.* New York: Knopf, 1969.

DUHL, L. J. *The urban condition.* New York: Simon and Schuster, 1969.

FINNEY, J. C. *Culture change, mental health, and poverty.* New York: Simon and Schuster, 1970.

FROMM, E. *The revolution of hope.* New York: Bantam, 1968.

HAVIGHURST, R. J. *Human development and education.* New York: McKay, 1953.

——, and B. L. NEUGARTEN. *Society and education.* Boston: Allyn, 1967.

HODGES, H. M., JR. *Conflict and consensus: an introduction to sociology.* New York: Harper, 1971.

MILLS, C. W. *The sociological imagination.* New York: Oxford U.P., 1959.

RECOMMENDED FURTHER READING

BOSSARD, J. H. S. and E. S. BOLL. *The sociology of child development.* New York: Harper, 1966.

COLES, R. *Children of crisis: a study of courage and fear.* New York: Dell, 1967.

DEUTSCH, M. et al. *The disadvantaged child.* New York: Basic, 1967.

——, I. KATZ, and A. R. JENSEN (eds.). *Social class, race, and psychological development.* New York: Holt, 1968.

DOUGLAS, J. D. *The relevance of sociology.* New York: Appleton, 1970.

ELKIN, F. *The child and society: the process of socialization.* New York: Random, 1960.

ERICKSON, E. H. *Childhood and society.* New York: Norton, 1963.

FRIEDENBERG, E. Z. *Coming of age in America.* New York: Vintage, 1965.

FROST, J. L. and G. R. HAEKES (eds.). *The disadvantaged child: issues and innovations.* Boston: Houghton, 1970.

KARLIN, J. *Man's behavior: an introduction to social science.* New York: Macmillan, 1967.

HANDEL, G. (ed.). *The psychosocial interior of the family: a sourcebook for the study of whole families.* Chicago: Aldine, 1967.

McNEIL, E. B. *Human socialization.* Belmont, Calif.: Brooks-Cole, 1969.

MARTISON, F. M. *Family in society.* New York: Dodd, 1970.

MERTON, R. K., L. BROOM, and L. S. COTTRELL, JR. (eds.). *Sociology today: problems and prospects.* New York: Basic, 1959.

REISSMAN, L. *The urban process: cities in industrial societies.* New York: Free Press, 1970.

SANFORD, N. *Self and society: social change and individual development.* New York: Atherton, 1966.

SUSSMAN, M. B. (ed.). *Sourcebook in marriage and the family.* New York: Houghton, 1968.

Multi-
disciplinary
Perspectives

Biological Perspectives

Prelude
Basic Theory and Research
  Heredity
  Variability of Behavior
  Stability, Change, and Potential
Implications
  Understanding Yourself and
    Others
  Living and Working with Chil-
    dren, Adolescents, and Adults
  Developing Positive Models

PRELUDE

THE DEVELOPMENT of a biological perspective for understanding childhood is particularly important because most of the studies on human development have focused only on environmental influences and their results. Psychologists in the past had to content themselves with studying the environmental inputs surrounding the child and the subsequent behavioral outputs omitting the further complexities of hereditary and physiological factors that intervened between input and output. We now realize that human behavior can be produced or modified by internal processes as well as by external environmental processes. Furthermore, recent research in genetics, biochemistry, psychobiology, and brain research promises a major breakthrough in our understanding of the biological foundation of developmental behavior.

The biological domain is broadly defined in this text to include the following: (1) the study of heredity, that is, the totality of physical and mental influences transmitted by the parents to their children; (2) the study of physiology, defined as the relationships between bodily processes and behavior; (3) the study of psychomotor development that involves physical behaviors resulting from physical maturation and learning; and (4) the study of the physical self-concept that includes all the psychological effects of the body and its functions on the individual. Table 6–1 summarizes and elaborates on some of the influences of the biological domain on human development. Although the importance of the biological domain on human development and behavior is lifelong, it has its greatest impact during the early formative years as suggested in Figure 6–1.

FIG. 6–1.
Relative importance of biological, environmental, and learning factors as a function of time. As the influences of the biological domain on development and behavior decrease with the passage of time, the importance of the environment and the learning processes increases.

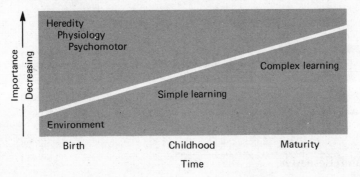

BASIC THEORY AND RESEARCH

HEREDITY

A biologically unique individual is created when the male sex cell, the sperm, unites with the female sex cell, the ovum.* Each of the parents' sex cells contributes twenty-three genetic information units, called chromosomes, to the fertilized egg. Each of the twenty-three chromosomes is made up of approximately twenty thousand genes, the trait-determining carriers. The

Multi-
disciplinary
Perspectives

* The exceptions are identical twins (monozygotic) who develop from a single fertilized ovum and share the same genetic endowment. Fraternal twins (dizygotic) develop from separate fertilized eggs and, therefore, have different genetic endowments.

TABLE 6–1
SOME INFLUENCES OF THE BIOLOGICAL DOMAIN ON DEVELOPMENT

Biological Components	Influences
Heredity	Physical characteristics: eye, skin, and hair colors; physique, height, and weight. Potentials for behavior: intellectual, special talents.
Physiological	General physical and mental health, resistance to disease, level of physical and mental vigor, emotional sensitivities, regularity of bodily functions such as sleep and hunger.
Psychomotor	Large and small muscle coordination, balance, motor skills, eye-hand coordination, learning and playing physical games.
Physical Self-Concept	Body as symbol of self; many separate and changing components: appearance, competencies, endurance, health, strength, and defects.

uniting of the genes from the mother with those from the father is a random process and because of the large numbers of genes (approximately 1 million) available, a practically endless number of combinations is possible.

Individual genetic inheritances, then, are determined largely by chance factors operating within this fantastically large genetic pool. Since the single sperm that successfully unites with the single ovum is only one of millions of sperms produced by the father, uniting with only one of hundreds of eggs produced by the mother, this randomization of genetic links is even further complicated.

Nevertheless, it is just this genetic linking process that accounts for the resemblances found within families as well as the unique differences among individuals.

Yet we must be careful not to assume that the role of heredity is completed at the moment of conception. Such an incorrect interpretation may lead to the old notion of preformationism that believed that the sex cell (male) contained a fully developed but miniature human being, as illustrated in Figure 6–2. The role of heredity in human development, as yet not fully understood, is far more complex and pervasive in its influence. Actually the complexities and their underlying biochemical processes are beyond the scope of this book, but a brief overview of the heredity process may provide us with the necessary perspective for further study.

Chromosomes are made up of deoxyribonucleic acid (DNA for short). DNA is the basic substance of heredity; it contains the genetic code or set of instructions for genetic development that will usually unfold predictably under proper environmental conditions. The complete set of genetic instructions for an individual is uniquely written for him in his own twenty-three "DNA volumes" represented by the twenty-three pairs of chromosomes given to him from his parents. The genes represent the sentences used in genetic writing. The instructions contained in most of the genes are best understood only in the context of the rest of the sentences, paragraphs, chapters, and volumes. Although no one has been able to read the genetic

Biological
Perspectives

85

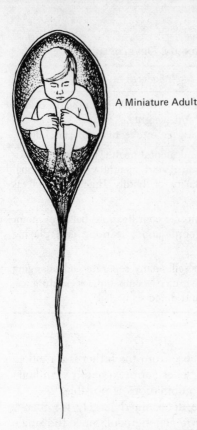

A Miniature Adult

Fig. 6–2.
*Preformationism.
Until the 18th
century scientists
believed that the
male sperm con-
tained a complete
human in minia-
ture, as shown in
this illustration
from a treatise of
1694. The female's
role during preg-
nancy was to
nourish and protect
the preformed
fetus.*

code as yet, recent research has succeeded in identifying all twenty-three pairs of chromosomes—a discovery of major importance because the chromosomes contain the genes that carry instructions for mental and physical traits (Birns 1965).

In general the gene-carried instructions are not dogmatic, as if written in indelible ink and never to be modified, changed, or deleted. Rather genes tend to work in varying degrees and in varying ways as teams, although, at times, a single major gene seems to determine a particular trait. Even a seemingly simple physical trait, such as eye color, usually results from the interaction of several genes, although it is usually a single dominant gene that determines the main outcome. When two genes for a single trait, such as eye color, carry different instructions, one gene may be dominant (brown eyes) over the weaker recessive gene (blue eyes). For example, if a child should receive just one dark "eye-color" gene from one parent, no matter what color gene he receives from the other parent—green, gray, blue, or albino—he will have dark colored eyes, although he will be a carrier of a "hidden" green, gray, blue, or albino gene for eye color. (Even the matter of eye color can be complex. In blue eyes alone it has been estimated that there are nine color classes that can be inherited in forty-five possible combinations.) At other times many genes may work together to help determine, at least in part, such complex characteristics as body shape, susceptibility to certain diseases, and intellectual potentiality.

The great impact of heredity on very early development can be observed in the behaviors of newborn infants. Table 6–2 presents some of the motor activities of such infants. As we can see newly born infants come to us with

Multi-
disciplinary
Perspectives

a large reservoir of responses. In later chapters we discuss additional infant behaviors and their gradual development and modification as environmental forces and learning become increasingly important determinants of human development.

TABLE 6–2
SOME MOTOR BEHAVIORS OF THE NEWBORN INFANT

1. Head Movements:
   Upward and downward movements
   Turning head from side to side
   Head shudder in response to "bitter" stimuli
   Balancing head in response to body changes

2. Head and Arm Responses:
   Closing hand in response to stimulation
   Arm flexion in response to sudden tap on the head
   Rubbing face in response to noxious odors
   Arm play
   Startle response of arms in response intense and sudden stimulation

3. Trunk Reactions:
   Arching the back in response to nose pinch
   Twisting of the trunk when head is rotated
   Abdominal reflex in response to needle

4. Reproductive Organ Response:
   Cremasteric reflex (raising of the testes) in response to stimulation of inner thigh
   Penis erection

5. Foot and Leg Responses:
   Knee jerk and Achilles tendon reflex
   Flexion of leg in response to foot or leg stimulation
   Extension of the leg in response to gentle push
   Protective reflex—when one foot or leg is stimulated the other pushes against the source of stimulation
   Kicking
   Stepping movements when held upright with feet touching a surface
   Toe extension when sole of foot is stimulated

6. Coordinated Responses:
   Resting and sleeping positions (unique for infants)
   Stretching, shivering, and trembling
   "Fencing position" when head is rotated
   "Springing position" when held upright and inclined forward
   Startle response (Moro reflex) when "frightened"
   Crying and unrest
   Creeping movements when placed in prone position
   Supporting bodily weight by grasp
   Attempts to lift head and rear quarters (when held horizontally under the armpits)

7. Facial and Mouth Responses:
   Opening and closing mouth; lip movements; sucking
   Smiling; pushing objects from mouth when "undesirable"
   Grimaces; yawning, swallowing; vomiting; coughing
   Hiccoughing; cooing; holding breath

8. Eye Responses:
   Opening and closing of eyelids in response to a variety of stimuli
   Pupillary response (widening and narrowing of the pupils)
   Pursuit movement (following visual stimuli) and *saccadic movement* (quick, jerky movements as in adult reading)
   Coordination of eyes
   Convergence of eyes (in some infants)

Adapted from W. Dennis, "Historical Beginnings of Child Psychology," *Psychological Bulletin,* 1949, 46, 224–235.

VARIABILITY OF BEHAVIOR

If we had to use a single term to describe the total effects of the biological domain (heredity and constitutional factors) on human development, it

Biological
Perspectives

87

would be *variability*. Variability is the *sine qua non* (the indispensable characteristic) of human behavior. The range of individual differences resulting from genetic factors alone is enormous. The variability of behavior becomes even more marked because of varying environments and learning abilities. For example, a genetically gifted child may greatly enhance his original potential if he is also blessed with rich, vigorous, and exciting surroundings. On the other hand, a genetically weak or defective child may find his handicaps increased as a result of dull and impoverished existence.

As indicated in Table 6–2, the newborn infant is a complex organism. He can kick, stretch, "defend himself," yawn, tremble, turn his head, go through the motions of creeping, track visual stimuli, pretend he's "fencing" or about to "spring forward," suck, salivate, excrete, cry, grunt, sigh, and much more! However, even at birth babies have distinctive styles for expressing the same behaviors. For example, vigor of physical expression is consistently higher among some babies. These babies appear more autonomous and capable of doing and getting what they want. Some babies are very sensitive and give startle responses to even slight sounds. They may cry and whimper even when hit by sunlight. Some infants tend to be relatively stable emotionally and not easily aroused by impinging stimulation. Others tend to overreact to minor delays and discomforts that may be early signs of a "nervous child" (Richmond, 1955). Furthermore, variations in constitutional make-up may account for marked differences in ability to develop, cope, and recuperate from physical disorders and psychological upsets. Thus a change in routine may produce a colicky episode, a sleep disturbance, or just a smile. Along this line, some babies are very lovable and cuddlesome, and return affection given them by cooing and smiling. Table 6–3 indicates some variations in the behaviors of newborn infants and their possible implications for present parental interactions and future behavior.

TABLE 6–3
Some Newborn Infant Variations in Behavior and Their Implications

Behavior Responses	Implications
1. Vigor of physical responses	1. A possible measure of physical health and strength; introvertedness or extrovertedness.
2. Excitability and soothability	2. May influence interactions with parents; may lead to liking or disliking the infant.
3. Physiological reactions (heartbeat, muscle tone, respiration, reflex actions, etc.)	3. Related to emotional expression and feeling; a measure of resistance to stress and disease.
4. Crying; sensitivity	4. Some relationship to later speech development and intelligence test scores; may be more self-assertive; may get reputation of "cry baby" or "little man."
5. Sensory development: vision, hearing, taste, smell, thermal, pain, cutaneous, and kinesthetic	5. May be related to various kinds of intelligent behaviors, emotionality, sensitivity, and levels of awareness.

STABILITY, CHANGE, AND POTENTIAL

The lifelong effects of heredity on human development can best be examined in terms of *genotype* and *phenotype*. Genotype means the totality of an individual's genetic inheritance and phenotype is the extent to which that inheritance has been measurably or visibly fulfilled. A person's phenotype, at any particular time of his life, is the result of the total interaction of (1) his unique genetic code; (2) his environmental influences before and after birth; and (3) his self-concept—the individual's perception of himself as a distinct person and as an important determiner of his own behavior.

Phenotypes can be grouped into three major classifications: (1) physiological phenotypes, which include measures of the nervous system, receptors, and endocrine glands (see Figure 6–3); (2) morphological phenotypes, which include measures of physique or body build; and (3) behavioral phenotypes, which include anything the individual does or reports. We know that infant phenotypes are often complex and variable. However, such physiological phenotypes as heartbeat, respiration, and glandular functions are important in measuring consistent, high level, and prolonged excitement to mild upsets, and may indicate higher than average vulnerability to the normal stresses of life. Long-term studies in which the same infants were studied over a two-year period found that such psychophysiological predictions were possible. Other studies support the generalization that such phenotypes as hyperactivity, hypoactivity, sucking, and reactivity are relatively stable and begin very early in life. (Thomas et al., 1960.)

Physical growth patterns and physical characteristics such as body shape, weight, and eye color are also relatively stable. What concerns most of us are the little differences that mean a great deal. A few inches more or less in height or ten pounds either way in an adult may lead to such labels as "short" or "tall," "fat" or "skinny." A quarter of inch on the nose, an inch off the chin, and five inches off the "vital statistics" differentiate a young lady as a gorgeous "dream" or just another "plain Mary." Certainly how people react to a baby's "beauty" or lack of it may have far-reaching effects on the present and later development of her physical self-concept.

Although most physiological and morphological traits are relatively stable, it is the plasticity of behavioral and attitudinal phenotypes that are of greatest concern to us. The ability to change our behavior to meet the requirements of an ever-changing environment is one of the great hallmarks of human nature. In the words of James C. Coleman (1950):

> In the universal struggle for survival and growth, many different adjustive patterns have emerged in the animal world. Some species manage to survive by sheer number of offspring; others rely heavily upon defensive armaments such as poisons, camouflage, or speed. Though widely different, these various patterns have one thing in common: They rely upon "built-in" adjustive know-how. While most animals are capable of some learning, their behavior is determined primarily by adjustive patterns that are instinctive. We might say that they come factory equipped with adjustive know-how.
>
> With man, however, nature has tried out a dramatically different solution to the problems of adjustment. Endowed with superior mental capacities, man has few, if any, instinctive behavior patterns beyond the level of

Biological
Perspectives

the simplest reflex. He must rely instead on his ability to learn and reason in working out the most satisfactory mode of adjustment, continually modifying his behavior to meet the demands of new situations. The superior mental gifts and, consequently, the superior adaptability of man have enabled him to become the unchallenged master of the animal kingdom and to go far toward conquering his physical environment. But man's unique gifts have also created unique problems, for man alone is faced with the responsibility of determining his own behavior—of evaluating and choosing the "best" course of action and of developing the competencies of skills essential for carrying it out. In short, man is faced with the necessity of *self-direction,* and this places a heavy demand upon him to determine the type of creature he is and the basic "role" he should play as a human being.

It is the lack of fulfillment of behavioral phenotypes that accounts for the great differences between what the infant, child, and man are and *what they all could be.* The fulfillment or partial fulfillment of this potential probably underlies our continuous struggle for a better life for our children and ourselves. The struggle is revealed in our continuous attempts to improve the world psychologically, biologically, and sociologically.

IMPLICATIONS

UNDERSTANDING YOURSELF AND OTHERS

None of us are, or ever will be, at all times completely satisfied with ourselves or with others. We could blame this dissatisfaction on "divine discontent" or we could try to better understand the influences of the biological domain as one important determiner of human nature. Perhaps the most basic insight is the view that behavior is initially and inherently variable from birth because of the uniqueness of genetic pools. This, in turn, leads to differences in morphologies and physiological mechanisms underlying behavior. If this is true, the argument for "no fault" or "born innocent" is irrefutable in accounting for early behavior and appearance. To dislike an infant for being overly sensitive, restless, or failing to meet our expectancies of the "ideal baby" is like blaming nature for making water wet or trees green.

In evaluating ourselves and others, we must be careful to distinguish between characteristics that reflect relatively stable phenotypes and those that are within the realm of change or modification. A person cannot readily change his susceptibility to disease, physical prowess or strength, skin pigment, or reaction sensitivities. On the other hand, man is not just a product of his heredity and environment or a thing manipulated by forces beyond his control. We take the view that man is capable of choosing, judging, and directing or redirecting much of his behavior. He can strive for self-growth and improvement. This potential for self-enhancement can be more readily fulfilled by positive encouragement and proper education to enable man to choose and behave more wisely.

Multi-
disciplinary
Perspectives

90

Living and Working with Children, Adolescents, and Adults

Since the genotype must interact with the environment to bring about the phenotypes, everyone who has the responsibility for socializing, training, and educating children is involved in the process of enhancing or changing behavior. For example, we know that children from deprived backgrounds score well below middle-class children on standardized measures of school achievement and that this gap increases with age; we know that infants who never received loving care never learn to speak, to walk, or to feed themselves; and we know that children from an impoverished social background and biological inheritance thrive when placed in a better environment.

The promise offered here is that adults who live and work with children have the exciting challenge of being architects—not of roads, bridges, and building, but of human beings.

Developing Positive Models

Someday we will be able to fully read the genetic code and remedy such defective heredity traits as some forms of mental retardation (Down's syndrome, cerebral sclerosis, and phenylketonuria), hemophilia, certain kinds of visual and auditory deficiencies, as well as other diseases suspected of having hereditary origins. How far genetic intervention should go is a complex legal, religious, and philosophical question. In the past there have been advocates of selective human breeding in attempts to improve the genetic pool. This process of mating is called eugenics, and its greatest success has been with matings of lower organisms. Attempts with humans have been very limited, and apparently unsuccessful.

Nevertheless, we may have to come to grips with the problem of genetic intervention within our lifetime. Of greatest concern to us are psychological phenotypes that are only indirectly and vaguely under the influence of heredity. No psychological trait is ever directly inherited. Therefore, the first research question that needs to be answered is how much of any particular psychological trait is influenced by heredity and how much by environment? We must also determine which human traits are most valuable and, therefore, to be given the greatest probability of occurence, and by what combination of heredity and environmental interventions the chosen traits are to be enhanced. Finally, we must learn how and by whom the success or failure of such programs are to be evaluated.

At the present time the most promising form of genetic intervention seems to be in the form of counseling the community-at-large, expectant couples, and potential parents. Such genetic counseling would begin with the dissemination of prenatal information through mass media and the school systems. Such information would include the fact that the single most important factor contributing to the healthy development of the fetus is probably the proper nutrition of the mother. Postnatally, the single most important factor would be the proper nutrition of the growing child; other information that would be provided includes the need for good obstetrical care during pregnancy and good medical and psychological care from the dates of birth of the future mother and father; the fact that marijuana, LSD, uppers, downers, and others drugs, even common ones such as aspirin and barbiturates, may have detrimental effects on the fetus; and that the chances of giving birth to

Biological Perspectives

children with chromosomal abnormalities, such as mongolism, increases steeply for mothers over the age of forty. (Montagu, 1962.)

Private genetic counseling would be essential for individuals interested in detecting any heartbreaking genetic defect before or during pregnancy.* The bases for such counseling would come from information gathered from family case histories, blood tests, or intrauterine diagnosis of the amniotic fluid that surrounds the fetus. For certain genetic defects, the counseling may be restricted to racial groups. Sickle-cell anemia is found almost exclusively among blacks, whereas Tay-Sachs disease, in which children usually die by age five as a result of brain damage, is found almost only among Jews. A person may be a carrier of a disease although he shows no signs of the disease himself, and may pass it on through the genes to his offspring.

Although the actuality of wiping out all genetic defects is probably still in the distant future, we are now in the process of developing sufficient knowhow to prevent and to treat an increasing number of genetic ailments. At times, information and common sense together can reduce the number of children so afflicted. For instance, if two sickle-cell anemia carriers marry each other, theoretically 25 per cent of their children will have the disease, 50 per cent will be carriers like their parents, and 25 per cent will not be carriers.

CHAPTER REFERENCES

BIRNS, B. M. Individual differences in human neonates' responses to stimulation. *Child Development*, 1965, 30:249–256.

COLEMAN, J. C. *Personality dynamics and effective behavior*. Glenview, Ill.: Scott, Foresman, 1960.

DENNIS, W. A. A description and classification of the responses of the newborn infant. *Psychological bulletin*, 1934, 31:5–22.

MONTAGU, M. F. A. *Prenatal influences*. Springfield, Ill.: Thomas, 1962.

RICHMOND, J. B. and S. L. LUSTMAN. Autonomic function in the neonate: implications for psychosomatic theory. *Psychosomatic medicine*, 1955, 17: 269–275.

THOMAS, A., S. CHESS, H. BIRCH, and M. E. HERTZIG. A longitudinal study of primary reaction patterns in children. *Comprehensive psychiatry*, 1960, 1:103–112.

RECOMMENDED FURTHER READING

ASIMOV, I. *The human body*. New York: Signet, 1963.

BARRINGTON, E. J. W. *The chemical basis of psychological regulation*. Glenview, Ill.: Scott, Foresman, 1968.

BUTTER, C. M. *Neuropsychology: the study of brain and behavior*. Belmont, Calif.: Brooks-Cole, 1968.

CANDLELAND, D. K. (ed.). *Emotion: bodily change*. New York: Van Nostrand, 1962.

CARTER, C. O. The genetics of common malformation. In M. Fishbein (ed.), *Congenital malformations*. New York: International Medical Congress, 1964.

FOSS, B. M. (ed.). *Determinants of infant behavior*. New York: Wiley, 1961.

FULLER, J. L. and W. R. THOMPSON. *Behavior genetics*. New York: Wiley, 1960.

Multi-disciplinary Perspectives

* Anyone wishing to know where genetic counseling is available in the United States or Canada should write to the Medical Department, The National Foundation— March of Dimes, P.O. Box 2000, White Plains, N. Y. 10602.

GERARDIN, L. *Bionics*. New York: McGraw-Hill, 1968.

HIRSCH, J. Individual differences in behavior and their genetic basis. In E. Bliss (ed.), *Roots of behavior*. New York: Harper, 1962.

HODGSON, E. S. *Neurobiology and animal behavior*. Glenview, Ill.: Scott, Foresman, 1968.

KALLMAN, F. J. and L. F. JARVIK. Individual differences in constitution and genetic background. In J. E. Birren (ed.), *Handbook of aging and the individual*. Chicago: U. of Chicago, 1959.

————. *Heredity in health and mental disorder*. New York: Norton, 1953.

MCCLEARN, G. E. Genetics and behavior development. In M. L. Hoffman and L. W. Hoffman (eds.), *Review of child development*. New York: Russell Sage, 1964.

MILLER, H. L. (ed.). *Education for the disadvantaged*. New York: Free Press, 1967.

PIAGET, J. *Biology and knowledge*. Chicago: U. of Chicago, 1971.

PRIBRAM, K. H. (ed.). *On the biology of learning*. New York: Harcourt, 1969.

SCHILDER, P. *The image and appearance of the human body*. New York: Science Editions, 1950.

WOOLDRIDGE, D. E. *Mechanical man: the physical basis of intelligent life*. New York: McGraw-Hill, 1968.

Biological
Perspectives

Psychological Perspectives

Prelude

Basic Theory and Research

Historical Sketch of Child
Psychology

Some Contemporary Trends in
Child Psychology

What Child Psychologists
Actually Do

Implications

Understanding Yourself and
Others

Living and Working with Children, Adolescents, and Adults

Developing Positive Models

PRELUDE

B Y NOW it should be apparent that understanding human development can be greatly enhanced by gaining an interdisciplinary perspective in such diverse areas as history, philosophy, anthropology, sociology, and biology. It is becoming increasingly clear that one area of knowledge is insufficient to grasp the beauty and the complexity, the frustrations and the joys, or for that matter the meaning of these various periods of our lives.

Another major area of human knowledge and understanding that contributes to a better view of the landscape of human development is that of psychology, and this is the major focus of the remainder of the text (with, of course, the interdisciplinary emphasis intertwined). It is the function of this chapter, then, to give you some insight into the research by psychologists as they study the growing individual and, more important, the application to life of their findings.

BASIC THEORY AND RESEARCH

Most of you, having been children and adolescents and having probably taken an introductory psychology course, already know that many psychologists spend a great amount of their time working with children who have special problems. For example, child psychologists work with children in clinics and mental hospitals, the school psychologists administer tests to children and counsel with their parents, and other psychologists work with handicapped children in special education programs in public schools, special clinics, and hospitals. Yet, you may not be aware of the contributions that psychologists make indirectly through their research efforts as they study the many facets of human behavior.

You may also not know of the historical development of child psychology and that it has become one of the most important research areas of contemporary psychology. And you may not be cognizant that different areas of human behavior and functioning are studied by psychologists separately and are then integrated with theories of human development.

Too, you may not be fully aware of the significance of research findings, theories, and applications in child psychology as one of the hopes of solving some of man's most pressing personal and social problems.

Finally, you may not have a grasp of the social significance of some of the "frontier" research areas of child psychology in which ways to extend the human potentialities of children and adolescents are being carefully explored.

HISTORICAL SKETCH OF CHILD PSYCHOLOGY

In the nineteenth century and before, a few "voices in the wilderness" argued for the study of children and respect for their individual differences. But the ears of the world were not "tuned in." As we pointed out in Chapter 3, philosophers such as Plato, Aristotle, and Rousseau recognized individual differences in the abilities and interests of children. Educators such as Comenius and Dewey recognized the need for child study as a separate field. Literary figures such as Thackeray, Sir Walter Scott, and Charles Dickens wrote about the various psychological and social needs of children, although whether they did so intentionally is not known. Biologists such as Darwin, who published his *Biographical Sketch of An Infant* (1877), argued

Psychological Perspectives

95

for the study of child development to test his hypothesis that man, like lizards and lions, had descended from animals.

According to Wayne Dennis (1949) there were two important landmarks in the early development of child psychology. The first was the publication of Preyer's *Die Seele des Kindes*, in 1882. This was the first account of mental development in the child, and was based on Preyer's observations of his son. The second landmark occurred in the following year, 1883, with the publication of Hall's *The Content of Children's Minds*, which attempted to describe the concepts and thought processes possessed by a child entering the first grade.

A milestone in the history of child study came in 1907 when Binet and Simon in France were given the task of identifying schoolchildren who were not mentally capable of doing regular schoolwork. From their research came the first intelligence test. Regarding the importance of this pioneering effort, Anderson (1956) had this to say:

> Why is Binet's work so important? Clearly it substitutes for the onus of moral blame, a measurable phenomenon within the child's resources, which is to be studied henceforth in its own right. The repercussions were tremendous. Bright children, normal children, handicapped children, retarded children, deafened children, blind children; all types and kinds of children everywhere were measured and studied in the years that followed. But, more than that, Binet made psychologists everywhere so highly aware of the relation of chronological age to mental processes that henceforth almost every investigation on children contains some analysis of the results in terms of chronological or mental age. Moreover, Binet's techniques spread widely and rapidly over the whole world. It is impossible for us, unless we lived through the period, to recapture the enthusiasm, discussion and controversy that the Binet tests started.

In the United States, the intelligence test for children was introduced in 1916 by Lewis M. Terman, who revised the Binet-Simon tests.

The work of E. L. Thorndike, of Columbia University, on learning and learning theory influenced American educational practice and inspired learning research throughout the world for the first four decades of the century. Thorndike was also important because of his studies in the measurement of school performance of children, and was a pioneer in establishing the S-R reinforcement theory of learning as contrasted with the cognitive learning theory (Misiak and Sexton, 1966). Both theories are explained in detail later in this book. For now, it is sufficient to state that Thorndike explained learning as trial and error with no consideration of the conscious influence of the individual being taught, whereas cognitive theorists emphasized the conscious efforts of the learner through insightful relationships.

The field of psychological testing, which originated with the measurement of performance by children, was given greater impetus with the advent of World War I. Group tests were developed and data was collected on many human characteristics, both physical and psychological. After the war, these techniques were applied to children and much normative data was compiled. Such data provided information to see if a child's behaviors were what would be normally expected at various stages of his development. Studies such as these were typical of this period.

Multi-disciplinary Perspectives

In 1917, the Iowa Child Welfare Research Station opened and began to publish surveys of physical and mental growth rates in children. In the early 1920's, Gesell opened a child study unit at Yale University that continues in operation today. Similar groups were started at Harvard University and the University of Chicago. All of these studies emphasized the physical and mental growth of children.

In 1918, only three psychologists in this country were actively and primarily working with children. By 1937 that number had increased thirty times, and today there are more than one thousand members and fellows of the section on child study of the American Psychological Association.

Another significant event in the historical development of child study was the establishment of the White House Conferences. Anderson (1956) traces their development as follows:

> In discussing the development of the field some attention must go to the White House Conferences. The first of these called in 1909 by President Theodore Roosevelt concerned itself mainly with what the national government should do about children. Out of it came the U. S. Children's Bureau, which has been active ever since. The Conference in 1919 dramatically brought to the fore the physical and mental deficiencies revealed by the draft in World War I. The Conference in 1929 pooled substantial amounts of research from all the agencies in the United States (including much data from the Institutes), conducted various surveys on its own, and issued a substantial series of publications which are still significant. The Conferences held in 1940 and 1950, however, were much more concerned with the practical and social aspects of the problems presented by children rather than with research findings.

To trace all the important trends, events, and men who have contributed to the field of child psychology would take several chapters. In order to become aware of some of the trends in the present-day field of child psychology, we have summarized some of the important recent events in the field in Table 7–1. Some of the events are referenced so that you may do further reading if you are interested.

TABLE 7–1
SOME SIGNIFICANT EVENTS IN THE HISTORY OF CHILD PSYCHOLOGY
SINCE THE 1920's

1920—Establishment of Committee on Child Development, National Research Council.
1926—Establishment of National Association of Nursery Education and National Council on Parent Education.
1931—Publication of *Manual of Child Psychology* (1st ed.).
1933—Establishment of Society for Research in Child Development.
1946—Establishment of Division of Childhood and Adolescence within the American Psychological Association.
1960—Golden Anniversary White House Conference on Children and Youth.
1970—White House Conference on Children and Youth.
1970—Revised Manual of Child Psychology (Mussen, 1970).

Psychological
Perspectives

To visually depict the growth of one important area of child psychology in four countries, Brackbill (1967) compared the average number of publications produced each year on research in the field of infant behavior from 1890 to 1962. Figure 7–1 shows the results of her study.

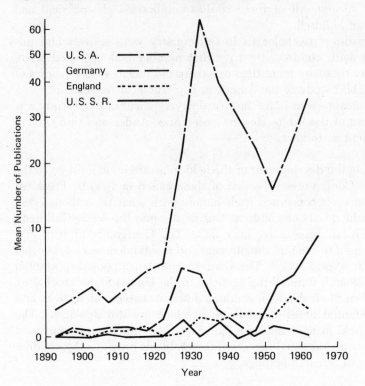

FIG. 7–1.
Average number of publications per year on research in infant behavior for the four most research-productive countries during a 73 year period. (The last entry is based on a three-year interval, 1960–62. The entries on which this figure is based come from data, part of which is published in Y. Brackbill (ed), Research in Infancy and Early Childhood: A Cross-Indexed Bibliography.) Reprinted by permission of © The Williams & Wilkins Co., Baltimore, 1964.

In commenting on this graph, Brackbill (1967) points out the following:

1. That during the 73-year period the United States has done five and one-half times as much infant research as the research output of Germany, Britain, and the USSR combined.
2. That the United States has a much larger number of trained psychologists than all of Europe combined.
3. Only since 1960 have psychologists in the USSR been permitted to use infants as subjects.
4. That the large increase in research in the late 1920's was due to the availability of financial support from private sources such as the Rockefeller Foundation which was then directed by a significant contributor to the psychological research on children, Dr. Lawrence K. Frank.
5. That the graph does not reveal the changes in types of infant research over the years. Brackbill notes a distinct shift from pure "observational-diary type accounts" to more of an emphasis on basic psychological processes such as concept formation, sensory and language development, etc.

Multi-disciplinary Perspectives

SOME CONTEMPORARY TRENDS IN CHILD PSYCHOLOGY

Child psychology is characterized today by a number of trends that account for its attractiveness as a field of study. It has developed rapidly,

98

particularly during the past ten years. Experimental and comparative psychological research has been performed with children only since 1950. Cross-cultural aspects of child behavior did not become commonplace until the mid 1960's. The developmental interactions with other fields of study, such as sociology, anthropology, and clinical medicine are only now being explored.

The field of child psychology is thus characterized today by a broadening from a local and regional focus to a cross-cultural one, from a single disciplinary approach to a multidisciplinary approach, and from a heavy stress on observational and descriptive type studies to more experimental and predictive type studies.

Efforts to Improve Child Welfare. Another significant trend in child psychology today has been an increased concern by child psychologists as well as all social scientists for some of the human problems of the day. The modern psychologist can express his concern through his work. First, he can use his research time and efforts to determine and describe the basic social problems and processes. Second, he can experiment to find possible solutions to these problems. Third, he can implement and help evaluate the results of possible solutions. Applied research programs such as Head Start are examples of this third kind of social-psychological activity.

The need for psychologists to become more involved in applied research areas is becoming more evident every year. The federal government has recognized this need and provided funds for socially relevant research through the Office of Education, the Office of Economic Opportunity, and the Department of Housing and Urban Development. These and other agencies have developed the following programs (Morrisett, 1970):

1. The Regional Laboratories for Research and Development, seven of which are specifically concerned with preschool learning and compensatory education;
2. The National Laboratory on Early Childhood Education, involving at least six universities in research and development in preschool and primary grade programs;
3. Project Head Start, which, in fiscal year 1969, helped over 600,000 children in academic year and summer programs at a cost of $275 million;
4. Project Follow Through programs, of which there were 91 in fiscal year 1969 affecting over 15,000 children. (p. 198)

This brief summary of some of the federal programs does not begin to list many of the state and local efforts, which, together with the federal programs, make up a massive national commitment to early learning and compensatory education.

Another recent trend in the broad area of child psychology has been the development and expansion of organizations and agencies whose sole purpose is to help children and adolescents through research, work with parents, treatment of children with problems and/or the prevention of children's problems. The authors have been overwhelmed by the vast number of such public and private organizations involving thousands of persons whose sole aim in life is to help children and adolescents become more fully functioning individuals.

Psychological
Perspectives

What Child Psychologists Actually Do

Some child psychologists work with the "whole child," whereas others work with only segments of child and adolescent behavior.

In studying, teaching, and doing research in developmental psychology, one must "take the child apart" for purposes of analysis and discussion. For instance, we dissect child behavior and then classify it in various ways (e.g., cognitive, affective, biological, and social). We discuss growth and development during different stages (e.g., the prenatal, infant, early childhood, later childhood, adolescent, adult, middle age, and old age stages). This method presents a dilemma to us, since we run the risk that you will lose sight of the uniqueness, the individuality, and the authenticity of the whole child. We partially resolve our dilemma by "bringing the child back together" in the various application sections of each chapter.

This same dilemma occurs in the field of child psychology. A child psychologist focuses his time and energy on one area of the child or he specializes in the study or treatment of children or adolescents of a certain age or at a particular stage of development. Yet, most child psychologists rely heavily on the research and accumulation of research findings and theories from other disciplines. The first five chapters of this section have given you some insight into these contributing fields.

The child psychologist also uses the findings from other areas of psychology. Table 7–2 gives a listing of all the divisions of the American Psychological Association. In a sense, it is a breakdown of the different areas of research and study and application of psychology.

TABLE 7–2
MEMBERSHIP DIVISIONS IN THE AMERICAN PSYCHOLOGICAL ASSOCIATION

1. General	12. Industrial and Organizational	21. Consumer
2. Teaching		22. Philosophical
3. Experimental	13. Educational	23. Experimental Analysis of Behavior
4. Evaluation and Measurement	14. School	
5. Physiological and Comparative	15. Counseling	24. History of Psychology
6. Developmental	16. Public Service	25. Community Psychology
7. Personality and Social	17. Military	26. Psychopharmacology
8. Society for the Psychological Study of Social Issues	18. Adult Development and Aging	27. Psychotherapy
	19. Engineering	28. Hypnosis
9. Psychology and the Arts	20. Psychological Aspects of Disability	29. State Affairs
10. Clinical		30. Humanistic Psychology
11. Consulting		

Multidisciplinary Perspectives

Psychologists vary in their approach to the field of child psychology from "pure research" to pragmatic application.

Another way of characterizing the field today is in terms of the goals of the work being done. Some child psychologists feel that they can contribute

100

most by conducting laboratory studies on some basic areas of child and adolescent behavior. The work of Bruner in the cognitive domain of children is an example (see Chapters 17 and 18).

Other developmental psychologists find most satisfaction "on the firing line," working there with parents, children, and adolescents. They attempt to solve specific problems in the family, in the school, or in the community.

Other child psychologists do both highly abstract, theoretical research as well as work with children and families.

The authors, for example, have several child-psychologist colleagues who work part time in a child guidance clinic, teach a graduate course for psychology majors at the local state college, carry on a part time private practice, and conduct research studies. Such work patterns are common among professional persons. They see that research and application tasks are highly interrelated; that is, performing one task helps the psychologist grow and develop in the other.

Some child psychologists develop theories about children and adolescents. One of the important tasks of any science is to accumulate data about its sphere of study. In the behavioral sciences, this means the accumulation of data or research findings about man. In child psychology, one of the important jobs that some workers do is to make some sense (often purely hypothetical) out of the mass of research findings that are published yearly.

These "theoretical child psychologists" develop tentative explanations about certain classes of child and adolescent behavior. These hypothetical explanations are called theories. Theories often generate more research—to test them out, refine or change them, which in turn sets in motion a whole new set of research projects. Such "snowballing" continues and is one of the important functions of science.

Some contemporary examples of "theoretical models" of child and adolescent behavior include the work of Piaget, Erikson, and White (see Part IV).

Child psychologists are trained to use certain methods to observe, study, and treat children and adolescents. An important part of the training of a child psychologist (which at present requires the attainment of at least a master's degree; however, the doctor of philosophy is fast becoming the necessary credential for research and/or work with children) is the study of ways to observe and treat children.

Such training involves taking advanced courses, gaining supervised internship experience in a clinic or hospital, and conducting specialized research studies (a master's thesis and/or a doctoral dissertation) about children or adolescents. Child psychologists are thus trained to conduct research studies using different research methods or strategies. They are also trained in clinical methods of diagnosis and treatment of exceptional children (children with problems or handicaps). Table 7–3 briefly summarizes some of these methods.

Child psychologists often study or specialize in different *development stages*. As the field of child psychology develops, the complexity of the developing child and adolescent becomes more apparent. Research studies in child psychology have increased markedly in the past ten years. In order to keep up and to attempt significant research in the field, many child psychologists are finding it necessary to specialize in one or more developmental

Psychological
Perspectives

TABLE 7–3

SOME METHODS USED BY CHILD PSYCHOLOGISTS TO STUDY, OBSERVE, EVALUATE, AND TREAT CHILDREN AND ADOLESCENTS

Method	Brief Description
Cross-sectional Studies	Groups of different aged children studied to determine patterns of behavior at certain stages of life.
Longitudinal Studies	Study of same group of children over a long period of time.
Survey Methods	A series of questions developed to elicit responses that will measure attitudes, opinions, and/or beliefs about a certain issue, value, person, or type of behavior.
Case History Method	A detailed analysis of background information. In child psychology these are used extensively in the diagnosis of children with problems and often survey areas of behavior found in the cognitive, affective, biological, and social domains.
Interview Methods	Used to elicit information on a more personal basis than a survey. A series of questions (interview schedule) is asked of a respondent and the answers are written down or tape recorded.
Observation Methods	Used to observe field type situations where no interference by the experimenter is crucial. In child psychology, this method is often used with "one-way" mirrors to observe children's interactions.
Experimental Method	A highly and carefully structured method of studying behavior where a high degree of control over most variables is important. The most powerful method in terms of making predictions about behavior.
Testing Method	Used to measure a number of behavioral variables: aptitudes, intelligence, interests, personality, motivation, attitudes, etc. Used by child psychologists in educational and clinical settings for diagnosis.
Cross Cultural Method	Used to compare methods of child rearing and behavior among different cultures. Child psychologists use data from these studies that are usually conducted by cultural anthropologists.

stages. Table 7–4 gives a breakdown of these stages, with the approximate age range for each stage. There are widespread differences about the number of developmental stages, the exact ages, and how significant each period is for later development. However, most child psychologists would not disagree markedly with this general breakdown.

Most child psychologists are concerned with the different *developmental domains* of the growing child and adolescent. Another part of the world of the child psychologist covers the areas of behavior he chooses to observe or study. Not only do child psychologists often specialize in a particular stage

Multi-disciplinary Perspectives

TABLE 7–4

SOME STAGES WITHIN WHICH DEVELOPMENTAL PSYCHOLOGISTS DO
RESEARCH AND STUDY

Name of Stage	Approximate Age Range
1. The Prenatal Stage	Conception to Birth
2. The Infant Stage	Birth to Two Years
3. The Early Childhood Stage	Three to Five Years
4. The Later Childhood Stage	Five to Nine Years
5. The Adolescent Stage	Ten to Eighteen Years
6. The Adult Stage	Eighteen to Thirty-nine Years
7. The Middle-Age Stage	Forty to Sixty Years
8. The Old-Age Stage	61+

of development but many select a specialized area of behavior within that
stage.

There are many possible ways to look at human behavior systematically.
The authors have selected one of many possible ways to talk about and
discuss research findings. Table 7–5 presents the four major domains of
human behavior that the child psychologist may observe, study, or work
with. These four basic domains also provide the background throughout the
remainder of the text as the development of the child through the various
growth stages is discussed.

TABLE 7–5

MAJOR DEVELOPMENTAL DOMAINS OF THE CHILD PSYCHOLOGIST

Domain	Examples of Types of Behavior Included
Cognitive	Thought Processes, Language Development
	Learning Processes
Affective	Feelings, Emotions, Motivation
Biological	All Biological Processes and Their Psychological Implications
Social	Effect of Institutions on Human Development
	Effect of Society and Groups on Developing

In viewing these four major domains, it should again be emphasized that
they are being used only as a means of systematically studying the central
areas of human behavior as they develop. These domains or systems are in
no way independent, separate systems, but are highly interrelated and interactive. One sphere influences another, and it in turn has an impact on the
rest. The reader is cautioned to keep this in mind as he reads each section
separately. Hopefully, toward the end of the book he will be able to grasp
the "gestalt" or "whole" child and these domains will disappear as he experi-

Psychological
Perspectives

ences the significance, beauty, and aliveness of the growing, fully function-ing, and emerging child.

Child psychologists study the behavioral dynamics of the growing child and adolescent. In addition to being concerned with the basic development domains, child psychologists are concerned with the effects on the person as he comes in contact with the world around him.

Thus, how a person views the world (perception), how a person becomes attracted to a goal (motivation), how a person solves problems (thinking), how a person learns about his environment (learning), and how a person feels about his world (emotions) are all of interest to the child psychologist. We also study these basic behavioral processes during the different stages of growth.

Some child psychologists do research and develop theories about the *mentally healthy or fully functioning* child and adolescent. A recent develop-ment in the area of psychology in general (which has generalized to the specialized field of child psychology) is that of the research on self-actualiz-ing, mentally healthy, or fully functioning persons. The work of Maslow, Rogers, Allport, and other "humanistic psychologists" has played a key role in this development. Also, the philosophical writings of the existentialists such as Kierkegaard, Nietzsche, and others have had an impact on this movement.

The authors feel that the implications of this research and theory (how-ever tentative it may be) are so profound that we have incorporated them into our next section (Part II) as a means of setting down possible models for people who will be living and working with children as parents, teachers, nurses, child psychologists, or social workers. In other words, we use this research to raise such questions as: What kind of a world would it be if we could fully develop the potential of every child—their cognitive, affective, psychological, and social domains? What kind of models do we need for parents and professional workers to help children and adolescents become fully functioning members of the world of tomorrow? How can we help develop the models for a loving child, a creative child, a compassionate child, and a healthy child? It is such questions that Part III of the text tries to help you answer.

Some child psychologists specialize in research and/or treatment of chil-dren and adolescents with specific barriers that prevent them from becoming fully functioning persons. The field of child psychology also focuses on spe-cific problems of children. The need for trained child psychologists to help children with various problems in all domains is so great that many child psychologists spend a portion of their time in this area. For example, some psychologists may specialize in working with neurologically handicapped children, while others may help those with emotional problems. Chapter 21 discusses some perspectives on the diagnosis, treatment, and prevention of these barriers.

This lengthy chapter introduces you to the field of study about which this book is written; it invites you to consider some major concepts that reoccur in the remainder of the text. To better visualize the field of child psychology, think of the child psychologist as working along a continuum as Figure 7–2 illustrates.

Continuum

Study of a small segment of behavior (molecular approach). Study of "whole child" (molar approach).

"Pure research" and theory building activities.	More applied type work.
Some specialize in working with and studying children and adolescents with barriers to becoming fully functioning person.	Some specialize in working with and studying fully functioning children and adolescents.
Some make observations about single child (observation and case study research methods).	Some make observations and generalizations about many children (experimental and survey methods).
Some specialize in the study of one developmental stage (e.g. prenatal, infancy, etc.)	Others specialize in study of entire developmental span.
Some specialize in the study of one developmental domain (cognitive, affective, etc.)	Others specialize in study and interrelationship of all domains.
Some specialize in study of one of the basic behavioral processes (e.g. thinking, perceiving, learning, etc.)	Others specialize in all basic behavioral processes.

FIG. 7–2. *Some dimensions in the field of child psychology.*

IMPLICATIONS

UNDERSTANDING YOURSELF AND OTHERS

Child psychologists are now firmly convinced that what happens early in life makes a significant difference in a person's future personality. (Thousands of scientists from many disciplines devote their entire life to studying often minute aspects of an infant, child, or adolescent.) One of the tasks of this section is to lead you into an exploration and a testing of this proposition in respect to your own early developmental history.

One of the authors remembers that a significant event in his first psychology course was completing a case history form regarding his family background and early childhood experiences. It was partly through this experience (and partly through being older) that he began to look at himself, his brother and sister, and his parents from a different perspective. He found that he felt and reexperienced some of the frustrations that his parents must have felt during the Depression; some of the joys of spending a week's vacation at the beach; how hard it must have been at times for his father, a machinist, to have to go to work every day whether he felt well or not; how unfair his parents were to his brother, who was the oldest.

The result was that the author began to establish a different relationship with his parents and siblings because he could, for at least a moment, sit back and reflect and recreate early experiences that had shaped him.

You might begin a similar analysis by thinking about positive and negative events during your own developmental stages. Then, you might ask each of your parents (independently) to do the same thing. Last, you could compare the results and see how interesting they are and how useful they can be.

Psychological Perspectives

105

Another insight that we hope you have developed, as a result of reading this section, is that human behavior is a highly complex process. It is the result of forces (domains) that keep interacting over all the years of life. The four domains discussed earlier include the major variables upon which most of our behavior is based.

Another way of experiencing the implications of these four domains is to reconstruct a developmental history within your own life history. Since much of this material has been forgotten, you will be better able to reconstruct your history through discussions with your parents.

As a result of thinking about your development during the different stages and domains, you may have become aware of some barriers that may still be preventing you from becoming a fully functioning person. By exploring some of these, you can gain further insight into yourself and your parents.

When you have thought about, as well as discussed, your developmental history with your parents, your brothers and/or sisters, and/or friends, a striking thought will probably occur to you. It is that all of us have similar classes of experiences in the various domains during our developmental histories. The specific details may be different, but the types of events are quite similar: financial troubles, serious illness, problems in school, jealousy of a newborn sibling, a wonderful vacation, a first boyfriend or girlfriend, or falling in love with a teacher are examples.

Knowing this should give you a feeling of compassion and empathy for your fellow man. You will come to realize that some groups of individuals—because of racial differences, financial or educational inequalities, or just the period of time they were born—have experienced large numbers of barriers that have prevented them, right on into adulthood, from becoming fully functioning individuals.

Think of the barriers that children develop during the war years. Think of the barriers that the children of impoverished families experience. Think of the children of families of minority groups, where the seeds for the growth of barriers are planted early. How to eliminate these barriers later in life, and more important, how to prevent the development of these barriers, is a task to which many of you may wish to devote your professional lifetime.

LIVING AND WORKING WITH CHILDREN, ADOLESCENTS, AND ADULTS

The field of child psychology is a broad area of human study that overlaps with many other disciplines. We hope that you now have some idea of the contributions it has made and continues to make in helping understand children and adolescents whether it be on the theoretical, research, or applied level. Being aware that there are theories, studies, and research findings available on all stages and domains of child and adolescent development, you can find some answers to specific questions that may arise as you live and work with children and adolescents. Hopefully, by the time you finish studying this book, some of these questions will be partially answered, and you will know where to go for more definitive answers. You can continue to study with the bibliographies that are provided.

The fact that there are literally hundreds of agencies, clinics, and foundations concerned with childhood and adolescence should help you realize

Multi-
disciplinary
Perspectives

106

that if you go into child psychology or related fields, you will have many resources near at hand to assist you in your efforts.

Being aware of local, regional, national, and international resources should help you realize the multidisciplinary aspects of working with children.

Being exposed to some of the "exploratory" research on the "fully functioning child and adolescent" will help you to experiment in certain directions with your own children and/or those with whom you will be working.

DEVELOPING POSITIVE MODELS

The field of child psychology has come a long way over the years, from a few early philosophers and "child biographers" to its development into a complex study of all facets of human development. The implications of the research in this expanding field for developing positive models (while still evolving) are striking. For example, for the first time in the history of man, we are in a position to begin to define the important factors in the development of more fully human persons.

Putting it another way, as a result of some of the following factors, the field of child psychology should produce within the next several years information that will help us develop positive models in the four domains of man's development: (1) The powerful research methods and computer technology; (2) The extensive support of public and private funds for research in this area; (3) The availability and exchange of cross-cultural research on human development; (4) The application of psychological principles to the prevention and overcoming of barriers to developing into a more fully human person; (5) The increasing emphasis on a multi-disciplinary approach to the study of human development, and (6) The increasing awareness among parents and teachers for the need to seek the advice of a child psychologist when problems arise early in childhood.

CHAPTER REFERENCES

ANDERSON, J. E. Child development: an historical perspective. *Child Development,* 1956, **27**:181–196.

BRACKBILL, Y. (ed.). *Infancy and early childhood.* New York: Free Press, 1967.

DENNIS, W. Historical beginnings of child psychology. *Psychological Bulletin,* 1949, **46**:224–235.

MISIAK, H. and V. SEXTON. *History of psychology.* New York: Grune, 1966.

MORRISETT, L. N. Early learning and compensatory education. In F. F. Korten, S. W. Cook, and J. I. Lacey, *Psychology and the problems of society.* Washington, D.C.: Am. Psychological Assn., 1970.

MUSSEN, P. H. (ed.). *Carmichael's manual of child psychology,* 3rd ed. New York: Wiley, 1970.

RECOMMENDED FURTHER READING

AMERICAN PSYCHOLOGICAL ASSOCIATION. *Careers in psychology.* Washington, D.C.: The Association, 1969.

———. *Proceedings of the 79th annual convention of the American Psychological Association.* Washington, D.C.: The Association, 1971.

ANASTASI, A. *Fields of applied psychology.* New York: McGraw-Hill, 1964.

Psychological
Perspectives

BRECKENRIDGE, M. E. and M. M. MURPHY. *Growth and development of the young child*. Philadelphia: Saunders, 1969.

CROW, L. D. and A. CROW. *Child psychology*. New York: Barnes & Noble, 1953.

FROST, J. L. (ed.). *Early childhood education rediscovered*. New York: Holt, 1968.

HARRIMAN, P. L. *Handbook of psychological terms*. Totowa, N. J.: Littlefield, Adams, 1969.

HILL, J. P. (ed.). *Minnesota symposia on child psychology*, vol. 4. Minneapolis: U. of Minnesota, 1970.

HOSELITZ, B. F. (ed.). *A reader's guide to the social sciences*. New York: Free Press, 1970.

KESSEN, W. *The child*. New York: Wiley, 1965.

MEDINNUS, G. R. (ed.). *Reading in the psychology of parent-child relations*. New York: Wiley, 1967.

MISIAK, H., and V. S. SEXTON. *History of psychology*. New York: Grune, 1966.

MUSSEN, P. H., J. J. CONGER, and J. KAGAN (eds.). *Readings in child development and personality*. New York: Harper, 1965.

REESE, M. W. and L. P. LIPSITT. *Experimental child psychology*. New York: Academic, 1970.

SUPER, D. E. *Opportunities in psychology careers*. New York: Universal Publishing and Distributing Corp., 1968.

Multi-
disciplinary
Perspectives

PART III
Life Goals

AN *anonymous student once wrote the following to his teacher:*

Sometimes I feel like all the world is just a big movie theatre, and everybody on earth is just acting a role and I'm just an observer. After sitting for a long time and watching people (which I do quite often) I feel isolated and invisible. But I want to scream and run up to some kind face and say: "Please communicate with me; I don't know how to start but I'll help if you go first." It's so frustrating because I have nice things, but it seems that I have lived my life away from everyone. It's like I'm sitting on a big hill and just parasitically drawing from society. Just using people.

This statement dramatically focuses on one of the major dilemmas that face mankind in the modern world—alienation, a feeling of helplessness, a lack of power to feel much at all.

There are many symptoms of this alienation as can be seen in the statistics in the daily newspapers. Our suicide rates are increasing (particularly among youth). Our drug abuse rate has increased markedly (also particularly among the young). Our crime rates have soared (again particularly among the younger generation). Incidence of mental illness has increased. The number of alcoholics has increased (particularly among the older generation). Minority peoples throughout our land are not satisfied with the lives they are forced to live.

Simply put, all is not well with Americans today. So many people lead crippled and miserable lives. The explanation seems to lie in a complex of psychological and social factors.

What can be done about these problems that cause so much pain and misery for millions of persons? There are, of course, those ready-made simplistic answers:

"Build bigger jails!"

"Construct more mental hospitals!"

"Put drug users and pushers in jail or in the gas chamber!"

"Sterilize all criminals!"

"Make everyone go to church on Sundays!"

We must note that these are means of treating only the symptoms of the "illness." Furthermore, the history of the use of these approaches shows quite convincingly that they just don't work! Let us then suggest another way, one that involves the exploration of a great mystery. It is a mystery that has triggered a search so vast in scope, and so monumental in its significance, that it often overwhelms those who are involved with it. It is a search that may never end, and yet, it must be pursued.

The exploration involves many areas of human existence, yet essentially it is a search for the basic nature of man . . . not just any man, but a special breed of man. Some call him a "self-actualizing man,"

Life Goals

others a "fully functioning man," some an "authentic man." We will call him a "more fully human person."

This search, then, is what this section is about. It is going on in all domains: the biological, cognitive, affective, and social. It is hoped that by the end of this section you will be able to grasp more fully the reason it is so important to discuss this search before studying the development of the child into a man.

At the outset, let us say that we believe that society cannot afford to build more jails and mental hospitals. The human price is far too high to pay. Nor can we afford to live for today and forget about tomorrow while rearing our children. We cannot ignore the research pouring out of universities and special centers about the nature of children, man, and society.

We must listen and understand. We must begin to develop some positive models of human sanity now if we and our children are to live in ways that foster the growth of the human species, rather than its destruction.

In a sense, we are "sticking our necks out" because psychologists are not supposed to discuss values. However, one of the reasons we decided to write this book was that most social scientists have not taken a stand regarding positive, growth-producing, and humanly beneficial aspects of their research.

In the figure that follows we have summarized some dimensions of the more fully human person. Notice that this model involves a series of satellite patterns, many of which are still unknown. Thus, it is a temporary model, to be added to and subtracted from as the search continues.

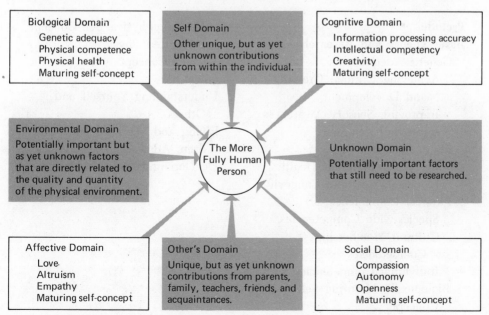

Biological Domain
  Genetic adequacy
  Physical competence
  Physical health
  Maturing self-concept

Self Domain
Other unique, but as yet unknown contributions from within the individual.

Cognitive Domain
  Information processing accuracy
  Intellectual competency
  Creativity
  Maturing self-concept

Environmental Domain
Potentially important but as yet unknown factors that are directly related to the quality and quantity of the physical environment.

The More Fully Human Person

Unknown Domain
Potentially important factors that still need to be researched.

Affective Domain
  Love
  Altruism
  Empathy
  Maturing self-concept

Other's Domain
Unique, but as yet unknown contributions from parents, family, teachers, friends, and acquaintances.

Social Domain
  Compassion
  Autonomy
  Openness
  Maturing self-concept

Some factors involved in contributing to a more fully human person.

Life Goals

The Biological Domain

Prelude
Basic Theory and Research
  Genetic Adequacy
    Achieving Optimal Growth
    and Development
    Improving Sensory Awareness
    Improving Learning
  Physical Health
    Increasing States of Health
    Increasing Zest and Longevity
  Physical Competence
    Species-wide Competencies
    Cultural Membership
    Competencies
    Individual Competencies
  Biologically Maturing Self-
  Concept
  Positive Physical Self-Concept

Realistic Physical Self-Concept
Integrated Physical
  Self-Concept
Implications
  Understanding Yourself and
  Others
  Living and Working with Chil-
  dren, Adolescents, and Adults
  Developing Positive Models

PRELUDE

THE INTRODUCTION to this section of the text emphasizes the need to uncover the mystery that will enable man to become more fully human; that is, to become superbly healthy psychologically, biologically, and sociologically. At the present time such a goal sounds like the impossible dream. But, then so did the idea of man walking on the moon until July 20, 1969.

The first step toward helping man become more fully human is the development of proper goals by those concerned with the welfare of children. We admit that some parents and teachers who have no stated goals for their children do a fine job of rearing them, but we submit that those who have definite goals will do a better job.

BASIC THEORY AND RESEARCH

Except for certain treatable genetic defects, diseases, and physical malformations, medical science has made little progress toward establishing a high degree of "wellness" in our population. Although there is a vast uncharted territory between what we know about human biology and our observations about human behavior, it is clear that there is much that we can do to aid the developing human individual to realize his full biological potential.

Figure 8–1 illustrates the four areas in which man's human biological potential may be more fully developed.

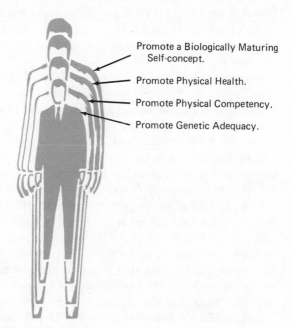

Promote a Biologically Maturing Self-concept.

Promote Physical Health.

Promote Physical Competency.

Promote Genetic Adequacy.

FIG. 8–1.
Life goals in the biological domain.

GENETIC ADEQUACY

The genetically adequate man as defined is not merely a person who lacks known genetic defects but one whose biological potential for superior well-being has been brought to a maximum level throughout the stages of life.

The Biological Domain

Achieving Optimal Growth and Development

Growth, in general, refers to the observable increases in the size of the body and its parts. Technically, growth refers to increases in cells and intercellular substances, as well as corresponding changes in their physical and chemical structures and functions. Development, a product of both growth and learning, refers to changes in behavior and attitudes that occur as the infant progresses to adulthood. Both growth and development include the physical, cognitive, emotional, and social domains. In the biological domain especially, development is governed essentially by genetically determined time schedules. The sequence of development is the same for all children, but the rates of development and the end-products vary from child to child.

We discuss growth rates at a later point in this book. However, information about expected sequences and rates of growth and development provide adults who work with children with a basis for understanding the individual child. Thus, goals can be set ahead of time in light of the child's maturity and his rate of development, and obstacles that are beyond his capacity to cope can be removed. Equipped with this understanding, adults can enhance the child's chances for achieving optimal growth and development.

Many factors may interfere with the individual's achievement of his full genetic potential for growth and development. Obviously, nutritional and vitamin deficiencies can produce retarded growth and weak development. Not so obvious are some other considerations. Heroin addiction in a pregnant woman may result in her having a heroin addicted baby. More than eight thousand of these infant "junkies" were born in the United States in 1971; most suffered some degree of drug withdrawal symptoms during the first few days of life. With proper medical treatment, 60 to 80 per cent of these babies can be saved. However, it is too early to say just what long-term effects this fetal heroin addiction may have on the child's growth and development.

For the present, we will have to be satisfied with a definition of optimal growth and development as that which falls within the normal range for individuals of the same age and background. Our present knowledge does not, for the most part, allow us to establish goals for development under improved or ideal conditions. There is, however, some evidence that man's genetic potential may be changing. This is not surprising when we consider that man, like other animals and most plants, is an adapting organism and his species is constantly undergoing evolutionary change.

Observations of man's performances at athletic events clearly shows that today's champion athletes are superior to champions of twenty to fifty years ago. Even when we discount the improvements in equipment, training and coaching techniques, and superior psychological preparation, it is difficult to account for the fact that any one of the finalists in the girls' free-style swimming events at the 1972 Munich Olympics routinely swam these events in better times than the male gold medal winners in the 1936 Olympics.

In 1956, Roger Bannister broke the fabled four-minute barrier in the mile run. At this writing the world record has been lowered to approximately three minutes and fifty-one seconds, and physiologists who study human performance indicate that it may be within the genetic potential of man to further drop this record to approximately three minutes and twenty-five seconds.

Life Goals

114

Perhaps as child psychologists move toward lifelong behavioral studies using experimental manipulative techniques, the frontiers of genetic potential may be redefined for other areas of human endeavor.

Improving Sensory Awareness

Our first criterion for defining genetic adequacy is optimal growth and development because the most fundamental ability of life is the ability to grow. Our second criterion is improving sensory awareness because the senses are the channels of information into the human systems. To develop optimally, the infant must be able to perceive as fully as possible his physical

Fig. 8–2.
Sensory input.

and social environment. The infant has five ways to learn about the world around him: he can see, smell, feel, hear, and taste. In order for the infant to become fully human, these five channels must be effective transmitters of information. Table 8–1 indicates that most newborn infants can demonstrate various degrees of awareness in the different sensory modes. After birth, the development of sensory awareness proceeds rapidly, and there is increased responsiveness to external and internal stimulation.

Improving Learning

Another early sign of a genetic adequacy is the ability to learn. Basically learning involves changes in one's behavior as a result of new experiences. Learning is a principal reason for the continuous changes in the infant's responses.

According to Illingworth (1971), the first general signs of learning occur sometime during the first four weeks of life when the infant begins to watch his mother as she speaks to him. He becomes quiet, opens and closes his mouth, and bobs his head vertically. Babies smile frequently during the

The Biological Domain

TABLE 8–1
SENSORY DEVELOPMENT OF NEWBORN INFANTS

Sensory Modalities	Behaviors
Vision	Almost always responds to light. Some indication of color vision. Large minority are capable of pursuit of object (sequential order: fixation, horizontal, vertical, then circular following). Preference for complex patterned stimuli rather than homogeneous.
Hearing	Can detect sounds less than 70 decibels (just above normal conversation). Some evidence for frequency discrimination. Continuous stimuli of low pitch and moderate intensity tend to inhibit activity (a mother's lullaby).
Taste	Relaxes and sucks in reaction to sweet solutions and grimaces, rejects, and ceases to suck in reaction to salty, sour, or bitter substances. Hungry infants are more likely to accept foods with new texture and taste than moderately full infants.
Smell	Difficult to investigate, probably a poorly developed sense.
Feel	Not as sensitive to pain as adults when given electric shocks or pin pricks; sharp changes in temperature increase activity level. React readily to touch, rotation of body, and motor movement; females more sensitive than males to mild electric shock and stimulation of abdomen by air jet.

first month, however, in the absence of any apparent external stimulus (Buhler, 1930).

In the second month, the child responds to the attention of others; one can observe genuine smiling in response to the voice and glance of the parent. By the twelfth week, other general signs of learning can be observed, such as recognition of mother, interest in surroundings, and excitement when presented with toys. Table 8–2 presents some additional behaviors that are indicative of developmental learning during the first year of life.

More precise evidence for the existence of *early* infant learning comes from experimental studies of conditioned response behavior. Table 8–3 presents some of these results in the sensory modalities of feeling, smelling, hearing, and seeing. Examples of these conditioned responses can be readily observed in the behaviors of growing infants. A baby sucks when a nipple is placed between his lips, but this sucking response is not assumed to be learned behavior because it is present at birth. Eventually, however, the baby will start sucking movements at the mere sight of the nursing bottle. This sucking behavior at the sight of the bottle is called a conditioned response because it was not present at birth and because it was elicited only after experience. In his original studies Ivan Pavlov found that dogs could be trained to salivate to a variety of previously neutral stimuli such as a bell, the sight of food, or a touch on the paw. Pavlov concluded that events that occur repeatedly together tend to be connected in such a way that in the future the happening of one event will increase the likelihood that a certain type of response will occur.

The road to achieving genetic adequacy begins long before the baby is
Life Goals   born. The roots lie in the health and well-being of the parents. Proper

TABLE 8–2

SOME BEHAVIORS INDICATIVE OF LEARNING DEVELOPMENT
DURING THE FIRST YEAR OF LIFE

12 weeks	Turns head away when nose is cleaned. Emits squeals of pleasure. "Talks" a great deal when spoken to.
16 weeks	Anticipates and excites when prepared for feeding. Shows interest in strange room. Laughs aloud.
20 weeks	Smiles at mirror image.
24 weeks	Expresses displeasure at removal of toy. Holds arms out to be picked up. Seems to like and dislike. Vocalizes at mirror image. When he drops cube he looks to see where it has gone. Shows excitement on hearing steps. Beginning of imitation. Laughs when head is hidden in towel.
28 weeks	Shows expectation in response to repetition of stimulus. Imitates acts and noises. Tries to attract attention by coughing. Enjoys peeking games. Responds to name. Keeps lips closed when offered food that he doesn't want.
32 weeks	Reacts to cotton wool swab by grasping his mother's hand and pushing it away. Reaches persistently for toys that are out of reach. Responds to "No." Imitates sounds.
36 weeks	Compares two cubes by bringing them together. Puts arms in front of face to avoid having it washed.
40 weeks	Pulls clothes of mother to attract attention. Waves bye-bye. Patacake. Repeats performance when laughed at. Looks around corner for object. Responds to words, *e.g.* "Where is daddy?" Holds object to examiner, but won't release it.
44 weeks	Drops object deliberately, to be picked up. Helps to dress.
48 weeks	Rolls ball to examiner. Will give toy to examiner. Anticipates body movements when nursery rhyme being said. Interest in picture book. Plays peeking by covering face. Shakes head for "No."

Adapted from R. S. Illingworth, *The Development of the Infant and Young Child: Normal and Abnormal.* Baltimore: Williams & Wilkins, 1971.

medical supervision during pregnancy and delivery can ensure that the newborn child is not subject to birth-related accidents that would hamper his efforts to achieve full genetic potential. Proper attention to the growth and development rates of the child can point out possible areas of deficiency in the child. Providing the child with ample sensory and learning stimuli

The Biological
Domain

TABLE 8–3
SOME CONDITIONED-RESPONSE LEARNING IN VERY EARLY INFANCY

Sense Modality	Conditioned Responses
Feeling	Mouth opens in response to moving his arm upwards after arm movement has been paired with Babinski reflex (pressure on palm of supine infant produces opening of mouth). Infant ceases to respond to air jet on skin after repeated presentations.
Hearing	Changes in skin resistance to sound after sound has been paired with electric shock. Premature infants grimace, blink, swallow, and suck to sound after sound has been paired with ammonia. Infants turn head to left upon a sound after the sound has been paired with milk.
Smelling	Infant continues to suck in presence of noxious odor after odor was paired with pacifier in mouth.
Visual	Infant closes eyes to vibrations on foot after vibrations on foot were paired with flashes of light. Three-month-old infant smiles upon sight of mother.

can contribute to the development of his general awareness and increase the chances that the child will realize his genetic adequacy.

PHYSICAL HEALTH

In advancing an adequate definition of a physically healthy person, we cannot overlook his mental and social health. Our major life goal of the development of more fully human persons is not solely concerned with physical potentials. We expect the physically healthy, however perfect their bodies and coordination may be, to learn to use their minds and to live harmoniously with their fellow men. Therefore, we accept as our first criterion the concept of an *integrated state of health* as defined by the World Health Organization (1947). "Health is a state of complete physical, mental, and social well-being, not merely the absence of disease and infirmity." Note that the definition includes well-being in mind and body, in family life, and in community life.

Increasing States of Health

By increasing states of health, we mean that we do not stop being concerned with our physical well-being once a disease or a discomfort has been cured. Rather, it means that we are constantly searching for higher or more positive levels of physical well-being. We feel that Halbert L. Dunn, M.D. (1961) has captured the essence of the concept of increasing states of health in the following passage:

Personally, I have become deeply interested in wellness, and find it more absorbing than sickness. When we become interested in wellness as a condition, we discover that the state of being well is not just a drab, static one. Quite the contrary. Wellness has many levels. It is ever-changing in its characteristics. In fact, it is an interrelated panorama of life itself.

Life Goals

118

Well-being calls for *zest* in life. Often, we confuse zest with something that gives us a very momentary "lift." For instance, we may indulge in cocktail parties to get this lift. Some go further in their search for "kicks": drug parties, using heroin or marijuana. But alcohol and drugs are temporary excitants. At the very best, they give a bang which is followed by a pretty severe hangover. Such excitement is not uncommonly succeeded by depression.

On the other hand, a high level of well-being brings its own lift, and has its own bang, yet it does not result in a hangover. It usually leaves a state of affairs inside of us which makes us reach for an even more zestful life, later on. We can enjoy life more because of what we *have* enjoyed.

Apart from the obvious evidence for the need for early prenatal care, physical fitness, proper nutrition, and medical attention, it is difficult to find research that was designed to enhance physical well-being. Perhaps, when medical science changes its focus of attention from disease, disability, and death, to goals in line with the development of superhealthy people, we will be better able to specify the characteristics of a high level of physical well-being.

Table 8–4 shows some of the key relationships between the nervous system and behavior as well as the structures essential for physical and psychological well-being. The better this system functions the greater are the chances that the person will receive full benefits from both inner and outer experiences. Oddly enough, when the nervous system receives continuous stimulation, it becomes increasingly more capable of handling, storing, and integrating information (Dubos, 1968). For example, during the evolutionary emergence of man, there was an enlargement of the neocortex, that part of the brain that is intimately related to the handling of increased complexity in physical and social relationships (Young, 1960).

TABLE 8–4
THE CENTRAL NERVOUS SYSTEM AND BEHAVIOR

Structures	Behaviors
Cerebral cortex	Centers for learning, thinking, language, abstract thought, memory, and dreaming.
Cerebellum	Centers for bodily movements and physical balance.
Thalamus	Receives all sensations except smell and relays them to appropriate parts of the cerebral cortex.
Hypothalamus	Centers for hunger, thirst, sex, body temperature control, and preparation of the body for fight or flight in emergencies.
Pituitary	Influences general metabolism, chemical balance, and secondary sexual characteristics.

INCREASING ZEST AND LONGEVITY

If we had to choose between a short, happy life and a long, miserable one, most of us would probably choose the former. A long, happy life, however, is

The Biological Domain

119

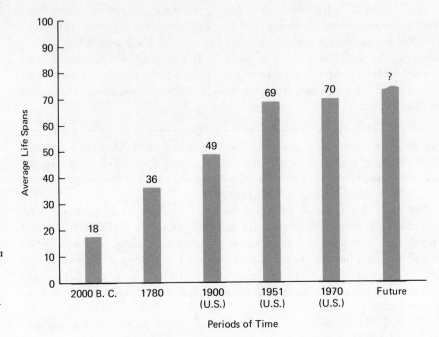

Fig. 8–3.
The average human life span has been increasing sharply during the course of recorded history. (Compiled from Hellman, 1971.)

the ideal, for we would all like to add life to years as well as years to life.

That man has succeeded in adding years to life can be readily demonstrated; the average life span in the United States has increased by twenty-one years, from age forty-nine to seventy, in the period from 1900 to 1970. (Figure 8–3) In ancient Greece, the average life span was only twenty-two years (Hellman, 1971). Apparently the advancements of the medical and social sciences have enabled us to live longer and healthier lives.

Because the body is a self-repairing mechanism, the life span of man is theoretically unlimited. The ever-increasing life span suggests that fewer of us are dying at earlier ages from diseases. According to Prehoda (1969), if all major diseases were eliminated, the average life span would be extended into the gray area shown in Figure 8–4, but there would be no significant extension of the *maximum* length of life. Such an extension of the human survival curve is, of course, dependent on providing people with optimal nutrition, exercise, and relaxation, together with hormone replacement. If gerontologists succeed in their efforts to slow or halt the processes by which the body ages, then perhaps the life span may extend well into the two-hundred-year range as illustrated in Figure 8–5. Finally, if all causes of aging could be prevented or corrected, man could conceivably live for one thousand years or more as suggested in Figure 8–6.

To add life and zest to years is a worthwhile but difficult goal. Even though we may not agree totally with the hedonistic philosophy, there is much to be said for increasing human happiness. There lies before us, if we choose to be aware of it, a wondrous world of sensation for us to interpret and enjoy. The world—full of sights, sounds, tastes, and feelings—can play symphonies within us if only we would tune ourselves to the harmony and beauty around and within us. The brain itself contains far larger pleasure than pain centers. Perhaps we need to have more joy than we are having. It would be difficult, we believe, to deny that the sight of a happy

Life Goals

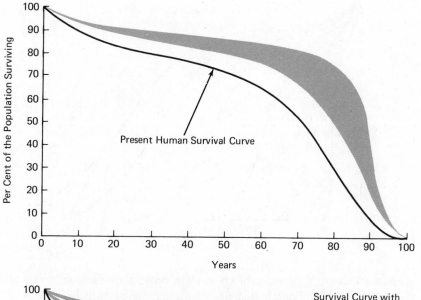

FIG. 8–4.
*If all major
illnesses, including
cancer, heart
disease, and strokes
were eliminated,
the human lifespan
would be extended
into the gray area
shown here. But
there would be no
significant exten-
sion of the maxi-
mum length of life.
(Prehoda, 1969.
Reprinted by
permission of the
World Future
Society,
P.O. Box 30369,
Washington, D.C.
20014.)*

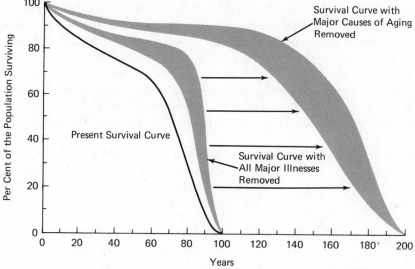

FIG. 8–5.
*Control of the
major causes of
aging would cause
a significant
extension of the
maximum length of
life, perhaps toward
the 200-year mark.
(Prehoda, 1969.
Reprinted by
permission of the
World Future
Society,
P.O. Box 30369,
Washington, D.C.
20014.)*

child who is glad to be alive, glad to be himself, and glad to be doing what he is doing is not the *sine qua non* of the more fully human child.

Physical Competence

Our definition of the physically competent child includes three criteria: (1) species-wide competencies such as crawling, sitting up, and walking; (2) competencies necessary to be considered normal by his social groups such as playing ball and riding a tricycle; and (3) competencies that are unique or fairly unique to the individual such as hobbies, special talents, and vocational skills.

Species-Wide Competencies

The term *species* refers to a single class of living organisms whose essential sameness distinguishes them from all other organisms. Man represents only one of the more than 1.2 million different species of living things. Man,

The Biological
Domain

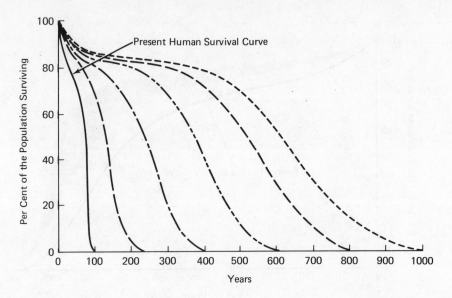

Fig. 8–6.
*If all causes of
aging can be cor-
rected, the life-span
might be progres-
sively lengthened
until people might
conceivably be
living longer than
Methuselah's 965
years. (Prehoda,
1969. Reprinted
by permission of
the World
Future Society,
P.O. Box 30369,
Washington, D.C.
20014.)*

no matter where he lives, exhibits certain basic sequences of physical behavior from birth to death that are characteristic of only his species.

It is probably safe to assume that the potentials for species-wide physical
competencies reside in the common genetic pool of mankind and develop
chronologically and sequentially under a wide range of favorable environmental conditions. Studies by Shirley (1931), Bayley (1935), and Gesell
(1940), using different samples of children in the United States, support the
idea that the early development of physical and motor abilities follows an
invariable sequence. Table 8–5 lists selected physical competencies and
their approximate time of appearance. Perhaps more important than the
sequence of development is the accumulative building of more complex
skills upon the more simple ones. We can observe this phenomenon of
growth competency as a function of maturity in other areas of physical
ability such as running speeds, throwing distances, and throwing velocities
(Keogh, 1965; Glassow and Kruse, 1960).

Cross-national studies of growth and physical competencies are not common, but where they do exist they suggest a similar pattern of constant
improvement with age until certain limits of performance are reached
(Dennis, 1935). If we accept continuous growth in height and weight as
valid indicators of ability to perform increasingly more complex physical
tasks (see Figure 8–7), we can develop the hypothesis that there are certain
species-wide competencies that develop sequentially and that these improve
as a function of age with little apparent influence by other persons, especially during the very early years. However, the statistics on the mean
height and weight for children, aged six through eleven, in the United
States, United Arab Republic, and India suggest that the ages for the onset
of physical competencies may occur earlier depending on such environmental factors as nutrition and medical care (Public Health Service, 1970).
Attempts, so far, to measurably alter some early species-wide physical behaviors before age two have not met with success (Dennis, 1935; McGraw,
1935). Thus, we may conclude that the time of appearance for certain
motor behaviors and their subsequent improvement are more dependent
Life Goals   upon the development of the nervous system than upon early practice and

TABLE 8–5
GROSS MOTOR ATTRIBUTES IN EARLY CHILDHOOD

Approximate Time of Appearance	Selected Behaviors
1 year	Walking unaided
	A rapid "running-like" walk Will step off low objects
2 years	Walking rhythm stabilizes and becomes even Jumps crudely with two-foot take-off Will throw small ball 4–5 ft.
	True running appears
	Can walk sideward and backward
3 years	Can walk a line, heel to toe, 10 ft. long
	Can hop from two to three steps, on preferred foot Will walk balance beam for short distances Can throw a ball about 10 ft.
4 years	Running with good form, leg-arm coordination apparent, can walk a line around periphery of a circle
	Skillful jumping is apparent
	Can walk balance beam
5 years	Can broad-jump from 2–3 ft. Can hop 50 ft. in about 11 seconds Can balance on one foot for 4–6 seconds Can catch large playground ball bounced to him

Adapted by permission from Sigmund Grollman, *The Human Body*, 2nd Ed. Copyright © Sigmund Grollman, 1969. New York: Macmillan Publishing Co., Inc.

exercise. If the acceleration of species-wide physical competencies is deemed as an important life goal, then research will have to focus on means for achieving earlier ripening of the neural structures.

Cultural Membership Competencies

Cultural membership competencies are those motor activities that an individual may or may not develop and that depend substantially upon appropriate practice and timing. It is one of the glories of mankind that each growing individual can draw competencies from unfolding innate potentials, from his own cultural life styles, and by means of modern communication and facile transportation from a wide variety of different cultural life styles and traditions.

Ideally, it would seem, one should begin cultivating those complex physical competencies suggested by the species-wide activities and sensitivities

The Biological Domain

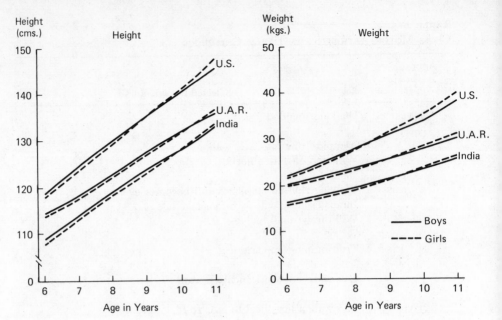

FIG. 8–7.
*Mean height and weight for children aged 6 through 11 years, by sex and single year of age: United States, United Arab Republic, and India.
(Public Health Service, 1970)*

with which a particular child has been endowed by heredity. As mentioned in Chapter 6, individual differences form the essence of biological potential and fulfillment. We can learn to accept genetic differences by recognizing and building upon the individual's innate pattern and by encouraging each child's unique contribution to the world.

Once decisions have been made regarding cultural membership competencies (whether child-oriented or based on social, economic, religious, sex, or moral considerations), timing and training programs become of paramount importance. Since training programs are beyond the scope of this text, we focus instead on the problems of timing or readiness. The problem of determining the important effects of maturation and learning upon the more advanced motor tasks is complex. The problem is to determine *when* a particular child is ready to learn new skills such as playing a musical instrument, writing, or reading. It is important to realize that the child must be ready not only physically (with adequate strength, coordination, and perception) but psychologically and socially as well.

Individual Competencies

In addition to the usual repertoire of physical skills required of most members of a particular social or cultural group, there are also skills that are uniquely cultivated by individuals for either vocational or avocational reasons. The opportunity for the development of such individual skills has been greatly enhanced by the advent of modern technology; it has reduced the need for monotonous manual labor and long working hours, and has created the time and money for increased avocational activities. In other words, one of the blessings of modern technology is the increased freedom it provides for exploring one's potentials with no economic strings attached.

Perhaps sooner than most of us expect, it is projected that 2 per cent of the American population will produce *all* of the necessities of life for the entire country (Fabun, 1967). What then will the other 98 per cent of the population be doing? The prospects are enormously exciting. Man should

Life Goals   be more free to engage in people-oriented work such as teaching, learning, social welfare, ecology, nursing, and general service to others. Furthermore, man will also be free to engage in a wide variety of physical and psycho-motor activities (those involving a part or some parts of the body) that may serve no social need. Man will be free to do things just for the pure joy of doing them. For example, a person who enjoys painting may be able to paint without feeling that he must have some extraneous purpose for doing so. His paintings would not have to be sold or be produced for the pleasures of others. Painting for the sake of painting would be sufficient justification.

BIOLOGICALLY MATURING SELF-CONCEPT

Much of what a person does or refuses to do in any area of life depends substantially on his own evaluation of his competencies. Furthermore, this estimate of his talents, or lack of talents, will influence his performance regardless of the degree of truth underlying this self-evaluation. Therefore, the first step in helping a child move toward a biologically maturing self is to help him to develop a positive *physical* self-concept.

Positive Physical Self-Concept

Anything that significant people in a child's life can do to help him to establish positive feelings about his body, its appearance, and its functions is highly important; it is the body that acts, that is seen by others, and that shows competencies and reveals emotions. The body is the single most significant avenue for expression of the child's total self.

FIG. 8–8.
*Development of a
positive self-concept
is due in large
part to the child's
own assessment
of his capabilities.*

125

Thus, a positive cycle may be nurtured. A child who feels and shows that he is physically competent will solve more problems and engage in more activities than his counterpart who feels and shows inadequacies and shyness. Success makes a child feel good about his physical self-concept, which in turn encourages him to develop further in his motor competencies.

Realistic Physical Self-Concept

A positive physical self-concept must also be realistic if a child's potential for achieving success is to be realized. Children may often be better judges of what they are capable of doing than their elders, because the signs of developmental readiness of the child may be overlooked or hidden from adult view. Furthermore, occasional misjudgments of abilities may be of value; children need to test reality on their own, face the consequences of their actions, and then make appropriate adjustments by learning new competencies. Such experiences may lead to more realistic views of themselves and their ability to cope with the external world.

All children need feedback from their relatives and friends because of lack of experience, and because defense mechanisms can warp their self-perceptions. In one study each member in a group was asked to rate himself on certain personality characteristics. At the same time close friends were asked to rate each individual on the same scale. The results showed clearly that most children were unaware of a significant number of shortcomings in

FIG. 8–9.
A *child's physical self-concept must also be realistic.*

Life Goals

themselves (Frenkel-Brunswick, 1939). Differences between what we think about ourselves and what others believe should be carefully considered and plans should be made to take constructive measures to improve one's competencies. The level of one's self-esteem and, consequently, one's chances for future success are thereby increased.

Integrated Physical Self-Concept

Children actually construct varying physical self-images depending on their stage of development. The total of these self-images includes both ideal images of what could be and realistic images based on past experiences. Together these images make up an integrated physical self-concept, which is but one component of the total self-concept. In the following chapters we discuss self-concepts of the cognitive, social, and emotional domains.

In keeping with our holistic orientation to human development and behavior, we must keep in mind the essential interplay of biological forces with psychological and social ones. The growth, learning, and viability of practically all biological systems and activities are dependent on their environments for acceptance, support, and guidance. To speak of a child as growing toward biological maturity without a discussion of the parallel psychological and social growth is, in our opinion, a rather meaningless undertaking.

IMPLICATIONS

UNDERSTANDING YOURSELF AND OTHERS

As adults we should not feel that we have achieved biological maturity, but rather we should feel that we are still in the process of becoming biologically mature. We can still add years to our life and, more important, life to our years. There are many unexplored physical and psychomotor skills that we could develop in such diverse fields as crafts, music, and the culinary arts. We could further the stimulation of our sensory potentials of sight, sound, touch, movement, and taste.

As biologically more mature persons we should realize that such matters as physical defects, physiques, physical appearances, skin color, and facial characteristics are genetically random processes; they are "skin-deep" and not the fault of the owners. If we seek to evaluate others, we should do so based on their actions, feelings, and intent.

LIVING AND WORKING WITH CHILDREN, ADOLESCENTS, AND ADULTS

There is an old story about a famous gunfighter who claimed that he never missed his targets. When asked to demonstrate his marksmanship, he gladly obliged. He fired six shots at an old barn, walked over, and drew circles around each bullet hole. "There," he said, "they are all bull's-eyes!"

In a sense, this is what many parents and educators do when they observe admirable qualities in their children or in young adults. Although we cannot take credit away from parents for a job well done, we present, in this section, the case for the selection, whenever possible, of desirable life goals *before* and not *after* the facts.

We believe that people will feel and perform better when they have some

The Biological Domain

worthwhile goals to work toward, and when they have some things to look forward to and to believe in. Anticipation of what *could be* may well be one of the greatest motivating forces behind man's continuing progress and his desire to create a better world for himself and for his children.

The arrival of a child brings together for the first time the reality of the plans of the parents and the demands of the infant. Although far removed from any measure of mastery over his body or of the physical world, the newborn is endowed with an appearance and responses that are appealing to adults and that promote in the parents the need to care for and to caress him. This first encounter marks the beginning of a long series of interactions that will modify and change some of the life goals of the parents. It is wise to remember that although a perfect balance may exist in all areas during developmental stages between the needs of the child and the parent, the antics of a "tom-boy," for instance, may frustrate all the coping skills and patience of some parents. During these times a neighbor or a brother-in-law may be able to be more objective than the parents, and compromises of some of the original life goals may have to be made.

Because we now live in a world that, like a sleeping giant, has been awakened by informational, technical, and change explosions, we can no longer feed to all children the same diet of information and goals at all stages of their development. There will be times when we, perplexed, will turn to our children for guidance and ask them to discuss with us what they believe is best for them. At this point we will have made a start in the important direction of the promotion of more self-directed persons that should be one of our ultimate goals of child-rearing.

DEVELOPING POSITIVE MODELS

Possibly the principal role of biologists in the future will be to manipulate the heredity of man in positive ways. Future children may thus be saved from crippling genetic defects and malformations. Mothers who wish may be spared the pain and hardship of childbearing as artificial wombs are perfected. Our children may live for much longer periods of time and be freed from the sufferings of disease while at the same time being able to enjoy the extra years of life needed to explore all of their potentials.

Another approach for developing superhealthy people is the humanistic biology model proposed by Abraham Maslow (1971). He suggests that since all desirable traits are positively related, the healthiest 2 per cent of the population, the middle 2 per cent, and the least healthy 2 per cent of the population should be studied. From these assays of biologically sound and biologically unsound specimens, the best that the human species has to offer may be discovered. However, Maslow makes it clear that the actualization of the highest human potentials is possible only within the framework of a good society and that we shall have to develop a theory of a good society.

Until other models are developed, and until child welfare becomes our top national priority, those who work with children will need much assistance from the child experts in the fields of medicine, genetic counseling, psychology, education, and sociology. Parents must learn as much as possible about normal and abnormal child growth and development, and, as expertise is developed, they can then relax, be themselves, and provide a loving accepting atmosphere in which children can prepare themselves to enjoy competent self-actualized lives.

Life Goals

BAYLEY, N. The development of motor abilities during the first three years. *Monographs of the Society for Research in Child Development*, 1935, **1**, no. 1.

BUHLER, C. *The first year of life*. New York: Day, 1930.

CRATTY, B. J. *Perceptual and motor development in infants and children*. New York: Macmillan, 1970.

DENNIS, W. The effect of restricted practice upon the reaching, sitting and standing of two infants. *Journal of Genetic Psychology*, 1935, **47**:17–32.

DUBOS, R. *So human an animal*. New York: Scribners, 1968.

DUNN, HALBERT L. *High-level wellness*. Arlington, Va.: Beatty, 1961.

FABUN, D. *The dynamics of change*. Englewood Cliffs, N.J.: Prentice-Hall, 1967.

FRENKEL-BRUNSWICK, E. Mechanisms of self-deception. *Journal of Social Psychology*, 1939, **10**:409–420.

GESELL, A. *The first five years of life: a guide to the study of the preschool child*. New York: Harper, 1940.

GLASSOW, R. N. and P. KRUSE. Motor performance of girls age six-fourteen years. *Research Quarterly*, 1960, **31**:426–433.

HELLMAN, H. *Biology in the world of the future*. New York: Hayden, 1971.

ILLINGWORTH, R. S. *The development of the infant and young child: normal and abnormal*. Baltimore: Williams & Wilkins, 1971.

KEOGH, J. F. *Motor performance of elementary school children*. Monograph, U. of Calif., L. A., Physical Ed. Dept., 1965.

MASLOW, A. H. *The farther reaches of human nature*. New York: Viking, 1971.

MCGRAW, M. B. *Growth: a study of Johnny and Jimmy*. New York: Appleton, 1935.

PREHODA, R. W. Our children may live to be 200 years old. *The Futurist*, 1969, **3**, no. 1:4–6.

PUBLIC HEALTH SERVICE. *Height and weight of children in the United States, India, and the United Arab Republic*. No. 1000, series 3, no. 14. Washington, D.C.: H.E.W., September, 1970.

SHIRLEY, M. M. The first two years: a study of twenty-five babies, vol. 1, Postural and locomotor development. *Institute of Child Welfare Monograph Series, No. 6*. Minneapolis: U. of Minnesota, 1931.

WORLD HEALTH ORGANIZATION, 1947, vol. 1, no. 1–2:9–43.

YOUNG, J. Z. *Doubt and certainty in science*. New York: Oxford U. P., 1960.

RECOMMENDED FURTHER READING

Early diagnosis of human genetic defects: scientific and ethical considerations, no. 72–25. Washington, D.C.: Supt. of Documents, 1972.

FRANCOEUR, R. T. *Utopian motherhood*. Garden City, N. Y.: Doubleday, 1969.

GAVER, J. R. *Birth defects and your baby*. New York: Lancer, 1972.

HANNA, T. *Bodies in revolt*. New York: Holt, 1970.

NATHAN, P. *The nervous system*. Philadelphia: Lippincott, 1969.

OTTO, H. A. *Explorations in human potentialities*. Springfield, Ill.: Thomas, 1966.

RUTHERFORD, F. W. *You and your baby*. New York: Signet, 1971.

SCHILDER, P. *The image and appearance of the human body*. New York: Wiley, 1950.

SINGER, R. N. *Motor learning and human performance*. New York: Macmillan, 1968.

STUART, H. C. and D. G. PRUGH (eds.). *The healthy child*. Cambridge, Mass.: Harvard U. P., 1960.

TIGER, L. and R. FOX. *The imperial animal*. New York: Holt, 1971.

WARSHOFSKY, F. *The control of life in the 21st century*. New York: Viking, 1969.

The Biological Domain

The Cognitive Domain

Prelude
Basic Theory and Research
  Information Processing
  Intellectual Competency
    Intellectual Potential and
      Functioning
    Multi-intellectual Talents
  Creativity
    Characteristics of the
      Creative Person
    Creative Thinking
  Maturing Cognitive Self-Concept
Implications
  Understanding Yourself and
    Others
  Living and Working with Chil-
    dren, Adolescents, and Adults
  Developing Positive Models

PRELUDE

IT IS probably true that the basic competencies needed for living have always been the same—the ability to work, to love, and to play. However, it is in the quality, quantity, and priority of these competencies that the changes necessary for living more effectively in the future will have to be made. Because of vastly improved technology we will have the additional time necessary for establishing more intensive and extensive relationships in love and play. But the same technology that has provided increased freedom to love and play has placed on us the increased challenge in the area of work. We need to assess, master, and improve the technology and its by-products of an information explosion, a shrinking world, and an expanding universe. We need to increase our potential to think effectively and creatively if we are to prevail.

BASIC THEORY AND RESEARCH

Figure 9–1 is a diagrammatical representation of primary life goals in the cognitive domain. The four overlapping models of man are these: the person who is processing information accurately, the person who is developing his intellectual competencies, the person who is exploring his creative competencies, and the person who is forming a cognitively maturing self-concept.

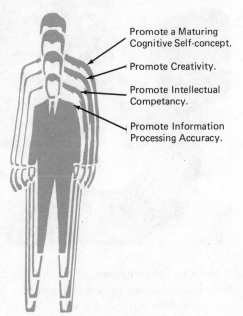

Promote a Maturing Cognitive Self-concept.

Promote Creativity.

Promote Intellectual Competancy.

Promote Information Processing Accuracy.

FIG. 9–1.
Life goals in the cognitive domain.

INFORMATION PROCESSING

A fairly safe assumption is that the first requirement for developing competencies in any area of life is the ability to process information accurately, by which we mean the ability to receive information as given, to integrate it with previous information, and to store, retrieve, and synthesize the information with the requirements of daily living as well as with our

The Cognitive Domain

131

individual personality characteristics. Figure 9–2 illustrates that the clear channels of communication necessary for processing information efficiently depend on the source of the information, the nature of the information and how it is presented, and the biological and psychological states of the learner.

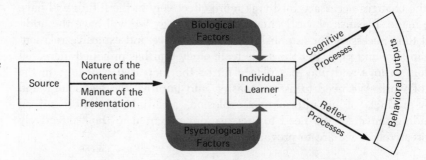

FIG. 9–3.

Even in the profession of teaching, educators have been unable to specify the characteristics of a good teacher. Educators do agree, however, that, since children represent a wide variety of personal needs and abilities that vary further with developmental stages, any one teacher cannot be expected to be equally proficient in teaching all children at all levels in all subjects.

Nevertheless there is general agreement that a good teacher has an adequate grasp of the subject matter, is familiar with the cultural backgrounds of the learners, respects general as well as individual patterns of development, and is able to establish rapport with his students. In addition, those who live and work with children usually realize quickly that not all

Life Goals   subject matter is of equal importance at the same time. Some information

132

is learned more rapidly because it is more necessary to the present needs of particular children. In general, the closer the match between the input of information and the needs of the receiver, the better are the communication and the learning.

Newly discovered ways of organizing the contents of the knowledge explosion will facilitate and accelerate the production of the highly educated persons needed for living successfully in the world of tomorrow. Students will not have to spend most of their time memorizing endless lists of facts, dates, and numbers. Instead principles will be emphasized that will help them to understand the many facts that previously had to be memorized. For example, in the new mathematics the role of rote learning of number operations is deemphasized in favor of the basic assumptions that underlie the mathematics taught in kindergarten through grade twelve. Furthermore, modern technology is supplying the teacher of children with such instructional aids as programmed learning, television, language laboratories, and computer-aided teaching.

FIG. 9–4.
Teaching machines and other modes of presentation can facilitate effective information processing.

As emphasized in Chapter 8, the foundation for learning is a healthy nervous system. A healthy nervous system requires receptors that pick up the stimulation accurately, a brain that copes with the information accurately, and transmitters that carry decoded information to the effector organs. The effector organs, that is, the extremities, and vocal mechanism, convey the information accurately to the outside world in the form of behavior. Any defect in the input or output channels blocks or distorts information processing. The importance of such a healthy neural system is illustrated by research reported in Smith and Dechant (1961) with elementary schoolchildren and by Lugo and Hershey (1969) with high school and college students. Both studies revealed that approximately 40 per cent of the stu-

The Cognitive Domain

dents tested had visual problems that were directly related to the reading difficulties. It is informative to note that none of the older students tested were aware of their visual handicaps as contributing factors to their reading difficulties, and neither were their reading teachers.

A second important determinant of effective information processing is a state of psychological health. If an individual's understanding of reality is radically distorted from that commonly held by his society, the individual is often considered to be mentally ill. For example, this distortion of reality may be of the kind that has been called an *ego defense mechanism* by Freud. It operates in such ways as to cause repression (previously acknowledged events or motives are suddenly "forgotten"), rationalization (logical reasons are made up for behaviors whose real motives have been repressed), and projection (accusing others of possessing one's own undesirable attributes).

INTELLECTUAL COMPETENCY

In the preceding section we discussed the first stage in the development of the cognitively healthy person; that is, man as an effective information-processing organism. This analogy of human learning to a computer model seems to imply a simple process and that all that is required is to look, listen, feel, taste, and smell. In reality, intelligence as measured by learning ability is a highly personal process, involving our past experiences, emotions, motivations, and conscious and unconscious processes. Intelligence, therefore, must be regarded as a manifestation of personality as a whole.

Intellectual Potential and Functioning

We believe that intellectual potential—what man is theoretically capable of knowing and doing—is not fixed rigidly by heredity at birth. Rather, the original genetic limits, whatever they happen to be, can be extended through favorable (although as yet unspecifiable) environmental conditions. It is more accurate to conceive of intelligent behavior as a product of living instead of as a fixed determiner of how we are to live. If we can accept this newer view of the nature of man, then we are open to the highly exciting challenge of becoming active human architects instead of passive recipients of the "inevitable" unfolding of human nature.

Perhaps we can explain the view that inherited potential may be extended by comparing it with past, present and future views of intelligence as diagrammed in Figure 9–5. The past view, which is still held by many persons, has been that the limits of intelligence were fixed at birth and could not be changed; potential and functioning were the same thing; intelligence was only of one kind, and either a person had much, some, or little intelligence. In other words, intelligence was predetermined and there was nothing anyone could do about it. The prevalent view today is that although potential is fixed, intellectual functioning can be improved through enriching experiences. Further, more people today are accepting the idea that there are many different ways of demonstrating intelligent behavior; they realize that intelligence tests do not measure all areas of the intellect. The present view of intelligence suggests that human nature holds considerably more promise, implying that it is possible to extend human functioning only up to the limits imposed by heredity. It is a view based on the idea that we can improve human nature not so much by working on man's biological inheritance

Life Goals

as by working on ways of improving his social inheritance. It holds that the factors underlying intelligence, whether inborn or created by experiences, are as varied and numerous as the factors underlying any other major area of human existence. The future view of intelligence, as suggested by some recent research, indicates the exciting possibility that both functioning and potential may be extended beyond our fondest expectations.

Historical View of Intelligence

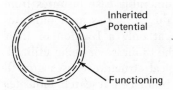

Inherited Potential

Functioning

1. Intellectual potential is fixed forever by heredity.
2. Since intellectual potential is known through and determined by intellectual functioning (present level of behavior), both intellectual potential and functioning are fixed forever by heredity.
3. Only one common factor underlies all intelligent behavior.

Present View of Intelligence

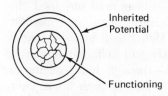

Inherited Potential

Functioning

1. Intellectual potential is fixed forever by heredity.
2. Positive and enriched experiences will improve intellectual functioning up to the limits set by heredity.
3. There are many factors which underlie intelligent behavior.

Future View of Intelligence

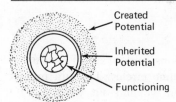

Created Potential

Inherited Potential

Functioning

1. Intellectual potential can be created beyond the limits set by heredity.
2. The process of improving intellectual functioning can be markedly accelerated to limits hitherto undreamed of.
3. The number and variety of factors underlying intelligent behaviors is far greater than we had ever imagined; there are literally endless unique ways of being "smart."

FIG. 9–5. *Three views of intelligence: historical, present, and future. The circles with the double lines represent inherited intellectual potentials. The circles with broken lines represent intellectual functioning at the present time. The circles with jagged lines represent created potential during life.*

The importance of the differences among these views of human potential and functioning may be enhanced by reading the following descriptions representative of the past, present, and future:

PAST VIEW

By intelligence, the psychologist means inborn, all-round, intellectual ability. It is inherited, or at least innate, not due to teaching or training; it is not emotional or moral, and remains uninfluenced by industry or zeal; it is general, not specific, i.e., it is not limited to any particular kind of work, but enters into all we do or say or think. Of all our mental qualities, it is the most far-reaching; fortunately, it can be measured with accuracy and ease. (Burt, et al., 1934)

PRESENT VIEW

The infant as a potential is thought to be a bundle of largely inherited latent traits of emotionally expressive abilities for achieving goals, which can only be realized gradually as the child develops and which may be influenced by training and growth. . . . Children may have a high or low

The Cognitive Domain

potential for the development of certain skills or personality traits. The combination of a high potential and the best environmental influence is thought to be essential to the greatest success in achieving the goals offered to the adult. (Fisher and Fisher, 1963)

FUTURE VIEW

The human being as a biological organism has an unexplored capacity for plasticity, self-transformation, adaptation, change, organismic regeneration and organismic self-destruction. Innumerable case histories from the annals of medical science substantiate this. . . . Research indicates that man's neurological structures function at only a fraction of their capacity. There is evidence that one-half of the brain is not being utilized. There is also evidence that use of neurological structure causes growth and extension to take place. For instance, brain cell research indicates that *function seems to create neurological structure.* (Otto, 1966)

If man believes that his intellectual capacity has been predetermined, that is, set in concrete, then all he can do is to measure, argue, and meditate about the varying sizes of the concrete blocks. But if man believes that he can change his capacity, then he can consciously and deliberately start to work on improving his own destiny. As man—through his capacity for awareness of himself and the world around him and through his capacity for modifying both—accepts this new view of his intellectual potential, he can start to create the desired changes within and without himself in ways commensurate with this new view.

Multi-intellectual Talents

There are currently different theories, definitions, and means of measuring intellectual potential and functioning in academic circles. The full impact of the issues involved becomes apparent when we find out what the IQ tests and testers say about our own intelligence. More shaking is the moment when a child's teacher, trying to be nice, says to the child's parents that the youngster is "not up to par," "just doesn't have the ability." Evaluations so sweeping can be devastating, especially in our society in which a person's future depends to an unprecedented degree on his achieving within the school system.

Possibly the greatest concern for those who live and work with children is that IQ (Intelligence Quotient) tests fall far short of measuring all of the child's intellectual functioning and potential. The most widely used tests, such as the Stanford-Binet and the Wechsler scales, are really measures and predictors of school success and only test in terms of the present system. Even worse, these results usually are reported as *one* score, obtained from *one* intelligence test. These common practices have given rise to the false belief that intelligence is of one kind and that IQ tests measure each individual's total capacities in all areas of life.

This now-prevalent idea that all intelligence was of one kind developed in 1904 after Binet and Simon were commissioned by the Minister of Public Instruction in Paris to draw up guides for predicting *school* success of children who were either feeble minded, or dull, or who simply lacked proper motivation for learning what was being taught in the schools. Binet and Simon's first step was to observe the skills and knowledge demonstrated by

Life Goals

children at different age levels while the children were progressing through the grades. They next constructed a series of sequential subtests to measure the developmental skills observed. The underlying assumption was that the children who had developed more skills and information at a given level were more intelligent than those who had not, provided that all of them had equal opportunity to learn (the assumption of equal opportunity was and is still open to question). For easy administrative placement of children, Binet and Simon unfortunately used a single score to describe a wide range of different skills and information, even though they specifically stated that their test was measuring independent abilities (Peterson, 1925). This unfortunate practice of summarizing a fairly wide range of behaviors into a single score is still a prevalent practice today.

The analysis of scores obtained on the various subtests of the most commonly used IQ tests does show that there is some evidence for generalized or homogeneous intelligence (G-factor). That is, people who score high overall, also on these tests, tend to score high on the subtests, such as those in vocabulary, information, analogies, and reaction time.

There is evidence for viewing functional intelligence as consisting of both G-factors and a number of more specific abilities (S-factors). The latter factors are not measured by the commonly used IQ tests. At the level of everyday experiences, we are all aware of the existence of individual differences. For example, a person may be very adept with his hands but relatively nonproficient verbally. A mathematical whiz may be insensitive to music, art, and other aesthetic activities. Recent psychological research thus provides us with arguments against a strict homogeneous interpretation of intelligence. There are numerous cases of *idiots savants* who, although mentally retarded, were able to perform prodigious feats of memory. For example, in one study, two identical twins, who were classified as *idiots savants*, could not add or subtract, but could give the day of the week for any date over a period of time extending back over centuries (Horowitz et al., 1965). In short, although these people have achieved a high degree of competency in one area, they remain essentially incompetent in all others.

Research in the field of intelligence testing indicates a strong and growing interest in breaking down general intelligence into smaller factors each of which measures distinct abilities or clusters of abilities. Viewing the component parts of intelligence was made possible by statistical methods known collectively as factor analysis, which indicated that all responses on IQ tests could be broken down further into separate categories. Use of this technique enabled the Thurstones (1941) to identify seven general factors and subsequently to construct tests to measure these.

The most promising of the factor analytic models of intelligence is that developed by Guilford and his associates. It seems to encompass most of the presently testable abilities considered as indicators of human intellectual functioning. Guilford's model, called *Structure of Intellect*, proposes that there are at least 120 different variables of intelligence. Although still in the experimental stage, research, thus far, has uncovered nearly 70 different components of intelligence (Guilford, 1967). A brief summary of Guilford's theory is presented in Figure 9–6, which is a three-dimensional model in which each of the 120 intellectual abilities are described in terms of the contents involved, the types of operations employed by the individual handling the information, and the variety of end-products that result.

The Cognitive Domain

137

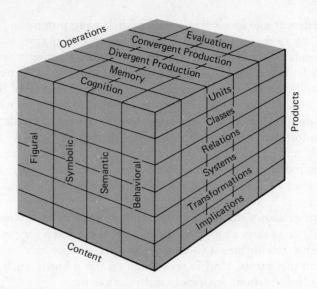

Operations   The kinds of things a person does with the raw materials of information:

      Cognition – Discovery or recognition of information.

      Memory – Retention of information in the same form as was originally learned.

      Divergent Production – Using information to produce new ideas or products; the creative use of information.

      Convergent Production – Using information to arrive at conclusions.

      Evaluation – Comparing the results of one's thinking with known information or standards.

Products   The various forms in which the information is organized or conceived by the individual:

      Units – Singular information; such as, one word, one symbol, one figure, or one idea.

      Classes – Information that occurs in sets or concepts; related objects, events or persons.

      Relations – Information that is processed in relation to other classes or systems; e.g., the semantic relations of the analogy that *ground* is to *air* as *automobile* is to *airplane.*

      Systems – Information that is organized into a complex of interrelating parts such as the structure of language, arithmetic reasoning, or comprehending a social situation.

      Transformation – Information that is reorganized, changed, or redefined. Very often this involves conceiving the information in a different or novel way or applying it to a seemingly unrelated situation.

      Implications – The ability to forsee the expectancies, predictions, and consequences of information.

Content   Types of information grouped by virtue of their common properties:

      Figural – Concrete information involving visual, auditory, and motor senses.

      Symbolic – Information such as numbers or letters.

      Semantic – Information in the form of the meaning of words, both spoken and written.

      Behaviorial – Information about other's attitudes, intentions, and actions.

Fig. 9–6. *Guilford's structure-of-intellect model. (After Guilford, 1967)*

If we view intelligence not as a simple concept that can be expressed by a single score but rather as a complex concept with almost innumerable faces, we can ask such interesting questions as: In what areas is a person "intelligent" and in what areas does he lack "intelligence?" Is his verbal ability as good as his memory? Does he use the knowledge gained with good judgment and in ethical ways? If so, in what kinds of situations and in solving what kinds of problems does he use his knowledge? Acceptance Life Goals of Guilford's model reopens the question of what intelligence is and allows further questioning and research. In short, we have not as yet developed the instruments to measure man's actual intellectual functioning or his potential; knowledge of IQ scores supplies us only with what an individual can do in a specific testing situation, not what he would do if sufficiently motivated in a variety of real life situations.

CREATIVITY

Most examples of creative thinking have come from the works of recognized scientists and artists such as Newton, Fleming, da Vinci, Cervantes, and Shakespeare. These great creative geniuses have, of course, been extensively studied. But today psychologists are also concerned with creativity in the average person—the newsboys, clerks, mechanics, engineers, teachers, and students. This is because creativity is no longer thought of simply as a gift, or luck, or an invariable characteristic of intelligence.

In discussing creativity, it is convenient to follow Maslow's distinction between "special talent creativity" that requires special skills and training as well as unusual inborn capacities and "self-actualizing creativity" that is related more to psychological health. According to Maslow, mentally healthy persons seem to approach most of their activities in a creative way. They have a good feeling about themselves, which generates trust in oneself. They tend to be more autonomous, less dependent on what others expect of them or on what their culture demands. Maslow (1956) puts it this way:

> This creativeness appears in some of our subjects not in the usual forms of writing books, composing music, or producing artistic objects, but rather may be much more humble. It is as if this special type of creativeness, being an expression of healthy personality, is projected out upon the world or touches whatever activity the person is engaged in. In this sense there can be creative shoemakers or carpenters or clerks. Whatever one does can be done with certain spirit which arises out of the nature of the character of the person performing the act. (p. 186)

Intelligence and creativity are not synonymous. In relation to mental health it should be stressed that even though there have been creative people who were neurotic, the available evidence indicates that they were creative in spite of, rather than because of, their neuroticism. The research of both Kubie (1967) and Roe (1959) discredits the image of the neurotic creator. Getzels and Jackson (1961) gave high school students tests of intelligence and creativity. The results indicated that some students scored very high on intelligence but not as high on creativity, whereas other students scored very high on creativity but not as high on intelligence. Illustrative of the low positive relationship between creativity and IQ is the fact that if the highest 20 per cent of the high school scores on IQ tests were selected this would leave out 70 per cent of those who were among the highest 20 per cent on creativity (Taylor, 1959).

Other related studies tend to support the view that intelligence and creativity can be considered independent but not mutually exclusive characteristics (Maslow, 1956). For example, it is important to realize that although highly intelligent persons may also tend to be more creative than persons of average intelligence, high intelligence in itself is no guarantee of

The Cognitive Domain

creativeness (Taylor, 1959). Nevertheless, a specifiable minimum IQ is probably necessary for engaging in creative activities. In a related study with schoolchildren, Wallach and Kogan divided the children into separate groups based on their scores on intelligence and creativity tests. They observed some of their behavior and came up with the following descriptions (Wallach and Kogan, 1965):

1. *High creativity-high intelligence.* These children show both control and freedom as well as adult-like and child-like kinds of behavior.
2. *High creativity-low intelligence.* These children are in angry conflict with themselves and their school environment and have feelings of unworthiness and inadequacy but can flower in certain situations.
3. *Low creativity-high intelligence.* These children are described as "addicted" to school achievement. Academic failure to them would be extremely painful, and they constantly strive for excellence.
4. *Low creativity-low intelligence.* These children are bewildered and engage in various defensive maneuvers such as passivity or psychosomatic symptoms.

Characteristics of the Creative Person

It has been said that the creative person is both more primitive and more cultivated, more destructive and more constructive, and a lot madder and a lot saner than the average person. The creative person seems to be as evasive as the will-of-the-wisp. So let us hope that our preliminary probes into the domain of creativity will enable us eventually to locate, recognize, and develop what should be our single most valuable human resource. This we know: (1) If we wish to understand the characteristics of the creative person more fully, we must look well beyond the boundaries of the IQ tests. The typical intelligence test probably does not measure significantly more than a half-dozen of the many variables involved in creative behavior. (2) Creativity, just like any other important human characteristic or activity, is not composed of a single component or a static list of smaller components but rather tends to be a complex and dynamic mixture of components. These depend on the individual's personality and the nature of the products. In other words, we should rarely expect the same person to be equally creative in the arts, the sciences, the social sciences, and in psychomotor skills. Research nevertheless indicates that creative persons may have certain common outstanding qualities. It is to these qualities that we now turn our attention.

Creative Thinking

In Guilford's model thinking is divided into two basic kinds, convergent and divergent production. Convergent thinking is characterized by learning and thinking according to authority. (Authority may be a parent, a teacher, a book, an expert in the field, or the majority opinion.) Such abilities are characterized by the operations of recognition, memory, and local thinking. On the other hand, creative thinking is characterized by divergent thinking (e.g., fluency, flexibility, originality, and elaboration). The creative thinker must first engage in the learning process if he is to have a stock of information to use in being creative. In divergent thinking, the person tends toward the novel, the speculative, the unique, and the flow of diverse ideas. Creative transformations involve the improvising and adapting of information and

Life Goals

ideas to new or unusual uses. Creative evaluations consist chiefly of noting inconsistencies, missing elements, absurdities, and unexpected problems and dilemmas. Even within the various abilities involved in creative thinking there are significant individual differences.

Youthful Attitude. One common attribute of creativeness seems to be a continuously youthful and fresh attitude toward life and problems. In Maslow's opinion the creative person is possessed with a continuous freshness of experience; e.g., the thousandth baby he sees is just as miraculous a product as the first one he saw. In such a state, one tends to be more flexible in his approach to learning and thinking and more willing to try almost anything. Such a person is also more apt to notice that something is in need of improvement. According to Guilford, increased awareness of beauty or the correctable imperfections of life may start the creative person on his way to creative production.

Self-Confidence and Autonomy. In the process of spotting imperfections and in trying to improve the general state of affairs of the society, the creative person will probably encounter, by necessity, much failure. Those about him may, in turn, make him feel that such natural and healthy failures (scientists call similar failures in research or experimentation negative results) really mean personal inadequacy. To shed the effects of these negative criticisms, the creative person must be highly self-confident and unusually self-assured; he lives according to the truth as he sees it.

If we accept the assumption that failure lies within the person failing, rather than in the newness of the situation, in looking at an old situation from a different perspective, or as a necessary condition for exploring the unknown, then the creative person, in addition to cultivating feelings of self-confidence, is then forced to become more or less independent of other people's judgments. This quality of autonomy, although facilitating creativity, may also alienate people around him such as parents, teachers, and peers (Barron, 1968). Some creative people tend to become so involved in the world of new ideas that they become somewhat "absent-minded" about the world of people not included in their present frame of reference. Nevertheless, this apparent indifference of creative individuals toward some people is temporary and somewhat understandable in light of their serious dedication to the tasks at hand.

Openness to Experience. Apparently, feeling good about oneself (a sign of good mental health) allows the creative person to permit more and varied experiences to enter directly into consciousness (Rogers, 1961). This process is just the opposite of defense-oriented behavior in which certain experiences are perceived as threatening and are blocked out or distorted before they are allowed to enter consciousness. Openness to experience provides the potential creator with more information because he also weighs contradictions. Shulman (1966) confirmed this positive relationship between creativity and openness to experience with tests among fourth grade children.

Toleration of Ambiguity. Openness to experience implies a high degree of toleration for ambiguity, confusion, contradictions, and disorder. In fact, when given a choice between simple and well-organized tasks and those that are complex and disorganized, creative individuals tend to select the latter. Apparently they are challenged by disorder and complexity and wish to redefine or reorganize at a different or higher level of thinking. This

The Cognitive Domain

avoidance of easy or safe answers provides further support for all the characteristics listed so far: youthful attitude, self-confidence, autonomy, openness to experience, and tolerance of ambiguity.

Humor. Getzels and Jackson (1961) found that high school students who scored high on creativity had a strong sense of humor. Coleman (1969) in his book *Psychology and Effective Behavior* states that "a sense of humor is an important adaptive resource. The person who can remain objective enough to appreciate the incongruities of a situation is less likely to be overwhelmed by it." Thus, the presence of a high degree of humor adds credence to the idea that it is fun to create, to explore, to discover, and to put things together in unique ways.

Childlike. Creative work is often characterized not only by humor but also with playfulness, relaxation, a lack of rigid or preconceived categories of thinking, and a general feeling that it is all right not to know all the answers (Taylor, 1959). The creative are like natural explorers, tending to receive new experiences with open minds, open hearts, and open arms (Maslow, 1956). A possible explanation for this display of childlike or infantile behavior (regression) among creative adults is that creative people tend to feel sufficiently adequate about themselves so that they can let their hair down even at the risk of ridicule from others (Kris, 1952). The basic idea is to return to a childlike state without losing control of one's thought processes.

Just as every baby is both unique and typical, so are creative people. Maslow implies that creativity is a fundamental property of human nature, present in all people at birth but lost in varying degrees by most in the process of socialization. Therefore the spark of creativity lies dormant in all of us. It is only in the study of extremely creative persons that the typical characteristics stand out in bold relief. However, the range of uniqueness in creativeness is probably extremely wide and elusive, as suggested by Golann's (1963) review of the literature. We must be careful not to try to form neat pigeonholes as standards for judging creativity, as we still do with the measurement of intelligence.

Creative Potential. The crucial question is whether creativity can be taught. The vast majority of authors and researchers state or imply that this is the case. Presently there are a number of studies that indicate improvement in creativity following a period of training (Torrance, 1970). Furthermore, if Maslow's hypothesis about the innateness of creativity is correct, then the major task is to study the family and sociological backgrounds of highly creative people. Such a study should reveal useful creative models for others. We shall examine such studies later when we discuss the development of creativity.

MATURING COGNITIVE SELF-CONCEPT

By our definition, there are three major aspects to a cognitively maturing self-concept: (1) a person who has abilities to learn and to appropriately apply all the physical, social, and psychological competencies necessary for working, loving, and playing in the present world; (2) a person who can maintain the flexibility and openness to new experiences necessary for coping with life in a rapidly changing society; and (3) a person who has the abilities and characteristics for sustaining a creative life while at the

Life Goals

same time participating authentically in social experiences. This last point is a plea for encouragement of distinctive and unique individuals.

IMPLICATIONS

UNDERSTANDING YOURSELF AND OTHERS

Practically all of us have some specific ideas about how intelligent we are supposed to be and, rightfully or otherwise, we tend to behave in ways that fulfill the prophecy. We probably obtained these notions through knowledge of some IQ tests or, more significantly, through daily direct but often subtle interactions with others, particularly teachers. However, if we accept the multifactor intellect model of Guilford and others, we are free to reconsider the question of how smart we are. For many of us and for those with whom we associate, this could mean the removal of an enormous psychological burden. We would be free to say to ourselves, "Only God really knows how smart I am, and in what ways, and in dealing with what kinds of different problems . . . and He is very discreet." Such intellectual emancipation from current means of measuring intelligence could be tremendously exciting and rewarding both personally and in living with others.

A rather sad example of the psychological damage that can be caused by the old views of intelligence occurred in the experience of one of the authors when he was organizing a remedial reading program in a college. The students' counselor refused to admit one particular student into the reading clinic. Upon investigation the counselor stated that the student's IQ was too low for him to benefit from reading instruction. An IQ test had been administered to this twenty-two-year-old college student when he was in the first grade, and he scored low. Now fifteen years later he was still being denied the full opportunity to learn and grow intellectually.

Probably one of the great challenges that we all face in life is to find areas of competencies where we can more fully develop our intellectual and creative abilities. The same author recalls a fifteen-year-old boy who came to a university psychological clinic for academic assistance. He could barely perform the basic skills of reading, writing, and arithmetic, Yet his nonplussed father informed us that his son could perform marvels with his hands. For example, the boy constructed, without assistance or blueprints, complex miniature bridges with matchsticks that were strong enough to support electric toy trains. This boy's use of figural information to transform a spatial visualization (bridges) into three-dimensional concrete models is an intellectual feat of the first order.

LIVING AND WORKING WITH CHILDREN, ADOLESCENTS, AND ADULTS

There is a growing awareness among psychologists that intelligence and creativity are not simply unchanging gifts of nature. More and more we are accepting the notion that intelligence and creativity can be inculcated as a result of special kinds of experiences. Certainly, as the research literature indicates, children reared in impoverished environments tend to think and behave in impoverished ways. If early ideas are ill-defined and vague when learned, subsequent behavior will also tend to lack precision. On the other

The Cognitive Domain

hand, as we foster stimulating, loving, and challenging environmental conditions, we can then expect behavior that is more commensurate with our goals for cognitively maturing children.

A basic assumption in helping children to grow cognitively is that their abilities will develop more fully when the children are motivated to do well. We do not develop, for example, problem-solving ability in children by passively observing them. We should teach and encourage them when they are ready to solve problems; we should create challenges for them and set up situations for practice. A dramatic example of the encouragement process is reported in a study where the average IQ went up twenty-five points when the same group of youngsters was tested in two different situations (Torrance and Strom, 1965). In one situation, the children were motivated to behave intelligently; in the second situation no efforts were made to do so.

DEVELOPING POSITIVE MODELS

Regardless of the skills or attitudes that we wish our children to share, there are two basic kinds of teaching: (1) formal models in which the desired competencies are taught directly; and (2) informal models where children learn by watching others or through the encouragement of behaviors already in the children's repertoires. Because society and the schools in particular have not yet accepted the development of multiple intelligences and creativity as major goals, parents and child workers must rely principally on informal models. Although we have very little comparative data for evaluating the two kinds of models, we believe the impact of everyday incidental learning from friends and relatives may very well be of greater importance than formal education. The following description by Torrance (1970), who has made intensive studies of the developmental pattern of creativity throughout the elementary grades, seems to add support to the view that encouragement by parents may be very important:

> Albert Einstein also suffered a great deal because of his proclivity for asking questions about things which puzzled him. His mother apparently loved and encouraged this tendency. His father was occasionally somewhat exhausted by it, but nonetheless accepted it and responded with liveliness and understanding. Young Einstein found no such response in the German schools that he attended, however, and he disliked school rather intensely until, at a later time, he found a school in Switzerland where his questions were respected. But at the Luitpold Gymnasium in Munich, teachers did not like him because he asked so many questions, and they sometimes thrashed him for this offense. (pp. 16–17)

Admittedly, it is difficult for parents to encourage ideal models of multiple forms of intelligence and creativity in their children when most of our social institutions are still not ready to accept the complexities and occasional discomforts necessary for their nurturance. Nevertheless, we need multiple talent and creative thinkers today as never before. Our complex social problems and the constant threat of nuclear extermination can be solved only by solutions embodying the very highest orders of intelligence, creativity, and altruism.

Life Goals

144

BARRON, F. *Creativity and personal freedom.* New York: Van Nostrand, 1968.

BURT, C., E. JONES, E. MILLER, and W. MOODIE. *How the mind works.* New York: Appleton, 1934. In J. McV. Hunt, *Intelligence and experience.* New York: Ronald Press, 1961.

COLEMAN, J. C. *Psychology and effective behavior.* Glenview, Ill.: Scott, Foresman, 1969.

FISHER, J. L. and A. FISHER. The New Englanders of Orchard Town, U. S. A. In B. Whiting (ed.), *Six cultures: studies of child rearing.* New York: Wiley, 1963.

GETZELS, J. W. and P. W. JACKSON. Family environment and cognitive style: a study of the sources of highly intelligent and highly creative adolescents. *American Journal of Sociology, 1961,* 26:351–359.

GOLANN, S. E. Psychological study of creativity. *Psychological Bulletin,* 1963, 60: 548–565.

GUILFORD, J. P. *The nature of human intelligence.* New York: McGraw-Hill, 1967.

HOROWITZ, W. A., C. KESTENBAUM, E. PERSON, et al. Identical twins—"idiots savants"—calendar calculators. *American Journal of Psychology,* 1965, 121: 1075–1079.

KRIS, E. *Psychoanalytic explorations in art.* New York: International U. P., 1952.

KUBIE, L. S. The utilization of preconscious functions in education. In E. M. Bower and W. G. Hollister (eds.), *Behavioral science frontiers in education.* New York: Wiley, 1967.

LUGO, J. O. and G. L. HERSHEY. Analysis of junior college reading problems. In G. L. Hershey and J. O. Lugo (eds.), *Teaching psychology at the two-year college: innovations and problems.* Monograph No. 1. New York: Macmillan, 1969.

MASLOW, A. H. Self-actualizing people: a study of psychological health. In C. E. Moustakas (ed.), *The self: explorations in personal growth.* New York: Harper, 1956.

OTTO, H. A. (ed.). *Explorations in human potentialities.* Springfield, Ill.: Thomas, 1966.

PETERSON, J. *Early conceptions and tests of intelligence.* New York: Harcourt, 1925.

ROGERS, C. R. *On becoming a person: a therapist's view of psychotherapy.* Boston: Houghton, 1961.

ROE, A. Personal problems and science. In C. W. Taylor (ed.), *The 3rd. University of Utah research conference on the identification of creative scientific talent.* Salt Lake City, 1959.

SHULMAN, D. Openness of perception as a condition for creativity. *Exceptional Children,* 1966, 33:89–94.

SMITH, H. P. and E. V. DECHANT. *Psychology of teaching reading.* Englewood Cliffs, N. J.: Prentice-Hall, 1961.

TAYLOR, C. W. (ed.). *Research conference on the identification of creative scientific talent.* Salt Lake City: U. of Utah, 1959.

TORRANCE, E. P. *Encouraging creativity in the classroom.* Dubuque, Ia.: Brown, 1970.

————, and R. D. STROM, (eds.). *Mental health and achievement.* New York: Wiley, 1965.

THURSTONE, L. L. and T. G. THURSTONE. Factorial studies of intelligence. *Psychometric Monographs,* 1941

WALLACH, M. A. and N. KOGAN. *Modes of thinking in young children: a study of creative-intelligence distinction.* New York: Holt, 1965.

The Cognitive Domain

ANDERSON, H. H. (ed.). *Creativity in childhood and adolescence*. Palo Alto, Calif.: *Science and Behavior*, 1965.

————. *Creativity and its cultivation*. New York: Harper, 1959.

BERGSON, H. *Creative evolution*. New York: Modern Library, 1944.

GETZELS, J. and P. JACKSON. *Creativity and intelligence*. Wiley, 1962.

GHISELIN, B. (ed.). *The creative process*. New York: Mentor, 1952.

HAEFELE, J. W. *Creativity and innovation*. New York: Reinhold, 1962.

HUNT, J. McV. *Intelligence and experience*. New York: Ronald, 1961.

LEHMAN, H. C. *Age and achievement*. Princeton, N.J.: Princeton U. P., 1953.

MacIVER, R. M. (ed.). *The hour of insight*. New York: Harper, 1954.

MOONEY, R. and T. RAZIK, (eds.). *Explorations in creativity*. New York: Harper, 1967.

OSBORN, A. F. *Applied imagination*. New York: Scribners, 1960.

REED, S. C. The evolution of human intelligence. *American Scientist*, 1965, **53**: 317–326.

SEIDEL, G. J. *The crisis in creativity*. South Bend, Ind.: U. of Notre Dame, 1966.

TAYLOR, C. W. and F. BARRON, (eds.). *Scientific creativity: its recognition and development*. New York: Wiley, 1963.

————. *Creativity: progress and potential*. New York: McGraw-Hill, 1962.

VERNON, P. E. (ed.). *Creativity*. Baltimore: Penguin, 1970.

VIAUD, G. *Intelligence: its evolution and forms*. New York: Harper, 1960.

VINACKE, W. E. *The psychology of thinking*. New York: McGraw-Hill, 1952.

Life Goals

146

The Affective Domain

Prelude
Basic Theory and Research
  Love
  Altruism
  Empathy
  Maturing Emotional Self-concept
Implications
  Understanding Yourself and
    Others
  Living and Working with Chil-
    dren, Adolescents, and Adults
  Developing Positive Models

PRELUDE

As discussed in earlier chapters, the development of full human potential is partly the result of achieving competency in the biological and cognitive domains. Important as these areas are, the failure to achieve growth in the affective domain may be the most serious failure of all.

History describes in the unkindest terms the monstrous acts of individuals such as Adolph Hitler, the Emperor Claudius, and Henry VIII of England, who displayed such gross lack of affective development that they were capable of incredible acts of savagery.

Deficiency in affection robs the individual of the most precious and most necessary human qualities of feeling and emotion, and if this deficiency becomes a widespread human condition, it leads to a society of "robots."

In light of this, it is important to note the fact that the number one form of mental illness in our society, schizophrenia, essentially involves a splitting of the affective and cognitive domains within the individual, with a pronounced subordination of the affective domain. The results of this process may be manifest in a wide spectrum of psychotic behavior ranging from the "mechanical-man" symptoms of autism to the "godlike" intellectual superiority of megalomania.

Before discussing the establishment of goals in the affective domain, we must consider that here we are concerned with living, growing, responding, and ever-changing human beings. We are dealing with the very fiber of human existence, namely feelings and emotions. To reduce all possible combinations and varieties of subjective experience into four models and to establish worthwhile goals for human development are at best difficult and arbitrary tasks.

Selecting the four models of the affective domain included the following considerations:

1. Developments in our own affective domain.
2. Emerging societal changes and their implications for the affectivity of the individual and his children.
3. Affective models, where some have been developed.
4. Theories, with some research findings to support them.
5. Affective characteristics that seem to be common to established "models of human sanity" or models of "mental health." Many of these characteristics come from such diverse areas as philosophy, religion, sociology, anthropology, biology, psychiatry, psychoanalysis, and psychology.

Figure 10–1 visually describes four levels of life goals in the affective domain.

BASIC THEORY AND RESEARCH

At this stage of the text, we are describing the parameters (boundaries) of these goals. The process of working toward these goals and of what parents and child workers can do to attain some of these goals are discussed in subsequent sections.

LOVE

Love is a very personal thing. It defies conventional scientific examination and it transcends traditional academic description. Love's existence is tangi-

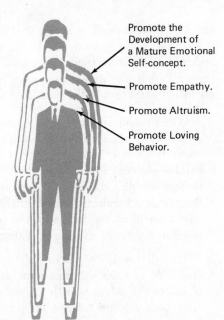

Fig. 10–1.
*Life goals in the
affective domain.*

ble, yet immeasurable; its qualities are vital to human survival, yet these qualities cannot be conserved. Love is a condition that we feel to be unique to the human species, yet without the physical contact that we associate with motherly love certain lower animals fail to thrive.

The fact that we all need love is well established in our history and literature. The fact that the fully human person also needs to give love is only now becoming apparent.

Motherly Love. This type of love is characterized by its unconditional nature (Fromm, 1956). That is, it is given no matter what the love object does. Motherly love has no strings attached and it is considered to be the foundation for all other types of love. We usually think of motherly love as having two facets. The first serves as the basis for the assumption of responsibility for the care and protection of the love object. It is this aspect of motherly love that assures the survival of the species and provides the foundation for growth in all other domains.

The second aspect of motherly love, which transcends the first, serves as the motivation for instilling a sense of worth in the love object. It is this aspect of motherly love that says "for me, you are someone special . . . you are irreplaceable."

The individual who is capable of giving motherly love of both types must be happy, well adjusted, and have a well-developed affective domain. The effect on the individual who receives this type of love is to produce these same qualities in kind.

As we have said, motherly love seems to form the foundation for all other

* In considering the topic of love we use some traditional categories as the basis for our discussion. The first two categories, motherly love and fatherly love, carry with them certain sex role connotations that are unfortunate in terms of today's society. Quite obviously, the type of love described under the category of fatherly love is not necessarily limited to that possessed by the male parent, and the same is true for motherly love and the female parent. We use these terms in order to provide continuity for those students who wish to do further reading and study in this area.

The Affective
Domain

149

kinds of love; indeed, it seems that it is so important that at least at birth it is a matter of life or death. In the early 1900's, a majority of hospitalized children died before they were one year old (Chapin, 1915). Doctors of the time called it marasmus, a wasting away. Montagu (1966) describes how doctors found clues to the causes of the deaths:

> When intensive studies were undertaken to track down its cause, the discovery was made that babies in the best homes and hospitals were most often its victims, babies who were apparently receiving the best and most careful physical attention, while babies in the poorest homes, with a good mother, despite the lack of hygienic physical conditions, often overcame the physical handicaps and flourished. What was wanting in the sterilized environment of the babies of the first category and was generously supplied in babies of the second category was motherly love.

> This discovery is responsible for the fact that most hospitals today endeavor to keep the infant for as short a period as possible. The best place for the infant is with its mother, and, if its own mother is not available, with a foster mother, for what the infant must have is love.

Since that time, many other studies have demonstrated the critical need for this type of maternal love and stimulation in the first months of life (Casler, 1961).

Fatherly Love. Although motherly love toward the love object is unconditional (does not have to be earned and is always available), fatherly love is based on conditionality (it must be earned by fulfilling certain conditions). Fatherly love says, "you have my love because you are thus and so." Obviously there are some negative aspects to this type of love.

Fatherly love may be withdrawn if the love object fails to deserve it. The positive aspect to fatherly love is that it provides the love object with the motivation to learn a sense of values and responsibilities. Fatherly love can be earned and kept. For the child, there is a strong need for fatherly as well as motherly love.

Thus, whereas motherly love involves more the development of emotions such as caring and feeling accepted and wanted, fatherly love develops more in the area of attitudes and values. In a sense, a person who experiences both of these kinds of love will develop these facets of human experience as a part of his own personality. In fact, Fromm (1956) believes that this development is one criteria for a mature person.

Up to the age of about six years, the child relies heavily on motherly love to sustain him and provide the basic growth conditions. Past the age of six the child begins to transfer some of these love needs to the fatherly type, where he finds the conditions for developing his coping patterns and his value system. Success in achieving this transfer is fundamental to the development of good mental health, whereas failure to do so may lead to the later development of neurosis.

Self-Love. Another significant development in becoming a loving person is the experience of feeling good about yourself as a unique individual. It appears that this feeling can take place early in the development of a child, when he discovers that he is separate from his mother and from other persons in his world. Freud called it the development of the "ego" or self-identity (Hall, 1954).

Life Goals

TABLE 10–2
DEVELOPMENTAL STAGES AND TYPES OF LOVING RELATIONSHIPS *

Developmental Stage	Relationship	Type of Love
Prenatal	Husband and wife	Mature love (hopefully) Erotic love
Infancy	Mother and child	Motherly love
Early childhood	Father and child Child and himself	Fatherly love Self-love (early forms)
Later childhood	Child and peers	Brotherly love (early forms)
Adolescence	Adolescent and opposite sex	Erotic love (early forms)
Adulthood	Adult and spouse Adult and fellow man Adult and self	Mature love (hopefully) Brotherly love (hopefully) Self-love (hopefully)
Middle age	Expansion of above	Expansion of above
Old age	Expansion of above	Expansion of above

* For detailed description of the "objects of love," see: Fromm (1956, pp. 46–62).

FIG. 10–3.

ALTRUISM

In this section we are concerned with the question: Does man have any basic tendencies toward fostering the well-being of all humanity, or is most of his life a big "ego trip" during which his own selfish goals are pursued regardless of others?

The argument is not a new one; in fact, it goes back for centuries. For example, in the fifteenth century, an Italian nobleman named Machiavelli wrote the following:

The Affective Domain

> A man who wishes to make a profession of goodness in everything must necessarily come to grief among so many who are not good. Therefore, it is necessary . . . to learn how not to be good, and to use this knowledge and not use it, according to the necessity of the case.

Other writers have suggested that man, rather than being selfish and egoistic, is driven by a basic tendency to help others. One of the earliest proponents of this theory in the nineteenth century was Auguste Comte, who coined the word *altruism*. It has come to be defined as "an unselfish concern with the welfare of others." In his writings, Comte advanced the idea that all social teaching should be devoted to the promotion of altruism over egoism.

Although we do not pretend that this section fully answers the broad questions of man's basic nature, we believe that altruism and its various components will continue to be critical to an alive and growing person, today as well as in the future. Indeed, the fact that our earth is becoming a smaller and smaller interdependent planet makes the development of more altruistic persons one of the factors upon which our very survival may depend.

Rationality. One of the traits of the altruistic person is that he faces each situation rationally. He carefully considers how his behavior will affect not only himself but others as well—not only here and now, but in the future as well. In fact, Peck and Havighurst (1960) coined the term "rational-altruistic" to describe the highest level of moral maturity.

Such a person does not blindly follow his principles or impose them on others. He lets circumstances alter his actions. When confronted with decisions, he studies the situations carefully and mentally experiments with alternate solutions and their implications before deciding on the most appropriate course of action. His final actions depend on what he believes to be morally right in light of careful study, not because it is "the thing to do."

Realistic. Along with a rational approach to life, altruistic persons are realistic. They tend to maintain objectivity about life and their interactions that allows them to automatically assess any decision on the basis of human good as well as the future consequences of the decision. It seems that they are better able to perceive the world and situations requiring moral judgment. Hence, their behavior tends to be consistent, in the sense of making decisions that generally tend to be for the good of people.

Considerate. Altruistic persons are considerate in that they truly take into account the needs of their fellow man in most of their actions. As Peck and Havighurst put it, "He is as much concerned with assuring the well-being of others as with assuring his own" (p. 8). Peck and Havighurst describe the rational-altruist in another way: "He enjoys seeing others live a full life, and his efforts to aid them are based on what they need and want" (pp. 8–9).

Responsible. The altruistic person is responsible in that he not only desires to help others but he carries this through into constructive action. That is, he "responds" behaviorally by doing something with his good intentions. Thus, in his various roles in the family, community, and world, he does his part. He stands up for his principles, yet does not prevent others from expressing their own points of view.

Life Goals

Cooperative. Liking and accepting himself, the altruistic person is able to "get close to others." He is able to work with others in various ways from social action to recreation activities. There is no dichotomy between his public and private world. That is, what he says he believes—and does. His values in working with all others are the same as those he uses in relating to his family and close friends.

Many of the characteristics just discussed overlap with the characteristics of the loving person, which were discussed earlier. This is consistent with our overlapping model. That is, these models are not distinct but are components of the whole person's behavioral characteristics, feelings, and traits. It is not surprising to realize that a loving person is also an altruistic person. So, an altruistic person shares many of the dimensions of a loving person. He knows himself well and therefore gets to know others well. He cares about people, he is responsible in his relationships with others, and he respects the uniqueness and individuality of himself and others.

In the concluding chapter to their book, Peck and Havighurst (1960) state:

> If man is by nature a social being, as seems an inescapable fact, then he cannot stand to be rejected or continually frustrated by other people. No matter what disappointed cynics may protest, or psychopaths try to overlook, it is an observable fact that friendly, considerate treatment by others is essential to the genuine happiness of every human being. (p. 20)

Fig. 10–4.

Obviously the need for developing altruistic behavior is of high concern to all of us. We should keep in mind that an "ideal model" of man has been presented and that probably no man lives up to this model. Yet, all of us can grow in some of these directions. Especially, we can provide the kinds of early experiences and relationships with our children that may increase the chances of producing more altruistic feelings and behavior in them.

EMPATHY

There is a fine, but important, distinction between the altruistic and the empathic person. Our definition of the altruistic person focuses primarily on his rationality and ability to perceive realistically with consideration and responsibility for other humans. Our definition of the empathic person, in contrast, focuses more on the "feeling tone" aspect of the person. That is, his ability to "feel with," or put himself in another's position, emotionally— through the processes of identification and projection.

Many persons "feel and experience" the needs and problems of others. Many of us have heard others (and sometimes ourselves) say: "This situation is so terrible and sad, but what can I do, the problem is too big!" We have also heard others discuss very intelligently and rationally how to solve some of man's basic problems, but in doing so, without revealing one degree of feeling. That is, the person may not really understand or feel the plight of his fellow man. He may merely approach it as an intellectual "game" with little or no affect through which he might grasp the human meaning of the dilemma.

It is in the combination of altruism and empathy that we find a person who not only feels for humanity and his fellow man but goes a step further and does something about it through the use of rational and responsible judgment.

Some Early Views of Empathy. It is interesting to briefly trace the historical development of the term *empathy*. First introduced by Lipps in 1907 as a concept called *Einfühlung* (feeling oneself into), the actual translation of the concept into the word empathy was proposed by Titchener (Murphy, 1949; Allport, 1954).

During more recent years a renewed interest in the term has developed, particularly in developmental and clinical psychology. Although very few experimental studies have been conducted, the concept seems to be increasingly recognized as an important variable in the moral and social development of a person, as well as in therapeutic relationships.

There is evidence (Hoffman, 1970) that the development of empathy, as part of the process of socialization, is an important prerequisite to the development of morals. The ability to put oneself into another's position in order to experience the consequences of one's actions toward him is valuable in learning moral rules and the control of impulsive behavior.

The role of empathy in counseling and theory is important, because it allows the therapist to experience the client's anger, fear, or confusion as if it were the therapist's own. The therapist can thereby communicate a clearer understanding of these conditions to the client (Rogers, 1961).

Recently the importance of empathy has been studied as an element in such diverse situations as: mother-child relationships (Schachtel, 1959), teacher-student relationships (Gage, 1968), accurate perception of others

(Steiner, 1955), employee-employer relationships (Haire, 1955), and successful family relationships (Foote, 1955).

The importance of the empathetic process in reducing intergroup tensions (Cottrell and Dymond, 1949), racial prejudice (Toch et al., 1968), as well as cross-cultural perception (Bagby, 1968) has also been explored. It thus appears that this process (even though it is a rather difficult concept to define) may be a key variable in the development of full affective potential.

Identification. The empathic person has the ability to identify himself with others in such a way that he can intellectually "put himself in the other person's or persons' situation." This element, then, refers more to the cognitive domain of the person than to the affective. It is one dimension of the empathic person, but it must be integrated with the other affective characteristics of "feeling with" another person.

Emotional Projection. The empathic person can also "feel with" and experience many of the feelings of another person. It is the ability to figuratively place himself in another's shoes and *walk with him* that the empathic person displays—very readily—in his relations with others.

This process, then, actually involves projecting oneself into another's frame of reference or, putting it another way, the ability to look out of another's "perceptual window" and view the world as he does.

Accurate Perception of Others. Having the ability to readily identify with others and to emotionally project his feelings into another's situation, the empathic person generally perceives other persons in a more accurate manner (Toch and Smith, 1968). He is able to experience more of the world of other people since his interactions with them are based on the reality of the relationship rather than on inaccurate perceptions of another person.

Trust. The very actions of the empathic person exemplifies a basic trust in his fellow man. This trust, the roots of which appear to develop in the mother-infant relationship, generalizes to all persons. Thus, the person is able to allow himself to enter into another's realm of existence, even momentarily.

Warmth. The empathic person tends to approach human relationships with a high degree of warmth, openness, and readiness to respond. He tends to like others (not that he isn't capable of disliking others for behavior that goes against man); he tends to accept others as they are, wherever they are in their development. Often, he tends to work in occupations where he can use his empathic ability to help his fellow man: teaching, social work, nursing, medicine, or psychology.

Self-Love. Perhaps one of the key variables in the empathic person is the fact that he likes himself. In fact, he is "in love" with himself. Just as with altruism, it is this cluster of attitudes and feelings of self-love that allow the empathic person to extend himself into the realms of existence of his fellow man. Without this self-love, he would not extend himself beyond his own sphere of existence, because to do so would be too threatening.

All of us have been touched by that rare person who shows empathy and love at just the moment when we doubted that anyone understood or cared for us. Experiences where we have been touched by another person, deeply touched and understood, even for an instant, give life validation and meaning; without such experiences, life becomes empty and meaningless.

The Affective
Domain

157

MATURING EMOTIONAL SELF-CONCEPT

We are not sure that there is such a thing as an "emotionally mature person." That is, there are some people who react "maturely"—(whatever that is)—most of the time, but we all act immaturely—(whatever that is)—some of the time.

This leads us to another dilemma. In writing the last sentence, we almost wrote "childish" in place of "immaturely" . . . (maybe children are emotionally mature and adults are immature).

What is maturity and immaturity? Is maturity an end point we reach at a certain stage of life? Is it to be defined by my standards, or yours? Is it more of an ongoing process? Or can we, in fact, define it at all?

With these questions left hanging, let us go ahead and do the best we can with the most humanly descriptive words (perhaps this may be a major part of our problem—when we try to describe alive, growing, becoming persons with words, we lose these qualities through semantic abstraction).

Some Dimensions of a Maturing Emotional Self

We use the term *maturing* because it denotes movement, aliveness, growth, and spontaneity. Rather than an end point, as the term *mature* denotes, *maturing* suggests the process of becoming. This does not mean that mature persons always act in an emotionally competent and responsible manner, but that their "life style" tends to reflect mature behaviors more often than not.

We use the term "maturing emotional self" because we are discussing that part of the person, his emotional self, that involves all the affective areas of his behavior. In other models, we referred to other facets of the person's total self (his biological self, his cognitive self, and later, his social self). We do not spend time defining the "self-concept" since it is explored throughout the book in a developmental sequence as the various parts of the emerging and growing person are discussed.

Freedom to Feel. The emotionally maturing person's behavior is typified by a sense of free-flowing emotions that are related to how the person feels at the moment. These people do not "hold in" their feelings over a long period of time, as many of us tend to do. There seems to be a relatedness and congruence between their feelings and behavior.

This freedom to feel includes the entire range of emotions, from expressions of joy, love, and happiness, to emotions of fear, anxiety, anger, and hate. One might get the feeling that these people are tender, fragile people who go around with smiles on their faces all the time. On the contrary, they are capable of deep feeling as well as strong expressions of emotion whenever they feel them.

Appropriateness of Emotional Expression. Being able to freely express themselves at the moment they experience various feelings, the behavior of emotionally mature persons tends to be related more to the reality of the situation at hand. Thus, their behavior and emotional expression is more often appropriate than inappropriate. It is the person who withholds his emotions and who later explodes at a minor irritation who has problems with others because his emotions seem inappropriate to the situation.

Authenticity of Being. The emotionally maturing person's life reflects an authenticity of being that is refreshing to experience. All facets of the lives of these individuals seem to reflect an honest and vital part of their existence

Life Goals

158

—from emotional expression to such areas of life as their occupation and how they carry out their job, their home and family relationships, their hobbies and interests, and their personal and private world.

Bugental, in his humanly insightful book, *The Search for Authenticity* (1965) defines the term this way:

> Authenticity is a term used to characterize a way of being in the world in which one's being is in harmony with the being of the world itself. To say it differently, we are authentic to that degree to which we are at one with the whole of being (world); we are authentic to the extent that we are in conflict with the givenness of being. Clearly, I am here seeking to characterize an ideal or ultimate condition of authenticity with the recognition that we are always somewhat less than fully authentic. (p. 33)

Spontaneity. The behavior of emotionally maturing people is not rigid and compulsive. They can approach new situations without planning in advance how they are going to respond. Having this freedom to feel as well as being in tune with their own authentic self, they can spontaneously live in the here and now.

This also means that these individuals do not tend to dwell in the past or live for tomorrow. They can live for the present and respond as they feel at the moment. This might imply an irresponsibility, yet these people are very ethical and moral because they feel good about themselves and therefore have little need to be mean to or hurt others.

Sense of Humor. The emotionally maturing person has the ability to look at himself and others and smile at the often absurd nature of life and our behavior. This is not a hostile or sadistic sense of humor that one finds in disturbed persons; rather, it is an open, accepting, and warm smile about the absurdity of life at times.

Jourard (1974) believes that a sense of humor and a healthy personality are closely related:

> The capacity to see humor in situations and to respond with laughter is regarded by some experts as an indicant of wellness. Indeed, it may be true that loss of the ability to laugh at oneself and at comic situations is one of the early symptoms of more serious personality disorders. When a person can laugh even in potentially grim situations, it implies some degree of freedom from the press of fate and circumstances. Prisoners in the Nazi concentration camps during World War II could even find something to laugh at, though they lived but a hairsbreadth from torture and death. (p. 102)

Ability to Handle Stress. The emotionally maturing person is able to face stressful situations in a direct manner without falling apart. His ability to handle the frustrations of life is well developed. One might say that he has a high "frustration tolerance" (the ability to tolerate emotional tension and anxiety).

This is not to imply that he is cold and unemotional in stressful situations, but rather that he is in control. Nor is this intended to say that he does not cry in times of sorrow and sadness, or get angry when there is justification. There is also an acceptance in such individuals of the fact that stress and

The Affective
Domain

159

anxiety are a part of living. Emotionally maturing people don't fight stress-ful situations nor do they try to avoid any disagreements or situations that may produce anxiety and tension. It is the emotionally immature person who "is in a rut" and refuses to open himself up to new situations or ideas that may make him anxious and produce tension. Therefore, he plays it safe and stays with the same pattern of life, the same ideas and thoughts, and the same job no matter how miserable he may be.

Emotionally Maturing Person and Other Affective Models. As you might have suspected by now, there is a high degree of overlap among the four models we have been discussing. In fact, as you might have also guessed, it may seem that all along we have been talking about the same person.

In a sense we have been, because, as was mentioned earlier, these models are all part of a syndrome or constellation of traits that are often found in a single person. (*Note:* This "hypothetical person" appears later in Chapter 12. He is called many different names by different theorists, as you will see, but we will focus on the late Abraham Maslow's model of the "self-actualiz-ing man.")

Thus, there is a high probability that once you find one of these charac-teristics in a person, you will also find the others. Perhaps the most basic trait (and a prerequisite to all the others) is the self-love found in the loving person. It seems that the ability to love oneself (based upon the quality of motherly and fatherly love received) gives one the courage to be truly concerned with others (altruism); to be able to become emotionally involved with the world of others (empathy); and to be able to express himself emotionally in spontaneous, authentic, and appropriate ways (emo-tional maturing).

Thus, the importance of the early loving relationships is again emphasized and will continue to be.

IMPLICATIONS

UNDERSTANDING YOURSELF AND OTHERS

If you are like many of the students with whom we have discussed such qualities of the fully human person, you may feel very inadequate and personally lacking. We, too, feel this way when we write about the hypo-thetical "fully human person." Very few persons ever reach that level of human existence. Why, then, do we talk and write about qualities that very few of us ever fully experience in our daily lives?

Erich Fromm, in a seminar that one of the authors had with him at Michigan State University, gave a partial answer in the form of an analogy. He began by asking if any of us had ever contemplated a seed. A seed, he said, is a miraculous thing. Some seeds are as small as pinpoints, and yet so much potential for growth lies wrapped up in that small bundle.

Fromm then said that you might think of a newborn as a seed—a flower seed, for example. Now you could plant a flower seed (in the spring at least) most anywhere, and cover it with dirt, and water it occasionally. It would grow and probably bloom. But it would be small, its flowers faded, with pale green leaves and in all probability, it would be invaded by insects in the soil and on the leaves. All in all, it would end a stunted and rather puny plant, with flowers that probably few people would want to pick.

Life Goals Now, Fromm went on, if you were to take the same seed, or one of the same variety, and select a proper place to plant it, prepare the soil with the correct mixture of ingredients, plant it at just the right depth, water it, fertilize it, and spray it to protect it from infestation of insects and diseases . . . you would find a tall plant with brilliant and fully developed flowers, lush green leaves with no infestation . . . you would be seeing a plant that had grown near to its full potential.

It is so sad, Fromm concluded, pointing to himself, that most of us are like the stunted flower—that most of us die never having come close to developing our full potential. Most people feel that cancer and other physical diseases, mental illness, or the possibilities of atomic annihilation are the most serious human problems. It may be that history will record as most tragic that millions of humans live and die without ever reaching even a fraction of their full human potential.

Fromm added that the process of allowing our potential to blossom forth begins within ourselves through knowing ourselves, caring for ourselves, assuming responsibility for ourselves, and respecting our unique human qualities. This, of course, ultimately means learning to love ourselves.

Thus, we too feel that we are all capable of developing more of our potential during our lifetimes. We believe that some of the qualities we have discussed in this chapter will allow you to free yourself to develop your own unique potential. As Fromm mentioned, begin within yourself, with self-knowledge, caring, responding, and respecting—with the development of self-love.

Fortunately, most of us have had some experiences (particularly as infants) that gave us some degree of self-trust and love. We can build on this foundation. Although there is no simple way to learn to know and love yourself, we believe that the processes involved in working toward the models of the fully human person offer you ways to help yourself grow and your children as well.

LIVING AND WORKING WITH CHILDREN, ADOLESCENTS, AND ADULTS

Hopefully, the affective models of the fully human person can be translated into daily living in whatever spheres the person moves. We believe that the qualities of love, altruism, and empathy as well as emotional maturing can be generated among those relationships where the person spends the greater part of his life: the family, community, society, school, and work.

People working with children who generally share these qualities are usually much more effective in their relationships whether these be in the role of teacher, parent, minister, or employer. These sensitive people have been called by such names as "therapeutic helpers," "growth producing people," "human facilitators," or just plain "warm and loving people." Jourard (1974) speaks of this type of person, calling them "therapeutic people":

> These therapeutic people may simply be good, sympathetic listeners. Or, they may be busy people, strongly committed to the pursuit of some goal, as for example artists, scientists, or politicians. Whatever their vocation, they tend to inspire hope and imagination in the persons around them, such that the latter feel more fully alive and strongly motivated to cope with problems outside themselves. They feel better for having known these people. (p. 459)

The Affective Domain

Developing Positive Models

The implications of this chapter for developing positive models are clear. In summary, we believe (and the research evidence strongly suggests this to be the case) that a truly loving person tends to produce loving relationships among those people with whom he interacts. Thus, loving mothers or fathers will tend to relate to each of their children with dimensions of care, responsibility, respect, and knowledge, which in turn will tend to produce a loving family. The family will eventually emerge out into the community and hopefully produce a more loving community, which in turn will tend to affect the school and world of work, which in turn will affect society as a whole. This pattern could be followed in the other models of altruism, empathy, and emotional maturing. It is a simplified model, to be sure, yet it does give some clues for developing positive models that have far-reaching implications. Figure 10–5 shows a diagram of this possibility.

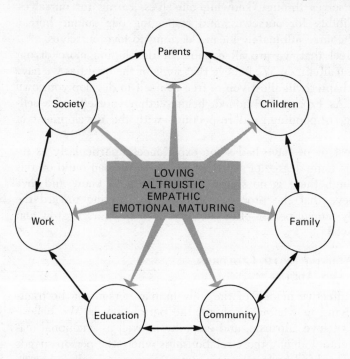

FIG. 10–5. *A visual picture of how positive models may generate changes in other segments of the world. The cycle can begin anywhere and can move in both directions. Thus, some communities may decide to foster more altruistic behavior through community action, which in turn has an impact on the family, the schools, and the business community. Or some college may wish to foster more loving behavior among its students, faculty, and administration; this in turn may have an impact on the surrounding community, employers, and families.*

In concluding this chapter, it is interesting to note that the *Report to the President* from the 1970 White House Conference on Children includes the following recommendation:

> Identity is the totality of one's thoughts and feelings about the universe —one's self, one's surroundings, others, and the unknown. As a child develops, he or she will become aware of and relate to more and more of a personal universe. The child will develop a positive, healthy identity only if capacities to think and feel are guided towards knowledge and love. Knowing and loving must expand with awareness, and a child must come to know and to love self and others. Only if these capacities continue to expand will the child be able to fulfill his or her human potential and become his or her true self. If this expansion of knowledge or love is frustrated or blocked, the child will remain unhappy, unsatisfied, even disturbed. (p. 21)

Life Goals

162

ALLPORT, G. W. *Pattern and growth in personality.* New York: Holt, 1961.

————. Historical background of modern social psychology. G. Lindzey (ed.), *Handbook of social psychology.* Reading, Mass.: Addison-Wesley, 1954.

BAGBY, J. W. A cross-cultural study of perceptual predominance in binocular rivalry. In H. Toch, and H. C. Smith (eds.), *Social perception.* Princeton, N. J.: Van Nostrand, 1968.

BUGENTAL, J. F. T. *The search for authenticity.* New York: Holt, 1961.

BURNS, E. M. *Western civilizations: their history and their culture.* New York: Norton, 1963.

CHAPIN, H. D. A plea for accurate statistics in infants institutions. *Transactions of the American Pediatric Society,* 1915, **27**:180.

CASLER, L. *Maternal deprivation: a critical review of the literature.* Monographs of the Society for Research in Child Growth and Development, 1961, vol. 26, no. 2.

COTTRELL, L. S. and R. DYMOND. The empathic processes. *Psychiatry,* Nov. 1949, 11, no. 4: 355–359.

FROMM, E. *The art of loving.* New York: Harper, 1956.

GAGE, N. L. Explorations in teacher's perceptions of pupils. In H. Toch and H. C. Smith (eds.), *Social perception.* Princeton, N. J.: Van Nostrand, 1968.

HAIRE, M. Role-perceptions in labor-management relations. *Industrial and Labor Relations Review,* January 1955, vol. 8, no. 2.

HALL, C. S. *A primer of Freudian psychology.* New York: World Publishing, 1954.

HOFFMAN, M. L. Moral development. In P. H. Mussen (ed.), *Carmichael's manual of child psychology.* New York: Wiley, 1970.

JOURARD, S. M. *Healthy personality.* New York: Macmillan, 1974.

————, and R. M. REMY. Perceived parental attitudes, the self, and security. *Journal of Consulting Psychology,* 1955, **19**:364–366.

LIPPS, T. Das Wissen von fremden Ichs. *Psychologische Untersuchungen,* 1907, **1**:694–722.

MACHIAVELLI, N. *The prince.* New York: Mentor, 1952.

MONTAGU, A. *On being human.* New York: Hawthorn, 1966.

MURPHY, G. *Historical introduction to modern psychology.* New York: Harcourt, 1949.

PECK, R. F. and R. J. HAVIGHURST. *The psychology of character development.* New York: Wiley, 1960.

ROGERS, C. R. *On becoming a person.* Boston: Houghton, 1961.

SCHACHTEL, E. G. *Metamorphosis.* New York: Basic, 1959.

STEINER, I. D. Interpersonal behavior and accurate social perception. *Psychological Review,* 1955, **62**:268–273.

TOCH, H. H., A. I. RABIN, and D. M. WILKINS. Factors entering in ethnic identifications. In H. Toch and H. C. Smith (eds.), *Social perception.* Princeton, N. J.: Van Nostrand, 1968.

————, and H. C. SMITH, *Social perception.* Princeton, N. J., 1968.

WHITE HOUSE CONFERENCE ON CHILDREN. *Report to the president.* Washington, D.C., Supt. of Documents, (O-414-184), 1971.

WYLIE, R. C. *The self concept.* Lincoln, Neb.: U. of Nebraska, 1961.

RECOMMENDED FURTHER READING

BERKOWITZ, L. and J. MACAULAY. *Altruism and helping behavior.* New York: Academic, 1970.

The Affective
Domain

BETTELHEIM, B. *The informed heart*. New York: Free Press, 1960.

———. *Love is not enough*. New York: Macmillan, 1965.

BRIGGS, D. C. *Your child's self-esteem*. Garden City, N. Y.: Doubleday, 1970.

FROMM, E. *The heart of man*. New York: Harper, 1964.

FROMME, A. *The ability to love*. North Hollywood, Calif.: Wilshire, 1963.

HARLOW, H. F. *Learning to love*. San Francisco: Albion, 1971.

JOURARD, S. M. *The transparent self*. Princeton, N. J.: Van Nostrand, 1971.

KAY, W. *Moral development: a psychological study of moral growth from childhood to adolescence*. London: Allen & Unwin, 1968.

MAY, R. *Love and will*. New York: Norton, 1969.

MOUSTAKAS, C. *Personal growth: the struggle for identity and human values*. Cambridge, Mass.: Howard A. Doyle, 1969.

SEARS, P. S. and V. S. SHERMAN. *In pursuit of self-esteem*. Belmont, Calif.: Wadsworth, 1964.

SOROKIN, P. A. *Forms and techniques of altruistic and spiritual growth*. Boston: Beacon, 1954.

STOTLAND, E., Exploratory investigations of empathy. In L. Berkowitz, *Advances in experimental social psychology*, vol. 4. New York: Academic, 1969.

———, S. E. SHERMAN, and K. G. SHAVER. *Empathy and birth order*. Lincoln, Neb.: U. of Nebraska, 1971.

WILSON, J., N. WILLIAMS, and B. SUGARMAN. *Introduction to moral education*. Baltimore: Penguin, 1967.

Life Goals

The Social Domain

Prelude
Basic Theory and Research
  Compassion
  Autonomy
  Openness
  Maturing Social Self-Concept
Implications
  Understanding Yourself and
    Others
  Living and Working with Chil-
    dren, Adolescents, and Adults
  Developing Positive Models

PRELUDE

Having explored some dimensions and life goals of the fully human person in the biological, cognitive, and affective domains, we are now ready to translate these qualities into the realities of daily life. For it is here, in the arena of the social domain, that the person may (or may not) *express* such worthwhile human goals as health, zest, creativity, altruism, and empathy.

The importance of establishing goals that contribute to the development of a socially effective individual can be seen when we consider the future. It is in the future that today's children will be living and working, and the task of determining how to raise today's children to live full and meaningful lives can be one of today's most socially relevant activities.

It is difficult to predict just what qualities will be needed for living a more fully human life in the world of tomorrow. The acceleration of social and technological change is so great and the nature and scope of these changes so complex that it is staggering to the imagination.

To give an idea of the rapidity and enormity of changes that man has undergone during much of his existence, we use Toffler's (1970) fascinating analogy of man's eight hundred lifetimes.

Toffler divides man's existence during the last fifty thousand years into lifetimes of about sixty-two years each. Thus, there have been approximately eight hundred such lifetimes. He then explains the major events in man's existence according to these lifetimes. These are illustrated in Figure 11–1.

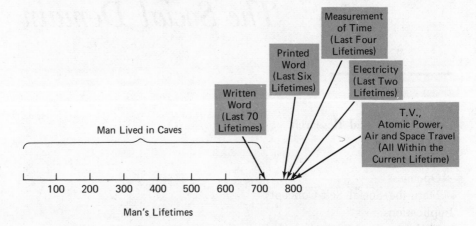

Fig. 11–1.
*Man's 800 Life-times. (Adapted from Alvin Toffler,
Future Shock.
New York:
Random House,
1970.)*

As you can see from this figure, nearly all of man's major technological advantages have come about within the scope of one lifetime. If we further analyze this situation we will see that the greatest number of these changes have occurred within the last twenty-five years of this current lifetime, and more technological change has taken place in the last decade than in the thirty years that immediately preceeded.

It is this ever increasing *rate* of change that has led Toffler to suggest that we may be reaching the point where man can no longer adapt to change rapidly enough to keep up with the rate of change. To illustrate this concept let us use a relatively insignificant analogy: suppose that you are just now getting around to deciding that you should buy an electric toothbrush. Isn't

Life Goals

166

it a bit worrysome to you to find out that some manufacturers have already gone through four different generations of electric toothbrushes? How does it strike you to find out that electric toothbrushes may be obsolete in a few short years, when ultrasonic teeth cleaning devices reach the market? Maybe you should put off buying an electric toothbrush. But on the other hand, how do you know that ultrasonic toothbrushes won't be replaced by something else in three more years?

Fig. 11–2.
Things around us change at an ever increasing rate.

It is this rate of change that is challenging man's ability to adapt. When the change becomes so rapid that man can no longer accommodate to the change, he loses his feel about *his* place in the world. Just as with our electric toothbrush buyer, man becomes plagued with indecision regarding a course of action when he is faced with a too rapidly changing set of social alternatives. Under these conditions man suffers a paralysis of will.

We see other signs of the human effects of these rapid changes: social and political unrest among the racially and culturally different in this and other countries; a demand by the youth that the "establishment" not lag so long in changing and reexamining social, political, religious, and economic values; changes in the meaning, structure, and functioning of the family unit; and vast and rapid changes in the goals and functions of the educational system.

What kind of man will be needed to cope with both "present" and "future shock?" We believe that four of the essential dimensions that will increase the chances of living a more fully human life in the world of tomorrow as well as today are compassion, autonomy, openness, and the development of a socially maturing self-concept providing skills and attitudes that allow entrance into the society while retaining personal identity and capacity for growth. Figure 11–4 presents these four models.

The Social Domain

167

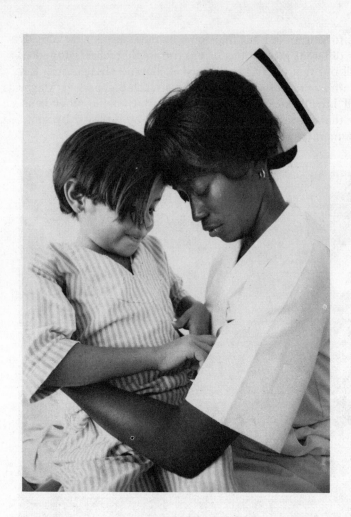

FIG. 11–3.
A compassionate
relationship.

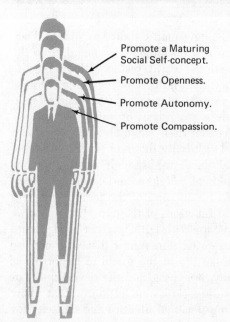

Promote a Maturing
Social Self-concept.

Promote Openness.

Promote Autonomy.

Promote Compassion.

FIG. 11–4.
Life goals in the
social domain.

BASIC THEORY AND RESEARCH

Compassion

There are many everyday experiences in which people are touched by compassionate persons: the lady who comes to the aid of the little girl lost in a supermarket, the man who stops his car to allow the child to retrieve his baseball, the teacher who puts her arm around a student who has just had a bad experience in school, the husband who gives his wife a hug after her hard day with the family.

We all have our own ideas about what compassion is, or what compassionate persons are like. These ideas of compassion are generally expressed in terms of kindness, thoughtfulness, helpfulness, and sympathy. No doubt the concept of compassion entered your mind as you read the material dealing with love, altruism, and empathy. The dictionary defines compassion as: "Sympathetic consciousness of other's distress together with a desire to alleviate it." From this you can see that compassion is closely related to altruism and empathy.

The key difference between compassion and altruism and empathy, for the purposes of our discussion, and the reason that compassion is included within the social domain rather than the affective domain, is that compassion involves the element of action. Compassion carries the affective processes of altruism, empathy, and love one step further into the realm of social action.

Another reason for including compassion in the social domain is that two of the three developmental components of compassion arise from the process of socialization. (The third component springs from the affective domain.)

Humanly Socialized. One of the first dimensions of a compassionate person is that he has been reared in such a way that he learns to value not only himself, his parents and his brothers and sisters but also his fellow man as well. He is "for man" and the full development of man's potential.

The process through which the compassionate person learns to value himself and others is called the socialization process. We have discussed this process earlier in the text but we shall review the definition again (Elkin, 1960):

> We may define socialization as *the process by which someone learns the ways of a given society or social group so that he can function within it.* Socialization includes both the learning and internalizing of appropriate patterns, values, and feelings. The child ideally not only knows what is expected of him and behaves accordingly; he also feels that this is the proper way for him to think and behave. The term *socialization,* in itself, refers to learning the ways of any established and continuing group—an immigrant becomes socialized into the life of his new country; a recruit into the life of the army; a new insurance agent into the patterns of his company and his job. Socialization of the child has a broader application —the child ultimately becomes an adult human being who has learned the ways of the ongoing society. (p. 4)

As can be seen from this definition, no values are attached to socialization. That is, as long as the person learns the ways of a given society or social

The Social Domain

group and can function within it, he is considered to be "socialized." This definition is fine for a more objective and scientific discussion; however, for our use here it is too limited and must be amended.

Thus, we are joining the word *humanly* along with *socialized* because merely "adjusting" to the norms of any society or any group is not sufficient, or in some cases even desirable. A fully human person is not necessarily one who accepts all of the values of a society and just "functions well within it." Adjusting to the norms of a head hunting tribe or the norms of Nazi Germany during World War II certainly are not the acts of a fully human person.

Indeed, one of the dilemmas facing our country today is that many sub-groups do not want to "adjust" to, or "function well" within our society because it often dehumanizes, disenfranchises, and downright damages the psychological as well as the physical growth of members of these groups. This is, in part, what many young people and such diverse groups as the poor, the culturally different and even the aged, are saying.

Thus, a "humanly socialized" person is one who has been reared to value life and growth for other human beings. He values life and growth not only for "United States Man" but for all those in other parts of the world; those who may "wear" different colored clothes, skin, and minds, as well as those who live in different ways, eat different foods, play different games, worship different gods, and buy and sell differently, and whose plays, novels, and television programs are different from his own.

Social Interest. Another dimension of compassion that overlaps with the first is that of social interest. This concept was originally developed by Alfred Adler (1964). Although he uses the terms in a slightly different way and for a different purpose, Adler indicates that man is born with a social feeling, an innate kinship bond with his fellow human. It is through the process of socialization that social interest is developed from this inborn tendency. According to Adler, a lack of social interest in society, or in the particular family into which one is born, is a root cause of mental illness and social deviance in the individual.

The compassionate person, then, has developed this feeling of "social interest," which means that he is concerned for the welfare of his fellow man and exhibits this in his style of life.

Hall and Lindzey (1970) summarize this concept as follows:

> Adler, who was an advocate of social justice and a supporter of social democracy, enlarged his conception of man to include the factor of social interest. Although social interest takes in such matters as co-operation, interpersonal and social relations, identification with the group, empathy, and so forth, it is much broader than all of these. In its ultimate sense, social interest consists of the individual helping society to attain the goal of a perfect society. (p. 125)

Fellow Feeling. Another dimension of the compassionate person is related to the affective domain or feeling component of man. We use the term *fellow feeling* because it conveys the tone and meaning of what we are trying to describe. The compassionate person displays many characteristics of the altruistic man, particularly his feelings of concern for his fellow man. Thus, he feels this sense of oneness with the rest of humanity, so that, when

Life Goals

there is a serious tragedy or a joyful event in another part of the world, he feels this sorrow or joy, even though he may be thousands of miles away and may never have visited that part of the world.

AUTONOMY

Although the compassionate person displays social interest and feelings of fellowship with all mankind, there is another dimension of the more fully human person that at first may seem to be the opposite of such socially positive feelings. We are referring to the strong tendencies toward independence and self-containment found in the more fully human person. These persons seem to be able to rely more on their own "inner voices" (as Abraham Maslow described it (1962)), rather than on listening to the chorus of society.

We have indicated in our earlier discussions of the cognitive domain that independence is a component of creativity and a maturing cognitive self-concept. Autonomy, then, is considered part of the social domain because it implies *functional* independence accompanied by social responsibility. We discuss the latter concept developing from a maturing social self-concept a bit later. Functional independence arises from the process of socialization during which the child should form a *positive self-concept* encompassing the following dimensions: inner centeredness, authenticity, and trust.

FIG. 11–5.

171

This trend toward autonomy, many believe, begins early in life and has lifelong implications for the individual. Erikson (1971), for example, believes that it begins as early as twelve to fifteen months of age:

> The sense of trust once firmly established, the struggle for the next component of the healthy personality begins. The child is now twelve to fifteen months old. Much of his energy for the next two years will center around asserting that he is a human being with a mind and will of his own. (p. 124)

Positive Self-concept (Identity). This early developing autonomy seems to arise from the individual's sense of his own identity as a person. The autonomous person must first develop a sense of his own selfhood, his "being in this world," his uniqueness as an alive and growing person. This process is called *identification* and essentially involves the child's early imitative behavior of those people who are important to him, particularly his parents. From the reactions of his parents, the child comes to recognize that he is separate from them and that he is a unique being.

Reisman and others (1953) believe that to a certain extent we are all "victims" of the expectations and traditions of our parent's values and those of society. The person with a positive self-concept is less a victim because he tends to rely more on his own inner feelings of what is right or wrong, rather than depending entirely on codes established by others. This person possesses an *inner centeredness* to which he often turns for approval or disapproval, standards, and guidance.

A significant part of inner centeredness is *authenticity*. A person can rely on inner centeredness as long as he possesses an awareness of being and his thoughts and feelings are consistent with his state of existence. It is the perspective or awareness of the relationships between the real world, its activities, and his existence that characterizes the authentic person.

The autonomous person displays a basic *trust*. He trusts himself and his own impulses and feelings, and he tends to trust his fellow man.

OPENNESS

The fully human person tends, too, to be an "open system" rather than a "closed" one. That is to say he continues to be an alive, growing, self-renewing, becoming, and responding individual rather than merely a "dead-end" person. This element is described by Kelley (1962) as "seeing oneself as a part of a world in movement—in process of becoming."

The open person is one who is also not afraid to "unmask" himself in front of others. Jourard (1971) originated the term *self-disclosure* to describe this ability to reveal our real feelings, intentions, and being to another *significant* individual. According to Jourard, self-disclosure is a basic component of the healthy personality.

The open person tends to have developed a basically *democratic personality* pattern in his approach to life in general and other persons in particular. That is, he tends to accept others as they are, is willing to tolerate ambiguous situations, does not tend to view others in categories, and tends to question authority, especially when it is irrational and inhuman.

The opposite of this pattern, the authoritarian personality, was studied a number of years ago by Adorno (1950) and his colleagues, who determined

Life Goals

the characteristics of highly prejudiced and humanly intolerant persons. Although the study was criticized by some, it did stimulate some further studies.

Hodges (1971) summarizes a number of these findings about the "authoritarian man":

> According to Christie, the authoritarian personality is inclined to be relatively "punitive and condescending toward inferiors . . . less sensitive to interpersonal relationships, and given to assuming that most people share his own . . . hierarchical orientation toward life." He is submissive toward authority, admires power and toughness, and is highly conventional, and he seems driven by something that Newcomb calls a "threat orientation." Beset by a deeply rooted, pressing, yet almost entirely subconscious sense of insecurity, the authoritarian seems in Gordon Allport's words "fearful of himself, of his own instincts of his own consciousness, of change, and of his social environment." Because he apparently cannot live comfortably with himself and with others, he works out a distinctive style of life—in effect, a crutch—to ward off the free floating anxieties which plague him. One of the more central of the several defensive measures which he uses is repression, a form of selective forgetting in which the painful or unpleasant is excluded from consciousness (yet remains, bottled up, beneath the surface). (pp. 507–08)

The open person is also receptive to change in himself, others, and in his environment. He is open to himself and his growth processes, and therefore, he views life in the same way, as a process of new and unexplored territory and experiences.

He values the unfamiliar and the new. He exposes himself to new ideas and experiences. He may even welcome change just for the challenge involved. Such acceptance of change means that he can afford to take risks in his life. He is like the poker player with a large pile of chips. He can gamble quite freely.

The open person is in a continual process of what some have called *becoming* and others have called *self-renewal*. He is always in the process of discovering within himself new feelings, abilities, interest, passions—resources for extending boundaries of self-awareness and insight.

MATURING SOCIAL SELF-CONCEPT

We again use the term *maturing* to indicate an ongoing process rather than one that has reached its end-point, maturity. The social self-concept can be thought of as the individual's own view of his capacity to interact effectively with his social environment. As with the other developing self-concepts, the social self-concept is the result of the individual's perception of the degree of success or failure in his social experiences. As we gain competence during our process of socialization, our social self-concept undergoes transformation and begins to mature.

Social scientists in this country and abroad point with concern to areas in which individuals and groups are not given an opportunity to develop adequate *social competencies* to allow them to become participating members of the society. Youth, cultural minorities, and the aged are some of the groups that presently seem to recognize this problem of being excluded from

The Social Domain

certain socialization processes with the result that the social self-concepts of some of the individuals within these groups fail to mature. This failure to mature inhibits the individual's and hence the group's psychological, economic, and political growth.

It may seem that we are playing the same record over and over again. However, this characteristic does seem to be a major variable in many areas of the fully human person. The socially competent person feels good about himself; he believes that he can make a difference in the world, that he can function successfully in the world. The term *self-esteem* has been used by some to describe this pattern.

Clausen (1968) uses the analogy of the "vicious" versus the "benign" cycle of success experiences in the world to illustrate the significance of this positive self-feeling: "Launched on the right trajectory, the person is likely to accumulate successes that strengthen the effectiveness of his orientation to the world while at the same time he acquires the knowledge and skills that make his further success more probable." (p. 277). Figure 11–6 illustrates this notion.

FIG. 11–6. *"Vicious" and "benign" circles involved in the development of competent and incompetent people. (Adapted from J.A. Clausen (ed.), Socialization and Society, Boston: Little, Brown and Co., 1968, p. 277.)*

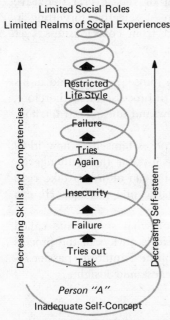

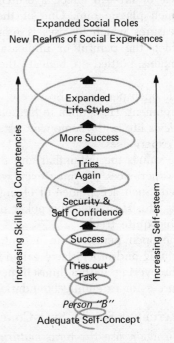

Closely related to the positive feelings about one's self is an active or *positive life orientation* combined with a sense of hopefulness about the self in the world. That is, an approach toward life that takes the posture: "I can do something about my environment. I can help shape a part of the world (even though I may be controlled by many social forces)."

Such characteristics have been found, for example, by Smith (1961) in a study of competent Peace Corps teachers. Through a series of extensive interviews and other research methods, the following characteristics seemed to emerge consistently: self-confidence, responsibility, a feeling that his life is important and that it matters what he does, openness to the world, tolerance and ability to articulate well his situation and problems.

Life Goals

Clausen (1968) cites another study by Coleman and others (1966) of 645,000 pupils in elementary, junior, and senior high schools in which a major finding was that the degree to which a person feels he has some control over his life and future is directly related to his school achievement (even more than the traditional criteria of school achievement: grades, teacher recommendations, or scholastic achievement tests).

Similar findings have been recorded in a study of effective helpers in teaching, the ministry, and among student nurses. Combs (1969) summarizes the characteristics of effective helpers as having a positive view of their subjects and a belief in the capacity of man to save himself. They see themselves as one with their fellow man, and tend to view themselves in positive ways.

Ability to Face Reality. The socially competent person, feeling good about himself and actively engaging the world around him, can tolerate reality. That is, he does not tend to fool himself about the world around him. He is able to test reality and respond to the consequences.

As a result, behavior of socially competent persons is far more efficient than those who cannot tolerate reality and live half of their lives in fantasy. Thus, they can efficiently relate to their roles and status in life in a knowledgeable manner. They know that living in a complex society there are many games they will be playing. They, therefore, do not tend to get lost in the games. They constantly know that they are playing these games and therefore don't get caught up in all the petty aspects of worldly "gamesmanship."

IMPLICATIONS

UNDERSTANDING YOURSELF AND OTHERS

These characteristics of the more fully human person represent goals that we might set for ourselves and our children. Probably no one will ever achieve these goals to a complete degree—but they can serve as "bench marks" or guides toward a richer and more complete life.

Most of us have been reared to a degree like that "stunted plant" that Erich Fromm described in Chapter 10. But "stunted plants" can be stimulated to further growth by a number of techniques.

Changing Your Environment. It is amazing how a scrawny, dying house plant, for example, may come alive and become a beautiful, lush, green plant when it is moved to a new location. We are not suggesting that you move away from your neighborhood and community (although that often helps). What we are suggesting is that you purposely expose yourself to new social settings.

We have been amazed how much compassion has been shown by many of our (often egotistically oriented) students who become involved in volunteer work with the elderly, children, or people in hospital settings.

Adding Extra Stimulants. Sometimes dormant plants need a "shot" of fertilizer to break into a new growth cycle of blooming and flowering. Sometimes, too, we all need a certain amount of new stimulation to redirect and reappraise our state of being.

We have seen emotionally insulated and bored students suddenly come

Fig. 11–7.
Could this plant
have been saved?

alive as they read some new ideas or theories about man. Sometimes, conducting a research study or working on a project with other students may help revitalize the person. Maybe you remember such experiences when a new stimulus came into your life and triggered off a whole new way for you to view the world.

Removing Sources of Infestation. Sometimes plants (particularly roses) are not fully alive and growing because their strength is being sapped by dead branches. Humans are often hampered in their growth because of "psychological infestations" that literally sap their strength. Fears, anxieties, compulsions, and unvented hostilities may force us into a state of complete exhaustion and depression. If it is so serious that we are incapacitated, we are forced to seek professional help from psychologists or psychiatrists.

One of the major purposes of such help (a common form called psychotherapy) is to help the person uncover these hidden "infestations" or negative feelings. Once these are uncovered the person is free of these forces and often becomes renewed for living and feels like a new person.

We are not suggesting that everyone needs therapy; however, we all have certain (often unconscious) forces at work that drain us of our human energy. Sometimes just talking to a good friend, teacher, counselor, minister, or even parents or relatives may uncover some of these hidden areas of your emotional life.

Life Goals

176

Living and Working with Children, Adolescents, and Adults

All the horticulture and garden books say the same thing: it is much easier to raise a healthy plant by proper preparation and nuturing while the plant is forming its basic nourishment for growth (roots) and its basic strength (trunk or stem).

In living and working with children, it is far easier to prepare the environment (home, school, nursery, day care center, or hospital setting) to nurture such fully human qualities as compassion, autonomy, openness, and social competency. It essentially means that the parents or those who work with children in various settings truly love children and respect their individuality, care for their welfare, get to know the child, and assume responsibility to carry out human interactions so that the child may develop his full potentialities.

This is no easy course of action for parents or those who work with children, for in the day-to-day existence, it is hard to think in such lofty terms while your child has just pulled the cat's tail and is sitting on the floor screaming at you and the cat. But, we believe such "lofty" goals can be approximated by every parent as well as child workers.

The most important thing that parents and child workers can do is to increase their level of self-understanding and self-acceptance. The evidence seems overwhelming that those who understand and like themselves (positive self-concept or image) tend to relate with others in ways that foster positive human growth.

Specifically, this means that they will tend to relate to children with respect, knowledge, care, and responsibility, which, in turn, will tend to produce this behavior in the children. This, in turn, means that there is a high probability that they will relate to others with compassion and openness, as well as feeling autonomous and developing into generally more socially competent people.

The next thing that one can do to increase the chances of developing this more fully human person in the social domain is to prepare the setting (seed bed) in which the most significant years of growth will occur . . . the years when the "roots" and "trunks" of the child will be formed.

This means first having a mother and father who are feeling good about themselves. This means that they will communicate openly with each other; which means that when the child is born, he will have a "seed bed" to begin his growth which is open, alive, and humanly sensitive to promote his maximum growth.

It means providing models of human interaction that exemplify care, respect, responsibility, and knowledge for others. From this kind of soil the child will develop roots of compassion, a strong autonomous trunk, as well as feeling free to disclose his branches to the world, with leaves that completely "breathe" in and out as a full participating member of nature.

Developing Positive Models

It becomes apparent that man can no longer tolerate the human unfairness, suffering, and basic loss of dignity that have been so common throughout history. The time has come when we must all work together to ensure a genuine sense of "community" and "fellow feeling." We need each other;

The Social Domain

we depend heavily upon each other; we are truly living in an interconnected and interdependent world. Combs and Syngg (1959) dramatically point this out in the following passage:

> The greatest problems of our time are no longer the problems of production and control of "things" but of communication and cooperation among people. Having won control over our physical world, we find ourselves confronted with a new problem, the problem of how to control ourselves! (p. 3)

With this high degree of interconnectedness comes a high degree of social responsibility. This point is well illustrated by Frazier (1970):

> The Nuremberg trials set forth the principle that each man is accountable before a court of universal justice that transcends loyalties to any lesser tribunal. Man can no longer justify his behavior by the claim that he was following the orders of a superior or that he felt himself powerless in the midst of other compelling circumstances.

> What this seems to many to mean is that everyone must read as well as he can what is absolutely just and try as he can to live by his understanding. Faith comes through belief that as each man lives his life righteously, life altogether will become what it ought to be. Community in its truest sense will be born. (p. 75)

One who feels a sense of community with his fellow man must first feel this within himself and his family. It is this kind of positive model—a sense of "reverence for life"—my life, my wife and children's lives, my fellow man's life—that will nuture and eventually produce such humanly beautiful blossoms as: growth, life, joy, aliveness, emotional freedom, and compassion. Let us begin preparing the soil in our own lives so that the seeds may flourish in those of our children.

CHAPTER REFERENCES

ADLER, A. *Social interest: a challenge to mankind.* New York: Capricorn, 1964.

ADORNO, T. W. et al. *The authoritarian personality.* New York: Harper, 1950.

CLAUSEN, J. A. (ed.). *Socialization and society.* Boston, Mass.: Little, Brown, 1968.

COLEMAN, J. S. et al. Equality of educational opportunity. Washington, D.C.: U.S. Office of Education, Supt. of Documents (FS 5. 238.38001), 1966.

COMBS, A. W. et al. *Florida studies in the helping professions.* Gainesville, Fla.: U. of Fla., 1969.

————, and D. SNYGG. *Individual behavior.* New York: Harper, 1959.

ELKIN, F. *The child and society: the process of socialization.* New York: Random, 1960.

ERIKSON, E. H. A healthy personality for every child. In R. H. Anderson and H. G. Shane, *As the twig is bent.* Boston, Mass.: Little, Brown, 1971.

FRAZIER, A. The quality of life and society in the United States. In Association for Supervision and Curriculum Development, NEA, *A man for tomorrow's world.* Washington, D.C.: N.E.A., 1970.

HALL, C. S. and G. LINDZEY. *Theories of personality,* 2nd ed. New York: Wiley, 1970.

Life Goals

Hodges, H. M., Jr. *Conflict and consensus: an introduction to sociology.* New York: Harper, 1971.

Jourard, S. M. *The transparent self.* 2nd ed., New York: Van Nostrand, 1971.

Kelley, E. C. The fully functioning self. In A. W. Combs, *Perceiving, behaving, becoming.* Washington, D.C.: N.E.A., 1962.

Maslow, A. *Toward a psychology of being.* New York: Van Nostrand, 1962.

Reisman, D., N. Glazer and R. Denney. *The lonely crowd.* New York: Doubleday, 1953.

Smith, M. B. Explorations in competence: a study of Peace Corps teachers in Ghana. *American Psychologist,* 1961, **16**:299–306.

Toffler, A. *Future shock.* New York: Random, 1970.

RECOMMENDED FURTHER READING

Allport, G. *The nature of prejudice.* Reading, Mass.: Addison-Wesley, 1954.

Baier, K. and N. Rescher. *Values and the future.* New York: Free Press, 1969.

Brown, H. *The challenge of man's future.* New York: Viking, 1954.

Bugental, J. F. T. *The search for authenticity.* New York: Holt, 1965.

Christie, R. and M. Jahoda (eds.). *Studies in the scope and method of the authoritarian personality.* New York: Free Press, 1954.

Combs, A. W. A perceptual view of the adequate personality. In A. W. Combs (ed.), *Perceiving, behaving, becoming.* Washington, D.C.: N.E.A., 1962.

Coopersmith, S. *The antecedents of self-esteem.* San Francisco: Freeman, 1967.

Gardner, J. W. *Self-renewal: the individual and the innovative society.* New York: Harper, 1963.

Gergen, K. J. *The concept of self.* New York: Holt, 1971.

Kahn, H. and A. J. Weiner. *The year 2000.* New York: Macmillan, 1967.

Reich, C. A. *The greening of America.* New York: Random, 1970.

Rogers, C. R. *On becoming a person.* Boston: Houghton, 1961.

Rosenberg, M. *Society and the adolescent self-image.* Princeton, N. J.: Princeton U. P., 1965.

Smith, M. B. Competence and socialization. In A. J. Clausen (ed.), *Socialization and society.* Boston: Little, Brown, 1968.

The Social
Domain

12

The More Fully Human Person:
Some Models and Processes

Prelude

Basic Theory and Research

  Some Models of the More Fully
    Human Person

    Arthur W. Combs (The
    Adequate Person)

    Hubert Bonner (The
    Proactive Person)

    Carl R. Rogers (The Fully
    Functioning Person)

    Abraham H. Maslow (The
    Self-actualizing Person)

  The Process of Becoming a More
    Fully Human Person

  The Psychoanalytic View

  The Behavioristic View

  The Humanistic View

  Some Conclusions about the
    Three Approaches

Implications

  Understanding Yourself and
    Others

    Understanding Your
    Self-concept

  Living and Working with Chil-
    dren, Adolescents, and
    Adults

  The Psychoanalyst

  The Behaviorist

  The Humanist

  Developing Positive Models

PRELUDE

Thus far, in our efforts to help you to develop major life goals for you and your children, we have analyzed the biological, cognitive, affective, and social domains. In this chapter, we try to synthesize, putting the child back together, by discussing four models of the more fully human person. Although these models are still tentative and open to change, they provide us with additional dimensions upon which to base our children's growth and development in the world of today as well as tomorrow.

In addition, we want you to think about the process of becoming more fully human through an examination of three basic frameworks: the psychoanalytic, the behavioristic, and the humanistic. We conclude the chapter with a reemphasis on the unique person as expressed through his emerging self-concept.

BASIC THEORY AND RESEARCH

History is replete with descriptions of man's intentions and efforts to improve the human condition. Nevertheless, in perspective, compared with other living organisms, man as a species is little more than a newborn infant. Yet, as a relative neonate, man did bring to the world for the first time, as far as we know, the ability to reflect on what he could be and on what he could become. Imagine the thoughts of a caveman reflecting on the future of man. Imagine now what man will be like a million years from now. In essence, it seems that man's awareness of himself and his imagination have combined to formulate such questions as: "What can man become? What would it be like if man could fulfill all his potentials and then some?" We will refer to the end-products of man's dreams as "self-actualization" and to the processes leading to fulfillment as "becoming more fully human."

Some Models of the More Fully Human Person

Psychologists, particularly in recent years, have focused more attention on these aspects of man. As a result, a few tentative theories have emerged regarding the characteristics of the more fully human person. Figure 12–1 shows the basic dimensions of four theories of the more fully human person. They are useful at this point because these models are based on a particular theory about man and his growth. Because of space limitations, we do not present these theories in detail. It is hoped that the reader will go beyond these sketches to some of the original sources for what we guarantee will be some extremely fascinating and humanly stimulating reading.

Arthur W. Combs (The Adequate Person)

Combs in his address to the California Association for Supervisors and Curriculum Development in 1962 stressed the need for goals in education. He emphasized that all people needed goals that would define where they stood, what they should work for, and what they could commit their lives and those of their children to. Regarding his research into the nature of these goals, Combs (1970) had this to say:

> As a result of the thinking and study of scholars and researchers, little by little, the picture begins to unfold. We begin to get some inkling of

The More
Fully Human
Person: Some
Models and
Processes

181

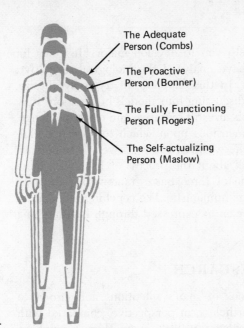

Fig. 12–1.
*There are different
views of the more
fully human person.*

The Adequate
Person (Combs)

The Proactive
Person (Bonner)

The Fully Functioning
Person (Rogers)

The Self-actualizing
Person (Maslow)

what the fully functioning person is like. This is no average man they are describing. Who, after all, wants to be average? This is a Free man with a capital F. This is a goal for us to shoot for, a picture of what can be and might be. Here is a concept of a free man that lifts our sights to what, perhaps, one day man may become.

What is more, a study of the characteristics emerging from the studies provides us with a blueprint for education practice. I believe the work of these people in defining the nature of self-actualization is certainly among the most exciting steps forward in our generation. For me, it has provided new meaning in life. It provides new goals, and direction for me, not just in times of crisis, but in the quiet hours between, and in my professional work as well. (p. 563)

In essence, Combs believes that man is capable of becoming far more than he ever dreamed he could be, that intelligence and potentials can be created, and that we now know enough about people who are superhealthy psychologically to make the goals of self-actualization real ones in the educational systems. Some of these goals are as follows:

1. *Self-directed citizens* who can assume the major responsibilities for learning, living, and their own destinies. The key concept here is the fostering of uniqueness. Combs feels that the world has become far too complex to continue teaching the same ideas and coping skills to all the students in an authoritarian way. Such an education reduces students to passive followers of established patterns and repeaters of answers long established to questions answered long ago. If we really want to produce self-starting and self-directing citizens, then we must make learning and living in the schools a highly personal matter, individual and unique.

2. *People who tend to see themselves in essentially positive ways* have tremendous advantages. Their inner strength and personal integrity permit them to cope with the challenges of life with far less fear than the rest of us. Combs (1970) stresses that:

Life Goals

182

It is in this factor of how the individual sees himself that we are likely to find the most outstanding differences between well-adjusted and poorly adjusted people. It is not the people who feel about themselves that they are liked and wanted and acceptable and able and so on who fill our jails and mental hospitals. Rather, it is those who feel themselves deeply inadequate, unliked, unwanted, unacceptable, unable, and the like. (p. 563)

3. *Openness to experience* depends upon inner security that leads to broader and more accurate views of reality. Self-actualizers tend to have such a high degree of trust in themselves that they are able to look at all kinds of information, including that which is derogatory to them, without distorting the information to make it congruent with their fears or desires. They can, for example, admit they're "stinkers" or "got an *F* in English" but they can do so without resigning to remain unchanged.

The search for a more complete definition of these adequate persons is important because such criteria will serve as goals and as guidelines for all people engaged in helping children to develop optimally during their lifetimes.

Hubert Bonner (The Proactive Person)

For Bonner, author of numerous texts in psychology, the self-actualizer is the "proactive person"—that is, a person who has developed forward movements in a variety of different life situations to an unusually high degree. Although all people possess some at birth, proactivity, just like intelligence and creativity, can be facilitated or suppressed by the particular world in which one lives and by one's courage to confront unpredictable circumstances. Some of the characteristics of the proactive person are as follows:

1. *Free to make own decisions.* All of us experience mixed feelings of anxiety and hope during moments of decisions. However, the proactive person because of his strong desire for new experiences (openness) and his capacity for coping effectively with anxiety is freer to make more and broader decisions. Such experiences increase his chances of finding greater satisfaction in life especially when he realizes that he has become "the captain of his own ship." In Bonner's words, "He can say truly of himself that he *lives* instead of *being lived*. He can now view life not as a 'useless passion' but as something he can love and enjoy."

2. *Aesthetic view of life.* The aesthetic view of life admits that objectivity can be of value but that it requires that we look at people and events coldly and dispassionately. This artificial separation of facts from humanity is anathema to the self-actualizing person. Facts alone may satisfy computers or robots but rarely a truly human person. Facts must be allied with aesthetic judgment and feelings to make them true, meaningful, and memorable. Let us make this point more personal by considering the following question: If we said that we could be objective about your children but not ours, would you want us to teach your children?

3. *Idealization.* All of us have some notions about our ideal selves, that is, ideals toward which we can strive in the future. Proactive idealization is the envisioning of ourselves as being different from what we are. It is a process by which proactive individuals, in particular, become more self-actualizing, and by which generally psychologically healthy persons become even more healthy. It is important to emphasize that both the proactive and the healthy

person base their idealization models on valid or near-valid analysis of what they are and what they would like to become. Although neurotics also use idealization, in their case it takes on the form of self and social deceptions. The maladjusted, in the perpetuation of their negative life cycles, strive to appear to be what they are not. Again, the chances are that the neurotic will meet failure, and again he must bolster his defenses to protect even more so his battered self-concept.

4. *Creativity.* Bonner agrees with Maslow that creativity cannot be limited to special talents or creations. Creativity is a much broader term. It is an essential characteristic of the proactive person, but, at the same time, creativity is a process for making the life style of the proactive person even more fully human. First and foremost, the creative person, already a unique individual, is constantly striving for greater individuality. He is different from most other people because in his pursuit of uniqueness and excellence, he will tend to reject the common place. Therefore, although psychologically

Fig. 12–2.

Fig. 12–3.

Fig. 12–4.

184

healthy, he is often in a state of emotional and intellectual turmoil, because he must frequently adjust to a world that is increasingly his own creation.

5. *Self-transformation.* Basically the proactive person is striving arduously to make himself into a work of art. Not satisfied with what he is, or was, he seeks to improve himself into whatever he can become. His orientation to life is one of optimism with a capital *O.* He believes that his future is largely in his own hands and then proceeds heartily to confirm this belief in real life. As Bonner states: "Many a person, born in humble and culturally impoverished circumstances, has outgrown his past and become an individual of exceptional character and achievement" (1965, p. 65).

With his proactive people, Bonner brings to us models of men who have tremendous faith in their abilities to master their own destinies in order to become increasingly better human beings.

Carl R. Rogers (The Fully Functioning Person)

Further insights into the characteristics of self-actualization comes from an unsuspected source: troubled and emotionally ill people. Carl Rogers, through many years of experience as a psychotherapist, found that after a period of time in a situation of basic trust and honesty, the disturbed person changed. The changes produced a more healthy person. Let us study some of these changes.

1. *Willingness to Accept What He Experiences.* The healthier person seems to be more aware of his own feelings and attitudes. He does not try to run away from himself or disguise his real feelings. In addition, he begins to look at the world in a more realistic way. He doesn't respond to life rigidly with preconceived ideas; rather, he looks at the world as it is. In his relations with others, he is also more realistic.

2. *Trust in Himself.* The improving person begins to accept and trust the *impulses* (action without thought) and feelings that he finds emerging. He actually finds he fears himself less and less. He even develops an affection for all of his own feelings.

3. *Self-Reliance.* The improving person next develops a greater reliance on his own feelings and *attitudes* (how he feels and thinks about something) of right and wrong. There is less reliance on what society expects, on what friends and relatives expect. As Rogers puts it: "He recognizes that it rests within himself to choose; that the only question that matters is: 'Am I living in a way which is deeply satisfying to me, and which truly expresses me?' This I think is perhaps the most important question for the creative individual."

4. *Willingness to Continue to Grow as a Person.* The more healthy people tend to understand the idea that being alive means allowing oneself to grow and to change as a person, rather than reaching some end point and standing there.

As one of Rogers's 1961 patients put it: "I haven't finished the job of integrating and reorganizing myself, but that's only confusing, not discouraging, now that I realize this a continuing process. . . . It is exciting, sometimes upsetting, but deeply encouraging to feel yourself in action, apparently knowing where that is."

Abraham H. Maslow (The Self-Actualizing Person)

Maslow's model of self-actualization comes to us basically from persons who are or who were (historical figures) superbly healthy psychologically.

The More Fully Human Person: Some Models and Processes

185

Maslow first set up his standards of psychological excellence and then set out to find subjects who fit these requirements to the fullest for further study. Incidentally, his subjects included three thousand college students, only one of whom met his standards. Before discussing the major characteristics of his theory, let us present some of his underlying assumptions about the nature of man (1968):

1. We have, each of us, an essential biologically based inner nature, which is to some degree "natural," intrinsic, given, and, in a certain limited sense, unchangeable, or, at least, unchanging.
2. Each person's inner nature is in part unique to himself and in part species-wide.
3. It is possible to study this inner nature scientifically and to discover what it is like (not invent—discover).
4. This inner nature, as much as we know of it so far, seems not to be intrinsically evil, but rather either neutral or positively "good." What we call evil behavior appears most often to be a secondary reaction to frustration of this intrinsic nature.
5. Since this inner nature is good or neutral rather than bad, it is best to bring it out and to encourage it rather than to suppress it. If it is permitted to guide our life, we grow healthy, fruitful, and happy.
6. If this essential core of the person is denied or suppressed, he gets sick sometimes in obvious ways, sometimes in subtle ways, sometimes immediately, sometimes later.
7. This inner nature is not strong and overpowering and unmistakable like the instincts of animals. It is weak and delicate and subtle and easily overcome by habit, cultural pressure, and wrong attitudes toward it.
8. Even though weak, it rarely disappears in the normal person—perhaps not even in the sick person. Even though denied, it persists underground forever pressing for actualization.
9. Somehow, these conclusions must all be articulated with the necessity of discipline, deprivation, frustration, pain, and tragedy. To the extent that these experiences reveal and foster and fulfill our inner nature, to that extent they are desirable experiences. (pp. 3–4)

In other words, Maslow believes that all people are born with a potentially self-actualizing nature that will invariably unfold *if* permitted by appropriate conditions, because this inner nature is not strong and can be easily overwhelmed by cultural pressures and wrong attitudes. In a sense, all we have to do to find the characteristics of self-actualization is to study what we are really like as human beings. Possibly, Maslow has already provided us with some clues as to what human nature is really like, deep down.

Although Maslow's list is lengthy, fortunately many characteristics overlap. We believe that there are essentially eight characteristics that should be of practical importance.

1. *An Ability to Accept Oneself, Others, and Nature.* Maslow found that the mentally healthy tend to accept themselves. In fact, they like themselves. Putting it another way, they have a positive *self-concept;* they tend to view themselves as people who are acceptable and able living in a world where they can make a contribution.

Maslow also found that these people tend to accept others. Feeling good about themselves, they can accept the other person even if he is different. In general, mentally healthy persons seem to have the ability to accept people and the world. This ability can often be seen in children, who experience life as it is, and, sometimes, to the embarrassment of parents, tell others how it is.

2. *More Profound Interpersonal Relations.* Another quality of these people, Maslow found, is that they tend to get closer to people. Because they feel good about themselves, they can afford to have deep human relationships with others. It must be noted that Maslow also found that these strong ties were usually to only a few people, for a deep involvement with even one person takes considerable time and emotional energy.

Furthermore, the extremely mentally healthy tend to be kind to and patient with people, especially with children. They both possess and show *compassion* (sympathetic feelings for others) for their fellowmen.

3. *More Efficient Perception of Reality and More Comfortable Relations with It.* It seems that the truly emotionally healthy do not have to fool themselves about the world and the people in it. Again, having a good self-concept, these people do not have to hide behind a mask through which they filter reality.

Their *perceiving* (how one sees the world) the world as it really is and people as they really are means that these people are operating with valid information. The result is that they tend to get more done—they don't "spin their wheels." When a problem arises, they can solve it more efficiently because they can make their decisions in terms of how things really are, rather than on how they wish they were.

4. *Continued Freshness of Appreciation.* People like Maslow's subjects also tend to continually find enjoyment and appreciation in just being alive. They tend to respond to many more things in life as if they were doing each for the first time.

5. *Autonomy, Independence of Culture, and Environment.* Having a good feeling about oneself generates a trust in oneself. The most emotionally healthy individuals rely on their own insights about what is right and what is wrong, and about what should be done in a given situation. Thus, they tend to be more *autonomous* (independent in thought or action) relying more on their own standards of behavior and values rather than always overemphasizing what others expect of them or what their *culture* (the ways of living of a group of people) demands.

Nevertheless, as a matter of course, these people tend to follow routine social customs on a regular basis except when social injustice occurs; that is, when the basic human rights of a nation, a group, or an individual are violated. During these times, they tend to remove their "light cloaks of conventionality" and to become effective fighters for human rights and dignity.

6. *A Democratic Character Structure.* A by-product of being a mentally healthy person is the development of a democratic character structure (a consistent way of behaving). This always involves an appreciation and respect for the rights of others, a willingness to listen and learn from others, and a reverence for uniqueness and differences in other persons.

Maslow (1968) expresses the point as follows:

The More
Fully Human
Person: Some
Models and
Processes

187

They find it possible to learn from anybody who has something to teach them—no matter what characteristics he may have. They give this honest respect to a carpenter who is a good carpenter; or for that matter to anybody who is a master of his own tools or his own craft. (pp. 182–183)

7. *Peak Experiences.* Peak experiences are moments of great joy, ecstasy, overwhelming oceanic feelings that are impossible to put into words. Most of us have had peak experiences, moments of joyous mysticism such as a haunting melody during a beautiful moment, a bird saying "hello" to a sunset, a flower bathing in the moonlight, or an orgasm that somehow transcends the sex act and appears to be the entire world since its beginning. Such moments are for the self-actualizer more common than they are for us.

8. *Resacralizing.* Resacralizing is being a believer in something greater than one's self, a believer in the eternal and the sacred. Perhaps holding a newborn baby for the first time may bring forth such feelings of sacredness or the feeling that life is a poem that stretches into eternity. Or perhaps we may have the feelings when observing beauty and goodness such as a mother nursing, a person teaching, or a nurse easing pain, that beauty and goodness extend beyond what we are presently observing.

It is well to remember that Maslow's theory of self-actualization, although

TABLE 12–1
SOME OTHER THEORIES OF THE MORE FULLY HUMAN PERSON

Name of Theorist	Major Emphasis in Theory	Characteristics
Fromm (1955)	Productive orientation	Able to love self; love others; uses reason to understand the world; can do productive work.
Adler (1927)	Social interest and feeling	Lack of competitiveness in relations with others. Views fellowmen as worthy.
Sullivan (1963)	Accurate perception of people	Ability to view others as they are. Effective interpersonal relations.
Rank (See Thompson, 1950)	Affirmation of one's will	Courage to be a unique person. Courage to express your differences from others. Courage to be creative.
Tillich (1959)	Courage to be	Knowing one's feelings, opinions, beliefs. Willingness to accept consequences of your own behavior.
Tournier (1957)	Man as a person	Treat others as persons, not as objects, tools, or instruments.
Buber (1955)	I-thou relationships	Ability to live in dialogue with fellowmen.

Life Goals

the most complete we have so far, was based on one man's investigation and reflects his bias. We need more research. As we wait, we should be examining other ideal models of man (see Table 12–1). Since all these models were based essentially on members of Western cultures with all kinds of built-in biases, we also need to study models of self-actualization based on cross-cultural samples.

THE PROCESS OF BECOMING A MORE FULLY HUMAN PERSON

Our long survey (Chapters 8 through 12) of criteria for becoming more fully human brings us to the crucial and controversial question of how we achieve these criteria. We have established some valuable and humanly fulfilling life goals. We must now turn to the complicated and partially unknown task of how to help our children to achieve some of these goals. The answers are not easy or always readily available in all of the domains of man.

Underlying almost all descriptions of the processes involved in becoming a more human person (see Table 12–2 for a brief description of some of these processes) are three basic theoretical orientations that have been used in the study and explanation of man's growth.

These three views of man each have made significant contributions in the

TABLE 12–2
EXAMPLES OF SOME MAJOR BEHAVIORAL PROCESSES IN BECOMING A MORE FULLY HUMAN PERSON

Basic Processes	Major Domains Involved	Description
Learning	Cognitive and Affective	How one grows and changes behavior from life experiences.
Maturation	Biological	The unfolding of basic biological tendencies in the developing person (e.g., build and size).
Perception	Biological, Affective, Cognitive, Social	Learning to become aware of one's surroundings via one's sense organs (hearing, sight, touch, smell, and taste).
Motivation	Biological, Affective, Cognitive, Social	The process whereby an individual's behavior is aroused (through biological or social factors) and channeled toward a goal.
Emotion	Biological, Affective, Cognitive, Social	Processes involved in arousal of an individual (biological) accompanied by feelings (affective).
Thinking	Cognitive	Ways that the person symbolizes the world in order to solve problems, create new ideas, find different relationships, and integrate concepts.

The More Fully Human Person: Some Models and Processes

historical as well as contemporary development of psychology. Much of what we now know about human behavior is directly related to the insights and theoretical framework that these views provide. These three approaches have been labeled differently by psychologists; we use the following terms in discussing them: the psychoanalytic view, the behavioristic view, and the humanistic view. Let us look at these three points of view to determine the design and construction of the "window frames" they provide as we observe "man in process" walking the "sidewalks of life" outside. (See Figure 12–5.)

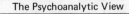

The Psychoanalytic View

Man driven by unconscious forces.

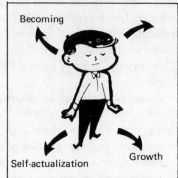

The Humanistic View

Man in process of growth and change.

The Behavioral View

Man, the result of various patterns of stimuli which condition him to respond in predictable ways.

FIG. 12–5.
Three "windows" through which psychologists have explored man's behavior.

The Psychoanalytic View

The psychoanalytic "window" provides psychologists with a "third dimensional" analysis of man and his development. That is, it tends to be more of an "in depth" view.

When Freud first wrote about his discoveries, he shocked many people because it was a time when man was considered to be an extremely rational being. Here was a Viennese medical doctor suggesting that man was driven by all sorts of instinctual life (sexual) and death (aggressive) tendencies, as well as a host of unconscious conflicts that were hidden (repressed) during childhood.

Life Goals

190

Freud added a "third dimension" to man and his behavior that had not existed before. The details of Freud's system are too complex and detailed to go into here. We have outlined many areas of his contributions in Table 12–3. Again, we hope that you will turn to some of the references we have provided for a more detailed study of this fascinating and highly influential view.

As far as forming the underlying theory to help us understand some processes in becoming a more fully human person, Freud gave us some key insights into such processes as the unconscious aspects in many areas of man's behavior (particularly in such areas as motivation and emotions). That is, we know that many times we want to do something for supposedly one reason, when, in fact, we are doing it for another (unconscious motivation). Freud believed that man develops a whole series of unconscious devices to protect himself (his ego) from feeling inadequate or insecure.

We also know that our emotional reactions are often out of proportion with the immediate situation. Many times we are really reacting to some earlier frustration or we are reacting in a manner similar to the way we reacted during childhood (Freud called this process regression).

One of the problems with this view is that it did not present a very positive image of man. Bonner (1965), for example, comments on some positive as well as negative aspects of psychoanalysis:

> In view of what we have said here and elsewhere, it is clear that we hold Freudian psychology in high esteem. Its penetration into the deeply embedded and indirectly accessible motives of human conduct, is in our humble judgment as yet unequalled. Freud's grasp and delineation of the dramatic conflict within every individual has been exceeded only by a few great dramatists and poets. What gives them the power and authenticity is Freud's observation of them in living and suffering individuals, with an unsurpassing clinical mind.

> We begin our verdict with the strong conviction that, first, although psychoanalysis goes far indeed in describing man's personality, it does not go far enough; and second, that, although the human being it portrays is indeed an animal driven by blind forces to which he responds mechanically, it completely neglects those qualities of man which enable him to transcend his crippling past to create a healthy future. (p. 42)

The Behavioristic View

The behavioristic view has proven to be one of the most scientifically productive areas of human exploration. This view focuses on the overt dimensions of man; that is, those factors that impinge on him in his environment (stimuli) as well as man's reactions to these forces (responses). Thus, this approach is often referred to as S-R Psychology. (See Table 12–3).

Originated in this country with the work of Thorndike and Watson (discussed briefly in Chapter 6) and based upon Pavlov's original studies in Russia, the emphasis on studying objective, observable behavior has led to the accumulation of many concepts and principles involved in the learning process.

Although there are many criticisms of this approach as being too me-

The More
Fully Human
Person: Some
Models and
Processes

191

chanistic or as turning man into a "rat in a maze," there is no doubt that it provides psychology with a way to study how man learns the many things he learns during his development from birth onward.

Behaviorism's strength, that is, the use of the carefully controlled experimental procedure to define, predict, and control behavior is also its chief weakness. Many subjective areas of human behavior are outside the scope or the ability of current experimental techniques.

B. F. Skinner (1971), the most widely known contributor to behaviorism, presents a plea for the design of environments so that man may achieve his full potential.

Early versions of environmentalism were inadequate because they could not explain how the environment worked, and much seemed to be left for autonomous man to do. But environmental contingencies now take over functions once attributed to autonomous man, and certain questions arise. Is man then "abolished?" Certainly not as a species or as an individual achiever. It is the autonomous inner man who is abolished, and that is a step forward. But does man not then become merely a victim or passive observer of what is happening to him? He is indeed controlled by his environment, but we must remember that it is an environment largely of his own making. The evolution of a culture is a gigantic exercise in self-control. It is often said that a scientific view of man leads to wounded vanity, a sense of hopelessness, and nostalgia. But no theory changes what it is a theory about; man remains what he has always been. And a new theory may change what can be done with its subject matter. A scientific view of man offers exciting possibilities. We have not yet seen what man can make of man. (p. 215–216)

The Humanistic View

Humanistic psychology (a more recent development) actually developed as a reaction against the earlier two prevailing models of man: the psychoanalytic and the behavioristic. More and more psychologists believed that these views left man in a very precarious position; he seemed a "puppet" on a string being controlled by an oversexed and very angry puppeteer.

Whereas the psychoanalytic model exposed us to a historical dimension of man's existence, and behavioristic psychology provided insights into variables in man's overt world (the stimuli and responses that man made), the humanistic view provided us with a more realistic picture of existing man in the everyday, real world.

Humanistic psychology is sometimes called "third force" psychology because of its position in relation to psychoanalytic and behavioristic psychologies. The basic formalizing of humanistic psychology into a valid school of thought can be traced to Maslow's work in the late 1950's, although many other psychologists pioneered in its development.

As originally set up by Maslow, humanistic psychology offered an approach to the study of certain areas of human activity that had no systematic place in either psychoanalytic theory or behavioristic psychology. Included are such topics as creativity, love, self, growth, basic need gratification, higher values, objectivity, autonomy, responsibility, and identity.

Life Goals

The latest brochure of the Association for Humanistic Psychology lists the following four elements as basic to the humanistic orientation:

1. A centering of attention on the experiencing *person*, and thus a focus on experience as the primary phenomenon in the study of man. Both theoretical explanations and overt behavior are considered secondary to experience itself and to its meaning to the person.
2. An emphasis on such distinctively human qualities as choice, creativity, valuation, and self-realization, as opposed to thinking about human beings in mechanistic and reductionistic terms.
3. An allegiance to meaningfulness in the selection of problems for study and of research procedures, and an opposition to a primary emphasis on objectivity at the expense of significance.
4. An ultimate concern with and valuing of the dignity and worth of man and an interest in the development of the potential inherent in every person. Central in this view is the person as he discovers his own being and relates to other persons and to social groups.

Some Conclusions about the Three Approaches

In order to better understand the processes involved in becoming a more fully human person, we need to employ all three perspectives. We need the insights to man's unconscious; to his irrational self. We need the perspective that the psychoanalytic view gives us about the different stages of development and the conflicts they produce in children.

We also need to know how people learn to walk, to talk, to think, to read, to write; all competencies needed to get along in the world. We need to be continually aware that much of our behavior *is* conditioned by social and parental reinforcement.

We further need to know that behavior *can* be changed: that the disturbed child can unlearn conditioned fears; that the handicapped child can learn to cope with his environment; that parents can learn to become more effective in rearing more fully human children.

Above all, we need to know all we can about how to foster such feelings as love, joy, compassion, and empathy.

In short, we need to know all we can about the processes fostering self-actualization, creativity, intelligence, altruism, and social competence.

It is easy to criticize one or more of these points of view as inadequate or in error. Yet, the facts are that man is a very complex organism and psychology is a relatively young science. We must consider all leads, all hints, all ideas about the nature of man if we are to help solve the great human dilemmas facing man today and his children tomorrow.

In order to give an overall comparison of the three views, we have summarized them in the following tables. Table 12–3 presents a detailed summary of the three views in terms of assumptions, concepts, principles, processes, methods, contributions, criticisms, and basic references. This table is very complex and detailed. Its major purpose is to give an overall comparison of the three views so that you may more fully understand and visualize the processes for becoming a more fully human person and may appreciate their underlying basis.

The More Fully Human Person: Some Models and Processes

TABLE 12–3
A COMPARISON OF THREE BASIC ORIENTATIONS USED BY PSYCHOLOGISTS IN
STUDYING AND DESCRIBING THE PROCESSES INVOLVED IN
BECOMING A MORE FULLY HUMAN PERSON

Underlying Assumptions

Psychoanalytic View	Behavioristic View	Humanistic View
1. Man is not as rational as he may believe. 2. Much of man's behavior is controlled by unconscious forces. 3. Man is born with certain basic instinctual tendencies (life and death instincts); these produce much of man's life energy. 4. These instinctual tendencies must be channeled by the parents and society.	1. All behavior is lawful. 2. All behavior can be objectively studied. 3. All behavior (eventually, when we know enough about it) can be accurately predicted and controlled.	1. Experience is the most important variable to study about man. 2. Psychologists should study meaningful areas of human experience even though they cannot be completely and scientifically defined yet (e.g. love, happiness, joy, creativity, humor, friendship, empathy, and others). 3. Man is born basically "good." 4. Man does have some "degrees of freedom" in his life. 5. Man must be looked upon as "in process" and as a growing, becoming organism; not as a stable and fixed being. 6. We can learn much about man through the study of the "healthy man" or by asking the question: What can man become?

Basic Concepts *

1. Basic personality structure:
    id
    ego
    superego
2. Stages of development:
    oral
    anal
    phallic
    latency
    adolescence
    maturity
3. Process of psychoanalysis:
    free association
    repression
    identification
    transference
    libido
    fixation
    regression
4. Defense mechanisms
	1. Classical conditioning
	2. Operant conditioning
	3. Reinforcement
	4. Secondary reinforcement
	5. Schedules of reinforcement
	6. Generalization
	7. Extinction
	8. Shaping
	9. Social learning theory
		1. Self-actualization
		2. Becoming
		3. Peak experience
		4. Growth
		5. Existentialism
		6. Sensitivity
		7. Encounter
		8. Being
		9. I-thou
		10. Creativity
		11. Choice
		12. Will
		13. Love
		14. Spontaneity
		15. Play
		16. Warmth
		17. Courage
		18. Authenticity
		19. Self-disclosure
		20. Hierarchy of needs

* For location of further discussion of these concepts see index at end of text.

Psychoanalytic View	Behavioristic View	Humanistic View
1. Man's basic personality structure is formed very early in life (before the age of five).	1. Much of our behavior (including such diverse behaviors as attitudes, values, interests, skills, and basic personality patterns) has been developed as a result of the learning process (changes in behavior as a result of rewards and punishment).	1. Man has far more "degrees of freedom" than he (or psychologists) ever thought possible.
2. The structure of the child's personality is related to his relationship with his parents.		2. Man's potentialities are far greater than man has ever imagined.
3. Events in these early relationships with our parents are often forgotten; yet, they continue to affect our behavior even in adult life.	2. Behavior that is rewarded tends to be repeated.	3. It is important for man to use his sources of stimulation as much as possible (e.g. his senses, his emotional responses, his intellectual stimulation, and his basic biological processes) in order to continue his growth toward self-actualization.
4. Children, in order to become healthy adults, must successfully pass through the various important stages of development.	3. Behavior that is not rewarded tends not to be repeated.	
	4. The persistence of behavior is a function of the type of, amount of, and consistency of rewards.	4. Man is basically "alone" in this world; once he faces this fact, he frees himself for more meaningful encounters with himself and others.
5. Man's basic personality can be understood by using the concepts of the id, ego, and superego.	5. Behavior can be changed through proper planning and control of rewards.	5. Man will die; he must face this realization before he can face life.
6. Many problems can be alleviated through a relationship of trust and confidence (with a psychoanalyst) wherein we talk freely about our feelings and thoughts.	6. Behavior that is punished is hard to predict but generally tends not to be repeated.	6. Man cannot love others until he loves himself.
		7. The only important thing is to live for the moment; the here and now.
7. Very often the relationship to the therapist (analyst) will reveal insights into the relationships we had with our parents.		8. Expression of feelings is important for continued human growth and aliveness.
8. Dreams and slips of the tongue are clues to our unconscious world.		9. When people are in a situation where they feel secure and accepted, they will tend to lower their defenses and will grow toward their true nature; they will become more themselves.

Basic Processes

1. Processes involved in mental illness.	I. The learning process (includes the acquisition of all forms of behavior under each domain).	The process of becoming more authentically human; this involves all four domains.
2. The process of the development of the ego (one's self-concept or self identity).	1. Biological Domain: How we learn such things as ways of walking, coordination, and psychomotor skills.	1. Biological Domain:
3. Unconscious processes as they may affect: motivation, learning, forgetting, emotions, and perception.		a. Interactive effect of basic physiological functioning on well-being of person and vice-versa.
	2. Cognitive Domain: The process of learn-	b. Processes of sensory stimulation.
4. The process of human de-		

Psychoanalytic View	Behavioristic View	Humanistic View
velopment from birth onward.	ing such things as modes of thinking, certain styles of problem solving, attitudes, and (to a degree) learning capacity.	c. Process of need gratification.
5. Dream processes.		d. Process of developing a "biological self-concept."
6. Interaction processes between parents and their children.		2. Cognitive Domain:
7. Problem areas during childhood (toilet training, weaning, sexuality) and processes used by the child and parents in coping with these situations.	3. Affective Domain: Ways of expressing emotions, ways of expressing our mood variations, ways we feel about our parents, siblings, and peers, and ways we feel about ourselves.	a. Creative processes.
		b. Process of creating "open minds."
		c. Process of developing a "rational self-concept."
	4. Social Domain: How we learn to relate to others in our environment, how we learn to relate to the various institutions (family, church, school, government, and business), how we become members of a social group and learn the appropriate behaviors (rules, customs, roles, values), how we become socialized.	3. Affective Domain:
		a. Emotional processes (particularly love, warmth, joy, anger, and ecstasy).
		b. Emotional expression (how it is fostered).
		c. Process of developing an "emotionally maturing self."
		4. Social Domain:
		a. Encounter processes.
		b. Dialogue processes.
		c. Processes of developing a sense of "community" within a group of humans.
		d. The self-disclosure process.
		e. The process of developing a "social self-concept."
	II. Processes involved in the management of learning.	
	1. Processes of learning more efficiently.	
	2. Processes involved in forgetting.	

Basic Methods

In process of psychoanalysis:	In psychotherapy and counseling:	In psychotherapy and counseling:
1. Free association	1. Behavior modification methods	1. Client centered methods
2. Transference		2. Gestalt therapy methods
3. Historical approach		3. Sensory awareness methods
4. Case history method		4. Encounter methods
In research studies:	In research studies:	
1. Case history	1. Experimental method	In research studies:
2. Hypnosis	2. Comparative method	1. Observation method
3. Correlational studies		2. Case study

Psychoanalytic View	Behavioristic View	Humanistic View
4. Projective testing		3. Self-report (diaries, self-introspective writings) 4. Q-sort technique 5. Semantic differential 6. Historical biographical data (e.g. Maslow's original studies of self-actualizing) 7. Questionnaires and surveys 8. Interviews 9. Projective testing

Basic Contributions

Psychoanalytic View	Behavioristic View	Humanistic View
1. Stimulated beginnings of the study of child development.	1. The first truly scientifically verified area of psychological prediction and control of human behavior.	1. Importance of expression of emotions for greater mental health.
2. Convinced many that mentally ill persons could be helped.	2. Explains well how persons learn all forms of behavior in all domains.	2. New therapy techniques (individual and group therapy).
3. What happens early in life is vitally significant for later personality health and/or illness.	3. Can help persons unlearn self-defeating behaviors (e.g. fears, negative self-concepts, and phobias).	3. Emphasis on dynamic aspects of man as a growing organism.
4. Many important things are forgotten (repressed) during childhood; these continue to affect our behavior in later life.	4. Has contributed to our understanding of how students learn.	4. Importance of studying the unique, creative person. 5. Development of "growth centers" for human development.
5. Broke the image of man as being completely rational; man is often irrational and driven by unconscious forces.	5. Development of programmed and individualized learning (e.g. teaching machines, self-pacing devices, auto-tutorial learning).	6. Formation of Association for Humanistic Psychology and Journal of Humanistic Psychology.
6. Our relationship to our parents is a crucial variable in the development of our ego (self-concept), as well as the development of our superego (conscience), as well as how we handle our basic instinctual tendencies of the id (our sexual and destructive tendencies).	6. Development of behavior modification techniques to help persons overcome inadequate ways of relating to themselves and others. 7. Development of social learning theory to explain how we learn very complex social behaviors.	7. Shifted psychological studies away from reliance on animal and human pathological data. 8. Emphasis on healthy man. 9. Concept of self-actualization. 10. Emphasis on man's subjective experience.
7. Dreams may offer significant insights into our unconscious world.		11. Concern for and encouragement of studies about relevant human concerns: love, joy, loneliness, death.
8. Children grow through "critical periods"; the way in which they successfully		12. Development of experimental programs in humanistic education.

Psychoanalytic View	Behavioristic View	Humanistic View

complete these "stages" has much to do with their mental health later in life.

9. Stimulated wide research and theory building efforts in all social sciences as well as fields of education, art, literature, business, and religion.

Basic Criticisms

Psychoanalytic View	Behavioristic View	Humanistic View

1. Concepts too hard to objectify for scientific study.
2. Psychoanalysis too long and costly a process.
3. Not necessary to relive one's past to gain understanding of current problems.
4. Too much emphasis on sexual repression as major problem area.
5. Freud's theories based on subjective data such as case studies and personal hunches.
6. Concepts too hard to define and therefore cannot be studied scientifically.
7. Little statistical data to support theories.
8. Did not emphasize effects of society on individual.

1. View of man is negative; man is highly manipulative organism.
2. Artificiality of laboratory experiments (often based on animal studies).
3. Questions of who will do the controlling and predicting of man's behavior.
4. Views man as having little freedom or choice.
5. Difficult to explain and study such important experiences as growth, actualization, creativity, joy, and human will.

1. Theories based on nonscientific data (much of it comes from personal impressions and observations).
2. Difficult to define major concepts adequately.
3. Difficult to measure major concepts with precision and consistency.
4. Leads man to believe that he has lots of freedom, when, in fact, he is a product of conditioning all the time.
5. Unrealistic emphasis on expression of personal feelings, the modern world will not tolerate much of this.

Basic Names and References for Further Study

Some Primary References:	*Some Primary References:*	*Some Primary References:*

Adler, A. (1927, 1953, 1955, 1960, 1963)
Freud, S. (1953–64, 1953, 1955, 1960, 1963)
Jung, C. G. (1953)

Pavlov, I. P. (1927)
Thorndike, E. L. (1911, 1932)
Watson, J. B. (1925)
Skinner, B. F. (1938, 1953, 1961, 1969, 1971)

Allport, G. W. (1955)
Bonner, H. (1965, 1967)
Bugental, J. F. T. (1967)
Maslow, A. H. (1965, 1967, 1969, 1970, 1971)
May, R. (1969)
Moustakas, C. (1971)
Murphy, G. (1958)
Rogers, C. R. (1951, 1961)

Psychoanalytic View	Behavioristic View	Humanistic View
Some Secondary References:	*Some Secondary References:*	*Some Secondary References:*
Blum, G. S. (1953)	Bandura, A. (1969)	Combs, A. W. (1962)
Freud, A. (1945, 1946)	Bijou, S. and Baer, D. M.	Combs, A. W. and Snygg, D.
Fromm, E. (1941, 1959, 1955)	(1966)	(1959)
Horney, K. (1939, 1950)	Hall, C. S. and Lindzey, G. (1968, 1970)	Goble, F. (1970)
Jones, E. (1953, 1955, 1957)	Holland, J. G. and Skinner,	Severin, F. T. (1965)
Monroe, R. (1955)	B. F. (1961)	Sutich, A. J. and Vich, M. A.
Sullivan, H. S. (1947, 1963)	Mowrer, O. H. (1951)	(1969)
	Rachlin, H. (1970)	
	Wolpe, J., Salter, A. and Reyna, L. (1964)	
Some Applied References:	*Some Applied References:*	*Some Applied References:*
Erikson, E. H. (1963)	Bandura, A. (1969)	Combs, A. W., Avila, D. L., and
Hall, C. S. and Lindzey, G. (1968)	Blackham, G. J. and Silberman, A. (1971)	Purkey, W. W. (1970, 1971)
Hall, C. S. (1954)	Bradfield, R. H. (1970)	Frick, W. B. (1971)
Hilgard, E. R. (1968)	Cohen, H. L. and Filipczak, J. (1971)	Hershey, G. L. and Lugo, J. O. (1970)
Rapaport, D. (1959)	Dollard, J. and Miller, N. E. (1950)	Jourard, S. M. (1963, 1971)
Shakow, D. and Rapaport, D. (1964)	Miller, N. E. and Dollard, J. (1941)	Otto, H. (1966, 1968)
Sullivan, H. S. (1947, 1963)		Neill, A. S. (1960)
		Peterson, S. (1971)

IMPLICATIONS

UNDERSTANDING YOURSELF AND OTHERS

The three views of man can be thought of as microscopes with which we can magnify and examine certain parts of man's behavior. The psychoanalyst enlarges the individual's historical development, the behaviorist contributes to our understanding of the ways in which we learn through reacting to the world, and the humanist provides glimpses of man's growing and striving activities as he loves, creates, wishes, and dreams.

Understanding Your Self-Concept

One concept that has been used with increasing emphasis in psychology is the concept of *the self*. It is through the use of this concept that one "puts man back together again," for it includes all facets of man: the unconscious, the learning, and the feeling.

Total self-concept refers to a self that is biologically, cognitively, affectively, and socially maturing. It refers to all that a person calls his; his body and movements, his information and ways of thinking, his feeling and values, and all of his social contacts and competencies as well as his characteristic ways of relating to others. The total self has two major characteristics. It is dynamic and continuously changing as it incorporates new

The More
Fully Human
Person: Some
Models and
Processes

199

ideas, attitudes, and ways of coping with future events. It is relatively static because it provides the individual with stability and a sense of security in a changing society. In these respects, it resembles a gyroscope that provides orderly balance during moments of turmoil. The self serves as a basic frame of reference for evaluating new experiences and selecting appropriate ways of behaving in different situations. In the last analysis, the self is all a person has and he must value it to maintain his mental health regardless of its objective or subjective worth, or whether it is valued by others or not.

For teaching purposes, the self is often broken down into major components, but it is well to remember the holistic nature of the self. The self is unified and even when it is temporarily separated, as in some forms of mental illness, it is always striving to put itself back together again.

This section is concerned with the processes involved in the development of a fully human self. Through a study of the different domains of the self and with the goals provided by the various models of the self, we hope we have provided the reader with a greater appreciation and feeling for what it means to become a more fully human person.

Figure 12–6 provides a summary of the interactive aspects of the different components of a person's self. Think about these aspects of your self. Make a list of the major characteristics that typify you as a unique person. (Do your own *self* analysis.)

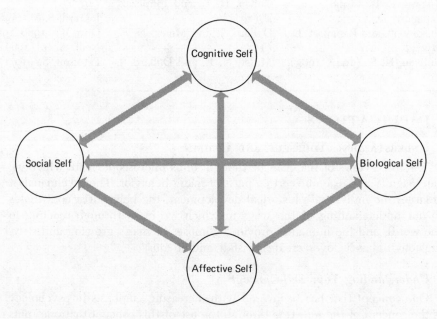

FIG. 12–6. *Interaction among the major components of self. The total self always behaves as an inseparable unit. Whatever happens to one component of self affects the remaining components. Therefore, success in one area may initiate a positive cycle that will affect other areas and reverberate feelings of success back to the original area. Similarly, failure may produce a negative cycle that can cause far-reaching and self-defeating attitudes.*

LIVING AND WORKING WITH CHILDREN, ADOLESCENTS, AND ADULTS

The models that we have presented suggest what it means to be a fully human person. Along with the three psychological views of man, they offer many insights into how we as "gardeners of growth" might cultivate more "beautiful blossoms" from the seeds we plant during our lives as parents

Life Goals of children, friends or relatives, teachers, nurses, or childcare workers. To bring these implications to life, let us listen in on a series of talks to parents given by a psychoanalyst, a behaviorist, and a humanist.

The Psychoanalyst

Good evening, parents. I want to tell you about a house that is being built. The basement is already there, the main part of the house and the beams of the roof are still under construction, but the architect has already designed the basic structure. In this house, it is too late to make changes.

Where is the house? What does its construction have to do with you? Who will live in this house?

1. The house is being built right under your own noses; right inside your own home.

2. You, as parents, are the architects.

3. Your children will reside in this house for the rest of their lives.

What did you say? Oh, please sit down and stay. No, I'm not one of those "nutty" analysts that you see on TV. I'm "deadly" serious. And what I'm talking about is the most important job you have in the world: the design and construction of your child's "inner world," the architecture involved in building your child's lifetime residence—his "Freudian house." Let me explain.

Fig. 12–7. *The basement of the Freudian "house."*

You see, Sigmund Freud sketched the outline of the universal "human place of residence" for all mankind. I call it a Freudian house.

The first and most important part of this house is the basement (see Figure 12–7). It is a hole in the ground with two parts. One is dark and damp with poisonous snakes and spiders. The other part is like a recreation or "party room"; it is light, and a lot of music is being played there (often sexually sensuous in nature).

The part of the house that Freud called the id—the unconscious or hidden parts of man's personality—contains life (sexual) and death (destructive) impulses. We all have these impulses; in fact, we are born with them. The id produces the energy that keeps us alive and growing as unique persons. The id is also the repository for all sorts of feelings and experiences that we have during childhood. Thus, this basement gets very cluttered as we grow up.

Now on top of this basement is the main part of the house (see Figure 12–8). It is through these doors and windows that the child engages the "real world."

Freud called this part of the human personality the ego or conscious part of the person. It is the "cognitive domain" of the person since it has to do with such things as ability to plan, to think, and to intellectualize the world around us.

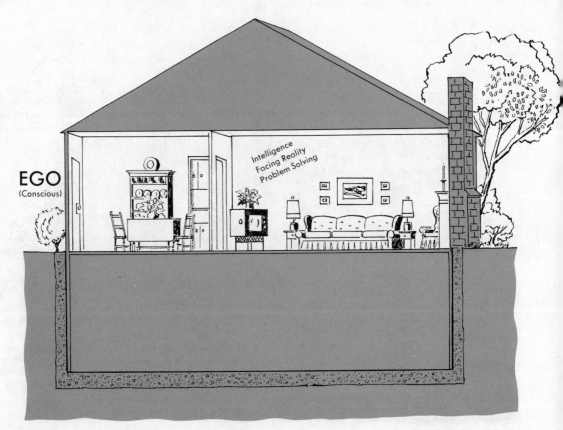

Life Goals Fig. 12–8. *The ground floor of the Freudian "house."*

Some persons have large doors and clear windows (a high degree of ego strength) through which they interact with the world, whereas others have small doors and blurry windows that prevent them from seeing reality very clearly (little ego strength).

On top of this house, naturally, is a roof (See Figure 12–9). This roof is made of shingles. The "roofers" on this house are many: your parents, the church, the school, all the institutions that have anything to do with providing restraints.

Freud called this the superego—the morals and values that we all develop during the "socialization" process.

One more feature of this house and our "construction job" is complete. There is a trapdoor that allows access to the basement (see Figure 12–7). This trapdoor is under the control of the ego whenever it is strong enough. The ego also has to carry the burden of the roof. If it is too heavy, it may "squash" the main part of the house. This roof also exerts pressure on the trapdoor. Thus, how freely the trapdoor opens and closes is also a function of the amount of pressure from the roof.

Well, there you have it. A house that you are designing and didn't

FIG. 12–9. *The roof of the Freudian "house."*

know it! By the way, you have one of these "inside you." Your parents built it!

OK. Time for a few questions. Yes, madam? How can you design a strong house for your child? Good question. The best thing you can do is to get to know how *your* house is built. What is hidden in *your* basement? What kind of windows and door do *you* see reality through? What is *your* roof made of?

By examining your own house, you will be more free to allow your child to build his own roof with values that he feels are important— rather than your own fears. It is not easy to examine your own house, particularly your basement. Many people go to psychoanalysts for years to learn about their house.

Another question?

What is the trapdoor for?

Oh, yes! The trapdoor.

That trapdoor is one of the most important parts of your house. You see, in the "healthy person" the trapdoor is well oiled and can be opened and closed by the ego to let out some of these snakes and spiders as well as sexual impulses. But in the "sick person" that trapdoor may actually be sealed shut, because those snakes and spiders would scare the "hell" out of the person if they emerged. Besides, the roof may be so heavy that it exerts tremendous pressure on the trapdoor.

Thus, you as parents can help allow your child's trapdoor to open and close freely, and this really depends on the flexibility of your own trapdoor. And if it isn't free to open and close, then your child's will be sealed as much as yours.

Similarly, if your roof is heavy and burdened with all sorts of morals and values (many of which you may not be even aware of), then your children will pick these up and place them on their roof as well.

One more question. Yes, sir?

What did you say? You don't believe this; you think it is all an invention of a "crazy man." Well, thank you for telling us. I guess you're ready for the next speaker, Dr. Behaviorist. Perhaps you'll find him more credible.

The Behaviorist

Wow! Am I glad to get a chance to speak. Those snakes and spiders were getting to me!

Now look, let's get back to reality. . . . It is really all very simple, and you don't even need to construct any "Freudian house."

You, as parents, are really architects. That's about the only thing that the psychoanalyst said that made any sense. Maybe a better word than architect is planner. Like a city planner. Only you are "people planners." You have the power to plan for and create the kind of child you want through the use of the basic tools of all "people planners": reward and punishment.

You see, we know that people learn how to behave (not from any snakes or spiders in a hypothetical basement) but from what happens to them when they behave. Thus, the child says or does something, and the parents hug and kiss him and make all kinds of "songs and dances" (in such situations as when he says his first words or goes "potty" for the first time), then the child has been rewarded and will tend to repeat these behaviors.

If the child does something else (such as saying a "dirty word" or going "potty" on the floor), then parents may yell and scream or even spank the child. Generally, although not always, a child will tend not to repeat these behaviors.

It is all so simple and based essentially on the principle of reinforcement. It is up to you what behaviors you want to reward. Of course, if you're not sure of what kind of child you want, you may reward the child at one time and punish him later for the same behavior. Then, you've got problems. Inconsistent reinforcement only confuses the child and produces confused people.

All right, time for one or two questions.

Dr. Behaviorist, how can I help my child develop into a good student? I never went to college and I really want my child to go.

If you're really serious about it, really feel that this is an important goal for your child, then there are many things that you can do to increase the probability that he will like learning and school.

Of course, you can't be 100 per cent certain that he will turn out as you wish, but you certainly can improve his chances.

This will take some "human engineering," you know. It may mean beginning very early in life by associating positive experiences with books. Introduce him to fairy tales. Spend time reading to your child. Take him to the library early in his development. Have well-illustrated children's books around the house. Let your child observe his parents and older siblings reading and discussing books.

When he begins school, make sure that he has positive experiences early in kindergarten and the early first few grades. Give him praise when he receives good marks or when he creates something new.

I could go on, but I'm sure you get the idea.

Now there is a difference (and a child will spot it) between parents who really don't care about learning and try to "con" the child into liking learning and school and the family who truly values books, ideas, learning, and growth. Out of this latter family you certainly would increase the chances of producing a "gifted" child who will become involved with ideas and lifelong learning.

One more question? Yes, madam?

The More
Fully Human
Person: Some
Models and
Processes

205

I'm mad, you sound like a "con" artist yourself. It isn't right for a parent to manipulate a child. The child is a unique person and his potentialities will unfold naturally. You don't have to treat him like a rat in a maze, as you seem to suggest.

Pardon me, madam, but you are actually giving part of our next speaker's talk. With your permission I would like to withdraw in favor of Dr. Humanist.

The Humanist

Thank you, Dr. Behaviorist, and thank you madam for setting the theme for my talk.

I feel a little uneasy being the last of the speakers because I represent a point of view that is so new. There have been literally thousands of research studies conducted using the other two views as the theoretical base, whereas the humanistic view is supported in only a few recently published journals. In many journals, humanist-based research still isn't even acceptable.

At any rate, I am going to discuss with you as parents and fellow humans some ideas about children that the humanistic view stresses.

Basically, the humanistic position was developed because many psychologists felt that the two prevailing views of man, even though they offered many insights, actually left an incomplete picture of man. They gave the impression that man is easily manipulated or oversexed and highly aggressive, and that you have to learn to control him.

These views were passed on to parents and teachers who were told to control their children's impulses when they were young or they would end up with little monsters on their hands!

The humanistic position believes that a newborn is born basically "good," that he has a tremendous growth potential, and that he has a basic inner nature that is striving for actualization. So we believe that the best thing a parent can do for a child is nothing! That is, stay out of the child's way and let him unfold and become. This, of course, means that you, the parent, do the same thing yourself, that you allow yourself the freedom to be and become.

Another implication of this view is that parents experience their children not as end-products or goals that parents have set but that they look at their children as beings in the process of growing and becoming. This means accepting them wherever they are.

This, in brief, is the central "message" that humanistic psychologists like myself have to offer. Where does it leave you? In a "scary" position, I'll admit, because it means that parents must have courage and trust in themselves and in their children, trust that their children will develop *without* parents on their own.

We have time for a few questions. Yes, sir?

Life Goals   Is there any research to support your views?

Well, yes, but it is a different kind—more of an observational or clinical type of research. That is, it is based more on subjective, personal observations, rather than on highly controlled experimental-statistical studies.

The largest amount of research comes from therapy where psychologists find that when people are free to "be," free to express their feelings, free to be their authentic selves, they tend to become less neurotic and afraid and become more healthy and self-actualizing.

Other research comes from schools, of which Summerhill is the most prominent example. There the students are given total freedom, but with *responsibility*. They can do whatever they feel like doing as long as it doesn't infringe on the well-being of others. It seems that in this kind of setting most students learn well. They turn out all right in later life. Not all of them become scholars, of course, but they all experience more personally satisfying lives, no matter what field they enter.

Next question?

Your views are too general. Won't you please give us a more specific outline, such as Dr. Behaviorist did?

No. I won't, because I can't! You see, what we're talking about deals with experience. You can't define it, because it's different for different persons. All I can say is for you to let yourself go. Become more free flowing, a person who is not compulsively living life according to a schedule. When this happens in you, it will begin to happen in your child.

DEVELOPING POSITIVE MODELS

Research provides us with information on two levels, description and theory. By description we mean information about what is true for most children most of the time as they grow or change over time. Theories provide information for explaining and understanding descriptions, for integrating new information with the old, and as a means for developing and evaluating new ideas. What we lack with most research is the information about the unique and different. It is here where we can gain insights for developing more positive models.

Uniqueness is somewhat of a problem for science because the student is constantly asking general laws of behavior and established normative data, "Hey, what about me?" The researcher, using statistical terminology, usually replies, "We know all about you. You are our error term, the unaccountable variance in our results. That's who you are." These replies are simply polite ways of saying, "We don't know who you really are."

Parents and child workers are constantly faced with this dilemma of difficult-to-predict individual behavior. There are a number of reasons for our inability to understand unique behavior: (1) As yet, we don't know all of the forces converging upon a particular child at any point in space or time, (2) as yet, we don't know the full impact of all the cumulative forces that converged on a particular child during his life span, (3) as yet, we don't know the end-products of the almost endless combinations of

The More
Fully Human
Person: Some
Models and
Processes

207

past and present forces, and (4) as yet, we haven't fully appreciated the extent to which a child's self-concept, conscious or with any degrees of unconsciousness, may transform known external forces into unique or symbolic ones.

For the time being, and perhaps for all time, if we really wish to know more about the uniqueness of an individual we will have to spend the time necessary to be with him, to observe him, and try to see and feel the way he does (at least for a period of time). Even then, we must be ready for the unexpected. Perhaps unpredictability is an essential characteristic of human nature because life could become awfully dull if we were to know exactly what others were going to do next.

The theories of the more fully human person and the three views of man presented in this chapter are beginnings; they offer clues to our search for developing positive models. It is through further study and refinement of these and other models that we can extend our vistas of the individual as well as all mankind.

CHAPTER REFERENCES

ADLER, A. *Practice and theory of individual psychology*. New York: Harcourt, 1927.

ALLPORT, G. W. *Becoming*. New Haven, Conn.: Yale U.P., 1955.

BANDURA, A. *Principles of behavior modification*. New York: Holt, 1969.

BIJOU, S. and D. M. BAER. Operant methods in child behavior and development. In W. Honig (ed.), *Operant behavior: areas of research and application*. New York: Appleton, 1966.

BLACKHAM, G. J. and A. SILBERMAN. *Modification of child behavior*. Belmont, Calif.: Wadsworth, 1971.

BLUM, G. S. *Psychoanalytic theories of personality*. New York: McGraw-Hill, 1953.

BONNER, H. *On being mindful of man*. Boston: Houghton, 1965.

———. *The proactive personality*. In J. F. T. Bugental (ed.), *Challenges of humanistic psychology*. New York: McGraw-Hill, 1967.

BRADFIELD, R. H. (ed.). *Behavior modification: the human effort*. San Rafael, Calif.: Dimensions, 1970.

BUBER, M. *Between man and man*. Boston: Beacon, 1955.

BUGENTAL, J. F. T. (ed.). *Challenges of humanistic psychology*. New York: McGraw-Hill, 1967.

COHEN, H. L. and J. FILIPCZAK. *A new learning environment*. San Francisco: Jossey-Bass, 1971.

COMBS, A. W. Fostering self-direction. In D. E. Hamachek (ed.), *Human dynamics in psychology and education*. Boston: Allyn, 1970.

——— (ed.). *Perceiving, behaving, becoming*. Washington, D.C.: Association for Supervision and Curriculum Development, National Education Association, 1962.

———, D. L. Avila and W. W. Purkey. *Helping relationships*. Boston: Allyn, 1971.

——— and D. SNYGG. *Individual behavior*. New York: Harper, 1959.

DOLLARD, J. and N. E. MILLER. *Personality and psychotherapy: an analysis in terms of learning, thinking and culture*. New York: McGraw-Hill, 1950.

ERIKSON, E. H. *Childhood and society*, 2nd ed. New York: Norton, 1963.

FREUD, ANNA. *The ego and the mechanisms of defense*. New York: International Universities P., 1946.

Life Goals

————— et al. (eds.). *The psychoanalytic study of the child.* New York: International Universities P., 1945.

FREUD, S. *The standard edition of the complete psychological works,* vols. 1–23. J. Strachey (ed.). London: Hogarth, 1953–1964.

—————. *The interpretation of dreams.* In *Standard edition,* vols. 4 and 5. London: Hogarth, 1953. (First German ed., 1900.)

—————. *The psychopathology of everyday life.* In *Standard edition,* vol. 6. London: Hogarth, 1960. (First German ed., 1901.)

—————. *Three essays on sexuality.* In *Standard edition,* vol. 7. London: Hogarth, 1953. (First German ed., 1905a.)

—————. *Introductory lectures on psycho-analysis.* In *Standard edition,* vols. 15 and 16. London: Hogarth, 1963. (First German ed., 1917.)

—————. *Beyond the pleasure principle.* In *Standard edition,* vol. 18. London: Hogarth, 1955. (First German ed., 1920a.)

FRICK, W. B. *Humanistic psychology: interviews with Maslow, Murphy, and Rogers.* Columbus, Oh.: Merrill, 1971.

FROMM, E. *Escape from freedom.* New York: Holt, 1941.

—————. *Sigmund Freud's mission.* New York: Harper, 1959.

—————. *The sane society.* New York: Holt, 1955.

GOBLE, F. *The third force.* New York: Grossman, 1970.

HALL, C. S. *A primer of Freudian psychology.* New York: World, 1954.

————— and G. LINDZEY. The relevance of Freudian psychology and related viewpoints for the social sciences. In G. Lindzey and E. Aronson (eds.), *Handbook of social psychology,* vol. 1. Reading, Mass.: Addison-Wesley, 1968.

HERSHEY, G. L. and J. O. LUGO. *Living psychology: an experiential approach.* New York: Macmillan, 1970.

HILGARD, E. R. Psychoanalysis: experimental studies. In D. L. Sills (ed.), *International Encyclopedia of the Social Sciences,* vol. 13. New York: Macmillan, and Free Press, 1968.

HOLLAND, J. G. and B. F. SKINNER. *The analysis of behavior: a program for self-instruction.* New York: McGraw-Hill, 1961.

HORNEY, KAREN. *Neurosis and human growth.* New York: Norton, 1950.

—————. *New ways in psychoanalysis.* New York: Norton, 1939.

JONES, E. *The life and work of Sigmund Freud.* vol. 1, 1953; vol. 2, 1955; vol. 3, 1957. New York: Basic.

JOURARD, S. M. *Personal adjustment: an approach through the study of healthy personality.* New York: Macmillan, 1963.

—————. *The transparent self.* New York: Van Nostrand, 1971.

JUNG, C. G. *Collected works,* vols. 1–9, H. Read, M. Fordham, and G. Adler (eds.), Princeton, N. J.: Princeton U. P., 1953.

MASLOW, A. H. A philosophy of psychology: the need for a mature science of human nature. In F. T. Severin, *Humanistic viewpoints in psychology.* New York: McGraw-Hill, 1965.

—————. *Motivation and personality,* (2nd ed.) New York: Harper, 1970.

—————. *Self-actualization and beyond.* In J. F. T. Bugental (ed.), *Challenge of humanistic psychology.* New York: McGraw-Hill, 1967.

—————. *The farther reaches of human nature.* New York: Viking, 1971.

—————. *Toward a psychology of being,* 2nd ed. New York: Van Nostrand, 1968a.

MAY, R. (ed.). *Existential psychology,* 2nd ed. New York: Random, 1969.

MILLER, N. E. and J. DOLLARD. *Social learning and imitation.* New Haven: Yale U. P., 1941.

MOUSTAKAS, C. *Personal growth.* Cambridge, Mass.: Doyle, 1971.

MOWRER, O. H. *Learning theory and personality dynamics.* New York: Ronald, 1951.

MUNROE, RUTH. *Schools of psychoanalytic thought.* New York: Dryden P., 1955.

The More
Fully Human
Person: Some
Models and
Processes

Murphy, G. *Human potentialities.* New York: Basic, 1958.

Neill, A. S. *Summerhill: a radical approach to child rearing.* New York: Hart, 1960.

Otto, H. (ed.). *Explorations in human potentialities.* Springfield, Ill.: Thomas, 1966.

———— and J. Mann. *Ways of growth.* New York: Viking, 1968.

Pavlov, I. P. *Conditioned reflexes.* G. V. Anrep, trans. London: Oxford U. P., 1927.

Peterson, S. A. *A catalog of the ways people grow.* New York: Ballantine, 1971.

Rachlin, H. *Introduction to modern behaviorism.* San Francisco: Freeman, 1970.

Rapaport, D. The structure of psychoanalytic theory: a systematizing attempt. In S. Koch (ed.), *Psychology: a study of science,* vol. 3. New York: McGraw-Hill, 1959.

Rogers, C. R. *Client-centered therapy: its current practice, implications and theory.* Boston: Houghton, 1951.

————. *On becoming a person.* Boston: Houghton, 1961.

Severin, F. T. (ed.). *Humanistic viewpoints in psychology.* New York: McGraw-Hill, 1965.

Shakow, D. and D. Rapaport. *The influence of Freud on American psychology.* New York: International Universities P., 1964.

Skinner, B. F. *Beyond freedom and dignity.* New York: Knopf, 1971.

————. *Contingencies of reinforcement: a theoretical analysis.* New York: Appleton, 1969.

————. *Cumulative record.* New York: Appleton, 1961.

————. *Science and human behavior.* New York: Macmillan, 1953.

————. *The behavior of organisms.* New York: Appleton, 1938.

Sullivan, H. S. *Conceptions of modern psychiatry.* Washington, D.C.: William Alanson White Psychiatric Foundation, 1947.

————. *The interpersonal theory of psychiatry.* New York: Norton, 1963.

Sutich, A. J. and M. A. Vich. *Readings in humanistic psychology.* New York: Free Press, 1969.

Thompson, C. *Psychoanalysis: evolution and development.* New York: Hermitage, 1950.

Thorndike, E. L. *Animal intelligence: experimental studies.* New York: Macmillan, 1911.

————. *The fundamentals of learning.* New York: Teachers College P., 1932.

Tillich, P. *The courage to be.* New Haven: Yale U. P., 1959.

Tournier, P. *The meaning of persons.* New York: Harper, 1957.

Watson, J. B. *Behaviorism.* New York: Norton, 1925.

Wolpe, J., A. Salter, and L. Reyna. *The conditioning therapies: the challenge in psychotherapy.* New York: Pergamon, 1964.

RECOMMENDED FURTHER READING

Bandura, A. and R. H. Walters. *Social learning and personality development.* New York: Holt, 1963.

Combs, A. W. What can man become? In D. E. Hamachek (ed.), *The self in growth, teaching and learning.* Englewood Cliffs, N. J.: Prentice-Hall, 1965.

Eysenck, H. J. *The structure of human personality.* London: Methuen, 1960.

Hall, C. S. and G. Lindzey. *Theories of personality* (2nd ed.). New York: Wiley, 1970.

Harlow, H. F. *Learning to love.* San Francisco, Calif.: Albion, 1971.

Hilgard, E. R. and G. Bower. *Theories of learning,* 3rd ed. New York: Appleton, 1966.

Life Goals

Hook, S. (ed.). *Psychoanalysis, scientific method and philosophy.* New York: Grove, 1960.

Horwitz, L. *Theory construction and validation in psychoanalysis.* In M. H. Marx (ed.), *Theories in contemporary psychology.* New York: Macmillan, 1963.

Lundin, R. W. *Personality: a behavioral analysis.* New York: Macmillan, 1969.

Maslow, A. H. *Self-actualizing people: a study of psychological health.* In C. E. Moustakas (ed.), *The self explorations in personal growth.* New York: Harper, 1958.

Stein, J. *Effective personality: a humanistic approach.* Belmont, Calif.: Wadsworth, 1972.

The More
Fully Human
Person: Some
Models and
Processes

PART IV
The Life Cycle

In the first two sections of this text we attempted to define the study of human development and provide some broad perspectives for understanding the discipline. Selected aspects were examined from the viewpoints of the historian, philosopher, anthropologist, sociologist, biologist, and psychologist.

In the third section we attempted to identify the components that make up a fully human person and pointed out the interrelated nature of these factors. Hopefully, the intrinsic value of the goal of becoming self-actualized became apparent to you as you read the material. We attempted to introduce you to new words and phrases, (or at least new meanings for familiar words), and we tried to emphasize the importance of models to the developmental process.

The balance of this text focuses on the chronological development of the individual, from womb to tomb. As in the previous sections, the main avenues for analyzing the individual are the biological, cognitive, affective, and social domains. The major unifying theme continues to be the holistic nature of growth and behavior, pointing toward the development of a more fully human person.

The Life
Cycle

*What occurs during
the preconception
stage increases
the chances of
developing a more
fully human person
in the prenatal
and neonatal stages.*

The Preconception Stage

Prelude
Basic Theory and Research
  Biological Domain
    General Health Factors
    Birth Defects
    Unwanted Babies
  Cognitive Domain
    Self-fulfilling Prophecies
    Ethnic Group Intelligence
      Bilingualism
    Socioeconomic Factors
  Affective Domain
    Transition into Parenthood
  Social Domain
    Family Planning
Implications
  Understanding Yourself and
    Others
  Living and Working with Chil-
    dren, Adolescents, and Adults
  Developing Positive Models

PRELUDE

WHY DO we have babies?

Perhaps this question seems inane or too profound. Some consider this question to be meaningless, such as asking "Why do we breathe?" Others consider it beyond answering, such as asking "What is the purpose of life?" Nevertheless, let us consider some replies:

1. Some couples need babies the way that they need spaghetti.
2. I hadn't noticed. I just assumed that babies and marriage went together.
3. We didn't ask why we were born. Why should we answer that question about our babies?
4. Having babies is the only significant way to affirm life and to deny death.
5. Life without babies is not truly life. True life is continuity with the past, the present, and the future. Whoever breaks the eternal chain has not really lived at all.

We believe that parents who want and who plan enthusiastically for the arrival of their babies will be better able to provide them with the "milk and honey" necessary for optimal development. We can't help believing that parents who welcome their newborns with great love will be better able to make peace with the spilled milk and the mud, for of such things is the kingdom of childhood.

BASIC THEORY AND RESEARCH

BIOLOGICAL DOMAIN

As mentioned in Chapter 6, the notion of preformationism was once popular. It was believed that the baby was primarily the creation of the father who implanted the complete seed for the baby in the mother. The mother merely supplied room and board. The more feminist view, however, argued that the primary creator was the mother. The father's seed according to this view merely triggered off the egg that contained all the necessary ingredients for the baby's development.

Today we know that, except for its gender, each parent contributes equally to the total genetic inheritance of the newborn. Of the twenty-three pairs of chromosomes, one pair determines the sex of the newborn. In the female this pair of chromosomes are alike and are referred to as XX, whereas the male has an X and a Y chromosome pair. Thus the division of the female sex cell always yields an ovum containing the X-chromosome, whereas the spermatozoon carries a Y or X chromosome. When a Y-bearing sperm fertilizes an egg a male is formed, but if an X-bearing sperm fertilizes an egg a female is born. Since no one can tell ahead of time whether the egg will be fertilized by a spermatozoon with an X or Y chromosome, sex determination is essentially a matter of chance.

Just as the baby's genetic inheritance is a joint venture of the parents, so are all the factors that produce a successful preconception period in preparation for pregnancy and childbirth.

General Health Factors

The Life Cycle

Nutrition. Stated succinctly, biological growth depends on food. A physically healthy mother is like a well-stocked food market, ready to provide the growing conceptus with a wide variety of essential nutrients for optimal growth. On the other hand, seriously malnourished mothers produce far more stillborn and premature babies. Up to 75 per cent of all infant mortality in the first month of life is the result of immaturity. The crucial importance of nutrition during pregnancy as well as during preconception is stressed by Montagu (1962) as follows:

> Were they called upon to name the most important factor in contributing to the healthy development of the human conceptus, most authorities would unhesitatingly declare for the good nutritional welfare of the mother. This means not merely that her nutritional welfare during pregnancy is the important requisite, but that her own nutrition during her whole life, including the period of her sojourn in her own mother's womb, shall have been adequate. . . .
>
> Good *preconceptional* care is as necessary for the potential mother as good *antepartum* care is necessary for the actual mother. It is important to recognize that many things happen prior to pregnancy that have a significant influence upon both mother and infant. Rickets acquired in infancy or in childhood may so affect the development of the pelvis of a female that her later reproductive history and the fate of her children may be seriously affected. Rickets is largely a disorder of nutrition. (pp. 57–58)

In other words, the best time to start feeding the baby is prior to conception. Proper nutrition is probably the single best factor in ensuring a healthy baby at birth and for the child's later life.

Age of the Parents. During recent years it has become apparent that there is a high relationship between difficulties during pregnancy, birth, and birth defects, and the fact that the mothers were either too young or too old. The optimal age range for childbearing seems to be between twenty and thirty (Prenatal Care, 1970). Of course, many thousands of younger and older women have successful pregnancies each year, but the maternal records of these women are generally poorer (Pasamanich and Knobloch, 1966).

The age of the mother is a major variable responsible for an increase in the likelihood of miscarriages, stillbirths, prematurities, and malformations. To increase the chances for the health of the baby and the mother, it is best to plan pregnancies for the period of time when the mother's reproductive system is optimally ready.

A major problem among younger women, especially adolescents, is that they are most likely to have the poorest diet in the family regardless of their socioeconomic level. Although the number of mothers of all ages suffering from malnutrition is much higher among poverty stricken families, many affluent teen-agers also suffer from poor nutrition. A common reason for poor diets among teen-age girls is probably the current feminine ideal of a svelte figure carried to the point of emaciation (Livingston, 1971). However, there may be other factors, notably inadequate education regarding proper nutrition, because many obese girls as well as boys with varying physical figures have been found to have improper diets (Hampton et al., 1967). Underscoring the need for improving nutrition of teen-agers is the fact that according to the 1968 Census about one-fourth of young women in the United States marry and bear their first child before the age of twenty (Joint Commission

The Preconception Stage

of Mental Health of Children, 1970). Countries such as Sweden and New Zealand that emphasize nutrition education and maternal and child health programs have lower maternal and infant death rates than the United States (Smart and Smart, 1972).

As the age of the mother increases, there tends to be a significant increase in maternal and infant problems. The number of maternal deaths increases with age. The firstborn of mothers over the age of thirty-five have the highest rate of prematurity (Illsley, 1967). The chances for producing infants suffering from mongolism or Down's syndrome, a common form of mental retardation, increases with the age of the mother. In one study, the odds of having a mongoloid child went up from one in a thousand births for women in the age group twenty to twenty-four, to 125 in a thousand for women in the age group forty-five to forty-nine (Montagu, 1962). Approximately one in every 500 births in the United States is a mongoloid (Brenda, 1960). Similar results, as well as the increased probability of other abnormalities, have been reported in the United States, England, and Japan for older women (Penrose, 1954). Practically all available studies regarding the age of the father indicate no apparent negative influences. Even if there is some relationship between the age of the father and birth problems and defects, it is far less marked then that concerning the age of the mother.

Venereal Disease. With the advent of antibiotics, along with the increase in the number of states that require premarital physical examinations, and the increased stress on good prenatal care, fewer people now seem to take venereal disease seriously. Nevertheless, venereal disease, particularly syphilis, still poses dangers for the unborn. Prior to birth, the baby is well protected against a wide variety of viruses, but venereal viruses are one of the few exceptions. Nearly 40 per cent of syphilitic mothers pass the disease to their unborn infants unless treatment is begun prior to the fifth month of pregnancy, in which case the frequency of the disease in the baby is reduced to less than 2 per cent. Although the majority of cases of syphilis go unreported, it has been estimated that there are 1 million untreated syphilitics in the United States (Brown, 1960). Moreover, recent studies report great increases in the incidence of both syphilis and gonorrhea among our young people (Metropolitan Life, 1969). One possible reason for this increase is that young people today seem to be more sexually active prior to marriage (Adelson, 1970). A recent study prepared by the President's Commission on Population Growth and the American Future (1972), based on a sample size of 4,611 unmarried women, concluded that 13.8 per cent of unmarried girls at age fifteen had experienced sexual intercourse, whereas this percentage rose to 46 per cent by age nineteen. In one year, 1964, 275,000 babies were born to unwed mothers in the United States, and, of these, 40 per cent (110,280 babies) were born to mothers between fifteen and nineteen years of age (National Council on Illegitimacy, 1968).

Unwed mothers, who often do not receive proper prenatal care, probably represent the single greatest syphilitic danger to the unborn. The only fully adequate approach to syphilis is prevention or early detection and treatment. According to Coleman (1964), once the spirochetes or spores of syphilis have entered the body, either through sexual intercourse or direct contact with open sores, there are four fairly well-defined stages of the disease. The first stage, a sore at the area of contact, appears ten to forty days after contact. The sore will disappear within five weeks or so even if untreated.

The Life
Cycle

The second stage is marked by a generalized copper-colored rash that appears within three to six weeks. The rash may be mild or severe, and may be accompanied by such symptoms as fever, headaches, and indigestion. Subsequently, there may be further recurrances of the symptoms for the next ten to thirty years. It is during this third stage that the virus begins its destructive work on the blood and nervous systems. During the last stage, the results of cumulative damage is revealed in heart attacks, severe mental disease, blindness, loss of motor coordination, and death.

Drugs. Although relatively little is known about the effects on the newborn of some drugs taken by parents during the preconception period, we should not confuse *knowing little* with *caring little.* Certainly the tragedy of thalidomide, in which an apparently mild tranquilizer caused major physical malformations in thousands of infants, should serve as a warning against complacency.

Lysergic Acid. Lysergic acid or LSD is probably the most commonly used hallucinogen, a drug that produces sensory distortions ranging from euphoria to psychosis. One study concluded that one side effect of LSD was *possible* chromosomal damage and damage to unborn children (Jones et al., 1969). The conclusions reached by the National Foundation-March of Dimes are more positive (Birth Defects). They concluded that "LSD can damage chromosomes and investigations are continuing to determine the effect of such broken chromosomes on the developing fetus." These findings were supported by additional research published in *The Journal of the American Medical Association* (1970). If further research clearly confirms that LSD damages the germ cells of either the female or the male or both, we will have genetic defects that may stretch out into untold generations.

Drug Addicts As Future Parents. With the exception of heroin, there is no evidence that the use of other narcotics prior to pregnancy will produce direct damage to the unborn. However, the case against the use of narcotics cannot rest there because of the following reasons: (1) Since most pregnancies are not planned, it would be very difficult for habitual drug users to cease their practice immediately upon conception. In fact, it is very likely that such mothers will continue their dependency on drugs well into the prenatal stage. (2) There is an apparent increase in the use of narcotics not only in colleges but also in high schools throughout the United States (Sebald, 1968). Findings released in 1972 by the National Commission on Marihuana and Drug Abuse revealed the following projections based on a sample size of 3,186 Americans (Marihuana & Drug Abuse, 1972): (1) About 1 million people of high school age, and approximately 700,000 adults, have tried heroin at least once. (2) About 9 million people have tried hashish. (3) About 4.7 million people have tried one or more of the hallucinogenic drugs, LSD, peyote, or mescalin. (4) About 3 million people have tried amphetamines. Personality studies of drug addicts—those with a compulsion to take drugs and who are psychologically and physically dependent on them as well as habitual users—reveal many undesirable characteristics. Most drug addicts suffer from character disorders. They are often described as immature, inadequate, or passive-aggressive individuals who are frequently involved in criminal behavior. Although there is no single personality description that fits all drug addicts and habitual users, they tend to be persons who are passively avoiding their problems instead of actively trying to improve their conditions. What does seem certain is that addicts who depend on chemical substitutes to avoid the realities of life, and other persons who seek fleeting moments of euphoria through artificial means, are not likely to be parents who will produce more fully human, self-actualizing, and self-directing children.

Fig. 13–1. *Prevalence of common birth defects in the U.S. (From Facts, March of Dimes, White Plains, N.Y.)*

Birth Defects

Nothing is quite as sad as seeing an infant born blind, deaf, mentally retarded, or physically crippled. As loving parents we would gladly exchange our healthy organs for their defective ones. Yet every year about 250,000 American babies are born damaged in some way. One infant in fourteen comes into this world with a significant mental or physical defect. Every other minute a child with a defect is born—seven hundred babies a day. Nearly half of all chronic childhood disabilities are caused by birth defects. An estimated 15 million Americans of all ages suffer daily from the effects of one or more birth defects (*Birth Defects, Facts*). As concerned human beings we must do all we can to understand, prevent, and ameliorate such suffering. The following list summarizes some of the more common birth defects and their frequencies (*Birth Defects*).

1. Birth defects kill about 500,000 unborn babies and 60,000 children and adults each year.
2. About 1.17 million Americans under age 20 have mental retardation of prenatal origin.
3. About 600,000 Americans under age 20 have congenital blindness or deafness or some degree of impairment of one or both senses of sight and hearing.
4. About 400,000 Americans under age 20 suffer from muscular dystrophy or congenital heart and/or other circulatory diseases.
5. About 120,000 Americans under age 20 are clubfooted.
6. About 100,000 Americans under age 20 have cleft lips and/or palates.
7. One in 500 babies is born with some degree of hydrocephalus (water on the brain).
8. One in 250 babies is born with some form of urinary tract defect.

A birth defect can be defined as an abnormality of structure or function produced during the prenatal period by defective genes, environment, or both. Birth defects produce miscarriages, stillbirths, congenital defects that appear at birth, and abnormalities that appear in later life. Late-appearing birth defects are particularly insidious; for example, Huntington's chorea, a hereditary brain disease, usually appears between ages thirty and fifty. It is characterized by involuntary, irregular twitching, jerking movements. Huntington's chorea usually ends in severe mental disorder and eventually death. Figure 13–2 presents late-appearing birth defects and the corresponding age ranges of clinical detection.

It has been estimated that about 20 per cent of all birth defects are primarily the result of defective heredity and that about 20 per cent of birth defects are the result of factors that influence the environment of the developing fetus while it is inside the mother's womb. The majority of birth defects, however, are the result of the interaction of environmental and heredity factors (*Facts*).

We can no longer accept the idea that a healthy baby is the result of only chance factors that are outside of our control. Much can be done today to reduce the risks of infant death and morbidity during the peridevelopmental period. There is evidence that the intrauterine environment can be influenced, both negatively and positively, by such seemingly external factors as medicines and variations in diet, health, emotional states, glandular secre-

The Preconception Stage

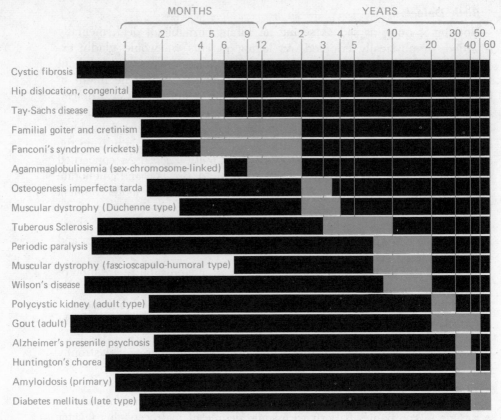

FIG. 13–2. *Late-appearing birth defects. These conditions include many which may be unfamiliar to laymen. All, however, are documented in medical literature in sufficient number to be significant. For more syndromes, age at onset varies widely. Ranges shown are those in which a majority first manifest clinically detectable symptoms. (From* Facts, March of Dimes, White Plains, N.Y.)

tions, and other factors that influence the blood chemistry of the mother. The genetic composition of the developing fetus can be influenced through genetic counseling, radiation, and drugs prior to and after pregnancy.

The interchanges of substances between the mother and the developing fetus point out the great importance of the physical and psychological states of the mother before and during pregnancy. The actual transmission mechanisms for these interchanges are explained in some detail in the following section on prenatal development. In this section we limit our discussion to factors that influence the developing fetus during the preconceptual stage only.

Blood Incompatibility. Most people have an element in their blood known as the Rh factor. Those who have it are referred to as Rh positive. Those people without this factor are called Rh negatives. The presence or absence of the element itself makes no difference to the health of the individual. It is only when one parent is positive and the other is negative that blood incompatibility *may* occur in the unborn child and produce such results as miscarriages, mental retardation, or heart defects. The probability of Rh incompatibility between mother and the unborn child is about one in two hundred.

The Life Cycle

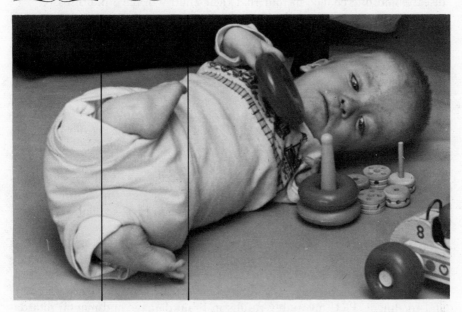

20% Heriditary	20% Environmental	60% Interaction of Heredity & Environment

FIG. 13–3. *Some genetic defects may not necessarily be hereditary. (Courtesy The National Foundation—March of Dimes.)*

Ideally every couple should have a blood test for the Rh factor prior to marriage or pregnancy. If blood incompatibility is found, preventive measures can be taken for the potential mother or the newborn child can be given treatment after birth. However, the treatment of the child is more difficult and dangerous because it requires a complete blood exchange in the newborn child.

Hemophilia. Hemophilia, a disease involving about 100,000 persons in the United States, is a defect in the ability of the blood to coagulate that results in excessive bleeding even from minor bruises and cuts. Approximately four out of five hemophiliacs are aware of a history of bleeding in their families, although the disease can occur without such positive histories (Gaver, 1972). Since the defective gene is carried by women who rarely have the disease themselves, those women who are aware of such histories should seek genetic counseling as a possible basis for selecting a marriage partner and for information about medical care of the infant. For further information, the interested reader should contact The National Hemophilia Foundation.

Ethnic Related Diseases. As mentioned in Chapter 6, there are genetic diseases that are limited almost exclusively to members of certain ethnic groups. *Sickle cell anemia,* for example, affects about one in every four hundred blacks in the United States (Gaver, 1972). During pregnancy sickle cell anemia can produce miscarriages, stillbirths, and other abnormalities. The disease lowers resistance and is often fatal. Presently the federal government's National Institute of Health is supporting major research efforts directed at alleviating this disease. For the time being it is well to remember that about 10 per cent of the blacks in America are carriers of the disease by virtue of their possession of one abnormal gene, even though they themselves rarely exhibit any of the symptoms. When two carriers of the

The Preconception Stage

223

disease conceive, there is one chance in four that their offspring will be unafflicted, two chances in four that their offspring will be carriers of the disease, and one chance in four that their child will have the disease.

Fortunately, a simple and inexpensive screening test has been developed for *Tay-Sachs disease*, which is found in about one of every thirty persons of Jewish ancestry. If two carriers of this disease conceive, their baby will be abnormal and die prior to its fourth or fifth birthday. At the present time, the only way to avoid Tay-Sachs disease is to prevent conception by two carriers.

Cooley's anemia primarily affects the children of people of Latin or Mediterranean descent. It is a lifelong debilitating disease that discolors the skin and produces abnormal bone structure (Gaver, 1972). Obviously, this disease tends to limit a child's physical and social activities. As with sickle cell anemia, the basic treatment for this disease consists of frequent, sometimes monthly, blood transfusions for the life of the victim; but fortunately, as with Tay-Sachs disease, there is a simple screening test available to determine carriers of the disease.

Phenylketonuria (PKU) is yet another tragic metabolic error transmitted by a recessive gene. It occurs equally among males and females; is rare among Jews, blacks, and Japanese; and is most common in Northern European countries (Centerwall and Centerwall, 1961). Without early diagnosis and treatment, PKU invariably results in brain damage and mental retardation. It has been estimated that PKU accounts for 1 to 3 per cent of all cases of mental retardation in the United States and that it affects about one in every 40,000 births (Shaw et al., 1961).

For a child to be affected by PKU, both parents must be either carriers or have the disease. To date there is no screening test for carriers, but there are several simple and inexpensive tests to detect it in the newborn. (In some states these tests are required by law.) The treatment for PKU consists of special diets, is lengthy, and relatively expensive, and must begin as soon as the baby begins to ingest proteins. PKU does not begin before birth because the metabolism of the mother protects it from occurring in the unborn.

In summary, one in twenty American families knows the tragedy of a child born less than perfect. Furthermore, the final results are not just handicapped children but handicapped families and a handicapped society. Although much remains to be done to reduce the number of birth defects, and much is being done by private and public agencies, it is up to us to take full advantage of *what has been done* to safeguard the health of our unborn children even before they are conceived.

Genetic Counseling. Genetic counseling consists of the detection, prevention, and treatment of certain identifiable genetic defects. This form of counseling is relatively new because it has been estimated that 90 per cent of the genetic information available today has been uncovered since the end of World War II. Nevertheless, today there are more than 150 genetic counseling clinics in the United States. The 1969 edition of the *International Directory of Genetic Services* lists 427 centers throughout the world.

Now for the first time in history, we have the means to prevent and treat more than fifty inherited disorders. As geneticists sharpen their diagnostic tools and as physicians learn how to handle genetic problems, there may be a dramatic reduction in birth defects that are wholly or partly caused by genetic illnesses and misfortunes.

Unwanted Babies

"Unwanted" here refers to those babies who were wanted by their parents but who were born at the wrong time as well as to those babies who were unwanted at any time. Each child who comes into this world is seen as either a possible source of enrichment for its parents and for all mankind or as a threat to the well-being of the parents or of a society that may feel that the newborn poses a danger to their food, space, air, water, and other resources.

For whatever reasons, we know that there are many babies who were and who are going to be unwanted by their parents even before their conception. Even in the United States, where until recently abortions were illegal, it is still estimated that 1 million abortions are performed each year. Furthermore, the number of parents in this country who reported that they had more children than they wanted is relatively high. The National Institute of Child Health and Human Development reported that in 1960 20 per cent of the married couples, in which the wife was between the ages of eighteen and thirty-nine, had not wanted their last child. Such attitudes span all socioeconomic levels but are more common among families of low socioeconomic status. For example, among wives with less than a high school education, 32 per cent reported that they had not wanted another child at the time of their last pregnancy, whereas only 10 per cent of those wives with a college education felt that way (Frost et al., 1968).

The question of abortion is a complex one because it involves the rights of adults to choose, after conception, whether or not to have a baby. The moral sentiments of the individuals, society, and the rights of the unborn to life must be considered. What is clear is the right of the unborn to be cared for and loved in an environment that will contribute to its healthy development. We see two possible solutions to the problems of unwanted babies. The first is to provide counseling and assistance to those parents who have already conceived in order to change their attitudes toward the unborn and to ensure that the baby will have proper medical care, nutrition, clothing, and shelter. The second remedy is to provide birth control information and services for those couples wishing to avoid unwanted pregnancies.

COGNITIVE DOMAIN

To discuss such matters as learning, education, and intelligence before the unborn are even conceived may seem premature. We believe, nevertheless, that there are some valid reasons for doing so. In the words of the noted child psychologist Jerome Kagan (1972), "Contemporary American society uses intelligence as one of the bases for ranking its members. We celebrate intelligence the way the Islamic Moroccans celebrated the warrior-saint." Kagan goes on to state that most Americans believe that intellectual capacities are genetically determined, and based on inheritance, some children are destined to assume positions of power and prestige. A smaller number of Americans believes that the right combination of early experiences and motivation account for such later successes in life. Presently both views can be supported through selected research findings.

The Preconception Stage

Self-fulfilling Prophecies

The more popular belief in the primacy of inherited intellectual capacities as being crucial to "success," combined with recent evidence that if children are expected to do poorly they will do poorly, makes a discussion of the cognitive domain during the preconceptualization period germane to our goal of developing more fully human persons. In other words, if future parents were to be convinced, somehow, that their offspring had less chance than others of being born with average or higher intellectual capacities, then there is a distinct possibility that their children will fall victims to such a "self-fulfilling prophecy." This hypothesis has been tested experimentally by Rosenthal and Jacobson (1968). They gave to teachers the names of pupils who had allegedly scored high on a test of "intellectual promise" and informed them that these pupils would probably demonstrate striking gains during the school year. The names of pupils in the control group, who actually had scored equally high, were not given to the teachers. Eight months later both groups were retested on the same intelligence test. The experimental group revealed significantly higher gains in IQ than did the pupils whose names had not been given to the teachers. Rosenthal and Jacobson concluded that a person's expectation for another person's behavior can unwittingly become a more accurate predictor simply for its having been made.*

Ethnic Group Intelligence Testing

The great French psychologist Alfred Binet warned back in 1905 that intelligence tests could be used as an estimate of intellectual capacity only if the individuals or groups tested had substantially the same opportunities to learn about the questions asked on the tests. Nevertheless, many people including some psychologists have ignored this warning, and some still continue to do so. Note, for example, the following historical statements that illustrate that a genetic explanation for differences in intelligence test scores can be mistaken (Light, 1972).

In 1925, Karl Pearson, one of Britain's most creative and methodologically sophisticated statisticians, wrote about Jewish immigrants: "Taken on the average, and regarding both sexes, this alien Jewish population is somewhat inferior both physically and mentally to the native population." The context of Pearson's assertion was that this alleged inferiority was genetic. In both America and Britain today, however, it is quite well known that Jews score as high on intelligence tests as the majority non-Jewish population.

Prior to 1960, Catholics in America scored lower than non-Catholics on standardized intelligence tests. In the 1930's a genetic explanation was put forth to account for the observed differences. Since 1960, however, the distribution of intelligence-test scores for American Catholics has duplicated the non-Catholic score distribution almost exactly.

* As often happens when measuring complex human relations, the final results often vary depending on subjects, time, and place. Fleming and Anttonen (1971) did somewhat similar research but found no significant differences when the IQ test was re-administered. It is comforting to realize that educational failure and success is not always nor solely attributable to a teacher's expectancies.

Examination of the research on American black-white differences among older children receiving IQ tests reveals that blacks rarely scored higher, sometimes the same, but most often lower than whites (Kennedy et al., 1963). A study of forty-week-old infant intelligence test scores between white and nonwhites, however, revealed no statistical differences between the races (Knobloch and Pasamanich, 1960). According to researchers the major reason for this observable difference is socioeconomic influence; the nonwhites had fewer advantages and less stimulation than the whites. It has been also demonstrated, first by Klineberg in 1935, later by Lee in 1951 and Klineberg in 1971, that the longer black children attended schools in the North the higher were their IQ scores. By the third generation the black children in their samples matched those of white children, whereas the test scores of similar black children in the deep South remained substantially lower than the national average.

An indication of the wide differences in intelligence test scores within the same racial group when members are exposed to different environments is seen in the test scores of black children in rural Tennessee, who averaged 58 and those in Los Angeles, California, who averaged 105 (Klineberg, 1971). Nevertheless, there is still a need to improve the quality of education and living conditions for the majority of black youngsters. Based on the 1966 nationwide survey of James S. Coleman and others, 85 per cent of black elementary and high school students scored below white averages on tests of intelligence and achievement. In its desegregation decision of 1954, the Supreme Court held that separate schools for black and white children are inherently unequal. Nevertheless, according to the Coleman report, blacks are still the most segregated minority group in the nation. For example, 65 per cent of black first graders attended schools that were 90 to 100 per cent black.

The case in point is not one of heredity *versus* environment, because all existing evidence indicates that both heredity and environment play a part in determining *intelligence* (no matter how the word is defined). The degree to which each component influences intelligence test scores is probably not fixed; that is, under severe conditions of environmental deprivation, no degree of genetic "loading" can compensate enough to allow the individual to function to his full potential. By the same token, under conditions of extreme mental retardation, no environmental advantages will offset the individual's lack of functional ability. Considering the social differences that exist between being black and white in American society, it is quite likely that this factor alone is sufficient to account for the differences observed in intelligence as measured by IQ tests with all their limitations.

Bilingualism

Although English is the national language of the United States, there are many minority group members who lack sufficient mastery of English to do well on intelligence tests. Since most of the intelligence tests in general use are verbal in character, their use with those limited in their command of English results in significantly lower test scores (Darcy, 1963). Furthermore, even members of such ethnic groups who have a sufficient mastery of English to understand the tasks often lack the necessary experiential background to perform well on these tests.

In a Canadian study, where true bilinguals (persons equally skilled in two

The Precon-
ception Stage

227

languages) were compared with monolinguals from similar socioeconomic backgrounds, bilingual children scored markedly higher in both verbal and nonverbal intelligence (Peal and Lambert, 1962). Other studies of bilingual Welsh and Jewish children in London and New York City showed either no retardation or slight superiority on intelligence test scores when compared to otherwise similar monolingual children (Arsenian, 1945). A possible explanation is that bilinguals may develop greater flexibility in thinking because they are constantly switching from one language track to another. Thus, they approach problems with two sets of hypotheses and develop unique conceptualizations beyond the scope of most monolinguals.

Socioeconomic Factors

The evidence for the relationship between socioeconomic levels and intelligence test scores is fairly clear-cut. The higher the socioeconomic membership level of the child the higher the intelligence test scores tend to be, and the lower the membership level of the child the lower the intelligence test scores also tend to be. Socioeconomic level is usually determined by such factors as family income, father's occupation, cost of the home, and neighborhood characteristics. The usual correlations between measures of parental socioeconomic levels and children's intelligence test scores are low to moderate and range from about +.30 to +.50. The magnitude of the correlation is given by the number. For example, a correlation of +.50 means that when we know the social index of a group of parents, we can predict about 25 per cent of their children's intelligence test scores *on the average.* If we wish to account for the remaining 75 per cent of the intelligence test scores, we must examine many other factors such as motivation of the children and their parents for school success, quality of education, and personality characteristics.

Individuals, regardless of their socioeconomic status, who plan to be parents should consider the word *average* to be of primary importance when evaluating the correlation between their social status and the partially predicted intelligence-test scores of their offspring. Indicators of social status provide rough estimates at best, and no group defined by social status can be considered homogeneous. In addition to the well-known individual differences to be found in any social group, the present measures of social class ignore many important qualities and subtleties of home life that may have significant bearing on intellectual functioning and potential. However, in view of the finding that lower socioeconomic groups obtain lower average scores on intelligence tests than higher social classes, future parents with low membership status should take more care to provide their children with a wide variety of different and stimulating environments.

In summary, it is presently impossible to assign specific weights to the roles of heredity and environment in determining intellectual development. Intelligence tests do not in themselves permit us to separate what is the result of innate capacity and what is the result of environmental influences. The nurture-nature issue is further complicated when the spiral of racial, social, linguistic, and cultural differences is introduced. Until new research methodologies succeed in separating all of these interacting forces into their appropriate compartments of responsibility, the individual parent, regardless of ethnic, racial, and social class, can favorably facilitate the intellectual growth of his children by avoiding the effects of negative prophecies.

The Life
Cycle

AFFECTIVE DOMAIN

We have all heard sad and shocking tales about bizarre behavior and tragic acts committed by individuals who were reared in affectionless homes. To a certain extent, stories such as these place an undue emphasis on the unusual; the vast majority of people who were raised under emotionally deprived conditions turn out to be "normal." In this text, however, we are not exclusively concerned with the "normal" (i.e. average) individual, but with the "supernormal" individual, the more fully human person.

There can be no doubt that the newborn infant has a much greater potential, and a much greater chance to develop this potential, if he is born into an emotionally stable home. Thus, the emotional relationship that exists within and between parents *before* conception and during pregnancy is one of the major variables that affects the newborn throughout his life.

Transition into Parenthood

Think about it for awhile and you will begin to sense the magnitude of adjustment and mutual growth as two very unique individuals (not only differing in psychological and biological makeup but in many cases differing in family sociological background as related to such important variables as social class, ethnicity, father's occupation, income level, as well as religion) decide to sign a contract to live together for a very long time (usually the rest of their lives, at least in our society).

Thus, it seems only natural that a newly married couple will go through a period of growth and development together that involves such areas of human relationship as sexual behavior, monetary decision making, kinship relationships, family planning, and particularly emotional relationships involving the full range of human feelings: joy, depression, love, hate, anger, compassion, and altruism. Many other areas of mutual growth are further explored in our chapter on young adulthood. For now, our emphasis is on the importance of the emotional relationship between husband and wife prior to conception.

One of the major transitions that occurs in life is that from being married to conceiving and having your first child. For many couples this is a time of joy, excitement, and eager anticipation. It is also, for some, a period of crisis, fear, worry, and a strain of the shifting role responsibilities for both the husband and the wife. A number of studies have found that many couples suffer a severe crisis at the beginning of pregnancy.

LeMasters (1957) found that 83 per cent of the couples that he interviewed indicated a profound disturbance in their marital relationship during the months following conception of their firstborn.

In interpreting his results, LeMasters suggests that:

1. Maybe parenthood instead of marriage is one of the most fantasized areas of life.
2. That schools and other institutions do not properly prepare you for the role of parents.
3. That one possible element in the crisis may be the fact that a two-person group seems to function more efficiently and easier than a three-person group.
4. That parenthood (not marriage) may mark the beginnings of maturity.

The Preconception Stage

229

5. That the degree of crisis to the arrival of the first child may only be the precipitating event, and that the emotional interactions and reactions to other stress *prior* to the arrival may be equally or more important than the event itself. (pp. 354–355).

Although more recent research indicates that the incidence of marital crisis may not be as high as LeMasters originally thought, there seems no doubt that for many couples the emotional impact of adjusting to the impending role of parents is high indeed.

Rossi (1968) in a highly creative analysis of the transition to parenthood also believes that it is a more demanding and abrupt transition period than either getting married or finding a satisfactory occupation. She specifically cites the following factors that add to the transitional problems during this time:

1. Cultural pressure on women to procreate as part of their female role.
2. Conception is not always a voluntary act. As Rossi puts it, "The inception of a pregnancy, unlike the engagement, is not always a voluntary decision, for it may be the unintended consequence of a sexual act that was recreative in intent rather than procreative" (p. 30).
3. Pregnancy cannot be easily terminated as can an engagement.
4. The extensive use of contraceptives allows newly married couples a period of time to make adjustments and for both to work. This early egalitarian relationship between husband and wife may allow a couple to work together more when children begin arriving.
5. Parents cannot divorce their children. As Rossi puts it, "We can have ex-spouses and ex-jobs but not ex-children" (p. 33).
6. Education for parenthood is most often insufficient.
7. The nine-months-pregnancy period is really not time enough to prepare a couple for parenthood.
8. The role of "motherhood" is abrupt: that is, you "graduate" with your "degree" at the end of the nine-months period, but you also begin your full time responsibilities as soon as the baby is delivered. Most "graduates" have a period of "on-the-job training" before they are given full responsibility.
9. There are few guidelines for becoming successful parents.

Social Class Variables. Jacoby (1969) studied some of the social-class factors that affect prenatal marital crises among the middle class and concludes the following:

1. *Middle-class expectation* standards may outstrip the income available for child rearing. Although middle-class parents have high expectations for their children (as high as upper-class parents), the financial burdens of parenthood often impose restrictions on their ability to provide advantages for their children. Children often create less of a problem for lower-class parents because the expectations and income of the parents are both low.
2. *Middle-class women place less intrinsic value on having children.* A working-class woman generally views the role of wife-mother as the most satisfactory way of increasing her status among her acquaintances. Middle-class women tend to use their occupational roles for this purpose.
3. *The principal sources of gratification for middle-class women are located outside the family rather than within.* The middle-class wife tends to develop

an existence outside the family, and the impending presence of a young child may be a source of frustration to her.

4. *Middle-class mothers are less experienced in child care.* Since middle-class women usually come from smaller families, they have less opportunity to observe small children and thus may experience some anxiety in this regard.

Building Marital Supports. A married couple can do much to reduce the probability of a "major crisis" in their lives *before* the child arrives if they are willing to prepare for this by building some supports together. These supports will help hold the relationship together under some of the stress and pressure of not only the birth of their first child but many other stresses and strains that are a part of living in the modern world: unemployment, death, divorce, temporary separation because of a job or military service, severe emotional or physical illness, and the like. That is, we believe that much can be done to prevent the problems associated with crisis in a marriage if the couple is willing to become involved with each other in growth and actualization.

Let us examine a few models (some of which we have already presented in earlier chapters) that we believe offer directions. They certainly do not offer step-by-step directions for a successful marriage—this is something that we believe a couple has to work out together—but they do offer an overall framework upon which a couple may build the kind of supports for growth toward a "self-actualizing family."

Basic Need Gratification. The family is one of the major institutions devised by man to meet the many human needs that must be fulfilled if he is not only to survive but if he is ever to reach some of the more important levels of human existence through self-actualization. Thus, any newly formed family unit must begin with planning for building supports that allow a family to become emotionally free of one of the most terrifying of all emotional experiences: the fear of not being able to provide food, shelter, and clothing for its family members. Fortunately, in this country most of us can provide this support to a relatively secure degree. Unfortunately, far too many families in our country still go to bed hungry or in doubt about their opportunities for jobs to provide the basic necessities for their children. In too many parts of the world, parents still have to make such humanly degrading decisions as to which member of their family they shall let starve to death in order to keep the other members alive to beg for food.

Safety and Security. Another emotional support a family provides to its members is a sense of security and safety. Husbands and wives provide this sense by establishing an atmosphere of emotional maturity and rationality in their daily interactions. Living in a community and nation where the basic dignity of human life is given prime consideration certainly helps build the emotional supports consisting of basic feelings of security.

Love. Any family can withstand tremendous amounts of stress and strain provided it has built a strong support based on mutual and mature love as well as a strong sense of belonging. Thus, any couple must begin to develop some of the dimensions of mature love (as defined by Erich Fromm) mentioned earlier (in Chapter 10).

As you remember, a prerequisite of mature love is self-love. That is, you must learn to know yourself, respect the uniqueness within yourself, and truly care enough about yourself, as well as assume responsibility for your own growth and actualization. Once you can learn to relate to yourself in these ways, you then can truly relate to your spouse in a maturely loving manner. You can also effectively develop the other forms of love toward your son or daughter (motherly and fatherly love) as well as your fellow man (brotherly love) more easily.

Self-Esteem. Another support that gives one an ability to withstand stress and even failures in life and marriage consists of those feelings of success and self-worth that are often referred to as self-esteem. A person who feels good about himself as a person, indeed, one who has learned to "love" himself in a mature manner can meet the pressures involved in the newly acquired marital roles of husband and wife and the future roles as mother and father.

Building self-esteem or a positive self-concept is a lifelong process for which many of the seeds are planted early in infancy and childhood (as seen in the following chapters). But a couple who come from family backgrounds built on "mature love" tend to have much more to build on.

Success experiences by the husband and wife in their schooling and/or job experiences also give one additional feelings of self-esteem. Developing social competencies with friends and/or relatives also builds self-confidence and feelings of self-worth. Groups of various kinds often help one learn to cope with interpersonal relationships and responsibilities. Hobbies of various kinds offer couples a chance to experience expertise and feelings of personal competency and success.

Values. A couple who know how they feel about certain value questions, as far as what is important and unimportant in their lives, are in a far better position to act in a more personally gratifying and often more mature manner than a couple that isn't sure where they stand on issues.

Many couples develop values around religious orientations, and others rely on their philosophical positions. These orientations may not be spelled out in detail and inscribed on a plaque that is hung in the living room, but they are implicit in how the married couple lives. These orientations may change with time; however, they do form the basis upon which the couple can later build and evolve into foundations and decisions. Many of the philosophical viewpoints discussed in Chapter 3 are indirectly related to many modern-day family philosophical views.

Self-Actualizing Family Supports. Many supports are provided to us in the "self-actualizing" model of the late Abraham Maslow. It seems that a couple who have developed their relationship to include many of the dimensions of the self-actualizing person will be in a far healthier position to handle family crises and stress in all its manifestations.

The characteristics of the positive self-concept—acceptance of others, more profound interpersonal relationships, autonomy, and basically a democratic personality structure—we believe, will allow a couple the freedom both in their inter- and intrapersonal relationships to continue their personal growth and yet to be flexible enough in their lives to handle the vast changes and stresses that modern-day families often experience. Again, many of the roots of self-actualization begin to grow in infancy and early childhood; yet many of the suggestions that we have provided in the Developing Positive Models and Implications sections of the text provide additional ideas for a couple to develop more of these characteristics in their relationship.

SOCIAL DOMAIN

Decisions involved in family planning (e.g., how many children to have, when to begin to have them, and so on) are not purely the result of a wife sitting down at the dinner table one night and saying to her husband (as wives do in many television and movie stories): "Darling, I think that we will be having a 'little visitor' in the house in nine months!"

Such a decision rests on a host of past, present, as well as future factors. Let us examine some of these now.

Family Planning *

The major considerations that come into play in family planning decisions stem from two areas. First, both the husband and the wife bring to the decision their own family backgrounds, and second, each is developing his own individual personality, interests, and values. Thus, it is difficult to predict with a high degree of accuracy how a married couple who were reared in different homes, whose fathers had different jobs and different incomes, and whose educational and ethnic backgrounds are different might make certain family planning decisions.

Social Change. Another influence on the married couple in the preconception stage as they begin family planning strategies has to do with the social situation at the time. As we mentioned earlier, in the United States, the last few generations in particular have experienced unprecedented amounts of social change during a relatively short period of time.

Thus, any couple must take some of the realities of the day into account in their family planning discussions. Some important considerations for any couple today have to do with some of the great social issues and trends that are being discussed with ever increasing frequency. Some of these include: the "population explosion" issue, the working wife, family mobility, and urbanization.

Population Issues. Most young married couples in their discussions of family planning today are somewhat aware of the question of the population increase and its related human problems. In science and health classes during school as well as in newspapers and magazines and on other mass media such as television and radio, this issue has been discussed with increasing emphasis.

The entire question of population expansion and control is a broad issue that has implications in areas such as religion, politics, war, as well as economics and the psychology and sociology of the individual. We are certainly aware of many persons who are for and against any form of

* It should be pointed out that there are many other things that a young married couple do besides talk about having children during their first few years of marriage. Our purpose in this section is to focus on those social domain factors related to the preconception stage. These other important factors (personality differences, financial problems, religious adjustments, are growth toward mutual self-actualization) involved in marital adjustment are considered briefly after we go through the process of growing up: as the person goes through the various stages of dating during adolescence, courtship, and finally marriage (if the person chooses to marry) during your adulthood.

population control, feeling that this is a personal issue that should not be left up to governments to legislate. Without expanding our discussion at this point, we would like to point out that our major purpose for including a discussion of population control here is that we, too, believe that it is a personal choice and that it should be included as an area of discussion for any young couple planning a family in this day and age.

The Changing American Family. Since the family plays a major part in helping prepare a newborn to live in a particular society, to play the roles required of him, and to develop some of the values considered appropriate, it is therefore one of the most important variables for the young married couple to consider as they contemplate parenthood. Since social change is also having an impact on the family (as well as all the established institutions in our country), let us examine some of the patterns or trends that seem to be influencing not only the structure but the functions of the modern American family.

The decline of the family as a basic institution within our society is being forecast by a number of scholars. They cite as evidence the high divorce rate (one marriage in every four ending in divorce with the rate of divorce in some densely populated communities running as high as 70 per cent), the falling birth rate (a decline from 30.1 live births per thousand population in 1910 to 17.7 births per thousand in 1969), and the increasing problem of teen-aged runaways (over 500,000 in 1970). In addition, increased family mobility, urbanization, the changing role of women, and other factors have all produced changes in traditional family functions.

The Role of Government. The impact of the institution of government on family planning is indirect in this country. Family planning efforts in many other countries, however, are more direct, with many governments not only providing birth control information but contraceptive devices and sterilization techniques as well. All of these efforts relate to the major concern for the population explosion.

In this country, the federal and local governments through their various welfare and child-assistance programs, day-care operations, and finding of basic child-oriented research projects exert a degree of control over the potential parent's attitude about the future of his children. The individual who feels comfortable with his relationship to his government, who feels that the governmental process is responsive to his needs and mindful of his child's future needs is more likely to give positive consideration to family planning.

More and more courses in high school are concerned with family living. Indeed, many school districts have elaborate courses in "sex education" or "family life," where such topics as premarital intercourse, masturbation, contraceptives, marriage and divorce, unwanted pregnancies, and abortion are freely studied and discussed.

Although there is little evidence as to the long-term effects of these courses, they seem to provide a model for a more knowledgeable approach to marriage and family planning.

Future Considerations. One future consideration for any couple should be what they want out of life. They should do this before they begin conceiving children. In other words, they should determine what is important and unimportant to them and how do children and rearing a family fit into their values.

We believe that many couples in their family planning are really the victims of several myths about children. These couples are, therefore, very unrealistic about children. In many other instances when they operate on false information and make a mistake, they can do something about it and start all over again. With children, one cannot "send them back" as you would a pair of pants that didn't fit. We believe, as well as LeMasters (1970), that an exposure of this folklore will give young couples some ideas to think about individually and to discuss together. Table 13–1 summarizes the common folklore and some reasons why it is considered folklore and

TABLE 13–1
A SUMMARY OF SOME COMMON FOLKLORE ABOUT PARENTHOOD *

Folk Belief	Analysis of Belief	Supporting References
1. Rearing children is fun.	Rearing children is hard work. Rearing children involves great responsibility, takes a great deal of ability, and once started you can't stop.	Ask any parent
2. Children are sweet and cute.	They are sometimes, but they are also demanding, crabby, and even mean at times.	LeMasters (1970) Green (1946)
3. Children will turn out well, if they have good parents.	Usually this is true, but children are unique; society is so complex that children are influenced by a variety of sources.	Indirect evidence (from children of famous persons who have not always turned out well). Problem in defining criterion "turn out well."
4. Girls are harder to rear than boys.	Girls are supervised more closely than boys (because of parents' concern of premarital pregnancy) but, boys are prone to more serious problems such as alcoholism, approaching marriage in unrealistic manner, greater chance of failure as marriage partners. Women are "superior" to men in many biological and psychological respects.	Komarovsky (1950) Burgess and Wallin (1953) Montagu (1968)
5. Child rearing is easier to-day.	It probably is much more difficult because of rapid technological change, the varied roles mothers must play (worker, cab driver, social groups); also, changing functions of the family, and awareness of psychological responsibility put on parents to rear children free from neurosis.	Frieden (1963) LeMasters (1957) Lewis (1968) Patai (1967)

* Compiled from LeMasters, 1970.

Folk Belief	Analysis of Belief	Supporting References
6. There are no bad children—only bad parents.	Children today are often influenced greatly by other factors such as the peer group, mass media, siblings, and education.	Lerner (1957) Brim (1959)
7. That two parents are always better than one.	One-parent families, although they do pose problems for children, are not always predisposed to pathology. More research is needed.	Kadushin (1968) Bell (1967)
8. That love is all a parent has to give the child.	Love (a minimal level) is a prerequisite, but this must be supplemented with knowledge, insight, and self-control.	Bettelheim (1950)
9. That all married couples should have children.	Biological parenthood does not automatically mean that a couple has other qualities needed to be an effective parent. There is too much pressure on couples to begin families early. Couples with no or one child rated their marriages higher (in terms of compatibility) than did couples with two or more children.	Bell (1967) Burgess and Cottrell (1939) Burgess and Wallin (1953)
10. That children improve a marriage.	The rate of divorce among childless couples is almost double that for couples with children. Thus, children seem to stabilize a marriage. But, there is little or no evidence to show that children *per se* improve a relationship between husband and wife. More studies are needed.	Cavan (1969)

also provides additional references for those of you who wish to explore this more fully.

IMPLICATIONS

UNDERSTANDING YOURSELF AND OTHERS

When the myriad of factors that interact prior to conception are considered, we may be inclined to favor a deterministic philosophy of life. It seems that so much has already been determined that the conceptus-to-be will have very few degrees of freedom for possible future change. The conceptus-to-be will arrive on a prearranged stage, with previously selected actors, to mingle with a preselected audience, to play roles for which he did not audition.

The Life Cycle

As adults we cannot change what was, but in understanding what was we can shed additional light on our past and present conditions. Through

236

changes in our present attitudes achieved through greater understanding of the past, we can perhaps implement changes in the future management of our lives. At the same time our better understanding of our preconceptual conditions may provide us with some insights into the behaviors of other people in light of their particular circumstances.

In addition to uncovering the "ghosts" from the past that set the tone for our own existence, it may help to magnify their importance for creating the best possible stage for our own children-to-be, which is the basic objective for the study of this chapter.

LIVING AND WORKING WITH CHILDREN, ADOLESCENTS, AND ADULTS

We believe that parents-to-be, deep in their hearts, want to do the best possible job. To do so they want and need guidance, instruction, and reassurance. The ideal time for learning how to be a parent, for learning about the most complex task known to man—the care and guidance of human actualization—is prior to pregnancy. During pregnancy, and particularly after birth, the focus of attention and time shifts from the parents to the growing child, and it becomes increasingly more difficult to play the dual roles of teacher and learner at the same time.

Parents who are knowledgeable about the different stages of life from the peridevelopmental stage to adulthood are better prepared to anticipate and to meet graciously the demands, joys, and exigencies of parenthood. They are better prepared to accept the fact that they cannot do it all perfectly at every stage of development for every child, and that there will not always be a match between their needs and those of their children. Informed parents are also better prepared to learn more, to seek help during difficult times, and to know when to "hold back" in order to let their child grow more toward independence.

Such parents, being more aware of the importance of prepregnancy needs, are more likely to prepare themselves biologically, psychologically, and sociologically. During this period they are more likely to build emotional competencies and supports, to ensure proper nutrition and physical health, to avoid the inception of negative self-fulfilling prophecies, and to better understand how the institutions of their particular society will help them in some ways to prepare their child for the world of tomorrow and for self-actualization.

DEVELOPING POSITIVE MODELS

Before conception, ideally, there should be two self-actualizing parents who have learned to live together while still maintaining their own integrity as separate individuals and who reside in a society whose primary priority is the development of self-actualizing persons. Perhaps, then, we could specify with considerable confidence the specifications for ideal models for the preconception period. For the time being we will have to imagine what the models would be from the bits and pieces that are now available.

This we know: we want the kind of preconceptual education and programs that will maximize the chances for each conceptus to meet successfully the challenges of pregnancy, birth, and development. We assume that a strong early foundation will increase enormously the chances for later

The Preconception Stage

237

successful growth at each stage of development. These are the tentative specifications for the models:

Holistic Framework. A state of optimal health in one domain increases the likelihood of similar states of health in the other domains because of the holistic nature of human functioning. Thus the benefits achieved by extra efforts in one domain are enhanced considerably beyond the original effort because of their effects on the remaining domains. On the other hand, negligence or misfortune in one domain negatively affects the entire scope of human growth.

Affective Domain. The state of mature love between two parents is the result of a long-term learning process. Ideally, future parents must work for its development prior to serious thoughts about parenthood.

Biological Domain. The fetus' total environment is the mother's body. Care for the health of the mother's body begins the day she was born.

Cognitive Domain. Preconceptualization attitudes that include faith and confidence in the conceptus' future well-being will tend to increase the odds that positive self-fulfilling prophecies will result.

Social Domain. Cooperation, support, and guidance should be actively solicited from private and public segments of society especially from the members of the immediate and extended families. For example, other children if any, in-laws, friends, and employers should be involved in the early phases of planning for parenthood so that they will be more likely to become active partners during and after pregnancy.

CHAPTER REFERENCES

ADELSON, J. What generation gap? *New York Times Magazine*, Jan. 18, 1970.

AMERICAN MEDICAL ASSOCIATION. "Clinical genetics" gain notice. *The Journal of the American Medical Association*, September 28, 1970, 13:213.

ARSENIAN, S. Bilingualism in the post-war world. *Psychological Bulletin*, 1945, 42:65–86.

BELL, R. B. *Marriage and the family interaction.* Homewood, Ill.: Dorsey, 1967.

BETTELHEIM, B. *Love is not enough.* New York: Free Press, 1950.

BRENDA, C. E. *The child with mongolism.* New York: Grune, 1960.

BRIM, O. G. *Education for child rearing.* New York: Russell Sage, 1959.

BROWN, W. J. Current status of syphilis in the United States. *Public Health Report*, 1960, 75:990–993.

BURGESS, E. W. and L. S. COTTRELL. *Predicting success or failure in marriage.* Englewood Cliffs, N. J.: Prentice Hall, 1939.

—— and P. WALLIN. *Engagement and marriage.* Philadelphia: Lippincott, 1953.

CAVAN, RUTH. *The American family,* New York: Thomas Y. Crowell, 1969.

CENTERWALL, W. R. and S. A. CENTERWALL. *Phenylketonuria.* U. S. Dept. of Health, Education, and Welfare, Children's Bureau, 1961.

COLEMAN, J. S. et al. *Equality of educational opportunity,* U. S. Dept. of Health, Education, and Welfare. Washington, D.C.: U. S. Govt. Printing Office, 1966.

DARCY, F. B. Bilingualism and measurement of intelligence: review of a decade of research. *Journal of Genetic Psychology*, 1963, 103:255–282.

FLEMING, E. S. and R. G. ANTTONEN. Do teachers get what they expect? The self-fulfilling prophecy revisited. *Childhood Education*, May 1971, 431–452.

FRIEDAN, B. *The feminine mystique.* New York: Norton, 1963.

FROST, J. L. and B. L. PAYNE. Hunger in America: scope and consequences.

Nutrition and intellectual growth in children, Bulletin 25-A. Washington D.C.: Association for Childhood Education International, 1968, 5–18.

GAVER, J. R. *Birth defects and your baby.* New York: Lancer, 1972.

GREEN, W. The middle-class male child and neurosis. *American Sociological Review,* 1946, 11:31–41.

HAMPTON, M. C. et al. Calorie and nutrient intakes of teen-agers. *Journal American Dieticians Association,* 1967, 50:385.

ILLSLEY, R. The sociological study of reproduction and its outcome. In S. A. Richardson and A. F. Guttmacher (eds.), *Childbearing—its social and psychological aspects.* Baltimore: Williams & Wilkins, 1967.

JACOBY, A. P. Transition to parenthood: a reassessment. *Journal of Marriage and the Family,* Nov. 1969, pp. 720–727.

JOINT COMMISSION OF MENTAL HEALTH. In *Crisis in child mental health.* New York: Harper, 1970.

KADUSHIN, A. Single-parent adoptions. (Unpublished paper) Madison, Wis.: School of Social Work, University of Wisconsin, 1968.

KAGAN, J. The concept of intelligence. *The Humanist,* 1972, 32:1, 7–8.

KENNEDY, W., V. VAN DERIET and J. WHITE. A normative sample of intelligence and achievement of Negro elementary school children in the United States. *Monograph of the Society for Research in Child Development,* 1963, 28: no. 6.

KLINEBERG, O. *Negro intelligence and selective migration.* New York: Columbia U. P., 1935.

———. Race and I. Q. *The Courier,* Nov. 1971, 5–32.

KNOBLOCH, H. and B. PASAMANICH. Exogenous factors in infant intelligence. *Pediatrics,* 1960.

KOMAROVSKY, M. Functional analysis of sex roles. *American Sociological Review,* 1950, 15:508–516.

LEE, E. S. Negro intelligence and selective migration: A Philadelphia test of the Klineberg hypothesis. *American Social Review,* 1951, 16:227–233.

LEMASTERS, E. E. Parenthood as crisis. *Marriage and Family Living,* 1957, 19: 351–360.

———. *Parents in modern America.* Homewood, Ill.: Dorsey, 1970.

LERNER, M. *America as a civilization.* New York: Simon and Schuster, 1957.

LEWIS, E. C. *Developing woman's potential.* Ames, Ia.: Iowa State U. P., 1968.

LIGHT, R. J. Intelligence and genes. *The Humanist.* 1972, 22:1, 12–13.

LIVINGSTON, S. K. What influences malnutrition? *Journal Nutrition Education* Summer, 1971, 3:1, 18.

Marihuana & Drug Abuse. Washington D.C.: U. S. Govt. Printing Office, March, 1972.

METROPOLITAN LIFE INSURANCE COMPANY. Patterns of venereal disease morbidity in recent years. *Statistical Bulletin,* 1969, 50:5–7.

MONTAGU, A. *The natural superiority of women.* New York: Macmillan, 1968.

MONTAGU, M. F. A. *Prenatal influences.* Springfield, Ill.: Thomas, 1962.

THE NATIONAL COUNCIL ON ILLEGITIMACY. *Unmarried parents and their children.* New York, New York, 1968.

THE NATIONAL FOUNDATION-MARCH OF DIMES. *Birth defects.* White Plains, N. Y.

———. *Facts.* White Plains, N. Y.

PASAMANICH, B. and H. KNOBLOCH. Retrospective studies on the epidemiology of reproductive casuality: old and new. *Merrill-Palmer quarterly,* 1966, 12: 7–26.

PATAI, R. (ed.). *Women in the modern world.* New York: Free Press, 1967.

PEAL, E. and W. LAMBERT. The relation of bilingualism to intelligence. *Psychological Monographs: General and Applied,* no. 546, 76(27), 1962.

The Preconception Stage

PENROSE, L. S. Mongolian idiocy and maternal age. *Annals of the N. Y. academy of sociology,* 1954, 57:494–502.

Prenatal care. Publication no. 4. Washington, D.C.: Children's Bureau, 1970.

PRESIDENT'S COMMISSION ON POPULATION GROWTH AND THE AMERICAN FUTURE. As in *Los Angeles Times,* May 10, 1972.

ROSENTHAL, R. and L. JACOBSON. *Pygmalion in the classroom.* New York: Holt, 1968.

ROSSI, A. S. Transition to parenthood. *Journal of Marriage and the Family,* Feb. 1968, 26–39.

SEBALD, H. *Adolescence: a sociological analysis.* New York: Appleton, 1968.

SHAW, K. N. F., R. KOCH, S. SCHILD, N. RAGSDALE, K. FISCHLER and P. B. ACOSTA. *The clinical team looks at phenylketonuria.* U. S. Dept. of Health, Education, and Welfare, Children's Bureau, 1961.

SMART, M. S. and R. C. SMART. *Children development and relationships.* New York: Macmillan, 1972.

RECOMMENDED FURTHER READING

BRICKLIN, B and P. M. BRIKIN. *Strong family, strong child.* New York: Delacorte, 1970.

CHRISTENSEN, H. T. (ed.). *Handbook of marriage and the family.* Chicago: Rand McNally, 1964.

GREY, ALAN L. (ed.). *Class and personality in society,* New York: Atherton, 1969.

GUTTMACHER, A. F. *Pregnancy and birth.* New York: Viking, 1962.

HESS, R. D. and G. HANDEL. *Family worlds: a psychological approach to family life.* Chicago: U. of Chicago, 1959.

HODGES, HAROLD. *Social stratification.* New York: Harper, 1971.

KEPHART, W. M. *The family, society, and the individual,* 3rd ed. Boston: Houghton, 1972.

LANE, CLAYTON W. *Permanence and change in social class.* New York: Harper, 1971.

LOURIA, D. B. *The drug scene.* New York: McGraw-Hill, 1968.

UDRY, J. R. *The social context of marriage.* Philadelphia: Lippincott, 1971.

The Life
Cycle

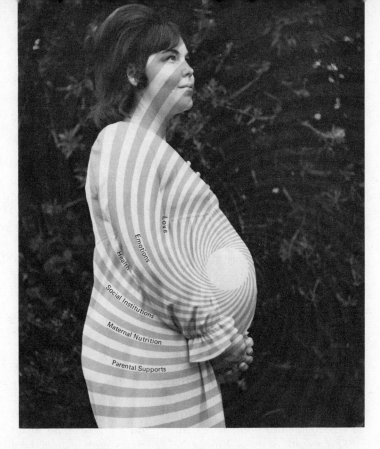

Love
Emotions
Health
Social Institutions
Maternal Nutrition
Parental Supports

The Prenatal and Neonatal Stages

Prelude

Basic Theory and Research
  Biological Domain
    Developmental Stages
    Prenatal Influences
  Cognitive Domain
    Early Learning
  Affective Domain
    Affective Dimensions of the
      Birth Process
    Maternal-Neonate-Affective
      Interactions

Social Domain
  Institutional Factors
  Social Class and Childbearing
Implications
  Understanding Yourself and
    Others
  Living and Working with Chil-
    dren, Adolescents, and Adults
  Developing Positive Models

PRELUDE

To CONTINUE our metaphor of the flower garden, the "seed bed" has now been prepared and the "seed" planted. This chapter concerns itself with the further care of the seed bed, that is, the environmental conditions that play such an important role in contributing to the growing and developing fetus.

Prior to conception, a couple will hopefully have developed their relationship to such an extent that there will be sufficient supports for withstanding the stresses produced during the nine months of pregnancy. Although much more research is needed in the area of the emotional life of the wife and husband during the prenatal period, the evidence is quite strong to convince one that the emotional reaction of the wife during pregnancy can have an effect upon both the experience of the pregnancy and the developing fetus.

BASIC THEORY AND RESEARCH

BIOLOGICAL DOMAIN

This section discusses the developmental sequence in the biological domain. As with the preconception stage, the major focus is on presenting information to minimize problems and defects and to maximize optimal health. During this critical period of time a human being is more susceptible to environmental influences than he will be ever again in his life.

The growth of every human being begins with a special cell, the fertilized ovum. Although the diameter of the ovum is approximately 1/175 of an inch and its weight is about one 20-millionth of an ounce, all the genetic potentialities for the complete development of a human being are contained within it (Corner, 1944). From this microscopically small cell, a baby composed of about 200 billion cells of different kinds will develop during the next nine months. This striking phenomenon of growth is common in all human beings. Montagu (1962) put it this way:

> The total population of the earth at the present time is 3,000,000,000. Allowing an ovum and a sperm to each individual as responsible for his existence, we have a grand total of 6,000,000,000 germ cells. This number could be contained in two and a half quart bottles. The spermatozoa could all fit into an aspirin tablet with plenty of room to spare, while the chromosomes of ova and spermatozoa, the actual bearers of the hereditary particles, the genes, could all fit into less than half an aspirin tablet! In short, the developmental materials of the whole human species living at the present moment could be contained within the space of half an aspirin!

Developmental Stages

The prenatal period can be divided into three major stages. First comes the ovum period, then the embryonic, and then the fetal. The normal period for development of a full-term baby is approximately 280 days although it is possible for a baby to survive after having spent only 180 days in the mother's body.

The Life
Cycle

242

The Ovum Stage. The ovum period, which lasts about a week, begins with the fertilized egg, called a zygote. The first cellular process, a single *multiplication,* is completed within three days when the zygote has divided itself into two smaller but identical cells. From then on there is rapid multiplication in the form of geometric progression, one cell divides into two, then into four, and so on. On the fifth day the second cellular process, movement, begins. The cells begin to organize themselves into clusters. For example, some cells group together to start the formation of the placenta, a permeable membrane and filter that will be created between the fetus and uterus, while other cells begin to form the embryo.

Multiplication and movement together set the stage for the third cellular process of *differentiation.* Differentiation involves the development of specialized cells for nerves, muscles, and bones that, eventually, will form the complex organs and systems of the body. The process of differentiation, which is just beginning at the ovum stage, is difficult to explain and is not fully understood as yet. An interesting question is how can identical cells produce specialized cells with different structures and functions? An important (and, possibly the key) answer lies in the interaction of the genes with the cellular environment. As emphasized in Chapter 6, the end-products of the continuous chain of development are the results of the interplay of heredity and environment. Possibly the same genes interacting with different cellular (environmental) conditions produce the tremendous varieties of cell structure.

During this first week or so the ovum has been moving from the Fallopian tube, in which the sperm united with the ovum, to the uterus (womb). It is now about the size of a pinhead, but it has used up all the food supply contained within the female egg. The ovum must now find a new supply of food or perish. By the tenth day the ovum implants itself deeply into the wall of the uterus where it will receive nourishment from the mother and where it will remain until birth. The process of fertilization, the movement of the ovum, and its implantation into the uterus is graphically depicted in Figure 14–1.

The Embryonic Period. With the physical unification of the ovum to the

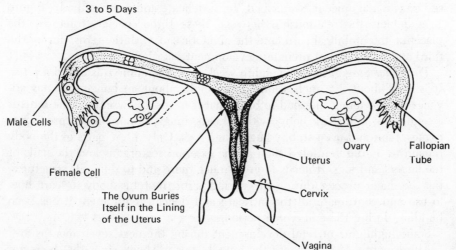

FIG. 14–1.
The process of fertilization and movement of the ovum through the Fallopian tube into the uterus.

(Adapted by permission from Sigmund Grollman, The Human Body, *2nd ed. Copyright © Sigmund Grollman, 1969. New York: Macmillan Publishing Co., Inc.)*

243

mother's uterine wall, the embryonic period begins. This period will last until the eighth or ninth week of uterine life. Growth is the major process during this stage whereas in the ovum period the major process was increased complexity. By the end of this period, the embryo will be almost two inches long and weigh about two-thirds of an ounce. This growth represents a 2 million per cent increase in size since fertilization.

In addition to rapid growth, the embryonic period includes the beginnings of three structures essential for protection and nourishment of the embryo: the placenta, the umbilicus, and the amnionic sac. The *placenta* develops at the point of implantation of the ovum to the uterine wall. This vascular organ contains channels for the exchange of fluids, water-soluble substances, and water-transportable substances. The incoming maternal blood contains nourishment, oxygen, antigens (substances needed to produce antibodies for destroying harmful bacteria), and hormones, whereas the outgoing blood essentially contains waste products. Because there is no direct connection between the maternal and embryonic bloodstreams, the two-way transmission of material occurs by osmosis, diffusion, filtration, or engulfing.

Vital to the welfare of the embryo and later of the fetus is the fact that the placenta also serves as an effective protective filter. Under normal circumstances no bacteria can pass through the placenta; however, certain viruses that can produce defects, illness, and death are able to pass through the placenta. The consequences of these viruses are discussed in some detail subsequently in this chapter.

The *umbilical cord* is a tubelike vascular (blood vessels) organ that connects the growing placenta to the abdominal wall of the embryo. Its length, which varies from ten to twenty-two inches, and its flexibility permit considerable activity during the fetal period. The maternal-embryonic exchanges occur through this ropelike structure. The *amniotic sac,* a nonvascular transparent membrane, completely encloses the embryo except at the point where the umbilical cord projects itself into the placenta. The amniotic sac protects the embryo from possible friction against the placenta and the uterine wall. Furthermore, it contains its own fluid that acts as a buffer against jars and shocks; it is an insulator against loud noises, and it serves as a magnificent "water bed" for a delicate and growing body. Figure 14–2 depicts the relationship between these three special structures, the placenta, the umbilical cord, and the amniotic sac, with the fetus, during the third and final stage of prenatal development.

The Fetal Stage. After the eighth week or so the embryo is called a *fetus.* It is now about 2½ inches long and weighs about an ounce, but has advanced so far along the road to birth that it needs a new name. The fetus is essentially a miniature baby, with a heart, lungs, brain, spinal cord, sense organs, face, and even stubby fingers and toes. Only a few parts of the body remain to be differentiated such as the external sex organs and the nails of the fingers and toes. It needs to grow much more and to refine its structures, but the major process during this period is for the fetus' body to learn how to use and coordinate all the intricate and delicate equipment it has been building during the embryonic period.

Some highlights of fetal development during the next seven months are:

Third month. In this month the fetus begins to shows signs that he is not only human but an individual. Distinctive physical characteristics can be observed in body shape and structures. Fetal activity increases in which

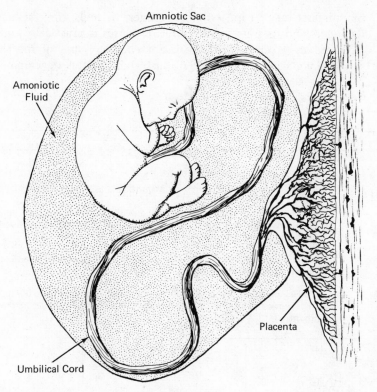

Amniotic Sac

Amoniotic
Fluid

Placenta

Umbilical Cord

individual differences can be noted. Respiratory movements have been reported, and urea has been detected in the amniotic fluid indicating kidney
functioning.

Fourth month. The fetus is now about nine inches tall, having reached
half the height it will have at birth. The entire reproductive system has
been formed. The repertoire of activities includes thumb sucking, hiccuping,
and all the reflexes found in the normal newborn infant except for vocal
responses and functional respiration. Almost all the body's surface is sensitive to tactile stimulation. For example, it will curl its fingers when its palm
is tickled and it will curl its toes when it is tickled on the soles of its feet.

Fifth month. The fetus is now about a foot long and weighs about a
pound. Its movements by the end of this period can be real kicks. Because
it is floating around in its fluid-filled sac, the fetus has marvelous ease and
variety of movements. Sometimes it lies on one side and then on the other,
sometimes it floats with its head down and sometimes with it up. By this
time the fetus may have developed favorite positions and activities. The
variability of fetal movements is marked. Some are noticeably active 75 per
cent of the time, whereas others are active only occasionally.

Seventh month. Fetuses born during this period have a fair chance for
survival but only with tender care. The fetus has already acquired some
immunities and some fat for warmth in preparation for the outside world,
and its nervous system is sufficiently developed for independent functioning.
The rate of fetal activity will increase until the final month when the snug
fit in the uterus will limit freedom of movement.

Eighth and ninth months. During this period the fetus begins to look more
and more like a full-term baby. The fetus is making the final preparations

The Prenatal
and Neonatal
Stages

for this first major trip. Its hair is longer; its nails grow beyond the tips of its fingers and toes; its repertoire of responses is practically complete.

Figure 14–3 summarizes the major characteristics of the three prenatal stages along with some pictorial illustrations of this developmental process.

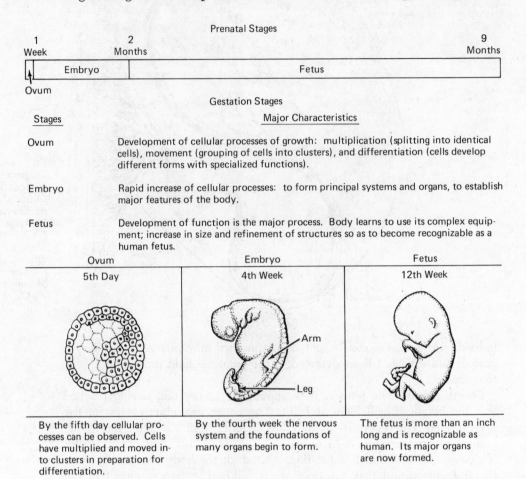

Stages	Major Characteristics
Ovum	Development of cellular processes of growth: multiplication (splitting into identical cells), movement (grouping of cells into clusters), and differentiation (cells develop different forms with specialized functions).
Embryo	Rapid increase of cellular processes: to form principal systems and organs, to establish major features of the body.
Fetus	Development of function is the major process. Body learns to use its complex equipment; increase in size and refinement of structures so as to become recognizable as a human fetus.

Ovum	Embryo	Fetus
5th Day	4th Week	12th Week
By the fifth day cellular processes can be observed. Cells have multiplied and moved into clusters in preparation for differentiation.	By the fourth week the nervous system and the foundations of many organs begin to form.	The fetus is more than an inch long and is recognizable as human. Its major organs are now formed.

FIG. 14–3. *Prenatal development.*

Preparation for Birth. Biological preparations for the birth process by both the fetus and the mother's body begin prior to the delivery day, which is usually 266 days after conception or about 280 days after the last menstrual period for a full-term baby. Up to the moment of birth, the mother's body has carried on all the vital life functions for the fetus including the provision of food, water, air, elimination, and warmth, and protection against many diseases. Although well provided for, the fetus is nevertheless making independent preparations for its own survival outside of the womb. For example, although all of the fetus' oxygen is amply provided for it from the mother's bloodstream through the placenta, the fetus has been practicing the movements of respiration. The heart, beating since about the third week of life, has been pumping blood through its circulatory system, including the as yet unfunctioning lungs. In apparent anticipation of its eventual need to react to external stimulation, the fetus by the second month will respond physically to a variety of sounds (Sontag et al., 1934). Although not ready

The Life
Cycle

to be used, the taste buds appear as early as the third month. By the seventh month the fetus' repertoire of responses is so similar to that of the newborn that if it is thrust prematurely from the womb it may be able to survive. In other words, like advanced technical systems of today, the developmental process is not just geared to meet the needs of the present time, but also to the needs of the immediate future.

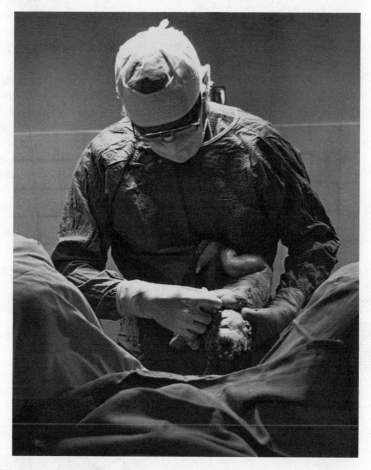

FIG. 14–4.
The moment of arrival.

The mother's body has also been making changes and adjustments in anticipation of delivery. The uterus has been contracting, even though slightly, throughout the pregnancy. During the last three months these contractions become firmer and can be felt rhythmically by the mother. The uterine cervix, the necklike exit from the uterus to the birth canal, becomes softer and flatter. The muscles and connective tissues of the pelvic area become more vascular (cushioned with blood), elastic tissues increase, and the pelvic joints become somewhat extended. All this and more takes place to make the fetus' four-inch journey a safer one.

The Birth Process. The fetus could probably benefit from the greater maturity obtainable by remaining longer in the uterus as is the case with whale, horse, and elephant fetuses, but because of the narrowness of the human birth canal and the largeness of the human head the process of birth must commence before the head becomes too large for safe passage. The

The Prenatal and Neonatal Stages

247

onset of birth itself is set off by a complex series of sequential chemical and physical interactions that are as yet not fully understood. In the first stage, there is a sharp drop in the oxygen level of the placenta followed by a decrease in its hormone, progesterone, whose function is to maintain the state of pregnancy. Now, the contractions known as "labor pains" begin to exert enormous pressure on the contents of the womb. The uterus, which in pregnancy is the largest and most powerful organ of the human body, begins to force the fetus into the birth canal. The further stretching of the cervix may cause the amniotic sac to burst and release its flow of "waters." With the opening of the cervix, the first stage of the birth process is over. The total birth process usually lasts about fourteen hours for first births and about eight hours for future ones.

The second stage usually begins with the head-first passage of the fetus into the birth canal. Fortunately the birth canal has a tremendous ability to stretch, and since the bones of the fetus' skull have not yet knit together, the head serves as a pliable instrument for widening the cervix and the vagina. During the slow passage, the fetus' body receives enormous pressure and stimulation on all sides from the contracting uterus and the ligaments, muscles, and bone surface of the pelvic area. Montagu (1962) states that

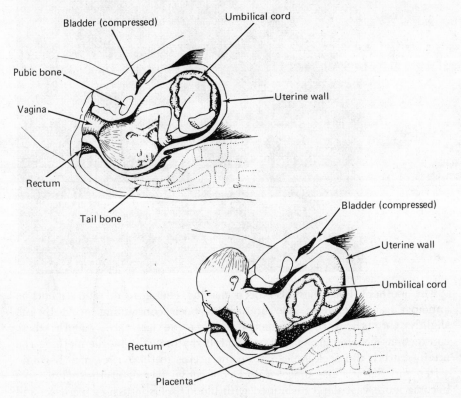

Fig. 14–5.
The birth process. (Adapted by permission from Sigmund Grollman, The Human Body, 2nd Ed. Copyright © Sigmund Grollman, 1969. New York: Macmillan Publishing Co., Inc.)

the function of prolonged and intensive stimulation during birth activates the vital functions of the newborn in his respiratory, gastrointestinal, and genitourinary systems. He cites as partial evidence the medical practice of slapping the buttocks of newborns who fail to breathe properly and the fact that many newly born animals such as mice, rabbits, and dogs die apparently

The Life Cycle

248

of gastrointestinal and genitourinary failures unless they are stimulated by their mothers immediately after birth. The contractions of the uterus will continue during the third stage until the placenta and membranes of the amnionic sac are ejected and the surrounding blood vessels are squeezed shut.

Postbirth Processes. The mother's body will gradually return to its preconception condition. The uterus will return to its normal size, the tissues and bones of the pelvic area will tighten again, and with time and exercise the abdominal walls will regain their firmness. Breast-feeding immediately after birth can help the mother because the sucking will set up biochemical reflexes that speed up the process of returning the body to its prepregnancy state. Furthermore, early breast-feeding will also help the newborn. Although the actual production of milk in the breasts (lactation) does not begin until about the third day after birth, the breasts at this time contain a liquid called colostrum that is rich in proteins and nourishes the baby until milk is formed. Colostrum acts as a laxative to remove prenatal substances from the infant's gastrointestinal tract and prevents diarrhea from developing. The greatest benefit of breast-feeding, however, is the immunization that it provides against certain infectious diseases through the action of the antibodies in the colostrum. Thus early breast-feeding is mutually beneficial, physiologically, to mother and child. In addition, the process itself enhances closeness for two humans who were once one and who will remain in a state of psychological oneness for some time to come.

A full-term baby will weigh between five and a half and ten pounds and its length will vary from 19 to 22 inches. For a while its head may be a bit out of shape because of the molding during birth. Its body may be covered with a white, creamy substance, and its general appearance may be that of a wrinkled, scrawny, little "old man." After it is cleaned up and its lungs have begun to function fully, it will begin to look like the picture-baby the mother may have had in mind.

During this period the very important consequences of negative preconception and prenatal influences can readily be seen. The results of poverty, malnutrition, drugs, genetic misfortunes, and so on can be summarized in the single statistic of infant mortality during the neonatal stage. Prematurely born infants, the single most common consequence of inadequate prebirth conditions, account for 70 per cent of all infant deaths during the first thirty days of life, and about 75 per cent of all infants who are going to die do so during this period of adjustment to the outside world. This evidence further helps to clearly document the crucial importance of proper care *before* birth (Falkner, 1969).

To further reduce the number of deaths of infants in the United States will require additional efforts by private, local, state, and national agencies. It is very disappointing to note, as illustrated in Figure 14–6, that the infant mortality rate is higher in the United States than in many other major countries. (It is also disappointing to learn that there are twice as many deaths in the state with the highest infant mortality rate than the state with the lowest —Falkner, 1969.) Although the majority of the victims of high infant mortality rates have lower socioeconomic membership, the absolute risks exist for all mothers. It is encouraging, on the other hand, to note that we have the knowledge and capacity to reduce infant mortality and morbidity. The im-

The Prenatal and Neonatal Stages

mediate solutions are to make these services available to all mothers, especially those of high risk and to increase their awareness and motivation to take full advantage of these services and related information.

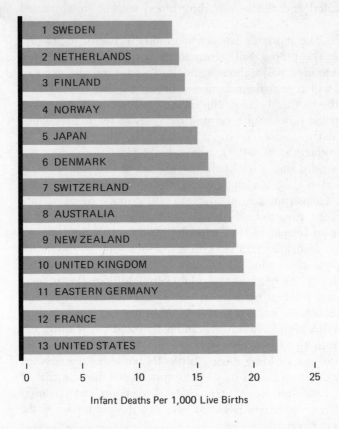

FIG. 14–6. *Infant mortality is higher in the United States than in many other major nations. (Falkner, 1969)*

1 SWEDEN
2 NETHERLANDS
3 FINLAND
4 NORWAY
5 JAPAN
6 DENMARK
7 SWITZERLAND
8 AUSTRALIA
9 NEW ZEALAND
10 UNITED KINGDOM
11 EASTERN GERMANY
12 FRANCE
13 UNITED STATES

Infant Deaths Per 1,000 Live Births

Prenatal Influences

In evaluating the importance of influences during the prenatal period whether they are biological, medical, social, racial, or economic, it is well to remember that it is by far the most important period of human growth and development despite its comparatively short length. Nevertheless, research did not begin to focus on its crucial significance until just prior to World War II. According to Pasamanick and Knobloch (1958), "To pure environmentalists, infants at birth were nondifferentiable except for some unimportant physical details, and to the pure hereditarians, they remained unchangeable products of genetic combinations which took place at conception. . . ." It has been only fairly recently that embryologists and biologists discovered and explained how the intrauterine environment and the environmental forces exerted on the mother could influence prenatal development. From the time before fertilization to that of birth, the mother's conditions psychologically, physically, and socially serve as the total environment for the developing organism. If she is healthy, comfortable, and happy in all three areas and receives proper prenatal medical care, the chances are overwhelming that she will have a healthy baby. By discussing prenatal factors that may influence the embryo and the fetus detrimentally, we are trying to increase the chances for giving birth to a healthy baby.

Maternal Nutrition. The expectant mother who regularly eats the right

The Life
Cycle

250

foods before and during pregnancy is more likely to have a normal pregnancy and less likely to have complications during birth than one who does not. The wisest course of action is for the mother to see a physician as soon as she suspects that she is pregnant because prenatal care includes advice on proper diet and weight gain for the next nine months. Minimal requirements of proper daily diet include the three different kinds of essential building materials: proteins for the growth and repair of the body, minerals and vitamins for growth and keeping the body in good working condition, and fats and carbohydrates for energy. Table 14–1 lists some of the foods needed during the peridevelopmental stage.

TABLE 14–1
SOME OF THE FOODS NEEDED DAILY DURING, BEFORE AND AFTER PREGNANCY

Food Item	Before and During the First Half of Pregnancy	During the Latter Half of Pregnancy	While Nursing the Baby
Milk, pasteurized—includes whole, nonfat, evaporated, reliquefied dry, or buttermilk	1 pint	1 quart	1 quart or more
Lean cooked meat, fish, poultry or meat alternate. Use liver or heart frequently	1 serving (2–3 ounces)	1–2 servings (5 ounces)	3 or more servings
Egg	1	1	1
Dark green or deep yellow vegetables	1 serving	1 serving	5 or more servings
Fruits and vegetables rich in vitamin C Good sources: citrus fruit or juice, cantaloupe, raw strawberries, broccoli, peppers	1 serving or	1 serving and	1 serving or
Fair sources: other melons, asparagus, brussels sprouts, raw cabbage, greens, tomatoes or juice, fresh or canned chili, potatoes cooked in jackets	2 servings	1 serving	2 servings
Other vegetables or fruit	1 serving	2 servings	2 servings
Whole grain, restored, or enriched cereal	1 serving	1 serving	4 or more servings
Whole grain, restored, or enriched bread	2–3 slices	2–3 slices	3 slices
Butter or fortified margarine	Amount as caloric level permits	Amount as caloric level permits	Amount as caloric level permits
Vitamin D		Use according to physician's instructions	Use according to physician's instructions

Adapted from *Nutrition During Pregnancy and Lactation,* rev. 1960. Berkeley, Calif.: California State Department of Public Health, p. 18.

The evidence for the importance of the relationship between diet and the health of the mother and the unborn is clear-cut. In a study among certain African tribes, mothers with enriched diets had infant mortality rates of about one-half of those who retained their usual diets (Hammer, 1962). In a similar study in Canada with mothers from low socioeconomic

The Prenatal and Neonatal Stages

status, it was revealed that mothers provided with supplementary foods had better prenatal records, fewer miscarriages, fewer infant deaths, and healthier babies during the first six months of life. (Ebbs et al., 1942).

These results were later confirmed in a study in the United States in which the records of mothers with good and excellent diets were compared with those with poor diets (Burke et al., 1943). The results of this study were described by Montagu (1962) when he indicated that every stillborn, every infant dying during the first few days after birth, with the exception of infants with major congenital defects, was born to a mother who had a poor diet during pregnancy. In contrast with this, 94 per cent of the infants born to mothers who were on good or excellent diets during pregnancy were in good or excellent condition at birth. A follow-up study on the same group of women who again become pregnant, at a later date, revealed that those women whose diet had become worse during the intervening years had correspondingly poorer maternal records with their new child. Furthermore, those whose diets had improved since the earlier pregnancies gave birth to babies who were in better condition than the previous ones (Montagu, 1965).

Infant mortality among poverty families in the United States is two to three times as high as it is in middle-class families. This relationship between levels of poverty and quality of diet is seen clearly in Table 14–2. The per cent of low-income families with good diets is much smaller than that for higher income families. In effect, malnutrition, high infant mortality and morbidity rates, and high prematurity rates coexist as a constellation of abnormalities centering around poverty. The extent of this problem in the United States is revealed by the statistic that there are 5 million women of childbearing age presently living in poverty (Falkner, 1969). The extent of the same problem on a worldwide basis is graphically depicted in Figure 14–7. As can be seen by the statistics, the less developed regions of the world have been and are still producing more children than their more developed counterparts (Unicef News, 1971).

TABLE 14–2

PER CENT OF HOUSEHOLDS WITH DIETS AT THREE LEVELS OF QUALITY BY INCOME

Income	Good Diets [1] (%)	Fair Diets [2] (%)	Poor Diets [3] (%)
Under $3,000	37	27	36
$3,000–4,999	43	33	24
$5,000–6,999	53	29	18
$7,000–9,999	56	32	12
$10,000 and over	63	28	9

1. Good diets: meet Recommended Dietary Allowances (1963) for 7 nutrients.
2. Fair diets: ⅔ R.D.A. for 7 nutrients but below R.D.A. for 1–7.
3. Poor diets: ⅔ R.D.A. for 1–7 nutrients; is not synonymous with serious hunger or malnutrition.

The Life Cycle

From: *Dietary Levels of Households in the United States,* Spring 1965, Agricultural Research Service, USDA, p. 5.

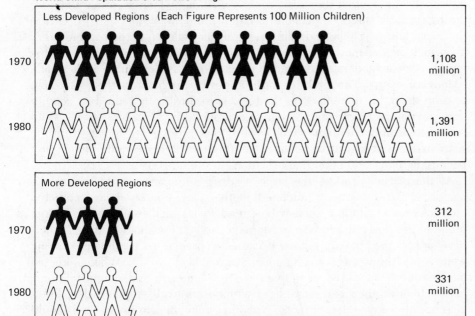

FIG. 14-7.
World child population 0-15 years of age. (Adapted from UNICEF News, 1971.)

Drugs and Other Chemical Agents. All drugs are capable of crossing the placenta and affecting the embryo or the fetus (Montagu, 1962). In general, medicinal drugs such as antibiotics taken by the pregnant mother are not harmful to the fetus but because some drugs are known to be potentially dangerous (such as large doses of quinine for malaria, which can produce deafness during the fetal stage), they should be taken only under a physician's supervision.

Even the intake of apparently mild substances such as aspirins, barbiturates, alcohol, and cigarette smoke may produce complications and undesirable side effects. There is evidence that pregnant mothers who smoke have a prematurity rate that is about twice as high as nonsmokers (Simpson, 1957). Mothers who smoke more than one-half pack of cigarettes daily have the highest prematurity rates, light smokers have a lower rate, and nonsmokers have the lowest rate. Even the effects of smoking only one cigarette can be detected in the activity of the fetal heartbeat (Sontag and Wallace, 1935). Alcohol intake has no known direct influence on the unborn. However, alcoholic addiction may endanger the healthy development of the

The Prenatal and Neonatal Stages

unborn if the mother ignores proper nutrition, which is often the case during the later stages of alcoholism. Later in life the mother may jeopardize the social and psychological adjustment of her children if she continues her abnormal dependency on alcohol. If the mother plans to breast-feed her infant, even a moderate consumption of alcohol is detectable in her milk (Montagu, 1959). The intake of barbiturates by pregnant mothers may help to calm them, but the effect on the fetus is to drastically reduce its activity even to the point of almost complete immobility (Hooker, 1952). With regard to aspirin, Montagu (1965) warns that aspirins fed to rats from the sixth to the last day of pregnancy resulted in high mortality rates, cleft palates, harelips, and other malformations in the fetuses.

At the extreme end of the scale of drug and chemical intake are the narcotics. Babies born to addicted mothers are almost always addicted themselves. In addition, such babies tend to be smaller in size and more prone to develop other illnesses (Montagu, 1965). Fortunately, drug addicts have a low rate of conception because of premature menopause among women and impotence among men (Carmichael, 1954). When addicted mothers are hospitalized in preparation for childbirth and cannot take any more narcotics, their babies are born with withdrawal symptoms that disappear in a few days (Baker, 1960). A mother who plans to breast-feed should be aware that narcotics taken during this time will appear in her milk (Lichtenstein, 1915).

Infectious Diseases. Any illness in the mother that is caused by virus, especially during the first three months of pregnancy, may injure the unborn. Among such illnesses are smallpox, mumps, scarlet fever, chicken pox, as well as one of the major causes of severe birth defects, *rubella* or German measles. Rubella poses a threat to the growing embryo during the first three months of pregnancy and commonly produces miscarriages, stillbirths, blindness, deafness, mental retardation, and/or congenitally damaged hearts. Now that a safe rubella vaccine has been developed, the virus can be wiped out. The main targets for the rubella vaccine are children aged one to twelve who are the main carriers of the virus. It cannot be used for inoculating pregnant women or those of childbearing age because its effect on the maternal organs are not known. Perhaps in the future there will be a vaccine for women during these critical years. For the present time the only protection is to vaccinate as many children as possible against rubella. There are immunizations for other infectious diseases for which prospective mothers should consult their physicians.

Maternal Emotions. The emotional states of the mother during pregnancy can have significant influences on the development of the embryo and the fetus. Emotions, especially intense ones, produce profound bodily changes that are regulated in complex ways by the central nervous system and the endocrine glands. The relationship of the autonomic portion of the central nervous system and the endocrine glands with the emotional states of the mother is particularly important because emotions largely act through the chemical and neural actions of these systems. During emotional states the autonomic nervous system activates the endocrine glands, which, in turn, secrete hormones directly into the bloodstream. The hormones, especially epinephrine (also known as adrenalin), act to produce many of the symptoms found in emotional states. Very often these hormones reach the unborn through the placenta and, in turn, produce symptoms of emotional states in the fetus. Thus, we can see how maternal emotional states can be converted into embryonic and fetal emotional states through this rather complex transmission mechanism. The mother and the unborn are thus tied together physically as well as emotionally. Furthermore, there is a relationship between the intensity of maternal emotional states and those of the unborn. Research has demonstrated that mothers with higher levels of autonomic activity measured by such responses as heart rate, respiration rate, blood pressure, skin conductance, face temperature, and so on had correspondingly higher levels of fetal activity (Jost and Sontag, 1944). The duration of fetal emotional activity, however, tends to be much longer than that of the mother (Sontag, 1944). This means, in the case of negative emotions for example, that once the threat is over the mother can begin to relax, but the fetus, having no way of knowing this, continues to respond to the chemistry of emotional reactions (Turner, 1956).

Newborn babies with records of high fetal activity as a result of severe and prolonged maternal tension have a greater than normal rate of postnatal adjustment difficulties (Ferreira, 1960; Grimm, 1961). Such infants tend to weigh less than the average baby, are more active, more finicky about eating, vomit more, are more diarrhetic, cry more, and squirm more (Sontag, 1946). They are, in short, very pesty infants. Investigations of mothers who typically produce pesty infants reveal a background of severe emotional disturbance during pregnancy.

Although it has not been proved that severe and prolonged maternal stress will produce damage to the fetus, there is some evidence that the frequency of cleft palates (cracks or openings in the roof of the mouth) may be related to severe emotional crisis at the time of the formation of the fetal mouth. In one study, women with unusual emotional stress had a higher rate of cleft-palated firstborn infants than those with less stress (Strean and Peer, 1956). A possible genetic variable was introduced when investigation revealed that 25 per cent of the high stress mothers had family histories of cleft palates or harelips. More dramatic results were obtained by the same investigators with rats. They injected pregnant rats with cortisone (a hormone secreted during emotional stress that in turn releases adrenalin) during the critical days when the palates were developing. Of the one hundred mice in the experiment, eighty-seven were born with cleft palates. Other experiments with rats have reported similar results (Montagu, 1965).

There is evidence of the possibility that wars and political crises may also be responsible for a variety of birth defects in newborns. Malformations, miscarriages, and stillbirths are explicable through the effects of malnutrition, but less appreciated is the possibility that psychological shock may also be a factor. Montagu (1965) in his analysis of a long-term study of infant malformations in Germany has provided us with some important, but indirect, evidence. The pre-Hitler rate of infant malformations was about .07 per cent. The Hitler prewar rate was 1.7 per cent, the wartime rate was 2.6 per cent, and the immediate postwar rate was 6.5 per cent. Thus, we can see a continuous relationship between increased states of anxiety and shock and increased rates of malformations among newborn. Montagu was careful to point out that malnutrition in Germany during all these periods was not the major causative factor.

Research into the relationship between maternal states of emotional stress and complications during pregnancy have thus far yielded conflicting or ambiguous results, although related studies with animals have shown definite negative effects (Ader et al., 1963). A recent comprehensive study, however, has shown that women with high measures of psychological and social stress both *before* and *during* pregnancy had complication rates one-third higher than comparable women with low levels of stress (Nuckolls, et al., in press). Apparently, in some women, the cumulative effect of continuous, varied, and severe stress is related to increased medical complications during pregnancy.

Pregnant women, like all other people, experience a wide range of emotions from mild to strong, from temporary to prolonged, and from panic terror to euphoria (see Figure 14–8). Strong negative emotions may have detrimental effects on the mother and her child. The case for minimizing negative emotions or facilitating pleasant emotions is argued for by evidence of the lack of pregnancy complications for both mother and child. The case for prolonged and intense happiness before and during pregnancy has yet to be presented. Research may someday tell us what it means for both mother and child when the mother experiences intense joy before and during pregnancy.

Other Influences. There is ample evidence that *radiation* is detrimental to present and future generations. The major sources of radiation are X-rays, nuclear reactions, and cosmic rays. Presently X-rays are the single largest source of man-made radiation. The effects of too much radiation include stillbirths, maldevelopment and malformations, some forms of mental retardation, and genetic damage, which may result in birth defects far into the future (Montagu, 1962). Abnormalities occurred in the unborn who were exposed to atomic bombs in Hiroshima and Nagasaki (Plummer, 1959). Pregnant women exposed to heavy dosages of radiation in these bombings had an infant mortality and morbidity rate of 60 per cent, whereas those exposed to a light dosage suffered a 10 per cent rate. These figures contrast with the normal Japanese rate of 6 per cent.

There is some evidence that children of the fifth or higher *birth order* run greater risks of death; however, their parents are usually from lower socio-economic status, which, by itself, often means inferior medical care, malnutrition, and inadequate shelter. It is difficult to separate the effects of birth order from low economic standing when both occur simultaneously in the same families. The deleterious influence of possible cumulative effects of such factors as frequent births, low socioeconomic status, and brief time intervals between pregnancies may yield the single greatest damage to the unborn and to infants. Data from the Maternity and Infant Care Project in New York City reveal that the neonatal death rate is thirty-five per one thousand for deliveries occurring within one year after a preceding delivery. For births with an interval of one to two years, the neonatal death rate goes down to seventeen per one thousand. If the interval is two to three years, the neonatal death rate goes down to seven per one thousand (Falkner, 1969).

In summary, although there is a tremendous gap between the great amount that is known about prenatal influences and that which needs to be discovered, it is the *effective gap* between what is presently known and that which is applied that concerns us most at the moment. It has been estimated by a panel of interdisciplinary consultants to the National Institute of Child Health and Human Development that we now have sufficient knowledge if it were rigorously applied to save over one hundred seventy thousand infants during the next five years (Falkner, 1969).

Our primary objectives should include the reduction of infant mortality as well as the creation of conditions that will assure that every child is well-born and will be reared in conditions that will enable him to fulfill and possibly extend his genetic potentials. To help accomplish these goals prospective parents should take full precautionary measures in light of currently available evidence. Comprehensive medical care should be readily available to all, and we must take steps to improve the quality of life at all socioeconomic levels.

Nevertheless, there are some encouraging signs. There is an increased awareness of the problems of providing maternal and child care, and more agencies at the local and national level are allocating funds to research and personnel training. Infant mortality in the United States, although still too high when compared to other major countries, decreased 12 per cent from 1964 to 1967 (Falkner, 1969). In 1972, the Food and Drug Administration announced that exposure of human reproductive organs to medical X-rays had been reduced by one-third since 1964 (Los Angeles *Times*, 1972). There have been promising developments recently in techniques for diagnosis and the treatment of defects and diseases even before the fetus leaves the uterus. For example, the greater use of amniocentesis (a technique that permits a sample of amniotic fluid to be withdrawn from the pregnant mother) allows for detection of some possible abnormalities including chromosomal and metabolic defects. Such information can aid parents and doctors in making important decisions regarding the health of the mother and the infant during the entire peridevelopmental stage.

COGNITIVE DOMAIN

Of all newborns, the human is the most helpless at birth. Lower animals arrive with a vast array of built-in information and know-how; man, however, arrives with only a relatively small number of reflexes and no instincts, but large reservoirs of potential. These circumstances provide both advantages and disadvantages. Cognitively, animals get off to a head start because of their "factory-installed" instinctual behaviors and early advanced neurological development that permits more rapid learning at first. Animals make fewer mistakes than humans because they are governed principally through instinctual behaviors. Animal learning potential, however, is largely restricted by the demands of a much larger body in relation to brain size, less need to learn because of instinctual patterns, and a lack of sophisticated language development.

The human neonate, well protected and provided for during infancy, will more than double its brain size by the end of the first year. Having no known instincts, man must rely solely on learning and reasoning to find adequate or superior ways of living.*

* We say that man has no known instincts because a behavior must meet all three of the following criteria to qualify as instinctual: (1) is present in all members of the species; (2) is invariably brought about by particular cue or set of cues, and (3) the elicited behavior must be fairly complex and not simply a reflex action. No known human behavior meets all three prerequisites.

Early Learning

Until recently it was believed that the cerebral cortex, the main center for learning, was nonfunctioning in the newborn. Recent evidence has demonstrated, however, that the neonate is capable of learning at least at the level of the simple conditioned response (which is suggestive of limited cortical activity). Two- and three-day-old babies have been taught to turn their heads in response to a sound. To teach this response, strokes on the cheek, sweet water to drink, and the sound were presented sequentially. After numerous repetitions, the sound by itself elicited head turning. Babies of three to five days have been taught to turn their heads to the sound of a tone but not to the sound of a buzzer (Lipsett, 1967). Similar findings have been reported using the sense of smell. Years ago it was widely believed that newborns could see literally nothing. Now there is evidence that two-week-old babies can not only attend to objects visually but can also discriminate among rather similar patterns (Fantz, 1965). These rather startling indicators of early learning during the neonatal stage suggest a remarkable sensitivity to the outside world that is as yet not widely known or appreciated. The new evidence indicates that the humanization process, which is basically a learning process, begins far sooner than we had previously thought possible.

AFFECTIVE DOMAIN

We have previously discussed the importance of maternal emotions on the fetus and newborn. The beginnings of emotional development of the infant in relation to such affective variables as maternal love, empathy, contact, and stimulation are the subject of an increasing number of theories as well as highly sophisticated research programs. For the most part, we put off our discussion of this topic until the next chapter.

In this section, we discuss two important affective interactions that have implications with regard to modeling and shaping the infant's behavior; the affective conditions that prevail during the pregnancy and delivery and the affective interactions between mother and newborn.

Affective Dimensions of the Birth Process

The affective conditions surrounding pregnancy, birth, and even the nature of delivery are the result of a complex series of variables related to such things as the mother's childhood experiences, her personality, her overall health, and her social class and ethnic background. One of the most important variables is the emotional meaning of birth and the birth process in a particular society.

Although there are no definitive studies regarding the interplay among these variables in our complex society, we can study contrasting preliterate cultures. Newton (1970) summarizes a number of studies showing the extreme differences in cultural attitudes and emotions toward sex, pregnancy, and childbirth with their resulting outcomes among the Cuna Indians of Central America (De Smidt, 1948; Marshall, 1950; Stout, 1947) and the Siriono Indians of Bolivia in South America (Holmberg, 1950; Tichauer, 1963).

The Life
Cycle

Ideally, the Cuna girls did not learn of the existence of either coitus or childbirth until the final stages of the marriage ceremony. Pregnancy was seen by the Cuna as a time of anxiety and rising fear of childbirth. Each day the pregnant woman went to the house of the medicine man, who specialized in prenatal care and childbirth, for a cup of freshly brewed medicine tea. Labor, however, was too "hidden" for the medicine man to attend. Children and men, even husbands and medicine men, were excluded from the labor area. The midwives kept the medicine man informed of the progress of the labor. He chanted and supplied medications in response to the labor progress reports. Labor under these circumstances was frequently prolonged and so extreme that unconsciousness of the laboring woman occurred at times.

In contrast to this, the Siriono patterned birth as an easy, open process, in keeping with their relaxed sexual attitudes. Birth took place in a communal hut and was a public event freely witnessed by men as well as women. The mother labored in a hammock while groups of women gathered, gossiping about their own labors and wondering whether the coming baby would be a boy or a girl. No help, however, was given to the mother during the usual normal labor. She herself tied the childbirth rope over her hammock to pull during contractions. She dug the earth under the hammock to cushion the baby's fall. The grunts and groans of labor did not appear to bother others within earshot. When the baby was born it slid over the edge of the hammock, dropping a few inches to the ground. (Newton, 1970, p. 86)

Imagine the emotional differences felt by women in those two tribes as they approached pregnancy and childbirth! Contrast these examples with the pregnancy and birth experiences in our own society and the differences are apparent. Despite some of the "crisis" studies relating to the poor preparation we have for parenthood, the women in our society and many other modern societies do not have to enter the birth process with quite so many complex and mystical rituals and beliefs that often trigger off a number of negative emotional patterns.

Ideally, the expectant mother has participated in a prenatal health program of dietary planning as well as regular physical examinations. In most cases, the mother delivers in a hospital with several nurses and a doctor as well as ample supportive medical services for any complications occurring during delivery. The husband and members of the family are available for emotional support after the birth (and in some cases *during* the birth), and the mother usually gets a few days' rest in the hospital before returning home.

Maternal-Neonate-Affective Interactions

Just how do cultural and psychological variables influence maternal emotions that affect the early behavior of the neonate? Yarrow (1963) has noted a definite difference in the manner in which mothers respond to their newborns, not merely as a function of the mother's social and psychological background but also as a function of the differences in emotional responsiveness of the infant himself. He points out these differences in the observations of a foster mother and her relationships to her two foster boys, Jack and George:

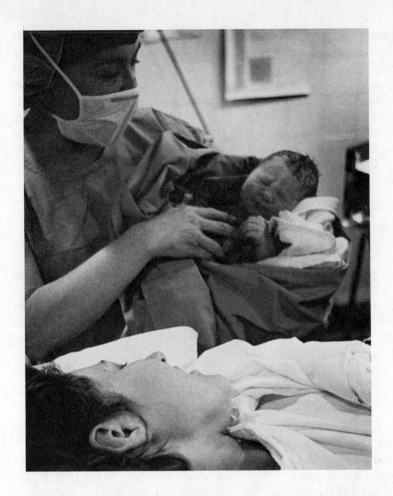

FIG. 14-8.
The first "formal"
introduction.

The one infant, Jack, was, from early infancy, a passive baby, with a low activity level and a generally low level of responsiveness to environmental stimuli. He usually accepted environmental frustrations without overt protest. He tended to wait quietly if he was not fed immediately when hungry. Even at three months, much of his day was spent in sleeping. He was not much interested in food, and ate without much zest. By three months, he could be encouraged to respond socially with a smile or a mild increase in activity, but only after very strong stimulation. At five months he still showed no initiative in social interaction. He did not reach out toward people or make approach responses. He enjoyed his thumb, and when awake spent much of his time in a state of passive contentment, sucking his fingers or thumb.

In marked contrast to Jack, George was a vigorously active infant. He ate with great zest and sucked on the bottle with exceptional vigor. By three months, he was showing much initiative in attempting to handle and master his environment. He actively went after objects, expressed his needs directly, was very forceful in demanding what he wanted, and persisted in his demands until he was satisfied. By six months, he was showing a high degree of persistence in problem situations. George was highly responsive to social stimulation and took the initiative in seeking social response from others. (p. 109)

The Life
Cycle

Yarrow then describes the differences in the mother's reaction to the two infants. George received a great amount of physical stimulation, he interacted as a family member, and he was held and played with by all members of the family. Jack, on the other hand, spent most of the day lying in the playpen, with little family interaction, since he demanded little. The foster mother even called him a "poor little thing," and when he was three months old, she verbalized hostility and rejection of Jack.

Yarrow (1965) pointed out that the relationship between mother and newborn is a complex one and is as much dependent upon the infant's basic response patterns, predispositions, and individual sensitivities as upon the mother's behavior. Table 14–3 indicates some of the major interactions that occur between mother and infant. A positive response from the infant often ensures and promotes a continuing maternal interest and activity.

TABLE 14–3
SOME MAJOR INTERACTIONS BETWEEN MOTHER AND INFANT

Some Basic Needs	Maternal Action	Positive Infant's Response
Food	Feeding; water.	Contentment; proper elimination; growth.
Shelter and Security	Provision of quiet, dry environment; safety precautions.	Physical health.
Warmth	Clothing; environment.	Quietude; contentment.
Physical contact	Holding while feeding; bathing; etc.	Recognition; contentment.
Affection	Sound of voice; holding; rocking; petting; etc.	Attention; recognition; smiling; "gurgling."
Stimulation	Visual environment; toys; sounds; etc.	Alertness; movement of head; etc.
Elimination	Correct foods; cleanliness.	Sufficient rest; contentment.
Hygiene	Doctor's visits; cleanliness; dry environment.	Physical health.
Exercise	Provision of large, flat surface; encouragement; freedom from restraint.	Increased physical skills.

SOCIAL DOMAIN

Institutional Factors

Quite obviously, the influence that society exerts upon the intrauterine life of the developing fetus is modified by the mother's body. Social factors that have direct bearing on the mother's health, well-being, and emotional state are all important to the baby within. In this section we discuss some of society's institutions, their influence on the parents, and the resulting ramifications for the fetus and newborn.

Education. One of the major problems facing the childbearing family is

The Prenatal and Neonatal Stages

that current educational programs have, for the most part, been inadequate in preparing the couple for their new roles as parents. The focus of their educational experience has been directed toward career training and has all but neglected the important facets of successful family life such as sex, child care, home maintenance, and personal financial management. In our society, we tend to assign responsibility for training in these areas to the individual's home, with the result that most new parents are seriously deficient in basic family skills (Rossi, 1968; Senn, 1968).

Many educational programs are being carried out by national and local public and private agencies such as the Family Service Association, YMCA, YWCA, and others to provide some basic information for young married couples in the process of family planning and prenatal care. Unfortunately, far too many of these programs focus solely on the biological domain as far as the "well-being" of the child is concerned. One of the authors remembers taking a class for prospective parents with his wife prior to the birth of their first son where the major focus was on diaper changing, feeding and bathing the child, and the showing of a live birth movie (in color) that proceeded to raise the anxiety level of both husband and wife considerably. Only one class meeting was devoted to emotional problems or how the pregnancy was affecting inter- and intrafamily relationships.

The situation may well be improved if a major recommendation of the 1970 White House Conference on Children is eventually carried out. This recommendation calls for the establishment of a "National Institute for the Family." Among the many institute goals is the establishment of a nation-wide community based family life education program.

Government. We have mentioned in previous discussions the role of the various governmental agencies in promoting social welfare, child care, educational programs, and in regulating food and drug standards. All of these have important consequences for the family and the developing individual.

TABLE 14–4
LAWS AFFECTING FAMILY LIFE

Marriage
Establishment of legal age for marriage.
Prohibition of bigamy.
Prohibition of incestuous marriage.
Prohibition of marriage between mentally deficient individuals.
Licensing and premarital venereal disease examination requirements.
Property rights and inheritance.

Divorce
Establishment of legal grounds for divorce or annulment.
Establishment of custody rights.

Child Rearing
Establishment of legal responsibility for children and child care.
Prohibition of the exploitation of children.
Establishment of the responsibility for illegitimate children.
Establishment of responsibility for financial obligations of children.
Prohibition of child abuse or child neglect.

The Life
Cycle

Historically, government has provided strong supportive legislation aimed at strengthening the family institution.

Although most laws are intended to act as a means of enforcing society's values, recent legislation and court rulings have reasserted the individual's right to self-determination. One of the most important examples of this tendency is the recent Supreme Court ruling that *in effect* makes abortion a matter of individual choice for the woman. Aside from the obvious family planning implications of this ruling, the woman who desires an abortion no longer need be subject to the physical danger that has so often accompanied the illegal abortion.

Religion. Religion as a social institution often plays a major role in influencing the attitudes and values of the family regarding pregnancy, illegitimacy, abortion, contraception, miscarriages, handicapped children, and many other aspects of family life. As such, religion and its primary agency, the church, often play a critical role in forming the social environment for the fetus and newborn.

Economic Institutions. One of the important functions of the "expectant" family is to provide an adequate financial framework for the growth and development of the newborn. In a recent survey, the median first-year costs of having a baby (including delivery) was $1,651. A U. S. Department of Agriculture study in 1969 estimated that the overall cost of rearing a child to his seventeenth year was $22,690.

As you can see, the costs involved in raising a child are substantial enough to warrant careful consideration in family planning especially when one considers that pregnancy and childbirth usually means that one of the parents must give up his income-producing job for at least a year or more (Pennock, 1970).

Social Class and Childbearing

The degree and the direction to which an individual is influenced by his interactions with social institutions is partly a function of the following:

1. Who you are (your social class and ethnic background).
2. What is happening (such as the type and extent of technological and social change going on during the period).
3. Where you live (urban or rural setting).

Table 14–4 illustrates some of the different reasons that people give for having children. The reasons are as varied as the social classes to which they belong (Richardson and Guttmacher, 1967).

IMPLICATIONS

UNDERSTANDING YOURSELF AND OTHERS

By talking to your own parents and other relatives, and determining the background of their family situation during the time of your prenatal development, you can perhaps gain some insight into the reasons for your own existence at this point in time. By now you realize that many factors were brought to bear upon your parents, and all of these played some part in your own life.

Perhaps one of the things that this chapter might do is to stimulate, within you, an appreciation for the complexity and continuity of human life. The

The Prenatal
and Neonatal
Stages

TABLE 14-5
WHY PEOPLE HAVE CHILDREN

Male College Students *	City Couples *	Kenya †	India †
1. Companionship. 2. Perpetuate family line. 3. Satisfaction in creating new life. 4. Companionship in old age. 5. Fulfilling social obligations.	1. Pleasure, emotional satisfaction. 2. Companionship for parents. 3. Gives life purpose. 4. Makes family stronger. 5. Brings husband and wife closer. 6. Security for parents.	1. Females bring cattle into the family. 2. Males help bury their mother. 3. To take care of mother when old. 4. Son's wife can help his mother. 5. Sons can build houses and repair fences. 6. Several sons give mother high status.	1. Having children guarantees a good afterlife (childless mothers become ghosts). 2. Boys preferred to girls. 3. Sons can uphold family name. 4. Sons needed for father's funeral. 5. Girls a financial liability (family must provide dowry). 6. Minimum of one girl needed for father to give away in marriage (Hindu tradition).

Compiled from: * LeMasters (1957)
                † Whiting (1963)

vast multiplicity of factors within the four domains that influenced the total environment surrounding your prenatal development and birth were in large part responsible for shaping your early life. You, because you are partly a product of your parents and their environment, carry these things with you and pass them on to your own children.

LIVING AND WORKING WITH CHILDREN, ADOLESCENTS, AND ADULTS

It should be clear by now that there is much that a couple can do as they make plans to conceive a child. These "support systems" were discussed as an integral part of the preconception stage. Now, we are finding that the prenatal period, too, is more than a time of "sitting and waiting" for the newborn. What the husband and wife do or don't do during this period may have long-lasting implications for the infant.

From the affective domain, the implications are evident. Maternal emotions seem to indirectly affect the fetus, but maternal emotions are but a reflection of other areas of a woman's life during this period. They reflect, for example, her relationship with her husband and the amount and quality of communication that is going on between them. Maternal emotions are also a reflection of how the mother's parents (particularly her own mother) viewed pregnancy and childbearing as a part of their lives.

Implications in the social domain depend upon the ways in which the childbearing family is related to its extended family as well as other institutions. What kind of job and how much money a husband earns has a lot to do with the availability of certain prenatal services (both medical and psychological). The couple's religion as well as the amount of education it has had also plays an important role in the family's approach to childbearing. Of importance also is the general availability of community and governmental agencies concerned with human welfare.

The Life
Cycle

Some implications in the realm of the biological domain can be summarized as follows:

1. Expectant mothers must eat the right kinds and amounts of food in order to increase their chances of bearing healthy infants.
2. Certain chemical agents and drugs are potentially dangerous to healthy fetal development.
3. Prevention of various diseases is of prime consideration for expectant mothers.
4. Prolonged maternal stress may produce damage to the fetus.

Research findings in the cognitive domain imply that the intellectual and learning competencies of a person may be at stake during this critical early period of neurological development. Such events as premature births certainly increase the chances of producing a less intellectually competent human being.

DEVELOPING POSITIVE MODELS

The major theme of Chapters 13 and 14 has been developed around the notion of increasing the chances of conceiving, developing, and bearing a human being who has all the ingredients for becoming a more fully human person. It is among the interaction of factors in the social, affective, cognitive, and biological domains during this stage of human development that one can find the various positive models that underlie the birth of a healthy and responsive human being. To repeat these models again would be repetitious. Suffice it to say that parents who demonstrate some of the qualities of the cognitively, affectively, socially, and biologically maturing selves certainly have a better chance of approaching the peridevelopmental period with a more realistic and humanly gratifying attitude than those who have not reached some of these goals.

On a broader level, it is gratifying to see large-scale efforts by both private and public agencies to establish means to meet the many needs that families have at this important early period of human development. For example, in the *Report to the President* from the 1970 White House Conference on Children, the following programs and accomplishments were outlined:

Infant mortality has been significantly reduced in urban ghettos. In the past three years, the nation's infant mortality has decreased more than twice as much as in the decade from 1956 to 1965, and mortality reductions in major cities were greater than the national average. The maternity and infant care programs in many large cities are making a major contribution to these reductions.

Comprehensive health services have been delivered to children and pregnant women in low income areas which have few medical practitioners.

In implementing the national policy to make family planning services available to women from low income groups who want these services, 425,000 women received family planning services in 1968.

High quality medical care was provided last year for 425,000 children who are crippled or have conditions which may lead to crippling. This

The Prenatal and Neonatal Stages

265

includes care for 30,000 children born with congenital heart disease, many of whom were cured or greatly helped through open heart surgery.

Specialized diagnostic, evaluation, and treatment services were provided to 45,000 mentally retarded children in 150 clinics in 1968.

More than 100 special programs for unmarried pregnant girls of high school age have been initiated and are demonstrating that repeated out-of-wedlock pregnancies can be reduced by perhaps 60 per cent. There has also been a major breakthrough in community attitudes and action, and in the programs for school-age girls now in operation, teenage unmarried mothers are helped to complete their high school education and are provided health and counseling services.

The 59 new comprehensive health care projects for children and youth make preventive health care available to children from low-income families so they may avoid develping serious health problems. Currently, over 400,000 children are registered for comprehensive care in this program.

The Office of Economic Opportunity and several voluntary organizations have developed 55 neighborhood health centers with new and imaginative ways to reach people in economically deprived areas and to make services available and accessible.

Another example of the scope and range of programs was given by Keith P. Russell in a speech before the National Congress on the Quality of Life (1972). In his speech, Russell outlined an ideal maternal and infant care program as follows:
Goals:
   1. Education in parenthood.
   2. Maintain and improve prepregnant state of health.
   3. Wellborn healthy baby.
   4. Prevention of problems prior to conception.
Means to achieve goals:
   1. Classes before and during pregnancy.
   2. Abortion clinic.
   3. Rubella vaccine program.
   4. Venereal disease detection.
   5. Genetic counseling.
   6. Fetal monitoring.
   7. Nutrition program.
   8. Research and development.

It is from programs such as these that we hope to build better models of human growth and well-being that in turn will help parents rear more fully human persons.

CHAPTER REFERENCES

ADER, R. and E. W. HAHN. Effects of social environment on mortality to whole body x-irradiation in the rat. *Psychological Report*, 1963, **13**:24–215.

BAKER, J. B. E. The effects of drugs on the foetus. *Pharmacological Reviews*, 1960, **12**:37–90.

BURKE, B. S., V. A. BEAL, S. F. KIRKWOOD, and H. C. STUART. Nutrition studies during pregnancy. *American Journal of Obstetrics & Gynecology*, 1943, **46**: 38–52.

CARMICHAEL, L. The onset and early development of behavior. In L. Carmichael (ed.), *Manual of child psychology*, 2nd ed. New York: Wiley, 1954.

CORNER, G. W. *Ourselves unborn: an embryologist's essay on man.* New Haven: Yale U. P., 1944.

DESMIDT, L. S. *Among the San Blas Indians of Panama.* Troy, N. Y.: the author, 1948.

DIETARY LEVELS OF HOUSEHOLDS IN THE UNITED STATES. Agricultural Research Service, USDA, Spring 1965, p. 5.

EBBS, J. H., A. BROWN, F. F. TISDALL, W. J. MOYLE and M. BELL. The influence of improved prenatal nutrition upon the infant. *Canadian Medical Association Journal*, 1942, **46**:6–8.

FALKNER, F. (ed.). Key issues in infant mortality. National Institute of Child Health and Human Development, Washington, D. C.: U. S. Govt. Printing Office, 1969.

FANTZ, R. L. Visual perception from birth as shown by pattern selectivity. *Annals of the N. Y. academy of science*, 1965, **118**:793–814.

FERREIRA, A. J. The pregnant woman's emotional attitude and its reflection on the newborn. *American Journal of Orthopsychiatry*, 1960, **30**:553–561.

GRIMM, E. R. Psychological tension in pregnancy. *Psychosomatic medicine*, 1961, **23**:520–527.

HAMMER, J. H. The cultural aspects of infant mortality in Subsaharan Africa. Unpublished doctoral dissertation, Northwestern U., 1962.

HOLMBERG, A. R. *Nomads of the long bow: The Siriono of Eastern Bolivia.* Washington, D. C.: Smithsonian Institution, Institute of Social Anthropology, publication 10, 1950.

HOOKER, D. *The prenatal origin of behavior.* Kansas: U. of Kansas, 1952.

JOST, H. and L. W. SONTAG. The genetic factor in autonomic nervous system function. *Psychosomatic Medicine*, 1944, **6**:308–310.

LEMASTERS, E. E. Parenthood as crisis. *Marriage and Family Living*, 1957, **19**: 352–355.

LOS ANGELES *Times*. Less x-ray exposure eases genetic threat. April 7, 1972.

LICHTENSTEIN, P. M. Infant drug addiction. *New York Medical Journal*, 1915, **102**:905.

LIPSETT, LEWIS P. Learning in the human infant. In S. Stevenson, E. Eckhard, and H. Rheingold (eds.), *Early behavior: comparative and developmental approaches.* New York: Wiley, 1967.

MARSHALL, D. S. *Cuna folk: conceptual scheme involving dynamic factors of culture, as applied to the Cuna Indians of Danien.* Unpublished manuscript, Department of Anthropology, Harvard U., 1950.

MONTAGU, M. F. A. *Life before birth.* New York: Signet, 1965.

———. *Prenatal influence.* Springfield, Ill.: Thomas, 1962.

———. *Human heredity.* New York: Harcourt, 1959.

NEWTON, N. The effect of psychological environment on childbirth: combined cross cultural and experimental approach. *Journal of Cross-Cultural Psychology*, Spring 1970, **1**, 1:85–90.

NUTRITION DURING PREGNANCY AND LACTATION, rev. 1960. Berkeley, Calif.: Calif. State Dept. of Public Health.

NUCKOLLS, K. B., M. B. CASSELL, and B. H. KAPLAN. Psychosocial assets, life crisis and the prognosis of pregnancy. *American Journal of Epidemiology*, (in press).

PASAMANICK, B. and H. KNOBLOCH. The contribution of some organic factors to school retardation in Negro children. *Journal of Negro Education,* 1958, **27**.

PENNOCK, J. L. Cost of raising a child. *Family Economics Review,* March, 1970, **16**.

PLUMMER, G. Anomalies occurring in children exposed in utero to the atomic bomb in Hiroshima. *Pediatrics,* 1959, **2**:659–661.

PRENATAL CARE. Office of Child Development, U. S. Dept. of Health, Education and Welfare, 1970.

RICHARDSON, S. A. and A. F. GUTTMACHER. *Childbearing: its social and psychological aspects,* Baltimore: Williams & Wilkins, 1967.

ROSSI, A. S. Transition to parenthood, *Journal of Marriage and the Family,* Feb. 1968, 26–39.

RUSSELL, K. P. What is a good m and i program? Speech Delivered at National Congress on the Quality of Life. Chicago, Ill., March 22–25, 1972.

SENN, M. J. and C. HARTFORD. *The Firstborn: experiences of eight American families,* Cambridge, Mass.: Harvard U. P., 1968.

SIMPSON, W. J. A preliminary report on cigarette smoking and the incidence of prematurity. *American Journal of Obstetrics & Gynecology,* 1957, **73**:808–815.

SONTAG, L. W. Differences in modifiability of fetal behavior and physiology, *Psychosomatic Medicine,* 1944, **6**:151–154.

———. Some psychosomatic aspects of childhood. *Nervous child,* 1946, **5**:296–304.

———. The significance of fetal environmental differences. *American Journal of Obstetrics & Gynecology,* 1941, **42**:996–1003.

———. War and fetal maternal relationship. *Marriage and Family Living,* 1944, **6**:1–5.

——— and R. F. WALLACE. Preliminary report of the Fels Fund: study of fetal activity. *American Journal of Disturbed Children,* 1934, 48, 1050–1057.

——— and ———. The effect of cigarette smoking during pregnancy upon the fetal heart rate. *American Journal of Obstetrics & Gynecology,* 1935, **29**:3–8; 77–83.

STOUT, D. B. *San Elas Cuna acculturation: introduction.* New York: Viking Fund Publications in Anthropology, 1947, no. 9.

STREAN, L. P. and L. A. PEER. Stress as an etiologic factor in the development of cleft palate. *Plastic and Reconstructive Surgery,* 1956, **18**:1–8.

TICHAUER, R. The Aymara children of Bolivia. *Journal of Pediatrics,* 1963, **62**: 399–412.

TURNER, E. K. The syndrome in the infant resulting from maternal emotional tension during pregnancy. *Medical Journal of Australia,* 1956, **1**:221–222.

UNICEF NEWS. 1971, **68**:8.

WHITE HOUSE CONFERENCE ON CHILDREN. *Report to the President,* Washington, D. C.: U. S. Govt. Printing Office, 1971 (0-414-184).

WHITING, B. B. (ed.). *Six cultures: studies in childrearing.* New York: Wiley, 1963.

YARROW, L. Research in dimensions of early maternal care. *Merrill-Palmer Quarterly,* 1963, **9**:101–114.

YARROW, L. J. and M. A. GOODWIN. Some conceptual issues in the study of mother-infant interaction. *American Journal of Orthopsychiatry,* 1965, **35**: 473–481.

RECOMMENDED FURTHER READING

BEADLE, G. and M. BEADLE. *The language of life.* New York: Doubleday, 1966.

ELKIN, F. and G. HANDEL. *The child and society: the process of socialization,* 2nd ed. New York: Random, 1972.

The Life
Cycle

FLANAGAN, G. L. *First nine months of life.* New York: Simon & Schuster, 1962.

GLASSER, PAUL H. and LOIS N. GLASSER. *Families in crisis.* New York: Harper, 1970.

GOODRICH, F. W. *Infant care.* Englewood Cliffs, N. J.: Prentice-Hall, 1968.

GUTTMACHER, ALAN F., WINFIELD BEST, and FREDERICK S. JAFFE. *Birth control and love.* New York: Macmillan, 1969.

INTERNATIONAL CONFERENCE ON ABORTION. *The terrible choice: the abortion dilemma.* New York: Bantam, 1968.

LEWIS, ABIGAIL. *An interesting condition: the diary of a pregnant woman.* Garden City, N. Y.: Doubleday, 1950.

McWILLIAMS, M. *Nutrition for the growing years.* New York: Wiley, 1967.

MARTIN, E. A. *Nutrition in action,* 3rd ed. New York: Holt, 1971.

MINTURN, L. and W. W. LAMBERT. *Mothers of six cultures: antecedents of child rearing.* New York: Wiley, 1964.

NEUBARDT, SELIG. *A concept of contraception.* New York: Trident, 1967.

PATAI, R. (ed.). *Women in the modern world.* New York: Free Press, 1967.

PRESIDENT'S COMMITTEE ON POPULATION AND FAMILY PLANNING. *Population and family planning.* Washington, D. C.: U. S. Dept. of Health, Education and Welfare, 1968.

RAINWATER, LEE (ed.). Family planning in cross-national perspective. *Journal of Social Issues,* October 1967, **23**, (4).

RIVERS, P. My baby's book of child health. Oberlin, Oh.: Crane, 1971.

RUTHERFORD, F. W. *You and your baby.* New York: Signet, 1971.

SALTMAN, J. *Your new baby and you.* New York: Grosset, 1966.

SENNETT, RICHARD. *Families against the city.* Cambridge, Mass.: Harvard U. P., 1970.

SMITH, C. A. *Physiology of new born infant,* 3rd ed. Springfield, Ill.: Thomas, 1959.

WEISER, E. *Pregnancy: conception and heredity.* New York: Blaisdell, 1965.

WHITE HOUSE CONFERENCE ON CHILDREN. *Report to the President,* Washington, D. C., 1970.

WHITING, B. B., (ed.). *Six cultures: studies in child rearing.* New York: Wiley, 1963.

The Prenatal
and Neonatal
Stages

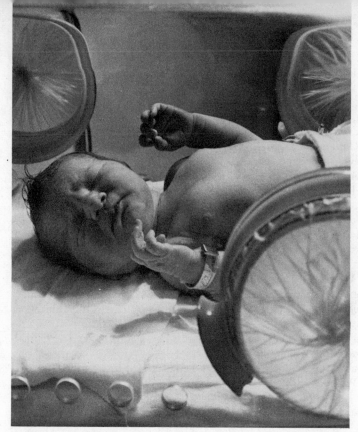

Infancy

Prelude
Basic Theory and Research
  Biological Domain
    Development and Organization
      of the Brain
    Basic Reflexes
    Basic Principles of Early
      Development
    Sensory and Perceptual
      Development
    Motor Development
    Nutrition
    Toilet Training
  Cognitive Domain
    Basic Learning Processes
    Learning Development
    Piaget's Theory of Cognitive
      Development

Language Development
Creativity
Affective Domain
  Basic Infant Responses
  Variability and Continuity in
    Emotional Development
Social Domain
  Basic Social Goals
  Trust
  Maternal Influences
Implications
  Understanding Yourself and
    Others
  Living and Working with Chil-
    dren, Adolescents, and Adults
  Developing Positive Models

PRELUDE

T HE FETUS, prior to birth, had been actively rehearsing some of the activities required of him after birth, such as respiratory exercises, circulation of blood, gross body movements, and the grasping reflex. He thus arrives with a fairly complex set of behaviors necessary for biological survival. However, he is quickly confronted with relentless demands from his changing physical and social environments. There is increasing evidence that the quality and quantity of these infant experiences are of very great importance for all the changes that follow. In the social domain there is evidence that the restricted interpersonal experiences during infancy form the basic psychological structures and attitudes for subsequent social experiences in later life. In the affective domain there is evidence that the origins of mature adult love develop during infancy and that if one hasn't learned to love during this critical period, one may never learn to love at all. In the cognitive domain there is evidence that during infancy there is a dramatic transformation from a reflex-oriented and one-tracked organism to a highly complex and multitracked human being. In the biological domain there is evidence that during infancy there are a series of transformations of the underlying organic structures that are responsible for supporting increasingly complex social, affective, and cognitive functioning.

This chapter attempts to present a coherent picture of the infant's behaviors in response to critical recurrent demands, to explain some of the mechanisms or reasons underlying these behaviors, and to suggest ways for maximizing their success. Unfortunately, in so doing, we find many gaps between what we need to know in order to achieve these objectives and what is actually known about the hows and whys of infant behavior and development.

BASIC THEORY AND RESEARCH

Although the newborn is a fairly complex organism, his behavior is primarily reflexive and stereotyped. By the third month of life, there is a major shift to a variegated and increasingly complex style of life. By the end of the second year he has developed the ability to represent himself and the world as separate entities in the form of mental images. He can now think out solutions to simple problems before acting on them.

How does this transformation of learning ability occur? One level of explanation lies in the biological domain. We know that information processing depends on the ability of healthy receptors to receive stimulation accurately (eyes, ears, nose, skin, and muscles) the versatility of affector organs (motor acts and later language), and what goes on between receiving and acting (the nervous system). In this section we concentrate on the gross development and functioning of the human brain and the behaviors that correspond with its growing parts.

BIOLOGICAL DOMAIN

Development and Organization of the Brain

Simply and functionally, the brain can be divided into three major parts, the lower or stem, the midbrain, and the cerebral cortex. The stem consists

Infancy

Fig. 15–1.
Sucking reflex.

of the cerebellum, the medulla, and the part of the spinal cord that enters the brain. The stem is basically concerned with such survival functions as reflexes, breathing, digestion, body balance, coordination, and metabolism; the midbrain essentially contains pathways between the stem and the cortex; the cerebral cortex controls such functions as learning, remembering, thinking, consciousness, and motor and sensory responses. The cerebral cortex is divided into two symmetrical hemispheres, one on the right side and the other on the left. Almost all of the functions of the left side of the body are dominated by the right hemisphere, and control of the right side of the body is dominated by the left hemisphere. Each hemisphere is divided into four lobes: the occipital lobe or visual area, the parietal lobe or body sensory area, the frontal lobe or motor and speech areas, and the temporal lobe or auditory area. Although each hemisphere is capable of functioning independently, normally both halves cooperate and are in direct communication regarding most major functions. (An important exception is language, which is normally located in the left hemisphere for right-handed persons and in the right hemisphere for left-handed persons.)

About three-fourths of the cortex, however, is not as well mapped as the lobes. It is, nevertheless, assumed that this section of the brain, known as *association* areas, is responsible for organizing, processing, and storing information for such high level intellectual tasks as learning, thinking, and language (Wenger et al., 1956). Figure 15–2 depicts schematic representations of the major parts of the brain and the four lobes.

The brain develops sequentially from the stem to the cortex. The cortex, far from being mature at birth, is the slowest part of the nervous system to develop. For some time it was believed that the newborn's cortex was non-

The Life
Cycle

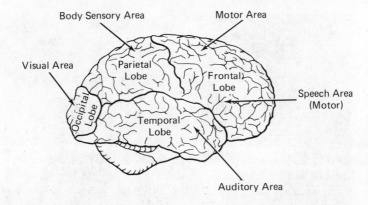

FIG. 15-2.
The human brain showing the main subdivisions and their major functions.

functioning at some time after birth (Robinson, 1969). Perhaps it was such evidence that led to the severe underestimation of the learning abilities of infants. Although the infant's behavior up to about the twentieth week is mediated primarily by the spinal cord and lower brain, there is increasing evidence that those parts of the brain, irrespective of location, necessary for the survival of the baby develop first during the fetal period (Robinson, 1969; Anokhin, 1964). For example, animals born and reared in the dark develop vision later and auditory and olfactory senses sooner in order to meet the special demands of their particular environment. At seven to nine months of age, the midbrain begins to function and new areas of competencies begin to appear. By the end of the first year the cortex is starting to play the dominant role; by the end of the second year most cortical maturation has been completed, and by the end of the eighth year practically all areas of the human nervous system's growth have been completed except for some maturation that continues until the middle of adolescence.

Basic Reflexes

The basic initial equipment for responding to external and internal stimulation during very early infancy is the reflex. A reflex is a relatively automatic or inborn response to a certain type of stimulation. As in all major developing functions, there is a period of anticipatory responses that precede the fully operative function. In fact, all reflexes found in the newborn can be traced back to fetal activities except for actual breathing (there are prebreathing exercises while still in the womb) and vocalization.

Oral Reflexes. Tactual stimulation applied to the infant's cheek or to the side of the mouth elicits the rooting reflex, the baby turns his head in the direction of the stimulation. Objects placed in the infant's mouth gradually elicit the sucking and squeezing activities known as the *sucking* reflex. With practice, the oral reflexes become better coordinated and more efficient.

In addition to their vital role in feeding, the oral reflexes serve important roles in "tranquilizing" and "explorative" functions. Sucking reduces general body activity and leads to a quieting effect on previously overactive infants (Wolff and Simmons, 1967). Furthermore, sucking can serve as a pain reducer and some hospitals commonly use pacifiers during circumcisions.

Moro Reflex. The effective stimuli for the Moro reflex are sharp blows to objects surrounding the infant, raising the head while the baby's on his back (supine position) and quickly releasing the grip on the head, and gently   Infancy

273

Figs. 15–3.
Basic reflexes:
(a) Tonic-neck
reflex, (b) Moro
reflex, (c)Labyrin-
thine righting
reflex, (d) Grasping
reflex.

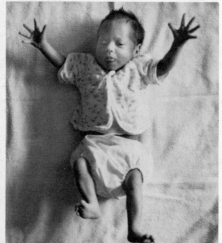

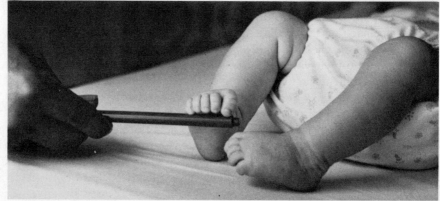

The Life
Cycle

raising him by his hands and then quickly letting go. This reflex will cause the baby to spread his arms and, to some extent, his fingers and legs; subsequently, he will return his arms and legs to a flexed position against his body. His arms are now in a position preparatory to embracing someone. We don't know whether this "embracing" behavior after a "frightening" experience is a signal for comforting by mother or others. The Moro reflex, seen as early as the ninth week after conception, disappears by the second or third month after birth.

Grasping Reflex. Touching, stroking, or placing objects on the palms of the hands and the front parts of the bottom of the toes leads to flexion of the hands and feet. This reflex, which is strong at birth and during the next few months, begins to weaken about the sixth month and disappears by the end of the first year. Some babies are able to remain suspended by the grips of their hands and feet (Illingsworth, 1971).

Tonic-Neck-Reflex. When the head is turned to one side, the infant assumes a "fencing" position. The arm, facing the head, is extended and the opposite leg and arm are flexed. While resting or sleeping the infant often assumes the "fencing" position during the first few months of life. This reflex develops during the twentieth week after conception and is utilized by obstetricians during normal deliveries in which the fetus comes out head first. By turning the head from side to side, the infant's torso and limbs also turn, thus facilitating the birth process.

Labyrinthine Righting Reflex. Toward the middle of the first year when the infant is held up by the shoulders, his head will maintain an upright position even though the body is being tilted in different directions. This reflex is first seen during the second month after birth when the infant tries to lift his head while lying on his stomach. By the fourth month he extends his arms to keep his head up longer (as if doing a push-up).

Positive Supporting Reflexes. Precursors to later complicated behavior such as walking, climbing, and crawling can be observed at birth or very shortly afterward. It is important to realize that these behaviors are reflexive and not under voluntary control. The "walking reflex" can be induced in many two-week old infants by holding an infant upright and letting the soles of his feet press against a horizontal surface, moving the infant forward, and tilting the body slightly to one side. Alternating the tilting while in forward motion can produce "walking" movements from the hip down. Using similar procedures, an infant can "climb" stairs or even "walk" on a ceiling while held upside down (Cratty, 1970). The "crawling reflex" can be induced by alternating pressure to the bottom of the feet. All of these reflexes, developed during the fetal period, terminate by about the fifth month.

"Swimming Reflex." Reflexive swimming movements can be induced by placing the infant in water when he is about two weeks old; the head must be supported during this time (McGraw, 1966). This reflex usually lasts until about the age of five months.

These reflexes in the behavior repertoire of the infant, and many more not mentioned, serve such functions as diagnostic signs of a healthy and developing nervous system, as survival mechanisms for an organism with minimal learning abilities, and as a major foundation for more complex behaviors as the underlying neurological structures proceed from subcortical levels as the infant interacts with the environment to stimulate and to facilitate neurological growth and functioning.

Infancy

Basic Principles of Early Development

Holistic Principle. What we see developing, even at the reflex level, is a positive growth cycle because of the powerful interactions between the biological domain and the environment as both cooperate to enhance optimal development. Any negative interference, whether from the "inside," such as neurological defects or hormonal imbalances, or from the "outside," such as lack of stimulation or proper diet, can alter the positive growth cycle into a negative one.

Mass to Specific Activity. At first, mass activity typifies infant behavior. A pinprick on a finger elicits not only hand and arm movements but also movement of the head and shoulders. If excited about something, the infant's whole body may move wildly around. For example, a hungry infant seems to be hungry all over; his ears, his toes, his fingers, and his whole body literally "cry" for nourishment judging by his massive all-inclusive reactions to hunger pangs. Gradually mass activity is replaced by specific individualized and coordinated responses.

Differentiation-Integration. The process of replacing mass with specific activity is known as *differentiation.* After an area of behavior has reached a certain stage of differentiation or specificity, the trend toward *integration* begins. That is, the small units of behavior start to combine and to coordinate into larger, more functional units. For instance, when hunger strikes, instead of a massive "catastrophic" reaction, we may see a sequence of meaningful attempts to obtain nourishment: mild crying, searching for food, reaching for the bottle or breast, and placing it directly into his mouth.

Cephalocaudal and Proximal-Distal Sequences. In general, from conception to maturity, growth proceeds in the direction from the head to the toes, the *cephalocaudal* sequence, and from the center of the body outward to the extremities, the *proximal-distal* sequence. Examples of cephalocaudal development are that at birth 25 per cent of the infant's body control resides in his head movements and the first step toward walking begins in head and neck control. A proximal-distal sequence is seen in the development of reaching. At first, the major activity centers around the torso and shoulders and then gradually to the arms, hands, and fingers.

Different Rates of Growth. Every time we state that a certain behavior or characteristic appears at a certain age we are merely providing the reader with an approximate time guideline for the average of a large number of subjects. It is well to remember that variability around the average or individual differences is the *sine qua non* of human development and behavior. Furthermore, important differences in rates of growth are also found within the development of any individual. For example, in the biological domain, growth of the reproductive organs is very slow compared to general body growth, whereas neurological growth is very rapid. In other words, although knowledge of a child's chronological age is helpful because we know what to expect in a general way, it isn't really sufficient information for us to appreciate his uniqueness as a human being. The following anecdote by Gesell illustrates the importance of intraindividual differences in rates of growth (Gesell and Ilg, 1943):

Then there is the story about the very modern boy, not much higher than a table, who wore a pair of horn-rimmed spectacles. A kindly lady leaned over and asked him tactfully, "How old are you, little boy?" He removed his horn-rimmed spectacles and reflectively wiped them. "My psychological age madam, is 12 years: my social age is 8 years; my moral age is 10 years; my anatomical ages are respectively 6 and 7; but I have not been apprised of my chronological age. It is a matter of relative unimportance." Thereupon he restored his horn-rimmed spectacles. (p. 69)

Sensory and Perceptual Development

Sensation refers to the ability of an organism to register what is happening in the external world and to some degree what is happening inside of him, in order to respond to it either through learning or reflex action. To do so the organism must have specialized receptors that are sensitive to the impinging stimulation. *Perception* refers to the process of converting the "meaningless" neural and chemical stimulations into information. Learning is the process by which we classify and store information, and thinking is the process by which we use the stored information in a variety of ways to solve problems. We now introduce the three major avenues through which we receive information from our external and internal worlds. They are proprioceptors or near senses, interoceptors or deep senses, and exteroceptors or distance senses.

Proprioceptors. Proprioceptors include smell, taste, and cutaneous or skin receptors. Smell is involved in detecting differences in the gases reaching the nose; taste is involved in detecting differences in the liquids and solids stimulating the taste buds. Both the smell and taste senses work closely together in detecting specific flavors within the primary tastes of sweet, sour, salty, and bitter. The cutaneous senses are involved in the sensations of touch, pain, warmth, and cold.

Smell. Since a necessary condition for a substance to have a smell is that gaseous form of the substance reach the olfactory receptors in the lining of the nasal cavity, we have no direct evidence that the fetus is capable of smelling; however, evidence for the very early ability, although primitive, to detect strong noxious odors is revealed by the violent reactions of some premature infants especially to ammonia (Peterson and Rainey, 1910). Similar results are found with infants from birth to three weeks of age indicating that the sense of smell is poorly developed at first (Pratt et al., 1930). One of the major reasons for difficulty in experimenting with olfaction is that the human sense of smell is much more sensitive than the chemical tests used to analyze the odors in the first place (Wenger et al., 1956). It has been estimated that most adults can detect about four thousand different odors.

Taste. The sense of taste, or gustatory, is not well developed in the newborn although he responds favorably to milk and sweet substances and negatively to strong solutions, which are salty, sour, or bitter (Pratt, 1954). By the second or third month there is a distinct increase in the infant's ability to disclose pleasure or displeasure regarding his food preferences (Watson and Lowrey, 1954). Research indicates that reactions to the same food by infants, young children, and adults differ, possibly because of a decreasing number of taste buds as a function of age up to adolescence (Laird and Drexel, 1939). This conclusion probably coincides with the experience of mothers with their children during meal time as they grow.

The Cutaneous Senses. The skin, our largest organ, is sensitive to mechanical, electrical, thermal, and chemical stimulation and can literally engulf us, hopefully, in varied and tingling pleasures.

Pressure, Touch, and Pain. Fetuses during the last few months and new-born infants are sensitive to pressure, touch, and pain (Carmichael, 1954). However, none of these senses is well developed nor differentiated, and a stimulus such as pain must be strong to elicit any response especially during the first few days after birth (Gullickson and Crowell, 1964). At first, the infant responds to irritation with immediate and generalized body movements. Gradually there is a delay in responding, and by the first year or so the infant becomes capable of directly locating the source of irritation with his hands or by sight (Jensen, 1932).

Thermal Sensitivity. There is abundant evidence that newborns are sensitive to temperature changes (Pratt, 1954). The presence of sensitivity to changes in temperature probably depends on the age of the newborn. Infants who have become accustomed to a certain milk temperature are likely to protest change in the temperature. On the other hand, in one study with newborns, the range of individual differences before reacting to differences in milk temperature was from 50 to 85 degrees Centigrade and for cold milk the range was from 5 to 32 degrees Centigrade (Jensen, 1932). These results indicate that newborns have a wide range of tolerance for temperatures considerably above and below that of normal body temperature and demonstrate, again, the singular need for adults to treat even the newborn as unique individuals.

That newborn infants may be less sensitive to cold than we had previously realized or that they may be able to become rapidly accustomed to it has been demonstrated by some recent studies. In one study premature babies were fed milk directly from a refrigerator whereas a similar group was fed with milk at body temperature. After over two thousand feedings a careful medical examination of both groups of infants revealed only one significant difference—a temporary drop in body temperature immediately following feeding for the infants who were given cold milk (Holt et al., 1962). Similar results were reported earlier in a study with one hundred and fifty infants who were fed cold milk formulas. Here we may conclude that either infants are much more resilient physiologically or that learning and habituation occur much earlier than we had previously believed. In either case, before recommending cold milk feeding we would first like to see the results of long-range research with a large number of normal, premature, and exceptional infants.

Interoceptors. The interoceptors or deep senses are of three types. The kinesthetic includes receptors in the muscles, tendons, and joints that provide information about body movements; the vestibular includes receptors in the inner ear that provide information about location and movement of the body in space; and the organic includes receptors in the inner organs that provide information about such bodily functions as need for food and water, temperature changes, and sensations related to sex.

Kinesthesis. Kinesthesis is the sense of active movement, and in many respects physical movement is almost akin to the feeling of being alive. The continuous flow of sensations that comes to us from the different parts of the body provides us literally with a "symphony of information" about what we are doing and learning physically. The following description gives us some idea of what life would be like without kinesthesis (Sanford, 1961).

There is a disease known as *labes dorsalis* which involves a destruction of the neural tracts carrying muscular sensations to the brain. With this disease, an individual can still move his muscles, for the pathways running to them are intact. But he cannot control his movements except by watching very carefully what he has just done. If he shuts his eyes, he cannot walk. Nor can he stand erect with his eyes shut, for what we know as standing still involves a constant pattern of learning albeit one way, correcting for it, learning the other, correcting for it, and so on. Such small speedy and constantly needed correctives cannot be made on the basis of visual and static sensations alone. If the damage in *labes dorsalis* is high up in the nervous system, the individual is unable to touch his face or his ear without watching carefully his every move, and if the damage is in the brain itself the delicate muscular co-ordinations necessary for speech become difficult and the patient's speech may become almost completely unintelligible. (p. 256)

There is evidence that the fetus has been exercising kinesthesis well before birth (Carmichael, 1954). Naturally the fluid fetal environment was conducive to physical freedom and, hence, considerable movement.

Vestibular. In addition to kinesthesis and vision, our ability to sense body positional changes and movement in space (from the horizontal to the not-so-vertical to the vertical, forward, backward, and sideways movements and so forth) depends on the proper functioning of the vestibular apparatus that is mediated by the three semicircular canals in each ear. Fortunately, there is a reliable neurological test for proper vestibular functioning that can be used with newborn infants (Lawrence and Feind, 1953). The test consists of a rapid rotation of the infant's body and observation of the presence of nystagmus—the slow movement of the eyes in the direction opposite the rotation and their rapid return to central fixation. Nystagmus can be readily demonstrated in newborn infants.

Organic. The internal physiological security of the body is maintained and regulated in a fairly automatic fashion by homeostatic mechanisms that: (1) maintain relative stability in such things as nourishment, water, temperature, and blood salt, acidity, and glucose; (2) regulate the endocrine glands that influence body growth and functions by secreting hormones directly into the bloodstream. These glands include the pituitary (growth), thyroid (body activities), parathyroid (tissue activity), adrenals (maintenance of life, emotions, sex differences), pancreas (sugar), ovaries (feminization), and testes (masculinization); (3) provide inner defenses against disease and physical damage by the production of high temperatures, antibodies, and coagulants.

Because of the nature of its functions the organic sense may be considered to be "the inner voice" of the body. Lack of homeostasis or balance usually produces symptoms or messages such as body tension or feelings of distress. When nourishment or water is needed, the "message" usually comes through very loud and clear. At other times the signals that all is not well within the body and that help is needed from the outside (medicine, surgery) may or may not be interpreted correctly by the individual. Infants and young children need the assistance of a perceptive interpreter for the signals coming from within the body.

Exteroceptors. Exteroceptors include the two senses that give us information of distant objects, audition and vision. Audition or hearing is the ability to respond intelligently to the almost infinite variations and combinations of sounds. Vision is the ability to translate correctly the complex physical characteristics of light transmitted from almost endless objects in different and varying positions in space under changing and subtle conditions of illumination.

Audition. As mankind has become more and more socialized his sense of hearing has become correspondingly more important for living and working together. Life today centers more about a people-world than an object-world. Try to imagine the nature of your daily existence while living in a highly crowded city if you could not hear a sound! Try to imagine how understanding people would be toward you if you continually ignored their comments, requests, and warnings!

Both fetuses and newborns respond to fairly high levels of auditory stimulation. This apparent early inability to respond to lower levels of sound could be attributable to the presence of mucous in the inner ears or to the fact that the newborns are merely reacting to reflex hearing (Whetnall, 1958). Comprehension hearing will gradually develop as the higher centers of the brain gain control over the lower reflexive ones. The inability of newborns to respond to low frequency sounds led some investigators to conclude that newborns were deaf (Spears and Hohle, 1967). Neonates respond readily to sounds such as whistles, bells, hand clapping, and the clanging from tin cans or pans. By the tenth day some infants react to voice sounds. By the fifth and sixth month most infants turn their heads in the direction of sounds that are visually out of their range (Gesell, 1925). However, more recent research suggests that neonates only twenty-three to one hundred hours old have a capacity for sound localization (Leventhal et al., 1964). This finding is important because it suggests that cortical development is more advanced than was previously indicated by research.

During verbal "communication" with newborn infants, the characteristics of infant hearing should be considered. For example, research supports the common practice of talking or singing to distressed infants in low-pitched monotones to calm them down (Thompson, 1962). Infants, like all individuals, undergo a reduction in responsiveness with prolonged stimulation. Research suggests that auditory stimulation of about ten seconds produces optimal reactions (Haller, 1932). It has been found that as sound durations increase beyond ten seconds there is a tendency for infants to become less responsive (Pratt, 1954). Thus, if we wish to repeat certain sounds over and over again we should do so for ten-second periods with ten-second intervals in order to evoke maximum responses.

Thus far there has been little auditory research with older infants, but since learning to hear must precede learning to speak it seems logical that parents should maintain verbal "communication." Furthermore, there is some evidence that older infants respond more to familiar words than to new ones, which suggests some accommodation to the sounds of the human language (Mussen et al., 1969). We know that infants are soothed by familiar lullabies. Recent research indicates that this is also true even for two-year-olds. In one study, in which the sleep-inducing qualities of metronomes, heartbeats, and lullabies were compared, it was found that heartbeats were significantly more calming (Salk, 1961). Perhaps the wisdom of cuddling and embracing is not just a romantic notion after all. What greater security can there be than to hear again the rhythmic sounds that we heard at the dawn of our own creation?

Vision. For centuries many romanticists have viewed vision as the "mirror of the soul." But for most scientists and parents, infants' vision was considered to be essentially nonexistent or a mass of visual confusion and blindness. Recent research reveals that infants, even at birth, can see far more than the most romantic poets imagined. Even before birth all the basic parts of the eye necessary for vision are completely formed except for the still-developing fovea (Peiper, 1963). This means that the newborn's world is not formless and chaotic, and that the newborn can see objects rather clearly. In fact, two-day-old infants prefer to fixate on more complex patterns than simpler ones when given various choices of what to look at, such as when shown a schematically drawn face, a bull's-eye pattern, a section of newsprint, a plain white circle, a fluorescent yellow circle, and a red circle, the newborn's order of preferences was the face pattern, the bull's-eye, and the newsprint. In just four short months infants are able to accommodate (make adjustments to objects at varying distances) almost as well as adults (Fantz, 1963).

Sustained visual fixation, which is absent at birth and rudimentary within a few hours, becomes operational by about the fourth or fifth week (Ling, 1942). During the first six to nine weeks sharp and complex contours are attractive to infants especially where the contrasts are created between black and white (Salapatek and Kessen, 1966). Infants also tend to pay more attention to moving objects as early as thirty-six hours after birth when they will visually pursue a light in a dark room (Sherman and Sherman, 1925). In a lighted room infants will demonstrate horizontal visual pursuit at about fifteen days, vertical pursuit at about thirty-five days, and circular visual pursuit at about one hundred and five days (Jones, 1926). In addition, research on fixation shows that up to age six months infants prefer the human face to nonsocial stimuli (McCall and Kagan, 1967). Since infants show a strong preference for the human face or anything resembling it, familiarity is a most important determinant of visual preference.

Apparently "divine discontent" with the old and renewed attraction to the novel also typifies much of infant visual behavior. With continued repetitions of the small stimuli the fixation time of infants tends to decrease (Fantz, 1964) even though it does increase with such familiar things as the human face. In an attempt to resolve this contradiction, McCall and Kagan tested infant males and females just prior to the fourth month with a discrepancy hypothesis (McCall and Kagan, 1967). This hypothesis stated that stimuli that represent a moderate discrepancy from the ones being presently perceived will elicit maximal attention, whereas those stimuli that are very similar or very different will elicit minimal attention. The discrepancy hypothesis was supported by female infants but not by the males. To explain the failure of the males to support the experiment the researchers raised the possibility that visual development may be more advanced for girls than boys. Perhaps future research will support the discrepancy hypothesis for male infants who are slightly older but, nevertheless, there is validity in the idea of presenting infants with slightly different stimuli in order to attract and to maintain their attention. This sustained effort by the infant toward novel stimuli is explained later in this chapter in the discussion of the theories and findings of Jean Piaget, the great Swiss child psychologist.

Infancy

Monocular vision (seeing with one eye at a time) characterizes infant vision during about the first eight weeks. The infant fixates one eye on an object and closes or relaxes the other eye (Gesell, 1950). Gradually the infant demonstrates rapid alternation from one eye to the other. "Crossing" of the eyes or strabismus is fairly common at this stage and coordination of both eyes improves rapidly during the first few days of visual practice (Sherman and Sherman, 1929). During these early weeks we can observe the first joining of an eye to a hand either during the movements produced by the tonic-neck-reflex or in the normal resting position as the eye fixates on the extended arm and hand; however, it will not be until the fifth or sixth month that true visually directed reaching of objects will emerge.

Binocular vision, which develops with foveal maturity, occurs when the two eyes simultaneously team together to focus on an object of interest. The first signs of binocular fixation, which permits far more accurate judgments of distance and depth, can be observed in infants between the sixth and eighth week. Up to this time, vision has been essentially monocular, reflexive, and limited to fairly large objects within a distance of about two feet. From the fourth month on there is evidence that the infant is achieving cortical control, and hence voluntary control, over his visual activities. Now, with rapid improvement in visual acuity and binocular vision, the infant's grasp of the visual world expands significantly.

After the first year, infant vision is basically similar to that of an adult except that the infant lacks the language skills necessary for thinking through complex visual problems, the richness of previous associations with the visual world, and constancy and accuracy when perception involves geometric figures and their characteristics such as shape, size, and solidity. For example, a two-year-old may appreciate the differences among forms of objects, but he can be readily observed placing a triangular cover on a square pot. Some size constancy is detectable as early as the tenth week and in most infants by six months (Cruikshank, 1964), but two- to four-year olds still may confuse "big" and "small" and especially the concept of "middle-size" (Thrum, 1935). Size constancy, as displayed by adults, is not reached until about age ten.

Much of the variety and richness of early sensory and perceptual experiences comes about through the combinations of information received by means of the various senses. For example, an infant's notion of an apple consists of visual, taste, olfactory, and tactile feedbacks. If he throws the apple, he receives kinesthetic feedback, and, when it lands he may receive auditory information. It is the totality of all these bits of information that enables the infant to take a hold of and to make sense of his expanding world.

Motor Development

The development of *locomotion* involves an orderly sequence of maturational events and appropriate exercises that eventually result in voluntary, controlled, and well-coordinated walking (fifteenth month), running (second to sixth year), and skipping (sixth year). By the fourth week, the infant can lift his chin; by the sixth week, when held up in the prone position, he can maintain his head level with his body; by the twelfth week, the supporting reflex permits him to hold his head and shoulders up from the floor. By the sixth month he can hold up his chest and upper abdomen. At this time the cerebellum, which is concerned with balance and posture, begins its rapid growth period that will last until the eighteenth month (Gesell and Thompson, 1934). The infant can now roll from the prone position to the supine, and, within a month, from the supine to the prone (Illingsworth, 1971). By the ninth month, most babies can sit steadily without support for about ten minutes, lean forward, and recover their balance (but not if they lean sideways).

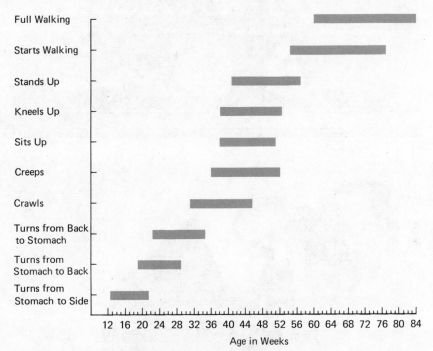

FIG. 15–4.
Age range for motor development. (Reprinted by permission from Emmi Pikler, Learning of Motor Skills on the basis of self-induced movements. In J. Hellmuth, ed., Exceptional Infant, Vol. 2. New York: Brunner/Mazel, Inc., 1971.)

*Crawling.** At this stage, between the fourth and seventh month, the infant is "putting all his resources together" (integration) to engage in a more complex process that is under his *voluntary* control: reflexes, maturation of the brain to higher levels, visual perception, and psychological motivation. When placed in a prone position, the labyrinthine and supportive reflexes permit him to raise the front part of his body so that he is able to locate desired objects. In the process of crawling toward the desired goal he will now put to use the movements he has previously used in the reflexive movements known as the tonic-neck-reflex. With the abdomen touching the floor, the infant begins to crawl slowly forward propelled by the friction caused by his arm movements. Additional friction is provided when the legs begin to move with the arms. The head faces the side in which the arm and the leg are flexed in a forward position, and then the entire body is reversed along with the corresponding arm, leg, and head direction. Thus crawling is a *homolateral* activity, one side operates first and then the other. These movements can also be observed when the infant is lying on its back. When the head is turned, he will flex the corresponding side of its body and then alternate when the head is turned to the other side.

* Some writers use the terms *crawling* and *creeping* as synonyms whereas still others use crawling for creeping and creeping for crawling. In this book crawling is defined as distinct from and prior developmentally to creeping.

Infancy

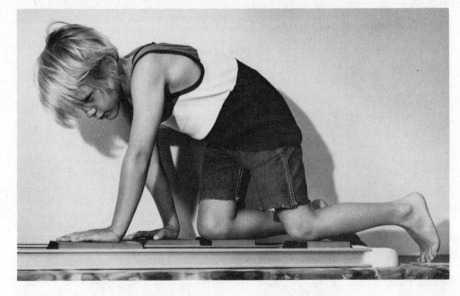

FIGS. 15-5.
(a) Homolateral
creeping. Note that
the left arm and
left leg are both
forward. (b) Bi-
lateral creeping left
arm and right leg
are forward.
Bilateral creeping
begins after about
nine months.

Further evidence of the homolateral nature of infant activity is observable in the visual and auditory areas during actual crawling according to Dela-cato (1966). As the infant locomotes he uses his right eye for right move-ments and his left eye for left movements. During this stage he has difficulty locating sounds in space because his ears are not working together as a stereophonic system. Other studies emphasize that infants can follow moving objects with both eyes as early as the first week of life and can locate sounds by turning their eyes at one month (Nelson, 1966). This apparent disagree-ment is probably one more example of the single-track undifferentiated nature of very early infant attention.

Creeping. Creeping develops from crawling at about nine months. In this form of locomotion the body is carried up from the floor and the infant moves on his hands and knees. At first the pattern is still homolateral, that is, movement begins with a single arm and a knee from the same side of the body advancing at a time. Smooth and efficient creeping begins when he

The Life
Cycle

284

starts to locomote in a *cross-pattern* fashion. At first the left hand will move forward with the head pointed at it and both eyes focused on it, followed by the right knee; then the entire process will be reversed using the other hand and knee. With practice the sets of alternate hands and knees will make contact with the floor at the same time.

At this stage, the infant for the first time has become a *bilateral* being, that is, he is now capable of using both sides of the body in concert. Furthermore, he has now become capable of using both eyes in concert while engaging in a complex activity; he can now be labeled as being fully *binocular* in addition to being *binaural,* that is, capable of using both ears simultaneously. The infant has become far more capable of judging the distance of objects by stereoscopic vision and the location of sounds by stereophonic hearing.

Variation in human locomotion is observable during these early stages prior to standing and walking without support. Among these forms of progression are (Illingsworth, 1971):

1. The infant may become proficient at getting around by rolling.
2. The infant may lie in the supine position and elevate the buttocks and the entire lower part of the body from the ground, progressing by a series of bumps on the buttocks.
3. The infant may hitch or shuffle—getting about on one hand and one buttock, or on both hands and both buttocks.
4. The infant may crawl backward.

Standing and Walking. Standing alone is the next step in the development of walking, although some infants walk almost as soon as they can stand. Most infants, however, will begin to walk several weeks after being able to stand freely (Shapiro, 1962). Being able to stand with support normally coincides with the previous stages of crawling and creeping.

The average infant or toddler learns to walk during the first three months of the second year although it will be about another year before his walking approximates the smoothness, efficiency, and ease of adult walking. The first efforts at unsupported forward movement are often met with some frustration because of his own excitement, the outward direction of his feet, his relatively high center of gravity, his short, erratic steps, the high, unnecessary lifting of his legs, and so forth. In efforts to maintain balance, the infant's hands are usually held up above his head or out at his sides. With maturational changes in his body proportions, from stubby legs, long trunk, and large head and abdomen, the center of gravity is lowered, and with the development of his neuromuscular system, he gradually develops the strength and coordination necessary for walking in a normal cross-pattern fashion that is an extension of cross-pattern creeping. For example, as the left arm and right leg move forward, the head and neck will turn slightly toward the extended arm, and then the entire process is reversed to the left side of the body as the right arm and left leg move forward.

For the toddler, the advent of walking probably brings tremendous feelings of joy and power. He can now extend himself to most everything in his horizon. He may even feel the way Julius Caesar felt when he said, as he observed the world at his feet: "Veni, vidi, vici." (I came, I saw, I conquered). For the parents the advent of baby walking may be like "seeing the pyramids move." Their doll can really walk! It works! Now the parents may see actual proof that someday the infant will be really able to continue

Infancy

to walk "in their shoes onto eternity." Nevertheless, the parents will now have to protect "moving baby" more than before because his ability to explore, manipulate, and to get into things far exceeds his awareness of potential dangers: a yank on a dangling tablecloth could precipitate an avalanche, a finger in an electric outlet is a "shocking" thing, and the sight of a hungry dog eyeing his empty plate is sad to behold.

Manipulation. The emphasis thus far has been on how the external world operates on the internal world of the infant to help him to accomplish the developmental tasks expected of him biologically and psychologically. In this section, we are concerned primarily with the development of ways by which the infant operates on the external world in order to understand it, change it, and come to terms with it. As in all facets of growth, we see the gradual development of complex skills from the combinations of more fundamental and often anticipatory ones, through the processes of differentiation and integration. In other words, through the study of manipulatory skills, we are able to see that simpler systems of behavior gradually become coordinated into superordinate systems that integrate what were previously distinct, separate, and simple functions. In addition, in this section we review some evidence that the infant's ability to process information is greater than his ability to use it, or to put it more succinctly, the infant is smarter than the impression given by research and casual observation up to this time.

Integration of Separate Functions. The infant takes hold of the world with his eyes and mouth months before he can do so with his hands and arms. During the first two months, his hands remain tightly closed and his arms are limited in the variety of positions that they can assume. During this period, hand and arm activities are basically controlled by the grasping and tonic-neck reflexes, respectively. Thus, for the first eight weeks, the infant's "manipulatory" activities are visual—looking, staring, seeking, groping—and sucking, tasting, swallowing, and rejecting. Nevertheless, it has been recently discovered that, even at this very early stage, the infant is capable of integrating vision and sucking into a more powerful system for manipulating the environment.

By about the third month the liberation from reflexes is seen as the infant develops more voluntary control over his activities. The development of the first voluntary physical prehensile activity is that of swiping at objects, an activity that indicates the beginning of visually guided motor movements. At this time, the infant's preference for looking at three-dimensional objects exceeds that for two-dimensional viewing. By the fourth month reaching toward an object develops although not the grasping of it. Visually, the infant can be observed alternating between looking at his hand and the object. The next developmental stage is visually guided manipulation of the hands. Here we see the unification of touch with vision. Between the fourth and sixth month, the period during which sitting without support develops, the infant is starting to coordinate all the preceding manipulatory skills into visually guided, tactual-motor grasping activities. Here the independent and semi-independent functions combine together to provide the infant with visually directed reaching and grasping. When grasping an object, the infant routinely looks at it and feels it before bringing it to his mouth.

At about six months and after, the infant seems to say "I've waited a long time to show my stuff. Now watch me do my thing." He now tears, crumbles, rubs, squeezes, and pushes appropriate objects. He drops and throws things.

All these activities permit him to integrate visual, tactual, kinesthetic, and auditory inputs (Uzgiris, 1967). Toward the end of the first year he seems to say "Well, I've been self-centered. Let me now show you my goodies." The infant will now extend an object to another person but will resist efforts to take it away. By age two, he is more willing to share in the process of give and take. In these activities we can see the beginnings of passive and active social manipulations.

Nutrition

Now, more than ever before, special attention is being paid to the biological, psychological, and social well being of infants because it is there where the foundations for healthy adults are formed. The importance of nutrition during infancy and early childhood is much greater than it is during the adult years, because the major parts of the body, especially the nervous system, undergo their greatest growth during this period. The far-reaching impact of poor nutrition is well documented. Biological and cognitive retardation, irritability, lack of alertness, sleeplessness, apathy, diminished motivation, and so on have been reported.

Early research had established that undernourished infants tend to develop smaller head sizes than their more nourished counterparts. Later research, however, has revealed that smallness of head size was correlated with smallness of brains in undernourished infants in addition to retardation in physical, motor, sensory, and psychological development (Stoch and Smythe, 1967). It is important to realize that the rest of the body—heart, lungs, muscles, and so on—also develops sequentially. The timing of growth of the organs differs but the end results are roughly similar. If the early growth of an organ is stunted, the chances of reaching maximum development is diminished.

The deleterious effects of malnutrition on the human brain have been reported on a world-wide basis—Africa, Chile, Indonesia, India, Lebanon, and the United States—and the same dismal thread of limited mental and physical development appears in all studies (Heard et al., 1961). The more elaborate analysis of the effects of malnutrition permitted by animal experimentation not only supports the human findings but also reveals additional complications. Studies of the effects of diets that are low in good quality protein on the development of baby dogs and pigs reveal not only retardation of physical growth and brain size but also structural as well as functional abnormalities of the nervous system (Heard et al., 1961; Lowrey et al., 1962). Such abnormalities in the nervous system, the central switchboard for body and mental functions, can be responsible for pervasive chemical and neurological disturbances throughout the body. To guarantee infants the full growth of their brains and bodies is the extraordinarily important function of proper nutrition during the first year. They will not get a second chance because cellular growth in the brain stops at approximately the same time for undernourished as well as for properly nourished infants.

Birth to Third Month. The most obvious characteristics of infant feeding during this stage are the unmitigated demands for instant feeding and irregularities and short intervals of the hunger cycle. Hungry adults tend to get grumpy if food is delayed, but infants literally turn into "masses of screaming hunger." This is because hunger sensations are subcortically con-

Infancy

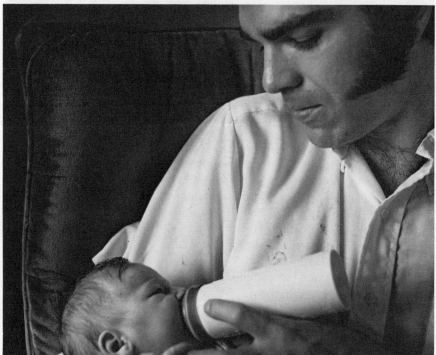

trolled, and it will not be until the fourth month or so before the cerebral cortex will start to exert some control and inhibition over hunger pangs. Since demands for food based on physiological rhythms will not become regular for some months, babies are usually placed on a self-regulation or

The Life
Cycle

"self-demand" feeding schedules. Most babies will demand food every two to four hours (Aldrich and Hewitt, 1947). Babies who are fed on demand seem to be well nourished, especially when they are capable of vigorously expressing their needs (Simsarian, 1948). For passive babies some kind of flexible or variable schedule may be more suitable than self-regulation. Based on one comprehensive study of fifty newborns, more than one-third of the total crying of newborns is for food, and another one-third for physical discomfort. The reasons for the remaining crying time could not be accounted for (Aldrich et al., 1945). By the end of the first year most infants will have adjusted to the various adult feeding schedules.

Before considering the management and details of feeding, or any other area of child development, it is essential to realize that it is the total relationship between parents and infant that is paramount. The truth of this statement is supported again and again in research findings dealing with parent and adult-child relationships. For example, a loving tender mother who bottle feeds her baby on a rigid schedule will, in all probability, do a better job than an indifferent mother who mechanically administers "the best techniques known to science." But imagine the results of a loving mother who practices recommended techniques and who modifies them to meet the special changing individualized needs of her infant.

The contents of colostrum are remarkably matched to the nutritional needs of the newborn and it also supplies defenses against disease (Committee on Nutrition, 1960). Human milk, after the colostrum stage, supplies all the nutrients required for the next few months, except for vitamin D if the mother's diet is adequate. During lactation the mother's dietary needs are greater than those during pregnancy because of the increased nutritional needs of the growing infant. A vitally important difference between breast- and bottle-feeding is that breast-feeding, because of its intimate nature, guarantees emotional support for the infant whereas bottle-feeding will only provide emotional support if the infant is physically supported during feeding. Research, which is discussed later in this chapter, stresses the tremendous importance, sometimes a matter of life or death, of early handling and cuddling. This information is particularly important for mothers living in the United States because American mothers nurse less often and for a shorter period of time than do mothers in Europe, Asia, and Africa (Aitken and Hytten, 1960). The frequency of breast-feeding among mothers in this country, however, is reported to be higher for those in the upper social class as compared to those in the lower social class (Salber and Fernleib, 1966).

Third Month to Second Year. By about the third month, additional amounts of food, vitamins, and minerals are needed to satisfy the baby's growing needs and increased activities. Semisolid, puréed foods should be added to the milk diet. The timing for the gradual introduction of these new foods depends on the individual infant's physiological and psychological readiness to receive and to manipulate solids from the front to the back of the mouth. At first, it may be best to place the food well back on the tongue. Psychological readiness for new foods is assured by having made the infant's first three months of feeding pleasant and enjoyable.

Weaning from sucking to drinking from a cup usually begins some time during the last quarter of the first year. Weaning in fact has been going on since the fetal stage from nutrients supplied by maternal blood, colostrum, milk, vitamin drops, and semisolids. Some babies wean themselves; most require patience and understanding during this process. A delay of several months, if it helps the infant to establish positive attitudes toward feeding, is certainly worthwhile—unless the mother is breast-feeding and the infant has exceedingly strong jaws and a full set of teeth that may develop before age one. Most infants' teeth, however, begin to erupt between the fifth and eighth month.

Sucking for nonnutritive purposes occurs even at birth. As sucking becomes more proficient, almost any handy object may become an oral target. Such sucking is a normal activity and an important avenue of learning for the infant as discussed later in this chapter. Even sucking a thumb or a pacifier for years falls within the normal range. However, if sucking continues after the secondary teeth have appeared, usually around age five, then there are grounds for concern because of possible dental malformations (Lewis, 1937).

Many infants are ready to share, within limits, the family menu by about age two when their digestive systems have matured sufficiently to digest most of the foods prepared for adults.

Toilet Training

Most problems related to readiness for training such as weaning, toilet training, reading, and writing would probably be lessened if we waited until all children reached the age of fifteen. The point we are trying to make is that one of the greatest dangers to a child's health physically, psychologically, and socially is to force him to do things when he is not ready holistically. Perhaps all norms or records of expected behaviors at certain ages should be destroyed or a sign should be posted on them stating, "Warning: It has been determined that use of this information is dangerous to your health and that of your child." Perhaps, then, both parents can relax, be themselves, and continue on happily with the business of helping children to grow up without constant insidious and invidious comparisons with the "marvelously precocious achievements of others."

Bowel and bladder control, like creeping and walking, is best learned when the infant is ready neurologically, physically, and psychologically. The same logic which inhibits parents from punishing an infant for not walking early or for occasionally falling and tripping as he masters the complex skills of upright locomotion applies to toilet training and its frequent mishaps. For the first year or so, elimination is reflexive, automatic, and uncontrollable by the infant because toilet functions are still under subcortical influence. Voluntary control, hence trainability, appears when the cerebral cortex begins to coordinate the activities of the subcortical areas.

Usually the infant will provide subtle cues as to when toilet training should begin with such telltable signs as regularity of elimination needs, anticipatory physical movements, or repetition of words or sounds used by the parents during these processes. When training is adapted to the infant's growth pattern and personality characteristics, the chances are high that toilet training will require little, if any, "training."

Expected ages for the achievement of bowel control vary considerably. In one study most children achieved such control by age two and one-half, the percentage being higher for girls (Roberts and Schoelkopf, 1951). Some children, however, do not achieve full control until ages four or five. Bladder control generally follows bowel control. As with most developmental tasks related to neural maturation, much patience is necessary if optimal success is to be achieved. Figure 15–7 illustrates the success factors when two twins were started on bladder control training at different times (McGraw, 1940). Training for the first twin was started far too early, whereas training for the second twin was profitably delayed until about the end of the second year. It is encouraging to note that there seems to be a trend toward postponing beginning training. In 1935, Fries reported that the initial age for bowel training was six months with an average time of one to two months for the majority of infants (Fries, 1935). In 1957, Sears, Maccoby, and Levin found that eleven months was the average beginning age with an average time for completion of training of about seven months (Sears et al., 1957).

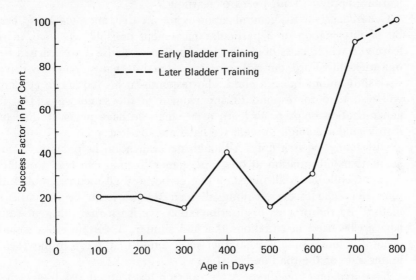

FIG. 15–7. *Bladder control training should begin when the individual infant is neurologically ready. Efforts to achieve control prior to maturational readiness may lead to failure experiences for both infant and parents. (Adapted from McGraw, 1940)*

COGNITIVE DOMAIN

Basic Learning Processes

In general, learning is said to occur when there have been changes in behavior as a result of experiences as distinguished from changes in behavior resulting from such nonexperiential factors as genetic inheritance, maturation, or physiological changes caused by disease, drugs, or extreme fatigue. Two basic learning processes are referred to as classical and instrumental (operant) conditioning.

Classical Conditioning. Classical conditioning is the simplest form of learning and is considered by many psychologists to underlie the earliest learning in fetuses and newborns. It later continues as a basic form of learning throughout life.

In 1927 Ivan Pavlov found that dogs could learn to salivate to a variety of previously neutral stimuli such as tones, bells, touches on the body, or upon the sight or sound of the person who normally fed them. Pavlov found, for example, that if he repeatedly rang a bell and then presented food to a hungry dog, soon the ringing of the bell alone was enough to produce salivation in the dog. The major point is that events that occur repeatedly together tend to be connected in such a way that in the future the happening of one event or stimulus will increase the chances of a certain type of   Infancy response to occur again. Through classical conditioning, responses to a great variety of new stimulus situations are often changed without the awareness of the organism involved.

Instrumental Conditioning. In contrast to classical conditioning where things are done to the subject, in instrumental or operant conditioning the subject must produce the desired behavior independently before receiving a reward (positive reinforcement) or punishment (negative reinforcement). In other words, in instrumental conditioning the subject must be active; it must produce the desired behavior such as naming an object correctly, reaching for a cup, writing a letter, and so on before reinforcement.

Although instrumental conditioning can lead to more complex, varied, and novel behaviors than classical conditioning, the following principles of learning apply to both forms of learning.

Generalization. By generalization is meant that once we have learned a bit of information or a particular movement or skill, we have, in reality, learned a whole class of similar information or skills. If we learned to drive in a stick-shift Ford, our skills are generalized so that we can now drive most stick-shift automobiles; a child who responds to his mother in certain ways will also tend to respond to any woman in the same ways. The fact of generalization helps us to learn even what we have never studied or seen if it is similar enough to what we have already learned.

Discriminative Learning. Although generalization helps us to learn large amounts of information at one time, generalization can lead to difficulties. A young child loves all men to a degree because all men resemble father to some degree. However, calling all men "Daddy" can be embarrassing to mother. By the process of discrimination, we learn that different responses have to be used in situations that are similar. A certain siren sound may mean it is lunch time, but another siren sound may mean to move your car to one side of the road and to stop.

Reinforcement Schedules. After a person has learned a skill efficiently, we want him to retain the skill for a long time without the need for constant reteaching or rewarding. A mother wants her child to become independent of her training, and a teacher wants students to work on their own. The essential procedures for long-range learning are described as follows (Skinner, 1938):

1. *Continuous Rewards.* Begin to train by providing the proper reward after the person has produced the proper response. For example, when the child starts to read for the first time, tell him what a good boy he is *every time* he starts to read in order to establish a new habit.

2. *Intermittent Rewards.* After the child has started to form the habit, praise him every other day or so. Studies indicate that learning under intermittent rewards lasts longer than learning under continuous rewards.

3. *Variable Rewards.* After the child's habit is well established, praise him irregularly so that he never knows when he is going to be rewarded. In life, rewards are given occasionally, not every time. Research indicates that learning under variable rewards lasts longer than learning under intermittent rewards.

4. *No Reward.* In order to develop persistent and possibly lifelong habits, the dependency on external rewards must be gradually removed. If the first three steps are followed, then rewards are no longer always neces-

sary because the learned behavior tends to become self-rewarding. Self-rewarding behavior feels good and the child too "wants to keep it up." He has now developed a habit and it becomes, hopefully, an automatic part of his way of living.

As a rule there is relatively little creativity in conditioning behavioristic learning. As mentioned in Chapter 12, learning by association is often referred to as S-R or stimulus-response learning (sometimes referred to as behavioristic learning) in which the individual is essentially molded by the external forces impinging upon him. Nevertheless, both kinds of conditioning account for a great deal of learning, whether conscious or unconscious, up to about age four and then decrease in importance thereafter.

Imitation and Identification. In this type of learning the desired behavior comes from watching or hearing other persons who deliberately or inadvertently demonstrate the responses. Learning by imitating the behaviors of others is common, but the most "contagious" models are those with whom the child can readily identify, namely, parents, siblings, playmates, and

Fig. 15–8.
An example of imitative behavior.

others who play prominent roles in his everyday life. Furthermore, learning by imitation often occurs without apparent reinforcement—that is, tangible rewards or punishments. Perhaps, in older children, reinforcement is self-provided, or those with whom they identify have reinforcing powers as a

Infancy

result of their close associations with such primary reinforcers as food and reduction of pain.

Cognitive Learning: Insights, Reasoning, and Creative Imagination. Conditioning and imitation learning are essentially models for teaching or reinforcing responses that are already available to either the learner or the teacher or both. To account more readily for new responses to new problems, the models offered by cognitive learning seem to be more suitable for explaining the development of complex innovative behaviors. This point of view is especially appealing to psychologists who view man as an active, striving, self-directing organism (often referred to as humanistically oriented by psychologists). By insights is meant the sudden acquisition of new relationships or answers to problems after a period of study or effort. Reasoning usually refers to the active seeking of underlying explanations or causes for behaviors. Creative imagination is usually synonymous with divergent thinking.

All higher forms of learning include thinking that is some attempt at problem solving. Thinking usually involves ideas or symbols of events that are no longer present. The act of thinking, in turn, is usually followed by some appropriate action. In other words, cognitive learning is usually more than the gathering of information; it involves new ways of learning, wanting, acting and evaluating.

Learning Development

We have summarized various forms of learning and related key concepts. With this information in mind, we now discuss developmental learning from birth to age two beginning with the simplest form and going to the more complex for this age span.

Birth to Third Month. During this early period, infant learning is limited primarily to the attachment of existing unlearned responses such as reflexes, autonomic activities, random motor movements, and sensory adaptations to new stimuli through classical and operant learning procedures. In fact there is a fairly extensive history of infant conditioning going back as far as 1920 (Robinson, 1969; Anokhin, 1964). An example of classical conditioning involves the Babinski reflex, which consists of the extension of the big toe and extension and fanning of the other toes when the sole of the foot is lightly stroked. By presenting a mild tone just prior to stroking repeatedly, the Babinski reflex will now be elicited by the tone itself, whereas before conditioning only mechanical stroking could bring forth the reflex action. At this point, the Babinski reflex is called a conditioned reflex. With the passage of time, surrounding stimuli that initially produced no reactions such as mother's footsteps, vocalizations, and presence will become conditioned cues for predictable infant behaviors. Examples related to feeding are anticipatory sucking, mouthing, and turning the head toward the food supply. Conditioning of head turning illustrates the application of instrumental conditioning, because the baby must turn his head *before* he receives a reward.

Although conditioning can be demonstrated with infants very early in life, as outlined in Figure 8–4 in Chapter 8 and even before birth, such conditioning prior to the end of the second month is difficult to achieve and tends to be short-lived (Malakhovskaia, 1959). A plausible explanation for the lack of ease in establishing early conditioning in infants is that the task of adjusting from pre- to postbirth conditions takes up most of the baby's physical and mental resources. Another explanation could be the oversight on the part of some experimenters to control strictly for the infant's physiological and mental state at the time of the conditioning, which leads to the false conclusion that no learning had occurred (Connolly and Stratton, 1969). The difficulty in defining infant states is brought out clearly in the following statement (Lewis, 1972):

> Behind much of this difficulty of definition rests the general belief that the state of arousal continuum varies from a quiet sleep level (nonREM) through an alert level to a super-active level such as crying or extreme anxiety. The arousal continuum is a difficult and contradictory concept which necessarily does not have a one-to-one correspondence with state. For example, there may be more activity (level of arousal) during active sleep than during an alert-attentive period when no activity is present. (p. 96)

In other words, the state of the infant at any given moment may interact with conditioning stimuli to help determine not only the frequency of response and the kind of response but it also may determine if any response is to occur at all.

A third explanation is that the measurement of learning in young infants may require the development of new techniques designed to investigate changes in the coping mechanisms that are most readily available to the newly born. For example, infant sensitivity to light stimuli is well established even within one day after birth. In one study, 95 per cent of newborn infants reacted to almost 500 light stimuli. (Pratt, 1930) Furthermore, as reported earlier in this chapter, Fantz found that newborns, with a minimum of experience, respond selectively to complex visual patterns as compared to simpler ones. In light of this information, the following description of early infant learning may open the door to new research frontiers (Bruner, 1968):

> her infants varying from one month through three months in age are shown a picture that is initially out of focus on a large and close back-lighted screen. By sucking on a pacifier, the child can bring the picture into focus. If the distance from out-of-focus to in-focus be arbitrarily assigned the value of one clair, then each suck by the child improves the focus by .16 clair, and six sucks bring the picture into full focus. If sucking should fall below the rate of one per two seconds, the picture starts out of focus. The brightness remains virtually constant throughout. In a control condition, the picture is in focus, and sucking drives it out of focus at the rate mentioned above. Refraining from sucking at the prescribed rate lets the picture come back into focus.

> First let me say that a six-week infant can in fact learn to suck to bring the picture into focus and to desist somewhat when his sucking blurs the display. Infants plainly will work for visual clarity. What is especially interesting is how the child learns to *coordinate* the two ordinarily independent activities of sucking and looking. . . . (p. 23)

Infancy

What we see here is not the expected simple response to a specific stimulus but rather a remarkable adaptive sequence of organized responses. It would, therefore, seem logical to suppose that since perception, whether visual or others, comes prior to action, whether motor or language, we should stress perceptual stimulation and learning during the first three months of life as a major means of communication with the newborn.

Just how much difference an enriched, but not overwhelmingly stimulated environment can make for infants can be seen from the research of Burton L. White at Harvard University's Laboratory of Human Development, and Richard Held (1966).

The first step taken by White and Held was to find the normal age ranges for the development of such aspects of visual-motor development as visual attention, hand regard, and visually directed hand grasping. They then exposed experimental infants to various enriched environments in order to see if such added experiences contributed to the advancement of these fundamental sensorimotor behaviors when compared to other infants who were exposed to controlled stimulation. The first environmental enrichment consisted of twenty minutes of extra handling per day of infants from age six days to thirty-six days. As the apparent result of extra handling, there was a significant increase in visual attention but not in the other measures of visual-motor development. This result, although not as dramatic, is in line with some animal research in which small amounts of extra handling produced superiority in many physical and adaptive measures (Levine, 1957; Denenberg and Karas, 1959). In fact, such research with mice strongly implies that any kind of stimulation, even when painful, is far better for the future welfare of such animals than no stimulation at all. We use the term *implies* because the evidence from animal studies on the benefit of early stimulation on the course of development is not all clear-cut. Other studies with mice do not yield positive effects (Hunt and Otis, 1955; Goldman, 1964). At least for animals, we may conclude that the effects of stimulation vary for different kinds of animals and possibly within one family.

The second environment consisted of a massive enrichment including handling from day six through day thirty-six and increased motor movements and visual stimulation from day thirty-seven through day one hundred and twenty-four. To increase visual stimulation, a stabile, which contained a mirror, rattles, toys, and gaily colored decorations was suspended over the babies' heads. Even the plain designs of the bumpers on the cribs were changed to multicolored prints. The course of development for grasping and visual attention was dramatically altered after the enriched experiences. In less than one month, these babies learned how to reach out and grasp correctly—a coordinated skill that took babies in the normal environment three months to develop. Furthermore, they were able to efficiently grasp at about ninety-eight days—forty-five days sooner than the other infants.

The third environment was less enriched than the second because the babies in the second environment cried more than the control group. It occurred to the experimenters that perhaps an overly rich environment was actually ineffective and possibly even unpleasant. Extra handling was provided until day thirty-seven but there was one important modification from day thirty-seven until day sixty-eight. During this interval two pacifiers were mounted on a red and white pattern against a white background six to seven inches away from the infant's eyes. On the sixty-eighth day, the stabile replaced the pacifiers. These infants made the fastest gains of all.

From the studies reported by White and Held we can see that there is a remarkable elasticity present during the course of very early development and, in order to take full advantage of these opportunities, we must be careful to match the environment with the present needs and capabilities of the infants. For instance, we now realize that the quantity of stimulation that enhances aspects of visual-motor development in the three-month-old infant may overwhelm the nervous system of the two-month-old infant to the extent that he shuts out some of it. Furthermore, what amount of stimulation the baby should receive and for what length of time depends on the child's natural excitability, which is often evident from birth in his cries, bodily movements, and autonomic responses such as rates of respiration and heartbeat. Babies differ in their sensitivity to various forms of stimulations (Birns, 1965). We must therefore be careful in selecting stimuli for conditioning or learning purposes.

Another important variable that must be taken into account during early learning is *habitation,* that is, when an infant ceases to respond to a stimulus that previously attracted his attention.

Some babies respond to most stimuli and habituate very quickly (probably the more alert) whereas some do not habituate or do so slowly. Still other babies respond to few stimuli but habituate quickly, and some babies respond to few stimuli and do not habituate (Bridger, 1961). Furthermore, it is conceivable that a particular infant may not respond to a strong stimulus and be judged improperly because, unknown to the experimenter, there had been habituation to stimulus in the baby's past experience.

Fourth to Sixth Month. During this period the infant is still not ready to demonstrate his intelligence through clear-cut conditioning even though he has by now liberated himself from most of his reflex-oriented existence. In fact, he now behaves like a "liberated soul." The infant now indiscriminately smiles at people and even at inanimate objects. He is now much more alert. At birth he was visually alert less than 3 per cent of the time. At six months this alertness occurs almost 50 per cent of daylight hours (White and Held, 1966). The infant now seems eager to relate to himself, to others, and to objects. The enthusiasm of his actions seems to convey the message: "Here I am and I love it. I want to be a friend of everybody and everything."

By now, past experience must be added to maturation as important determiners of attention, action, and learning. Although the older infant possesses a wider range of capabilities for interacting with himself and others, reinforcements from past responses are already molding what he is likely to attend to and may influence the nature of his present responses. Such natural learning that results from everyday living can be observed in the ways the infant has learned to adapt to the more constant demands of his inner and outer environments. For example, food preferences, feeding schedules, and anticipatory movements and expressions in preparation for feeding have probably been heavily influenced by the particular routines of the family. By now we may be able to infer some of the traits that characterize caretaker-infant interactions. Infants who cry excessively may have failed to develop feelings of security that are related to delayed satisfaction of needs or inappropriate external stimulation (Stewart et al., 1954). And the pleasant nature of certain infants may be partly a result of the caretakers who have

Infancy

taken notice of the special nature and timing of needs and who may even anticipate needs before the infant feels the discomfort. To do so successfully calls for great individualization of care because of the great differences among infants. Truthfully, one cannot provide just average care and expect to promote good growth and optimal cognitive development.

One distinct advantage of even a few months in age is the dramatic reduction in learning time. In one study, the time required to learn a discrimination task was compared for infants in three age groups: 1.5 months, 3.5 months, and 5.3 months. The number of trials required for learning in each age group was approximately 225, 185, and 70 respectively (Papousek, 1967). Nevertheless, the fact that there is improvement in some behaviors with age should come as no surprise, but the important point demonstrated by these early infant learning studies is that the normal human infant is capable of conditioning and differential responses especially when the learning is related to survival and exploration of the novel in the environment. In other words, the infant can no longer be regarded as having no learning capacity or cognitive ability.

Seventh to Twelfth Month. During the second half of the first year the infant's rapid development of manipulative and visually directed grasping permits the use of more complex learning problems. In one study, such infants were tested with a two-choice discrimination problem involving yellow blocks in the shapes of a circle, cross, triangle, square, and an oval

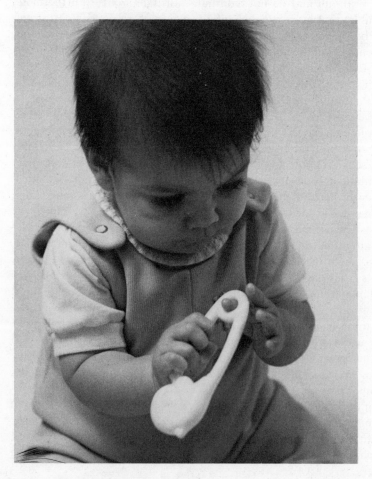

FIG. 15–9.
*Visual-directed
behavior in an
eight-month-old
infant.*

298

(Ling, 1941). The negative block was fixed to the tray, but the positive block was removable and coated with saccharine solution to provide a sweet taste as reinforcement for a correct response. For the first part of the experiment the yellow block was always correct and was always compared with one other block. The problem was considered solved when the infant made eight of ten correct choices. After solving twenty-seven such problems, the infants were given reversal training. The circle was now incorrect. This time the infants learned the reversal problems in approximately half the time. Later studies involving color discrimination and color and form discriminations have yielded similar results with most infants of this age span (Lipsitt, 1963; Hill, 1965).

Thus far, infant research studies have demonstrated simple conditioning over a wide variety of stimuli. Further insight into the why of the limitations of early infant conditionings might be explained in terms of object permanence and separation. At nine months of age, most infants begin to realize that objects and people can disappear and return again, and that they, as infants, have a separate existence from the world of objects and people (Hunt, 1965). The infant is now more interested in exploring his surroundings and eliciting social responses than in the continuation of his bodily explorations. Most infants may at this age have become somewhat habituated or bored about body manipulating and now focus their attention on things and people that disappear and return. We see here some definite signs of assertiveness in the form of preferred objects and activities. At this time, we should perhaps encourage the growth of autonomy and curiosity strivings. We should remember that the infant cannot learn what he has not experienced.

Second Year. The infant is now proceeding from interest in events that he did not cause to self-induced activities that result in new events. This shift from control by outer stimuli to increased influence from within based on past experiences indicates that the infant is becoming capable of representing his experiences in the form of mental images. These images are in turn used to mediate between the onset of outer events and subsequent actions (Gollin, 1965). For example, if the path to a goal is blocked or altered, the infant will now seek new routes. This ability to seek his own means to his own ends signals the beginning of insightful learning. The infant is no longer at the mercy of accidents, or chance, or a highly attentive mother for all his learning. The ability to find solutions to simple problems suddenly and by himself heralds the beginning of what we call thinking.

At the age of eighteen months, the infant reaches a peak of self-assertiveness. He behaves as if his powers were greater than they really are, and his ability to get into trouble exceeds his capacity to get out of it. According to Mahler (1968) this is because he still perceives his mother's help as an extension of his own powers. However, the fact remains that the infant's coping skills have improved dramatically. An important key to his rapid learning is the development of language, which is discussed later in this chapter. With language, the power to mentally represent one's self, one's memories, and one's present world are enhanced enormously. The very existence of these mental structures permits the growing infant to think out possible solutions before acting. Furthermore, infants seem to enjoy solving their newly discovered problems. They seem to find pleasure in the act of matching somewhat unfamiliar things with their own mental pictures. According to Kagan (1965), such discoveries and solutions produce an "aha" reaction in infants along with cardiac decelerations and smiles. Learning at this stage of life may be a long series of little, quiet, cognitive discoveries. If so, then normal learning depends upon slight mismatches between what the infant knows and the challenges presented by his environment. There must be sufficient incongruity to permit the infant to develop the interest to learn, but there must not be too great a discrepancy if his attention is wanted and his success in learning is to be assured. What the right degree of incongruity is depends on the individual infant. Furthermore, learning can be further enhanced if the desired challenges or activities are made to stand out clearly from the rest of the competing environment. In other words, it is the distinctiveness of the sufficiently different stimulation that is important and not just the sheer quantity.

At the present time there is a surprising lack of research using classical and operant conditioning during the first two years of life (Reese and Lipsitt, 1970). A possible reason for this lack is that "most early learning is neither purely classical conditioning nor of a purely operant variety, but is some sort of amalgamation of these." (Lipsitt, 1967) For the time being, we would like to offer the assumption that infants have not been too cooperative because they are not the relatively passive creatures that we once thought them to be. We believe that infants are really very active participants in their own learning process, and that, perhaps, we need to study them first in their "natural habitats" and to learn how they cope with their learning before we impose our standards and techniques on them. As we show later in this chapter, this approach has been demonstrated to be extremely useful in furthering our understanding of early infant learning and later cognitive development.

We can now begin to see evidence for the belief that our major task during early infancy is not teaching *per se*, but rather the preparation of the infant for later learning in the traditional sense. This line of reasoning is supported by the well-known physiological psychologist Hebb (1949), who states that the cortical association areas required for learning and memory are best established through a wealth of sensory-motor experiences during the first two years of life. Others, such as Hunt (1967) also argue for the priority of sensory-motor experiences because they believe that intelligence develops out of human experience, which in turn leads to the learning of more complex ways of coping with the environment.

Piaget's Theory of Cognitive Development

Cognitive development (learning and thinking) lies at the heart of Piaget's theory of development; other aspects such as social competence and moral development are considered to be dependent on cognition; still other important aspects, particularly in the affective domain, are ignored for the present. Cognitive development can be viewed in terms of physical and psychological stages. Each stage is unique although it depends on the previous lower level stages for its own development. The stages appear in a fixed invariant sequence although the time for their appearance varies depending on both biological growth and the extent and timing of experiences. The cognitive development of all human beings is basically the same if they are permitted sufficient interaction at each stage with increasingly complex experiences; however, for Piaget, intelligence is not fixed or predetermined at birth. The main stages of cognitive development, the expected ages of occurrence, and some of the major characteristics are summarized in Table 15–1.

TABLE 15–1
PIAGET'S STAGES OF COGNITIVE DEVELOPMENT

I. Sensorimotor stage	0–2 years	Infant's learning limited to the simplest aspects of motor movement and sensory perception: vision, touch, smell, taste, and sound.
II. Preoperational stage Preconceptual	2–4 years	Elaboration of these aspects; can retain image of absent objects; rudiments of language and symbols permit extension of experiences beyond the immediate (This stage is as high as animals can go.).
Intuitive thought	4–7 years	Characterized by childlike precausal thinking: egocentrism, phenomenism, lack of conservation, animism, and naïve realism.
III. Concrete operations	7–11 years	Begins to use elementary logic and to reason about size, volume, numbers, and weight; application of conceptual systems to concrete events; increasingly able to apply principle of conservation.
IV. Formal operations	12 years onward	Hypothetico-deductive reasoning: can formulate laws or general principles and apply them to possible classes of situations; can think in terms of alternative hypotheses and manipulate them symbolically to solve problems; has reached the highest level of cognitive development; equals that of mature adults.

Piaget is better understood in light of his biological background. Any living organism, whether animal or plant, manages to develop and, at times, to flourish because of a remarkable adaptability to the demands of its environment. This analogy is helpful for gaining an understanding of Piaget's interpretation of cognitive development. All living organisms have changeable adaptive structures (physical and psychological competencies) that interact with selected and changing aspects of their surroundings. Basically, cognitive growth is a function of the continuous interplay between the continuously changing internal structures of the organism with the continuously changing aspects of increasingly complex environmental forces. Hence the wider the range of the interactions, the more diversified will be the intellectual operations of the growing child.

Equilibrium. The term *equilibrium* refers to the state of the organism in which there is a balance between the internal and the external forces. Under this condition, there is a minimum of tension within the organism, a minimum of change in the environment, and, subsequently, a minimum of learning and thinking. In other words, the lack of equilibrium, whether Infancy from the inside or the outside, is a very important condition for learning and optimal cognitive growth—a child learns in the process of achieving equilibrium.

Adaptation. Adaptation to changes within the organism and to changes in the perceived environment is a two-way process: the organism changes internally to fit the environment and the environment is "worked" upon to make it fit the present characteristics of the organism through manipulation, selection, and modification. Adaptation to change depends upon the complementary processes of *assimilation* and *accommodation*. Assimilation refers to the actions taken on the environment to make it sufficiently meaningful for incorporation into the existing cognitive structures of the organism. For example, when a relatively new object is given to a year-old infant, he will probably engage in such assimilatory behaviors with the object as feeling, tasting, throwing, and banging it. Through such continuous activities, the infant will probably learn that such a large object cannot be placed into the mouth, that its taste is not palatable, or that loud sounds result when striking it against other objects. These realities of the nature of the environment act upon the organism to produce more complex and new ways of exploring and manipulating the world. Accommodation is the term for the changes in the organism that result from assimilatory activities or the changing of ideas to fit the new situation. The growing child, at any stage of development, learns more and more through active participation in the spirals of continuous adaptation, that is, through the processes of assimilation and accommodation as a result of constant states of disequilibrium. It is well to remember that assimilatory actions and resultant internal accommodations require a variety of experiences, repetitions, and time for practice.

Schemas. A schema is any activity or thought process that the organism is capable of performing whether a simple reflex, playing ball, driving an automobile, or reading a book. It is through maturation and the interaction with the environment that the original schemas at birth develop into elaborate or new complex schemas.

Intrinsic Motivation. In addition to the motivation provided by disequilibrium and the energizing effects of positive and negative emotions, there are intrinsic motivational factors caused by the nature of the schemas themselves. According to Piaget, developing schemas require much repetition, in slightly varying forms, to increase the generalization of the schemas to related situations. Infants and children can often be seen intensely repeating the same or similar actions over and over again; e.g. pouring water into a can, piling blocks, hammering, running around a tree, and so forth. Furthermore, old schemas regain their original motivational energies when they are in the process of being combined into more complex schemas, or when they are serving as means to some nearly desired end or purpose. Changes in schemas brought about by attempts at adaptation and reorganization brought about through intrinsic motivation together ensure schemas of greater complexity and hence intellectual growth.

Individual variations in intellectual competencies, the age at which any stage is reached, and whether a child develops into the more advanced stages or not depends on educational opportunities, cultural backgrounds, the degree of stimulation they receive, and heredity.

The Life Cycle

With these basic concepts in mind we now discuss some essential characteristics of the first major stage of cognitive growth. In this stage learning is organized around sensory and motor activities; at a later stage learning centers around concrete experiences, and finally it centers around abstract formalized thinking processes.

The Sensori-Motor Stage. The underlying feature of this stage, which lasts approximately two years, is that all the basic information dealt with involves sensory and motor experiences that will gradually transform the reflex-oriented neonate into a toddler capable of spontaneous and deliberate behaviors. The three major competencies developed during this stage are: (1) The ability to combine simple schemas into more complex ones. For example, he will learn to pursue objects visually; he will learn to handle objects; and he will then learn to look at what he is manipulating; (2) He will learn that the world exists even when he cannot see it. At first an infant behaves as if objects that disappear from the visual field cease to exist. Later, he will continue to search for objects or people who are no longer visible to him; and (3) By the end of infancy he will be able to relate schemas sequentially, experimentally, and purposively as means to achieving desired goals on a limited level. The three substages of the sensori-motor stage and their corresponding approximate ages are as follows (Piaget, 1952):

1. Primary circular reactions. 1–4 months. First signs of learning new schemas, discriminative learning, and generalization; continuous repetition of newly acquired behaviors.

2. Secondary circular reactions. 5–8 months. Activity is directed more to external rather than own body; begins to coordinate schemas as means to ends; beginning of imitation; continuous repetitions of newly acquired behaviors.

3. Tertiary circular reactions. 9–18 months. Active exploration and experimentation with environment; variation of approaches to old and new problems; more advanced form of imitation.

Primary Circular Reactions. The neonate has two classes of reflexes: those such as the knee jerk that are not influenced by experience and others such as sucking and grasping that are modifiable. It is basically from the elaboration of these inborn schemas that more complex ones develop. Through random trial and error the infant begins to participate actively with his surroundings, especially his body, and soon begins to repeat over and over again those acts that have been positively reinforced or that are the results of the intrinsic motivation provided by the modification of schemas through assimilation and accommodation. The infant gradually begins to "see" the connection between his activities and the results in his immediate environment; e.g. rapid movement of his legs also results in movement of objects hanging over the crib, keeping his head toward the breast will increase the probability of more sucking experiences and nourishment, and so forth. The beginning of coordination between schemas is now observable: one action (the means) leads to another (the desired end). By the end of this stage the infant becomes capable of imitating some simple observable behaviors.

Secondary Circular Reactions. The infant who was previously limited to repeating schemas, which had accidentally brought about interesting and desired changes, now begins to show signs of intentional and controlled behaviors. He may indicate that he wants something by repeating behaviors that were associated with that activity in the past. For example, he may direct his eyes toward a desired object, keep looking at an object that just Infancy

303

disappeared, or keep repeating activities associated with an object upon seeing it. He thus begins to show some signs of purposive behavior in addition to some awareness of the permanency of objects. The coordination of schemas now advances to the point where he can use objects to attain goals or push barriers aside. Simple imitation of observable behavior is now possible.

Tertiary Circular Reactions. The infant now ceases to behave in a "one-tracked fashion"; his reaction to familiar situations ceases to be predictable repetitions of old responses. He will now vary his responses by trying new approaches to old situations. Furthermore, he is now more active in exploring and experimenting with his surroundings. In a sense, we can now say that the infant is showing signs of "creative" behavior. He is attracted to the new, the novel, the unexplored; he will let objects fall to see what happens to them, knock objects, shake things, and so forth. On the other hand, his repertoire of imitative behavior increases and becomes more accurate and refined.

Up to this point the development of schemas has been strictly dependent on observable sensory and motor activities. Toward the end of this period or about age two years, the infant begins to show signs of becoming "liberated" from an existence that was entirely dependent on what was presented to his senses at the immediate moment of action. He is now becoming capable of representing himself and his relationship to his world in the form of mental images. For example, he will now readily go around detours blocking his path to a hidden object or go to the end of a sofa to catch his dog who just walked around the opposite side. The infant is now ready to enter the second major stage of cognitive development, the preoperational stage, in which he will engage in the beginnings of insightful behavior.

Language Development

In addition to its almost innumerable benefits, language competency is the third major force in the development of intelligence and creativity. The other two determinants are genetic endowment and the quality and quantity of life experiences. Language competency may be considered man's crowning achievement for various reasons: language permits man the enormous wealth of contemporary as well as historical knowledge that would be beyond his grasp if based solely on his personal experiences; language permits man a variety of efficient and subtle modes of communication for expressing his innermost feelings and thoughts ranging from the poetic and the musical, to the precise formulations of the mathematician; language permits man to liberate himself from the present and the concrete and to transcend time, space, and reality; language permits man to dream about what is really fair, great, or wonderful and to ask "If this could be, then why isn't it so?" Perhaps it has been the efforts to answer such questions that has driven man to progressively higher levels in the different areas of existence. In exploration we have gone from Mount Kilimanjaro, to Mount Everest, to earth orbit, to moon orbit, and to planetary orbit. In human justice we care more now than ever before for the sick, poor, and hungry no matter where or who they may be. In the search for human meaning we see ourselves more and more as indivisible parts of our family, community, country, world, and universe.

Aspects of our shared humanity are noted in that infant babbling seems to be a "universal language" shared by all infants throughout the world. Infants are capable of producing speech sounds that are not found in their native language. Some of these sounds are extremely difficult even for adult members to pronounce such as the French throaty trills, the Welsh *ll*, and the German umlauts. Infants, during their very early language development, do not seem to be affected by such "highly important cultural factors" as language spoken at home, birth order, socioeconomic status, and even whether the parents are deaf or hearing (Nakazima, 1962; Lenneberg, 1967). In their refusal to be so influenced, babies may have provided us with some insights into the realization of Utopian democracy—a world in which men are born equal if their *opportunities remain equal*. A simplified sequence for classifying oral language development during the first two years is prebabbling, babbling, word meaning, and expressive language.

Prebabbling. The general biological mechanisms of auditory receptors, vocal chords, and the central nervous system needed for language development are operative at birth and even before (Carmichael, 1964). In fact, the neonate is equipped for responding and differentiating among a wide variety of sounds within and beyond the range of human speech sounds (Eisenberg, 1964).

Crying to physical discomforts composes the infant's first utterances. Scientific analysis of these cries reveals that the vocal characteristics of a given infant are his and his alone (Menyuk, 1971). This evidence supports the claim of mothers who believe that they can tell their babies' crying from those of others. Within a few weeks after birth some mothers feel that they can "interpret" the distinct meanings of crying; that is, pain, hunger, discomfort and so forth. Actually such interpretation is much easier by the end of the second month when most babies have developed a large repertoire of crying sounds varying from whisper-quiet whimpering to shrill-piercing screams. Even then the interpretation of infant crying requires special efforts because the nature of the cries depends on the intensity of the infant's needs and not in the kinds of needs. It is important for adults to respond accurately and promptly to the baby's cries for help because of the following reasons: (1) excessive and prolonged crying can be damaging physically and psychologically especially for the very young who cry intensely, literally with their whole bodies and souls; (2) to begin to instill in the infant the values of noncrying modes of communication in preparation for the stages leading to language competency; and (3) to provide the infant with the tremendously important feelings that it is good to be alive and that someone will help him in times of need.

In addition to discomfort cries, there are comfort sounds or cooing. Both forms of vocalization are reactions to changes in body conditions. All early "verbal noises" should be considered as important precursors to language development not only because of the exercising of the biological mechanisms but also because prebabbling has private meaning for the infant and for those who are in close communication with him.

Babbling. The addition of babbling sounds to the infant's repertoire of linguistic skills usually begins about the sixth week and lasts until about the ninth month even though some infants continue to babble until about age two. Babbling is essentially language play. At first, babbling consists of the repetition of sounds previously made only to bodily conditions in the prebabbling stage, but that are now produced for no known reason except

Infancy

possibly sheer joy. The babbling infant seems to find contentment in hearing his own sounds and those of others because he will babble more in the presence of adults who talk with or who babble along with him. It is intriguing to note that the duration of early babbling sounds are similar to those of adult verbal units and that the intonations of later babbling will imitate the intonations of adult speech (Lenneberg, 1967). Hopefully, the pleasures of babbling will serve as a beginning for subsequent enjoyment of language development, both spoken and written.

The number and variety of sounds emitted by the infant increases with age primarily as a function of physiological maturity and increased control over the vocal mechanisms, but also as a result of increased reaction and imitation of human sounds including his own. Deaf infants, for example, reach the early stages of babbling but soon enter the world of silence as they lose interest in what they cannot hear. During the first few weeks the only incentive for imitation is the crying of other infants, but by the fourth week or so infants begin to respond to adult voices as judged by their bodily movements, smiles, and by their being soothed into quietness. By the third or fourth month infants begin to respond vocally to speech in terms of their own private language. This marks the beginnings of imitation; that is, the infant babbles when others talk. H. M. Lewis (1963), who believes this kind of imitation paves the way for language learning from adults, explains it this way:

We have to recognise that whenever we speak of imitation—in whatever field of behavior—we cannot make absolute correspondence our final criterion. Indeed if absolute similarity is our criterion we are forced into the absurdity of saying that a child of five who says *fing* for *thing* is not imitating, that imitation only begins when he can say *thing*. It is surely reasonable to say that the child's f is his imitation of th.

In a child's earliest months his vocal responses to our words do not closely resemble them. But there is usually a regularity in his responses to particular sounds: and it is this regularity which is the source of his ultimate ability to imitate. To take a typical instance: a child in his fourth month said *weh* when he heard somebody say *goo*—one of his own familiar sound-patterns. After a time this became quite regular; it is reasonable to say that at this stage *weh* was his response to *goo*—although *goo* often appeared in his own babbling. (p. 23)

Gradually in successive stages of approximation the infant's babbling will sound more and more like adult speech patterns if adults provide them with necessary language models and appropriate encouragement.

Word Meaning. The babbling stage usually ends by the first year depending on the infant's rate of maturation and the incentives provided for moving onward to more meaningful modes of communication. Soon there will be specific sounds or actions in response to specific words or situations. Now the parents may say to themselves "By golly he seems to be using words but we can't find them in the dictionary." We may refer to these utterances as "words" because there is some meaning attached to them by the infant and the persons close to him. Furthermore, the speech sounds and sequences are used consistently in the presence of particular persons and objects.

During this stage there is a gradual development of word meanings corresponding to the progressive increments in sound productions and sound-situation associations. Here we see definite signs of understanding some words and the utterances of the first linguistically meaningful words. Perhaps we tend to overestimate or underestimate the infant's skills by insisting that for language comprehension to be present the spoken words must be clearly understood by all adult members of his linguistic community as referring to clear-cut situations and that his responses to spoken words should refer clearly to unambiguous situations.

The first spoken words are usually similar phonetically. According to H. M. Lewis (1963) there are six basic sound-patterns derived from the babbling stage that form the basic beginning for spoken language for all infants regardless of the language spoken at home: These sound-patterns are *mama, nana, papa, baba, tata, dada* with but slight variations from place to place. Furthermore, since the early use of words serves multiple purposes, parents will still need to serve as interpreters of the infant's language. For example, at age one year the word *mama* is used in a wide variety of contexts—mother, father, objects, and so on. Eventually, perhaps in another year or so, the infant will learn to use *mama* appropriately if adult members respond consistently to his correct use of the term.

Expressive Language. From age eighteen to twenty-four months there is a rapid growth in expressive language. During these six months, vocabulary expands from approximately twenty to about three hundred to four hundred words including the appearance of two- and three-word phrases (Menyuk, 1971). This truly remarkable growth of language strongly suggests that the infant's learning of receptive language during the previous stages has been very great indeed. Again, evidence of this kind supports the very important notion that infants are capable of learning far more than what we give them credit for. It seems that infants lack the means for expressing their knowledge until they are maturationally capable of doing so. Too often we tend to equate learning only with measurable performance forgetting that learning can also be receptive, passive, and latent.

During this stage the interrelatedness or the holistic nature of human development can be noticed again. Expressive or verbal language is virtually nonexistent for the first eighteen months. At this time, when Broca's area or the speech center in the cortex develops, there is a rapid development of expressive language (McCarthy, 1954). Naturally, along with brain maturation there must be social and psychological stimulation because language develops only in the context of a linguistic community. Language development also coincides with motor development as summarized in Table 15–2. However, language development does not depend upon corresponding motor development as evidenced by the language competency of children who cannot walk or move their arms.

Creativity

As mentioned in Chapter 9, creativity seems to be a basic characteristic of human nature. It seems to be present in some respects in all at birth but, for most of us, it loses much of its spark during the process of socialization. Nevertheless, creativity probably lies dormant in all of us in a kindling stage ready, if the right conditions appear, to give birth to a new flow of ideas and activities.

Infancy

TABLE 15–2
RELATIONSHIP BETWEEN MOTOR AND SPEECH DEVELOPMENT

Approximate Ages	Motor Development	Speech Development
2–3 months	Holds head up independently	Cooing sounds: squealing-gurgling, spontaneous, unlearned, and universally found in infants even when deaf.
6 months	Sits independently	Cooing is now changing into babbling: increased number of sounds but no real meaning.
12 months	Stands alone	First meaningful words spoken; definite signs of understanding some words.
18 months	Walks alone	Begins to enlarge vocabulary—more than three but less than fifty words; combines two or three words into primitive sentences.
24 months	Runs; walks stairs up and down	Some can label most objects in sight; definite interest in language.

Compiled from Lenneberg (1963) and McCarthy (1954)

It is, of course, common sense that for the newborn everything about them is as new as they are. We see here a provocative situation in which the new confronts the new. During these early stages we can readily observe such characteristics of creativity as learning in the face of uncertainty, growth of new responses, and increased capacity for dealing with the new. Perhaps there is a closer relationship between intelligence and creativity in early than in later life because the infant, in dealing successfully with the new and varying conditions, is actively involved in fashioning his own learning competencies and intelligence. In this respect, creativity is both a learning tool and an active means of creating intelligence if we agree that increased competencies in handling novel situations is a form of intelligence.

A willingness to confront the novel in a playful manner is another characteristic of infant activity and learning once the immediate physical needs have been satisfied. To develop further this playful attitude, feelings of openness and hopefulness are needed. The growing infant must be provided with the opportunities, encouragement, and success experiences to continue to want to move into new and more complex situations. The importance of these healthy attitudes toward the novel become more apparent as the child starts to explore his neighborhood and when he is confronted with the novelties of school living and learning. According to a recent review of research "by the time the child is five years of age he will have solidified his modes of dealing with the new." (Lichtenberg and Norton, 1971). Others say that the modes for dealing with the novel are already established by three years of age (Murphy et al., 1962).

To produce an infant who is open, exploratory, playful, and searching while learning means that caretakers must be careful to avoid too many hurts and defeats that could lead to the avoidance of the novel and to constant repetitions of previously successful but now inappropriate responses. The Life Cycle Probably the three most critical moments for fostering the confidence needed

The Life
Cycle

for creative living are three months, nine months, and eighteen months. Developmentally, it is during these points that peaks in the infant's strivings for autonomy, independence, and self-assertiveness are reached.

AFFECTIVE DOMAIN

In discussing emotions in the infant, we must remember that the type of emotion and the degree to which emotion may be demonstrated by an infant are subject to adult interpretation. For example, an infant response that we as observing adults might consider to be intense pleasure may in fact be mild displeasure. It is very difficult, even for the baby's parents, to infer a particular emotional state based on an infant's nonverbal behavior.

As adults, we often tend to attribute very complex emotional responses to simple infant behaviors. There seems to be no firm evidence that babies are capable of experiencing complex emotional states such as joy, hatred, or even love. Most of the early infant emotional development stems directly from the biological reflexes that we have discussed earlier.

Nevertheless, Watson (1920) using observational techniques concluded that the newborn was capable of three basic emotional states: love—a response to tactile stimulation, fear—a response to loud noises, and, anger—a response to physical restraint. Further research has not shown that emotional states as complex as these do actually exist in newborns.

Bridges (1932) concluded that infants have only one emotional state, that of *generalized excitement.* Every behavior that we observe in early infancy lies at some point along a continuum from tranquility to agitation. According to Bridges, it is from the tranquility end of the continuum that pleasurable feelings eventually develop and from the agitation end of the spectrum that feelings of displeasure eventually spring.

During infancy there are a number of important behavioral events that occur fairly regularly that seem to act as a signal that "all is going well" in the emotional development of the infant. Although we are still studying and uncovering these and other clues to proper affective development, there are certain patterns emerging. The exact meaning and interpretation of these behaviors are the basis for certain theories of infant development. We examine these later.

Basic Infant Responses

One of the indications that an infant is responding to his environment is found in the visual responses that he makes toward others. Related closely to the physical development of the infant's eyes and nervous system (see the discussion of these under the Biological Domain) are his emotional responses to various objects and persons he perceives in his environment.

For example, the infant, early in life, is able to look at various visual stimuli. He may even smile and vocalize at these nonsocial objects (Rheingold, 1961; Salzen, 1963). As he grows older, he begins focusing on social objects, particularly his mother, and spends considerable time exploring others (Wolff, 1963).

At about the fourth month, the infant tends to prefer the sight of his mother's face and the sound of her voice (Ambrose, 1961).

Fear Responses. Another response that seems to indicate that an important affective development has taken place is when the infant, at about seven to nine months, reacts negatively to the presence of a stranger. Up to this time infants generally will smile at most human faces (with preference given to mother's face). But at this age the appearance of a strange face or person will trigger off a general fear reaction of crying, restlessness, and withdrawal (Morgan and Ricciuti, 1968).

Bowlby (1969) cites three phases of infant development that have been observed (Freedman, 1961; Schaffer, 1966; Ainsworth, 1967) to occur before a typical fear response (moving away from the stranger, whimpering, crying, and a negative facial expression) is given:

A. A phase during which he shows no visual discrimination between strangers and familiars;
B. A phase, usually lasting 6 to 10 weeks, during which he responds to strangers positively and fairly readily, though not as readily as to familiars;
C. A phase, usually lasting 4 to 6 weeks, during which he sobers at sight of a stranger and stares. (pp. 324–325)

Although the actual ages at which the fear response begins to occur varies, some observations of this phenomena have been made as early as twenty-six weeks of age, but most often it appears at about eight months (Freedman, 1961; Schaffer, 1966; Ainsworth, 1967). The peak of the fear response occurs somewhere around the age of nine to ten months (Ainsworth, 1967; Tennes, 1964).

Recent data from two longitudinal studies has shown some additional interesting findings about sex differences, onset, as well as implications of this fear response. In the Berkeley Growth Study the fear response (defined as crying during the monthly developmental examinations) was found in some infants as early as four months of age, whereas in some infants it didn't appear until the end of the first year. In Ainsworth's studies of the first year of life, the onset of the fear response (which was evoked by an observer present in the home and was defined as a delay in smiling, inhibited movement, and crying) was also observed to occur at about the identical age distribution.

Bronson (1970) used this onset of fear data to relate it to later measures of shyness. He found a significant relationship in males between an early onset of fear and a greater degree of shyness. This significant relationship held up to the age of three and one-half years and up to the age of eight and one-half, although not significant, the trend continued. In the data from Ainsworth's one-year study, Bronson found a similar finding: that an early onset of fear response was significantly associated with more intense fearfulness at age one.

This unexpected finding, that only males who display the fear response early in their development may be more shy and fearful later in life, has led Bronson to hypothesize that young males may be more affected by experiences in early infancy than females. This hypothesis remains to be tested (Bronson, 1971).

*Smiling Responses.** The infant's smiling response has increasingly been

---

* The infant's smile is typically considered a topic under the Social Domain, since it involves interaction with others. We are treating it as an affective response, however, which signals that an important emotional phase of development has occurred—the infant smiles only at a human face or voice.

the focus of much research (Freedman, 1964; Ambrose, 1960) and interest during recent years for a number of reasons. First, because it appears to be one of the earliest infant responses that tells the parent that the infant is satisfied and happy. Second, it is one of the responses that allows the parent to know that the infant recognizes him and can discriminate him from others. Third, it is one of the early responses that is generalized through learning to many other situations in later life. Fourth, it is one of those responses that portrays the developmental interaction of various senses: in the act of smiling to others, the adequate development of infant vision at that age is closely related with the cognitive ability to differentiate objects from persons. Fifth, smiling is a response that is interpreted by some as a link to our past (built-in inherited responses)—and others as an example of "pure social conditioning."

Although this response is still far from being completely explored, many studies give us a general view of its development. Gerwitz (1965), for example, describes the developmental sequence of smiling in three phases.

Phase I (Birth to Two Weeks—Reflex Smiling). This is the earliest form of smiling that involves brief episodes of smiling as a response to such things as internal stimulation (gastric smiles) or from outward sources such as smiles produced by stroking the face or cheeks. These first reflexive smiles have been reported as early as the first twenty-four hours of life (Wolff, 1959). Generally they are not "full" smiles in the sense of affecting the entire face.

Phase II (Two to Eight Weeks) "Social Smiling." The second phase of smiling begins somewhere between the second and eighth weeks, and continues to about the twentieth week. This phase is labeled "social smiling" since it is evoked through visual presentation of various stimuli, most of

Infancy

them social in nature (the human face and voice). During this phase, the smiling response is made less and less to inanimate objects and more and more to animate objects. Rheingold (1971) comments on some factors involved in this type of discrimination.

Two processes can account for the developing discrimination. First, the social object, being animate, possesses, and therefore more regularly presents, the set of effective stimuli. Second, the social object, being animate and *human,* that is, a member of one's own species, is *responsive* to the infant's smiling. The infant's smiling evokes responses from persons much of the time, from things not at all. A smile is often met with a smile, and sometimes also with words and touches. At the least, the human observer will move closer, stay longer, and pay attention. It is upon this characteristic of human interchange that Bowlby based his statement on the adaptive value of the infant's smile for his own survival. (p. 318)

Phase III "Selective Social Smiling." As the infant's biological and cognitive domains become more developed, he is able to differentiate sights and sounds more so that his smiling responses become more selective. Thus, after a period of relatively indiscriminate social smiling (to familiar as well as unfamiliar faces) he now carefully differentiates social stimuli and only smiles at familiar adult faces. Gradually, the sight of a stranger will not only fail to evoke a smile (as it did in Phase II) but will often produce withdrawal behavior, such as crying, and a general fear response. The age and quality of these fear responses to strangers vary considerably, but generally occur in a mild form (sober expression while staring at the stranger) between twelve and twenty-six weeks, and occur in very strong form (physi-

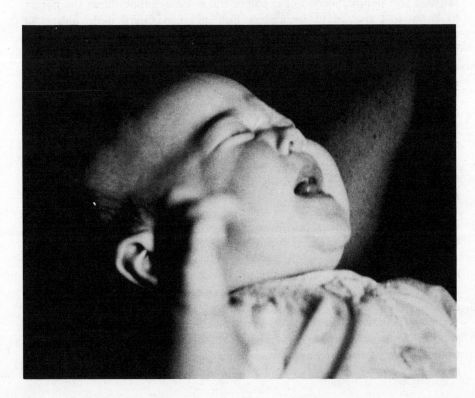

FIG. 15–11.
Crying response.

cal withdrawal and loud crying in most infants) by eight to nine months (Freedman, 1961; Schaffer, 1966; Ainsworth, 1967).

Crying Responses. Another emotional reaction that appears to serve many purposes for both the growing infant and mother is the cry. Crying can be viewed from its role as a signaling device and as an early indication of social recognition of mother.

Let us look at each of these functions briefly.

Crying As a Signal. One of the most important "instruments" of the infant for communicating with himself and others in his environment is his ability to vocalize. This often turns out to be a cry that is a signal of some distress or discomfort the baby is experiencing. Such common things as stomach contractions, symptoms of various illnesses, the uncomfortable feeling of soiled or wet diapers, sudden noises, movements, being too hot or cold, or irritating odors all may contribute to the infant's cry. Thus, one function of the cry is to inform the mother or caretaker that something is bothering the baby.

Early in the infant's development, some mothers can distinguish their own baby's cry from others within forty-eight hours of birth (Formby, 1967). It appears that newborn cries are so distinct that sound spectrograms show individual variations in "cry-prints" as readily as fingerprints (Wolff, 1969; Bowlby, 1969).

Bowlby (1969) cites various types of distinct crying patterns that may be caused from such things as hunger, pain, anger, coldness, and even nakedness. Many others are able to identify the cause of crying by being familiar with its sound.

Bowlby (1969) believes that the significance of crying, in the human infant at least, is that its termination, in most cases, requires stimuli involving human intervention. Such things as the human voice (Wolff, 1969), touching, moving, rocking (Gordon, 1966), and nonnutritive sucking (Newson and Newson, 1963) (e.g., using such things as a rubber pacifier or "dummy") all seem to help terminate crying, although some of these approaches appear to be more satisfactory than others.

For example, Wolff (1969) found that the stimuli for termination of crying progressed from more general stimuli (such as the sound of a rattle or bell) during the first week, to the human voice, to a female voice, and finally to mother's specific voice.

Crying As an Early Form of Social Behavior. Ainsworth (1964) believes that early crying is one of the first forms as well as signals of attachment behavior that lets the mother know that the infant can differentiate her from others. In her classic study of African babies, Ainsworth noted that babies of between eight to twelve weeks of age could actually discriminate between the mother and others (for example, infants were observed crying when held by a stranger and upon handing the child to the mother, the crying ceased in most cases). Or, when the baby is crying and continues to cry even though handed to a stranger who tries to comfort and console him, it was noted in most cases that, when transferred to the mother, the infant stopped crying.

The significance of the infant's cry and maternal behavior in response to it are summarized in the following quote from a fascinating study (Moss, 1967) that explored the relationship between the infant's emotional state and mother's response to these various states.

From these findings it is difficult to posit a causal relationship. However, it seems most plausible that it is the infant's cry that is determining the maternal behavior. Mothers describe the cry as a signal that the infant needs attention and they often report their nurturant actions in response to the cry. Furthermore, the cry is a noxious and often painful stimulus that probably has biological utility for the infant, propelling the mother into action for her own comfort as well as out of concern for the infant. Ethological reports confirm the proposition that the cry functions as a "releaser" of maternal behavior.

Thus, crying not only acts as a signal; it eventually has an effect on the quality and quantity of social interaction between mother and infant.

Variability and Continuity in Emotional Development

We have looked briefly at some important, specific emotional responses that occur fairly regularly during "normal infant development." We may have given you the notion that there is much regularity in the manner of expressing these infant emotional behaviors. This could not be further from the truth. It seems that there is great variability in the expression of basic emotional patterns. Many studies have demonstrated the extreme variability in infant-state or activity level (Brown, 1964; Escalona, 1962; Bridger, 1965).

The exact cause of such differences in emotional expression is still not clear, but the evidence seems to suggest that it is an interplay between the inherited genetic endowment and the environment in which the person is reared (learned responses as a result of his environment).

One of the most extensive studies to show this unique individuality in early infancy is the research of Thomas, Chess, and Birch (1970) who, for over 14 years, systematically studied 141 children in 85 families from birth to the present. Using a combination of interviews, observations, and psychological tests, their data strongly suggest that individual differences in temperament are observable in the first weeks of birth (irrespective of parent handling or personality) and continue to persist as the child matures. They cite the following two examples to demonstrate this relationship (Thomas et al., 1970):

Donald exhibited an extremely high activity level almost from birth. At three months, his parents reported, he wriggled and moved about a great deal while asleep in his crib. At six months he "swam like a fish" while being bathed. At 12 months he still squirmed constantly while he was being dressed or washed. At 15 months he was "very fast and busy"; his parents found themselves "always chasing after him." At two years he was "constantly in motion, jumping and climbing." At three he would "climb like a monkey and run like an unleashed puppy." In kindergarten his teacher reported humorously that he would "hang from the walls and climb on the ceiling." By the time he was seven Donald was encountering difficulty in school because he was unable to sit still long enough to learn anything and disturbed the other children by moving rapidly about the classroom.

Clem exemplifies a child who scored high in intensity of reaction. At four and a half months he screamed every time he was bathed, according to his parents' report. His reactions were "not discriminating—all or none." At six months during feeding he screamed "at the sight of the spoon approaching his mouth." At nine and a half months he was generally "either in a very good mood, laughing or chuckling" or else screaming. "He laughed so hard playing peekaboo he got hiccups." At two years his parents reported: "He screams bloody murder when he's being dressed." At seven they related: "When he's frustrated, as for example when he doesn't hit a ball very far, he stomps around, his voice goes up to its highest level, his eyes get red and occasionally fill with tears. Once he went up to his room when this occurred and screamed for half an hour." (p. 104)

The researchers believe that the child's basic reactions may be heightened, diminished, or modified somewhat by the environment. But, the basic temperamental patterns still remain later in life. In their study they found nine dimensions upon which infant temperamental differences could be observed and rated. (Note: They were only able to categorize 65 per cent of their subjects; the other 35 per cent showed a mixture of traits.)

Some specific examples of these categories are summarized in Table 15–3.

TABLE 15–3
NINE CATEGORIES OF TEMPERAMENT UPON WHICH INFANTS WERE OBSERVED TO DIFFER

Category	Description	Rating Index
1. Activity level	The proportion of active periods to inactive ones.	High–Low
2. Rhythmicity	Regularity of hunger, excretion, sleep, and wakefulness.	Regular–Irregular
3. Distractibility	The degree to which extraneous stimuli alter behavior.	Distractible–Not Distractible
4. Approach–withdrawal	The response to a new object or person.	Positive–Negative
5. Adaptability	The ease with which a child adapts to changes in his environment.	Adaptive–Not Adaptive
6. Attention span and persistence	The amount of time devoted to an activity and the effect of distraction on the activity.	Long–Short
7. Intensity of reaction	The energy of response regardless of its quality or direction.	Intense–Mild
8. Theshold of responsiveness	The intensity of stimulation required to evoke a discernible response.	Low–High
9. Quality of mood	The amount of friendly, pleasant, joyful behavior as contrasted with unpleasant, unfriendly behavior.	Positive–Negative

Compiled from Thomas et al., 1970.

Infancy

Basic Social Goals

Attachment. One of the most fascinating and controversial theories about the significance of infancy is reflected in the work of John Bowlby, who is Director of the Child Guidance Department, Tavistock Clinic, London.

Most of Bowlby's research and theory-building efforts evolved out of his early interest in infants and children who had lost or were separated from their mothers either permanently or temporarily. The "songs" these children sang and the effects of such separation will be described later. Much of what we know about these children was derived from Bowlby's significant summary of research and programs on homeless children which he conducted in 1950 for the World Health Organization and summarized in his now well-known report entitled: *Maternal Care and Mental Health* (1952).

As a result of this report, methods of care for homeless infants and children were changed dramatically and a series of research studies and controversial points of view were stimulated. As Bowlby himself admits, this report had one major limitation: it failed to discuss the actual processes whereby children become disturbed during and after separation from their parents.

After another series of studies of separated children with Robertson (1952), Bowlby became more convinced that the observed behavior of children six months and older who were separated from their mothers (such as anger, hostility, protest, despair, and detachment) was indicative of the loss of one of the most basic developmental phases in the growth of a human being. It is from these empirical studies that they derived their widely used principle that: "the young child's hunger for his mother's love and presence is as great as his hunger for food, and that in consequence, her absence inevitably generates a powerful sense of loss and anger" (Bowlby, 1969).

Since these early findings, Bowlby (1958, 1960, 1961, 1963) and others (Heinicke and Westheimer, 1966; Ainsworth, 1962, 1967; Ainsworth and Bell, 1969; Robertson, 1963) have refined their research from which Bowlby developed a theory that is elaborated in Volume One of a two-volume series entitled *Attachment and Loss* (Bowlby, 1969).

We do not go into the development of his theory (much of it based on Freud's writings as well as studies of animal behavior). The reader is encouraged to refer to the early chapters of *Volume One—Attachment* (Bowlby, 1969) for a fascinating look at theory integration and building.

Bowlby's Attachment Theory. Essentially, what Bowlby is saying is that the major task during the first three years of life is for the infant to form an attachment to at least one other human being. The process of making this attachment goes through a series of four phases during which the infant focuses more and more on one figure or person in his environment (usually mother or a mother substitute). If this process does not occur, that is, the child is separated from his mother or caretaker before this attachment process runs its course, the person may experience serious personality problems in relating to others for the rest of his life. Thus, how a person becomes attached to his mother influences how he becomes attached (or whether he can become attached) to other humans throughout his lifetime.

Normally a baby will go through four phases of developing an attachment. These are:

The Life
Cycle

Phase One (birth to eight or twelve weeks): During this phase, the infant uses his "built-in" behavioral systems that provide the "building bricks" for the latter development of attachment. These include at birth responses such as crying, sucking, clinging, and orientation; a few weeks later such responses as smiling and babbling; and months later responses such as crawling and walking.

In Phase One, the infant, although responsive to stimuli, is generally unable to discriminate one person from another. At the sight and sound of any human he may orient himself toward him, visually follow him as he moves, reach and cling to him, or smile and babble at him. Such behavior has an interactive quality to it. That is, these responses usually ensure that the person will stay around and interact with him more, and in doing so, the infant will tend to respond more.

Phase Two (twelve weeks to six months): Orientation and signals directed toward one (or more) discriminated figure(s). During this time the infant's behavior is still friendly to other persons, but gradually he responds more and more toward his mother or mother-substitute. Differential responses to mother's voice are evident at about four weeks and visual responses to her presence are observed at around ten weeks.

Phase Three (seven months to two years and sometimes into the third): Maintenance of proximity to a discriminated figure by means of locomotion as well as signals. This phase is evident in such infant behaviors as when he begins to become more selective in his responses; he is uneasy around strangers, he follows his mother when she leaves the room, he greets her on return, and uses her as a "safety base" from which to explore strange places or persons. He generally begins to perceive her as an independent object who comes and goes fairly predictably.

Phase Four (during second or third years) Formation of a Goal-Corrected Partnership: During this phase, the child gradually is able to cognitively infer some cause and effect behavioral sequences in relations with his mother. Gradually he develops insight into how his mother may feel or why she behaves as she does in certain situations. This phase, Bowlby believes, is the beginning of a true "partnership" relationship.

Trust

Erikson's Eight Stages of Life. Erikson (1959, 1963) believes that as man develops from birth, he is continually evolving through a series of eight stages that are closely related to his biological, psychological, and social development. During each of these eight stages the person must go through a particular type of conflict situation in which the demands of the individual are pitted against society's demands as reflected early in his life by his parents' attitudes and behavior. It is out of this struggle between the needs of the individual and society's demands that the person develops certain basic human qualities such as trust, autonomy, initiative, and industry. Table 15–4 presents a listing of these eight stages together with their particular psychosocial crises.

Erikson believes that how these crises are solved in one stage have an overlapping effect on one's ability to handle future stages. He also believes that these are overlapping phases, so that the ages are only an approximation. Erikson further inserts the words "a sense of" before these polar traits (e.g., a sense of trust vs. a sense of mistrust) because he believes they

Infancy

TABLE 15–4
ERIKSON'S EIGHT STAGES OF MAN

Stage	Approximate Ages	Basic Psychosocial Conflict	Scope of Human Relationships Involved	Successful Outcome of Dilemma Produces
I	0–2 (Infancy) Birth to 2 years	Trust vs. Mistrust	Mother	Hope
II	3–4 (Early Childhood)	Autonomy vs. Shame, Doubt	Parents	Will
III	5–8 (Play Age)	Initiative vs. Guilt	Family	Purpose
IV	9–12 (School Age)	Industry vs. Inferiority	Neighborhood, School	Competence
V	13–19 (Adolescence)	Identity vs. Identity Confusion	Peer Groups Leadership Models	Fidelity
VI	Young Adult	Intimacy vs. Isolation	Friends (Male and Female); Spouse	Love
VII	Adulthood	Generativity vs. Self-Absorption	Job Acquaintances—Family Interactions	Care
VIII	Mature Age	Integrity vs. Despair	All of Mankind	Wisdom

Compiled from Erikson, 1963, 1959, and Maier, 1969.

represent an actual feeling that the person is left with as a result of the outcome of these "developmental battles."

In this chapter we only discuss the first human "crisis"—trust versus mistrust. In succeeding chapters we explore the other stages (Erikson, 1963).

TRUST VERSUS MISTRUST

The first demonstration of social trust in the baby is the ease of his feeding, the depth of his sleep, the relaxation of his bowels. The experience of a mutual regulation of his increasingly receptive capacities with the maternal techniques of provision gradually helps him to balance the discomfort caused by the immaturity of homeostasis with which he was born. In his gradually increasing waking hours he finds that more and more adventures of the senses arouse a feeling of familiarity, of having coincided with a feeling of inner goodness. Forms of comfort, and people associated with them, become as familiar as the gnawing discomfort of the bowels. The infant's first social achievement, then, is his willingness to let the mother out of sight without undue anxiety or rage, because she has become an inner certainty as well as an outer predictability. Such consistency, continuity, and sameness of experience provide a rudimentary sense of ego identity which depends, I think, on the recognition that there is an inner population of remembered and anticipated sensations and images which are firmly correlated with the outer population of familiar and predictable things and people.

. . . The general state of trust, furthermore, implies not only that one has learned to rely on the sameness and continuity of the outer providers, but also that one may trust oneself and the capacity of one's own organs to cope with urges; and that one is able to consider oneself trustworthy

The Life Cycle

enough so that the providers will not need to be on guard lest they be nipped (pp. 247–248).

Erikson thus introduces the reader to the first and most basic of all human stages of growth, the infancy period when the infant faces the crisis of developing a sense of trust or of mistrust regarding not only important persons in his environment but of his self-image and bodily processes as well. It is out of these early experiences of trusting his psychological as well as physiological world that the child can allow himself to accept and experience novel experiences in the future. This increases his chances of accepting with more trust and favorable expectancy new experiences in the future.

Although the child never quite loses all the remnants of mistrust (any new experience for the infant always has both aspects of trust and mistrust), it is the faith of his parents that tends to "tip the scales" toward a more trusting and confident orientation to the infant's immediate environment.

Much of the infant's basic trust is tied to his biologically developing processes during infancy. During the first four months much of the child's behavior involves the "taking in" of nourishment through the sucking response. Erikson believes it is the mother's whole orientation toward the infant (e.g., how she holds him, talks to him, and her smile) in the feeding situation that determines the child's early trust in other humans.

As the other senses develop, the child "incorporates" and accepts (or trusts) the environment. Soon the child learns to receive and trust his system in relation to his mother's ways of caring for him.

Next, the child begins to receive his environment through such acts as mouthing objects for which he can reach.

Another phase of trust begins as the infant learns to grasp objects he can now see and hear better. As he develops, the child interacts more and more with his surroundings. He now tries to hold onto objects and cling to them. Often this desire is so intense that he may bite his mother in order to keep her close. Of course, he soon learns that this often results in her moving away very rapidly!

Thus, it is through a sense of identifying himself with the mother that the child learns (1) that his world is fairly stable and predictable; (2) that he can develop an inner reality and outer environmental regularity; (3) that he can project some of his own feelings upon his mother (this, by the way, reinforces the mother's desire to love her child and respond to him); and, (4) that his feelings of mistrust in his world and himself gradually and more readily give way to a sense of trust; this eventually produces in the child that most important ingredient that seems to keep man, societies, and civilizations from dying—it is called Hope.

Maternal Influences

As part of their approach in studying children in a preschool project at Harvard University, Burton White and his associates systematically observed children in kindergartens, nursery schools, and Operation Head Start programs (Pines, 1969). They were trying to find children whose behavior reflected either an overall competence or incompetence in dealing with their worlds of playing as well as learning. From their observations, they selected a total of 440 three- to six-year-old children—about half of them reflecting

Infancy

FIG. 15-12.

a high degree of competence (the "A" children) and the rest a low degree of competence (the "C" children).

Much to their surprise, they found many three-year-old children who were classified as "A" (highly competent). As E. Robert La Crosse, one of the project directors, stated—"We found that if you're talking about competence, the action comes before the age of three" (Pines, 1969).

They then shifted their focus and began looking at younger children one to three years of age. La Crosse and four associates went into the homes of thirty infants, and for months they followed the mothers around their houses and tape recorded their observations. Others in the research team did the same thing, focusing only on the infant's behavior in 170 different homes. After one-and-one-half years they began to summarize their results.

The preliminary results (a book is now available by White and Watts, 1973, summarizing the results) indicate that there is a close relationship between children's behaviors and how they relate to their mothers: La

Crosse believes that the data show five basic types of mothers. Table 15–5 summarizes these patterns of maternal behavior.

TABLE 15–5
SOME PATTERNS OF MATERNAL BEHAVIOR RELATED TO COMPETENCE IN CHILDHOOD

Types of Mothers	Description	Outcome
"Super Mother"	Occasionally intervenes to provide educational experience for child as he grows. Enjoys child as he is. Balance between mother and child-initiated activities. Child spends much time in "make believe" role playing.	"A" child. Highly competent in his ability to cope with his environment in all domains.
Smothering Mother	Constantly orders child around. Pushes child. Never accepts child at his present level of performance.	"A" child in cognitive domain but not in affective development (immature and shy child).
Almost Mother	Waits for behavior to be initiated by child. Difficulty in understanding and meeting his needs. Confused and fails to initiate intellectual input.	"B" child. Above average competence. Some difficulty in coping with environment.
The Overwhelmed Mother	Child spends much time sitting and doing nothing (forty-one times more than child of "super mother"). Little time to spend with her child because of problems of daily living. Home is disorganized. Siblings may care for child.	"C" child. Average competence—much difficulty in coping with environment.
Zoo-Keeper Mother	Household routine highly structured. Physically cares for her child very well. Leaves child alone in crib with educational toys. Little mother-infant interaction. Monitors child very little.	Probably a "C" child. A child who is unable to approach his behavior in flexible manner. Highly stereotyped behavior.

Compiled from Maya Pines, 1969.

These types of mothering seem to be generally unrelated to socio-economic level, although middle-class children seem to more often have "supermothers." It should be noted that these categories of "mothering styles" are not discrete, that is, there are some mothers who may reflect parts of two different styles. Also, as White warns, the study must be verified by others using different groups of parents and children.

The important point is that this study is one of the first to provide data on what mothers do with and for their children early in life that helps the children interact more effectively with their world later in life. In a two-year   Infancy follow-up study of the original "A" and "C" children, the same levels of competence were generally displayed in the two groups as they performed and interacted socially in school. It will be fascinating to follow these groups later in life to determine if these relationships remain.

Maternal Deprivation

Once upon a time there were two groups of infants who, for a variety of reasons, had to be placed in institutions to be cared for. One of these groups of youngsters was placed in a "nursery" and the other group was placed in a "foundling home."

Both of these institutions were about the same in most respects. That is, they were both located on the outskirts of large cities and surrounded by gardens. They were models of cleanliness (for example, all personnel and visitors were required to wear sterilized smocks and scrub their hands before entering the baby ward). The walls were painted in light colors, the food was prepared according to the needs of the individual baby, most of the infants were breast-fed or, if bottle-fed, the bottles were carefully sterilized, clean clothing was provided, and a well-regulated temperature was maintained in the rooms.

The foundling home babies had the advantage of receiving daily visits by a doctor and specialists when needed. In most cases they were placed in the foundling home because their mothers were unable to support them.

The nursery school, on the other hand, was actually located in a jail for delinquent girls where most of them were placed for a variety of reasons. Many of them, being pregnant upon sentencing, went to a nearby hospital, delivered their babies, and returned to prison (where their babies were placed in the prison nursery).

Now, along comes a doctor who decides to compare these two groups of babies. He gives them a series of infant tests that measure such areas of human development as perceptual ability, body mastery, social relations, memory, relations to inanimate objects, and intelligence. The foundling home babies scored higher (an average IQ of 124) than the nursery babies did (an average IQ of 101.5).

At the end of the first year, the doctor came back and gave these tests again. This time, the foundling home babies scored an average IQ of 72 whereas the nursery infants scored an average IQ of 105. This, in itself, is a remarkably significant decline in development, but even more significant is the fact that in the foundling home at the end of the first year there were about a fourth of the babies missing—they had died. In contrast, in the nursery, during that same period, no babies had died!

Also, at the beginning of that first year, in the older ward (ages eighteen months to two and a half years) in the foundling home, only two out of twenty-six babies were able to walk, hardly any of them could eat by themselves or say but a few words, and they all wore diapers and had to be changed.

At the nursery, in the older age group (only eight to twelve months of age) let's let the doctor, René Spitz (1945), describe what he found.

In sharp contrast to this is the picture offered by the oldest inmates in nursery, ranging from 8 to 12 months. The problem here is not whether the children walk or talk by the end of the first year; the problem with these 10-month olds is how to tame the healthy toddlers' curiosity and enterprise. They climb up the bars of the cot after the manner of South Sea Islanders climbing palms. Special measures to guard them from harm have had to be taken after one 10-month old actually succeeded in diving right over the more-than 2-foot railing of the cot. They vocalize freely, and some of them actually speak a word or two. And all of them understand the significance of simple social gestures. When released from their cots, all walk with support and a number walk without it. (p. 60)

What could account for such dramatic differences in the death and developmental rates of these two institutions?

As you may have guessed by now, the major difference between the two settings was that the infants in the "nursery" had their mothers there with them on a daily basis whereas the infants in the foundling home had "an eighth of a nurse."

That is, in the nursery, the infants' mothers (the delinquent girls) were with them daily from the beginning. Under the supervision of older nurses who helped and advised the mothers on child care, they fed, nursed, and cared for their babies. If, for some reason, the mother had to be separated from the infant, that baby was provided with a substitute mother (another mother or a pregnant girl who could relate well with the child).

Contrast this to the foundling home where there was a head nurse and five assistant nurses, responsible for the entire care of forty-five babies. Thus, they were forced to leave the infants in their cribs most of the day in order to spend a few minutes with each one for feeding and changing. Thus, efficiency rather than time for playing with and loving the child was the main consideration in the foundling home.

What are the long-term effects of this type of early deprivation experience? Spitz did a two-year follow-up study (1946) on these children. Despite some changes that had been instituted, the mortality rate over a two-year period was up to 37 per cent. The infants originally studied (now about two to four years older) were all significantly behind in the various areas of infant development. For example, of the original twenty-one babies still in the foundling home (many of them had already been placed in other institutions or foster homes), only five could walk unassisted, nine could eat with a spoon, only one could dress himself, fifteen were partially toilet trained, and only two could speak more than a dozen words! Not only were they behind in developmental categories, they were substantially below in physiological development as well. Of the twenty-one, only three had the normal weight for their age, and only two had attained the average height: all others fell below the normal height-weight standards. As Spitz notes: "The physical picture of these children impresses the casual observer as that of children half their age" (1946).

What about the nursery schoolchildren? What happened to them? In a similar follow-up study in which twenty-nine of the original group (much younger in age than the foundling home infants) were still there, Spitz (1946) observed the following:

In spite of this enormous difference in age, the nursery children all ran lustily around on the floor; some of them dressed and undressed themselves; they fed themselves with a spoon; nearly all spoke a few words; Infancy they understood commands and obeyed them; and the older ones showed a certain consciousness of toilet requirements. . . . In all these children, tests showed that the developmental quotients which in the 11th and 12th months had receded somewhat, not only came up to the normal age level, but in most cases surpassed it by far. (p. 113)

Regarding the death rate in the nursery school over the entire three and a half year study: *not a single child died!*

What is the significance of this classic study done over thirty years ago? It certainly is not an example of the "model experiment," in fact, it did have many weaknesses as a highly controlled study.

It was not the first study written about the fact that children die in institutions at a far greater rate than they do in homes.

But, it was the first "experimental type study" to show, for perhaps the first time, the drastic results of the lack of maternal love, maternal stimulation, and the human contact. Since this study, many others on maternal deprivation have found similar striking results.

Since these studies have, we believe, convincingly shown the importance of maternal (or maternal substitute) stimulation and interaction in early infancy, the question of whether a mother (or mother substitute) is needed in infancy has been answered and given way, in more recent years, to other, equally important, questions as:

What are the long-term effects of maternal deprivation?

Are these effects lasting and irreversible?

What can be done to reduce the effects of maternal deprivation when it occurs?

At what age is the most critical period for maternal deprivation to occur?

What are the factors in mother-infant interactions that make it so critical for the full psychological and physiological development of the child?

What are the responsibilities of mothers who must work and leave their infants in daytime or week-long nursery school settings?

What can institutions (such as hospitals and nursery schools) do to prevent the effects of maternal deprivation?

Maternal Separation. While René Spitz (1946) was conducting his study in the foundling home and nursery he observed another strange phenomenon. Among many of the foundling home babies and some of the nursery school infants he found this typical pattern:

She lay immobile in her crib. When approached she did not lift her shoulders, barely her head, to look at the experimenter with an expression of profound suffering sometimes seen in sick animals. With this expression she examined the observer. As soon as the observer started to speak to her or to touch her she began to weep. This was not the usual crying of babies which is always accompanied by a certain amount of vocalization going into screaming. It was a soundless weeping, tears running down her face. Speaking to her in soft comforting tones only resulted in the weeping becoming more intense, intermingled with moans and sobs, shaking her whole body. (pp. 314–315)

Now, among the foundling home infants this syndrome (which he labeled anaclitic depression) continued, deepened, and became so critical that the very health of the children deteriorated to such a point that they became extremely susceptible to disease and, as you recall, thirty-four of them died.

In the case of the nursery school infants, an amazing thing happened. In all cases, this strange pattern of behavior actually disappeared. But how? In all cases, the mothers (because of a variety of reasons) had left the infants for about two to four months. When the mothers returned, the children actually got well again, displayed more of the usual types of developmental behavior and—in a sense—became human beings again.

What is the significance of this part of Spitz's study? Again, he was one of the earliest researchers to clearly point out and dramatically show that:

1. Separation from mother during critical periods in infancy can have a devastating effect on the infant.
2. If a mother or mother-substitute is replaced within three months the child suffers little damage.
3. If, however, something isn't done, the damage to the child is irreversible.

We do not go into further details of this second phase of Spitz's classic study, except to present his final recommendations for therapeutic measures:

1. Prophylaxis: deprivation of infants, during the first year, of love objects for a prolonged period, should be strenuously avoided. Under no circumstances should they be deprived for over three months of love objects, during the second half of their first year.
2. Restitution: if infants have been deprived of their love objects during their first year for a prolonged period, restitution of the love objects within a period of maximally three months will enable them to recover, at least partially, from the damage inflicted.
3. Substitution: where neither prophylaxis nor restitution is possible, the substitution of the love object by another one is advisable.

   Particular attention should be given to the facilitation of the infant's locomotor drives in the largest measure possible, and to the supporting of its tendencies to choose actively its own substitutes for the love object of which it has been deprived. (pp. 338–339)

Other Dimensions of Maternal Separation. Since Spitz's original studies, the theme song, "Oh, Mother! Where Have You Gone?" has been sung by more and more children where the mother (having interacted with the infant in a focused relationship, and often having produced an attachment response on the part of the infant to her) has to be separated either temporarily or permanently from the infant.

Contemporary events such as World War II (when millions of children were separated from their parents), smaller wars (such as the Korean and Vietnam wars when thousands of orphans were left to roam the streets and fields), the high mobility and urbanization (where parents go to the city to work and come home on weekends in the rural areas), reduction on the emphasis on the expanded family where aunts and uncles often take care of the child, increase in working mothers as well as mothers who continue their education and professional roles, illegitimate children as well as abandoned and orphaned children caused by many factors, and children in hospitals either temporarily or on a long-term basis all have caused some degree of separation.

All of these situations, whether temporary or permanent, whether the result of environmental or situational factors, or of parents' intentional or unintentional separation, have an effect on infants. We are not exactly sure what all the variables are and how they interact with specific children in specific separated situations, but we do know that it has a definite effect. Yarrow (1964) in his extensive review of separation studies believes that such factors as determinants, duration, and repetition would relate to the specific separation effects on the infant. He proposes six different degrees of separation, as follows:

1. Single brief separation followed by reunion with the parents.
2. Repeated brief separations with reunion.
3. Single, long-term separation with reunion.
4. Repeated long-term separations with reunion.
5. Single permanent separation.
6. Repeated permanent separations.

In summarizing all the relevant research on the effects of separation on the infant, Yarrow (1964) maintains that the studies thus far (the need for research is still great) indicate the importance of at least seven major variables and/or conditions in the effects of separation on the infant. Table 15–6 summarizes these variables and their effects on the child as supported by the limited studies.

TABLE 15–6
SOME VARIABLES WHICH HAVE AN IMPACT ON THE CHILD WHO IS
SEPARATED FROM HIS MOTHER

Conditions and/or Variables	Some Effects	References
1. Age at time of separation.	Reactions less severe in early infancy before stable mother-infant relationship develops. Most severe reactions occur in infants separated from their mothers after a focused relationship has been established (around 6–8 months).	Yarrow (1956) Yarrow and Goodwin (1963)
	It appears that there may be a "critical period" when separation may have the most severe consequences.	
	If separation occurs before a focused relationship develops and the separated child never experiences an intimate human relationship, then he may be permanently impaired in the capacity to establish relationships in later life.	
2. The quality of the relationship with the mother prior to separation.	Children showing most severe reactions to separation had closest relationship with mother.	Spitz and Wolf (1946)
	Cultures where multiple-mothering is practiced produces less acute separation responses than those with single mothering relationships.	Mead (1963)
	Temporary separation (e.g., hospitalization) may be less traumatic where a close mother-infant relationship exists.	Prugh et al. (1953) Faust et al. (1952)

Conditions and/or Variables	Some Effects	References
3. The character of maternal care subsequent to the initial separation.	Much personality and intellectual damage to the infant can be avoided if a mother-figure is provided who can give adequate stimulation, can develop a warm relationship, and who is sensitive and responsive to the infant's particular needs. (Both for temporary and long-term separation situations.)	
4. The character of the relationship with the parents during temporary separation.	In temporary situations, if the child can maintain a relationship with his parents, the effects of the separation are less harsh than if there is an abrupt termination of relationship (e.g., hospitalization).	Maas and Engles (1959)
5. The duration of separation experience.	For temporary separation, severity of reaction related to duration.	Spitz and Wolf (1946)
	There may be time interval after which separation effects may be irreversible (3 to 5 months for infants).	
	Effects of duration of separation also related to child's age, previous experiences at being separated, and amount of stress or human deprivation he is experiencing. (More studies needed.)	
6. Subsequent reinforcing experiences.	Later favorable experiences after separation may modify or undo the earlier effects.	More research needed
	Children who have experienced separation may enter subsequent experiences with more trauma (because of being overly sensitive to this kind of experience).	Goldfarb (1944) Trasler (1960)
7. Constitutional factors.	Infants differ in basic overall biological response and sensitivity.	Chess, Thomas, Birch, 1959
	These constitutional differences are related to differential responses to different types of separations (exactly how is still not clear).	Alpert, et al. (1956) Bergman and Escalona (1949)

Compiled from Yarrow, 1964.

Disturbed Mothers. The studies on deprivation and separation in infancy may lead one to the conclusion that placing an infant in an institution or hospital setting is the "worst of all evils" and that an infant in a home situation is always much better off.

Today it is recognized that there are family situations that are far more damaging to the infant than the problems of separation discussed earlier. In fact, in some cases, the child may be far better off separated from his parents. This distinction was considered to be of such importance that, in 1962, the World Health Organization included this topic as a theme in a   Infancy major publication entitled *Deprivation of Maternal Care—A Reassessment of Its Effects* (1962).

In that publication Prugh and Harlow (1962) point out some of the problems in assuming that a home setting is always the best.

A further consideration that has sometimes been (erroneously) drawn is that any home setting is better than any institutional placement. Case studies by DuPan and Roth and by many other workers attest to the fact that the physical presence of a parent or foster parent does not guarantee emotional satisfaction to the child, especially if that parent is unable to tolerate any disturbance in behavior on the part of the child. If a foster-home setting is involved, a train of events leading to repetitive shifts in home settings, with serious emotional consequences for the child, may be set in motion. . . .

Finally, misplaced emphasis given to Bowlby's earlier statements can lead to the facile conclusion that any child at any age is better off in his own home than in a foster-home, hospital or other institutional setting. It is true that most children are happier with their own parents, no matter how disturbed or unsatisfying the parent-child relationships may be. However, recent experiences in nurseries and residential treatment centers, which have admitted disturbed children from physically intact but seriously disturbed families, have indicated that the home may not always be the most favorable environment for a child's development. On the contrary, it is sometimes seen that only when the child is removed from the home is he able to begin to mature and develop. (pp. 9–10)

Although many types of problems and dynamics are involved in "disturbed families" one of the most common is where the mother is unable to warmly relate to the child because of her "coldness" and indifference. Prugh and Harlow (1962) cite one example of such a mother:

A mother, an attractive but seriously inhibited and cold young woman felt completely unable to respond to her first-born infant, a boy. She went through the motions of his care, but was consciously aware that she felt no warmth towards him and took no pleasure in him at any time. Although she remained close to him physically, she let him play alone for many hours in his playpen during the first year of life, withdrawing into herself or reading and paying only occasional attention to his safety. During the latter part of the boy's second year, the father became alarmed at the child's lack of responsiveness or interest in the environment and upon psychiatric study, an autistic psychotic picture was apparent. (pp. 11)

Very often such mothers have been reared in a similar manner in a family with little warmth and caring.

Masked Deprivation. Prugh and Harlow (1962) in their article summarizing the various forms of this type of hidden or masked "deprivation" discuss two major forms it may take. Table 15–7 shows some of the forms that these relationships often take, along with their possible consequences for the child.

Factors in Healthy Mother-Infant Interaction. We have seen how some of the songs of infancy often lead to difficulties in the musical arrangements

TABLE 15–7
SOME FORMS OF "MASKED DEPRIVATION"

Type of Relatedness	Specific Examples
I. Distorted Relatedness	1. One or both parents cannot perceive child as being a unique individual. a. Child not clearly differentiated from parent. b. Either child's or parent's needs can only be met by others' response. 2. Parent perceives child as unique individual, yet still responds in terms of his or her needs. a. Parent projects a part of himself into child. b. Parents perceive child in distorted way because of previous experience or attitudes.
II. Insufficient Relatedness	1. Parent "coldness" and inability to relate "warmly" to child because of personal problems. a. "Cold" mother. b. Parents so involved in themselves, little emotions given to child. 2. Situational problems of parents during infancy produce emotional problems that interfere with adequate relatedness to child.

Compiled from Prugh et al., 1972. D. G. Prugh, and H. Harlow, masked deprivation. In *Deprivation of Maternal Care*. Public Affairs Papers No. 14. WHO, Geneva, 1962.

with such things as "sour notes," a dissonance, a harsh sound, or badly tuned instruments. We have seen, also, how these theme songs are often so loud and overwhelming that they interfere with the individual's ability to create his own variations later in life—they just sit there and repeat themselves over and over again, like a broken record—so that the person cannot even get away from them.

We have seen what happens when no life song is ever created, because there is no one there to "make music with"—so many people go through life singing a monotone or solo—they never learn the beauty in the give-and-take of a duet with another human being.

But, what about creating an overture to life that is melodic, alive, and beautiful to hear—a life "theme song" that is flexible and harmonious enough so that the infant, later in life, can expand and modify it as he grows into a unique and more fully human authentic person? What about creating an overture that is truly a mutuality—an evolving duet between mother and child? Is this possible? Do we know enough about this kind of "music making" to give some ideas and guidelines?

It is in this area of "musical" development that researchers are now frantically searching for clues. They, too, are now convinced that it is in these early months of mutual give-and-take between mother and infant that the first and most important human relationship of life is set. Many believe that it is out of the quality of this relationship (or this duet) that one essentially writes his lifetime "social melody."

Let us try and explore, with the limited research available, the following questions:

Infancy

1. What are the parameters (aspects) of this mother-infant interaction?
2. Which are the most important?
3. What are the best types of mother-infant relationships in terms of increasing the chances of the person becoming a more fully alive, self-actualizing human?

Mother-Infant Interaction During Feeding. The first and most important human relationship that an infant has in life is with his mother. How he learns to relate to her and how she relates to him—many researchers feel may offer clues to the development of individual human relatedness. Indeed, some believe that it is out of this early and first relationship that one sets a pattern in terms of how one relates to himself and others the rest of his life.

Now, what are some of the ways in which we can tell if an infant is beginning his early social development in a way that will increase his chances of becoming a more fully human person? Obviously, we cannot ask him, so we observe him and make deductions from these early observations.

Ainsworth and Bell (1969) and others believe that there are several sequential clues that allow us to deduct whether an infant is having a proper (satisfying) human relationship. Some of these behaviors are related to signals that babies give us, such things as crying, smiling, following, clinging, crying when mother leaves room, using mother as a secure base from which to explore the world, and using mother as a haven of safety against threat (e.g., a stranger in the room). Many of these signals of effective human contact (called attachment by Bowlby) occur later (after the first three months) in the infant's life. Ainsworth and Bell (1969) believe that the forerunners—the preconditions for effective human contact—are, however, laid down much earlier in the day-to-day mother-infant interactions in the first three months.

What do mothers and infants do together during those early months? Most of their interactions together have to do with meeting the basic biological needs—activities having to do with feeding, eliminating, and rest. It is here in the early feeding situation that Ainsworth believes that clues to primitive social development (styles of human relatedness to self and others) may be uncovered. It is to this end that she began a fascinating and highly creative series of studies of mother-infant interaction.

Let us look at the earliest reports of Ainsworth's longer study in detail because it reflects the kind of research in mother-infant observations that is so badly needed if we are to understand and isolate the significant variables in early infancy.

Mother-Infant Interaction: Patterns in the Feeding Situation. Ainsworth and Bell (1969) and their research colleagues studied in depth the feeding interaction of twenty-six babies of white, middle-class Baltimore families who volunteered to participate upon referral by their pediatrician. Repeated observations (lasting two to four hours) were made in their homes over a time period of the first three months of the baby's life.

The actual feedings were observed and data gathered on the following three characteristics of the feeding situation:

1. The timing of feedings.
2. Determination of the amount of food ingested at the end of the feeding.
3. Mother's handling of the baby's preference in kind of food.

In addition, nine patterns of mother-infant interaction were identified (four of them represent feeding by demand and five represent feeding according to a schedule). Figure 15–13 shows the nine patterns observed. Notice that the patterns run along continuously from number one (where the baby is much more of an active partner) to number nine (where the mother is dominant).

The nine categories were designed as a rough approximation to measure the degree to which the baby was permitted to determine the timing of the feedings, the amount he ingested, the order in which solids were given, and the pacing of his rate of intake.

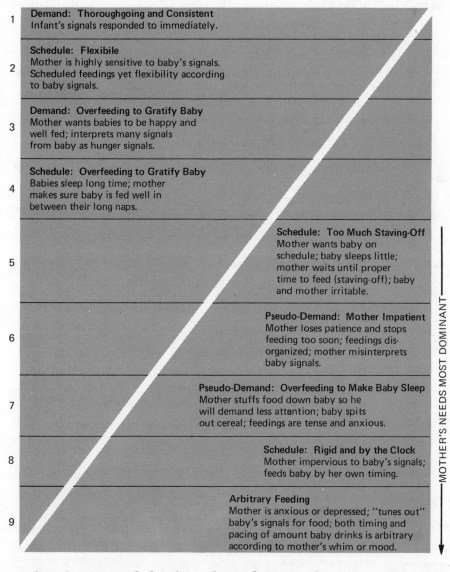

Feeding Pattern

1 Demand: Thoroughgoing and Consistent
Infant's signals responded to immediately.

2 Schedule: Flexibile
Mother is highly sensitive to baby's signals. Scheduled feedings yet flexibility according to baby signals.

3 Demand: Overfeeding to Gratify Baby
Mother wants babies to be happy and well fed; interprets many signals from baby as hunger signals.

4 Schedule: Overfeeding to Gratify Baby
Babies sleep long time; mother makes sure baby is fed well in between their long naps.

5 Schedule: Too Much Staving-Off
Mother wants baby on schedule; baby sleeps little; mother waits until proper time to feed (staving-off); baby and mother irritable.

6 Pseudo-Demand: Mother Impatient
Mother loses patience and stops feeding too soon; feedings disorganized; mother misinterprets baby signals.

7 Pseudo-Demand: Overfeeding to Make Baby Sleep
Mother stuffs food down baby so he will demand less attention; baby spits out cereal; feedings are tense and anxious.

8 Schedule: Rigid and by the Clock
Mother impervious to baby's signals; feeds baby by her own timing.

9 Arbitrary Feeding
Mother is anxious or depressed; "tunes out" baby's signals for food; both timing and pacing of amount baby drinks is arbitrary according to mother's whim or mood.

← INFANTS NEEDS MORE DOMINANT —

— MOTHER'S NEEDS MOST DOMINANT →

FIG. 15–13. *Nine patterns of mother-infant feeding interaction during the first three months. (Adapted from Ainsworth and Bell, 1969, pp. 144–48.)*

After observing and classifying the mothers according to one of the nine patterns of feeding, Ainsworth and Bell related the mothers in the nine patterns to three other variables: (1) the infant's crying, (2) the mother's

Infancy

attitudes and infant-care practices, and (3) the baby's reaction in a strange situation at the end of the first year. Let us see what surprising findings were obtained.

Infant-Mother Feeding Style and Infant's Crying Patterns. The researchers were interested here in the number of crying episodes and the length of each episode. In general, (there were a few exceptions) they found that the infants fed on consistent-demand and flexible schedule (feeding patterns one and two) cried less during feeding and cried less in overall time during the observations than the babies in pattern nine (arbitrary feeding). The overall tendency was for the babies in feeding patterns one through four (where the mothers reacted more to their infant's signals) to cry significantly less than the babies in patterns five through nine (where the mothers were generally less sensitive to their babies' signals).

Maternal-Care Variables. The researchers also observed the mothers' attitudes and behavior toward their infants. Six of the measures of maternal care are outlined in Table 15–8. Each dimension was rated on a nine-point scale. A high rating would represent a mother:

1. With a realistic perception of her baby.
2. Who takes delight in the things her baby does.
3. Who accepts her baby and does not resent his intrusion into her autonomy.
4. Who knows when and where not to intervene in her baby's current activity.
5. Who cuddles her baby and gives him much physical contact.
6. Who interprets her baby's cry accurately and responds accordingly.

TABLE 15–8

SOME MATERNAL-CARE VARIABLES MEASURED DURING THE FIRST 3 MONTHS

Variable	Descriptions
Mother's perception of the baby	Whether mother's perception of infant is distorted or based on accurate data.
Mother's delight in the baby	Mother's reaction to baby in specific situations.
Mother's acceptance of the baby	Degree to which mother accepts or rejects baby in terms of interfering with her autonomy.
Appropriateness of mother's interaction with the baby	What is mother's style of intervention with baby? Does she interrupt his activities? Does she know when to interact?
Amount of physical contact	How much physical contact is there between mother and infant in addition to the normal contact during routine care?
Effectiveness of mother's response to baby's crying	Does mother interpret and respond appropriately to baby's cry?

Compiled from Ainsworth et al., 1969.

Results of Relation Between Feeding Pattern and Mother Care Variables. As you might have predicted, the mothers who used feeding patterns one through four tended to have the highest maternal care ratings. Ainsworth and Bell (1969) characterize these mothers as follows:

> These are all patterns in which sensitivity to the baby's signals and a desire to gratify him are prominent. These mothers tended to be able to see things from the baby's point of view, to take delight in his behavior, and to accept him with little regret over the temporary surrender of their autonomy. (p. 156)

The lowest ratings on maternal care were associated with mothers who fed their babies either on rigid schedules or arbitrarily, when they felt like it. These mothers were described as follows:

> The mothers in these last two patterns tended to be distorted in their perceptions of the baby, to take little or no delight in his behavior, and to resent overtly or covertly the infringement of their autonomy by his demands. (p. 156)

Reactions to Babies in a Strange Situation. Another part of the experiment was conducted at one year of age to observe the infant's reaction to a "standardized strange situation."

This technique has been frequently used to measure degree of attachment of the child to his mother (Ainsworth et al., 1964). The "strange situation" consisted of observing:

1. What the infant would do in a room he had never been in (would he explore the room, using his mother as a "haven of security," or would he sit by her and watch her intently?).
2. The child's reaction during short periods when the mother left the room: one when the child was left entirely alone and another when the child was left with a stranger.
3. The child's reaction when the mother returned after being temporarily separated.

The findings in general (there were a few exceptions) revealed that the babies in feeding groups one through four (where the mothers tended to be more responsive to them) demonstrated more attachment behavior to their mothers than those in the other five feeding patterns (five through nine). That is, the infants who were treated with more sensitivity and responsiveness during the feeding situation (patterns one through four) tended to reflect attachment to their mothers by such behaviors as actively regaining and maintaining contact (by clinging to her) after the brief separation experience. The babies who were fed with less sensitivity on the mother's part after separation tended to either ignore the mother or engage in a combination of ignoring and contact seeking behavior.

Summary. The implications of this exploratory study, even though it has many limitations, we believe, are highly significant because they illustrate a number of changes and recent trends in the way we view early social development as it begins through the interplay of mother and infant—a sort of duet in harmony and rhythm.

Let us summarize some of the implications as seen by Ainsworth and Bell (1969):

1. In general, one could say that those mothers who could see things

from the baby's point of view tended to adopt infant-care practices which led to harmonious interaction not only in feeding but generally.

2. One could say further that babies whose behavior, social and otherwise, gave rise to consistently gratifying or interesting feedback tended to cry less, to learn modes of communication other than hard expressive crying, and to gain more frustration tolerance and more regular and predictable rhythms than babies whose behavior made little or no difference in determining what happened to them.

3. On the other hand, it is reasonable to believe that it is easier for a mother to interact harmoniously with a baby who is relatively easy to understand and to predict, and who responds with pleasure and interest rather than with frustration and distress. From the beginning, some of the babies in our sample may have been more difficult than others. . . . (p. 60)

IMPLICATIONS

UNDERSTANDING YOURSELF AND OTHERS

What does our discussion of infancy have to do with helping you understand yourself and others better? We believe it could provide additional insights into your own experiences during infancy through discussions with your parents regarding your birth and first two years. What kind of development in the four domains might have had an impact in your becoming a more fully human person? Was there adequate stimulation in your environment to foster competence in dealing with the world? Was there continuity in terms of general physical and social environment? What kind of mother-infant interaction did you experience? Was there opportunity for adequate learning and creative involvement with the world?

As far as understanding others, perhaps you now have more compassion for the young mothers who are placed in a situation of critical responsibility that may affect the infant the rest of his days. Maybe you can now see better the need for the building of adequate supports during the preconception stage so that the stress of mothering an active, growing, becoming infant is not so overwhelming. Maybe you can now sense the important role of a husband who is communicating with his wife during this important phase of life. We hope you realize the importance of an adequate environment for mothers and infants so that a feeling of trust may develop within this new person.

And, finally, maybe you can now sense the importance of those early "duets" between mother and infant. From this analogy we hope you get a feeling for the rhythmic and spontaneous interactions as the mother "sings" her songs to the infant, and how the uniqueness of the infant in turn produces his early melodies that in turn affect the mother's tempo and rhythms. This give-and-take in creative "music making" forms the basis for the give-and-take in "people making."

LIVING AND WORKING WITH CHILDREN, ADOLESCENTS, AND ADULTS

The Life Cycle

In general, the research is convincing that certain basic needs must be met during infancy in order to increase the chances of producing a more fully human person. Sally Provence, a professor of pediatrics at Yale University, summarizes some of these criteria of "good nurturing" as follows (1968):

1. Adequate nourishment for the child's growth and health: the prevention of physical illness through protective measures.
2. A speaking social partner.
3. An atmosphere that includes a reasonable amount of consistency and repetition.
4. Variety and contrast within the atmosphere created by consistency and repetition.
5. Toys and other playthings.
6. Physical handling through holding, cuddling, bathing, lifting, and touching.
7. Opportunities to move about, to play, and to utilize emerging skills and dispositions in a supportive and safe atmosphere.
8. Limits and prohibitions appropriate to the age of the child. The support of self-regulation and cooperative behavior from the child. (pp. 31–33)

The human implications of much of the research on infancy has led to a number of changes in practices in hospital nurseries and in community intervention and education programs. For example, many hospitals are encouraging mothers to "room in" with their babies immediately after birth, if no serious complications are evident. The effect of the atmosphere of the hospital nursery on the newborn is being studied. Changes in handling procedures and designs of cribs are being made so that the infant will receive adequate early stimulation.

Parent education classes are now being provided not just during the prenatal period but during those important first few months after birth so that they can learn how to better interact with their infants. In many cases, child-care workers are going into the homes to assist mothers to provide a richer emotional, social, cognitive, and biological environment for the infant.

Special plans are being made for the "vulnerable infant"; one who has been screened at birth and found to have a certain vulnerability for problems now or later in life. An environmental "prescription" is made for the parents to follow to reduce the risks for this infant.

Social agencies are now mobilizing to help mothers and infants who are too poor or too socially isolated to make use of existing services. Efforts to improve nutrition, handling procedures, and the integration of the family into their community are being made.

The results of studies on the effects of maternal deprivation and separation are being translated into practices of adoption agencies and infant day-care centers, as well as children's hospitals.

DEVELOPING POSITIVE MODELS

Much of the theory and research discussed in this chapter has already provided us with many positive models to think about: the "supermother," Erikson's notion of basic trust, the mother-infant "duet in harmony and rhythm," the importance of early physical and intellectual stimulation, and Piaget's theory. However, in order to relate the ideas in this chapter more specifically to our previously mentioned goals for developing a more fully human person, let us briefly look at these goals in the four domains.

Many of Fromm's ideas about a loving person seem to be supported by   Infancy our research and theories about infancy. It seems clear that a mother who cares about, knows about, respects the uniqueness of, and assumes responsibility for the care of her infant will tend to produce a child who is able to love himself and others. Many dimensions of the "supermother" as well as the trusting mother-infant "duet" imply these same dimensions.

Also, a mother who is truly concerned with another's welfare, who can view the world realistically, and who can carry out responsibilities is the kind of mother who will plant the early "seeds of altruism" that will increase the chances of growing in the lifetime of the newborn.

Similarly, a mother-infant relationship built upon an empathic feeling-oriented level, rather than a mechanistically based dialogue, will increase the chances of an empathically evolving human being who can "feel with" and for his fellow man.

Finally, it is out of these early emotional relations with others that an infant learns to accept and trust in his feelings. It thus tends to set in motion the evolving of an emotional self that is free (and not restrained), that can react appropriately to situations in the world, that is authentic to the person's state of existence at the time, that is spontaneous, that can allow the person to smile at himself, and that can tolerate stress and anxiety at times.

Although it may be difficult to observe and measure at such an early age, there is no doubt that these first two years form the foundations for our social domain models. Of course, the seeds of compassion, autonomy, openness, and social competence are planted in the first social relationship an infant experiences with his mother. Building upon this foundation, the child is able to grow in his social relations with others: his family members, his peer group, and later his schoolmates and the like. Ainsworth and Bell's (1969) research on early feeding patterns supports many of these social goals. They found that the more effective mothers in the feeding situation were also mothers who perceived their babies realistically, who respected the autonomy of the infant, who accepted the babies' state, and interpreted their signals correctly.

The holistic nature of growth and function implies that positive gains in one domain almost guarantees similar improvements in the other domains to varying degrees. Thus, if parents make special efforts to improve the infant's growth or competency in one area of life, they may be rewarded with positive reverberations throughout the other domains of the infant. For example, in general, there is a positive relationship between stimulation in one domain, whether it is in the form of tactile, kinesthestic, auditory, or visual modes and increased health, performance, and development. The major research problem now is to define the various conditions for stimulation and the differential inputs that should be optimal for different kinds of infants at different stages of their development in conjunction with the special and changing needs of the particular parent-infant combination. Meanwhile, there is much that we can learn from existing models that emphasizes the need for and the quality of early infant stimulation.

We have studied how much difference enriched sensory-motor experiences can make for the infant as well as the need to create the best possible match between the age and individuality of the infant with his particular environment. With this in mind we can study the stimulation model proposed by Doman and Delacato (1965).

MOBILITY. If the child is ever to have a playpen, give it to him now. Cover the floor of the playpen with a plastic mat and turn the little one loose on his tummy. Do not restrain him with tight clothes and heavy blankets. Dress the child in a light shirt and diaper so that he can move around as much as possible.

Encourage him to roll over, and as soon as he does turn him back over on his tummy (praising him, of course, for his mighty feat). It is at this time that he will begin his very first crawling movements. Do not put him on the carpet because the friction will prevent movement and discourage him.

SEEING. Babies receive their very first training for reading readiness when the doctor shines a light in his eyes to test the contraction of the pupils. It is not a gentle test, but babies' eyes do not need gentleness; they need stimulation, exercise, and use.

When it is dark outside, turn on the lights in the baby's room. You might keep a reasonable amount of light on all night. It won't disturb his sleep, and it will help his eyes exercise when he wakes up.

Just looking around won't provide contraction of the pupils, so you can turn off the light for a few seconds and on again several times in the evening. For these newborn eyes hungry for visual experience, that's a more thrilling experience than fireworks.

HEARING. When the doctor claps two objects together to test his "startle reflex," that is the beginning of his training for speaking. You can continue to stimulate this training by cooing, singing, laughing, talking to him. Let him hear lots and lots of music—especially with a strong, not-too-fast beat. Vary the beat, and make it good music.

FEELING. Cuddle baby's bare skin against yours. Let him learn through the powerful instrument of love what it feels like to feel. After you bathe him, gently rub his skin with soft, nubby towels. Tickle, squeeze, and gently pinch him. Put "feeling" objects into his hands—pieces of velvet, an old silk purse, a dry sponge. Things that are too big for his mouth, but small enough for two inquisitive hands. And at this stage don't bother with toys. That little stuffed duck may be the cutest thing in the world, but it means nothing to the baby, who has never seen a duck, except perhaps for a good "feeling" object.

TASTING AND SMELLING. Tasting and smelling are by far the most enjoyable experiences of the one-month-old infant. He delights in this stimulation during feeding, especially breast-feeding, when he is exposed to the sweet aroma of his mother's milk.

Keep him near the kitchen when you are preparing meals so he can smell the good smells of Mom's home cooking. And don't be afraid to take him outside on a warm day and let him smell the wonderful scent of fresh-cut grass.

Infancy

Second Month

MOBILITY. During the second month infants usually show signs of holding up their head and rolling from their belly to their back. If placed on a linoleum floor, he will be able to pivot part of a circle. It is at this time that he is close to this first important movement—the act of moving forward.

When he does start crawling along the floor, Mom must put him back in the middle when he reaches a wall, or he will become frustrated in his new adventure.

SEEING. If possible, move the child's crib once a week. Putting it in different spots in his room will give him something different to look at. You will know how he feels if you have ever been sick and restricted to lying flat on your back.

NEVER place the side of his crib against the wall. That position forces a child to look in only one direction, whichever is the most interesting. His eyes will learn to turn in only one direction. To supplement change of direction, you can place the baby with his head at different ends of the crib from day to day. And if you bottle feed your baby, hold him in one arm one time, and in the other arm the next, as though he were being breast-fed.

Hang a mobile in the baby's room. Get four or five (or make them) and change every few days. If there is no warm, gentle breeze, blow it yourself when you are in the room. Make his furniture brightly colored. Pastels are for weary, nervous adults who need soothing, not for babies, who need stimulation.

In line with the mobiles, you can cut out large shapes, squares, circles, etc. from brightly colored paper. These you can pin on the wall or hold before the child. They can also be incorporated into a homemade mobile.

HEARING. By the time the little one is two months old, any mother can distinguish two different cries. One is for pain or discomfort, and the other is just because he can cry. This crying is his first step toward language—he has used two different sounds to communicate two different needs.

You can make your own vocal sounds to stimulate him. Make soothing rhythmic sounds when rocking; happy, laughing, splashy sounds for bathing; delicious sounds for feeding, etc. Let him know that sounds are related to meaning.

Three to Six Months and Later

MOBILITY. During these months baby actually starts crawling. And unfortunately, this is the time when mothers put their child in a playpen. But if anything, they should get rid of it. The ideal crawling space is a piece of linoleum on top of carpet, so it is both warm and smooth. In baby's room keep the temperature up and remove threats of floor lamps, small tables, ash trays, doors that open inward, and uncovered electrical outlets.

When baby wants to creep, remove the linoleum. He now needs friction to creep. His feet should be kept bare so they have a chance to feel what it is like to be feet.

Above all, remember that this is the year to slow down. You want to encourage and stimulate neurological growth, but there is one thing you should not do. DO NOT MAKE BABY STAND UP AND WALK BEFORE HE IS READY. A playpen at this time will give him no alternative. When he is ready, and he will know, he will stand up all by himself.

SEEING AND HEARING. In this time the child is starting to combine skills. At age one he knows the meaning of many words before he can speak them. Use this advancement to stimulate both language and the eyes. Tell him to "look at Daddy." Help him to focus far and near (good exercise for reading readiness). This helps him to coordinate sound with sight and words with things.

Never say "Shhhhh. We have a baby." Don't stop other children in the family from making noise, and don't ask them to keep the TV down. Babies like to hear noise and activity. If you have a singing bird, put him in the baby's room. Let the baby crawl and creep in the dining room during meals so he can hear the tinkle and clatter and the hubbub of voices that accompanies meals.

When he speaks to you in nonsensical sounds, wait till he is finished and speak back to him just as seriously in either words or sounds. When he does start talking with real words, don't respond with baby talk. Include a little talk over his head so he has something to strive for.

Pikler (1971), in her model for fostering the development of gross motor skills, suggests that the infant should be an active participant in their own everyday affairs from the very beginning. Cooperative efforts are best achieved during activities that required the assistance of the caretaker such as bathing, feeding, and dressing. Ideally there should be intense and prolonged interactions during these activities with special efforts toward imitative behaviors. Imitative behaviors not only encourage autonomy but also prepare the infants for doing things on their own. Some conditions for increasing gross motor development are: (a) Nonrestrictive clothing that permits free activities during the different stages of development. For example, at birth the upper and lower limbs need freedom for bending and stretching. When the baby begins to turn, trousers are more suitable for rolling and tumbling; (b) Suitable space to facilitate movements when the caretaker is not needed and when the baby shows inclinations to play on his own; (c) Appropriate toys that can be successfully manipulated at respective levels of development without assistance of adults; and (d) No attempts should be made to force or encourage infants to do anything that they are not able to perform on their own. For example, if an infant is not capable of sitting up, he is never placed in this position for any reason. The underlying idea seems to be that infants will achieve optimal development on their own initiative, without the direct and systematic teaching of adults, if they are permitted to become active participants in their own development.

Implied in both models, as well as in most of the research reported in this chapter, is that lack of early stimulation stunts development and that enriched experiences enhance it. The evidence that enriched experiences also

Infancy

produce physically larger or functionally superior brains is, however, open to investigation because it is dangerous to extrapolate the results achieved with some animals to humans. The course of least error is probably to share our love and time with our babies while providing them with individually determined amounts of enriched and enjoyable experiences.

The Self. At birth, the totality of everything that defines an infant is the product of interactions: at conception it was the interaction of the genetic compositions of the parents, and during pregnancy, it was the interaction between the unborn and the physical and psychological conditions of the mother in which the father participated in important, but indirect, ways. After birth, the lifelong threeway interaction of the environment, the genetic endowment, and the self begins. From these three determinants emerge all the factors that describe what personality is. Working together, these forces shape infants into distinct but recognizable molds of human nature. However, with the passage of time, the self achieves a sense of its own identity and the infant begins to view each situation in terms of his own motives, feelings, and competencies. Thus, the effects of the environment and heredity become increasingly dependent on how it is viewed and experienced by the individual infant.

As the infant achieves a clearer sense of self-identity, he begins to evaluate himself as superior or inferior within the four overlapping domains of physical, cognitive, affective, and social competencies. Whether or not his feelings are positive or negative depend on his actual experiences or lack of them, his interpretation of them, and the experiences of his caretakers. These early evaluations of self-worth have a continuing and spiraling effect on personality development.

The development of the self depends primarily on the quality of the infant-parent interactions that in turn depend heavily on the harmonious matching of infant characteristics with those of the caretakers. Although all infants differ at birth, from the second month on the differences become more robust and can be displayed in varying degrees in such dimensions as quality of moods; responsiveness; adaptability; intensity of reactions; distractibility; activity level; and body rhythms in sleep, hunger, and elimination. In fact infants differ in their reactions to cuddling. Some babies resist efforts to cuddle them, but the question remains should we cuddle despite their vigorous protests because research strongly suggests that the need to be cuddled is a basic and universal need? Imagine if a mother, full of honey, were to give birth to a baby who was a noncuddler, somber, and with a high threshold for stimulation? Imagine, on the other hand, the impact on the self of an infant who was born a true cuddler, had a high degree of distractibility, and whose bodily rhythms were highly irregular but whose parents, besides being "cold fish," were to be inextricably occupied with other matters?

Researchers point out that these very early infant characteristics are not related to parental behavior and are determined more by heredity and constitutional factors at birth. Fortunately research with selected "nonmatching" couples indicates that most of these mothers were flexible and adapted their modes of care to the particular characteristics of the infant. However, we can readily imagine the negative consequences when all-powerful parents refuse to adjust to the infant's style and who may even interpret resistance as outright rejection.

AINSWORTH, M. D. *Infancy in Uganda: infant care and the growth of attachment.* Baltimore: Johns Hopkins, 1967.

————. Patterns of attachment behavior shown by the infant in interaction with his mother. *Merrill-Palmer Quarterly of Behavior and Development,* 1964, **10**:51–58.

————. The effects of maternal deprivation: A review of findings and controversy in the context of research strategy. In *Deprivation of maternal care: a reassessment of its effects.* Public Health Papers No. 14. Geneva: WHO, 1962.

———— and Bell, S. M. Mother-infant interaction in the feeding situation. In A. Ambrose, *Stimulation in early infancy.* New York: Academic, 1969.

———— and B. A. WITTIG. Attachment and exploratory behaviour of one-year-olds in a strange situation. In B. M. Foss (ed.), *Determinants of infant behaviour,* vol. 4. London: Methuen; New York: Barnes & Noble, 1967.

AITKEN, F. C. and F. E. HYTTEN. Comparison of breast and artificial feeding. *Nutrition Abstract and Review,* 1960, **30**:341–371.

ALDRICH, C. A. and E. S. HEWITT. Self-regulating feeding program for infants. *Journal of American Medical Association,* 1947, **135**:340–342.

————, C. SUNG and C. KNOP. The crying of newly born babies: the community phase. *Journal of Pediatrics,* 1945, **26**:313–326.

ALPERT, A., P. NEUBAUER and A. WEIL. Unusual variations in drive endowment. *Psychoanalytic Study of the Child,* 1956, **11**:123–163.

AMBROSE, J. A. The development of the smiling response in early infancy. In B. M. Foss (ed.), *Determinants of infant behavior,* vol. 1. New York: Wiley, 1961.

————. The smiling and related responses in early human infancy: an experimental and theoretical study of their course and significance. Ph.D. Thesis, U. of London, 1960.

ANOKHIN, P. K. Systemogenesis as a general regulator of brain development. *Progress Brain Research,* 1964, **9**:54–86.

BERGMAN, P. and S. ESCALONA. Unusual sensitivities in very young children. *Psychoanalytic Study of the Child,* 1949, **3–4**:333–352.

BIRNS, B. M. Individual difference in human neonates' response to stimulation. *Child Development,* 1965, **30**(1), 249–256.

BOWLBY, J. *Attachment and loss: volume 1—attachment.* New York, Basic, 1969.

————. The nature of a child's tie to his mother. *International Journal of Psychoanalysis,* 1958, **39**:350–374.

————. *Maternal care and mental health.* Geneva, Switzerland, WHO, 1952.

————. Pathological mourning and childhood mourning. *Journal of the American Psychoanalytical Association,* 1963, **2**:500–541.

————. Separation anxiety. *International Journal of Psychoanalysis,* 1960, **41**:89–113.

————. Separation anxiety: a critical review of the literature. *International Journal of Psychoanalysis,* 1961, **1**:251–269.

BRIDGER, W. H. Psycho-physiological measurement of the roles of state in the human neonate. Paper presented at the meeting of the Society for Research in Child Development, Minneapolis, April, 1965.

————. Sensory habituation and discrimination in the human neonate. *American Journal of Psychiatry,* 1961, **117**:991–996.

BRONSON, G. W. Fear of the unfamiliar in human infants. In H. R. Schaffer (ed.), *The Origins of human social relations,* Academic, 1971.

————. Fear of visual novelty: developmental patterns in males & females. *Developmental Psychology* 1970, **2**:33–40.

Infancy

BROWN, J. L. States in newborn infants. *Merrill-Palmer Quarterly*, 1964, **10**: 313–327.

BRUNER, J. S. *Processes of cognitive growth: infancy*. Worcester, Mass., Clark U. P., 1968.

———, R. R. OLIVER, P. M. GREENFIELD et al. *Studies in cognitive growth: A collaboration at the center for cognitive studies*. New York: Wiley, 1966.

BUYLEY, N. A study of the crying of infants during mental & physical tests. *Journal of Genetic Psychology*, 1932, **40**:306–329.

CARMICHAEL, L. The early growth of language capacity in the individual. In E. H. Lenneberg (ed.), *New directives in the study of language*, Cambridge, Mass: M.I.T., 1964.

———. The onset and early development of behavior. In L. Carmichael (ed.), *Manual of Child Psychology*, 2nd ed. New York: Wiley, 1954.

CHESS, S., A. THOMAS and H. BIRCH. Characteristics of the individual child's behavioral responses to the environment. *American Journal of Orthopsychiatry*, 1959, **29**:791–802.

COMMITTEE ON NUTRITION. Composition of milk. *Pediatrics*, 1960, **26**:1039–1047.

CRATTY, B. J. *Perceptual and motor development in infants and children*. New York: Macmillan, 1970.

CRUIKSHANK, R. M. The development of visual size constancy in early infancy. *Journal of Genetic Psychology*, 1941, **58**:327–351.

DELACATO, C. H. *Neurological organization and reading*. Springfield, Ill.: Thomas, 1966.

DENENBERG, V. H. and G. G. KARAS. Effects of differential infantile handling upon weight gain and mortality in the rat and mouse. *Science*, 1959, **130**: 629–630.

DOMAN, G., and C. DELACATO. Training your baby to be a genius. *McCall's Magazine*, March, 1965, **92**(6):65, 167–172.

EISENBERG, R. B. Auditory behavior in the human neonate: a preliminary report. *Journal of Speech and Hearing Research*, 1964, **7**:245–269.

ERIKSON, E. H. *Childhood and Society*, 2nd rev. ed. New York: Norton, 1963.

———. Identity and the life cycle: selected papers, *Psychological Issues* (Monograph). New York: International Universities, 1959, **1**:1.

ESCALONA, S. K. The study of individual differences and the problem of state. *Journal of Child Psychiatry*, 1962, **1**:11–37.

FANTZ, R. L. Visual experience: decreased attention to familiar patterns relative to new ones. *Science*, 1964, **146**:668–670.

———. Pattern vision in newborn infants. *Science*, 1963, **140**:296, 297.

FAUST, O. A., K. JACKSON, E. G. CERMAK, M. M. BURTT and R. WINKLEY. *Reducing emotional trauma in hospitalized children*. Albany, N. Y.: Albany Research Project, Albany Medical College, 1952.

FORMBY, D. Maternal recognition of infant's cry. *Developmental Medicine and Child Neurology*, 1967, **9**:293–298.

FREEDMAN, D. G. The infant's fear of strangers and the flight response. *Journal of Child Psychological Psychiatry*, 1961, **2**:242–248.

———. Smiling in blind infants and the issue of innate versus acquired. *Journal of Psychological Psychiatry*, 1964, **5**:171–184.

FRIES, M. E. The formation of character as observed in the well-baby clinic. *American Journal of Disturbed Children*, 1935, **49**:28–42.

GERWITZ, J. L. The course of infant smiling in four child-rearing environments in Israel. In B. M. Foss, *Determinants of infant behaviour*, vol. 3, London: Methuen, 1965.

GESELL, A. Infant vision. *Scientific American*, Feb. 1950.

———. *Mental growth and preschool child*. New York: Macmillan, 1925.

———— and F. L. ILG. *Infant and child in the culture of today.* New York: Harper, 1943.

———— and H. THOMPSON. *Infant behavior: its genesis and growth.* New York: McGraw-Hill, 1934.

GOLDFARB, W. Infant rearing as a factor in foster home replacement. *American Journal of Orthopsychiatry,* 1944, **14:**162–173(b).

GOLDMAN, J. R. The effects of handling and shocking in infancy upon adult behavior in the albino rat. *Journal of Genetic Psychology,* 1964, **104:** 301–310.

GOLLIN, E. S. A developmental approach to learning and cognition. In L. P. Lipsitt and C. C. Spiker (eds.), *Advances in child development and behavior,* vol. 2, New York: Academic, 1965.

GORDON, T. and B. M. Foss. The role of stimulation in the delay of onset of crying in the newborn infant. *Quarterly Journal of Exploratory Psychology,* 1966, **18:**79–81.

GULLICKSON, G. R. and D. H. CROWELL. Neonatal habituation to electrotactical stimulation. *Journal of Experimental Child Psychology,* 1964, **1:**388–396.

HALLER, M. The reactions of infants to changes in the intensity and pitch of pure tone. *Journal of Genetic Psychology,* 1932, **40:**162–180.

HEARD, C., A. MEYER, G. PAMPIGLIONE, R. STEWART and B. PLATT. *Proceedings of Nutrition Society,* 1961, **20:**1.

HEBB, D. O. *The organization of behavior.* New York: Wiley, 1949.

HEINICKE, C. and I. WESTHEIMER. *Brief separations.* New York: International U. P., London: Longmans, 1966.

HILL, S. D. The performance of young children on three discrimination-learning tasks. *Child Development,* 1965, **36:**425–435.

HOLT, L. E., JR., E. A. DAVIES, E. G. HASSELMEYER and A. O. ADAMS. A study of premature infants fed cold formulas. *Journal of Pediatrics,* 1962, **61:** 556–561.

HUNT, H. F. and L. S. OTIS. Restricted experience and "timidity" in the rat. *American Psychologist,* 1955, **10:**432.

HUNT, J. M. How children develop intellectually. In H. W. Bernard and W. C. Huckins (eds.), *Readings in human development.* Boston: Allyn, 1967.

————. Intrinsic motivation and its role in psychological development. In *Nebraska Symposium on Motivation,* Lincoln, Nebr.: U. of Nebraska, 1965.

ILLINGSWORTH, R. S. *The development of the infant and young child: normal and abnormal.* Baltimore: Williams & Wilkins, 1971.

JENSEN, K. Differential reactions to taste and temperature stimuli in newborn infants. *Genetic Psychology Monographs,* 1932, **12:**361–479.

JONES, M. C. The development of early behavior patterns in young children. *Journal of Genetic Psychology,* 1926, **33:**537–585.

KAGAN, J. Studies of attention in the human infant. *Merrill-Palmer Quarterly of Behavior and Development,* 1965, **11:**95–122.

LAIRD, D. A. and H. DREXEL. Sex and age alteration in taste preference. *Journal of American Dietetic Association,* 1939, **15:**549–550.

LAWRENCE, M. M. and C. FEIND. Vestibular responses to rotation in the newborn infant. *Pediatrics,* 1953, **12:**300–306.

LENNEBERG, E. H. *Biological foundations of language.* New York: Wiley, 1967.

LEVENTHAL, A. S., and L. P. LIPSITT. Adaptation, pitch discrimination, and sound localization in the neonate. *Child Development,* 1964, **35:**759–767.

LEVINE, S. Infantile handling and resistance to physiological stress. *Science,* 1957, **126:**405.

LEWIS, M. State as in infant-environmental interaction: an analysis of mother-infant interaction as a function of sex. *Merrill-Palmer Quarterly,* 1972, **18:** (2), 95–121.

Infancy

Lewis, M. M. *Language, thought and personality.* New York: Basic, 1963.

Lewis, S. J. The effect of thumb and finger sucking on the primary teeth and dental arches. *Child Development,* 1937, 8:93–98.

Lichtenberg, P. and D. G. Norton. *Cognitive and mental development in the first five years of life.* Rockville, Md.: National Institute of Mental Health, 1971.

Ling, B. C. A genetic study of sustained visual fixation and associated behavior in the human infant from birth to six months. *Journal of Genetic Psychology,* 1942, 61:227–277.

———. Form discrimination as a learning cue in infants. *Comparative Psychology Monographs,* 1941, 17, no. 2, 66.

Lipsitt, L. P. Learning capacities of the human infant. In R. J. Robinson (ed.), *Brain and early behavior.* New York: Academic, 1967.

———. Learning in the first year of life. In L. P. Lipsitt and C. C. Spiker (eds.), *Advances in child development and behavior,* vol. 1, New York: Academic, 1963.

Lowrey, R., W. Pond., R. Barnes, L. Krook, and J. Loosli. *Journal of Nutrition,* 1962, 78:245.

McCall, R. B. and J. Kagan. Attention in infants: effects of complexity, contour, perimeter, and familiarity. *Child Development,* 1967, 38:939–952.

———, ———. Stimulus-schema discrepancy and attention in the infant. *Journal of Experimental Child Psychology,* 1967, 5:381–390.

McCarthy, D. Language development. In L. Carmichael (ed.), *Manual of Child Psychology,* 2nd ed. New York: Wiley, 1954.

McGraw, M. B. *The neuromuscular maturation of the human infant.* New York: Hafner, 1966.

———. Neural maturation as exemplified in achievement of bladder control. *Journal of Pediatrics,* 1940, 16:580–590.

Maas, H. and R. E. Engles. *Children in need of parents.* New York: Columbia U. P., 1959.

Mahler, M. S. *On human symbiosis and the vicissitudes of individuation vol. 1: infantile psychosis.* New York: International U. P., 1968.

Maier, H. W. *Three theories of child development.* New York: Harper, 1969.

Malakhovskaia, D. B. Interaction between the conditioned and unconditioned plantar reflex in young children. *Pavlov Journal High. Nerv. Act.,* 1959, 38–44.

Mead, M. A cultural anthropologist's approach to maternal deprivation. In *Deprivation of maternal care,* public health paper no. 14. Geneva: WHO, 1962, 45–62.

Menyuk, P. *The acquisition and development of language.* Englewood Cliffs, N. J.: Prentice-Hall, 1971.

Morgan, G. A. and H. A. Ricciuti. Infants' responses to strangers during the first year. In B. M. Foss (ed.), *Determinants of infant behavior,* vol. 4, New York: Wiley, 1968.

Moss, H. A. Sex, age and state as determinants of mother-infant interaction. *Merrill-Palmer Quarterly,* 1967, 13:19–36.

Murphy, L. B. et al. *The widening world of childhood.* New York: Basic, 1962.

Mussen, R. H., J. J. Conger, and J. Kagan. *Child development and personality,* 3rd ed. New York: Harper, 1969.

Nakazima, S. A comparative study of the speech development of Japanese and American English in childhood. *Studia Phonologica,* 1962, 2:27–39.

Nelson, W. E. (ed.). *Mitchell Nelson textbook of pediatrics.* Philadelphia: Saunders, 1966.

Newson, J. and E. Newson. *Infant care in an urban community.* London: Allen & Unwin, 1963.

The Life
Cycle

Papoušek, H. Experimental studies of appetitional behavior in human newborns. In H. W. Stevenson, E. H. Hess, and H. L. Rheingold (eds.), *Early behavior: comparative and developmental approaches.* New York: Wiley, 1967.

Peiper, A. *Cerebral function in infancy and childhood.* New York: Consultants Bureau, 1963.

Peterson, F. and L. H. Rainey. The beginnings of mind in the newborn. Bulletin, Lying-in Hospital of N.Y.C., 1910, 7:99–122.

Piaget, J. *The origins of intelligence in children.* New York: Norton, 1952.

Pickler, E. Learning of motor skills on the basis of self-induced movements. In J. Hellmuth (ed.), *Exceptional infant,* vol. 2. New York: Brunner-Mazel, 1971.

Pines, M. Why some 3-year-olds get A's—and some get C's. *New York Times Magazine,* July 6, 1969, 4–13.

Pratt, K. C. The neonate. In L. Carmichael (ed.), *Manual of child psychology.* 2nd ed. New York: Wiley, 1954.

———, A. K. Nelson and K. H. Sun. *The behavior of the newborn infant.* Columbus, Oh.: Ohio State U. P., 1930.

Provence, S. The first year of life: the infant. In L. L. Dittmann (ed.), *Early child care.* New York: Atherton, 1968.

Prugh, D. G. and H. Harlow. Masked deprivation. In *Deprivation of maternal care.* Public Affairs Papers, no. 14. Geneva: WHO, 1962.

Prugh, D. G., E. Staub, H. Sands, R. Kirschbaum and E. Lenihan. A study of the emotional reactions of children and families to hospitalization and illness. *American Journal of Orthopsychiatry,* 1953, 23:70–106.

Reese, H. W. and L. P. Lipsitt. *Experimental child psychology.* New York: Academic, 1970.

Rheingold, H. L. The development of social behavior in the human infant. In S. Cohen, *Child development.* Itasca, Ill.: F. E. Peacock Publishers, 1971.

———. The effect of environmental stimulation upon social and exploratory behaviour in the human infant. In B. M. Foss (ed.), *Determinants of infant behaviour.* London: Methuen, 1961.

Roberts, K. E. and J. A. Schoelkopf. Eating, sleeping and elimination: practices of groups of two-and-one-half-year-old children. *American Journal of Diseases of Children,* 1951, 82:121–152.

Robertson, J. (ed.). *Hospitals and children: a parent's-eye view.* London: Gollancz; New York: International U. P., 1963.

——— and J. Bowlby. Responses of young children to separation from their mothers. *Courr. Cent. Int. Enf.,* 1952, 2:131–142.

Robinson, R. J. Cerebral hemisphere function in the newborn. In R. J. Robinson, (ed.), *Brain and early behavior.* New York: Academic, 1969.

Salapatek, P. and W. Kessen. Visual scanning of triangles by the human newborn. *Journal of Experimental Child Psychology,* 1966, 3:113–122.

Salber, E. J. and M. Fernleib. Breast feeding in Boston. *Pediatrics,* 1966, 37: 299–303.

Salk, L. The importance of the heartbeat rhythm to human nature: theoretical, clinical, and experimental observations. *Proceedings Third World Congress Psychiatry.* Montreal: McGill U. P. 1961, 1:740–746.

Salzen, E. A. Visual stimuli eliciting the smiling response in the human infant. *Journal of Genetic Psychology,* 1963, 102:51–54.

Sanford, F. H. *Psychology.* Belmont, Calif.: Wadsworth, 1961.

Schaffer, H. R. The onset of fear of strangers and the incongruity hypothesis. *Journal of Child Psychology and Psychiatry,* 1966, 7:95–106.

Sears, R. R., E. E. Maccoby and H. Levin. *Patterns of child rearing.* New York: Harper, 1957.

SHAPIRO, H. The development of walking in a child. *Journal of Genetic Psychology*, 1962, **100**:221–226.

SHERMAN, M. and I. C. SHERMAN. Sensori-motor responses in infants. *Journal Comparative Physiology and Psychology*, 1925, **5**:53–68.

——— and ———. *The process of human behavior.* New York: Norton, 1929.

SIMSARIAN, R. L. Self-demand feeding of infants and young children in family settings. *Mental Hygiene*, 1948, **32**:217–225.

SPEARS, W. and R. H. HOHLE. Sensory and perceptual processes in infants. In Y. Brackbill (ed.), *Infancy and early childhood.* New York: Free Press, 1967.

SPITZ, R. A. Hospitalism. In O. Fenichel, et al., *The psychoanalytic study of the child*, vol. 1. New York: International U. P., 1945.

———. Hospitalism. In O. Fenichel, et al. *The psychoanalytic study of the child*, vol. 2. New York: International U. P., 1946.

——— and K. M. WOLF. Anaclitic depression. In O. Fenichel, et al., *The psychoanalytic study of the child*, vol. 2. New York: International Universities P. 1946.

STEWART, A. H., I. H. WEILAND, A. R. LEIDER, C. A. MANGHAM, T. H. HOLMES and H. S. RIPLEY. Excessive infant crying (colic) in relation to parent behavior. *American Journal of Psychiatry*, 1954, **110**:687–694.

TENNES, K. H. and E. E. LAMPL. Stranger and separation anxiety in infancy. *Journal of Nervous and Mental Diseases*, 1964, **139**:247–254.

THOMAS, A., S. CHESS and H. C. BIRCH. The origin of personality. *Scientific American*, August 1970, **223**(2), 102–109.

THOMPSON, G. G. *Child psychology.* Boston: Houghton, 1962.

THRUM, M. A. The development of concepts of magnitude. *Child Development*, 1935, **6**:120–140.

TRASLER, G. *In place of parents.* London: Routledge, 1960.

UZGIRIS, I. C. Ordinality in the development of schemas relating to objects. In Herome Hellmuth (ed.), *Exceptional infant*, vol. 1. New York: Brunner-Mazel, 1967.

WATSON, E. H. and G. H. LOWREY. *Growth and development of children*, Chicago: Year Book Publishers, 1954.

WATSON, J. B. and R. RAYNER. Conditioned emotional reactions. *Journal of Experimental Psychology*, 1920, **3**:1–14.

WENGER, M. A., F. N. JONES and M. H. JONES. *Physiological psychology.* New York: Holt, 1956.

WHETNALL, E. The deaf child. In D. Gairdner (ed.). *Recent advances in paediatrics*, 2nd ed. London: Churchill, 1958.

WHITE, B. L. and R. HELD. Plasticity of sensorimotor development in the human infant. In J. F. Rosenblith, and W. Allinsmith, (eds.), *Causes of behaviour: readings in child development and educational psychology*, 2nd ed. Boston: Allyn, 1966.

WHITE, B. L. and J. C. WATTS. *Experience and environment*, vol. 1. Englewood Cliffs, N. J.: Prentice-Hall, 1973.

WOLFF, P. H. Observations on the early development of smiling. In B. M. Foss (ed.), *Determinants of infant behaviour*, vol. 2. London: Methuen, 1963.

———. Observations on newborn infants. *Psychosomatic Medicine*, 1959, 21, pp. 110–118.

———. The natural history of crying and other vocalizations in early infancy. In B. M. Foss (ed.), *Determinants of Infant Behaviour*, vol. 4. London: Methuen; New York, Barnes & Noble, 1969.

——— and M. A. SIMMONS. Nonnutritive sucking and response thresholds in young infants. *Child Development*, 1967, **38**(3):631–638.

WORLD HEALTH ORGANIZATION. *Deprivation of maternal care: a reassessment of its effects,* Public Affairs Papers, no. 14. Geneva: WHO, 1962.

YARROW, L. J. The development of object relationships during infancy and the effects of a disruption of early mother-child relationships. *American Psychologist,* 1956, **11**:423 (abstract).

———— and M. S. GOODWIN. *Effects of change in mother figure during infancy on personality development.* Progress Report, 1963. Family and Child Services, Washington, D. C.

————. Separation from parents during early childhood. In M. L. Hoffman and L. W. Hoffman (eds.), *Review of child development research,* vol. 1. New York: Russell Sage, 1964.

Early Childhood

JAMES O. LUGO, Ph.D.
Fullerton College, Calif.

STEWART COHEN, Ph.D. *
University of Rhode Island

Prelude
Basic Theory and Research
  Biological Domain
    Physical Growth and Health
    Perceptual-Motor
      Development

Theory of Neurological
  Organization
Cognitive Domain
  Language Development
  Variables in Language
    Development

* Dr. Cohen contributed the sections on the Affective and Social Domains.

Learning and Thinking
Creativity
Affective Domain
  The Development of Affect
  Play: An Avenue of Affective
    Development
  Theories of Play
  The Development of Play
Social Domain
  Socialization
  Theories of Social
    Development
  Theories of Psychosocial

Development
  Cognitive-Developmental
    Theory
  Social-Learning Theory
Implications
  Understanding Yourself and
    Others
  Living and Working with Children During Early Childhood
  Living and Working with Preschool Children
  Developing Positive Models

PRELUDE

THE IMPORTANCE of the infancy stage, that is, birth to the end of the second year, lies in the broad foundation it provides for the subsequent stage of life, early childhood. The scope and strength of this foundation lies in the nature of the biological factors present at birth and the interplay with the infant's particular environment. Toward the end of infancy we find two distinctive features of development: (1) the range of individual differences becomes more apparent and (2) there is a gradual shift in the range of activities from those dominated by biological forces to those influenced by the forces of the cognitive, social, and affective domains. The growing capacity of the nervous system to process incoming information appears to allow external forces to exert far greater influence in molding and shaping behavior. At the same time, the influence of these internal (biological) and external (cognitive, affective, and social) forces are coming under the control of the third emerging force of human life known as the *self*. Once the sense of self grows stronger, the child begins to behave in reference to it rather than to solely biological and external forces. Gradually, as the self becomes increasingly more important as the reference point for guiding and judging, the child begins to behave as an active participant in determining his own behavior.

As we enter the stage of early childhood, from the beginning of the third year to the end of the fifth year, we are able to see more clearly the total integration of the four domains into a holistic pattern. Together these factors determine the state of the individual at any particular period. Although we continue to present information from the four domains as if they were separate factors for ease of presentation and learning, the reader should always be aware of their dynamic and interrelated nature.

The importance of each isolated variable may not seem great at first, but the birth and development of each variable may be compared to a "trickle down a mountain slope" or a "small breeze in a canyon." Later, when it is perhaps too late, the "trickles" and the "breezes" come together to form a raging river or a hurricane.

Early
Childhood

349

BASIC THEORY AND RESEARCH

BIOLOGICAL DOMAIN

The gateway and the foundation for cognitive, social, and affective developments are rooted in the biological domain. Every facet of living appears in some way to be related to the nature and health of the body.

Many times during the life cycle positive or negative developments in the other domains seem to emerge from changing biological characteristics. In the social domain, first impressions, although not the most important, arise from physical factors such as height, weight, body build, and general body movements and vitality. For example, a sturdy, graceful child may develop broader ranges of interests, hobbies, and friends, whereas his weak or awkward counterpart may encounter more difficulties and limitations. Reactions from others to a child's physical appearance and competencies may influence the child's attitudes toward himself and others. Although a physically weak and poorly coordinated child who has a high level of self-esteem is likely to develop tolerance for his shortcomings or seek compensatory strengths in the other domains, the child with a lower level of self-esteem may reject his body and lower his self-esteem even further.

Bodily adequacies also influence the cognitive domain, perhaps more in this stage than later when higher mental processes will dominate the physical aspects. During this stage, physical explorations and manipulations are still major avenues for learning and developing. Learning ability develops as a function of the child's capacity to interact effectively with the environment, and a growing state of self-esteem results from success experiences and increasing competencies.

Although the full psychological impact of cumulative biological influences will not be felt until adolescence, it is during the early childhood stages that corrective action should take place to overcome physical limitations (Gough and Peterson, 1952).

Physical Growth and Health

Growth and Variation. By the time the child reaches the age of two, we can start making fairly accurate predictions about his eventual size at maturity. Prior to that time the genetic timetable for body growth is still making final preparations for its future growth trajectory. The evidence for the existence of this preparatory stage can be seen in the fact that the correlation between length at birth and eventual adult height is only about +.20 (about 4 per cent of adult height can be predicted). By age two the correlation between the relative heights of the individual increased significantly to about +.80 (about 65 per cent of adult height can be predicted).

Various parts of the body grow at different rates. Figure 16–1 shows some of the growth curves for different parts of the body. Many of the major tissues of the body, such as bone, muscle, lung, and kidney, follow the same pattern as the overall body dimensions. As can be seen from curve B the rate of growth is very rapid during infancy, slows down during childhood, and speeds up moderately around pubescence.

Other important organs and tissues have their own unique growth curves. The brain, spinal cord, and head size have a much more rapid growth rate as seen in curve A. The growth of the nervous system is extremely rapid

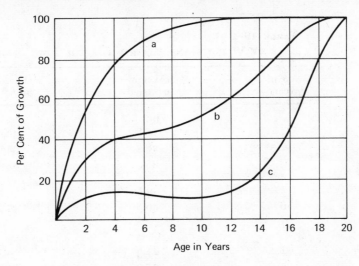

Fig. 16–1.
Differential rates of growth can be seen in (a) neural tissue including the brain, (b) body dimensions including some of the major internal organs, and (c) the development of primary sex characteristics. (Adapted from Harris, 1930.)

during infancy and then slows down dramatically during early childhood. By age nine, the skull and brain sizes have reached about 90 per cent of their full maturity. In terms of weight, the brain has reached about 25 per cent of its adult value at birth, 50 per cent by the middle of the first year, and about 95 per cent by age ten years. In contrast, the development of the reproductive organs and tissues shows a very slight growth in early infancy and then practically none until puberty, when the curve increases very sharply as shown in curve C.

Developmental Rates. Every child grows at his own rate. Although many children will closely approximate these general growth curves for height and weight, there are other growth patterns that must be considered. The speed of growth, however, is only one factor in the child's physical development. The important decision as to whether or not a child is progressing normally or optimally in the outside (physical dimensions) and in the inside (internal organs) is not an easy one to make.

Any measurement, such as growth rate, if it is to have real meaning should be evaluated in comparison with some standard of reference. Such standards are called *norms* and are based on similar measurements in groups of children with backgrounds and living conditions close to those of the child being evaluated.

Such norms of physical growth have been gathered by sampling sections of the United States during different periods of time. Table 16–1 shows norms for ages one to six taken from fifteen hundred boys and girls in Iowa City mostly from the upper economic and educational levels. Table 16–2 shows the norms for heights for ages two to six from a sample of sixty-six white boys and sixty-three white girls from the upper socioeconomic levels of Berkeley, California (Tuddenham and Snyder, 1954). You will notice that there is a difference between the heights and weights in the two samples. When evaluating any particular child, you must consider the characteristics of the sample group and the dates of the study.

Skeletal Age. A most valuable clue for comparing a child's development age with his chronological age can be obtained by measuring the ossification of his hand and wrist bone by X-ray photography. Ossification is the gradual step-by-step process by which cartilage hardens into bone. Again, a child's ossification age and rate should be evaluated in terms of standard measures taken on samples of similar children. This method is useful because it can

Early
Childhood

TABLE 16-1

AVERAGE WEIGHTS AND HEIGHTS FOR THE IOWA SAMPLE

Age in Years	Weight in Pounds	Height in Inches
	Boys	
1	22.8	30.0
2	28.5	34.6
3	33.3	37.8
4	37.7	40.7
5	42.0	43.2
6	46.0	45.7
	Girls	
1	21.3	29.3
2	27.3	34.3
3	32.4	37.5
4	37.0	40.3
5	41.1	42.9
6	45.2	45.3

Based on measurements made by the Iowa Welfare Station (Jackson and Kelly, 1945).

TABLE 16-2

AVERAGE HEIGHTS FOR BOYS AND GIRLS FOR THE CALIFORNIA SAMPLE

Age in Years	Boys' Height in Inches	Girls' Height in Inches
2	34.45	34.03
3	36.72	37.23
4	40.62	40.17
5	43.34	43.00
6	45.81	45.73

Based on measurements made in California (Tuddenham and Snyder, 1954).

be used at any age. Its sequence of development is not affected by illness, except for those of the hand bones themselves and the normal complexities and mysteries of bodily growth. A child may be called slow or fast-maturing if his skeletal age is 75 to 85 per cent below or above those, respectively, for children of his age and sex (Eichorn, 1972).

For most children, their skeletal age is very similar to other measures of their development age such as height, weight, and shape. Teeth, like bones, have their own developmental timetable and can be used as another index of developmental age. Deciduous or baby teeth begin to erupt by about the sixth month and continue until about the third or fourth year (Watson and Lowrey, 1958). Permanent teeth begin their appearance between the ages of six and thirteen. This early childhood period is then one of mixed deciduous and permanent teeth.

Sex Differences. As a group, females are physically smaller than males from birth to maturity except for their earlier adolescent spurt that results in girls being temporarily taller than boys. More important, however, is the fact that girls mature faster than boys. Skeletal ages taken throughout the early and late childhood stages show that girls are about 20 per cent ahead of boys of the same age. This sex difference is noted as early as the twentieth week of the fetal stage. Males lag about two weeks behind females at the start of life and continue with an apparent disadvantage that extends into such maturational competencies as early walking, toilet training, emotional control, and reading.

Family Influences. What the family provides or fails to provide in terms of diet, housing, medical care, and hygiene affects the rate and final stages of the child's physical growth. Children from higher socioeconomic levels tend to be accelerated in their total biological growth. Healthy and well-nourished children are physically larger and reach puberty sooner than children from disadvantaged families. Research, discussed in the chapter on adolescence, provides supportive data for the advantages and disadvantages for those with rapid or slow growth, respectively.

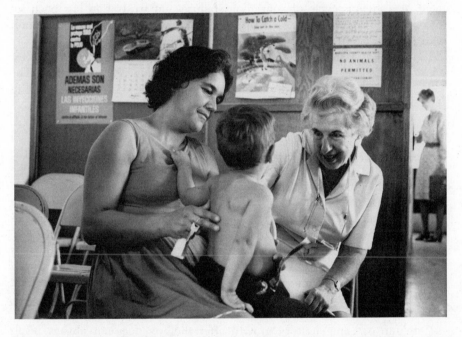

Fig. 16–2. VISTA *nurses frequently see children who have never before been seen by a doctor or nurse. There is a great need for health professionals to help develop rural health programs.*

Illness and Health. Illness in children has been shown to be associated with the phenomenon of catch-up (Prader and Tanner, 1963). In one study it was shown that children who were hospitalized for one or more illnesses during the first three years of life grew at a significantly slower rate than comparable children who were physically healthy. Nevertheless, several years later at the end of this longitudinal study, most of the hospitalized group had caught up with the nonhospitalized group (Falkner, 1966). As can be expected, there were exceptions to the rule of catch-up depending on the age of the child and the severity, length, and nature of the illness.

Although ordinary illnesses have fewer effects on the physical growth patterns of children if they receive proper treatment, certain severe illnesses may produce permanent damage. Furthermore, regardless of whether the

Early Childhood

illness is physical, mental, real, or imaginary, there exists the danger of long-term side effects.

An illness such as rheumatic fever may damage the heart, encephalitis may damage the brain, and rickets and poliomyelitis may cause bone deformities. Subsequent lack of physical activity results in some loss of body tone, flabby muscles, and fatigue. Early sickness may predispose a child to later illnesses by lowering his general resistance. The long-range side effects of illnesses may be physical, psychological, cognitive, and/or social in nature. A child who is prone to illness may develop a negative biological self-concept that could serve as a vulnerable point throughout his life. Since being physically ill is incompatible with psychological health, the sick child is more likely to be anxious and irritable. If those around him react in kind, the child is even more likely to view the world as cold and unaccepting. Even more important is the fact that such negative attitudes are known to linger beyond the period of illness and are bound to affect the child's emotional stability as well as his interpersonal relationships during these critical formative years. A sickly child is less likely to learn healthy patterns of behavior. At this point, the basic ingredients for the possible establishment of a vicious cycle of continuous failure and frustration has been set into motion. It is, therefore, not surprising that such children may encounter additional difficulties later, especially when they enter school.

By contrast, a state of good physical health is probably the single best guarantee that the growth of the child will continue to be normal. The following description provides some general characteristics of good health that may be observed easily by parents (Hurlock, 1964):

> The child's general health condition is shown in his appearance as well as in the quality and quantity of his behavior. In a *healthy* child, the mucous membranes (especially of the lips) are definitely pink; the facial expression is happy, often radiant; smiling is frequent; the eyes are bright and responsive; the skin is smooth and elastic; the limbs are rounded because of a sufficient layer of subcutaneous fat; the muscles are well formed, and their tonus is good; the stance is well balanced, erect, and graceful; the limb muscles are almost straight; the spine is straight; the shoulder girdles do not droop; the arches of the feet are well formed; and the movements of the limbs and body in walking and running are characterized by elasticity, vigor, and poise. (p. 143)

Catch-up or compensatory growth after therapy does not always result in consequences that are equivalent to no illness at all. Some of the children, in the previously mentioned comparison of hospitalized versus nonhospitalized children, did not catch up completely in their later physical growth. In another study performed with rats, the long-range effects of poor nutrition produced irreversible damage to normal growth (Widdowson et al., 1962). The malnourished rats when later supplied with limitless amounts of food caught up to some extent, but not enough to match the growth of the rats who were fed a normal diet.

Today, good physical care, proper nutrition, and improved medical practices have helped children of all ages to establish growth patterns that were never reached by preceding generations. A visit to museums containing armored breastplates of the fifteenth and sixteenth centuries readily confirms the fact that few adults of today could fit into those old costumes. This increase in normal growth rate is not limited to North America. Immigrants from European countries, for example, are usually taller and heavier than their parents and grandparents (Greulich, 1957). However, slow growth in height and weight have been reported for poorly nourished children all over the world (Woodruff, 1966).

How Healthy Are Our Children? As can be seen in Figure 16–3, children get sick frequently, and the younger the child the greater are the chances for his becoming ill. In fact, in 1961, the year these statistics were compiled, almost 170 million acute conditions were reported among children under fifteen years of age, that is, about three illnesses per year for each child. In this study, an acute condition was defined as a physical problem that required the service of a doctor, lasted less than three months, and/or restricted the child's normal activities for one or more days.

The most common causes for acute illness are shown in Figure 16–3.

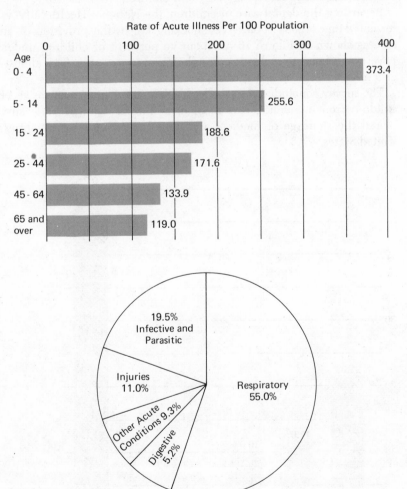

Fig. 16–3. (*Based on U.S. National Health Survey data for year ending June 30, 1961; from Schiffer et al., 1968.*)

Except for injuries, the highest incidence for all of these illnesses falls in the early childhood stage.

Figure 16–4 shows the rate and number of chronic conditions, those lasting

Early Childhood

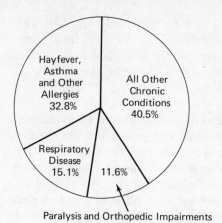

FIG. 16–4.
(From Shiffer
et al., 1968.)

Paralysis and Orthopedic Impairments

more than three months, in the childhood population. The frequency of chronic illness is about one in every four children.

Regarding the dental care of children, the National Health Survey (Schiffer and Hunt, 1968) reported a shocking lag in the provision of adequate care as shown in Figure 16–5. About 50 per cent of children under fifteen have never been to a dentist. For the age group under five, almost 90 per cent have never been to a dentist.

The survey concluded that the least adequate dental care was received by children from nonwhite, low income, and rural families. The survey deplored the shortage of medical and dental personnel and facilities in the United States.

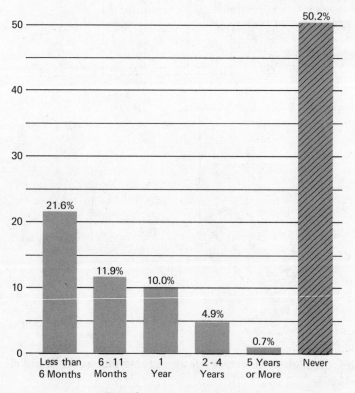

FIG. 16–5.
Half the children
under 15 in the
U.S. have never
been to a dentist.
(Based on U.S.
National Health
Survey data for year
ending June 30,
1958; from Shiffer
et al., 1968.)

Time Interval Since Last Dental Visit

Are We Getting Healthier? There have been dramatic increases in health and life expectancy in this century according to *Toward a Social Report* (1969) prepared for the President by the Department of Health, Education, and Welfare. A five-year-old child today can be expected to live twelve years longer than a child born at the turn of this century. Adults have increased their life spans by well over twenty years, from forty-seven to seventy years. But all is not equally well because the life expectancy for nonwhites is seven years below that of whites, and the disparity between the death rates of white and nonwhite children has actually increased over the years. In other words, white children have been living longer than nonwhite children, but now they can expect to live even longer. This fact alone points to the reality that the full pontential of our existing medical knowledge and resources for better standards of living have not reached all citizens. Furthermore, when different regions of the country were compared, it was found that a difference of five years in life expectancy existed between those states with the best records and those with the worst. Cross-national medical records also suggest that the United States is not making full use of its medical potential in that at least fifteen nations have longer life expectancies even though this country spends considerably more on medical care and is believed to be the leading nation in medical knowledge.

Improving the Health of the Young Child. Two pediatricians, Talbot and Howell (1971), concluded in their study of the causes and consequences of disease among children that:

> Health and happiness as well as disease and disability derive not only from man's bodily constitution and the physical environment in which he lives, but also from his psychological and behavioral interactions with the people who in his family, neighborhood and state comprise his social world. To thrive, human beings must draw upon certain "psychosocial supplies," such as attention, affection, approval and control. Without an appropriate balance of these supplies, the individual may suffer from forms of "psychosocial malnutrition" which can product results as disastrous to his health as is physical malnutrition induced by dietary imbalances. (p. 1)

Thus, although the direct evidence is primarily from the world of sickness, physical well-being can be increased with the aid of psychosocial supports. Children, because of their dependence upon adults, are more likely to benefit from living and growing in a situation where a high level of family wellness is present.

These psychosocial supports can be fostered if those around the child are aware of the individual's unique biological, psychological, and social development in relation to the expected norms of other growing children in that particular society or subgroup. For example, if certain socially accepted tasks, such as riding a tricycle or tying one's shoes, are not mastered at approximately the same time as other children of the same age, not only does the child's self-concept suffer but the child is likely not to accept the challenge of living a fuller and more exciting life. In later sections of this chapter, we examine the sequencing of perceptual-motor, intellectual, emotional, and social development during the preschool years.

Success breeds success, and continuous success breeds the "it's good to be

Early
Childhood

357

alive" feeling. Families that supply their children with adequate psycho-social supports are providing them with the resources for healthier living.

Perceptual-Motor Development

In Chapter 15 we divided sensory and motor developments into separate sections even though there is a gradual interaction between the senses and physical movements beginning early in infancy as illustrated by rudi-mentary visually directed grasping. In this chapter because of increased interaction we hyphenate the two forms of development. Perception is substituted for sensory because the term *perception* is more accurate than *sensory*. The older child has a sufficiently large storage of information to interpret, in varying degrees, most sensory inputs. Perception is, therefore, the process of gathering and interpreting the raw data picked up by our various sense modalities. Perceptual-motor is hyphenated because it is almost impossible to separate physical from perceptual activities in real-life situations. In Chapter 17 intelligence and motor are hyphenated because the higher levels of mental activities are concomitant with the more complex physical activities of later childhood.

In this section we discuss perceptual development, motor development, perceptual-motor development, and the Doman-Delacato theory of neuro-logical organization.

Perceptual Development. Perceptual ability is a developmental process that is far more dependent upon the world of experience and learning than it is on maturation processes. Unless the child undergoes relevant experi-ences, he will not develop the perceptual competencies necessary for intel-lectual growth and language mastery.

Everyday experiences reveal that we are handicapped by lack of experi-ence. It is difficult to distinguish individuals from a particular ethnic group with which we have had little visual experience. The young child may have difficulty recognizing his mother at the beach where everyone's clothing is similar. Animal research has shown the same dependence upon experience for perceptual growth. In one such study, rats from the same litter were reared under similar conditions except that one group had black triangles and circles painted on the walls of its cage (Gibson and Waik, 1956). At two months of age the rats with geometric experience were superior in solving problems involving the accurate perception of such forms than their litter mates who had no such experience. Further research with rats that have attended "nursery school" supports the holistic principle that we have emphasized so often. Autopsies performed on such rats revealed chemical changes in the brain that are associated with increased intelligence (Rosen-zweig et al., 1960). Although we have to be cautious when we apply animal findings to human beings, it appears, from the results of these tests, that the good we do in one domain of life seems to yield benefits in other domains as well.

Intellectual growth permits us to utilize increasingly more powerful learn-ing skills for organizing and interpreting the complex and changing mosaics presented to the senses. For a three-year-old child a brown cow is very different from a black cow, but for a six-year-old a "cow is a cow" regard-less of its color. When asked to group objects, the preschool child is very likely to classify on the basis of observable differences; the beginning

The Life
Cycle

358

schoolchild is more likely to place objects together based on their common use or function; the adolescent, however, can classify together such seemingly diverse objects as an elephant and a rose on the logic that both are living things.

Another important competency for interpreting the social and physical world is the development of language. Language provides the child with some verbal control over learning and perception. Its development beyond single words makes for rapid learning and greater generalization. Such beneficial effects of verbalization in young children have been found in a number of studies (Spiker, 1960; White, 1963).

Of course, perception is also influenced by such subjective factors as motivation, emotions, levels of consciousness, and the meanings the situations have for the individuals. These variables become increasingly more important with age and are discussed in the next chapter.

Visual Perceptual Development. The ability to see accurately and to organize what is seen in meaningful ways is a process that shows steady improvement with age and experience. Some trends from incompetency to competency are the shifts from the general to the specific to the integrated whole, from delayed to rapid responses, from gathering little to gathering much information from the same stimulus, and from the need for many and even redundant cues in order to perceive well to visual conditions that supply only minimal cues.

Form Perception. Form perception is important to understand the complex world of shapes. Furthermore, accurate form perception is the single most important visual skill required for learning how to read. The ability to see in a global manner (a whole word) as well as the details within (the letters) are basic to the reading process.

Whole and Parts. In general, there is a steady increase in preference for completed compact figures over large irregular ones especially from the fourth to the seventh year. Very young children seem to respond to entire forms without paying much attention to details, and it is only during middle childhood that they can respond simultaneously to both the whole and to its related parts (Werner, 1961). We may thus expect the five- or six-year-old to respond to a scene such as a playground in terms of specific objects, whereas the two-year-old may see it initially as a large mass of color, shape, and movement—until something strikes him as desirable. Wholeness responses tend to predominate for the very young child when the stimulus situation is relatively unknown and is vague as in the case of clouds and inkblots, or if the whole is composed of known parts in close proximity to each other (Meili-Dworetski, 1956). Global responses are further facilitated by heavy or clear-cut boundaries. However, after age four, specifics may predominate if known parts, such as candy canes or lightbulbs, are made to stand out within the whole. The ability to integrate wholes, that is, to relate parts to the whole, occurs more frequently about the middle of the sixth year.

Since reading is essentially the process of gathering information from visual symbols, we can see that the importance of encouraging the development of whole-part perception is necessary for learning the basic sight words, which compose about 50 per cent of our language usage and which must be learned by means of the "look-say" approach. Part perception is

Early
Childhood

359

necessary for learning word attack skills by means of the phonic method. Whole-part perception is necessary for achieving excellence in reading as explained in Chapter 17.

Size Constancy. The fact that objects do not really change in size as the distance from which they are viewed changes is known as size constancy.

Although some size constancy for known objects is present by the sixth month, it is not until about the sixth year that it can be considered a practical-everyday-competency. Adult equivalency, however, is not reached until about age ten. The fact that size constancy is developmental can be seen when young children on a bridge reach down to pick up the "toy" boats or automobiles, or when a child is observed stretching and reaching for the stars. With experience, children learn that familiar visual perceptions, such as friends, do not become miniature replicas at a distance even though their images on the retinas of the eyes are smaller. Children also learn that the size of an unfamiliar object can be judged by its relative size to familiar objects around it. Size constancy, even for adults, would tend to disappear if a strange object were placed in a strange surrounding with no familiar objects around it.

That size constancy is a function of increasing age and experience is demonstrated by Beyrl (1967). The subjects in this experiment, children age two to ten and some adults, were tested for size constancy by comparing varying size boxes and discs at varying distances from a standard box and a standard disc. Table 16–3 summarizes some of the findings of this experiment for three-dimensional comparisons for different age levels at varying distances from the standard box with dimensions seven by seven by seven

TABLE 16–3
THREE-DIMENSIONAL SIZE CONSTANCY

Age of Subjects	Comparison Distances in Meters			
	3	5	7	11
2	8.15	8.74	9.21	11.66
3	7.89	8.16	8.43	9.12
4	7.76	8.15	8.48	8.99
5	7.72	8.22	8.52	9.23
6	7.80	8.32	8.58	8.80
10	7.13	7.16	7.15	7.37
Adults	6.98	6.98	7.16	7.09

Size constancy improves as a function of age up to age ten when near adult equivalency is reached when the standard object is a seven-centimeter cube. Compiled from Beyrl, 1967.

centimeters. As can be seen, the accuracy of size judgments for three-dimensional objects increases gradually for all distances measured and for all age groups up to age ten when near-adult estimates are achieved. It is informative to note that young children tend to overestimate the size of objects. Table 16–4 shows similar trends for two-dimensional objects, but not the same degree of size accuracy. This finding is reasonable in view of the fact that the real world of objects is multidimensional whereas two-dimensional objects are further removed from the child's experiences. In view of the popularity of television, it might be informative to repeat Beyrl's experiment to determine if such intensive two-dimensonal experiences have altered the accuracy of size constancy for two-dimensional viewing.

TABLE 16–4
TWO-DIMENSIONAL SIZE CONSTANCY

Age of Subjects	Comparison Distances in Meters			
	3	5	7	11
2	13.48	15.17	15.81	18.02
3	11.91	13.24	14.26	15.93
4	11.26	12.95	13.48	14.96
5	11.12	12.25	12.84	14.93
6	10.91	12.11	12.81	14.11
10	10.31	10.40	10.28	10.34
Adults	9.67	10.17	10.24	10.46

Size constancy improves as a function of age up to age ten when near adult equivalency is reached when the standard object is a disc with a diameter of ten centimeters. Compiled from Beyrl, 1967.

Accuracy of size constancy, apart from its central value in making the world stable and reliable, is also important for learning how to read well. Once a child has been taught to recognize a letter or a word, whether it appears originally on the blackboard, television set, or book, he should recognize the letter or word again regardless of the print size or reading distance.

Object Constancy. Object constancy refers to the fact that objects are still recognizable regardless of their distance from the observer (size constancy), shape in space, color, and amount of light present. When we have become familiar with an object we tend to recognize its characteristics no matter where it is placed. Shape constancy is seen when we look at a circular object such as a plate. The plate always looks round even when it is placed on a table and seen at an angle although the image produced on the retina of the eye is an ellipse. Color constancy is seen when a black cloth looks black regardless of the light in the room.

Variation is the *sine qua non* of living and inanimate objects, but within that variation the most common variant is physical shape, which is almost limitless. The long-range purpose of object constancy is to permit the young child to stabilize the variability mentally so that he brings the logic of later intellectual development to bear on the world in forms of functions, transformations, and abstract thought.

Meyer (1940) tested preschool children up to age four for their ability to comprehend spatial relationships when there was some transformation produced by horizontal rotation. Based on these observations, Meyer proposed three developmental stages of objects: (1) Up to the age of about two the child seems oblivious to the reality of changing spatial relations among objects, because children respond to these changes solely in terms of their needs instead of in terms of the reality of the situation, Piaget called this the stage of "practical space." (2) The "empirical" stage is two to four years of age when the child begins to respond to the reality of

Early
Childhood

objects by adjusting his motions to the spatial relations of objects. As yet, however, he is not capable of decentering from his own needs sufficiently to respond objectively to the outside world. (3) From age four on, the "objective" stage, the child attempts to adjust his behavior to the positions of objects with some success, but the four-year-old is still not capable of coping with the more complex variants of object transformations.

The child's increasing skill in detecting similarities and differences in objects undergoing more complex transformations was illustrated by Gibson and Gibson (1955) with children from age four to eight. The standard for comparison was a letterlike form ‡ that was transformed in four different ways: (1) by separation of parts and closing of parts by adding connecting lines, (2) changing lines into curves, (3) rotations and reversals, and (4) changing angular and linear relations and sizes to produce more unusual variations. Actually many of these transformations occur in the alphabet as in *u* to *o*, *E* to *B*, *m* to *w*, *p* to *b*, and in the great variety of different writing and printing styles. The task of the child was to examine the standard form and then to look at a row that contained the standard along with the transformations of that form. The results are summarized in Table 16–5. It was

TABLE 16–5
DEVELOPMENT OF PERCEPTIONAL CONSTANCY

Age of Subjects	Transformations			
	Open and Close	Line to Curve	Rotations-Reversals	Perspective
4	18	38	47	80
5	10	23	23	78
6	10	23	15	79
7	6	13	5	75
8	5	7	5	58

Accuracy of perceptual constancy increases with age but at different rates for various kinds of transformations in terms of mean percentage errors. Compiled from Gibson and Gibson, (1955).

found that the number of errors of confusion decreased rapidly for all the transformations except for those in which accurate perspective perception is needed, such as when the observer is at a sharp angle to the material, because such transformations are generally not often detected even by eight-year-olds. Perhaps young children should not be seated too far to the left or to the right of the blackboard or to any visual object being studied.

This study was repeated with four- and five-years-olds using real letters with the first three transformations (Gibson, 1963). The correlation between errors on the first and second experiments was about +.60, which is moderately high. It thus appears that most children are ready to discriminate between letters when they first enter school, but some children are not ready and confuse letters such as *p* and *q* and words such as *was* and *saw*.

In one further modification of the original Gibson experiment, the effect of practice on the same transformations by kindergarten children was measured (Pick, 1965). The results of this test revealed a highly significant improvement for the practice group over the control group. We are reminded

FIG. 16–6.
*"Knowledge is
derived from action.
. . . To know an
object is to act
upon it and to
transform it."*
J. PIAGET

here of Piaget's (1970) advice, "Knowledge is derived from action. . . . To know an object is to act upon it and to transform it" (p. 27).

Decreasing Need for Redundancy. There is a developmental trend in the direction of decreasing reliance on an abundance of cues in order to recognize a familiar object. An older child can recognize a familiar object quicker and on the basis of less cues than a younger child. When four- and eleven-year-olds are given schematic drawings of sheep and rabbits with one or more body parts missing for placement into the two separate categories, about 60 per cent of the younger children could not do so whereas only 17 per cent of the older children failed in this classification task (Vurpillot, 1962). Four-year-olds also do poorly compared to seven-year-olds in recognizing partially masked faces of familiar children (Goldstein and Macember, 1966). Again the beneficial effect of practice in reducing the number of cues required for recognition has been demonstrated with children as young as three years of age (Gollin, 1960).

Probably the greatest importance for reducing the amount of information needed for recognition is proceeding from perceptual to conceptual thought; that is, the ability to classify seemingly different objects together based on a few common and essential characteristics. For example, the older child begins to notice common elements in "rain," "snow," and "ice," and soon classifies them all under "water." Similarly, the child learns that "father" and "mother" can also be "parents." Another value in reducing visual redundancy

Early
Childhood

may be illustrated by having the reader who is unfamiliar with Spanish distinguish *haciendo* from *hacienda*. In so doing he will probably regress to the slow, tedious visual scanning of the primary grade word-by-word reader. The smoothness and rapidity of the mature reader requires word and phrase recognition made possible by the ability to use only minimal visual cues for identification purposes.

Left-to-right Orientation. General spatial directional-orientation is a must for learning how to read and write. Prior to age six, however, there is only a slight improvement in this ability. Up to age six the ability to discriminate a standard figure that has been turned either to the left or to the right is difficult (Rudel and Teuber, 1963). This inability is understandable because in the real world it normally makes no difference whether we observe the same object from the left or the right *except for reading and writing, which are left-to-right activities in the English language.* During the early school years reversals resulting from a lack of adequate left-to-right orientation have been and still are considered to be normal. Unfortunately, this is a handicap for beginning readers and is a serious handicap if it continues after the second or third grade. Fortunately, directionality is susceptible to improvement. Practically all texts on how to teach reading include such exercises even for prereaders. In one experiment with kindergarten children, reward combined with appropriate arm movements (proprioceptive feedback) was found to be effective (Wohlwill and Wiener, 1964). We discuss this point later in this chapter.

Perceptual Integration. Gradually the child begins to bring together all his means for learning the world, including perceptual inputs from all his senses in addition to language symbols. This ability to integrate inputs from all sense modalities into "giant" perceptions provides tremendous impetus for the perceptual knowledge foundation for later, more complex learning and thinking.

The developmental nature of perceptual integration has been demonstrated in children between the ages of three and seven (Abravanel, 1968). First the children estimated the length of a bar with their hands and then they demonstrated its visual equivalency with a tape. As can be expected, marked improvement was noted as a function of age and experience. It is not, however, until about age six that children, by touching and handling alone, can distinguish complex forms such as stars and crosses (Piaget and Inhelder, 1956).

Auditory perception also develops as a function of age (maturation) and experience up to about age twelve or thirteen (Kidd and Rivoire, 1967). Similar developmental trends are reported for tactual sensitivity from ages three to fifteen (Fink and Bender, 1963).

A most valuable application of the total multiperceptual impact was the work of Grace Fernald (1943) of the Fernald Clinic, University of California at Los Angeles. She and her followers reported excellent results teaching reading to total nonreaders who could not be taught with the usual reading techniques. Basically, a child or an adult would learn to recognize and to pronounce a word through a tracing technique that combines visual, auditory, tactile, kinesthetic, and speech inputs simultaneously.

The full development of the richness of perceptual capacities and experiences is one of the exciting and rewarding tasks of preschoolhood. It forms the vital bridge between the sensory inputs of infancy and the complex internal thought processes of later life. A child who lags behind in perceptual ability and its resultant accumulation of information will be at a decided disadvantage especially in school learning. Such a child has to compensate for these weaknesses through greater intellectual and motivational efforts in a dual effort to learn what is new and to fill in the missing gaps from the past. On the other hand we have to be cautious about bombarding a child with more stimulation than he can cope with. To do so may be as harmful to his optimal development as deprivation.

Motor Development. Motor development refers to physical movements and skills that are more dependent on maturation than on learning or previously learned physical skills that have become automatic or semiautomatic in execution. Perceptual-motor refers to physical skills that are consciously or subconsciously directed and are, therefore, dependent upon perceptual processes for their exercise. A number of perceptual-motor skills are eventually called motor skills because, once mastered, they require a minimum of intervening perceptual processes. For example, consider the processes involved in riding a bicycle—judgments of distance, object constancy, spatial dimensions of the area, coordination of hands and feet, body balance, and the speed at which the feet are propelling the vehicle. After the mastery of these motor and perceptual skills, riding a bicycle becomes essentially a motor task.

The sequential improvement of motor skills in general body movements and hand manipulation with age are sufficiently similar from one child or group of children to another to support the belief that motor development is basically a maturational process. No significant differences are reported in sex membership or in relation to intelligence test scores except for a small positive correlation with hand dexterity from ages three through eight (Bayley, 1951). However, blacks as a group are reported to be advanced as compared to whites in motor development at birth and in maturation rate (Falkner, 1966; Ferguson et al., 1956).

Motor and perceptual-motor skills are usually classified into two overlapping categories, gross and fine coordination. Gross motor, or perceptual-motor, refers to behaviors that involve large muscles and most of the entire body, whereas fine coordination involves primarily the use of hands or manual dexterity. Table 16–6 describes some motor and perceptual-motor attributes for ages two to six involving both gross and fine motor and perceptual coordination.

Perceptual-Motor. During the first year of life, it is easy to separate perceptual (sensory) processes from motor action. Toward the end of the first year the infant becomes capable of integrating sensorimotor activities into coordinated activities such as visually directed grasping. As these activities became well established, the perceptual component tended to fade away. When confronted with new motor tasks to perform, the growing child must integrate again the emerging and more complex perceptual and motor abilities into higher order perceptual-motor sequences. Typically, it would seem, the perceptual images must precede the attainment of motor performance. A typical sequence for mastery of a new motor task might be as follows: (1) awaiting and encouraging the development of necessary perceptual and physical components; (2) developing specific perceptual know-how and motivation; (3) a "trying it out" session involving perceptual-motor coordination; and (4) a practice schedule until mastery is achieved and the

Early Childhood

365

TABLE 16–6

GROSS AND FINE MOTOR AND PERCEPTUAL-MOTOR ATTRIBUTES IN
EARLY CHILDHOOD

Approximate Time of Appearance in Years	Selected Gross Motor and Perceptual-Motor Behaviors	Selected Fine Motor and Perceptual-Motor Behaviors
2	Walking: even rhythm, up and down stairs, backward and sideward; true running, picks up object without falling.	Puts on shoes, socks; turns doorknob, unscrews lid; with pencil imitates vertical and circular stroke.
3	Can walk line, heel to toe, 10 ft. long; can throw a ball about 10 ft.; rides tricycle; stands on one foot for seconds.	Copies circle; unbuttons front and side buttons; builds tower with 9 cubes; variety of scribbling patterns.
4	Skips on one foot; goes down stairs one foot per step; running with good form and leg-arm coordination; can walk balance beam.	Can button clothes fully; copies cross and later square; crudely drawn human figures and houses.
5	Can catch large ball bounced to him; skips on both feet; can hop about 50 ft. in 11 secs.	Can tie shoelaces; copies triangle; animals drawn and refined houses.

Compiled from Cratty (1970) and Illingworth (1971).

perceptual component can be minimized (judging, hesitations, verbalization, and guidance). In other words, the development of a motor skill depends on the ability to use and to interrelate information from the several sense modalities. In so doing there is a gradual transition from conscious cognitive control to the more unconscious and automatic kinesthetic or motor control.

Intelligence and Self-Concept. There is a good deal of direct and indirect evidence that motor and perceptual skills are not related to intelligence (Abercrombie et al., 1964). Children and adults can spend hours mentally manipulating their environments independently of action. Nevertheless, such respected psychologists as Piaget (Flavell, 1963), Hebb (1948), and Kephart (1960) have emphasized that it is through physical exploration and manipulation that the infant first learns to deal effectively with the environment. Such early motor learning should develop the capacity to interact with the animate and inanimate environment. These people argue, despite the lack of significant correlations of motor ability with present and future intelligence test scores, that to an important extent the higher forms of learning develop out of and have their roots in motor development. Their arguments in regard to this relationship are, of course, theoretical. Piaget sees early thought as interiorized action; Hebb sees early thinking as the result of neurological and chemical changes resulting from sensory-motor experiences; and Kephart proposes that motor learning is the basis for all learning.

The Life Cycle

Regardless of the relationship to IQ, the preschool child is expected to perform a series of developmental motor tasks on time to keep up with other children as well as to meet the expectancies of the family. Success experiences in these important and highly visible skills improve the child's self-concept. Improvement in the child's feelings about himself is a justifiable end in itself. Furthermore, there is some evidence that the ability to control motor movements, such as walking, running, or drawing at different speeds, is positively correlated with intelligence test scores (Maccoby et al., 1965).

Fig. 16–7.
Many elements of perceptual and motor development can be seen here —gross motor skills, hand and eye coordination, a preschool educational situation, and self-concept. But no matter how much we analyze this situation, it is most obvious that the boy is totally engrossed and enjoying himself. He likes what he is doing and he likes himself.

Other Variables Related to Motor Development. Children engage in an enormous variety of physical activities, some in isolation, some in parallel to each other, and some in game situations. We offer partial explanations within the social, affective, and biological domains.

Social. Certain motor activities are common to all children such as sitting, standing, walking, running, throwing, and so forth. These are specieswide and are not very amenable to improvement through practice. Other activities are more common to particular cultures and their requirements for living. These later actions are more susceptible to improvement with practice. It is to be expected that what a culture values will be cultivated there.

If we entered a playground on a backstreet, we would be at first confused by the mass action. Once we adjusted to the situation, we would see many distinct activities, some reminiscent of our childhood play and some new. The familiar activities or variations of them are part of our heritage—hide-and-seek, blindman's bluff, leapfrog, or rope-skipping. The new activities reflect new materials, games, and equipment. In general, however, the equipment needs for the preschool child are simple: plenty of space to run, climb, and jump, and materials that can be manipulated, rearranged, and offer a challenge for resource activity.

Affective. Bodily movements whether emanating spontaneously from the inside or guided from the outside make for fun. Body movements seem to reward themselves whether they are just being learned or have already been gracefully mastered. In the same way that a beautiful song needs no justification for its existence, neither do the physical engrossments of children. The empirical evidence for these views are abundant. They are indelibly written on the faces of children, as they are permitted and encouraged to do their own thing.

Early
Childhood

We believe that such freedom of physical expression prepares children better for the eventual learning of the more enculturated physical skills that are ordained by society for later life.

Theory of Neurological Organization

Every living thing develops as a system in which every part is at once a means and an end in itself, a coordinated part of the whole and a future partner of the next emerging developmental stage. Neurological organization is defined as the optimal condition that the nervous system can achieve at each stage during its development. This condition is very desirable, of course, because the effects of the nervous system extend into practically all the other systems and control their function. We would like to enhance, therefore, the organization of the nervous system through its developmental stages as much as possible.

Although we do not know if neurological organization can be facilitated through manipulation of the environment, there is the theory of Doman and Delacato that claims to do so (1959, 1966). The medical profession as well as others have severely criticized this theory, but mostly in its application to the treatment of brain damaged and mentally retarded children (*Archives of Physiological Medical Rehabilitation*, 1969; Whitsell, 1967). Nevertheless, we are interested in those activities that may help children to develop their fullest capacities.

First Year. The basic recommendations for the development of the first stage of neurological organization were presented in the Implications section of Chapter 15. The Doman-Delacato theory holds that up to the twentieth week of life the nervous system is dominated by the spinal column and lower brain. During the remainder of the first year the midbrain functions begin and the infant's activities should be geared to this layer of the brain. For this reason cross-patterned creeping is emphasized. Cross-patterned creeping is a normal and expected development, but Doman and Delacato stress the activity because they believe that it will help to improve the child's intellectual and perceptual abilities during the next, or cortical, stage. In other words, if an infant does not have sufficient exercise related to this portion of the brain, there may be inadequate development later of the child's higher mental powers. Of course, this is theory and its validity will be revealed only when we have unraveled the intricate complexities of the human brain.

Second to Sixth or Eighth Year. The third and last task is for the child to establish as much one-sidedness as possible; that is, the dominant eye, hand, and foot should all be on the same side of the body. Most children accomplish this task from age one to ages six or eight without difficulty, but Doman and Delacato stress that to do so is of utmost importance if a child is going to become an efficient reader. However, the preponderance of evidence is that there is no relationship between lack of cerebral dominance and poor reading (Spitzer et al., 1959; Flesher, 1962; Stephens et al., 1967). Nevertheless, one of the authors who has had extensive experience teaching remedial reading from elementary school through college, sides with the minority viewpoint to the extent that the lack of cerebral dominance is a contributing factor in reading difficulties for a relatively small percentage of cases (Castker, 1939; Zangwill, 1962). For example, in one study of a college remedial reading class, Lugo (1969) found that about 25 per cent of the students had definite signs of cerebral mixed dominance. Let us suppose that only one child in a thousand suffered from this problem; statistically and scientifically this would be considered highly insignificant, but if the child is yours the significance could not be greater. Let us now consider some of the variables involved in developing laterality or cerebral dominance.

Hand, Foot, and Eye Dominance. The exact time to decide whether a child is right- or left-handed is not clear. According to Ames (1949) it is not until two years of age that the passive hand becomes passive as the dominant hand assumes more activity in the development of unilateral behavior. Hildreth (1949) reports a rapid increase in hand dominance up to ages three and four followed by a gradual increase up to seven or eight years. Hand as well as eye preferences are probably inherited as recessive traits. However, handedness as well as eyedness is also molded by cultural influence (Orton, 1943). The Doman-Delacato recommendation is to let the inherited hand tendency unfold naturally. Once the child has demonstrated a preference for the dominant hand as he scribbles, eats, throws a ball, or picks things up, then the parent should encourage the child's chosen hand. The same procedure applies to footedness, that is, the foot chosen by the child to step up or down or to kick, or by the leg used to power a scooter.

There is, however, a closer relationship between hand and foot preference than between hand and eye preference. Hildreth (1949) reports that from 20 to 40 per cent of the population show a lack of agreement between the dominant hand and the dominant eye. There are, of course, degrees of dominance, but we are concerned with those children who show a clear-cut lack of agreement.* The major guide for dominance is that of handedness so that footedness and eyedness should follow in the same direction. Eyedness can be tested informally by observing the preferred eye while aiming at a target, looking through a telescope, or observing which eye is used to see through a hole cut in the middle of a sheet of paper. Eyedness can be tested by use of a Telebinocular or Orthorater used by school nurses, or by asking an optometrist or opthalmologist. If a significant discrepancy is found between the preferred hand and eye, then the eye on the side of the dominant hand should be trained to become dominant. This training is offered by some reading clinics and by some eye doctors.

Another readily observable sign of neurological organization during the preschool period is cross-pattern walking, that is, a rhythmic alternation of the arms and the legs. As the right leg moves forward the left arm moves in unison with it, and the left leg moves with the right arm. Cross-pattern walking is illustrated in Figure 16–8 along with homolateral walking, which is a general sign of failure to achieve neurological organization.

COGNITIVE DOMAIN

During the past two decades there has been an increasing shift in research emphasis from social and emotional adjustment to language development, learning, thinking, and creativity. The underlying assumptions are that competencies breed success, success breeds greater self-esteem, and greater self-esteem breeds good mental and social health. The prevailing goals seem

---

* The Keystone View Company publishes a test for evaluating lateral dominance called the Leavell Hand Eye Coordinator Test.

FIG. 16–8.
(a) Crosspatterned,
and (b) homo-
lateral walking.

to be individual competence, creativity, and relevance in education. Our nation during its childhood resolved the conflict between individual freedom and societal needs in favor of social institutions in order to weld a heterogeneous population together; today we seek greater individuality and freedom to be from within because we have social foundations from which to spring outward and upward. There is thus a greater opportunity for our young people to become more altruistic, loving, and self-actualizing.

Child rearing practices and education procedures are now embarking on new voyages of discovery propelled by such forces as the belief that we can do a much better job of developing more fully functioning human beings, the realization that we need more creative and educated people for a society that has already switched from brawn to brain power, and the painful realization that a nation cannot continue to grow if any of its citizens are treated with less than brotherly love and remain unable to benefit from full membership in the mainstream.

Recent research has spotlighted what seems to be the most appropriate time interval for starting the new educational voyages—the first six years of life. Psychoanalysis has already pointed its pioneering finger to this stage of development for the establishment of mental health, but now there are new voices in the air. Bloom (1964), after a careful statistical analysis of school achievement and environmental factors, concludes that about 50 per cent of a person's intelligence test scores at age seventeen developed during the

The Life
Cycle

370

first four years of life (of course we do not know which half is more important, if any) and that about a third of the academic skills a person has at age eighteen were achieved before age six, that is even before he started first grade. *Equality of Educational Opportunity* by James S. Coleman (1966), the most comprehensive study ever done of our elementary and secondary educational systems, concludes that the major influence accounting for school success or the lack of it resides not in the schools but in the home environment. For our present system, the home environment offered by middle-class people is the single best predictor of academic success. Coleman writes, "It is well known that socioeconomic factors bear a strong relation to academic achievement. When these factors are statistically controlled, it appears that differences between schools account for only a small fraction of differences in pupil achievement" (pp. 21–22). However, a study by Dave (1963) demonstrated that it is what the parents *do* in the home rather than their socioeconomic status *per se* that is the powerful determinant of school success. From these reports it would seem that the roots for success in the cognitive domain, as measured in our present-day schools, resides principally in the family environment during the first six years of life.

The general pathways to cognitive wellness during the preschool stage seem to lie in the direction of greater language competency, readiness for learning and discovery, the acceptance of creativity as a part of all aspects of living, and the realization that relevance is found only in close interaction with the individual and his immediate culture, which is as important to the child as the air he breathes.

FIG. 16–9.

Language Development

Emerging Language Competencies. The child at age two is just entering the linguistic community. He has an active vocabulary of about three hundred to four hundred words, uses two- or three-word phrases, and demonstrates a definite interest in becoming a full member of the human race through language mastery. Although he will make mistakes, the three-year-

Early Childhood

371

TABLE 16–7
CHECKLIST OF COMMUNICATIVE DEVELOPMENT

Average Age	Question	Average Behavior
2 years	Can he follow simple verbal commands when you are careful not to give him any help, such as looking at the object or pointing in the right direction? *Example:* "Johnny, get your hat and give it to Daddy." "Debby, bring me your ball."	He should be able to follow a few simple commands without visual clues.
	Does he enjoy being read to? Does he point out pictures of familiar objects in a book when asked to? *Example:* "Show me the baby." "Where's the rabbit?"	Most two-year-olds enjoy being "read to" and shown simple pictures in a book or magazine, and will point out pictures when you ask them to.
	Does he use the names of familiar people and things such as *Mommy, milk, ball,* and *hat?* What does he call himself? Is he beginning to show interest in the sound of radio or TV commercials? Is he putting a few words together to make little "sentences"? *Example:* "Go bye-bye car." "Milk all gone."	He should be using a variety of everyday words heard in his home and neighborhood. He refers to himself by name. Many two-year-olds do show such interest, by word or action. These "sentences" are not usually complete or grammatically correct.
2½ years	Does he know a few rhymes or songs? Does he enjoy hearing them?	Many children can say or sing short rhymes or songs and enjoy listening to records or to mother singing.
	What does he do when the ice cream man's bell rings, out of his sight, or when a car door or house door closes at a time when someone in the family usually comes home?	If a child has good hearing, and these are events that bring him pleasure, he usually reacts to the sound by running to look or telling someone what he hears.

old will develop a speaking vocabulary of about one thousand words, an understanding of another one or two thousand words, and a grammatical structure that is roughly equal to that of ordinary adult language (Lenneberg, 1967). Now the child continues to improve his language ability rapidly. Instead of the short two-word sentences of the two-year-old, such as "that car" and "see baby," the young three-year-old may say "that big car" and "see baby eat." At the end of this year, he may say "I like baby" and "don't ever leave your truck."

By age four the child's language is well established and bears a strong resemblance to that which is spoken in the immediate environment. Active vocabulary at this age will increase to about two thousand words, but the greatest improvement comes in grammatical structure and voice control that matches the meaning of what is being said, and pronunciation. The child

The Life
Cycle

Average Age	Question	Average Behavior
3 years	Can he show that he understands the meaning of some words besides the names of things? *Example:* "Make the car go." "Give me your ball." "Put the block in your pocket." "Find the big doll."	He should be able to understand and use some simple verbs, pronouns, prepositions and adjectives, such as *go, me, in,* and *big.*
	Can he find you when you call him from another room?	He should be able to locate the source of a sound.
	Does he sometimes use complete sentences?	He should be using complete sentences some of the time.
4 years	Can he tell about events that have happened recently?	He should be able to give a connected account of some recent experiences.
	Can he carry out two directions, one after the other? *Example:* "Bobby, find Susie and tell her dinner's ready."	He should be able to carry out a sequence of two simple directions.
5 years	Do neighbors and others outside the family understand most of what he says?	His speech should be intelligible, although some sounds may still be mispronounced.
	Can he carry on a conversation with other children or familiar grown-ups?	Most children of this age can carry on a conversation if the vocabulary is within their experience.
	Does he begin a sentence with "I" instead of "me"; "he" instead of "him"?	He should use some pronouns correctly.
	Is his grammar almost as good as his parents'?	Most of the time, it should match the patterns of grammar used by the adults of his family and neighborhood.

From *Learning to Talk,* 1969.

may say "Daddy's coming home soon," indicating an ability to put words together as well as the meaning of past and future tense. Expressions such as "the tree is outside" indicates the ability to blend sounds together, which is important for learning how to read. Also by this time, the child begins to sound like a native speaker. A child from the South begins to sound different from a child in New England.

The five-year-old has a spoken vocabulary of about two thousand five hundred words and should be entirely understandable to adult members of his community except for a few slips in word pronunciation. Since words are the most important vehicles of learning about the world, it is to be expected that as the child broadens and deepens his contact with the world, the size of his vocabulary will increase in proportion. The average firstgrader knows about 2000 to 2400 words, whereas the high school freshman knows about 8000 words (Bryan, 1953; McCarthy, 1954).

Communication Disorders. The statistics for children with communication disorders are appalling according to the Subcommittee on Human Communication and its Disorders, National Advisory Neurological Diseases and Stroke Council (Learning to Talk, 1969). Their studies reveal that 500 out of 10,000 (5 per cent of children) have some type of speech disorder, twelve out of 10,000 are totally deaf, and perhaps as many as 300 out of 10,000 have severe hearing impairments. Altogether about 10 per cent of the nation's children suffer from some form of communicative disorder.* Although there are wide individual differences in language abilities, the check list of expected communicative behaviors at various age levels in Table 16–7 may provide parents with guidelines for future professional evaluation.

Variables in Language Development

Biological Domain. Maturation probably plays the dominant role in language development up to the age of two because of its close correspondence to motor development and its similar development among such children of this age regardless of language and the presence of a minimum of language experience. After age three learning seems to play an increasingly more important role, particularly as a result of its rapid progression, but the biological domain continues to play a role because of the continued strong relationship between language competency and intelligence test scores (Catalano and McCarthy, 1954). We are assuming that the foundation for intellectual growth is inherited and is, therefore, a component of the biological domain.

Further support for the significance of heredity comes from the well-known inability of present-day learning theorists to account for the complexity of language acquisition during early childhood (McNeil, 1970). Children's language at the various stages is systematic, rule-governed, and rarely directly imitative of adult language. It seems that children simply absorb the meaning and structure of their language in much the same way that the body assimilates nutrients. The chief proponent of biologically rooted language development is Chomsky (1958). Until further research we must accept a developmental interaction viewpoint; global language facilitation at first depends on biologically adequate "receivers" to pick up and to structure language, and gradually the "receivers" change their structures to pick up additional linguistic and psychological influences.

Sociological Domain. At every level, children from the upper socioeconomic groups are superior to those of the lower groups as measured by the onset of speech, size of vocabulary, grammatical correctness, and accurate enunciation and pronunciation (Entwisle, 1970). Because of the language model provided by their parents, the language competency of the advantaged children approximates standard English, the language of the better educated adults as well as the schools. Lower socioeconomic membership typically results in substandard or folk language competency, which is a distinct disadvantage for school learning. Unfortunately, most middle-class teachers view folk language as disorganized, vague, and undesirable. For example, note some of the differences between standard English and black substandard language:

* For further information about neurological and sensory disease problems, write for a guide of any of their fifty publications for parents to: Information Office, NINDS, National Institutes of Health, Bethesda, Maryland 20014.

Standard English	Black Substandard English
She is coming.	She . . . comin'.
Jane's brother.	Jane . . . brother.
I have ten pencils.	I got ten pencil.
I will go to school.	I'ma go school.

Linguists, persons who study languages scientifically, assume that no language is structurally better than any other language if the language meets the needs of the particular linguistic community. The black ghetto child's language may seem linguistically impoverished when compared to standard English, but in his environment he gets along remarkably well. Linguistic differences and not deficiency must, therefore, be considered in educating children who do not speak standard English. Supporting this viewpoint is a study comparing competency on word association tests. Black slum firstgraders in this study were found to be superior to the white middle-class suburban children (Entwisle, 1970). It appears that economically disadvantaged black children had greater word facility in their folk language than advantaged white children had with standard English usuage. Unfortunately, as could be predicted, the disadvantage of the middle-class children vanishes by the third grade. Practically all schools measure success in terms of standard English only.

Affective Domain. Linguists often refer to the language learned at home as the mother tongue. A mother tongue is a term of endearment. It is an inseparable part of a child's existence. To ignore the contents and style of a child's language is to ignore the child himself. If these things happen, then for the child, the world and school have become indeed irrelevant.

Cognitive Domain. Learning techniques are powerful tools for increasing language competencies. The most adequate descriptions of such techniques as conditioning and modeling are to be found in the works of Staats (1964) and Skinner (1957). *Classical conditioning* was originally demonstrated by Pavlov, who demonstrated that events that occur repeatedly tend to be connected in such a way that in the future the happening of one event will increase the chances of a certain behavior to occur more frequently. Parents and caretakers should take advantage of this technique. For example, when a thirsty child is given a glass of water, the water should be associated with words such as "water" or "We drink water when we are thirsty," depending on the child's level of language mastery. Once the child has paired the object with its name or description, he tends to repeat these when he is thirsty or upon the sight of water when desired. *Operant conditioning* is demonstrated when, from many sounds and words used by the child, the adult selects the desirable one for immediate reinforcement. A reinforcer is anything that when presented immediately *after* a desired response causes the same response to occur more frequently in the future. For example, if a child says "window" or an approximation of it for the first time, reinforcement should follow, such as a hug, a pat on the head, or praise with a repetition of the word while again demonstrating the object to the child, if possible. Another technique is *modeling,* which is a combination of operant conditioning and social imitation (Bandura, 1963). It has been demonstrated that young children can learn complex language skills by simply observing others, especially if the children are reinforced for correct responses. In one variation of modeling, two-and-one-half-year-old children were asked to look at pictures and to say anything they wished. Adults systematically expanded what the children said at a slightly higher linguistic level for thirty minutes a day, five days a week for three months. The language improvement of the children in the experimental group over those in the control group was evident (Cazden, 1965).

Further evidence for the beneficial effect of learning on language development is that children today possess larger vocabularies and employ more complex sentence structures than those of a generation ago (Templin, 1957). We assume that this improvement is the result of a more linguistically stimulating environment produced by television, more time spent by adults with children, and the increase in preschool education.

Thinking. We should not assume, because children use the same language that we do, that their thinking capabilities are the same as ours. To do so would be to revert back to the historically false concepts of preformationism and the miniature adult. For example, when children aged three to seven are asked "Why do clouds not fall?" a typical reply would be "The sky holds them up," and to the question "What makes clouds move along?" children may answer "They can move themselves because they are alive."

In the next section on intellectual development, the thought processes of preschool children, which are inseparable from their language usuage, will become clear to the reader.

FIG. 16–10.
*"Children operate
on the world in
order to understand
it so that they
may live in it."*
J. PIAGET

376

Learning and Thinking

Our presentation of learning and thinking begins with a continuation of Jean Piaget's theory of cognitive development. For ages two to seven the stage is entitled *preoperational*. At this point the student may wish to review the preceding sensorimotor stage and the key Piagetian concepts explained in Chapter 15. We have given Piaget priority because we believe that his theory is not only the most comprehensive but also because it has created a powerful "new look" at intelligence. The "new look" denies the old view that intelligence was fixed at birth and unfolded automatically. Rather Piaget provides us with the exciting recognition of the crucial role of experience in molding and creating intelligence from its original biological roots. The various lines of evidence seem to be coalescing and flowing favorably in the direction of Piaget. Partial support comes from such sources as Hunt's (1961) classic text, *Intelligence and Experience,* Bruner's (1960; 1966) challenge to educators included in *The Process of Education* and *Toward a Theory of Instruction,* and in many publications by Bronfenbrenner (1963). An objective evaluation of Piaget's theory is included in Reese and Lipsett's (1970) respected *Experimental Child Psychology* as follows:

> To a considerable extent the results Piaget has reported have been confirmed by other investigators all over the world. However, his interpretations of these findings, attributing the age changes in conversation, class concepts, and relation logic to the unfolding of mental operations, have been challenged by other workers. At present, there is no really clear-cut evidence that Piaget was wrong nor that he was right. His theories and research have, however, been tremendously fruitful and have produced a renaissance of the study of cognition. (p. 507)

The Preoperational Stage. For Piaget intelligence at any particular age is the totality of schemas available for use and for developing new schemas. In this sense, intelligence is a product (totality) and a process (a way of being more intelligent). Intelligence, in turn, depends upon learning of new and more complex schemas, but the learning of new schemas depends on the thinking processes of the child or person. It is precisely in his description of the different thinking processes that characterize the various stages of cognitive development that the genius of Piaget is reflected. If we know how little children think, then we understand better how they see themselves and the world, or in Piagetian terms "how little children operate on the world in order to understand it so that they may live in it." During the sensorimotor stage, learning, and therefore intelligence, depends on the infant's "thought process" that consisted of concrete action-oriented manipulations that matched somewhat his tiny reservoir of existing schemas. During the preoperational stage, the thought processes become more powerful as a result of the ability to mentally represent and to manipulate the external world in the form of images and linguistic symbols. Furthermore, the young child now has a larger reservoir of schemas to operate from and to build upon. The preoperational stage that lasts from about age two to six or seven is usually divided into two parts, the preconceptual stage (from two to four) and the intuitive (from four to seven).

The Preconceptual Stage. The child can now begin to "know" things with-

Early
Childhood

out a preponderance of dependency on direct action with the object. "Knowing," which is low level compared to that of adults, is limited to perceptual characteristics (size, color, texture) and motor characteristics (manipulable, turnable, throwable). The child is still tied down to the world of concrete objects and actions. He does not know how things operate internally or how things relate one to another (conceptual). Therefore, Piaget calls the child's thinking at this stage preoperational.

The two major characteristics and limitations of thinking at this stage are its egocentrism and its preconceptual nature. The major facilitating characteristic is the child's increasing ability to represent reality in symbols and to engage, therefore, in symbolic interaction with the environment and imaginative play. This ability to deal with more than what is present is the hallmark of representational intelligence.

Egocentric Thought. Egocentrism, the belief that everyone perceives and interprets the world in exactly the same way that one does, characterizes children's thinking up to about the eighth year.* The assumption that he has the "whole world in his hands" permeates the child's thinking: the moon follows only him around, and it is raining only where he is. This inability,

Fig. 16–11.
The preoperational child behaves as if he has the whole world in his hands.

not refusal, to see things from another person's view inhibits the development of such desirable behaviors as "fair play," "moral judgment," and "sharing." For the young child, egocentrism is not a matter of choice or lack of experience or training, it is simply the way a young child thinks. It is as much a part of his childhood as being physically small.

* Egocentrism can extend into later childhood and for some into adulthood. When members of a social group engage in egocentrism, we call it ethnocentrism because we assume that with enlightenment they will change. (When Piaget states an age level, he usually means that about three-fourths of those children will exhibit the behavior).

The Life
Cycle

Egocentrism is both a source of joy and consternation. We believe that young children are intrinsically lovable because they are so true to themselves. *In life they cannot pretend to be what they are not, because the only reality they know is their own.* Such naïvete is a thing of beauty and trust. We know that what we see is real. Little children cannot, as yet, wear "masks." On the other hand, their inability to see the consequences of their actions on others can be frustrating. Logic and reasoning do not work with the three-year-old who wants to play at the crack of dawn or who, while testing the sound effects of a club on objects, smacks another child on the head (1928). The other child's screams elicit more amazement than "sorrow."

FIG. 16–12.
The world revolves around the pre-operational child.

Egocentrism does, however, interfere with cognitive development since the child persists in the belief that his view of the world is the only one. There is a story about Piaget's amazement when he took his young son for an automobile ride and found that the boy could not recognize familiar mountains from a different location. A doll placed between children seated at opposite sides of a table would elicit a description that was appropriate to the side of the doll facing each child. Each child, when asked what the other child is seeing, would insist that the other child is seeing the same side that is facing him. Games, in which children imitate the physical actions of another person, elicit similar but reverse-sided actions. When the model

Early Childhood

379

faces left, the children face right; and when a right hand goes up, many left hands reach for the sky. Egocentric thinking will continue into the intuitive stage, during which the child will gradually "decenter" from himself as he becomes more involved with people and objects just the way he did during the first year of life when he gave up a facet of egocentrism as he realized the permanence of objects—out of sight was not out of mind any longer.

Preconceptual Thought. The use of concepts facilitates learning. Concepts result from the accumulation, combination, and elaboration of past perceptions with present perceptions so that certain definite or, at times, subtle aspects or qualities stand out so that the many perceptions can be grouped into one concept or "big idea." Concepts formation also requires symbolic thought because the child must remember situations or objects from the past as well as those in the present. For example, the child may recognize a triangle, a square, and a trapezoid, but to put them all together under the concept "geometric forms" is beyond the capacity of preconceptual thought.

The inability of the child at this age to handle multiple characteristics is one reason that Piaget called him preoperational. In order to form concepts, the child must be able to classify stimuli into logical or rational groups based on similarities and/or differences. The three-year-old, for example, has some classificatory abilities, but because he is so closely tied to the perceptual aspects he is unlikely to find a combinatory feature for several objects in order to place all under one label. For instance, if asked to classify seven wooden blocks, four of which are colored blue and three are colored red, he can do so based on their colors. If asked, however, are there more blue blocks or wooden blocks, he will probably answer that there are more blue blocks.

At this stage the child is not able to reason logically either by induction (from specific to general) or deductively (from general to specific). Instead, the child reasons by *transduction*, from specific to specific. In the example given, children of this age are so overwhelmed by the obviousness of the blue color of some of the blocks that they fail to attend to the more subtle wood composition of all of the blocks. As a further illustration, if a child is given a box containing a variety of differently colored geometric

Fig. 16–13.

380

forms and asked to pick out the similar ones, the child will, in all likelihood, classify either according to color or form. It is rare for a child this age to abstract an overall common property such as woodenness, weight, area, or volume.

Imaginative Play. For Piaget (1962), play is important for early cognitive development. Through play the child learns about and how to live in the world. Play experiences should be encouraged and respected, because play is, in many respects, the child's main job. One form of play, direct imitation, was observable as early as the sensorimotor stage. Through later "tertiary circular reactions," the toddler becomes capable of representational imitation (mental). He becomes capable of applying "familiar means to new circumstances," that is, the use of old schemas in a new situation. The following is one of the many examples provided by Piaget (1963) when his daughter was eighteen months old:

> for the first time Lucienne plays with a doll carriage whose handle comes to the height of her face. She rolls it over the carpet by pushing it. When she comes against a wall, she pulls, walking backward. But as this position is not convenient for her, she pauses and without hesitation, goes to the other side to push the carriage again. She therefore found the procedure in one attempt, apparently through analogy to other situations but without training, apprenticeship, or chance. (p. 338)

With an increasing development of mental images (nonverbal) and language, the three-year-old learns to make one thing represent another symbolically. When a child can play "sleeping," we know that he is no longer tied to concrete external action, because he can mentally represent his knowledge of sleeping in playful (symbolic) sleeping. At this point, the child can play games with his symbols: drink from a box, eat sand, drive a truck, and so forth.

The Intuitive Stage. The child between the ages of four and seven seems to cope adequately with the physical world, but actually he understands less than what his actions may indicate. The child intuitively acts as if he understood the complexities of the reality and logic that undergird his actions. In reality, his thinking processes are still preoperational, because his thoughts are still basically governed by the perceptual appearance of things, egocentrism, and illogical reasoning. Such ways of thinking are dramatically different from those used by adults. As a result of the child's increased ability to verbally describe his actions and reasons for them, the nature of early childhood thinking becomes more open for inspection and analysis. Some of the important characteristics are lack of conservation, decentration, irreversibility of thought, animism, realism, and phenomenalism.

Lack of Conservation. Everything, living and inanimate, is in a constant state of flux. As seasons change, people and objects change as well as the perceiver. For Piaget, stability is never given in the external world which so heavily influences the thoughts of our preschool child, but must be constructed gradually by the living organism. Conservation, the ability to compensate for external changes, implies an internal system of regulation (Furth, 1970).

Lack of conservation can be readily demonstrated with four- or five-year-olds. When two equal size glass jars are filled with water, children of this

Early
Childhood

age correctly state that the amount of water is the same in both jars. However, when the perceptual properties are changed by pouring the water from one jar into a differently shaped jar in front of the children, they will now change their minds and select the taller of the two jars. Children of this age believe that if things look different then they must be different. The same, seemingly incredible phenomenon can be demonstrated again with two lumps of equal size clay. At first, the children agree that both lumps are equal, but if one lump is separated into three or four smaller pieces as they watch, they will tend to insist that the separated pieces contain more clay. They will continue to do so even if the pieces are put back together and separated again. Why is this? Why can't the average five-year-old see what is so obvious to us? The two major reasons are lack of decentration and reversibility. Lack of *decentration*, which is a function of the presence of egocentrism, is essential for the achievement of conservation. Lack of decentration forces the child to concentrate on only one salient feature of an object at a time. At this age, that feature is length or height; a string of beads has "more beads" as a result of the simple process of increasing the distance between the beads. Thus, in the case of the water jars, the child centers only on the height of the water, whereas for clay and beads he centers only on the length. By age eight, the child realizes that with every change in height there is a corresponding change in width. He thus decenters and can concentrate on two dimensions simultaneously. The ability to handle three dimensions at a time will not develop until the child reaches the stage of formal operations.

At this time the reader can appreciate the importance of decentering for concept formation. How can the preoperational child develop adequate concepts when he cannot even classify what he sees accurately as a result of his one-dimensional system of analyzing? All people, all objects, all events are multidimensional.

To illustrate *irreversibility* in a young child ask one who has a brother "Do you have a brother?" He is likely to answer "Yes," but if asked "Does your brother have a brother?" he most likely will answer "Nope." To answer the second question correctly the child had to be able to reverse his thoughts, which he normally cannot do at this stage. Going back to the water jar and clay demonstrations, the acts of pouring the water back into the original jar and pressing the pieces of clay together again do not help the child because he is incapable of reversing his thoughts in order to arrive at the correct solution.

Reversibility is important for school learning, particularly for developing number concepts and manipulations. Basic arithmetic requires thinking forward for addition and multiplication, but for subtraction and division the ability to think backward is required. A relatively simple problem such as "If A is bigger than B and B is bigger than C, which is bigger, A or C?" would be too difficult for most children at the intuitive stage.

Animism, the belief that the world of objects is alive and empowered with purpose, is another function of egocentrism. Household objects, animals, mountains, and streams are endowed with human qualities. There are four stages in the decline of animism (Pulaski, 1971). During the intuitive stage there is a shift from attributing animism to all objects (ages four and five) to just moving objects. Later, the state of spontaneous movement must be present, that is, there is no visible propelling force. The fourth stage, in

Figs. 16–14. Various aspects of the intuitive stage are seen here. In (a) the boy may not realize that the same amount of sand in different containers can still be equal because he lacks a sense of conservation. (b) illustrates animism; the boy's beliefs about the moving bug can be applied to inanimate objects. (c) shows realism; that is, for the child the experience of cat and the word "cat" are the same. These characteristics, along with a lack of decentration, irreversibility, and phenomenalism, help us understand the way children operate on their world.

383

which only plants and animals are considered to be alive, does not develop until about ages eleven or twelve.

More important than knowing the existence of animism in children is the knowledge that the process may serve two valuable functions. First, since children are likely to project their feelings and attitudes onto personalized external objects, their expressions, whether verbal or nonverbal, may provide a rich source of information about children's psychological states. Second, the projection of internal feelings to external objects may assist children in their development from egocentrism to other-centeredness that is so essential for cognitive as well as for social competencies. For example, in calling a toy dog "naughty" the child is learning to objectify his own behavior (decentering from himself) and to see his own behavior from the viewpoint of others.

Realism, the belief that all things are equally real including objects, pictures, dreams, or words, is another expression of egocentrism (Piaget, 1969). For the preoperational child, words do not represent people, objects, or actions; names are as real as the things mentioned. Notice the total involvement of young children listening to an adventure story, or notice the face of a preschooler completely immersed in a television program. At this age, children are not able or have difficulty separating mental thoughts from the physical world.

Realism is one reason why adults should be careful about what they tell young children. A broken promise for a sensitive child may be equivalent to a "broken heart." Prejudicial remarks about ethnic or religious groups may leave emotional scars that cannot be removed by years of education. A casual remark to a mischievous child about "bogie man coming" may lead to sleepless nights or nightmares as the child awaits the reality for which the words stand. As with other Piagetian concepts, the influence is gradually reduced with age and experience. At first there is *absolute realism* in which the mind and the thing are one. For example, a cat is called a cat because it is a cat. In the next stage called *immediate realism*, there is a realization that names are arbitrary but are nevertheless real, as water is called water but could also be called wet. During *relative realism*, older children realize that names originate within us, are arbitrary, and bear no inherent relationship to what is named. In one study, only about half the children in a fifth grade class gave responses indicating that they had achieved relative realism (Jersild, 1968).

Phenomenalism, the belief that there is a causal relationship between two things or events because they occur close together, is still another expression of egocentrism. Examples of phenomenalism are: a child running into a chair and then striking the chair back; a child performing some actions or making a wish and then believing that his behavior will influence the event he either desired or feared; and a child, seeing a boat sinking while some birds are flying above, believing the birds to be responsible. An anecdotal illustration from Piaget (1969) follows:

A boy who lived in a somewhat lonely house was always very frightened on the evenings when his parents were out. Before going to bed he used to draw the curtains by unwinding a sort of roller. He had always the idea that if he could succeed in drawing the curtains very quickly the robbers would not come. But if the curtain took some time to unroll then the house was in danger. (p. 139)

Cognitive Development, Intelligence, and Learning. To learn something, according to Piaget, is to be able to perform operations on it mentally by manipulating its multiple characteristics, that is, knowing the thing from the outside (motor and perceptual) as well as from the inside (function, concept formation). The nature or quality of this learning depends, in turn, on the thinking ability of the child (process of adaptation including assimilation and accommodation). As we have just seen, the thinking of the preoperational child, even with the bright child as measured by intelligence test scores, is still characterized by the limitations of egocentrism, lack of conservation, and so forth. As the child proceeds through the four stages of cognitive development—sensorimotor (birth to two years), preoperational (two to seven years), concrete (seven to eleven years), and formal (eleven on up)—his ability to perform mental operation continues to develop until he can perform *mental operations on mental operations* and think in hypothetico-deductive terms (the highest level of human thought). These four stages and all they entail are cognitive development, learning is the process of acquiring knowledge, and intelligence is the totality of the information.

The reader must realize that cognitive development does not simply unfold by itself. Cognitive development depends principally on experience, learning, and education. Cross-national studies reveal that children who receive no or little formal education do not advance or are delayed as measured by tests on Piaget's cognitive stages (Bruner et al., 1966). Disadvantaged schoolchildren from Boston and San Francisco, for example, are not cognitive "brothers" with the economically advantaged in their own country, but, rather, with the unschooled "bush country" African child and the aborigine child in Australia. For example, children in the villages of Iran are about two years behind in cognitive development as compared to their counterparts in Geneva and Montreal.

Piaget and Learning Theories. Learning processes and theories are important parts of Piaget's total cognitive development theory. As we have shown in the previous chapters, the application of learning techniques is an extremely powerful tool for developing the child's repertoires of information, skills, and language. The major objection of the experimentally oriented learning psychologist to Piaget's work is Piaget's use of personally oriented clinical interviews and observations of his own children as the raw data for his theory. This objection is being overcome as a result of worldwide and carefully designed, statistically analyzed research with large groups of children employing Piagetian developmental tasks.

Stevenson, in his comparison of Piaget and learning theory, found some major points of similarities and differences (1962). The major similarities are (1) both see learning as being progressively modified by experience and recognize the importance of reinforcement or rewards (for Piaget reinforcement is an important source of motivation but for learning theory it is a cornerstone); and (2) although both use different terminologies, they are often referring to the same processes; for example, schemas are stimulus-response units, and circular reaction repetitions can be accounted for in terms of secondary reinforcers. The major differences between Piaget and

Early
Childhood

385

learning theory are: (1) Piaget sees the child as an active participant in his own learning, whereas learning theorists tend to view the child as reactive and passive; and (2) Piaget's theory is more dynamic in that learning involves action and changing relationships, whereas learning theory, because of its reaction orientation, is more mechanical. For further comparisons of the two views including psychoanalysis, the reader should study Langer's (1969) *Theories of Development*.

As can be expected, there is a positive but low correlation between scores on Piagetian tasks and learning theory tasks (using classical and operant conditioning), and intelligence-test scores.* Intelligence tests measure essentially what has been learned and not the tools for learning. The relationship between what has been learned and the nature of mental functions is revealed by the contents of the intelligence test that usually go from sensorimotor functions to the concrete to the abstract as predicted by Piaget's stages of cognitive development.

Predictions of intelligence test scores at age eighteen from test scores obtained during the same child's preschool years are unstable but the correlations do increase with the age at which the earlier scores were obtained (Bayley, 1951). For example, the correlation between ages three and eighteen is +.31, but between ages six and eighteen the correlation increases to +.61. One reason for the low correlation between very young children and teen-agers is that the tests for the young children contain many sensorimotor test items. Bloom, by removing these items, found a correlation of about +.65 between three and seventeen. *In other words, whatever produces intelligent behavior at age three is far more important than what we had previously realized because of the newly found high and positive correlations with later intelligence test scores.*

Preschool learning at the home. Children were learning before the first book was printed, before the first school was constructed, and before the name *teacher* was conceived. Today, even before the child starts schooling, he is in many respects "a little scholar" with a vast fund of knowledge and means for expressing it symbolically or physically. The family setting, the home, and the neighborhood are ideal environments for learning. We now turn to an analysis of some aspects of home learning in light of some of the important concepts of modern learning theory including reinforcement, timing of reinforcement, mass and distributive practice, aversive behavior, and method of successive approximations.

Reinforcement is a more specific term for motivation. It refers to any action, whether positive or negative, that increases the chances for a desired event to occur again. Learning theorists make a distinction between primary and secondary reinforcers. A primary reinforcer is anything that naturally motivates, such as food, water, sex, and removal of pain; a secondary reinforcer derives its motivating power through association with primary reinforcers. Adults, especially the mother, receive tremendous power as secondary reinforcers or motivators because of their constant associations with primary reinforcements. For a child, a mother's touch, a smile, or her praise are all great sources of satisfaction.

---

* An interesting exception is that children with a minimum understanding of English, as is often the case with bilingual children, score higher on conditioning tasks than on standard intelligence tests (Jensen, 1961).

A mother is a tremendously powerful motivator if she has taken care of her child. What she does, what she says, and what she values tend to become secondary reinforcers as well. If a mother values education, books, and learning, she will convey these secondary reinforcers to her children. Metfessel (1970) recently studied thousands of children who lived in poverty to see why some were high achievers in school, although the vast majority of them were not. The single most important correlate with school success was a mother who communicated her value of education to her child. Another study of disadvantaged schoolchildren and their family characteristics concluded (Havighurst, 1970):

> They lack a family environment that sets an example of reading and that provides a variety of toys and play materials of colors, sizes, and shapes that challenge their ingenuity with their hands and their minds.

> They lack a family conversational experience that answers their questions and encourages them to ask questions; extends their vocabulary with new words, in particular adjectives and adverbs; and gives them a right and a need to stand up for and to explain their point of view on the world. . . . (p. 15)

There is also evidence of the crucial importance of the entire family, the home environment, and the neighborhood for development of intelligence that is related to school success. Wolf's study, as reported in Bloom (1964), found that the following thirteen environmental variables correlated a remarkably high $+.76$ with intelligence-test scores:

A. Press for Achievement Motivation
   1. Nature of intellectual expectations of child.
   2. Nature of intellectual aspirations for child.
   3. Amount of information about child's intellectual development.
   4. Nature of rewards for intellectual development.
B. Press for Language Development
   5. Emphasis on use of language in a variety of situations.
   6. Opportunities provided for enlarging vocabulary.
   7. Emphasis on correctness of usage.
   8. Quality of language models available.
C. Provision for General Learning
   9. Opportunities provided for learning in the home.
  10. Opportunities provided for learning outside the home (excluding school).
  11. Availability of learning supplies.
  12. Availability of books, including reference works, periodicals, and library facilities.
  13. Nature and amount of assistance provided to facilitate learning in a variety of situations. (p. 78)

The preschool child has thus been busy learning the foundation for and acquiring the motivation for formal study. If this powerful motivation for learning is transferred to the school setting, the school setting itself becomes a powerful secondary motivating force from the very beginning.

When a child asks a question, the time to answer him is immediately.

Early
Childhood

The answer is a reinforcement for his curiosity. One of the authors, who taught for years at a well-known university reading clinic with a worldwide reputation for successful treatments of very difficult problems, is convinced that one of the major reasons for the success of that clinic was the very low ratio of teachers to pupils. Whenever a hand went up for help, the help was there almost instantly. Learning theorists have provided experimental evidence that learning is greatest when the time interval between the request or need and reinforcement is as short as possible (Perin, 1943). Since the ratio of parents to children is usually low, home learning should be remarkably efficient. In general, when we have to learn a large amount of information or a complex skill, it is best to distribute the total learning time into separate periods. This technique is known as *distributive practice*. In contrast, *massed practice* occurs when learning is continuous with no rest or interruptions. It seems that most parents, whether by necessity or intuition, teach their children through distributive practice. It would be an unusual mother who would tell her child "You have two hours in which to learn how to tie your shoes!"

A major problem with massed practice or learning, which is how children are taught in our crowded schools, is that too many learning trials tend to produce *aversive behavior* toward the learning itself. Aversive behavior refers to any activity that removes the child from the cause of his discomfort —daydreaming, scribbling, looking out the window, or feeling sick. Since a child cannot feel good and bad about learning at the same time, too much aversive behavior may eventually extinguish or reduce the original and the present motivation for learning.

Successive Approximations. When teaching a complex skill, the lessons are presented step by step in small parts with immediate rewards and feedback about how well the pupil is learning. A new step is taught only when the previous one has been mastered. Through this gradual procedure, successive approximations to the desired behavior are achieved.

Regarding preschool learning, we believe that most parents are doing a good job because they are employing many modern techniques in their everyday interactions with their children. We believe that educators could profit from studying how children learn in their natural habitats in order to improve their teaching and before early childhood programs are imposed on all preschoolers on the basis of the yet-to-be-proven idea that the earlier a child starts school the better. A mother who explains to her child why a ring forms in the bathtub after a bath probably doesn't need a psycholinguist to explain how to converse with a child. A father who explains the creation of life to his child by purchasing eggs and an incubator probably doesn't need a biologist to inform him about the origins of life. In the words of June Sale (1970), director of a community family day care center, "Let us not prescribe playdough where real dough is available."

Preschool Education. Some educators and legislators are pressing for earlier school education on the premise that schools and teachers can do more for young children than their parents. The major impetus for preschool education came from concern for our socially and economically disadvantaged children. According to Havighurst (1970), the disadvantaged children in the United States, or about 15 per cent of the total child population, account for 50 per cent of the educational failure. These statistics are startling! In 1965, President Johnson signed into law the Elementary and

Secondary Education Act to strengthen education in general, but especially to aid children in low-income areas. Congress authorized $1.3 billion for this program. The discovery that a child's intelligence grows as much during the first four years of life as it will grow in the thirteen years of school (Bloom, 1964) spurred the antipoverty crusaders who believed that early childhood education would be the most promising way to attack educational deficiencies among the poor. In 1969, President Nixon told Congress, "This administration is committed to a new emphasis on child development in the first five years of life." Later he called for a network of experimental centers to find out what would work best in early childhood education.

What works best for the disadvantaged child with low achievement scores is still not clear. The Information Retrieval Center on the Disadvantaged at Columbia University has well over eleven thousand documents in addition to the thousands listed in the issues of *Research in Education*. When the interim and final reports are analyzed, we may find that there is no one program that is best for all children of poverty who are failing. We will probably find that these children are just as heterogeneous as any other large group of children and that a great variety of different preschool programs will be required for them.

For working families who cannot take adequate care of their children, the answer may lie in small, personal, neighborhood programs that are often referred to as community-family day-care centers (Prescott and Jones, 1971).

For children of middle-class backgrounds, conventional preschool nurseries can be a splendid opportunity to enhance the values taught at home because most nurseries are oriented toward this segment of the population. Furthermore, such experiences can provide for a smooth transition into regular school and can serve as an intermediate testing ground for the social and physical competencies that the child has so far developed.

Creativity

Creativity seems to be a natural characteristic of early childhood. *Playfulness*, which we have included as a prerequisite for adult creativeness, is almost synonymous with the term *child*. For Piaget and others, imaginative play is an essential process for normal cognitive development. As early as the tertiary circular reaction stage (nine to eighteen months), babies perform action "to keep interesting things happening." They either *apply familiar means to new situations or they discover new means through active experimentation*.

From the third month, when infants begin to demonstrate their preferences, there is a gradual *emergence of initiative and autonomy;* at nine months, when infants have achieved object constancy and greater mobility, they tend to embark on *"voyages of discovery";* at about eighteen months of age the infants' *assertiveness* and ability to get into mischief exceed their judgment and ability to get out of their predicaments; by age three years, their degree of *autonomy* seems to stabilize and to become a more or less permanent personality characteristic.

From birth on, one of the major benefits of cognitive and physical development is the child's increasing ability to *creatively fashion his own world*. As a result of the almost overwhelming forces of egocentrism, the preschool child must *constantly modify and uniquely change whatever is out there to match whatever is inside* him already in the form of schemas. In

Early
Childhood

389

terms of creativity we call this process as being *open to new experiences from the inside as well as from the outside.* The young child cannot help being open to new experiences. The normal child is usually actively seeking new experiences to exercise the old schemas as well to construct new schemas. If we accept the view that children are naturally active participants in their own development, then we are forced to accept that creativity is just a part of total development. If we accept the more reactive view of children, then we should be somewhat amazed by their creative efforts to understand the world.

In view of what we know about children, it is rather sad to know that adults have to *reduce their fear of the unknown* in order to be more creative. Children, on the other hand, actively seek some discrepancy between what they know and what is happening. To do otherwise would be to create a state of equilibrium in which, according to Piaget, no or little learning could occur.

With the reduction of egocentrism and the emergence of new thought processes, the child must *revise his old ways of viewing* himself, people, events, and objects. With the emergence of reversibility and concept formation during the forthcoming concrete operational stage, the child must once again, *reorganize and refashion* his old world from the new perspective that is available to him for the first time.

After reviewing the intricate and necessary interactions of the growing child in order to learn how to live in a changing world, we would like to restate the original question asked in the previous chapters from "How can we encourage the development of creativity?" to "Whatever happened to our creativity?"

AFFECTIVE DOMAIN

Affect refers to the feelings and emotions that each of us displays in the course of our development. These attributes encompass a variety of psychological states as well as a range of expression. Moreover, these states are never constant; affect is a constantly changing entity. As we examine and try to account for individuality among persons, the expression of affect may serve as a primary reference point for the exploration of individual differences.

Affect is a multidimensional quality. People display a variety of feeling states. We experience anger and love, elation and depression, affection and apathy. Moreover, these feelings are not mutually exclusive. Among adults, a love object may elicit a variety of conflicting emotions in the loving party. For example, each marriage most likely experiences a variety of states, each of which is a function of the expressed feelings of its participants. No person is always loved or capable of loving.

A similar set of relations may be applied to the feelings of children. The thwarting of a momentary ambition by a concerned parent may create intense feelings of anger and frustration. Such feelings, however, will usually compete with a history of positive parent-child relations as well as emotions that have become part of the child's repertoire. Under these circumstances, conflicting or antagonistic feelings may develop, eliciting a further range of emotions, such as feelings of incompetence or worthlessness. Or, as is frequently observed, the child may experience within himself levels of intense negative emotion that are unlikely to be subject to successful personal resolution, but demand parental intervention. For example, the child having a tantrum, or who is emotionally upset, will usually be incapable of restoring individual emotional composure without the aid of an attentive adult. Or the angry child, who may be trying to punish his parents by disavowing his affection toward them, will find his feelings shifting as his parents fail to respond to his attempted rejection of them. As these illustrations indicate, the child is faced with the developmental task of learning to monitor varied and often contradictory feelings. Furthermore, the child must learn to appropriately adjust his emotions relative to his own behavior to situations of different character and demand.

In addition to variety, feelings are also subject to gradations of intensity. Each of us, often under unusual situational stress, has experienced and/or expressed strong emotion. Some of these feelings have been subject to personal control. Others are often expressed and likely regretted on some future occasion. Nevertheless, we find that the depth of human expression capable of being generated is a source of continuous surprise. In children, emotional control is less complete than in adults. Unlike the adult, the child is usually less capable of assessing the emotional tone of his feelings or of modulating his feelings relative to situational demands. Consequently, the child is likely to exhibit both inappropriate and excessive affect. This type of behavior may be found in both boys and girls. In the young boy, roughhouse behavior is often a very serious matter. Frequently, the parent who becomes involved in such behavior may find his children trading blows with him at a strenuous pace. Subsequently, in attempting to gain control over a roughhouse session, the parent may find it difficult to put an end to such behavior and to contain the emotions generated by the children. In girls, similar situations may be noted. Using crying, a socially approved emotional outlet for females, the young girl may extend her feelings of real or alleged hurt beyond the actual level of experienced hurt. In both physical and social circumstances girls, as boys, may employ inappropriate and intensive affect. As does her male counterpart, the young girl must learn to express her feelings in a manner and tone that are appropriate to the situation. Both boys and girls should be required to learn that the expression of feelings demands the implementation of intensity controls.

A further aspect of affect differentiating the expressed feelings of children and adults is the quality of exhibited emotion. The young child is limited in his range of potential emotions. Consequently, at times, his emotions seem inappropriate and of immature quality. In contrast, the adult may display the same emotion, but with greater finesse or variety of behavioral expression. To illustrate, the angry child will employ a limited range of aggressive behaviors in support of his feelings. Generally, his behavior will take the form of unprovoked physical aggression or outburst aggression (e.g., tantrum behavior). However, over time the child will acquire a variety of alternative techniques that may be used in service to expressed feelings of anger. In the realm of aggression, the older child or adult may exhibit direct verbal, written, or indirect (e.g., gossip) forms of aggression. (It appears sufficient to note that the adult will also be more capable of either avoiding anger or handling anger in a nonaggressive fashion).

Supplementing discussion of the physical dimensions of affect, the expression of feeling is a changing entity that may be observed to reflect developmental principles. Stated more simply, children and adults differ in terms of their capacity and willingness to express affect. The young child

Early
Childhood

391

possesses a limited and somewhat special repertoire of experiences. His relations with others have been restricted and are of unique character; during infancy and much of early childhood the child is largely a recipient of unrestricted care and attention.

These experiences, unfortunately, provide him with a narrow and distorted window to his environment. The child is generally unprepared to face or experience reality. In sum, the child neither possesses skills appropriate to effective interpersonal transactions nor, as a function of his experienced special status, may he be expected to express a willingness to acquire such skills. In contrast, the adult has accomplished the major task of transition from childhood to adulthood. He has been exposed to varied environmental climates, and through such experiences the adult has acquired the requisite skills for effective interaction and has acquired a positive incentive to continue initiated patterns of growth. Furthermore, he has developed an adequate concept of reality and perspective of himself relative to others, which enable and encourage his additional achievement. Through spirit, acquired skills, and a strong self-concept of himself, primarily as an effective member of society, the adult demonstrates a range of behaviors and related emotional states that are foreign to the child. Although these distinctions in accomplishment may appear to be of great distance and impossible attainment, particularly to the child, they more properly appear as a necessary challenge to his development.

The Development of Affect

Emotions develop through a variety of experiences. These include individual initiated patterns of growth (e.g. emotional interactions that occur primarily within the child) and group associated avenues of development (e.g., emotional exchanges that involve others such as family members, peers, and teachers). In other terms, development may be assumed to encompass the unique qualities that the individual contributes to growth in conjunction with the quality of experiences provided by others.

Historically, personally initiated patterns of growth have been accorded limited value. Traditional concepts of the young child have viewed him as inept, incompetent, and naïve. To illustrate, the young child has been perceived as: (a) passive relative to his environment; (b) unusually delicate and thereby requiring exceptional amounts of love and care for his development; (c) nondevelopmental, in the sense of being especially receptive to the impact of early experiences; and (d) noninteractive, behaving primarily as an object of externally initiated activity. These perceptions have been proven erroneous.

The young child has been shown to be neither passive nor compliant regarding his own development. As a constituent of varied environments, he is responsive to persons and events that surround his sphere of activity. Yet his response to events is neither unselective nor unchallenged. Some facets of his environment are acted upon, whereas others are rejected or ignored. That is, the child relates selectively to his environment, choosing those aspects of the environment that possess meaning to him and avoiding those parts of his surroundings that provide little opportunity for growth and development.

A second quality of human life that has been challenged both in theory and research is the notion of the young child as being especially fragile or subject to *permanent* injury through environmental neglect or mishap. Contrary to this thesis, physiological studies (from which psychological analogies may be drawn with caution) have demonstrated that children possess considerable capacity to withstand stress and are highly resilient relative to demands for body restoration after encountering injury. One illustration of the child's capacity for healing himself comes from the observations of young parents. While bathing a youngster the parent is often amazed to find the child's body covered with numerous bruises or scars. Yet, on further inquiry the parent will note that these injuries usually disappear within a relatively short time. Unfortunately, and to the parent's chagrin, an even further inspection of an old injury will often lead to the discovery of an alternative wound in lieu of earlier encountered damage. In the domain of emotional and psychological growth the effects of damage and cure, relative to injury, are less clearly assessable. The question of whether a child's emotions are offended and to what degree can not always be adequately determined. Yet, it is equally erroneous to assume that the child has little capacity for adaptation. To commit the child to this point of view is to deny him the critical role that he is to play relative to personal determination for the course of his development.

A third premise that has been questioned is that the child is primarily a product of his experiences, particularly those events that have transpired relatively early in his development. Yet, what is dismissed is that the child, perhaps less than the adult, is basically a person of the moment. What is of interest to the child is that which is immediate, that which he can touch, manipulate, or experience first hand. Moreover, the child, lacking necessary conceptual tools and extensive experience in the organization of material for the purpose of memory function, will forget much of what he has come to experience. Generally, the child, as the adult, will remember events and experiences that either serve some present purpose or have been subject to repeated exposure or overlearning. For example, the young child will exhibit within his immediate play area or the homes of familiar neighbors a rather remarkable ability in locating "hidden" candy or toys, but may forget to put on his underwear while getting dressed. Or frequently, when a parent will dispose of a toy that the child has not played with for years, the child will ask shortly thereafter where the "treasured" object has been placed. (Regarding the latter, most knowledgeable parents will conduct spring-cleaning operations in the absence of their children.) A second level of memory refers to events that have been subject to extensive reiteration. For example, currently employed language forms are not forgotten, whereas a second language, either of distant memory or disuse (e.g., high school French) will be lost. In general, what the child will remember is that which is viewed by him as useful, important, or which has been subject to frequent reiteration.

The fourth argument pertains to the role the child plays relative to others in facing the demands of development. In brief, it has long been suggested that the child is only capable of limited forms of interaction. Moreover, it has been assumed that the child's abilities in this domain are largely confined to the assimilation of experiences provided by others. Yet, extensive research findings have demonstrated that the child is not only acted upon in the course of development but acts upon others. Furthermore, dyadic interaction appears to be a representative facet of human relations in all phases of life.

Early Childhood

Rheingold (1966), in reviewing early mother-infant relations in humans, indicates a diversity of ways in which the infant may serve as an important element in social relationships. She notes that (1) the infant is attentive to social as well as physical stimulation, demonstrating an awareness of people as complex, multidimensional objects; (2) the infant is capable, through crying, smiling, touching, clinging, and later following, of initiating diverse social relations as well as responding to the initiated reactions of others; (3) the infant's behavior is subject to modification as a function of the prevailing social conditions that may surround him; and (4) the infant's social behavior, as indicated through crying and other mechanisms, serves as a stimulus for changes in the behavior of others. Regarding this latter observation, the arrival of an infant, as will be attested by parents, signals vast social changes in both the existing structure and functional properties of a childless marriage arrangement.

Our notes in this area indicate a somewhat different perspective of the child than has been evident in traditional psychological research. We find from developmental studies that the child, as the infant, is capable of initiating important growth patterns relative to himself and as an interactive element in a multifaceted environment. Infants, and by extension children, as indicated by Kessen (1963), are different, and are thereby able to exhibit varied forms of adaptation. Moreover, children are competent and hence capable of effective interchange even within a complex environment. In addition, children are active, which is in part responsible for the emergence of their growth characteristics. Finally, children are dyadic relative to their environment, providing evidence of their status as social objects who are able to relate in effective ways to their environment.

Play: An Avenue of Affective Development

Emotions develop through a variety of sources. As we have observed, a child's feelings generally reflect two spheres of influence, factors that seem to come from within the child and conditions that appear to have their origins apart or external to the child. These separate dimensions have been referred to as intrapersonal (within the person) and interpersonal (between persons) domains of influence surrounding development. Historically, early approaches concerned with the analysis of behavior and its development have attempted to view internal and external factors contributing to growth as independent and distinct entities (the nature-nurture controversy). However, developmentalists have come to believe that these domains are interactive, rather than exclusive or independent conditions of growth. Moreover, as our knowledge of development has increased, it has become more difficult to distinguish between intrapersonal and interpersonal factors contributing to the developmental matrix. In brief, the origins and conditions surrounding the initiation of human behavior, as well as factors contributing to the maintenance of established patterns of transaction, are more fluid than older viewpoints would lead us to believe.

Although these remarks indicate that the perspective of human development is interrelational, our comments should not be construed to imply that distinct facets of development or processes contributing to development cannot be identified and subject to examination. We find, for example, that certain facets of growth appear to stem primarily from internal forces, whereas other aspects of development are associated, at least in appearance,

The Life
Cycle

394

with discernible elements of the external environment. To illustrate, a child's activity level is probably derived from internal mechanisms, whereas the motive to achieve would reflect the influence of external social forces encountered by the child. Similarly, certain activities appear well grounded in terms of individual inclination or motive (e.g., athletic pursuits), whereas others are structured by community interest (e.g., school attendance). A primary vehicle of development in the young child, which serves as a link between individual internal growth factors and external social conditions, is play. As such, we turn our attention to an extended view of this important avenue of learning in the young child.

Our discussion asks two simple questions, what is play and what do children learn from it? Yet, as the reader will note, the brevity of our questions belies the complexity of the play process and its role in development.

The act of play has been defined variously. However, rather than concentrate our thoughts on an intensive review of this issue, which of necessity would incorporate a history of ideas, let us summarize some major concerns that have become associated with play. Play is a transaction; that is, play refers to a relationship into which the child enters with his environment. Furthermore, this relationship is an active one. It is a process of continuous action and reaction. Play may be described as a dynamic enterprise as a function of the quality and intensity of activity exhibited. Finally, play is a complete activity. Specifically, we may observe that the transaction of play forms a total behavioral episode. As do other serious activities, play may be said to possess boundary and continuity; the act of play consists of a series of sequential phases of experience including initiation, behavior pertinent to the course of action under engagement, and completion. It is through this complete cycle of experience that the child learns about himself and his physical environment.

Although this description provides some broad outlines of play, further inquiry may be attempted concerning how play, as a special activity, differs from other behaviors. For instance, it appears reasonable to question how one distinguishes a playful act from a nonplayful or work activity. In response, it may be suggested that play involves the implementation of certain distinct criteria. These include internal reality (i.e., fantasy), intrinsic motivation (i.e., personal instigation), and internal locus of control (i.e., individual determination of activity). In contrast, nonplay refers to conditions governed by external-reality considerations, extrinsic motivational arrangements, and external locus of control factors. The criteria established for play assumes that play implies freedom from external constraints, opportunity for exploration of one's environment without penalty, and allowance for the expression of possibilities. Nonplay usually assumes some form of restriction placed upon the child and his activities.*

---

* Three major distinctions may be drawn between work and play. First, both work and play are organized ventures. However, work is concerned with the attainment of goals established by parties or persons other than the participant. Play, in contrast, is organized by the actor. Furthermore, play is organized in process, that is, during the course of activity. Second, work is performed under order and is prestructured relative to goals. Play, however, is neither formally structured nor determined through prior arrangements. Third, the value of work is derived from objective criteria. Play, in distinction, is a subjective experience in which value and meaning are inherent in the activity or assume meaning relative to the player.

How do internal reality, intrinsic motivation, and locus of control enter play activity? Internal reality or fantasy represents a special attitude associated with play. Contrary to all other activities, play allows a special relationship between the child and his environment. During play the child may conform to or reject external reality. That is, he may choose to transform his environment into his personal will or sphere of interest. As such, the child is able to hold reality in abeyance. In play, the world becomes an expression of self. Rules, format, and responsibilities are unilaterally established and followed. Consequently, the child may experiment in a variety of ways usually restricted when the activity is task oriented.

FIG. 16–15.

Intrinsic motivation refers to self-motivation. Specifically, the child in play is an autonomous being. He engages in activity and demonstrates his involvement as a function of personal choice, rather than some overriding extrinsic factor. Primarily, he plays because play is fun. His reward for playing is the activity itself. We may contrast this attitude of the child at play with behavior exhibited by the adult at play. When the child plays, he is motivated to play as a function of the activity at hand. Furthermore, the child views that activity as the focus of his interests. In the adult, on the other hand, play is less distinguishable from other spheres of behavior. For example, play forms an extension of the adult's work activity, or a form of social commitment, or perhaps a personal challenge to be evaluated as other forms of achievement. Children rarely engage in passive play activity. Among adults, however, spectator recreation, usually associated with sporting events, consumes a far greater percentage of time than active participation. Adult involvement in games is often accompanied by betting activity, whereas children rarely associate play with wagers.

The notion of locus of control suggests that the governance of play rests with the player or players involved. That is, rules and format, where applicable, are personally determined in play. In distinction, in nonplay activity, the process and objectives of the game are guided by persons who are tangential to the action or spirit of activities associated with the players. It may be asked whether locus of control implies that a given activity must be under the exclusive control of any one player. In response, we note that the concept of locus of control does not refer to any single or distinct participant. Rather, locus of control suggests that the source of direction or point of origin of the activity at hand resides within the interests of the game. For example, in distinguishing the play activity of the young child, which is largely solitary, from the play activity of the older child, which is characteristically collaborative, the notion of locus of control is equally applicable. In both situations it implies that, irrespective of the quality of play being discussed, we may observe that control of the game lies within the arena of play and the grasp of the players.

Theories of Play

In addition to philosophical and historical references to play, a number of theoretical-developmental points of view have been constructed in evaluation of play. Three views of play, representing the ideas of Freud, Erikson, and Piaget, are presented here. These encompass Freud's discussion of play in terms of the emotional and social development of the child, Erikson's extension of psychoanalytic thought with regard to developing ego functions, and Piaget's definition of play through reference to the child's expanding intellect.

Freud's Views on Play. Freud's notion of play is conceptually a complex and multifaceted phenomenon. In play, Freud found what he felt to be a major vehicle of emotional-social development in the young child. According to Freud, play may be assumed to serve three distinct purposes: (1) the development of fantasy, (2) the testing of reality, and (3) the acquisition of mastery over one's environment.

Through play, Freud theorizes, the child is removed from reality. He is offered the freedom and opportunity to discharge ideas and emotions that in other situations would be subject to social prohibition or punishment. In play, the child may assume a variety of roles ranging from those representing family membership (e.g., baby, older sibling, mother, father, or grandparent) to roles associated with heroes and villains. We note, for example, that one of the most frequent and important facets of the play activity of children is the exercise of principles of dramatic play. Through role play the child can pretend to be another person. The boy may choose to assume the role of father or fireman, or jointly play both roles. The young girl may practice common tasks of motherhood through nurturant activity or aspire to assume the roles of teacher or doctor. Through such behavior, particu-

Early
Childhood

397

larly the imitation and practice of adult roles, the child gains an understanding and identification with adults and the future roles that he or she will come to occupy in society.

These examples indicate some of the roles that are open to the child through play. The illustrations offered, however, largely favor socially approved channels of expression. Yet, play also allows the child to demonstrate restricted or socially inappropriate roles. The young child may, for example, assume the role of a favorite or feared animal, or he may become an enemy of the social order. Young boys may play mother, become involved in homemaking chores, or assume roles usually stereotyped as feminine. Similarly, the young girl may become the daddy or be encouraged to experiment with tools usually considered to reflect masculine interests (e.g., carpentry). Expanding upon this theme, Freud views play as affording the child the opportunity for releasing hidden or feared emotions. Play, he observes, offers the child both a pleasurable emotional outlet as well as an experimental channel for the review of impulses or ideas that the child, in deference to his status, could not be expected to reveal freely within an adult-oriented society. Freud notes, for example, that the child may relive through play unpleasant experiences that previously represented unresolved conflicts. Through constant experimentation with themes, which in play are subject to personal control and individually chosen outcomes, the child is able to provide favorable solutions to existing problems.

Another aspect of play considered by Freud is its role in the child's development of mastery over his environment. Specifically, Freud recognizes that in order for learning to occur in the young child there must exist opportunities for practice and repetition of acquired skills. Correspondingly, Freud properly identifies childhood as a period of practice and preparation in which play allows for the mastering of experiences. This position has been supported by others, most notably Piaget (1962).

Erikson's Views on Play. The work of Erikson (1963) forms a critical amplification of Freudian theory. This contribution reflects Erikson's concern for the development of ego functions and his elaboration of the process of emotional growth originally described by Freud. According to Erikson, the ego is the major force and principal accomplishment of development. Consequently, in supplementing the traditional views of ego as primarily an adjunct of id and superego forces, Erikson postulates that the ego represents an independent source of experience. This position sees the ego as performing an integrative and balancing function that binds the child to society but also preserves his individuality. Specifically, Erikson's position, although based upon psychoanalytic principles, views the child as both a product of intrapersonal emotional growth elements (in accord with the traditional psychoanalytic perspective) and as an outcome of interpersonal social forces. That is, Erikson calls our attention to the duality of development, emphasizing the role of individual emotionality and social reality as confluent influences upon development. For Erikson, the ego is a driving, critical element in this scheme. Primarily, it is charged with the task of integrating energy factors inherent in the child, in accord with the child's developing internal psychological self and those external social conditions impinging upon him as a consequence of social membership. Play is assumed to facilitate the role of the ego in accomplishing this important integrative function.

The Life
Cycle

398

Play, according to Erikson, is the child's primary mechanism for learning to cope with his environment. Through spontaneous activity, for instance, the child is able to postpone reality or the pain of experience, in order to find more adequate solutions necessary for adaptation; the child escapes the boundaries of reality, which enables him to recreate situations and plan strategies for the resolution of situational difficulties encountered in living. As the child learns to master situations, the ego gains in strength and restores security to the self. Erikson finds that Western society commits a serious error in distinguishing between play as the sole preoccupation of children, from work as reality, and the exclusive province of adulthood. This separation suggests that play is largely an exercise in fantasy, a conclusion that appears unwarranted based on our observations.

Erikson's description of play conforms to criteria reviewed earlier. First, play is assumed to reflect the will of the child rather than the force of external demands. Second, it is argued that play is subject to personal criteria or intrinsic motivational principles. Third, Erikson believes that play is divorced from the production of given commodities. Specifically, he feels that the activity of play is the goal of play. Fourth, Erikson indicates that play usually involves some pleasurable element. That is, play frequently is fun, thereby sustaining individual interest. Finally, Erikson suggests that play is productive. In other words, play is assumed to perform a valuable function. As reported, this goal is to help the child encounter, cope, and master the problems of reality.

This commentary outlines Erikson's perspective of play by reference to its role in assisting the child in the performance of ego functions. Of equal significance, play is also regarded as an important aid to other facets of development. Specifically, Erikson suggests that elements of play may be equated with concepts of emerging selfhood, particularly facets of growth postulated by traditional psychoanalytic thought. Corresponding to the psychoanalytic formulation of personality development as consisting of a sequence of emerging intrapersonal-psychosexual stages, Erikson has extended this perspective to include reference to interpersonal-psychosocial elements in development. Each stage of growth, initially hypothesized to reflect the inclusive interests of biological adaptation, has been supplanted through association with a psychosocial corollary. During childhood, these references include the task of establishing basic trust versus basic mistrust, autonomy versus shame and doubt, initiative versus guilt, and industry versus inferiority. As is the case for intrapersonal facets of psychoanalytic thought, each of Erikson's stages appears in sequence and is built upon previous experience. Furthermore, with each challenge the child is faced with a problem of resolution and the acquisition of new mastery over his environment. Through play these challenges are reviewed and resolved.

Piaget's Views on Play. A third view of play is presented through the extensive writings of Piaget (1962, 1963). Although primarily recognized by his interests in cognitive or intellectual development in children, Piaget's contributions are of critical importance in understanding many facets of human development. The rationale for his inclusion here is twofold. First, in order to appreciate how children relate emotionally and socially to their environment, it is crucial that the reader understand something about how children think about their environment. Specifically, as we have endeavored to suggest throughout this text, development is a complex and intricate

Early
Childhood

399

process involving the interaction of all facets of human activity. Thought is an important aspect of such activity. Second, although Piaget has directed many research questions to the realm and study of thought processes, he has not done so exclusively. His writings have encompassed several important areas of interest to our understanding of social and emotional growth processes. These have included moral development, imitation, play, and dreams.

The development of thought, according to psychoanalytic theory, consists of two stages, a period of life characterized by primary processes (i.e., the exercise of fantasy under the influence of emotional needs) followed by a period of mature thought known as the secondary process (i.e., ego processes associated with reality). In play, Freud concentrates on the role of primary processes whereas Erikson attempts to deal with secondary processes. For Freud, play is a vehicle of fantasy. In contrast, for Erikson, play helps the child to cope and adapt to the demands of external reality.

According to Piaget, the development of thought, as facilitated through play, is accomplished through assimilation and accommodation. These two processes, in tandem, serve to monitor the quality and quantity of interaction that the child shares with his environment. As experience increases through such vehicles as play so does the range of assimilation-accommodation functions leading to the growth of intellect. Development proceeds from sensory-motor awareness, to a preoperational phase, to a level of concrete operations, followed by the emergence of abstract thought. During early childhood, approximately between the ages of two and six, the child thinks at the preoperational level of thought.

During the period of preoperational thought the child is primarily concerned with adapting himself to reality. Correspondingly, his thoughts are largely personally defined (i.e., subjective). Yet, through play, particularly its assimilative function (i.e., providing information about the environment), the child is able to strike a balance between his subjective conceptions of reality and the objective quality of reality. Furthermore, as the child begins to correct his perceptions, play becomes instrumental in aiding imitation, an accommodation function in which the child learns to adapt himself to reality. Through the assimilative (i.e., informational) and accommodational (i.e., imitative) functions of play, the child may act out past and present experiences, which leads to his acquiring a broader and more adequate concept of his environment and his own role within the environment.

In addition to his part in formulating the basic operations of play, Piaget has distinguished between a variety of play activities based upon the child's attained level of cognitive development. These include, in their developmental sequence or order of appearance, practice games, symbolic games, games of order, and constructional-type games. The practice game refers to generally orderless or random activity in which the activity is largely characterized by its assimilative function or is engaged in primarily for the purpose of amusement. Such activities are also usually of short duration. These activities will appear at the sensory-motor stage of development. The symbolic game refers to activities in which the child experiments with familiar objects and symbols by attempting to create new operations through varying arrangements or combinations. In brief, the form and content of the symbolic game is structured through the child's use of imagination. These games generally appear during the preoperational period of development but continue into later life. During the early period of concrete operations, approximately between seven and eight years of age, games referred to as games of order take on definite form and are characterized by the appearance of rules. Through such activities, the child acquaints himself with the notions of sharing and responsibility for cooperative effort. During the fourth type of activity the play is characterized by constructional-type games that are a faithful and objective reproduction of conditions that exist within the domain of reality.

The Development of Play

A number of attempts have been made to define the arena and developmental sequence of children's play. Two notable efforts in this direction are associated with Erikson (1963) and Parten (1932).

Paralleling the earlier efforts of Piaget, Erikson has observed that children's play may be conceptualized relative to emerging intellectual functions. Play, according to this perspective, reflects the child's changing views of himself and his understanding of his physical world.

In brief, Erikson postulates that children's play progresses developmentally over three dimensions of interpersonal space: namely, the autocosmic sphere, the microsphere, and the macrosphere. In autocosmic play, the child is concerned primarily with himself. Other people enter his sphere of activity primarily because they appear within his immediate vicinity. Play consists of repetitive sensory motor explorations that are requisite to his gaining mastery over his own functions and those within his immediate stimulus environment. In microspheric play, the child plays in the world of manageable toys and in simple gamelike activities. Finally, in the macrosphere, which occurs at the time of nursery school attendance, the child enters the world of others, learning to experience his world collectively and through sharing with others.

The distinction between individual and group play is finely drawn by Parten. She states that during individual play the child wanders about the room focusing on his own body movements and his own activities. Although the child will engage in microspheric activity, he will avoid macrospheric activity. He will manipulate toys and other materials such as clay. Moreover, he may be observed to visually explore his surroundings including the behavior of other children and adults. However, the child will make no physical or verbal contact with others. During group play, in contrast, there is both physical and verbal contact with others. Moreover, activity is extended to include a variety of tools and materials. In joint interaction, children employ blocks and dress-up clothes, play house, or use art materials. Such behavior is aided by sociodrama and role play.

The sequence of play that is exhibited among children in the course of development has been reported by Parten. She identifies six phases of play that are characterized by an increasing social awareness by the child. These include:

1. Unoccupied play: playing with one's one body, exhibiting random activity and movement.
2. Onlooker play: observing the activity of others without self-participation.
3. Solitary play: playing with toys at a distance from others, interest centered on own activity, independent activity.

Early
Childhood

401

Fig. 16–16. (a) Solitary play, (b) parallel play, (c) associative play.

4. Parallel play: independent play engaged in within the near distance of others, but nevertheless distinct from each other.
5. Associative play: the beginnings of group play in which common activity is evident and personal associations are formed.
6. Cooperative play: highly organized group activity in which there is a division of labor and common goals.

SOCIAL DOMAIN

The affective and social growth of the young child is a function of varied encounters reflecting a range of experiences. Previously, two spheres of influence contributing to this development were identified. We refer to the intrapersonal and interpersonal environments within which learning occurs and which, in effect, comprise the child's developmental life space. In the preceding section of this chapter, we looked at intrapersonal sources of experience contributing to affective growth. We now shift our attention to a review of theoretical models that stress interpersonal relations contributing to social development and conclude this section with an examination of four prominent theories of social growth.

Socialization

The Life Cycle

The role of interpersonal forces in the child's social development occurs within the framework of socialization processes provided him through membership within the social order. Socialization has been referred to as the process by which an individual acquires the knowledge, skills, and dispositions that enable him to participate as an effective member of a social group and a given social order. In less formal terms, socialization may be defined as the learning or acquisition of one's society and culture. The process of socialization, of course, is more complex than is suggested. In duration, for example, socialization forms one of the most extensive learning experiences that the individual will ever encounter. Socialization is a never-ending process. Since we all are continually learning about our culture and how to adapt to it meaningfully, each of us is subject to socialization procedures throughout our lives. What does socialization consist of and how is it translated to the child? In brief, socialization refers to the multitude of formal and informal social learning lessons that involve individuals and society, and that, over time, contribute to an acquired identification by the person as a member of a given social group.

Growth, as achieved through the process of social interaction, is based on the idea that the responsibility for social development, as least initially, should rest with a select number of people serving as the representatives of society. Usually, these people comprise the child's family of origin but may be members of a surrogate family or family of adoption. This primary group, which is later expanded to include peers and other significant persons (e.g., teachers), is charged with the task of training the young child in a developmentally appropriate sequence of growth in a manner leading to his assumption of the varied roles of society upon the attainment of adult status. Consequently, childhood serves as a period of learning and preparation for this achievement.

Theories of Social Development

Role Theory. Several ideas have been offered to account for the way in which society accomplishes the massive task of training the young child in the ways of his cultural heritage. One concept that appears especially appropriate to this question is the notion of role and its relation to development.

Role may be defined as the part or function an individual plays in relation to the position or status he or she is assigned or has acquired as a member of the group. In the case of complex societies, in which multiple group membership is common, individuals are required to play numerous roles within the social order. For example, a female adult may be a mother, a doctor, or a member of a professional order either at the same time or at different periods in her life.

These diverse roles, particularly with reference to those roles an individual selects or may be chosen to perform, share important similarities relative to the social order. First, all roles are prestructured or antedate the player. To illustrate, the role of mother, as a representation of a special type of family structure within the social order, exists previous to its assumption by a particular female. Similarly, occupational roles, such as teacher or surgeon, are socially structured previous to their formal adoption. Second, all roles are learned and require some degree of acquired competence for their performance. For example, whether skills are developed in the form of "on the job training," as is true in the case of parenthood, or through completion of the requirements of a college degree, as is true for the prospective teacher,

Early
Childhood

403

effective role implementation requires a discrete level of skill utilization relative to given role occupancy. Third, all roles require an acceptance of responsibility for their performance by members of the group assigned or trained to their occupation. In this context, role training will usually involve some form of social praise, personal esteem, or other reward of persons performing the functions assigned to them by the social order.

The task of society, according to role theory, is to train people to fill positions within the structure of group life. In its most primitive form, this view suggests that social adaptation may be measured in terms of how well people fit into the social structure. A good match allows for the optimal performance of functions associated with the attainment of each position. As such, from the perspective of society, training through socialization increases the approximation of this goal.

In accord with most theories of growth, the primary responsibility for socialization in role theory lies with the family. In terms of functional learning, it is believed that family membership provides the most effective and efficient source of training involving roles and role responsibilities. Through family structure and particularly by participation in family functions, the child directly experiences the lessons of status, role play, and reciprocity (i.e., shared responsibility). He learns that different members of the group occupy different positions and that each position entails certain responsibilities to the group. In addition, the child learns that the completion of each function (and often through his personal neglect resulting in the absence or failure to complete tasks) has consequences for individual and group survival. These experiences provide the critical backdrop for the assumption of roles in the larger arenas of group life.

A number of theories have been offered to account for the role of affective and social experiences in development. Although these theories differ, some common issues have been raised in their formulation. Specifically, three issues have been addressed: (1) the question of what constitutes critical experiences in development, (2) the problem of defining how the child organizes his experiences, and (3) the determination of what kinds of developmental-behavioral effects may be anticipated from these experiences. Four theories, representing the interests of psychoanalysis (the contributions of Freud and the amplification of his position by Erikson), cognitive-developmental theory, and social-learning theory have each attempted to review these issues.

The Psychosexual Theory of Development. In Chapter 12, the reader was introduced to Freud's concept of the dynamics of personality, including his discussion of id, ego, and superego functions. At this point, we attempt to review his treatment of the development of personality, including the formation of these three structural components of personality.

According to Freud, human growth is a developmental accomplishment based on a sequential set of intrapersonal experiences that occur during a long and arduous rite of passage. Over time, and through a progression of five crucial stages of life, the child passes through these experiences and comes to achieve an adult personality.

Initially, and approximately over the first five years of life, the child traverses three stages of development. These include the oral stage, the anal stage, and the phallic stage. Following this period of rapid growth the child enters the latency stage, when the dynamics of personality become stabilized

The Life
Cycle

for approximately five to six years. Consequently, and with the advent of adolescence, the child enters a final phase of development, the genital stage, that carries him through adolescence and into adulthood.

During the first five years of life, the child experiences largely pregenital forms of development in which behavior, although possessing long-range genital significance according to Freud, occurs primarily around nongenital sensual zones of the body. Originally, during the oral stage of development, activities center about the mouth, which becomes the focus of infant functioning and the infant's conduit to the world. Shortly thereafter, activity is transferred to the eliminative functions, and the child enters an anal stage of development. Finally, in early childhood, the child approaches the phallic stage in which the sex organs gain prominent attention and serve as an impetus to the critical problem of achieving proper sex-role identification.

The phallic stage differs for boys and girls. In the boy, sexual difficulties center about his mother (through the Oedipal Complex). In the girl similar, although somewhat less extensive, difficulties focus about her relations with her father (through the Electra Complex). After resolution of this phase, the child enters a period of organization of experiences through integration and personality consolidation. During this period, called the latency stage, biological impulses are muted and held in abeyance. Finally, under the stimulus of physiological demands, as evident in adolescent maturation, the child is thrust into the last period of development, the genital stage. We now turn to a more detailed review of each of these important aspects of development.

The Oral Stage. Freud views the newborn as a bundle of energy systems originating from the id and directed toward the seeking of immediate pleasure through gratification and stimulation. As such, he argues that the infant is an instinctively selfish creature who operates on the hedonistic principle of seeking gratification of needs through inherent-instinctive behavior patterns (e.g., sucking, swallowing, being held, touching, and being relieved of unpleasant sensations). Since much of the child's satisfaction and stimulation during this period is established through the mouth, Freud adopted the term *oral stage* to call attention to the sphere of development during the first year of life.

The Anal Stage. As the child enters the second year of life, rules and demands change; his experience of continuous and unquestioning nurturance through the attentiveness of caretakers is supplanted by a series of demands for personal behavior modifications. During this period of time the focus of activity is also shifted. In brief, the child moves from an incorporative phase to an eliminative-retentive period of development. The major focus of conflict occurs about the issue of impulse control with the exercise of infant and parent will as a means of conflict resolution playing a prominent role during this period of life.

In the anal stage the child is asked to exert bowel control with regularity and at the expense of personal pain (a consequence of retention) rather than seek, as was previously the case, immediate and pleasurable release of eliminative matter by means of instinctual mechanisms. This shift in parental attention places the child on notice that his parents will not continue to serve primarily for the purpose of gratifying his needs. Rather, through bowel training, parents demand accommodation in the child's behavior. As may be expected, this phase of development may lead to a battle of interests.

Early Childhood

A number of important clinical implications have been drawn from observations based upon the resolution of conflicting interests associated with the anal stage. Freud believes that the child's first lesson in external control of a previously natural and relief-producing inner tension produces lifelong character traits. Overly strict maternal reactions, he argues, produce a child who holds back his digestive wastes and becomes a stingy and compulsive person. Specifically, Freud refers to a triad of personality traits marked by obstinacy (i.e., stubborness), orderliness (i.e., excessive neatness), and parsimony (i.e., thriftiness) as an adult outcome of such child-rearing practices. In contrast, Freud believes that mothers who do not place severe pressures on the child, but rather praise the child's initial attempts, tend to produce a more open and flexible child. (The reader should note that the validity of these assertions has been severely questioned.)

Insofar as the child is confronted with the demands of reality, the anal period furthers the emergence of the child's ego. However, since the will of the parent may be exerted too forcefully, the development of superego functions is also enhanced. From this early encounter with reality, the child probably learns several important lessons of life. He finds that he is different from others, that his value as a person is not necessarily given (i.e., it must be earned), and that when he does things without regard for others (e.g., soiling his pants), his actions may elicit punishment from those he loves. Furthermore, through occasional toilet training failures or "slips," he may experience feelings of guilt, which leads to the development of the super-ego and conscience.

The Phallic Stage. As the child enters into the last phase of early childhood he traverses through the phallic stage. This period of life, according to traditional psychoanalytic theory, is of critical importance in the development of many human characteristics and conditions that will influence behavior throughout life. During this time the child explores and experiences his genital organs as pleasurable. These derived excitations, Freud believes, produce sexual fantasies involving the partner in his first love relationship, the child's mother. However, the child's emotional and sexual attraction for the opposite sex parent (the Oedipal Complex in males and the Electra Complex in females) is complicated by hostile and jealous feelings toward the same-sexed parent, resulting in an ensuing love-hate triangle.

In theory, the male child wants his mother for himself, but is confronted with the reality of his father's presence. He knows that "Daddy is bigger" and is more powerful than he. Furthermore, he recognizes that his father may harm him through castration. Consequently, he relinquishes his sexual fantasies in favor of a same-sex identification with the heretofore sexual competitor.

From this sequence of events, the manner in which the child resolves the Oedipal Complex is of considerable importance. Freud hypothesizes that out of this problem of emotional conflict, the child learns many lessons in building his superego. Furthermore, the child becomes identified with the like-sexed parent. This solution to his dilemma, Freud assumes, has many advantages for the growing child; through identification with his father he learns behaviors associated with the male sex role, he gains a vicarious sense of power through his father's successes, and he finds that he may express affection toward his mother without being afraid of his father or of his still unresolved pregenital sexuality.

The Life
Cycle

The Latency Stage. As a result of the phallic stage, the child goes through an expanding series of identifications characterized by a period of same-sex play and peer involvement. This is the time in elementary school when boys have their "buddies" and girls their special cliques. Moreover, the sexual feelings and behavior seen in the phallic phase are repressed and much of the libidinal energy is channeled through play, hobbies, and school achievements.

The Genital Stage. Having achieved close peer affiliations and adequate sex-role identification during the period of latency, the emerging person now channels his biologically renewed sexual desires in more socially acceptable avenues of expression. Thus, we find the adolescent and young adult expressing sexuality in a manner differing from the pregenital sexuality of the young child. Here sexuality, originally defined through self-purpose, is turned outward, directed toward helping and loving others for their own sake. Hopefully, with the successful completion of earlier stages of development, the person will place these energies into planning for a career and marriage.

Theories of Psychosocial Development

Whereas Freud endeavors to draw our attention to the role of intrapersonal elements associated with affective and social development, a number of revisions and extensions of his theory, reflecting the importance of interpersonal factors in development, have been proposed. One of these attempts, which has generally been accepted both within psychoanalytic circles and by wider audiences, is Erikson's theory of psychosocial relations.

Erikson's position follows the basic scheme and sequence of development proposed by Freud. For example, the oral stage is equated by Erikson with the concepts of trust versus mistrust, whereas the anal stage is associated with the notions of autonomy versus shame and doubt. Proceeding developmentally, we find that the phallic stage is equated with the ideas of initiative versus guilt and the latent stage is tied to feelings of industry versus inferiority. Finally, the genital stage is related to the question of achieving identity versus role confusion. Erikson's theory goes beyond Freud. Specifically, Erikson proposes three additional stages defining adulthood and old age. These include intimacy versus isolation, which is associated with young adulthood; creativity versus stagnation, relating to problems encountered in middle adulthood; and ego integrity versus despair, referring to achievements in the elderly. Although this discussion focuses on early and middle childhood, the interested reader is encouraged to examine Erikson's first and last three periods of development in order to derive a complete picture of his theory.

Autonomy versus Shame and Doubt. For Erikson, the child's first explorations outside the sphere of trust and attachment established with his parents involves a conflict between his desire to achieve independence and his fear of personal failure. On the one hand he strives to achieve autonomy, but on the other hand he doubts his ability to accomplish this task.

As the young child recognizes his existence as a separate and unique individual, he is thrust into a series of decision-making situations. These events require his independence and separation from others. He is asked to achieve personal control over bodily functions and to exhibit self-chosen behaviors. In addition, he is faced with acquiring a preliminary sense of

Early
Childhood

personal esteem and regard or continuing his dependence and need for support from others.

If the child is able to gradually overcome the doubt he has concerning his capabilities, and through proper parental support and encouragement is able to minimize the shame resulting from early failures to achieve independence, he develops a sense of will or self-determination that underlies many of his later personality and character traits.

The degree to which the child is able to successfully resolve conflicts at this stage of development depends, in part, upon his parent's encouragement and continued love. Failure to resolve the question of autonomy, according to Erikson, will produce self-retarding shame and doubt in the child, leading him to question his capabilities and his competence.

Initiative versus Guilt. Erikson proposes that the period from four to eight years of age is characterized by vigorous activity. That is, during this time the young child is an inquiring explorer. Through the maturation of biological and cognitive competencies, particularly in such areas as motor and language development, the child now intrudes through adventurous quest upon his environment. For example, he begins to roam the house and the neighborhood often at the fear and dismay of overprotective parents. Moreover, he begins to question many areas of the unknown with an incessant curiosity and verbal eagerness. However, he also lacks tact as well as patience. These liabilities are evident in a variety of ways. For example, in family conversations, the child attempts to become the center of activity and disregards the rights of others. In discussions with peers he demonstrates an eagerness in his tone of voice that demands attention and overwhelms others. Consequently, the child's curiosity becomes subject to the abuse of siblings and often the punishment of his parents.

Another important facet of this stage, according to Erikson, is the child's intense curiosity about human sexuality (paralleling Freud's phallic stage of development). Thus, the child may explore, with considerable candor, or show particular concern for the genitals of both sexes. Although this may be considered a normal and important phase of development through which children pass, it may be treated in a punitive manner by the child's parents and thereby create feelings of intense guilt in the child.

Coupled with the child's growing sense of behavioral initiative is a sense of social inappropriateness. Consequently, the task confronting the child at this stage of life is the need to acquire a sense of balance between adventure and curiosity and social order and propriety. The child must learn to monitor his behavior without loss of participation, but must avoid excessive and guilt-provoking (i.e., forbidden fantasy and exploration) activities leading to censure.

Erikson believes that the child at this stage requires family structure:

1. To teach the child where play ends and responsibility and purpose begin.
2. Where do's and don'ts are clearly defined with reference to words and actions.
3. Where a mutual, loving relationship characterized by a sense of basic worth and acceptance may develop between father and son as well as mother and daughter.

The Life Cycle

Correspondingly, for Erikson, the successful achieving of a balance between the powerful human emotions of initiative and guilt can produce a human being who feels a sense of purpose in life and who possesses a realistic sense of accomplishment.

Industry versus Inferiority. At the conclusion of the third stage, the developing child initiates inquiry into the various tools of his culture; he starts to ask how things come about and begins to seek knowledge of the means associated with industry. Furthermore, in an important expansion of selfhood, he becomes a direct participant, through technology and skill utilization, in a society of craftsmen.

This is the period, according to Erikson, when the child starts seeking and finding additional models of competence outside the immediate family. Thus, whereas the young child identifies with and readily imitates such observable figures as the father or the mother, or occupations close to the family unit (e.g., milkman, mailman, fireman), the older child seeks to know more distant and technologically sophisticated roles. Erikson observes that in preindustrialized society, where technology and tools were relatively simple, allowing early competence, the child entered this phase directly because adults acted as teachers from whom the child could learn directly. However, in the modern, highly technological society in which "abstract" tools and skills are to be mastered, one must first spend years learning to become literate (i.e., learning such basic skills as reading, writing, and mathematics) in preparation for the greatest number of possible careers. In addition, Erikson finds that our society presents numerous vocational ambiguities to the child. Since many of the "tools" needed for the highly changing technological job market are often vague and hard to define, identification is often illusory. As such, the child's drive for industry and productivity may become muted through confusion.

The critical danger during the period of industry is that the child's continuing sense of interest, if lost, may lead to alienation from himself as a doer. Subsequently, he will fail to develop a sense of standards to be applied to his work and will likely experience little mastery over his environment. This will lead to a sense of acute inferiority and low self-esteem. Erikson postulates that this situation is likely to arise under one or more of the following conditions:

1. The child may be highly dependent on family members for knowledge.
2. He may fear to acknowledge increasing independence from his family.
3. He may still maintain competition with his father by comparing his father's achievements with his own.
4. Family life may not have prepared him for adjustment to the external environment, particularly his participation in school-related activities.
5. The school situation is nonproductive since nothing he achieves provides him status with his peers, teachers, or parents.
6. The school may not be addressing itself to the potentials of the child thereby allowing little opportunity for meaningful success.
7. The child may find that the color of his skin or his parents' ethnicity rather than his performance or desire to learn are more critical to success than his own efforts.

In contrast to these conditions, Erikson believes that feelings of inferiority, which can have a devastating effect upon the person's long-range character development, can be reduced through loving and compassionate teachers and parents.

It is out of the school experiences of self-expression through freedom and

Early
Childhood

creative play, as well as the discovery of one's environment, that one experiences the learning of a new skill and its associated pride of accomplishment. From such opportunities, Erikson believes, two of the most important facets of development stem, namely, a feeling of personal competence and the exercise of mastery over one's immediate sphere of activity.

On a somewhat broader level of influence, the social implications of this period of development serve the good of society as well as specific facets of growth associated with the individual. Out of this stage, the child learns the way of his society as an organization of interrelated parts. He finds meaning in the notion of interdependence in which the divided and yet cooperative efforts and skills of many different persons make this world a more humane place to work and live. Out of these attitudes and experiences, Erikson suggests that the child learns a lasting basis for the development of cooperative effort and joint participation in productive adult life.

Freud and Erikson: A Comparison of Theories. A number of important distinctions between Freud's theory of development and the amplification and refinement of this theory by Erikson have been noted. For the reader's interest, these and related differences are summarized in Table 16–8.

TABLE 16–8
PSYCHOANALYTIC ORIENTATIONS

Freud	Erikson
Ages—infancy to adulthood	Ages—infancy to old age
Intrapersonal scope	Interpersonal scope
Biological-psychological orientation	Social-cultural orientation
Sexual emphasis	Social emphasis
Id oriented	Ego oriented
Primary process	Secondary process
Parent-child emphasis	Parent-child-cultural emphasis
Potential behaviors—clinical	Potential behaviors—social

In attempting to seek the source of divergence between the views of Freud and those of Erikson, the reader finds that the principal area in contention is reflected through their opposing views of society and social functions. For Freud, as presented in his *Civilization and Its Discontents* (1930), the major goal of society is to limit individual behavior through inhibition and sublimation (i.e., restructuring). This position is based on Freud's contention that the human organism is initially neither a social being nor, unless it is subject to environmental regulation, is it capable of becoming a member of the social group; in brief, for Freud, man and society are incompatible entities. It was for this reason that Freud introduced the concept of superego, whose purpose was to control and monitor those impulses whose uncontrolled expression would endanger the stability of society.

Erikson's contribution to basic psychoanalytic doctrine forms one of several major attempts at relating development to social and cultural life. As does Freud, Erikson postulates an emergent developmental structure characterized by stages and crises. However, in distinction to Freud, Erik-

The Life
Cycle

son views the roots of each crisis at each period of development as well as the consequences of crisis resolution in terms of its interpersonal significance as well as through reference to its individual importance for the purpose of personality structure. For example, as personal adjustment may be fixated (i.e., emotionally retarded or retained at a given stage of development) as a function of the individual's failure to respond adequately to biopsychological conflict, Erikson argues that similar processes are operative at the psychosocial level. The individual who has not achieved integration of self (i.e., identity) through a unification of self and social roles in adolescence will probably be unable to form lasting commitments to others through affiliation and partnership in young adulthood. As suggested by this thesis, the nature of each crisis and its requirement for solution is based upon child's successful balancing of inner needs with the particular demands of his increasingly complex social situation. Furthermore, it is likely that, to the degree to which both spheres of influence are consistently matched, the person will be in the process of full personality integration.

In addition to Erikson's efforts at emphasizing the contribution of cultural forces in the determination of personality, his view of the influence of external factors upon development appears expansive rather than restrictive. For Freud, society contributes to the limitation of biological potential. For Erikson, the resolution of each crisis adds a new flexibility and dimensionality to ego. Society, by creating challenges and requiring task mastery, provides the opportunity and motivation for the expansion of individual potential. Although the narrow demands of biological self will conflict with social tasks precipitating crises, the resolution of factionalism holds promise for the emergence of a less exclusive, more adaptive perspective of one's role and relations with his external world.

Cognitive-Developmental Theory

Cognitive-developmental theory differs from psychoanalysis and alternative theories of affective and social development in its emphasis on thought or intellectual factors as critical components of growth. The idea of thought serving as a factor in human affairs is, of course, not a recent development. Yet current attempts to specify the dimensions of thought affecting social processes have been unparalleled in the history of psychological inquiry. Furthermore, the idea of thought as an emergent, developmental factor affecting all facets of self-adaptation has provided considerable impetus and redirection in attempts to conceptualize developmental issues.

Cognitive-developmental theory refers to all interests or considerations of human behavior that assume some general cognitive principle or mechanism as an organizer of experiences. Specifically, these interests include play, moral development, sex-role development, and a variety of other facets of growth in which thought assumes some role in how a behavior is formed or expressed.

Cognitive theory is based upon several assumptions that differentiate it from the psychoanalytic and other approaches to the analysis of human interactions (Kohlberg, 1969). Development involves cognition and changes in thought in all forms and stages of life. Specifically, cognitive-developmental theory assumes that one cannot dichotomize life functions into distinct classes or areas, particularly categorization that excludes intellectual processes; in contrast, this theory assumes that cognition performs an um-

Early
Childhood

brellalike function in which all facets and systems are integrated through the exercise of thought.

A second related assumption of cognitive-developmental theory is that development and cognition form dual accomplishments. That is, cognitive-developmental theory assumes that the growth of thought is linked with the development of all life functions and their continued maintenance. Specifically, those principles of development used to define cognitive achievements are seen as being applicable to the definition of other life functions. Similarly, changes in cognition will require and precipitate changes in development.

The manner in which cognitive-developmental theory accounts for human development may be linked to two concepts: (1) the notion that behavior has form or structure, and (2) the idea that behavior is subject to both quantitative, and most critically, qualitative change over time. The notion of structural organization implies that behavior is a total entity that is not subject to reduction or partial analysis. Specifically, for cognitive analysis, behavior is relational, integrative, and interlocking. For example, a child's sex-role development will involve varied factors, both maturational and experiential, including affective, instructional, preferential, and judgmental properties. Hence, in asking how a child acquires a given sex-role identity we need to know more than if he is aware of sexual distinctions or whether he has been properly reinforced for sex-appropriate behavior. Similarly, in trying to account for parent-child relations, we must consider that the child is a changing entity who is constantly creating (through growth) changes in the system of social relations that he shares with his parents. Moreover, in understanding such relations from the parents' perspective, we need to note that the goals of parents may not correspond with their ability to provide the means for implementation. Or, we may find that the means appropriate for effective parent-child relations at one age are inappropriate at an advanced age of development. In sum, social interaction, according to the cognitive-developmental point of view, is a complex system of inter-related parts, each of which contributes in varying fashion to the sphere of action under scrutiny. Furthermore, since persons and situations comprising the behavioral life span change or are subject to changing conditions over time, we need to anticipate relationships within the context of flux.

The implications of cognitive-developmental theory for social and personality development are varied, ranging from a somewhat unique perspective of the nature of person-environmental interactions to the specification of processes responsible for continuity and change over time. Development, according to cognitive-developmental theory, is founded on interaction. As suggested, however, interaction is global in implication rather than specific or of limited range. This interchange refers to interaction between an organized system of responses that are characteristic of the organism and an established set of ordered relations that form his environment. This perspective differs from the maturational or learning theory approaches to behavior development. A comparison of this view with maturational theory reveals that cognitive-developmental theory assumes that development requires a rich exchange of experience in conjunction with physiological readiness as a prerequisite for growth. Moreover, cognitive-developmental theory not only presumes the necessity of exposure to certain experiences for proper development but argues against the notion of growth that is independent of external experiences.

Although the views of learning theory and cognitive-developmental theory may be presented and contrasted through varied reference, we limit our discussion to differences in perspective which involve conceptualizations of the role of environment. As maturational theory assumes the existence of an inherent system of basic mental structures, learning theory argues that mental function is derived from the patterning or association of events established in response to specific elements and experiences represented by the environment. From the latter point of view, individuals acquire their environment through specific experiences that are subject to modification by successive approximations leading to desired end states. In contrast, cognitive-developmental theory assumes that events are learned as a joint function of maturational status and their experiential appropriateness; understanding learning, or more specifically, how things are learned, requires analysis of the learner as well as appraisal of the environment in which learning occurs.

Social-Learning Theory

The final theoretical orientation to be considered in this section is social-learning theory. This position refers to an amalgam of different contributions that view the development of affect and social behavior in the child as a function of social learning principles. For the purposes of this discussion we contrast three facets of social-learning theory with schools of thought that have already been presented. These include: (a) the role of the environment in development, (b) the impact of learning on development, and (c) the importance of function in contrast to structure in development.

In distinction from the psychoanalytic theory of development, which views development primarily through the growth of intrapersonal resources, and cognitive-developmental theory, which assumes that development is a function of direct growth experiences, social-learning theory has attempted to offer a different interpretation of development. This view purports to account for development through appraisal of the arrangements and history of experiences prepared and screened by adults surrounding the child during the formative years of life. Initially, according to this position, the young child is highly dependent upon adult resources requiring the continuous attention of the adult environment for his survival. Consequently, over time, the presence and activity of the socialization agent in the role of caretaker serve as the child's primary means for knowing and acting within a complex, forbidding environment. The social agent, from this perspective, acts as a transducer and interpreter of experiences leading, at least initially, to the child's acquisition and performance of specified social roles and behaviors, prestructured and predetermined by the adult. However, over time, as the child increases in maturity, the role of the social agent in learning decreases in proportion to the child's ability to engage in independent decision-making activities.

A second level of distinction refers to the impact of learning on development. In social-learning theory it is assumed that the basic principles of learning theory, which account for the acquisition and performance of varied behavior, may be applied to questions of social development. Specifically, in contrast to the qualitative differences in emotional development

Early Childhood

413

stressed by psychoanalytic theory, and qualitative distinctions in cognitive maturity surrounding behavior, as suggested by cognitive-developmental theory, social-learning theory argues that development may be explained primarily through accepted vehicles of learning. As such, social-learning theory views the acquisition of stimulus-response patterns, particularly through modeling, and the performance of observed behavioral sequences through the regulation of reinforcement arrangements as primary forces in affective and social behavior development.

The third area of difference among these theoretical positions concerns the importance of structure and function in development. In contrast to psychoanalysis and cognitive-developmental theory, social-learning theory is astructural. That is, among social learning theorists the notion of underlying structure, structural change, and stages, as prerequisites to development, are considered superfluous concepts. Rather, social-learning theory argues that the primary factor in assessing behavior should be the issue of whether the behavior in question serves or has served some functional role relative to behavioral adaptation. Specifically, this approach sees development as a flexible, changing phenomenon subject to the changing environment in contrast to the changing organism.

IMPLICATIONS

UNDERSTANDING YOURSELF AND OTHERS

Pope wrote, "Just as the twig is bent, the tree's inclined." The comparison of plants to human development is not truly valid because children are not twigs and adults are not trees. Man can shape his own destiny. Those who have lived and worked with exceptional children and adults know, as a matter of routine, that human behavior can be modified, and often in dramatic ways, with care and treatment. An example of such behavior modification comes from the experiences of one of the authors who performed a psychological analysis for a student at a university reading clinic. This young man's behavior had been so consistently annoying that it had aroused the frustration and anger of his teacher to the extent that she was almost ready to give up. Investigation of the student's life revealed a history of despair and lack of love. At birth he was unwanted; as an infant he cried for hours and no one came; as a young child he had temper tantrums which culminated in his banging his head against the wall until it was bruised and bloodied; still no one attended to him. The psychological tests revealed that this rebellious and seemingly callous young man was really craving for love, for some attention. But how could he now ask for humanity after such a long history of asking and receiving no answer? His teacher, after hearing about his past, said to the author, "Now I understand. And I'm going to love and teach that boy no matter what he does or says!"

It goes without saying that this young man's behavior did not long continue in the same pattern.

LIVING AND WORKING WITH CHILDREN
DURING EARLY CHILDHOOD

That all of us are enormously influenced by our early experiences is readily supported by research, but to really understand and to feel empathy for others we must take time to make a concentrated effort to get "inside their skins," to see the world through their eyes, and then to try to help them directly or indirectly, perhaps by encouraging the procurement of professional assistance. This is what is meant by "love thy neighbor." To love means to care and to care means to take responsibility for others. Thus an important characteristic of a loving person is the ability to translate love and knowledge into effective remediation or prevention action because, at times, love is not enough.

We further believe that self understanding often precedes understanding of others. The roots of self understanding, however, often reside in childhood experiences long since forgotten. It was through promoting such self understanding that one of the authors prevented the divorce of a couple with five children. The wife's problem was her husband's deep distrust of her; on the other hand, the husband believed his distrust to be perfectly normal. After a number of counseling sessions, the husband called with the exciting news that he now knew why he distrusted his wife. While dining with his parents, he noticed that his mother tasted every portion of food on the table before his father would eat it. Upon inquiry his father explained that this was the only way he could be sure that his food was safe to eat. Later the same day he saw his father checking the odometer in the car. Subsequent conversation revealed that his father was checking for evidence of any possible excursions by his wife! Now, after so many years, this man finally understood the reason for his distrustful behavior, and no one was happier than he; this knowledge saved his marriage.

Living and Working with Preschool Children

It is an awesome yet extremely exciting feeling to realize that we can do so much for children during their formative years, and to realize at the same time that we must let children develop spontaneously. To create a balance between *doing* and *letting* is difficult because it requires intimate knowledge of the dynamically changing child and the equally changing demands placed on him. What is an adequate amount of doing for one child may be the creation of a prison for the more independent and outgoing child. What is adequate freedom for one child may be interpreted by a less mature child as a sign of neglect or indifference. Ideally, all children need individually-tailored programs of guidance combined with sufficient opportunities to find their own best ways.

We stress that planned-for guidance and freedom are better than unplanned guidance. Parents who have done their homework by studying child psychology and development in light of the unique characteristics of their children will tend to do a better job of helping children in their diverse pathways to maturity. The messages for parents, teachers, child-care workers, or any person involved with children during these early years are clearer than they have ever been before. Here are some of them.

Children need caretakers, especially parents, who are emotionally "together" during this critical period. Caretakers who truly exhibit all the dimensions of love—care, respect, responsibility, and knowledge—provide the best models for children at this stage of development. Such emotional stability is most essential at this stage not only to counterbalance the growing child's emotional states of immaturity and turmoil but also to provide a positive background for emotional development.

In rearing children toward greater self-actualization, it is important for

Early
Childhood

415

parents and caretakers to set realistic limits, to trust them, to use a democratically oriented family structure, and to base correction on a rational-consistent approach rather than on authoritarianism, harshness, and corporal punishment.

As children develop and experiment with new realities they often need crutches to see them through difficult periods. As soon as they have the knowledge, skills, and disposition, they will gleefully drop the crutches as they progress toward greater independence.

The first lessons in mastering social roles often occur in the safety of play. Play for children is an important and serious business. It really would not be preposterous for a parent to put up a sign next to her child's sandbox stating "Please do not disturb. My child is busy developing his schemata." For Piaget play is learning at its best because the child is *living* it. For Freud, Erikson, and others, play is literally the king's highway for the child's gradual mastery over his environment.

The indoor-outdoor environment should be one that enhances the child's natural curiosity and exploratory needs, as well as his perceptions and motor movements. The child's environment should be designed with his present and changing characteristics as guidelines for the architect, home decorator, and furniture manufacturer. Such planned ecology would permit children to explore their own potentials in a safe and challenging environment.

Piaget says that children need to be challenged cognitively, but they should not be pushed too rapidly. Instead, they should be permitted to develop their present schemas to the fullest extent. They will then move on to new and more complex schemas on their own if these challenges are made available to them. As parents or caretakers we prepare the environments, whereas children, as active participants, take care of their own learning. This viewpoint reflects a tremendous trust in children, a trust which will become reciprocal with time.

Bruner has succeeded, in our opinion, in reconciling the above recommendation by Piaget with American eagerness to get ahead faster. Bruner agrees that we should not push the child, but he also insists that we can teach a child anything if we have the decency to present the information at the child's present level of thinking. Many schools are following Bruner's suggestion, as evidenced by the "new math," "new language," and "new physics" now being taught in many primary and elementary grades.

Finally, children need children. They need the experiences of being, interacting, competing, fighting, and loving together. They need these experiences to test in their own world what they have learned in the adult world. It is out of such experiences that we increase the chances of producing more children with self-actualizing characteristics.

DEVELOPING POSITIVE MODELS

Children identify with and model much of their behavior and attitudes after their parents and caretakers. This means that if we desire children who are moving toward self-actualization, then we too must strive for greater self-actualization. If we want children who are moving toward rational-altruistic behavior, we must practice social justice for all. If we want children who are developing the capacity for brotherly love, we must learn to love the stranger, the unwanted, and even those whom we think we despise. Otherwise, how can we teach our children to be what we are not?

The Life
Cycle

416

The qualities inherent in a loving person or one with a maturing self-concept do not develop from limbo. They develop from one's having had many experiences of trust, care, and good will. They arise out of shared fantasy and play experiences with friends, out of a close relationship with a brother or sister. They are also produced by a father or mother who takes time to share joyful moments in the home, in the neighborhood, or on a trip together. They come from the love shown by the first-grade teacher who takes the time to give a frightened child his first lesson in the family car. They come from experiences with relatives, friends, and neighbors of all ages and ethnic backgrounds.

Love for animals and even the experience of taking care of a house plant can help to produce these qualities. All of these are ways we can increase the chances of developing more fully human children during early childhood.

CHAPTER REFERENCES

ABERCROMBIE, M. L. J. et al. Visual, perceptual and visiomotor impairment in physically handicapped children. *Perceptual and Motor Skills*. Monograph Supplement 3-v18, 1964.

ABRAVANEL, E. The development of intersensory patterning with regard to selected spatial dimensions. *Monographs of the Society for Research in Child Development*, 1968, 33:2.

AMES, L. B. Bilaterality. *Journal of Genetic Psychology*, 1949, 95:45–50.

BANDURA, A. and R. H. WALTERS. *Social learning and personality development*. New York: Holt, 1963.

BAYLEY, N. Development and maturation. In H. Helson (ed.), *Theoretical foundations of psychology*. New York: Van Nostrand, 1951.

BEYRL, F. On size perception in children. In Y. Brackbill and G. G. Thompson (eds.), *Behavior in infancy and early childhood*. New York: Free Press, 1967.

BLOOM, B. S. *Stability and change in human characteristics*. New York: Wiley, 1964.

BRONFENBRENNER, U. Developmental theory in transition. In H. W. Stevenson (ed.), *Child psychology*, 62nd yearbook of the National Society of Education. Chicago: U. of Chicago, 1963.

BRUNER, J. *The process of education*. Cambridge, Mass: Harvard U. P., 1960.

———. *Toward a theory of instruction*. Cambridge, Mass.: Harvard U. P., 1966.

———, R. R. OLIVER, P. M. GREENFIELD et al. *Studies in cognitive growth*. New York: Wiley, 1966.

BRYAN, F. E. How large are children's vocabularies? *Elementary School Journal*, 1953, 54:210–216.

CASTKER, B. M. Handedness and eyedness of children referral to a guidance clinic. Psychological Records, 1939, 3:99–112.

CATALANO, F. L. and D. McCARTHY. Infant speech as possible predictor of later intelligence. *Journal of Psychology*, 1954, 38:203–209.

CAZDEN, C. *Environmental assistance to the child's acquisition of grammar*, unpublished doctoral dissertation. Harvard Graduate School of Education, 1965.

CHOMSKY, N. *Language and mind*. New York: Harcourt, 1968.

COLEMAN, J. S. *Equality of educational opportunity*. Washington, D.C.: U.S. Gov. Printing Office, 1966.

CRATTY, B. J. *Perceptual and motor development in infants and children*. New York: Macmillan, 1970.

DAVE, R. H. *The identification and measurement of environmental process vari-*

ables that are related to educational success. Unpublished Ph.D. Dissertation. U. of Chicago, 1963.

DELACATO, C. H. *Treatment and prevention of reading problems.* Springfield, Ill.: Thomas, 1959.

———. *Neurological organization and reading.* Springfield, Ill.: Thomas, 1966.

THE DOMAN-DELACATO TREATMENT OF NEUROLOGICALLY HANDICAPPED CHILDREN. *Archives of Physiological Medical Rehabilitation,* 1968, **49**:183–186.

EICHORN, D. H. Variation in growth rate. In H. D. Behrens and G. Maynard (eds.), *The changing child.* Glenview, Ill.: Scott, Foresman, 1972.

ELKIND D., R. R. KOEGLER and E. Go. Studies in perceptual development: 2. Part-whole perception. *Child Development,* 1964, **35**:81–90.

ENTWISLE, D. R. Semantic systems of children: some assessments of social class and ethnic differences. In F. Williams (ed.), *Language and poverty.* Chicago: Markham, 1970.

ERIKSON, E. H. *Childhood and society.* New York: Norton, 1963.

FALKNER, F. The problems of estimating the effect of severe illness on physical growth of children. *American Journal of Diseases of Children,* 1960, **100**:587.

———. General consideration in human development. In F. Falkner (ed.), *Human development.* Philadelphia: Saunders, 1966.

FERGUSON, A. et al. Growth and development of Negro infants: 6. Relationship of certain environmental factors to neuromuscular development during the first year of life. *Journal of Pediatrics,* 1956, **48**:308–313.

FERNALD, G. *Remedial techniques in basic school skills.* New York: McGraw-Hill, 1943.

FINK, M. and M. B. BENDER. Perception of simultaneous tactile stimuli in normal children. *Neurology,* 1953, **3**:27–34.

FLAVELL, J. H. *The developmental psychology of Jean Piaget.* New York: Van Nostrand, 1963.

FLESHER, I. Ocular-manual laterality and perceptual rotation of literal symbols. *General Psychology Monographs,* 1962, **66**:3–48.

FURTH, H. G. *Piaget for teachers.* Englewood Cliffs, N. J.: Prentice-Hall, 1970.

GIBSON, E. J. *Child psychology.* Chicago: Natural Society for the Study in Education, 1963.

——— and R. D. WAIK. The effect of prolonged exposure to visually presented patterns of learning to discriminate them. *Journal of Comparative Physiology and Psychology,* 1956, **49**:239–242.

GIBSON, J. J. and E. J. GIBSON. Perceptual learning: differentiation or enrichment? *Psychological Review,* 1955, **62**:32–41.

GOLDSTEIN, A. G. and E. MACKENBER. Recognition of human faces from isolated facial feature: a developmental study. *Psychonomic Science,* 1966, **6**:149–150.

GOLLIN, E. S. Developmental studies of visual recognition of incomplete objects. *Perceptual and Motor Skills,* 1960, **11**:289–298.

GOUGH, H. G. and D. R. PETERSON. The identification and measurement of predispositional factors in crime and delinquency. *Journal of Consulting Psychology,* 1952, **16**:207–212.

GREULICH, W. W. A comparison of the physical and mental development of American-born and native Japanese children. *American Journal of Physiology and Anthropology,* 1957, **15**:489–515.

HAVIGHURST, R. J. Social backgrounds: their impact on children. In T. H. Horn (ed.), *Readings for the disadvantaged.* New York: Harcourt, 1970.

HEBB, D. O. *Organization of behavior: a neurological theory.* New York: Wiley, 1948.

HILDRETH, G. H. Development and training of hand dominance: characteristics of handedness; developmental tendencies in handedness; origins of handedness and lateral dominance. *Journal of Genetic Psychology,* 1949, **75**: 197–275.

HUNT, J. McV. *Intelligence and experience.* New York: Ronald, 1961.

HURLOCK, E. B. *Child development.* New York: McGraw-Hill, 1964.

ILLINGWORTH, R. S. *The development of the infant and young child: normal and abnormal.* Baltimore: Williams & Wilkins, 1971.

JACKSON, R. L. and H. G. KELLY. Growth charts for use in pediatric practice. *Journal of Pediatrics,* 1945, **27**:215–229.

JENSEN, A. R. Learning abilities in Mexican-American and Anglo-American children. *California Journal of Educational Psychology,* 1961, **12**:4.

JERSILD, A. T. *Child psychology.* Englewood Cliffs, N. J.: Prentice-Hall, 1968.

KEPHART, N. C. *The slow learner in the classroom.* Columbus, Oh.: Merrill, 1960.

KESSEN, W. Research in the psychological development of infants: an overview. *Merrill-Palmer Quarterly of Behavior and Development,* 1963, **9**:83–94.

KIDD, A. H. and J. L. RIVOIRE (eds.). *Perceptual development in children.* London: U. of London, 1967.

KOHLBERG, L. Stage and sequence: the cognitive-developmental approach to socialization. In D. A. Goslin (ed.), *Handbook of Socialization Theory and Research.* Chicago: Rand McNally, 1969.

LANGER, J. *Theories of development.* New York: Holt, 1969.

Learning to talk. Bethesda, Md.: National Institutes of Health, 1969.

LENNEBERG, E. H. *Biological foundations of language.* New York: Wiley, 1967.

LUGO, J. O. Analysis of junior college reading problems. In G. L. Hershey and J. O. Lugo (eds.), *Teaching psychology at the two-year college,* Monograph 1. New York: Macmillan, 1969.

MACCOBY, E. E., E. M. DOWLEY and J. W. HAGEN. Activity level and intellectual functioning in normal preschool children. *Child Development,* 1965, **314**(36):761–770.

McCARTHY, D. Language development. In L. Carmichael (ed.), *Manual of child psychology,* 2nd ed. New York: Wiley, 1954.

McNEIL, D. The development of language. In P. H. Mussen (ed.), *Carmichael's manual of child psychology.* New York: Wiley, 1970.

MEILI-DWORETZKI, G. The development of perception in Rorschach. In B. Klopter (ed.), *Developments, in the Rorschach technique: vol 2, fields of application.* Yonkers, N. Y.: World Book, 1956.

MERRELL, D. J. Dominance of eye and hand. *Human Biology,* 1957, **29**:314–328.

METFESSEL, N. S. and M. W. SENG. Correlates with school success and failure of economically disadvantaged children. In T. H. Hurn (ed.), *Readings for the disadvantaged.* New York: Harcourt, 1970.

MEYER, E. Comprehension spatial relations in preschool children. *Journal of Genetic Psychology,* 1940, **57**:119–151.

ORTON, S. T. Visual functions in trephsymbolia. *Archives of Ophthalmology,* 1943, **30**:707–717.

PARTEN, M. B. Social play among pre-school children. *Journal of Abnormal and Social Psychology,* 1932, **27**:243–269.

PERIN, C. The effect of delayed reinforcement upon the differentiation of fear responses in white rats. *Journal of Experimental Psychology,* 1943, **32**: 95–109.

PIAGET, J. *The child's conception of physical causality.* New York: Harcourt, 1930.

———. *The child's conception of the world.* Totowa, N. J.: Littlefield, Adams, 1969.

———. *Judgment and reasoning in the child.* N. Y.: Harcourt, 1928.

———. *The origins of intelligence in children.* New York: Norton, 1963.

———. *Play, dreams, and imitation in childhood.* New York: Norton, 1962.

Early
Childhood

————. *Science of education and the psychology of the child*. New York: Orion, 1970.

———— and B. INHELDER. *The child's conception of space*. New York: Humanities, 1956.

PICK, A. D. Improvement of visual and tactual form of discrimination. *Journal of Experimental Psychology*, 1965, **69**:331–339.

PRADER, A., J. M. TANNER and G. S. VON HARNACK. Catch-up growth following illness or starvation; and example of developmental canalisation in man. *Journal of Pediatrics*, 1963, **62**:646–659.

PRESCOTT, E. and E. JONES. Day care for children: assets and liability, *Children*, 1971, **18**:2.

PULASKI, M. A. S. *Understanding Piaget*. New York: Harper, 1971.

REESE, H. W. and L. P. LIPSITT. *Experimental child psychology*. New York: Academic, 1970.

RHEINGOLD, H. L. The development of social behavior in the human infant. In H. W. Stevenson (ed.), *Concept of development* (Monographs of the Society for Research in Child Development, Serial No. 107), 1966, **31**(5): 1–17.

ROSENZWEIG, N. R., D. KRECH and E. L. BENNETT. A search for relations between brain chemistry and behavior. *Psychology Bulletin*, 1960, **57**:476–492.

RUDEL, R. G. and H. L. TEUBER. Discrimination of direction of line in children. *Journal of Comparative and Physiological Psychology*, 1963, **56**:892–898.

SALE, J. S., C. W. MILICH, Y. L. TORRES, M. P. DAVIS, J. D. NICHOLIE and M. R. PEPYS. *Open the door-see the people*. Pasadena, Calif.: Pacific Oaks College, 1972.

SCHIFFER, C. G. and E. P. HUNT. *Illness among children*. Washington, D. C.: Children Bureau, 1963.

————, ————. *Illness among children*. Washington, D. C.: U. S. Department of Health, Education and Welfare, Children's Bureau Publication 405, 1968.

SKINNER, B. F. *Verbal behavior*. New York: Appleton, 1957.

SPIKER, C. C. Research methods in children's learning. In P. H. Mussen (ed.), *Handbook of research methods in child development*. New York: Wiley, 1960.

SPITZER, R. L. et al. The relationship between mixed dominance and reading disability. *Journal of Pediatrics*, 1959, **54**:76–80.

STAATS, A. and C. K. STAATS. *Complex human behavior*. New York: Holt, 1964.

STEPHENS, W. E., E. S. CUNNINGHAM and B. J. STIGLER. Reading readiness and eye-hand preference patterns in first grade children. *Exceptional Children*, 1967, **33**:481–488.

STEVENSON, H. W. Piaget behavior theory, and intelligence. In W. Kessen, and C. Kuhlman (eds.), *Thought in the young child*. Chicago: U. of Chicago, 1962.

TALBOT, N. B. and M. C. HOWELL. Social and behavioral causes and consequences of disease among children. In N. B. Talbot, J. Kagan, and L. Eisenberg (eds.), *Behavioral science in pediatric medicine*. Philadelphia: Saunders, 1971.

TANNER, J. M. The regulation of growth. *Child Development*, 1963, **34**:817–847.

TEMPLIN, M. Certain language skills in children, their development and relationship. U. of Minnesota: *Institute of Child Welfare Monograph Series*, no. 26, 1957.

Toward a social report. Washington, D.C.: U. S. Dept. of Health, Education, and Welfare, 1969.

TUDDENHAM, P. D. and M. M. SNYDER. Physical growth of California boys and girls from birth to eighteen years. *University of California Publication in Child Development*, 1954, 2:183–364.

VURPILLOT, E. Détails caractéristiques et reconnaissance de formes familières. *Psychologie Française*, 1962, 7:147–155.

WATSON, E. H. and G. H. LOWREY. *Growth and development of children*, 3rd ed. Chicago: Year Book Publishers, 1958.

WERNER, H. *Comparative psychology of mental development*. New York: Science Editions, 1961.

WHITE, S. H. Learning. In H. W. Stevenson (ed.), *Child Psychology*. Chicago: U. of Chicago, 1963.

WHITSELL, L. J. Delacato's neurological organization: a medical appraisal. *California School Health*, 1967, 3:1–13.

WIDDOWSON, E. M. and G. C. KENNEDY. Rate of growth, mature weight and life-span. *Proceedings of the Royal Society of Medicine*, 156, 96–108, 1962.

WOHLWILL, J. F. and M. WIENER. Discrimination of form orientation in young children. *Child Development*, 1964, 35:1113–25.

WOODRUFF, C. W. *Preschool child nutrition: Primary deterrent to human progress*. Washington, D. C.: Natural Academy of Sciences, 1966.

ZANGWILL, O. L. Dyslexia in relation to cerebral dominance. *Reading Disability*. Baltimore: Johns Hopkins, 1962.

RECOMMENDED FURTHER READING

ADLER, S. J. and R. C. TERRY. *Your overactive child: normal or not?* New York: Medcom, 1972.

ALMY, M. *Young children's thinking*. New York: Teacher's College Press, 1966.

BEADLE, M. *A child's mind*. Garden City, N. Y.: Doubleday, 1970.

BRIM, O. G. Education for child rearing. New York: Russell Sage, 1959.

BROWN, R. W. *Words and things*. Beverly Hills, Calif.: Glencoe, 1958.

COHEN, Y. A. *Man in adaptation, the biosocial background*. Chicago: Aldine, 1968.

HILDEBRAND, V. *Introduction to early childhood education*. New York: Macmillan, 1971.

MONTESSORI, M. *Spontaneous activity in education*. New York: Schocken, 1965.

PINES, M. *Revolution in learning: the years from birth to six*. New York: Harper, 1966.

TINKER, M. A. *Preparing your child for reading*. New York: Holt, 1972.

TODD, V. E. *The aide in early childhood education*. New York: Macmillan, 1973. ——— and H. HEFFERMAN. *The years before school*. New York: Macmillan, 1970.

Early
Childhood

Later Childhood

JAMES O. LUGO, Ph.D.
Fullerton College, Calif.

STEWART COHEN, Ph.D. *
University of Rhode Island

Prelude
Basic Theory and Research
  Biological Domain
    Physical Growth and Health
    Illnesses, Handicaps, and
      Accidents
    Motor and Perceptual-Motor
      Development
  Cognitive Domain
    Learning and Thinking
    Language Development

Bilingual-bicultural Education
Pathways to School Success
Creativity
Social Domain
  Social Factors in Development
Affective and Social Domain
  Identification
  Sex-Role Development
  Moral Development
  Aggression

* Dr. Cohen contributed the sections on the Social and the Affective and Social Domains.

Implications
   Understanding Yourself and
     Others
   Living and Working with Chil-
     dren During Middle Childhood
   Developing Positive Models

PRELUDE

THE CONCEPT of middle-childhood, as we learned in Chapter 2, is a fairly recent invention of Western civilization. Today the distinct and separate treatment of children from the ages of about six to twelve is common all over the world except for primitive societies in which children of this age are simply accepted as the youngest members of the adult society.

This realization of the recency of the concept of childhood, in addition to the different interpretations of what childhood means to contemporary societies both outside and within the United States, should make us aware of the diversity of behaviors that fall within middle-childhood. We must avoid the ethnocentrism that all children throughout the world behave in the same ways as children in our society with the naive but widespread assumption "that's the way children behave naturally." It was not long ago that it was "natural" for children to share with adults the same games, toys, drinks, and fairy tales.

Modern research into childhood has revealed many common development characteristics for this age period. In order to better understand childhood, we continue to turn our major attention to these underlying and common characteristics. We believe that it is better for the student of human development to concentrate on what is known about the basic psychological, biological, and sociological processes that undergird and modify behavior now and, later, to read about the fascinating, changing, and almost endless ways in which different children manifest these basic processes as reported by anthropologists, sociologists, and psychologists in other books.

BASIC THEORY AND RESEARCH

BIOLOGICAL DOMAIN

During the later childhood stage, the child is more concerned about actual physical growth and motor competency than he is with the psychological implications of the body image. During adolescence, however, a sharp increase in concern about the psychological significance of the body and its functions takes place.

The importance of physical competencies for cognitive development is revealed in that the three foremost theories of child development agree that motor skills are important for the advancement of learning and thinking in young school-aged children. Piaget believes that physical competencies are actually "action instruments" for assimilating new actions into new schemas in accordance with the newly emerging cognitive structures of the concrete

Later
Childhood

operational stage. In a similar light, learning theorists view the motor skills of the body in terms of their ability to produce new responses for conditioning purposes. In other words, by increasing the repertoire of motor responses we also increase the probability that new learning will occur. For Freudians, of course, the structure and functioning of the body literally determines the child's psychological destiny. Nevertheless, even for the psychoanalysts, this time of life is ideal for increased learning. The child is now entering the latency period when, at least theoretically, all will be quiet on the "sexual front." Because of the ego defense mechanisms, such as repression and sublimation, the sexual energies are partially channeled into substitute activities such as intellectual and cognitive interests. Thus the three major theories of child development stress the importance of the biological domain for cognitive growth during the period of early schooling.

In this section the major topics include physical adequacy, integrated health, motor development, and perceptual-intellectual motor development. The major focus is on a healthy biological domain for its own value and as a foundation for greater cognitive competency, which, in turn, should facilitate social and affective competencies.

Physical Growth and Health

The years from six to pubescence are characterized by slow but steady physical growth; that is, the gain per unit of time during this period is not as great as it was during the preschool period or as it will be during the adolescent period. The gains in height during this period are, however, not as great as the gains in the child's weight. The average six-year-old boy, about three and a half feet tall, will reach a height of about five feet by age thirteen (start of pubescence), a height reached by girls by age eleven (start of pubescence) (Nicolson and Hanley, 1953). By contrast, the average weight of the child doubles during the same time period from about forty to eighty pounds.

The basic pattern of body build also changes to the extent that there will be greater variation among the bodies of children at the end of this period than there were when it started. In both sexes, the trunk and arms lengthen and the trunk and hips broaden; the entire skeletal structure becomes bigger and broader. Up to the end of this period, it is very difficult to tell boys from girls solely on the basis of their body shapes and sizes. Sex differences, although present since birth, are further obscured because individual differences within each sex membership are greater than the average difference between the sexes.

During the early school years it is possible to recognize the general kind of physique a child is likely to have as an adult and to seek medical advice for the extreme cases. In addition, physique type may be important for predicting future personality, since, according to Sheldon (1944) there is a low positive but consistent relationship of about +.40 between physique and personality characteristics. The three basic components of physique, endomorphy, ectomorphy, and mesomorphy are present in all of us, although in some children one component may strongly dominate the other two. The endomorph is characterized by round body contours because of large amounts of fat and tends to be slow-moving, placid, jovial (at least on the surface), and obese. The ectomorph is characterized by thin bones, weak muscles, and tends to be introverted, sensitive, and restless. Ectomorphs tend to be the smallest children in the group until adolescence when they spurt up to be among the tallest of adults. The mesomorph is characterized by broad shoulders, heavy skeleton, and large, strong muscles. As expected, mesomorphs tend to be aggressive, action-oriented, and direct.

Although Sheldon's findings have been supported by some investigators, others have failed to replicate his findings. Nevertheless, common sense reveals that physique does play an important role in motor as well as in personality development. In one study with seven-year-olds, it was found that boys with weak muscular development displayed more anxiety; stocky boys showed greater ability to communicate and a higher degree of aggressiveness; and boys with above-average fatty tissue were more self-confident (Davidson, et al., 1957). Predictions about behavior from somatotypes of preschoolers, aged two-and-a-half to five, yielded the best results for mesomorphs in the expected direction, moderate success for ectomorphs, but failed in the case of endomorphs (Walker, 1962). When a group of psychologically healthy college students were compared with a group that had been advised to seek psychological help, the majority in the latter group tended to be ectomorphs and endomorphs (Parnell, 1957). On the other hand, research by Glueck and Glueck (1962) among juvenile delinquents and adults found a high incidence of mesomorphs.

It seems that children who have developed high levels of self-esteem, as a result of their feeling wanted and loved, will develop corresponding feelings about their bodies (Watson and Johnson, 1958). Thus, feeling good about one's self psychologically helps the child to also develop respect for the body. Naturally, as the child enters school, the adequacy of his body image may be challenged by the peer group, especially if his body form deviates too far from the local norms. What happens to the child depends on the strength of the individual's self-esteem and the consistency, force, and reality-contact of the critics' comments. The child may withstand the assaults successfully, or he may seek help to improve his body image.

A study of the children's wishes reveals the general ethos of this period of life (Cobb, 1954). Boys wish to be bigger and girls wish to be more attractive, but these wishes are rarely as powerful as the wishes to be successful academically and socially. Because young schoolchildren tend to be more concerned about social and psychological success than physical characteristics, caretakers may have to take more than the ordinary precautions about the physical well-being of their children.

Physical health primarily means the condition of the inner body. The evaluation of the health of the inner body is much more difficult than that of the visible body. Even though alert parents learn to become sensitive to minor physical cues and the accuracy of the reporting by their children, the final diagnosis of ill health requires medical opinion. The middle years, however, are fairly healthy despite the fact that, according to the National Health Survey (Schiffer and Hunt, 1968), 17.5 per cent of children under fifteen years of age have some chronic impairment and 1.5 per cent are restricted in their normal activities because of such illnesses.

Illnesses, Handicaps, and Accidents

Illnesses. Acute illnesses, which are by far the most common, are fairly stable throughout life, whereas chronic ones increase with age. Acute illnesses occur more often in females at all ages despite their longer life spans

FIG. 17-1.

(Whipple, 1966). For both sexes, however, the age of greatest vulnerability to disease is during the preschool period.

Respiratory diseases continue to form the bulk of acute illnesses during middle-childhood and throughout life. In one study of children, aged two through seventeen, over 45 per cent reported at least one cold per year (Bayer and Snyder, 1950). Infectious diseases, such as measles, chicken pox, whooping cough, and mumps, constitute the second most prevalent form of illness. In the 1950's, the incidence of infectious diseases continued unabated throughout life, despite the fact that if a child suffered one attack it tended to make him relatively immune from that disease. During the 1960's, as a result of immunizations, the incidence of measles and especially whooping cough has been significantly reduced. The third most frequent form of acute childhood illnesses is those of the gastrointestinal tract. However, this incidence declines very sharply after age two and then gradually until the start of middle childhood when it increases gradually until about age ten.

Handicaps. Physical handicaps are always potentially damaging psychologically. The extent of the psychological damage depends on such variables as: (1) type, durability, severity, and visibility of the handicap; (2) the age of the child at the onset of the handicap (the younger the child the easier will be the adjustment); and (3) the psychological integrity of the

The Life
Cycle

child and the amounts and kinds of psychosocial supports that are available.

The following handicaps afflict 9 per cent of all persons under age twenty-one (Harper, 1962): (1) seeing and hearing difficulties account for 1 per cent; (2) major speech defects account for about 1.7 per cent; (3) orthopedic problems including foot defects account for 1.7 per cent; (4) all grades of cardiac cases account for 1 per cent; and (5) all grades of mental retardation account for 3 per cent (usually IQ's below 70). Other handicaps such as cerebral palsy (.05 per cent) and epilepsy (.05 per cent) are included in the figure of 17.5 per cent given by the National Health Survey for chronic impairment in children under fifteen years of age.

Neither of these surveys includes the wide range of handicaps caused by acute and chronic brain disorders, which account for approximately 15 million cases in the United States, and emotional disturbance, which is the single greatest obstacle to optimal functioning for all human beings. Fortunately, the vast majority of these ailments do not involve serious disorders. However, within the classification of brain disorders, there are many school-aged children with *minimal brain dysfunction* who, despite their normal intelligence, have great difficulty learning in the school situation. The most common label for children with this kind of learning disability is the neurologically handicapped child.[1]

Neurological Handicaps. Although the final diagnosis depends upon a thorough psychological-medical evaluation, it is important for caretakers to be aware of some of the typical behaviors of these children in order to seek the necessary help. Like any normal group of children they are not mentally retarded, not emotionally disturbed, not physically crippled, and not gifted, although they can manifest some of these characteristics to varying degrees. It is difficult to estimate the number of children with neurological handicaps (NH) because of the recency of awareness of this problem and the lack of accurate studies. Estimates range from 1 to about 15 per cent. The New York Association for Brain Injured Children estimates that there are about 3 million such children in the United States.[2] All reports, however, agree that the problem is much more common among boys than it is among girls.

The following description of an NH boy is from the records of one of the authors. During the preschool period he was an alert boy, above average in intelligence, and markedly superior in physical coordination. After three years of schooling, the boy had not learned to read or write and was classified by the school authorities as mentally retarded and placed into a special program. The boy's parents were nonplussed about the fact that their alert and normal boy was classified mentally retarded. Five years later the boy, now in the eighth grade, still could not read or write. In desperation, the parents took him to a large university medical center. The diagnosis was neurologically handicapped with normal intelligence and no emotional disturbance. The author tutored him for one hour a day for one year with the techniques used at the Fernald School, UCLA. The boy gained over five

[1] Other names found in the literature include brain-injured child, child with dyslexia, hyperkinetic child, perceptually handicapped child, neurophysical immaturity, hyperactive child, and child with specific learning disorder.

[2] New York Association for Brain Injured Children, 305 Broadway, New York, New York 10007; California Association for Neurologically Handicapped Children, P.O. Box 604, Main Office, Los Angeles, California 90053; National Society for Crippled Children and Adults, 2023 West Ogden Avenue, Chicago, Illinois 60612.

years in reading, spelling, and arithmetic based on standardized test scores.

The official definition of the United States Office of Education of minimal brain dysfunction is (Ontario Association for Children with Learning Disabilities):

> . . . Under the term minimal brain dysfunction and learning disabilities shall be those children of near, average or above average ability with learning and/or behavior difficulties ranging from mild to most severe, which are due to subtle deviations arising from genetic variations, biochemical irregularities, perinatal brain insults, and/or illnesses and injuries sustained during the years critical for the development and maturation of those parts of the central nervous system having to do with perception, language, inhibition of impulses, and motor control. (p. 3)

In the early years, the symptoms of neurological impairment are not readily recognized by the average parent or teacher. After repeated failure the symptoms become more and more salient. A nationwide survey of professional centers and people working with NH children yielded the ten most commonly named characteristics (Clements, 1963):

1. Normal or above average general intelligence.
2. Specific learning deficits.
3. Perceptual-motor deficits.
4. General coordination deficits.
5. Hyperkinesis (or less frequently, *hypo*kinesis).
6. Impulsivity.
7. Emotional lability.
8. Short attention span and/or distractibility.
9. "Equivocal" or "soft" neurological signs.
10. Borderline abnormal or abnormal electroencephalograms (EEG).

All NH children will not demonstrate all of these symptoms, and there are additional symptoms such as lack of neurological organization (hand-and-eye coordination), more than usual reversals in reading and/or writing, difficulty in forming visual and oral discrimination of similar letters and sounds, and poor reading but adequacy in other school subjects (Kephart, 1963). Many of these children after treatment will be able to learn just like normal children with the usual school methods. Until the teaching of NH children becomes a part of the regular school program, it will be up to the parents or caretakers to trust their own opinions as to whether a child shows some of these symptoms and to obtain the required professional care, if necessary.

Accidents. In the United States, accidents are the single greatest cause of death between ages one and thirty-seven (McFarland and Moore, 1971). In one year, 1960, almost 70 per cent of children under age sixteen were injured in an accident. For the first year of life food and object poisoning produce the greatest number of fatalities. The next four major causes of deaths of infants are motor vehicle accidents, fires and explosions, drowning, and falls in that order, with deaths in automobile accidents increasing with the age of the child. In addition to fatalities, many children who survive are crippled and/or disfigured for long periods of time of for life as a result of accidents. Children between ages two and three are the most vulnerable to accidents, and those between five and six years are the second most accident-prone. About two-thirds of all childhood accidents occur before the age of nine, with accidents involving males exceeding accidents involving females at all age levels (Backett and Johnston, 1959; White, 1969).

As children become less egocentric the number of accidents in which they are involved are reduced. Perhaps an important preventative variable is the child's ability to internalize safety rules and to anticipate what could happen under certain circumstances. The need for adult supervision during these early years is revealed by the increased accident statistics when the mother or caretaker is ill, working, or busy with other children. A second important variable is probably the presence of unusual emotional stress that can lead to internal preoccupation instead of external vigilance. Studies of accident-prone children and adults support this hypothesis (Krall, 1953; Backett and Johnston, 1959).

In the final analysis, the heavy burden of responsibility rests on our shoulders—parents, caretakers, and concerned citizens. For example, the statistics that almost three hundred thousand children under the age of fifteen suffered nonfatal injuries in motor vehicle accidents in one year, and that motor vehicles are the single biggest killer of our children are unbelievably ghastly (Accident Facts, 1967). If our society truly loved its children, it would declare an immediate total war against that which hurts and kills them. We have the technology and the money to do so; the only real question is do we have the heart. Perhaps, someday, concerned citizens will consider the health and safety of our children to be the nation's top priority.

Integrated Health. As we have emphasized repeatedly, the soundness of body depends on more than just the prevention and treatment of diseases and injuries. The inner body is also psychological and social. In order to feel good on the inside, the child must come to good terms with the totality of messages coming from within whether they are physical, psychological, or social. If any of these internal cues elicits discomfort or anxiety, then the child is not living harmoniously with himself. A child, based on our holistic definition, is healthy only when he can successfully integrate all that comes from within with the realities of personal and social living. For example, if a child cannot cope adequately with hostile or erotic impulses and subsequently feels hopeless and frustrated, then the child cannot be considered to be in a state of integrated mental health.

Physiology and Stress. By age six the physiological processes of the child have stabilized considerably and will continue to do so during the school years. His pulse rate, for example, which was about 100 at age two will now range between 70 and 80. Physiologically, the entering schoolchild is better able to cope with stress whether it is biological or psychological.

Even at birth there are wide individual differences in physiological reaction to both normal stimulation and disturbing stress (Birns, 1965). Those children with low levels of physiological reaction to stress tend to react on the physical level with the use of their large muscles. Based on the research of Eysenck (1960) on the relationship of faulty development to autonomic activity levels, children or adults at the two extremes of physiological reaction levels are more prone to personality difficulties. Children who over-react are more likely to develop unnecessarily strong conditioned fears and anxieties, whereas those who underreact are more likely to lack the necessary precautionary attitudes and competencies to avoid and to prevent similar stresses in the future.

Faulty Adaptation to Stress. All of us know how we feel during moments of intense feelings, such as fear and anger, even though we may be less aware of the accompanying physiological counterparts. In all cases, but especially for those who overreact for prolonged periods of time, adaptation to stress is expensive in terms of suffering and wear and tear, as we are reminded by Selye, a well-known neurosurgeon (1956):

> It is true that immediately after some harassing experience, rest can restore us almost to the original level of fitness by eliminating acute fatigue. But the emphasis is on *almost.* Since we constantly go through periods of stress and rest during life, just a little defect of adaptation energy every day adds up—it adds up to what we call *aging.* (p. 274)

Furthermore, the presence of severe negative emotions tends to reduce learning capacity in the same manner that positive emotions increase reasoning and problem solving (Hinkle et al., 1957).

The overreactive child needs more psychosocial supports than the average child if he is to avoid too many psychological hurts and subsequent feelings of inadequacy. He should be protected against overwhelming stress until he can master sufficient problem-solving mechanisms. The underreactive child also needs more than average psychosocial supports, because such a child is less likely to worry about stress-producing situations and because of his tendency to respond more physically to stress. He needs to develop greater inner controls and social awareness by being better informed about what to expect and do in potentially stressful situations. He needs to talk about worries and problems with people he trusts in order to develop a certain amount of realistic anxiety that may motivate him to become apprehensive about illnesses, accidents, and failures.

Psychosocial Somatic Disorders. Children normally release emotional tensions as a result of severe stress whether it is produced biologically, psychologically, or socially through physiological reactions (with accompanying subjective feelings), and/or physical activities (sports, impulsive acts), and/or cognitive processes (talking, reasoning). In many children, however, the emotional release occurs through its conversion into physical ailments or symptoms with or without underlying organic pathology by unknown mechanisms. Such physical ailments and symptoms from which no part of the body seems to be immune are referred to as *psychosomatic, psychophysiological,* or *visceral disorders* when there is some organic underlying pathology and *conversion reactions* or *hysteria* when there is no organic involvement. In line with our holistic approach to sickness and health, we refer to all of these disorders as *psychosocial somatic disorders.*

The importance of psychological factors in all forms of illness is undeniable. As we have mentioned, "psychosocial malnutrition" can aggravate strictly biologically rooted diseases and injuries. In the case of psychosocial somatic disorders the consequences of social and psychological sufferings are revealed in an almost endless array of ailments including severe headaches, gastrointestinal disturbances such as ulcers, paralysis, skin problems,

The Life
Cycle

allergies, blindness, and so forth. Studies of such ailments typically reveal corresponding problems of adjustment (Hinkle, 1957).

There are a number of faulty parent-child relationships that may predispose children to such ailments. Anxiety over possible loss of parental acceptance may be seen in the "psychological crying" for nurturance by the asthmatic child. It would be, indeed, an extremely cold mother who would not respond, at least temporarily, to a child who is "gasping for life." In the case of one child with prolonged asthmatic attacks, it is not unusual for a second child to "join in" and develop similar symptoms (Starr, 1955).

A second faulty parent-child relationship is when a mother, who is domineering and overprotecting, overly restricts the child striving toward autonomy. The child, especially if he is a boy and if his father is passive and dependent, may have to cover up his justifiable anger and hostility (Goldberg, 1959). A third possibility exists when parents who value very high achievement have a child who cannot perform up to these standards. In the experience of one of the authors, these children are usually the second or third born after an academically very successful older child has set up the standards for the siblings to follow. Realistically, sometimes the only escape is an incapacitating "physical disorder" in order to become acceptable once again to the parents. Of course, pressure of this type may come from average-achievement parents when the child falls below standards. For example, one of the authors worked with a teenager who after many years of special lessons, was still a total nonreader. To the author's dismay, he was being confronted with his first failure in teaching remedial reading. In "desperation" a complete medical, psychological, and sociological examination was requested. The diagnosis, a fairly rare one, was periodical functional psychosocial somatic blindness. In other words, there were times when this boy could see, but there were other times when he could not see. The report of the social worker revealed an intense hatred for the boy by the father, a blue-collar worker, who sincerely believed that the heavy financial burden caused by the boy's failure to learn to read and frequent "unusual accidents," which probably were a result of his episodes of blindness, had ruined the father's chances for happiness in life. Fortunately, a state agency provided the boy with psychotherapy and sociotherapy (temporary separation from his father and free treatments).

As caretakers of children, we must be careful to see that such disorders are diagnosed correctly and the causes of excessive and prolonged emotional stress are removed. In many of these cases, in addition to medical care, some form of nonmedical therapy is required in the form of psychotherapy, which usually requires the inclusion of the parents, or sociotherapy, the remediation of undesirable social or family conditions. The accurate differential diagnosis between organic and psychosocial somatic disorder requires a holistic analysis by medical, psychological, and sociological personnel. Unfortunately such teamwork is fairly rare. Therefore, we would like to offer a few guidelines for developing hunches or guesses that a child's ailment is psychosocial somatic rather than organic:

1. The child's emotional state should match the severity of the illness. For example, a prolonged backache should elicit appropriate emotional concern. It is probably not normal for a child who cannot participate in everyday activities as a result of an incapacitating illness to react in a nonchalant or "contented" manner.

2. The child's present life situation should be studied. If there is evidence of an unresolved problem, the kind, severity, and extent of the ailment present may represent the biological solution to the psychological problem. For example, during World War II, it was found that under severe and continuous stress night fliers were more subject to night blindness, whereas those who flew daytime missions were more prone to failures in daytime vision (Ironside and Jorgensen, 1945).

3. There is repeated failure by the family doctor to cure the physical symptoms, because the excessive emotional stress remains unrelieved.

4. Sincere efforts should be made to help the child with unresolved problems. If this procedure does not work, a total-push effort should perhaps be started to make the child feel more wanted and loved. In some cases, such as enuresis, or bed-wetting after successful toilet training, the symptoms will disappear altogether. If the symptoms become somewhat less aggravated, this alone could be a sign that the problem is a psychosocial somatic disorder.

Health and Love. Just as the cognitive functioning of the child depends heavily on the richness of memories, so does his state of health depend heavily upon the child's history of being the recipient of love. During infancy, both the physiological and psychological systems are weak and unstable and therefore "easy game" for the ravages of stress. Early love and care are needed to protect both systems until they are strong enough to cope with the ordinary stresses of life. Freud taught us that a child is more prone to mental illness if his vulnerability to stress during early life was not carefully guarded. Grinker (1953) believes that the stage is set for later psychosocial somatic disorders if the infant's physiological defenses are attacked and weakened during its infancy stage of vulnerability. Levine's (1960) classical study with rats supports both Freud and Grinker in that early deprivation of love can reduce both physiological and psychological defenses against stress as well as learning ability. So it seems that the poets were right about love; that with love we flourish, that without it life withers.

Motor and Perceptual-Motor Development

During the middle-childhood years, several significant changes occur in the nature of and extent of gross and fine motor competencies. Motor competencies are increasingly being molded by the demands, values, and customs of society. Ultimately even the most liberally reared child must conform to most of the realities imposed by society on children of his age group.

In terms of pure pleasure there is a gradual decrease: in infancy, there seems to be sheer pleasure in doing and touching; in the preschool period, with its strong egocentric orientation, play and motor activities were the "child's work"; in middle-childhood elements of delight in motor play continue but it does not have to be necessarily strictly fun all the time. Children still play, but there is increasing concern with the effects of play on others, including the child's peers, parents, and teachers. The development of motor skills during this stage will now depend less upon spontaneous informal learning and more on the learning of rules of formalized, standardized, and even commercialized activities.

Perceptual and perceptual-motor competencies now develop very rapidly even though adultlike efficiency is not reached in all areas until very late in this stage or early in the adolescent stage. Intellectual ability and effort instead of perception will begin to play a major role in learning early in this stage. The relationship between school readiness and visual perceptual ability among kindergarten and first graders is about +.45, which is fairly high (Frostig et al., 1961), but by the second grade the correlation for perception is no longer significant. At this point, the positive correlation is between school success and intelligence test scores. Thus, during the preschool period we saw the switch from a primary emphasis on sensory to perceptual competency, and in the early school-age period we will see the switch from primary emphasis on perceptual to intellectual efforts.

Motor Development. The nervous system develops very rapidly during the early years. For all practical purposes, neurological maturity is reached by about age eight because subsequent growth is predominantly qualitative in character. Paralleling neurological development is the rapid expansion of both body and cognitive competencies. Furthermore, the physiological processes underlying these competencies have achieved a stage of maturity and stability that permits prolonged and strenuous physical exercises without causing exhaustion. Nevertheless, beginning school-age children are more physically ready in the use of large muscles than they are physiologically ready for sustained competitive athletics. Caution is required therefore to avoid unrestricted body-contact games.

Basic Motor Skills and Determinants. Basic motor skills from ages six to twelve improve steadily although not as rapidly as they did during the preschool years (Cratty, 1960; Cratty and Martin, 1969). By school entrance most children are proficient at jumping, skipping, hopping, and climbing a jungle gym with well-coordinated arm and leg movements. There are standardized measures of motor competency by which a child's progress can be compared with those of children his age and sex. Two such motor tests are the Lincoln-Oseretsky Motor Development Scale (Sloan, 1955) and the Kraus-Weber Test (Kraus and Hirschland, 1954). The first test, intended for children between ages six to fourteen, is mostly a measure of gross motor skills, although finger dexterity and eye-hand coordination are also included. The second test seeks to measure if the child has sufficient strength and flexibility to meet the demands of daily living and exercise.

Components of Motor Skills. When the great variety of motor skills are analyzed to account for poor or excellent performances, several basic components seem to stand out. One of these is strength, the amount of physical force exerted in terms of strength of hand grip. From ages six to twelve years there is a steady increase of such strength with consistent male superiority. Nevertheless, as Cratty (1960) stresses, measurements of strength based on only one part of the body can be misleading because muscular strength increases at different rates for the various portions of the body. For example, elbow flexion strength correlates only about +.40 with trunk flexion strength in boys from seven to nine years of age.

Reaction time, or the time interval between the presentation of a stimulus indicating the moment to begin a physical reaction and the length of time before the reaction begins, also increases steadily throughout the school years with boys reacting slightly faster than girls (Goodenough, 1935), except in fine motor movement reactions (Connolly et al., 1968). Cratty cautions that reaction time differs for the various parts of the body as well

Later Childhood

433

as the complexity of the motor tasks. Another difficulty is that there are many times when children and adults, very wisely, hesitate before they act. It is very difficult, therefore, to separate thinking time from reaction time. Among adults, thinking time may take ten times as long as reaction time.

Balance, the ability to maintain body control in static or moving positions, improves gradually during ages six to twelve as measured by beam-walking ability (Seashore, 1949). Although there are slight sex differences, girls between ages seven and nine are often superior to boys. By age six, most children can walk a beam that is at least two inches wide and can maintain static balance on one foot with their eyes closed (Cratty, 1960). Guilford (1958) in his analysis of psychomotor skills refers to additional components of motor abilities such as speed of movements for the body and its various parts, precision in terms of steadiness and aiming, smoothness of coordination of body parts, and flexibility as seen in bending and dancing.

Social Influences. To an important degree, what a particular society values will be cultivated there to a level of relative excellence. During the early 1950's the Kraus-Weber Test was administered widely throughout the United States, Austria, Italy, and Switzerland (Kraus and Hirschland, 1954). For all ages six through sixteen the European children were far superior to those tested in the United States in physical fitness as measured by strength and flexibility. Of course, there are other measures of physical fitness, but the publication of these results did result in an increased awareness of the need to improve physical fitness among children in the United States. The renewed interest even reached the White House, which established the president's physical fitness program. Perhaps, there has been a change of society's values; a repetition of these physical fitness studies may reveal significant improvements.

Socioeconomic influence on physical fitness is suggested by research that indicates that black American schoolchildren of both sexes demonstrate greater grip strength than their Anglo or Latin-American counterparts (Gross, 1968). It is understandable that blacks would seek to develop excellence in physical fitness to qualify for athletics where discrimination is minimal.

Motor Skills, Intelligence, and Perception. Practically all research reports indicate that there is little or no relationship between motor skills and intelligence test scores and academic achievement.

We would like to suggest, however, some reasons for the lack of correlation between physical fitness and intelligence and school achievement.

Children will seek success wherever they can most readily find it. Thus the intellectually gifted child may be more prone to seek success in the classroom, whereas the less gifted child may seek it in the playground or gym. Possibly, in later childhood, as play and games become more intellectually challenging, we may find a higher correlation between motor skills and intellectual achievement. A second reason is that a high correlation depends upon the existence of common elements in both conditions being compared. The contents of standard intelligence tests have nothing in common with gross motor skills and only very few elements similar to those found in fine motor skills.

Indirect support for the importance of motor activities for school achievement in terms of reading, writing, and arithmetic comes from a study by

The Life
Cycle

Ayres (1964) of one hundred school-age children who were failing in these school subjects because of visual perceptual deficits. Analysis of the reasons for these perceptual deficits led Ayres to conclude as follows:

> The finding is an indirect argument in favor of the theory that the development of visual perception is associated with tactile and kinesthetic perception. Since tactile and kinesthetic stimuli arise mainly from movement these data can be taken as support for approaches to visual training that involve gross motor activities. (p. 115)

In other words, if the possibility exists that motor activities facilitate visual perceptual development, which in turn is essential for learning how to read and write, then we should not hesitate in our efforts to assure children optimal motor development and exercise.

Switch from Perceptual to Intellectual Functioning. Perception, a midway process between sensory learning and learning by reasoning, becomes increasingly less important as a major avenue for learning during middle childhood. However, when there is a significant lag in perceptual development because of neurological handicaps, emotional disturbances, or a lack of appropriate experiences, the child is handicapped because he must make up for his deficit through increased intellectual and motivational efforts. It is a situation somewhat similar to that between figurative knowledge (perception) and operational knowledge (intelligence). Operational knowledge refers to information about a subject or object that is as complete as possible. Figurative knowledge is more like the imitation behavior of children that appears fullblown. The child may imitate a "doctor," but he cannot possibly understand what it means to be a doctor. Figurative learning is like perceptual learning in that both focus on the external surface characteristics of the world instead of the complex internal mechanisms and functioning that require active intellectual operations in the form of concepts, internal transformations, and logical judgments.

Since perceptual learning precedes and facilitates intellectual learning, we believe that all children entering school should be tested for lags in their visual perceptual development by school psychologists or counselors. The Gesell development examination for children aged five through ten years is described in detail in *School Readiness* by Ilg and Bates (1965). A second standardized examination is Frostig's Developmental Test of Visual Perception (1964). Children who score below recommended scores should receive special training in visual perception whether they are doing well in school or not. We realize that it sounds strange to recommend help for those children who are doing well, but these children are unduly compensating intellectually for their perceptual deficit. We suggest that these children are not happy in school because of the additional stress required to get grades that they could get with much less effort. By the second grade, most children have entered Piaget's third stage of cognitive development along with its increased ability to perform more complex intellectual operations. Children with perceptual lags need help so that they can dedicate all their intellectual energies to the tasks of doing well in school and living successfully in a more complex society. A truly happy child is one who can smile on the outside as well as the inside.

Later
Childhood

435

COGNITIVE DOMAIN

Concerning children, Burton L. White (1969) of the Laboratory of Human Development at Harvard University, has asked the question that no doubt has haunted the minds of all loving adults. "What specifically is human competence at age six?" *Nowhere in the literature could he or his associates find detailed descriptions of healthy well-developed six-year-old humans.* Of course, the same is true for children at all ages. For over five years, White has been trying to find observationally based measures of competence in the preschool child. Thus far White's best guesses as to competence at age six years are as follow:

SOCIAL ABILITIES

1. To get and maintain the attention of adults in socially acceptable ways.
2. To use adults as resources.
3. To express both affection and hostility to adults.
4. To lead and to follow peers.
5. To express both affection and hostility to peers.
6. To compete with peers.
7. To show pride in one's accomplishments.
8. To involve oneself in adult role-play behavior or to otherwise express a desire to grow up.

NONSOCIAL ABILITIES

1. Linguistic competence; i.e., grammatical capacity, vocabulary, articulation, and expressed language.
2. Intellectual competence
   a. the ability to sense dissonance or note discrepancies
   b. the ability to anticipate consequences
   c. the ability to deal with abstractions; i.e., numbers, letters, rules
   d. the ability to take the perspective of another
   e. the ability to make interesting associations.
3. Executive abilities
   a. the ability to plan and carry out multistepped activities
   b. the ability to use resources effectively.
4. Attentional ability
   the ability to maintain attention to a proximal task and at the same time to monitor peripheral events (called dual focus ability). (pp. 12–13)

In this section, in addition to the more well-grounded research, we offer additional "best guesses" for maximizing potential and happiness in childhood. When working with a child, we must do everything in our power to help even if it means trying things that are based on tentative findings or intuitive feelings. To do less, not to take risks until all the evidence is in, is to wait too long or to await eternity. Possibly the worst sin we can commit as caretakers of children is to permit a child's spirit to become mutilated while there is still a probability that some different or new approach may work.

The Life
Cycle

During the middle years, the child's capacity for thought and reasoning will change dramatically but it will not reach a level of mature adult capacity until formal operations begin to challenge the equilibrium of concrete operations beginning about age eleven and lasting throughout the life span. With the emerging cognitive competencies inherent in concrete operational thinking and increasing language facility, most children are ready to accept the challenges of formal education and increased peer contacts.

FIG. 17–2.

Learning and Thinking

We left the child at the preoperational stage of cognitive development in Chapter 16. He was then struggling to achieve equilibrium with an external world that would not bend or change despite his magical thoughts and precausal thinking. The preschool child tried to model the world after the only model he knew—himself—egocentric, wish-oriented, and full of life. Nevertheless, the physical world and people stubbornly refused to behave strictly according to his model. Now the schoolchild must accommodate to the complexities of the school situation, but he is developing powerful new mental operations and logic processes for doing so. Nevertheless, it will take several years or longer before he can replace egocentrism and preoperational thoughts as the only models for understanding the world.

The Concrete Stage. The hallmark of cognitive development during middle

Later
Childhood

437

childhood is the switch from dependency on perception as to how things look, to reasoning as the primary basis for conceptualizing the world. The child during this stage will learn to perform a variety of mental operations on concrete events, but the ability to think about thinking will have to wait until the development of formal operations. The characteristics of mental operations during the concrete operational stage—decreasing egocentrism, decentering, reversibility, and classificatory logic—will provide the child with the means for liberating himself further from the bondage of the physical world.

From Egocentrism to Other-Centeredness. According to Piaget, the process of moving from one cognitive stage to another depends on learning, and learning depends on establishing states of disequilibrium—a state of affairs with which the child's present schemas cannot cope. To establish equilibrium again the child must adapt to the new situation through the twin processes of assimilation and accommodation. In so doing he will develop new schemas and modify old ones. He is learning and, in the process of learning, he is creating more intelligence. Thus our major job as caretaker is to challenge the preoperational thinking of the child so that he may advance to a higher stage of cognitive thought.

The child's egocentrism must be challenged; if not, then theoretically it will continue unchanged into adulthood. Piaget warns us that this process of creating cognitive conflicts so necessary for new learning to occur requires many repetitions that actively involve the child himself. Otherwise the child merely imitates and fails to develop the intelligent operations (schemas) that we are seeking to teach. Piaget reminds us that assimilation requires active participation and that accommodation of the new to the old is a time-consuming process that should not be speeded up.

Normally there is a gradual lessening of egocentrism as the child passes from ages seven to eleven and as physical and social realities force the child to reflect and change his own assertions about the world. By about age seven a child becomes capable of maintaining a true dialogue or discussion. This behavior indicates that he is beginning to grasp the ideas that people have other points of view and that he is developing the language competencies for reflecting on ideas that did not originate directly from himself. By about ages seven or eight, moral judgments become more relativistic. Previously, according to Piaget (1932), the child was a moral *"realist"* in that he lived by the strict letter of the law instead of the spirit. *Relativistic* moralism means that mitigating and extenuating circumstances are considered prior to judging the degree of morality of an act. For example, the stealing of an apple by a very young and hungry child is a less serious offense than is the stealing of a crate of apples by a well-fed adult. Again, changes in children's ideas about morality and justice come about gradually through maturational and environmental influences.

Some research does not support Piaget's findings that most children develop such an advanced set of moral standards during later childhood (Kohlberg, 1963). Furthermore, the longitudinal study of moral development in children by Peck and Havighurst (1967) reveals that only about 25 per cent of their group achieved rational-altruistic morality by age seventeen. The rational-altruistic is the highest level of moral maturity and is indicative of the self-actualizing person. When confronted with moral decisions, such young people tend to study the situation carefully and mentally experiment with alternate solutions and their implications for others as well as themselves before deciding on the most appropriate course of action.[1] Naturally such mental operations are not reached until the stage of formal operations. Piaget may have confused imitation with true reasoning, with regard to moral judgments, during the early years of middle childhood.

Although most children by the age of six are aware of right and left orientations in regard to their bodies, the ability to imitate right and left movements of a model facing them begins at about age eight and improves gradually with a peak between ages twelve and fourteen (Boone and Prescott, 1969; Wapner and Cirillo, 1968). Success in such tasks requires a reduction in egocentrism in order to visualize mentally how things look to the other person. The development of handedness before entering school may be important because there is evidence that children who have difficulty identifying their left and right body parts are more likely to develop reading difficulties (Belmont and Birch, 1965). One procedure for helping the development of handedness is to avoid sitting young children opposite older children when both have the same handedness because the young will imitate in mirror-fashion the physical movements of the older children.

Growth of Conservation. As the child practices assimilation and accommodation with the realities of the external world, he begins to realize that seeing is not always believing. To come to terms with this "new reality" he must develop mental operations that will permit him to account for and to understand what is happening. He must account for the fact that the amount of water poured from one glass into another with a different shape does not really change the amount of water; he must account for the fact that as the shape of a lump of clay is changed the amount of clay actually remains the same; he must account for the fact that subtracting what was originally added actually leaves him with the same amount of the substance that he started with.

The two mental operations that permit physical conservation, the maintenance of the stability of an object despite some physical changes in its characteristics, are the ability to *reverse* the mental operations that represent physical realities and *decentration*, which is the ability to pay attention to more than one physical characteristic at one time. Reversibility of mental operations is essential for such important mathematical processes as subtraction, division, analyzing complex problems into component parts, and for understanding the reciprocals of quantities involving "more than" comparisons. In comprehending social relations, it is important to be able to go back mentally to the starting point in order to compare the past with the present situation. Being able to think backwards also helps in the development of concepts that require recalling absent objects as well as the various vital characteristics being used to classify objects and events into larger groups.

Increasing ability to decentrate is seen by age eight, when the child can conserve area even though its appearance may change provided nothing is added or taken away. To conserve area the child must be able to focus on both length and width simultaneously. The ability to conserve weight, which depends partly on judgments of size and partly on knowledge of the weight

---

[1] The major family correlates of rational-altruism are consistency, mutual trust, democratic family practices, and disciplinary controls that are neither harsh nor lenient.

Later
Childhood

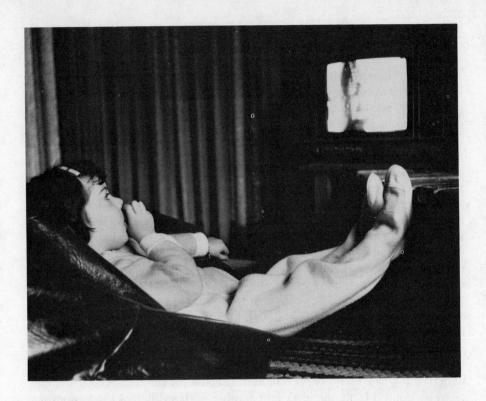

FIG. 17-3.

of different materials, does not appear until ages nine or ten, and the ability to conserve volume, which requires focusing on three dimensions, does not appear until about age twelve (Piaget and Inhelder, 1947).

Conceptual Thought. Conceptual thought can be regarded as one of the most important fabrics of mental life. A child hugs a stray dog and is bitten. What can he conclude? Should all dogs be classified as "dangerous animals" and avoided? Must the child repeat the activities leading to the dog bite over and over again or must he learn the critical cues necessary for differentiating the behaviors of different kinds of dogs? A child takes liquid from a bottle and becomes sick. How often must this happen before he learns differential classificatory skills regarding bottles containing liquids? The third grader, who after accepting a ride home from a total stranger is sexually molested, must decide from whom to accept or not to accept future invitations. In other words, the ability to develop concepts or generalizations and then to form subgroups and/or supragroups for discriminatory purposes makes life far more pleasurable, safer, and economical because the growing child is continuously being confronted with new phenomena that do not fit accurately into his previously successful but simplistic categories for anticipating behaviors.

Classificatory skills are one of the most important ways to help children improve their levels of concept formation. By a class we mean that a set of objects, people, or ideas share one or more common characteristics. During the preschool period, the child could engage in *simple sorting* based on a single perceptual property. Normally the emergence of *true classification* does not appear until about age nine when the child can form subclasses of objects and then include the subclasses in larger classifications (Inhelder, 1964). This ability, of course, requires decentration, conservation, reversibility, and the ability to mentally integrate separate events. To continue growth in concept formation as required in arithmetic reasoning, the child must understand the following characteristics of a number of classifications (Inhelder, 1964):

1. *Process of combination* or the ability to combine a certain number of elements in different ways. For example, if a child has two play garages and two cars, how many combinations of garages and cars can be made? By experimenting, the child should arrive at the conclusion that there are four possible ways to combine the garages with the cars. Older children can arrive at the same conclusion through mental operations, but it will not be until the stage of formal operations that they can arrive at the generalizations of the principles of permutations.

2. *Process of association* or the realization that the sum of a series is independent of its order. In arithmetic $(1 + 3) + 7$ is the same as $1 + (3 + 7)$. A more complicated form occurs with a series of overlapping classes such as boys and girls are children, children and parents are people, and people and animals are alive.

3. *Process of identity* or the realization that there is an identity operator that leaves unchanged any operation that it is applied to; in addition, adding of zero to any number leaves it unchanged; in multiplication, multiplying by one leaves it unchanged. In other words, identity leaves the original arrangement just the way it was. We can readily see that the realization "adding nothing and taking away nothing doesn't change anything" helps the schoolchild to escape some of the gross perceptual errors of classification of the preschool child.

4. *Process of reversibility* means that each element in the group has an inverse, which, when combined with the original, reverses the operation to its starting point. For example, the inverse of $+5$ is -5, and when both numbers are added together the result is zero.

By now the reader probably has recognized these terms or intellectual structures as those employed in the "new math." However, Piaget (Flavell, 1963) formulates far more complex structures or schemas. According to Pulaski (1971), these structures are "very long, very detailed, very difficult to follow except for the trained mathematician or logician." As an example, Pulaski presents one such organization structure:

$$(A \overset{a'}{\longleftrightarrow} \downarrow {}^bB)(B \overset{o'}{\longleftrightarrow} \downarrow {}^aC) = A \overset{a'}{\longleftrightarrow} \downarrow {}^eC$$

To the initiated, this represents a relationship such as the following: if A is the first cousin to the grandfather of B, and B is the brother of the father of C, it follows that A is the first cousin to the great-grandfather of C. (p. 57)

We may question the need for such complex processes to explain the seemingly simple mental activities of young schoolchildren. The focus, however, is on the word *seemingly* because children's thinking, if they are to achieve cognitive equilibrium with their world, must be as marvelously complex as the society and world in which they live. Piaget informs us that children must develop increasingly complex cognitive structures for coping with changing behaviors and increasing complexities. Today an increasing

Later
Childhood

441

number of schools are employing Piagetian educational models. For a review of such practices in early education in the United States see Lavatelli's *Piaget's Theory Applied to Early Childhood Curriculum* (1970). For a review of Piaget's recommendations to educators for helping the child's intellectual growth up to high school, see Piaget's *Science of Education and the Psychology of the Child* (1970). For a review of early education in England based on Piaget, read about the British Infant Schools (Feathersone, 1968). To learn about an exciting model for education, see Bruner's *Process of Education* (1960). Finally, regarding education, let us hear directly from Piaget himself (Ripple and Rockcastle, 1964):

> The goal of education is to create men who are capable of doing new things, not simply repeating what other generations have done—men who are creative, inventive, and discoverers. The second goal of education is to form minds which can be critical, can verify, and not accept everything they are offered. . . . (p. 5)

The Stage of Formal Operations. This stage, which develops for most adolescents who continue their formal education, represents the zenith of human thinking and, once developed, continues for life as the great organizer of mental life. The stage of formal operations represents internal freedom; it represents a psychological "Emancipation Proclamation," a "Declaration of Independence" of the human mind. It permits man to dream about what never was but could be. It permits the adolescent to become a dreamer about the good life, about social justice, about God, about the meaning or lack of meaning of life, about death, and about his finite existence.

Just as the onset of concrete operations brought about new ways of thinking, so will the onset of formal operations. There are some major differences in thought processes between the two stages. First, the adolescent rapidly develops the ability to readily use hypothetico-deductive reasoning as a means for solving problems. If given a fairly complex problem involving a number of variables and alternative solutions, he can mentally isolate each variable systematically to "see" *possible* consequences of the various combinations. In so doing, numerous hypotheses can be developed to account for various classes of consequences. In so doing, the adolescent's thinking resembles that of scientists trying to explain the complexities of the world. The middle-aged child is far more limited in developing mental solutions to problems because he is still basically tied down to the world of concrete events. Secondly, the adolescent becomes increasingly capable of employing *inductive reasoning* to discover principles or general rules from a number of specific events. The concrete-oriented child is more a prisoner of his constant need for many repetitions of specific examples to the point where a parent or teacher may say to herself "when will he ever learn the general principle that I am trying to teach him?" To do so, of course, would require that the child at the concrete stage go well beyond his own concrete experiences into the mental realm of "what could be." Finally, most adolescents can perform higher level operations than those just described; they can create *superhypotheses* and *superprinciples*. In other words, adolescents can think about the products of their own thinking.

The Life
Cycle

In summary, we can better understand the cognitive functioning of school-aged children if we understand the gradual changes in their thinking as

they progress toward the stage of formal operations. We can better understand ourselves if we remember that our thinking still contains elements of
thought that are characteristic of the sensorimotor, preconceptual, and concrete operational stages. In fact, the child within us cannot be denied biologically, cognitively, affectively, or socially.

Language Development

The mastery of the language used by the child's linguistics community is
essential for his full participation in it. The exact role of language, however,
in the development of intelligence is still an unresolved question. For instance, the intelligence test scores of deaf children do not differ significantly
from those obtained by children with normal hearing on the nonverbal
sections (Furth, 1966). In fact, many deaf children reason and solve cognitive problems very well. Piaget views language mastery principally as an
important vehicle for the expression of the intellectual schemas developed
during the progressive stages of cognitive development, whereas others view
language competencies as means for improving mental operations. Perhaps
as linguists, scientists who specialize in the study of languages, probe into
the issue of thought and language, they will be able to specify some of their
exact relationships.

Language and Thought. Piaget (1959), who believes that language improves only as mental operations become more logical, emphasizes that
efforts to improve language mastery without corresponding cognitive improvement will yield limited benefits. Nevertheless, there are some strong
arguments for the belief that language improvement plays an important role
in the development of thinking. Jerome Bruner (1971) contends that language competencies serve as amplifiers of intelligence, ". . . if language is
not freely employed in its pragmatic function of guiding thought and action,
then one finds forms of intellectual functioning that are adequate for concrete
tasks but not so for matters involving abstract conception" (p. 50). Bruner
et al. (1966), in a series of cross-national studies using Piagetian-type tests,
demonstrated very clearly the value of formal education, which is heavily
linguistically oriented, for achieving the more advanced stages of cognitive
competence. The unschooled child or adult tends to remain at the preoperational or the concrete levels. Studies of American children reveal similar
results in that many of our "culturally deprived" are also arrested in their
cognitive growth (Deutsch, 1965).

Research by the Russian investigators Vygostsky (1962) and Luria (1961)
is strongly supportive of Bruner. Their experiments suggest that children
develop more advanced ways of organizing mental activities through increased language competencies especially in the form of "inner speech" in
solving problems. Perhaps the best approach is one that combines language
training with training for logical reasoning, but only within the limits imposed by the prevailing stages of intellectual development. For children,
whose intellectual development is greater than their linguistic development,
additional language training may be the answer for improving their learning
competencies. In some respects, language is to thought what a number
system is to science—a most valuable and, perhaps, indispensable tool.

Linguistic Description. Linguistics is a highly technical field with many
specializations. The recent introduction of linguistics into the primary
grades in the form of "new language" suggests that as caretakers or future

Later
Childhood

443

caretakers of children, we have some understanding of this relatively new field. Table 17–1 summarizes some of the major domains of study of linguistics and some of the common terms used in this field. The recent and

TABLE 17–1
LINGUISTICS: SOME MAJOR DOMAINS AND COMMON TERMS

Major Domains:

Prelinguistics is concerned with the physiology of speech and the physics of sound. It contributes to our understanding of problems of speech and hearing pathology that constitute the work of the speech correctionist.

Microlinguistics is concerned with phonology, grammar, and semantics—those understandings that teachers need to improve children's instruction in reading, spelling, and English usage.

Metalinguistics is concerned with the study of language and culture and the influence of language on culture and personal interactions—those understandings of thinking and concept formation provided by the sociolinguist and the psycholinguist.

Contrastive linguistics is the comparison of two sound systems, whether languages or dialects, as to vocabularies, writing systems, and grammatical structures.

Common Terms:

Phonology is concerned with speech sounds, the differences in the manner of pronouncing a given word or phrase, and the differences in emphasis patterns over phrases and sentences.

Phonemes are the elementary or significant sound units of a language that do not by themselves have any meaning. About forty-five phonemes compose the sound system of English of which twenty-one are consonants, nine are vowels, and the rest are combinations of consonants and vowels.

Morphology refers to the rules for combining phonemes into meaningful sounds.

Morphemes are the smallest units of meaning; for example, both *a* and *elephant* are morphemes. Many morphemes are words, but often morphemes must be combined together by rules of grammar or syntax.

Syntax refers to the rules for constructing phrases and sentences. It is concerned with the patterns of sentences and the principles of arrangement of words and structures within the sentences.

Semantics refers to the meanings of words, including variations in significance, and the relationships of words to each other.

Lexicon refers to the dictionary definition of words, but also to the ability to handle complex terminology accurately and in detail.

Transformational-generative grammar refers to a system of rules that establish a relation between sound and meaning. The logic is that there are basic "kernel" sentences from which all other sentences can be generated if one understands the basic rules of grammar.

Kernel sentence is a simple, active, declarative sentence such as "He runs" or "I speak to you."

The Life
Cycle

Based partially on Shane's *Linguistic* (1967).

strong interest in new ways of teaching language and grammar developed after a growing conviction that the study of traditional grammar often left many students with no conceptual understanding of their own language. It is hoped that the new science of linguistics will provide entering school-children with new powerful language tools and an understanding of the logic and structure of their own language so that they may be able to better express the ideas, intellectual structures, and feelings that are developing "under their skins." For a linguistic view of the reading process, see Fries' *Linguistics and Reading* (1962). To better understand the relationship between spelling and sound, see Hail's *Sound and Spelling in English* (1961). For a clear explanation of the distinctive feature of structural grammar and of transformational grammar, see Thomas' *Transformational Grammar and the Teacher of English* (1964). For an analysis of social dialects, especially that of the black in urban areas, see Shuy's *Social Dialects and Language Learning* (1965). For an understanding of contrastive linguistics for teaching English to Spanish speakers, see Lado's *Linguistics Across Cultures* (1957).

Emerging Language Competencies and School Learning. Linguistics tell us that oral language development is primary and more nearly the "true language." Writing and reading are in turn dependent for their development on oral competency. Through the processes of writing and reading we are incapable of duplicating the richness of spoken language in the richness of meaning, emotional tone, and clarity that result from tone, intonation, and gestures. Regarding language development there may be a need to remind parents, teachers, and caretakers that "having been spoken first, then let it be written and read."

Research indicates that most seven-year-olds can articulate all English phonemes, the basic sound units. However, the need to provide special language training for those with articulation problems upon entering school is supported by a study of fifteen hundred kindergarten children that showed that such problems continued unabated for the next four years, for as long as the study lasted (Templin, 1966). Furthermore, those with the poorest scores in phonology also had the poorest scores in morphology (grammatical ability), throughout the primary grades (Templin, 1969).

At all age levels from preschool to adolescence there is an increase in the ability to apply language rules and to use more abstract words especially when there are good language models to imitate and caretakers who give rewards for correct responses (Liebert et al., 1969). Improvement in syntax, the ability to use complex sentences, is revealed in the increased use of complex, compound, and complex-compound sentences in written compositions and decrease in the frequency of simple sentences (Miller, 1951). Improvement in lexicon or vocabularies is noted in that the estimated size of vocabularies for first graders of about two thousand more than doubles by the sixth grade and quadruples by high school entrance (Bryan, 1963; McCarthy, 1954). A number of studies indicate that the extent of vocabulary is greater for children today at all ages than it was several decades ago (Menyuk, 1971).

The far-reaching and accumulative effects of oral language proficiency at the time of school entrance on later achievements in reading, writing, listening, and speaking was clearly demonstrated in the well-known study of language development of elementary schoolchildren by Loban (1963). This longitudinal research study followed the same children's language progress from kindergarten through the sixth grade. Loban concluded that competence in spoken language was basic for the development of competence in the other language skills. Probably the most important lesson that we can learn from Loban's study is that schoolchildren should not be taught reading and writing until they have developed sufficient proficiency in oral language. Children with low oral proficiency scores, typically from low socioeconomic status, can profit from a short period of intense exposure to a standard English dialect. Cazden (1970) found that lower-class black children in a Boston day-care center developed grammatically as well as middle-class white children normally do. In other words, Cazden's study suggests that many children from low socioeconomic status are not necessarily linguistically deprived but rather *linguistically different*. If the schools were to teach in the dialects of the linguistically different, the middle-class child, who is now the likely academic star, may find that he is in need of "special compensatory education" to make up his handicap.

Bilingual-bicultural Education

As discussed in Chapter 2, millions of Americans have limited English-speaking ability because they come from environments that differ linguistically from the language spoken in the core society. The educational system of the United States has thus far failed to educate properly millions of youngsters whose mother tongue is not English. In the case of the Mexican-American the statistics documenting this fact are particularly overwhelming because the vast majority are native-born American citizens who have received all of their education in the United States (Barrett, 1966). Mexican-Americans attain an average grade level of 7.1 compared to 9.0 for blacks and 12.1 for Anglo-Americans (Horn, 1966). In the five Southwestern states there are about 1.6 million school pupils with Spanish surnames, but of these nearly 1 million will not complete the eighth grade according to the National Education Association (1966). American Indian children, many of whom speak only their Indian tongue upon entering school, suffer from similar academic failure (Thompson et al., 1964).

It seems that many American educators and psychologists believe that bilingualism [1] is more of a handicap than an asset because of the long list of studies indicating how handicapped these children are linguistically, educationally, and often emotionally. There has been an increased awareness that it is almost impossible to teach children the basic school skills in a foreign language. In 1969, the United States Congress funded Title VII of the Elementary and Secondary Education Act, known as The Bilingual Education Act. In the same year, the United States Office of Education funded seventy-nine bilingual projects in the public schools. Although the Title VII programs affirm the primary importance of English, it also recognizes that the use of the child's mother tongue can have a beneficial effect upon his education. The mother tongue, used as the medium of instruction before the child's command of English is sufficient to carry the major burden of education, can help to prevent retardation in school performance. The Russian government adopted a similar policy in 1938 because only about

---

[1] Bilingual is a term used to identify a person who has any measurable competency in listening, speaking, writing, or reading in a second language. Any observable competency in any one of the four language skills is a sufficient condition for identifying a person as bilingual.

50 per cent of its population spoke Russian as its mother tongue (Cheavens, 1957). The task of teaching in a mother tongue first and then in the Russian language second was formidable because there are about one hundred different main languages spoken in the Soviet Union.

Bilingual Education. Bilingual education is a process by which all the pupils in the program, English-speakers as well as non-English speakers, are taught in their respective "mother tongues" as they learn to speak a second language. Subsequently, they can use both languages for instructional purposes. For the pupil whose mother tongue is not English, it is assumed that the strengthening of the mother tongue as a conceptual tool will enable him to learn through it, to develop a positive self-concept, and, in turn, to increase his ability and willingness to learn English. For the pupil whose mother tongue is English, bilingual education will provide him with the opportunities to conceptualize a second language and culture. For both the non-English speaker and the English speaker, it is fundamental that the best medium for teaching each child is his mother tongue. Research from other parts of the world indicates that the mastery of basic school skills in the mother tongue will transfer to the second language and that the pupils will attain higher levels of achievement in the second language as a result of earlier instruction in the mother tongue.

International Studies. After the American conquest of the Philippines, Filipino children found themselves being educated in English and punished for using their mother tongue. The recent Iloilo experiments demonstrated that children taught in Tagalog for the first two years, then in English, caught up with children who had received all their instruction in English (Davis, 1967). Consequently, Tagalog is today being used for the first two years and English is introduced as a second language. In 1925, the International Institute of Teachers College, Columbia University made a study with Puerto Rican children in Puerto Rico to see the relative effectiveness of learning through the mother tongue and English as compared with English-speaking children in the United States (1926). It was concluded that Puerto Rican children taught in English were markedly retarded in school learning as compared with children in the United States, but those who were taught in Spanish were markedly superior to their counterparts in the United States. In other words, Spanish-speaking children taught in Spanish learned more than English-speaking children taught in English. The major reason is that as a result of the nearly perfect correspondence of phonemes with written words, Spanish speakers learn to read faster and can start to learn subject matter considerably sooner than English speakers. Modiano (1966) found that Indian children in Mexico learned more Spanish when first taught to read and write in the Indian language than did Indian children who had received all of their instruction in Spanish.

The most elementary principles of learning and developmental psychology argue for the natural priority of the mother tongue as the first medium of school instruction. A. Bruce Gaarder (1966) of the United States Office of Education has given compelling reasons for making the mother tongue a language of school instruction:

1. The failure to dignify the mother tongue and its speakers by making it a school language will damage in some measure the child's concept of himself. I put it in these easy terms: for the little child language

Later
Childhood

447

is something like the air he breathes or the water the fish swim in. He is not truly conscious of it and how it works. Nevertheless, it is by far the single most important exteriorization of the self. To have the school, the all-powerful school, deny the manifestation of the self seems to have an effect over the years on the ego that many cannot recover from.

2. The failure to bring the mother tongue strongly into the schools as a medium of instruction will always weaken in some measure (and sometimes destroy entirely) the potentially reinforcing relationship between the school and the home. If the school alone or the home alone is the child's reality and the other simply something to be lived through "until I'm grown" the battle is half lost.

3. If the child reaches adulthood without having achieved strong literacy in his mother tongue, it will be practically useless for any technical or professional use where language matters, Thus, the single greatest potential advantage the child has—his competence in two languages—is destroyed, his mother tongue is not good for anything important, and the myth of the handicap of bilingualism is reinforced.

Peal and Lambert (1962) have noted that when true bilingual children equally skilled in two languages are compared with monolinguals from similar socioeconomic backgrounds, the bilingual children score markedly superior in intelligence test scores. They believe that because bilingual children have developed two sets of corresponding symbols and expressions for objects and experiences, their level of conceptualization has improved. Thus, they may approach problems with two sets of hypotheses and develop permutations that are beyond the scope of most monolinguals. Similar results have been reported tentatively from the bilingual project in Dade County (Gaarder, 1966). English-speaking children who have learned Spanish are scoring higher on English competency tests than English-speaking children who were taught only in English. Satisfaction from participation in bilingual education is reported also from more than 115 Spanish-speaking and English-speaking parents at the Nestor Elementary School in South Bay, California (Bilingual Education Project, 1972).

In order to develop separate conceptual systems for two or more languages, it is important that each language be kept as separate as possible in time and place during the learning stages (Ott, 1968). It is not clear as to how much time should be devoted to each language for optimal learning, but one must be careful not to give so little time to one language that the learning merely evaporates much like the efforts to fill a bucket of water drop by drop. Based on the neurological explanations of Penfield and Roberts (1956), the optimal time for teaching a second language is prior to age nine. The logic is to add a second language when the child's capacity for easy, natural, and unconscious language learning is still available (Anderson, 1960).

There is a prevalent attitude among educators that mother-tongue language maintenance is substandard when compared to the same language as spoken in the country of origin. Investigations reveal, however, that existing contrastive linguistic studies employed the language models of well-educated adults only. It would be difficult to convince English-speaking parents to permit their children to learn a new language if they believed that the variety taught would be substandard. To our knowledge, the first and only contrastive linguistic study of the Spanish spoken by Mexican-American children compared to standard Spanish was that of Yolanda Lastra (1969). Lastra reports that although there are some differences, the local dialect is sufficiently sound linguistically to permit its use as a language of school instruction.

Bicultural Education. Some educators, sociologists, and anthropologists do not consider that lack of English language competency is the major barrier to success in school. They point to the fact that there is a long successful history of educating immigrant children who entered school with little or no comprehension of English. A recent study by Lugo (1971) also suggests that the lack of English may not be the most important barrier to the school success of the Mexican-American child. Random samples of fifth-grade Mexican-American pupils were placed on a continuum from Spanish speakers only to English speakers only. School success, as measured by teacher grades and scores on the California Achievement Tests, was not achieved regardless of language spoken. That is, the majority of Mexican-American pupils did not succeed in school including those who spoke only English and who were born in the United States of native-born American citizens and who possessed normal scholastic aptitudes as measured by intelligence test scores. Furthermore, the fact that Spanish speakers of recent residency in the United States did not fall behind English speakers of Mexican ancestry suggests that positive identification with one's culture may be a more powerful motivator than competency in English. The harm done to linguistic minorities by denying them the use of their language in the schools may be exceeded only by the harm done to them as human beings when their cultural heritage is denied or demeaned.

Jacobson (1966), in a study of selected elementary school pupils, found that teachers showed preferential treatment toward Anglo-American pupils over Mexican-American pupils. He concluded that prejudice was in operation because Mexican-American pupils were constantly graded lower than their knowledge of subject-matter contents justified. Supporting Jacobson's finding is the ongoing research of Ackerman (1973) who reports a significant relationship between the academic achievement of Mexican-American pupils and their teachers' knowledge of their cultural heritage. These studies remind us of the long established truth that effective teaching requires understanding of the social, cultural, and linguistic characteristics of the children.

All that bilingual-bicultural education is saying is that we should educate schoolchildren who know little or no English in the same ways that we educate those who speak English. We need to use the mother tongue and curriculum contents that reflect their culture as the best approaches for teaching basic school skills, English, and an understanding and appreciation of both cultures. In other words, the world of the non-English speakers exists only in the language he speaks and is derived from the culture that his language represents. In the same way that a flower seeks the rays of the sun to sustain life, strength, and beauty, so does a language seek to retain its culture.[1]

[1] For a brief summary of a plan for the development and evaluation of a bilingual education plan for Mexican-American pupils, see *The Lingua Plan* by Libaw, Lugo, and Kimball. (1968)

Hopefully, some day bilingual-bicultural education programs will be standard in the United States. Such programs will permit our ethnic minorities to share their wealth with the existing culture and, in turn, to enrich their own. Such programs seem to offer cognitive enrichment that could not be attained in any other way and promise to unite many of the segments of our population while still permitting them to maintain their integrity.

Pathways to School Success

Education is basically an extension of society's efforts to socialize its children. Since our particular society is pluralistic, complex, and changing, the systems of education must parallel these characteristics if they are to be relevant to all its members, especially the minority groups. There must be a plurality of curriculum contents, methods, and definitions of what successful education means to match differences in social, affective, and cognitive styles. Adding to the need for diversity is the perpetual but increasingly important dilemma of meeting group as well as individual or self-actualization needs whenever they are different.

It is somewhat understandable that at the present time there is essentially a single major highway for school success designed and operated by the dominant middle-class social group. This highway represents the mainstream for successful socialization and is the major focus of our discussion on learning competencies. Nevertheless, there is increasing awareness that new roads are needed for school success for members of both the dominant and minority groups as well as for individual differences within all groups.

Home Education. Teachers cannot remedy by themselves all of the cognitive weaknesses that many children bring with them on the first day of school. It is worth reminding parents and caretakers of the claim by Bloom and others that fully half of a child's intellectual growth occurs between birth and age six, of the claim by Loban and others that adequate oral language development before entering school is the best predictor of academic achievement, and of the claim by Freud and others that mental health during the first five years of life is a tremendous reassurance of future mental health. A recent study by Kohn and Rosman (1973) supports the psychoanalytic hypothesis that a child's preschool social-emotional functioning is related significantly to academic functioning and intellectual achievement during the early elementary grades. In summary, parents and caretakers are the major educational and therapeutic agents during the preschool period.

Despite the importance of the early years, the child's future is by no means "set in concrete." Although we can hear the "cement mixer operating," it will continue to pour "soft cement" for many years. As concerned adults we can approach school-aged children with optimism and faith that we can do so much for them regardless of what has already transpired. Consider the following evidence for this positive point of view:

1. Of all living things, human beings have the greatest facility for reversing the effects of early experiences on their later lives. The entire fields of modern psychology, psychiatry, sociology, and anthropology are predicated on the basis that human behavior is changeable. To deny this is to admit that man is not even a higher level animal since even the erratic behavior of disturbed monkeys can be readily altered as demonstrated by the Harlows (1962).

2. Even if we accept the conclusion of Bloom that 50 per cent of intelli-

gence is developed by age four, the important question of which 50 per cent is the more important is not known. We would assume, based on the elegant work of Piaget and his followers, that later development of higher mental operations during the concrete and formal operational stages will supersede and compensate for lags in the earlier mental structures.

3. Sometimes the exceptions prove the rule. Although there have been few proven winners in the compensatory education programs for disadvantaged children from preschool through high school, the fact that some have succeeded proves that *it is possible* for the disadvantaged children to catch up with the more fortunate ones when the intervention is suitable. Hunt (1969), for example, states that compensatory programs that made a special effort to teach such cognitive skills as language and numbers showed success with children of poor families. He also notes that total-push extensive programs have as yet not been developed that take into account the background and the constitutional readiness of the children. Gordon (1969) reports that his program of having parents help their children has led to increased intelligence test scores, improved eye-and-hand-coordination, and improved personal-social relationships. In the more difficult cases, it may be necessary to start early, to involve the parents, and to go right through elementary school to obtain the significant and permanent gains that we are seeking.

4. There have been few consistent dramatic reports of changes in groups of children, probably as a result of the lack of long-term total involvement-intervention programs. Psychologists have been cautious, therefore, in their opinions about the beneficial effects of later positive experiences on the lags produced by early deprivations. In light of this, the following recent account by the noted child psychologist Jerome Kagan is significant (1973):

I have spent the last few years studying economically impoverished, isolated Indian children living in the highlands of Guatemala.

In one village, located on the shores of majestic Lake Atitlan, young infants, although they were loved, were kept in dark huts and neither talked to nor played with for most of their first year. As a result, the majority were seriously retarded in the rate at which they developed natural mental and motor skills. They were retarded in the absolute sense, as well as in relation to American children.

It is obvious that their restricted environment affected them seriously. If such a gross retardation during infancy is irreversible, as some psychologists have suggested, these children would remain mentally retarded for many years. However, we tested older children 5 to 11 years of age from the same village and compared their performance with that of middle-class children from the United States.

We found that by age 11 there was no essential difference between the Indian and American children on many natural capacities like quality of memory, ability to reason and make inferences from pictures or oral sentences, and perceptual analysis of pictures. Thus, it appears that a two-year-old who is seriously retarded in the absolute sense is able to recover normal intellectual functioning.

The major implication of this information is that early experience can, as psychologists have suggested, absolutely retard a child's intellectual

Later Childhood

growth. But that retardation seems to be more temporary than we have believed and children retain an enormous potential for recovery. (pp. 1, 7)

It is informative to compare Kagan's present views with those expressed by him and his coauthors in their psychology text *Child Development and Personality* (Mussen et al., 1969):

> Can the so-called compensatory education projects (such as Head Start, sponsored by the United States Office of Education)—designed to raise the educational level of economically and culturally deprived children— help him? Can enriched training programs, applied early, offset cognitive deficiencies? It is impossible to answer these questions definitively at this time, but a few studies suggest that it is possible, although difficult, to achieve such goals. (p. 315)

5. From research in creativity comes the exciting awareness that different kinds of children learn best when given a chance to learn in ways that are best suited to their particular abilities and motivations. As different teaching methods and techniques are introduced, different groups of children become the "academic stars" (Torrance, 1960). This kind of research has far-reaching implications for reaching and raising the educational levels of more of our children.

Reading Readiness. The prerequisites for learning how to read develop long before the child begins school. Probably most children would learn to read without any formal instruction in reading if they are given sufficient time and opportunity. At the risk of sounding facetious, we believe that there would be very few reading problems in the schools if we waited until age fifteen to begin teaching reading to those who had as yet not learned to read properly. However, the realities and urgencies of educational requirements argue that if children do not learn to read within the limits set by the school, they will become retarded in relationship to other children. Although most children seem to demonstrate their readiness by the end of the kindergarten year, there are still many children who are not ready because of developmental lags or environmental factors. Metfessel, from the University of Southern California, developed the following model for reading readiness based on his *Project Potential* research of school success and failure of economically disadvantaged children (1970):

1. *Perceptual-motor* These objectives stress the physical readiness of the child in terms of neurological input-output functions:
   a. Body image and differentiation of body parts
   b. Laterality and eye-hand coordination
   c. Directionality and eye-hand coordination
   d. Space-world perception; reality-centered observation skills
   e. Form perception; part-whole, figure-ground
   f. Sensory discrimination; tactile, auditory, visual, kinesthetic
   g. Muscle coordination; large, small
   h. Flexibility in motor control and ability to stop.
2. *Social-emotional* These objectives stress the readiness of the child in terms of independence and interaction functions:
   a. Group participation and sharing skills

b. Socially acceptable means of channeling expressions of feeling
c. Social interaction skills with adults and peers
d. Utilization of social-practical tools
e. Sensitivity to and expression of humor
f. Problem-solving attitudes in terms of perseverance
g. Skills in self-help and independence functions.
3. *Intellectual-academic* These objectives focus on the child's ability to approach the more formalized instructional processess of the regular school program:
   a. Receptive-language skills; understanding vocabulary
   b. Expressive-language skills; working vocabulary
   c. Problem-solving skills
   d. Ability to follow directions.

Home Environments. Deutsch (1964) and others have shown that the most significant variations in the child's cognitive growth and academic achievement is related to his socioeconomic background. Middle-class parents believe that eduation is the key to success in life. For example, a British study of seventeen thousand children reveals that by the time youngsters are seven years old, social class and the environment that comes with it has already separated the academic winners from the losers (*Today's Child,* 1972). A previous study of five thousand English children showed that between the ages of eight and eleven years, the working-class and the middle-class children grew further and further apart in tests of mental ability and school achievement (Douglas, 1964). Similar results have been well documented in the United States (Wolf, 1963).

As concerned parents and prospective parents, we are eager for knowledge of how to help our children develop the necessary competencies for experiencing some measure of success in school. We want to avoid the sadness, the fear, the frustration, the discouragement, and the humiliation that are born of school failure. Although there are very few studies describing the ways parents can help their children to develop the attitudes and behaviors that facilitate learning and working more effectively in school, perhaps we can identify and describe some major characteristics of parent-child relationships that are correlated with school achievement and intelligence test scores (Douglas, 1964; Wolf, 1963):

The Expression of Praise and Encouragement. Praise from their omnipotent parents is probably the single most powerful source of motivation known to children. Most of us can recall the sheer delight, the feelings of being "at least ten feet tall" when our mothers or fathers smiled their approval of our actions. Time cannot erase these precious memories that words cannot probably express. Among America's poor families, with the highest rate of school failure, this expression of faith and love in the child was the single best predictor of school success. Among the English families whose children were doing well in school, parental encouragement stood out as the single best predictor of academic achievement.

Knowledge about a Child's School Progress. This activity is an extension of feelings of high regard for the child. We want to know more about those we love. Such concerned parents are often seen talking to the teachers and principals. In the English study, 32 per cent of middle-class fathers as compared to only 12 per cent of working-class fathers visited the schools. Such

Later
Childhood

453

parents want to know about their children's progress, their strong subjects as well as the weak ones. They participated more in school activities as teacher aides, service givers, and facilitators. Knowledge about their children's strengths as well as their weaknesses helps parents to set academic standards for their children that are realistic and thereby avoiding the pitfalls of expectations that are either too high or too low.

Children will gravitate toward home educational resources and activities when they see their parents actively reading, discussing, and listening to the world of ideas, people, and objects. Parents should welcome and actively encourage children's participation in these social, affective, and cognitive activities. A central focus of these parent-child relations is the development of a growing active and receptive command of language skills. Parents, as they engage in mutually fulfilling and pleasurable actions, should make a conscious effort to provide the best model possible for their children.

A Labor of Love is to Create Disequilibrium. Parents should consciously, carefully, and deliberately create or select situations that will challenge the child's present mental abilities in order to increase his learning and cognitive growth. In so doing, the parents must provide the means for helping him solve the new problems and the incongruities that are forcing him to grow mentally. Such assistance includes a place to study; reference materials; opportunities to find the answers in trips to museums, zoos, and observatories; and ample time for open discussion with parents and others.

Children who read well and who do well in school, at home, and in life are those who have a *healthy self-concept.* They perceive themselves as adequate, lovable, valuable, and wanted. Such attitudes provide them with a deep sense of personal integrity, a love for life, and a desire to meet the challenges of life. Naturally, no list of what to do with children is effective, if the parents do not have their hearts in what they are doing, or if they apply them without any awareness of the child's own emotional climate. Effective parent-child relations are like a beautiful song, but the words (cognitive) must match the melody (feelings).

Creativity

One of the greatest joys of living and working with children is to watch them participating in increasingly complex mental activities. It is almost unbelievable to hear your child reading for the first time or to have a nonreader with whom you have been working for years walk down the hall reading signs such as "exit," "men's room," "stairs," or to hear him reciting from a menu for the first time "hamburger," "hot dog," or "ice cream." The look of absolute glee on his face and the happy sound of his voice are all the reward one can hope for. It is a wondrous experience to hear your child or a child you have known arguing for the first time with logical thoughts and cogent reasons. It is sobering to experience the first occasion when the child is right and you are wrong. These kinds of experiences indicate to both child and adult that the child is moving on the right track from dominance by the external physical and human environment to a greater reliance on his increased mental capacities.

The cognitive skills for acquiring information, solving problems, and creating new forms of ideas emerge gradually as the child actively incorporates new events, new ideas, and new objects. The child in the process of learning accomplishes two things: he increases his wealth of information and he increases his capacity for more efficient learning in the future. This tremendous insight, given to us by Piaget, that *the child's ability to learn creates intelligence that in turn creates more ability to learn is our greatest human resource*. To create intelligence, however, requires that the child undergo the twin processes of assimilation and accommodation, which require active participation in learning. Without active participation the young child tends to mimic without really understanding the logic of what he says or does.

Creating Cognitive Development and Intelligence. Piaget and Bruner believe that intelligence is shaped and created by the ways in which the mind is used. We have seen this process of intellectual growth in the way the infant organizes sensorimotor acts, in the way the preschooler organizes perception, and the way the schoolchild organizes his thoughts. At each level of development, mental thoughts are organized into more complex operations. The development of cognitive stages is a function of both maturation and learning. Learning, on the other hand, is provoked basically by the environment. A logical question to ask is how can we create cognitive development if it is a function of maturation that depends primarily on heredity? The answer, according to Bruner, lies in the evolution of human intelligence (1971). As man learned to use tools and to live cooperatively in ever more complex societies, the size and capacity of the cerebral cortex increased and the corresponding set of acquired mental abilities was passed on from the cultural pool to the human gene pool. Thus the *long-range creation* of inherited intellectual potential that was started in history is being created now and will be further enhanced in the future. In fact, we know that we now stand at the threshold of dramatic events that will change our ways of living and thinking just as events of the early part of the century produced radical changes in our present ways of living and thinking.

Learning, or the development of practical intelligence, is equivalent to creativity if we define learning in Piaget's terms.

Learning, or the creation of schemas (intelligence) for coping with the problems of living, is an everyday creative act. By definition, creativity is the emergence of an original process or product by the individual involved; by definition, the emergence of a schema is an original product that leads to original and changing mental processes. Of course, the passive acceptance of behaviors and the glib repetition of statements is not learning for Piaget and, therefore, not creativity. Perhaps this failure to differentiate learning from mere imitation is why intelligence test scores are often different from creativity test scores. If Piaget is right, then we must learn to value creativity scores as the truer measures of learning because learning and creativity are synonymous terms. This may be why teachers are fooled by the "model" behaviors and verbalization of some middle-class children into believing that these children comprehend more than they really do and into underestimating the mental abilities of disadvantaged children.

If we accept that learning and creativity are synonymous, then we can perhaps see the failure to learn as a result of living in a noncreative environment—one that fails to realize that individuals need an almost custom-designed environment to interact with if they are to undergo successfully the sequence of events necessary for optimal adaptation. All this means that effective learning is a highly personal affair and requires a teacher or parent who knows the learner intimately and who can continuously create a good

Later Childhood

455

match between the learner and the learning situation. To accomplish this kind of miracle, teaching requires the presence of a nonthreatening, stimulating, and experimentally oriented environment with a very low ratio of teacher-to-pupils. The teachers must be receptive to new experiences, childlike at times, blessed with a sense of humor, tolerant of ambiguity, playful, great believers in themselves and in their children's desire and ability to learn, and able to enjoy the excitement of divergent solutions to problems.

In the final analysis, a teacher or parent must come to grips with the realization that a good caretaker is one who eventually makes him or herself more and more unnecessary for the growing child. It is anticipated that as "mental and emotional and social nutrients" are provided at individually

TABLE 17–2
A COGNITIVE MODEL FOR LEARNING AND THINKING

Cognitive Levels	Environmental Activities	Activities of Child
Sensory-motor-perceptual (0–2 years)	Present a fairly stable world with salient features that change gradually; salient objects should be highly manipulable; physical freedom to select interesting objects and events at first and then gradually guidance toward essential features.	Seeing is believing but touch is divine; focuses on salient characteristics that appeal to the senses; requires time and practice to get "psychological" grip on learning.
Preoperational-intuitive (2–7 years)	Child needs a "reality" bridge between the external world and his internal thoughts to create gradual separation; learning by doing; needs encounters with objects, events, and people to force him to give up preconceptual and magical thoughts; encourage intuitive reasoning.	Begins to know things without direct action but not how or why; begins to be puzzled by the stubborn refusal of objects and people to behave according to his beliefs; can solve problems long before he can explain solutions.
Concrete operations (7–11 years)	Teach by showing, doing, verbalizing, and letting child repeat on his own; encourage many "mini" experiments; let child be free to explore, question, and discover; provide actual examples of principles; encourage formation of taxonomies, collections of objects and classes of objects.	Can reason about things but not about verbal propositions; can do mentally what was previously accomplished through actions; solutions to problems, although mental, are usually in terms of direct observable experiences.
Formal operations (11–adult)	Can teach deductively and inductively; can understand metaphors and satire; can perform true experiments; needs guidance and much contact with the realities of the world because of tendency to believe what he can create logically and conceptually.	Can reason about the actual and its relation to the possible and to the contrary-to-fact; can reason about his own reasoning; capable of coherent thinking about totality of relationships even when hypothetical.

propitious times, the child will develop through all the cognitive stages and then will be better able to spiral upward and outward by him or herself. Table 17–2 summarizes a possible Piaget model for teaching in the cognitive domain.

Piaget reminds us that the infant, the toddler, and the adolescent that we once were are still partially with us in our thinking and learning. Perhaps the process of beginning at the sensorimotor level of learning and proceeding upward to the operational level is still essential for true learning to occur for the adolescent as well as for the adult.

SOCIAL DOMAIN

This discussion represents a continuation of issues surrounding affective and social growth that we initiated earlier in Chapter 16. In this discussion we explore how various elements in the child's social milieu directly contribute to his development. In addition, we examine several modes of affective and social adaptation that are characteristic of the individual in his changing relations with his environment.

Social Factors in Development

As we have seen, individual development does not occur in a vacuum. Rather, all persons are subject to and are part of a system of interlocking social arrangements that serve to preface human events of all variations. Initially, stemming from birth (and experiences surrounding prenatal growth, such as maternal access to adequate nutritional and medical facilities), traversing the period of social initiation and education (where the obligations, responsibilities, and expectations of one's society are taught), to the attainment of adulthood (where acquired roles are played as well as transferred to a succeeding generation), human beings, above all other species, demonstrate the influence of social conditions and forces upon their development.

Socialization in terms of a particular culture encompasses two phenomena: (a) the learning of formal positions and roles characteristic of the person's society of membership (i.e., acquiring information pertaining to behavior of relative importance to varied membership in the social order), and (b) acquiring proficiency in the performance of roles that characterize the operations of social subunits (e.g., the family) and institutional practices (e.g., the ability to act in a manner associated with the common good such as through civic performance). These features of society, upon which socialization is based, have been referred to as the structural and functional properties of group life. In simpler terms, structure consists of the qualities of hierarchy and status generally identified with the positions people play in a social group (e.g., the family unit is normally defined as consisting of a mother, father, and a number of siblings representing both sexes). The concept of function provides reference to the idea of action or quality of operational interchange that characterizes how a given social unit and its members perform their assigned tasks. In terms of our interests in human development, the purpose of social function, relative to socialization, is that it provides the child an opportunity to practice roles and perform social obligations that are instrumental to his attaining complete adult status. This discussion is designed to explore some of the domains of structural influence

Later
Childhood

and functional opportunity within which individual roles are introduced, practiced, and lead to acquired proficiency on the part of the actor.

The Family. The family forms the most primary and pervasive of social and educational institutions in Western society. Initially, it serves as society's exclusive agent of social development, assuming extensive and complete control over the young child. However, over time, the family relinquishes its dominance over its growing members, providing adaptive learning opportunities that are preparatory toward effective functioning in the larger external community. Correspondingly, over time, through the achieved growth of its members, the family's role decreases in importance relative to its service to the individual. However, we also note that society is cyclical in its social arrangements. As such, one's ties with the family as a social unit are never completely severed. Rather such bonds are subject to regeneration as the child who, now as an adult, ventures forth to establish a similar but new unit through marriage and reproduction. As sociologists have observed, the family ensures a continuity of child care and social union that orients the child to his community and society, but also guarantees the primacy of certain forms of relationship among individuals (e.g., mother-child) that leads to their perpetuation.

In general, some accounts of the family have followed an individual descriptive approach characterized by analysis of its principal members. For example, parents, especially the child's mother, have often been conceptualized to serve as dominant stimulus agents in the exhibition and formation of behavior adopted by the young. This approach, which is essentially limited in orientation and scope, has led to the identification of important generational determinants (usually of adult initiation) that are responsible for distinctive patterns of family communication and interaction. However, this approach has also suggested a relatively simple parent-child, cause-effect model of behavior development that neglects both the rich interplay of intrapersonal factors that contribute to personality development as well as the child's participation, as an interpersonal factor, in the creation of conditions or states that elicit and effect parental and consequently the child's own behavior.

As an alternative to this approach, both sociological and clinical investigations of family life processes have argued for a more expansive representation of the family by the inclusion of all of its components. In addition, the notion of the family unit as possessing interdependent qualities, rather than serving as a composite of distinct but individual members, has been advocated. It has been observed in line with this position that the fact that the family is composed of separate personalities calls attention to the question of the merit of a cause-effect model that locates independent (i.e., stimulus) variables exclusively in the parents and dependent (i.e., response) variables exclusively in the children. In rebuttal, it has been suggested that at least minimal recognition of each family member as a source of autonomous action be considered.

The impact of the family may be viewed both in terms of its structural and functional properties. Such components as membership composition (e.g., number, spacing, and sex of children), role relations (e.g., division of labor and assumption of responsibility by husband and wife, parents and children, or distribution of authority and assertion of power by parents), and consolidations of membership (e.g., parental, conjugal, or child affiliations) serve to create joint structural and functional demands. These components, which are constantly in flux, represent a multitude of potential factors that may come to influence personality development. One illustration to this effect is provided in studies of ordinal position. For example, Schachter (1959), in pioneering studies of birth order, argues that firstborn children exhibit a variety of personality characteristics associated with position of birth. He found that firstborns, as group, experienced more inconsistent caretaking during their early years, which led to their greater responsiveness to anxiety or threat. He also noted that firstborns are more closely protected by their parents and experience frequent reinforcement. These conditions, Schachter assumed, helped to create greater needs in firstborns for affiliation, greater efforts toward conformity, and stronger needs for dependent relationships. As Schachter and others have observed, the number of children contributing to the size of the family unit forms a primitive, but nevertheless, critical component of group structure possessing strong structural and functional consequences. It is likely, for example, that the personality and social development of an only child will entail dramatic differences in child-rearing as compared to the child from a larger family unit. The nature of social encounters associated with the only child, as may be anticipated, will differ from that of a child with many siblings in both quality and quantity of opportunity of life experiences. In a large family, size alone necessitates a more careful allotment of available resources. In addition, the family size will also have important functional ramifications. The larger family unit will likely require stronger leadership, perhaps of a more authoritarian quality, more highly defined responsibilities and obligations on the part of its membership, and less opportunity for, or allowance of, deviations from delineated role demands. In addition, the older members of the large family unit will probably be required to assume a greater sharing of formal parental functions in traditional caretaking responsibilities, and to provide younger siblings with more plentiful, if less sophisticated, learning opportunities through observational learning of both child and parental roles.

The School. As a continuous vehicle of socialization, the role of the school in personality development probably ranks second only to that of the family. Although ostensibly confined to intellectual development, the school, nevertheless, provides numerous opportunities for the acquisition and performance of social behaviors required for mature development. In addition, by its explicit demands for achievement and academic excellence, conditions founded upon the attainment of independence and the acquisition of personal responsibility, the school serves to maintain family initiated patterns of growth and development.

The school, as the family, is an enduring institutional form serving to perpetuate the goals of society in a distinct fashion. In comparison with the family, structural features similar in form and mode of operation are noted in the school, although differing in content and manner of expression. For example, as in the family, the school is a relatively self-contained unit, characterized by leader-follower relations reflected by assigned status (which, as in the family, differentiate among the varied roles played by its members). To illustrate, young participants in school are required to fill externally dictated role functions commensurate with their assigned positions. As such, the child finds his behavior regulated through his status as a

Later
Childhood

student and the role attributes attached to this position. This system, however, is complementary. For example, whereas the student is required to play a subordinate role to the teacher, the teacher is required to fulfill a genuine learning function. The teacher is, ideally, responsible to the learner.

Supporting status and role distinctions, continued operation of the school, as the family, is based upon a normative system of recognition and rewards; an individual's behavior in his role as child and/or student is subject to reward and punishment relative to the degree to which personal responses conform or deviate from prescribed or acceptable behavior patterns. A second feature of the school, as the family, is that it is essentially a conservative unit. Both within the family and the school, yet unlike the peer group (or society of equals), for example, little significance is placed upon individual behavioral initiative, especially of youthful origin, in the formation or redefinition of structural properties that map group action. Rather, the purpose of family and school, previous to specific individual entrance and participation, serves as a conservative element preserving the integrity of the unit and contributing to its continuity across successive generations of membership.

Major interest in the school has been directed to a survey of its instructional-educative function. Correspondingly, less attention has been devoted to social structure within the classroom, the role of the teacher as a social agent, or the function of the educational enterprise as a more basic unit of socialization. There has been some recognition, however, that the school, particularly on the preschool and elementary school level, is a significant vehicle of social experience.

In assessments of the effects of early group experiences, important commonalities between the preschool and concepts of development expressed in Chapter 16 have been noted. It has been observed that the effectiveness of educational opportunity as an enduring consequence, as well as the significance of the school in social context, is contingent upon both the child's developmental level and the school's provision of experiences that supplement, rather than duplicate, the experiences the child is receiving elsewhere. In addition, reports on social development in educational settings provide some consensus concerning those elements of classroom practice and experience that appear instrumental in the course of development. Primary among these conditions is the role and influence of the teacher. As has been suggested by educational psychologists, the teacher may be the single most important factor in determining the nature of the school experience for the child. The teacher's ability to help the individual child improve in skill, in perceptiveness of social situations, and in his interpersonal relationships may well determine the progress he will make both in school and in other social settings.

Although the child's responsiveness to the peer group increases with age, the role of the teacher, nevertheless, appears to remain salient. It has been reported, for example, that in the elementary classroom the position of the teacher may serve as a focus of interpersonal interchange by affecting the socioeconomic climate of the classroom, the status of relationships among the children, individual behaviors, moral orientations, and intellectual performance levels. In addition, it has been found that the teacher may not only affect the object of her actions but those witness to her behavior as well. It has also been reported that such factors as the delegation of power and emotional acceptance of her students facilitates pupil-to-pupil interaction, reduces interpersonal conflict, and may stimulate autonomous work, independent thought, and personal responsibility.

Peer Relations. Peer relations form a third and highly important center of social activity and experience in the course of affective and social development in childhood. Although the family may be viewed as the primary influence in the initiation of individual patterns of behavior the child's activities in the company of age mates provides him with an opportunity to test the validity of previously formulated attitudes and behavior and to garner support for the maintenance, extension, or substitution of such responses. It is here that the functional component of behavior, formed through the influence of adults and adult-oriented social institutions, is most fully expanded upon and tested.

The peer society, as represented by the peer group, serves a unique and complementary function to the family and the school in both affective and social development. As an alternative social unit, the peer group, unlike the family or the school, is formed through the principle of egalitarianism; that is, status and leadership patterns are achieved through natural group processes. As such, the peer group offers the child his first experience in communal life, where positions, although formed through social enterprise, are achieved through individual skills rather than prior conditions or obligations. It is in this area through the expression of democratic procedures, rather than adult imposed or assumed directives, that the child is able to grasp and experience group life as an equal member of the community.

The peer group, paradoxically, is both of short and lasting duration. Specifically, although the peer group does not come into being through previous establishment or lasting commitment, it nevertheless acts as a model for later group affiliations by acquainting the individual with both formal and informal obligations required to sustain interpersonal relations and group membership.

Another feature of the peer group is that it is a voluntary rather than mandatory association. As such, the peer group represents both the individual's exercise of social choice and his acceptance of interpersonal bonds. Specifically, apart from his family, where membership is generated through birth (and thereby not selected) and is continuous in at least a structural sense (e.g., an adult, irrespective of age, is always a child relative to his parents), peer group participation is contingent upon the initiation and development of previously nonexistent interpersonal bonds as well as the maintenance of such ties through cooperative effort, conditions that are not requisite for continued family membership. Similarly, school attendance is a compulsory exercise, at least into the middle teens, whereas peer relations may be preserved or terminated at the discretion of the individual.

The significance of the peer group upon development may be traced through citation of its functional properties. According to Ausubel and Sullivan (1970), early group ties serve five basic developmental goals. They note that peer relations provide: (1) status and identity, (2) self-esteem, (3) a source of values and standards, (4) training opportunities, and (5) a forum for personal-social integration. That is, the group furnishes realistic standards for the comparison of one's behavior relative to age mates, a source for the confirmation or disconfirmation of self-judgments of competence and self-esteem, a differential frame of reference requisite for estab-

Later
Childhood

lishing acceptable behavioral standards, availability for role rehearsal and practice, and opportunity for matching particular or unique individual characteristics of development with special facets or styles of group membership.

Initially, the peer group appears as a marginal association of peripheral importance relative to the family and the school. However, peer affiliations assume increasing importance as the child grows older, supplanting both the family and the school with the attainment of adulthood. The peer group offers the growing person the opportunity to assess and integrate his social and personal self-systems as well as to extend himself into new realms of experience. As the child is socialized out of his family of origin and attains independence from mandatory school affiliations, he is socialized into the family of man. He becomes both a product and a legacy of society.

AFFECTIVE AND SOCIAL DOMAIN

Having reviewed the respective roles of various sources and agents of socialization in the child's life, we now turn to an examination of the different modes of adaptation that the child makes relative to his social environment. Our discussion concentrates on four facets of social and personality development including identification, sex-role development, moral development, and aggression.

Identification

A fundamental characteristic of human interaction is that in the course of interchange between individuals, persons come to affect each other. Although in most instances, the degree to which one person produces behavioral consequences in another is of momentary impact, certain select relationships result in substantial changes in personality. Some of these, in fact, appear to maintain themselves as relatively permanent characteristics of the individual over time. Identification is the psychological concept that refers to interpersonal situations and relationships in which one person serves as a lasting influence over another.

Although the concept of identification has been given many definitions by theorists of different persuasions a set of composite features have been observed. These are offered in order to direct attention to some of the more salient qualities that have been associated with this concept. First, identification refers to an acquired process of state of learning. That is, identification may be viewed as a learned outcome of interpersonal experiences that occur over the course of development as a function of the formation of human ties. Second, identification may be observed to reflect behavior or behavioral transformations. Specifically, the notion of identification, although possessing abstract meaning, is based on real and exhibited behavioral patterns. Third, identification may also refer to covert (i.e., unobservable) behavioral influences. In other words, we may find that one person may influence another person in indirect ways. To illustrate, people may be noted to possess attitudes, emotional qualities, and aspirational goals, which represent part of themselves that will influence their behavior but which we do not directly perceive. The process of identification, however, may be reflected in any of these avenues, as one person's relationship with another leads to some modification of a previously held attitude, emotion, or goal. Fourth, identification usually occurs within the context of a leader-follower relationship. That is, identification is unidirectional; in general, in the course of development we find that one person serves as the model for the adoption or change in the behavior of another. In the case of parent-child relations, from which we draw primary reference, the parent acts as the model whereas the child is the object of the identification process. Fifth, identification is neither a passive process nor is it affectless in character. Rather, the child identifies with the adult because the adult has assumed a particular emotional importance for the child. To adopt the behavior, attitudes, feelings, or goals of another is to try to be like that person. The motivation for the intense regard that is reflected in the child's wish to be similar to someone else is conveyed by the special affective status that the child has developed for the model of identification. Sixth, identification has been regarded as a total process reflecting a range of modeled behavior rather than limited elements or features that are characteristic of the model. To amplify, the notion of identification has been employed to suggest that the child seeks a complete or total emulation of the model rather than an imitation of fragments or isolated behavior traits. In sum, we find that identification refers to the notion of one human being, usually an adult, who has achieved a special affectional status, relative to a child that perpetuates the child's desire to be like him in as many ways as possible.

The major impetus to the study of identification is drawn from Freud. In essence, he argues that the child's initial identification with an adult (usually the same-sexed parent) serves as the child's chief means for achieving self-identification and sexual identity. Freud views this process within a developmental framework. Specifically, he suggests that the child passes through three states of identification. The first stage, established during infancy, consists of a primary asexual identification. This stage is based on the quality of nurturance (love) associated with the mother as caretaker. The second stage involves the formation of a love bond with the mother based upon the child's continued dependency and need for affection. The third stage, for girls, is associated with the child's efforts at intense emulation of the mother, assumed to be motivated by her daughter's fear of maternal abandonment (i.e., anaclitic identification). For boys, the third stage is assumed to involve a shift in love objects from mother to father motivated by the child's fear of the punitive, threatening father whom the boy initially perceived as a competitor for maternal affections (i.e., defensive identification). According to psychoanalytic theory, both boys and girls, through the successful resolution of the third stage of identification, achieve a broader perspective of themselves as possessing distinct character and specific role functions as man or woman.

The notions of anaclitic and defensive identification have been subject to varied discussion and inquiry. Anaclitic identification is based on the idea that the mother, in the course of her caretaking activity, begins to establish a different system of reciprocity relative to past practice as a function of the sex of the child. For boys, mechanisms contributing to the established primary identification are continued. However, for girls, the mother ceases to be nurturant upon demand. Rather, the girl is expected to conform to a series of interlocking and progressively more challenging role responsibilities. To illustrate, the young female is exposed to toys and tools as well as attire that tend to reflect, at least at a somewhat earlier age than boys, her future adult status as mother, homemaker, and woman. In addition, we find that

Later
Childhood

such adult-role attributes as responsibility and reliability, which are usually more critically applied to females than males, and at earlier ages, become associated with her continued role relations with the environment. According to Freud, these distinctions in child rearing, primarily associated with the sex of the child, account for differences in the process of identification in girls from boys. The young girl, previously accepted without regard for behavioral demands, is now thrust into adult society in which she is expected to assume an adult-role orientation. As a consequence, Freud hypothesizes that the emotionally dependent child has no recourse but to seek to imitate the behavior of her mother in order to ensure continued support and nurturance. Correspondingly, she comes to incorporate female personality attributes as her own.

As previously mentioned in males, the process of role achievement through identification differs dramatically from the situation described for females. First, the boy is required to shift identification from the female parent to the male parent. Second, the boy must establish a positive affective regard for the model of identification contrary to an earlier held view of his father as a competitor for maternal affection. Finally, through identification, the boy must resolve the Oedipal Complex and establish knowledge of parental sexual prerogatives. The motivation for male identification is twofold. First, the child, threatened by fears of castration anxiety derived from his assumption that his desire to possess the mother will lead to retaliation from the father, is required to accept the superior power and the prior claims of his adversary for maternal love. As such, he must relinquish a previously established relationship. Second, the child, in his review of paternal attributes begins to recognize that he is more like his father than his mother. Furthermore, it has been suggested that the young boy perceives that, through identification, he may aspire, with some hope of eventual success, to achieving the power and mastery over the environment already attained by his father. These factors appear to lead the young boy to accept his father as the proper figure for identification.

A number of alternative views of identification have been proposed. These consist of attempts to modify Freud's position as well as positions offered and based on other principles of development. In the former domain, Sears (1957), for example, attempts to place greater emphasis on the nurturant-dependency relationship established between mother and child as a primary force accounting for identification. Specifically, Sears sought to bring the concept of identification into closer proximity with traditional learning theory by focusing attention on the behavioral mechanisms that account for the child's development of affective ties with his mother. To this effect, Sears posited four stages leading to identification: (1) the establishment of the infant's biological dependence on the mother; (2) the occasional absence of the mother during times when the infant experiences need states; (3) interim attempts by the infant during the mother's absence to perform, through imitation, caretaking activities normally associated with the mother; and (4) receipt of gratification, through vicarious reinforcement, leading to the replication of similar behavior by the child in the future. According to this thesis, the child identifies with the mother in order to replace or restore dependency supplications. In predicting the child's behavior from this perspective, Sears assumed that the greater the degree of maternal affection offered the child, the greater was the likelihood that stronger dependency ties would develop. Moreover, under these circumstances, as the mother withdraws love-support from the child, either accidentally or intentionally (e.g., as a deliberate child-rearing practice), the bond of identification that may be anticipated on the part of the child becomes stronger.

An alternative view to the psychoanalytic position has been phrased in terms of the concepts of love and mastery. Kagan (1958) has described this point of view quite well. In brief, he argues that the process of identification is based on the child's perception of the parent as a source of power, which the parent may choose to exercise either through interpersonal relations (i.e., in his love or withdrawal of love from the child) or through his control over environmental resources (i.e., in his command of important goal states). The development of identification, Kagan suggests, is based on a sequence of experiences in which the child tries to incorporate elements of the parent's behavior in order to achieve love and mastery. Initially, the child perceives the model as possessing or controlling goals or conditions of satisfaction that the child desires. This wish to command the goal states controlled by the model leads the child to believe that if he were similar to the model he too would command these desired goals. As the child comes to imitate aspects of the model's behavior, he is told that elements of his behavior resemble those of the model, thereby reinforcing his continued efforts to identify with the model. Concurrent with this last phase of perceived similarity, and equally crucial in enhancing the child's adoption of identificationlike responses, is the environmental and model affective reinforcement of the child. That is, as the child's behavior approximates that of the model, he is also subject to the positive affective regard of the model and the modeling environment. In tandem, he is told that he is like his father and rewarded for adultlike behavior by his father or some other agent of socialization.

Although a number of additional theoretical approaches have been suggested in explanation of the process of identification, one additional perspective is offered here. This is the position advocated by Parson and Bales (1955) in their treatment of the family as a social structure associated with the child's acquisition of social roles. In brief, Parsons and Bales argue that identification is neither a singular process nor reflects the total internalization of another human being. Rather, they theorize that the child forms many identifications in the course of family interaction and that from each of these specific identifications, he incorporates both elements of other individuals as well as social standards to be applied to his own behavior. Furthermore, they suggest that identifications are successive. That is, as the child grows he identifies with specific behavior patterns and individuals, which change from original models, as a function of the level of maturity he has attained. The importance of this approach is that it tends to emphasize the role of social units, such as the family, in social behavior determination in conjunction with the developmental status of the individual.

Identification, as reviewed here, is a complex and difficult concept. The reader is confronted with a variety of differing points of view, each of which appears to hold some element of truth. As such, the reader may ask which perspective is most representative of the facts. Unfortunately, a simple answer to this inquiry is not available. The concept of identification, as evident by the diversity of approaches to this issue, has been viewed in a

Later Childhood

variety of ways. For example, even in his initial writings on this subject, Freud refers to identification in different perspectives, subject to situational variations. Freud views identification with an emphasis on overt action (i.e., with reference to matching behavior on the part of the child), as a motive (i.e., as an acquired drive state), and as process (i.e., as a psychological mechanism within which behavior and motives are learned). Consequently, later writers have tended to stress one or more of these independent facets of identification in order to create a more critical and succinct perspective of this concept.

Although we do not necessarily advocate one position over another, we do suggest that the reader need be aware of the complexities involved in reviewing conceptual differences and some of the apparent reasons for divergence in theory. The issues raised by various theories will probably not be quickly resolved. Furthermore, it is probable that the concept of identification will retain our interests for some time. Perhaps, as suggested by Stoke (1950), identification will become a more meaningful concept if each theoretical perspective would address itself to common criteria. Stoke suggests that the following factors influencing identification be applied to future considerations of this concept; (a) the biological fact of sex and its predisposition in influencing different forms of behavior; (b) the social pressures placed upon children to identify with their own sex; (c) the degree of affect shared by the person with whom identification is attempted; (d) the extent to which the child's needs are gratified by the person with whom identification is initiated; (e) the degree of acquaintance that the identifier has with the identified person; (f) the clarity of the role that is being imitated; (g) the attitude of persons toward whom identification is made; (h) the capacity of the child to form adequate identifications; (i) the temperament of the child relative to the object of identification; and (j) the existence of similar or conflicting needs of the child and the person to whom identification is attempted.

Sex-Role Development

The question of how boys and girls come to identify with the sexual roles of men and women has intrigued developmental psychologists for some time Mischel (1970). Although some evidence indicates, as suggested by Stoke, that biological principles are instrumental in the formation of a variety of traits (e.g., activity level, passivity) that have served to distinguish behavior patterns assumed by boys and girls (e.g., aggression, dependence), the acquisition of sex roles represents a complex and multifaceted growth process. Specifically, sex-role development has been viewed as an acquired behavioral outcome of social learning experiences that occur through the vehicle of socialization.

In the course of development, boys and girls learn to exhibit behavior patterns that because of their social association with a given sex and their occurrence at a high level of frequency come to be viewed as sex-typed (i.e., categorized according to sex). Such behaviors may be identified as responses that tend to serve as socially expected and sanctioned components of the child's personality. The process of sex typing refers to the manner wherein the individual comes to acquire, to value, and to adopt for himself sex-related behaviors, feelings, and attitudes. Our discussion focuses on how children acquire a particular sexual identity and some of the differences in sex-role orientation that have come to be associated with boys and girls, respectively.

Parent-Child Relations and Sex-Role Development. A major factor in sex typing and sex-role development is the child's parents. According to psychoanalytic theory, the child learns to become like the same-sex parent as a function of anaclitic or defensive identification processes. As may be anticipated, as the child strives to incorporate the behaviors, feelings, and attitudes of the same-sex parent, he or she also assumes the sexual identity of that parent. In conjunction with this theory, the respective roles played by parents primarily reflect the degree of success that the child has in resolving psychosexual problems, originally of intrapersonal origin, which confront him in the course of development. Supplementing this perspective, a number of other theorists, as well as research findings derived from other sources, have suggested that the processes of sex typing and sex-role development are more carefully defined than is suggested by psychoanalytic theory. These processes, it is held, are characterized by the active and direct learning of sex roles on the part of the child. Furthermore, it has been assumed that the impetus to sex-role learning may be more directly dependent on the environment and those social agents which structure learning opportunities and foster the child's attainment of sex roles corresponding to gender.

A second view of the role of parents in sex typing and sex-role identification is offered by Parsons and Bales. This approach, as suggested earlier, is based on the notion that the family and the pattern of interrelations that exists within the family unit form the prime source of social learning. Specifically, through the roles played by parents relative to their functions within the family, the child is provided with viable models for the purpose of sex-role identification. According to Parsons and Bales, parents assume complementary role functions within the family.

The mother plays the role of "expressive" leader, whereas the father exhibits the part of "instrumental" guide. The expressive mother represents the role of mediator and conciliator who strives to faciliate disputes, to reduce hostilities, and to provide affection, solitude, and warmth to her family. In other terms, the expressive role serves a supportive function that allows the family to maintain its integrity in the face of conflicting goals of personal dissension. Through her management of interpersonal tensions within the family, the mother is responsible for controlling ·the internal dynamics of the family.

The father, in complementary fashion, plays a role that primarily entails responsibility for guiding the family unit through the external community. In his role as instrumental leader, he is held accountable for the growth and survival of the family relative to the demands placed upon it by the outside environment. Correspondingly, he assumes an adaptive-instrumental function, characterized by pragmatic and decision-making behaviors. He leads the family by being responsive to changing demands in the economic, political, and social spheres of society. These complementary role functions serve to provide direction for the family by ensuring its survival, as well as important models for sex-role emulation. Through observing her mother, the young girl acquires an affiliative and nurturant behavioral life style that will be commensurate with her assumption of motherhood. In addition, she will acquire some of the facets of emotion, behavior, and attitude that Western society has approved as being appropriate to the female role. Similarly, the young boy observing his father will acquire a perspective of instrumental behavior and manipulative skills requisite to successful interaction with the external environment and his assumption of the role of father. Furthermore, he too will acquire emotional, behavioral, and attitudinal qualities that are assumed to be appropriate to his sex.

Cognitive-developmental theory holds that sex typing, as other facets of development, follows cognitive-developmental principles (Kohlberg, 1969). In the area of sex-role learning, the notion of cognition is translated into development in the following manner. The young child, in the course of development, is confronted with the fact that he or she possesses certain sexual attributes. These attributes, contrary to the child's previously held asexual status (i.e., as an infant), suggest to the child that he or she is a member of a distinct class of persons, either male or female. Consequently, the child begins to categorize himself as a male or female. This development, in turn, acts as an organizer of experience. Specifically, the child comes to evaluate events, relative to classification by sex, as appropriate or inappropriate to his or her self. To illustrate, the boy begins to relate to male objects, showing a strong disdain for girls and female attributes. A mother, for example, finds that her young son, who was once the recipient of her affections and sought her comfort during times of stress, now wipes off her kisses and impedes affectionate behavior with the approach of middle childhood. Similarly, the young girl at this time will stop playing an asexual, competitive role relative to her male counterparts. Rather, she will start to categorize herself as feminine, accepting those relationships that emphasize this distinction and avoiding those that do not.

Another view of sex typing is offered by social-learning theory. This perspective accentuates interpersonal influences in sex-role learning, whereas cognitive-developmental theory, in a fashion similar to psychoanalysis, emphasizes intrapersonal growth principles (i.e., within person attributes). According to social-learning theory, sex-role identification is acquired in a fashion corresponding to all facets of affective and social development. Specifically, the child achieves sex-role identification through a process of observational learning of salient models in which he learns and later adopts the attributes and actions of other people. This position, which has been subject to considerable research, suggests that the final nature of what is learned is determined by both situational and personal variables that enter into original learning or serve to maintain, primarily through reinforcement, such learning over time. For example, it has been found that such factors as the display of nurturance or positive regard for the child by the model, his power and control over available resources, and his similarity to the observer may serve to facilitate imitation and sex-role development. However, the process is also noted to be somewhat more complex than is apparent from our summary. For example, the characteristics of the model that exerts the greatest influence upon the observer depend in part on the type of behavior that is being modeled and on the conditions within which the observer must later rehearse or transmit such behavior. Furthermore, learned behavior will not necessarily be performed unless there is ample support by reinforcement for its continuance. That is, in order for behavior to sustain itself over time, there must exist some form of reward or acceptance of the behavior in question, either through internalization (i.e., self-reward) or external sanction (i.e., interpersonal reward). Parents, according to the social-learning position, serve as the principal models for observational learning of sex-appropriate behaviors, as well as the child's chief source of continued support and acceptance in the child's attempt to behave according to social sex roles.

Although these theories emphasize different perspectives of sex-role development, a number of ideas, particularly concerning the role of parents in this process, emerge and may be offered in support of the pivotal roles played by these social agents. From our review of various theories it seems that parents assist the child in sex-role development in at least three distinct ways. First, parents apparently serve to provide the child with sex-role standards. That is, the parent, as an agent of the social order through his role in the socialization process, will acquaint the child with information pertinent to behaviors, emotions, and attitudes that are appropriate to his or her sexual status. The parent will impart data concerning acceptable behavior relative to the child's sexual status. Second, the parent, as a member of a given sex, will present to the child a model of sex-appropriate behavior. In other words, the parent will, in fulfilling normal sex-role functions (e.g., playing the role of father or mother within the family) demonstrate for the child living examples of behavior to be imitated. Third, the parent will serve as the principal agent of reinforcement for sex-appropriate behavior in the child. As the child provides evidence in support of proper sex-role development, the parent is in an advantageous position to reward the performance of behavior that is indicative of correct gender identification. At this point in our discussion we turn to an examination of some of the differences in behavior, emotions, and attitudes which differentiate the performance of sex roles in boys and girls.

Sex Roles in Boys and Girls. Boys and girls behave differently. In general boys are more impulsive, aggressive, and independent. Girls are more reflective, nonaggressive, and dependent. Moreover, boys, in general, assume leadership roles more frequently than girls, but girls exhibit greater responsibility in a variety of independent settings. We are interested in knowing how such gross differences in behavior that are usually associated with each sex develop. One important account of these occurrences is provided by Lynn (1962, 1969).

In reviewing the nature and process of sex-role development for boys and girls, Lynn has proposed that the acquisition of sex roles in each sex reflects a distinct and differential referrent accounting for traits that are associated with one sex to the relative exclusion of the other sex. In girls, Lynn argues, gender identification is accomplished through a process of *parental identification*. However, sex-role development in boys is assumed to reflect a process of *sex-role learning*. For girls, the process of sex-role development is accomplished through the young child's initial and continuous identification with her mother. The young girl, through her relations with her mother, experiences a stable and consistent model of feminine behaviors in which the parent provides appropriate sex-role standards, a continuous and available model to be emulated, and a consistent and sex-appropriate source of reinforcement. In contrast, sex-role development for the boy is a more complex task requiring a different form of learning. Since he is not presented with a stable or continuous-singular model of masculine behaviors, coupled with the fact that his initial identification with his mother must be transferred to his father, sex-role identification in boys is unstable, inconsistent,

Later
Childhood

469

and discontinuous. As such, Lynn views sex-role development in boys as a more tenuous and ambiguous process, subject to a variety of influences, variations in accomplishment, and errors.

The process of identification for each sex, as suggested by Lynn, is characterized by a different learning process. For the girl, sex-role development involves mastering a lesson, whereas for the boy, sex-role learning is based upon the solving of a series of problems, each revolving about the issue of achieving a proper sex-role identity. With the lesson, the major issue facing the learner is the need to master stated objectives. In such situations, both the goals of learning (e.g., achieving femininity) and the means for addressing this task (e.g., the availability of the mother as a model) are known and available to the learner. The boy, in contrast, is charged with solving a more difficult issue. In attempting to solve the problem of achieving masculine identification, he cannot follow through imitation known behavior patterns as can his sister. Rather, since he is faced with an unavailable model for imitative purposes as well as a less completely defined task, the boy must first define the goal and then seek means appropriate to the attainment of the goal. In sum, the girl acquires her femininity through the formation of strong ties with her mother, which leads to her imitation and response to maternal femininity. In boys, however, the problem of achieving masculinity entails the establishment of a goal to be sought, a model or series of models to be followed, and the adoption of a strategy that may be implemented in striving to attain the goal. As a function of these differences in sex-role development, Lynn has derived a number of hypotheses relative to predicting sex-typed behavior in males and females. These involve differences in emotional and cognitive growth.

Since the girl learns the lesson of sex-role development through her mother, she must form a strong, personalized emotional tie early in life. Consequently, Lynn hypothesizes that in subsequent relations, affiliative bonds are likely to be highly instrumental in determining the course of the girl's later adjustment, particularly her associations involving others. Specifically, Lynn predicts that females will demonstrate a greater need for affiliation and tend to be more receptive to the standards of others in conflict situations (in order to avoid endangering emotional ties). In the cognitive domain, since the young girl is not actively challenged in the formulation of goals and strategies associated with sex-role learning, Lynn predicts that girls will be poorer problem solvers than boys. Furthermore, as a function of the particular circumstances surrounding sex-role acquisition in females, Lynn finds that girls are likely to rely more upon the judgment and direction of others in ambiguous situations.

In contrast, males are assumed to be less affiliative in orientation but more skillful in problem-solving situations. Since the boy does not establish the same early affective relationship that the girl forms, he is viewed as being less likely to be influenced in future relations by affiliative bonds. In cognitive attainment, however, the difficult problem of achieving a proper sex-role identification provides the child with training in the exercise of a variety of skills that leads to a superior ability to engage in abstract thinking and analytical problem-solving tasks.

The Life Cycle

Although the literature on sex differences supports the predictions offered by Lynn, there is some question concerning his explanation of how these differences in behavior and performance arise. In a somewhat different approach to this theme, Hoffman (1972) finds that:

> Since the little girl has (a) less encouragement for independence, (b) more parental protectiveness, (c) less cognitive and social pressure for establishing an identity separate from the mother, and (d) less mother-child conflict which highlights this separation, she engages in less independent exploration of her environment. As a result she does not develop skills in coping with her environment nor confidence in her ability to do so. She continues to be dependent upon adults for solving her problems and because of this she needs her affective ties with adults. (p. 147)

Moral Development

Through socialization and relations with a variety of social agents during the course of development, the child is placed in contact with rules that have come to govern the relationships of members of his social sphere of interaction and the order of society. These rules and the process within which the individual acquires them is the focus of this section.

As is the case of all social relationships and circumstances surrounding patterns of interaction, the principles of moral development are learned by the child. Originally, his knowledge and ability to act morally represents the will and control of his behavior by external social forces. Over time, however, the child begins to accept, through the internalization of moral codes, social dictates that are associated with his behavior. The problem of how children acquire the knowledge and orientation to act in accord with accepted moral principles has been of interest to developmentalists for some time.

The learning of moral behavior and the explanation of how acquired information becomes an integral part of the individual's working repertoire of behaviors is a multifaceted and complex issue. Children are, initially, neither moral nor immoral. That is, the child possesses no natural inclination to act in a moral or immoral fashion. His behavior in this domain, as is attested by variations in moral codes and behavior among different societies, is largely a function of the character of the society in which he is born and socialized. Specifically, adherence to a given form of morality is a function of social membership and social identification. Yet, the ability to act morally is neither simply an extension of the child's knowledge of moral principles nor his understanding of social dicta within a diversity of social situations. Rather, morality refers to an active process, where the child acquires responses to be practiced that eventually become internalized as a function of their judged degree of social appropriateness and their reflection of social morality. Morality is more than a process of social conditioning that is synonymous with the child's acquisition of knowledge of his social order. Rather, to act morally suggests that the child possesses information, intent, and responsibility for his choice of behavior. Furthermore, moral action implies that the child is capable of looking at issues demanding a moral judgment and that he is able to decide among alternative actions in a manner consistent with his understanding of the social order, particularly those facets of the moral code that transcend the specific situation in which he is required to make a judgment.

The child, initially, is neither required to adjust his behavior to the dictates of an external social structure nor to exhibit control over personal behavior choices. However, as suggested in the last chapter, the child, over time, becomes increasingly subject to the will of others. His free flow of behavior, his unrestricted command of social resources, his ability to act in the absence of standards, and his lack of restraint is terminated. In order to become a member of the group, he is required to relinquish his amoral status in favor of social responsibility.

In response to social mandates, the child begins to acquire information of appropriate behavior. These lessons are learned from a variety of sources: his parents, his school associations, and his peers. In scope, these lessons include attempts at formal instruction in morality (e.g., religious education) as well as experiential lessons derived from informal learning opportunities (e.g., play and games). Moreover, the child's experiences may range from specific individual encounter (e.g., an incident of childhood theft) to learning through vehicles open to all children (e.g., group games developed through the implementation of rules or related group decisions).

The acquisition of information is coupled with the child's growing perspective of himself as a social object. That is, the child comes to recognize that social rules are not abstract entities, but apply to behavior, including his own. This accomplishment stems from two sources. First, the child as a member of a given social group becomes subject to the rules guiding the behavior of members of the group. Second, as a function of maturation (i.e., internal growth functions) the child is able to perceive associations that are requisite to effective social relationships. That is, the child through cognitive growth begins to equate behavior with social consequences and in terms of cause-effect relations. In effect, he combines his knowledge of the social order with a developing sense of conceptual objectivity, leading to an ability to render moral decisions.

Inquiry into moral development has been offered in varied form. Three facets of morality have been extensively reviewed in theory and research. These represent the conceptualization of morality as: (1) conduct, with an emphasis placed on the child's demonstration of appropriate behavioral decorum; (2) an emotional response, with concern being directed toward the role of guilt and the child's formation of conscience; and (3) judgment, with the direction of inquiry shifting to the importance of cognitive elements involved in the child's learning of the social order and being able to make judgments relative to such information. These three interests reflect the theoretical views of social-learning theory, psychoanalysis, and cognitive-developmental theory.

Social-Learning Theory and Moral Development. The thrust of interest in moral development among social-learning theorists has been twofold, including concern for the child's acquisition of behavioral directives that may be applied to situations in which a moral decision is required (e.g., resistance to temptation), and interest in his development of internal controls over such behavior. As such, social-learning theorists have posited two views that coincide with the acquisition of moral behavior standards and the development of guilt reactions relative to the issue of internal control.

According to social-learning theory, the acquisition of morality as a behavioral dimension consists of the child's learning to express or inhibit specific acts that are defined by major socialization agents (e.g., parents) as good or bad, and that are rewarded or punished by these persons as they are performed by the child. This general format coupled with the child's ability to mediate initial learning opportunities to include, by means of generalization of experiences, other situations possessing similar stimulus properties prepares him to respond morally to a variety of problems.

In greater detail, the process is as follows. The child is originally instructed in specific behaviors. As he performs these acts (assuming they are positive) he is rewarded by social agents. As such reinforcement contingencies are extended in time and across situations, the same principles surrounding original learning will continue to prevail throughout life. Conversely, as the child behaves in a manner that is independent or contradictory to social standards, he is subject to punishment from social agents. Punishment, of course, may vary from physical hurt to a denial of privilege. In addition, punishment, as research inquiries have revealed, is a complex and often effective means of control. For example, human behavior may be subject to such facets of punishment as differences in frequency, timing, and intensity. Or the relationship between the punitive agent and the child will influence the effectiveness of punishment. In general the more loving parent is more effective as well as the parent of the same sex. Finally, we may note that the general efficiency of punishment has been associated with the degree or allowance of explanation accompanying punishment of the child's behavior.

This position is essentially one in which the child's behavior is externally monitored and is based primarily on the child's desire to receive reward and avoid pain. Supplementing this position are a number of additions to this theory principally reflecting the need to examine how self-control, relative to morality, is established. The focus of added inquiry has been placed on the child's fear of punishment and his internalization of such fears in the form of anxiety. It has been suggested that the child, in the course of experience, comes to realize (after transgression) that inappropriate behavior meets with punishment. In extension of this information, he also begins to approximate consequences. He is able to anticipate that future episodes of similar behavior on his part will likely meet with identical parental responses. As such, the child begins to equate (by means of cause and effect) the role of his behavior with the effects it elicits in the social agent or environment. As his anticipations (by means of anxiety) precede his behavior, he gains control (through inhibition) of the behavior in question and is able to make appropriate adjustments.

Psychoanalysis and Moral Development. A second point of view concerning moral development has been advocated by psychoanalysis. This position is based upon the child's development of guilt and conscience, with the focus of inquiry being directed toward the role of internal mechanisms that are instrumental in behavior regulation.

The psychoanalytic account of moral development reflects an intrapersonal framework. A simplification of mechanisms involved in this process is as follows. The young child through the experience of multiple needs, many of which fail to be satisfied, encounters numerous frustrations. In terms of interpersonal factors responsible for this condition, frustration is often mediated through his parents. Under these circumstances, the child develops intense feelings of hostility relative to his perceptions of his parents as frustrating agents. These feelings, in turn, create strong anxiety within the

Later
Childhood

child, particularly through anticipated punishment and abandonment, as well as the child's fear of the loss of parental love. In order to deal with these feelings of hostility the child represses open anger toward his parents and supplements such feelings in the form of good works. That is, in an effort to control repressed feelings, as well as to elicit parental affection (as a defense against punishment through abandonment or withdrawal of love), the child will adopt parental guides to behavioral conformity. In addition, the child will seek to emulate the parent in a variety of ways through the mechanism of identification. Finally, the child, as he comes in danger of violating parental approbations, will experience the dreaded sense of guilt that he has learned to associate with feelings reflecting the anticipated loss of parental support.

Cognitive-Developmental Theory and Moral Development. The last approach to moral development to be reviewed is that held by cognitive-developmental theory. This position reflects the initial proposals of moral growth postulated by Piaget (1932) and the amplification of those views by Kohlberg (1969).

The notion of morality, as suggested by Piaget, involves two facets of development; (1) the child's acquisition of respect for the rules of social order, and (2) his developing sense of justice through a growing concern for reciprocity and equality among individuals. These two concepts of development indicate a growth of respect for rules and persons as the dual components of social organization and unification. The processes involved in growth within this frame of reference include both maturational and experiential factors, whereas the quality of moral development is judgmental.

Piaget maintains that the acquisition of moral judgment involves a process wherein the child traverses through two broad stages of moral growth. In these stages the child exhibits an acquired respect for rules and a broadened sense of justice. The first stage in this sequence is called *moral realism.* In this period morality is heteronomous or external in orientation and scope. The child experiences justice as an obligation to comply with rules because he views rules as sacred and unalterable. For example, during a game he may refuse to play if someone suggests a change in the rules in order to speed up the game or to create greater interest among the players. During the period of moral realism the child judges behavior as being totally right or wrong, with little regard for the intentionality of the behavior in question. Furthermore, he thinks that everybody views behavior in a similar fashion. For instance, he will judge the correctness of an act or its inappropriateness on the basis of the magnitude of its consequences, or the extent to which it conforms exactly to established rules, or whether or not it results in punishment. His thinking at this stage of development is characterized by egocentrism (i.e., the belief that each of us thinks alike and views things within the same perspective) and realism (i.e., a confusion of subjective and objective circumstances surrounding an event). To illustrate, the child will exhibit egocentrism by assuming that an action in which he is a participant will be completely understood by others since it is understood by himself. Or the child will demonstrate realism by judging an accident as similar to an intentional act by suggesting that the punishment applied to each behavior be the same.

From moral realism the child advances to the stage of *autonomous reality.* This period is marked by a morality of cooperation and sharing. The child experiences rules as neither absolute nor unchanging, but as established through mutual accord and as being responsive to the needs of the group. In accomplishing this change in perspective, the child gives up his moral absolutism and begins to recognize a diversity of views concerning the rightness or wrongness of an act. Furthermore, his judgments of an action on the part of another are no longer solely determined by the consequences of that act. Rather, he begins to see behavior within the context of intentionality and personal consequences. Correspondingly, punishment is suggested relative to the quality of the behavior in question. To illustrate, an action will be judged relative to its human effects. Behavior leading to some personal harm will be viewed as being of more importance than an action in which replaceable property is lost. In this context, the child recognizes that morality should reflect the needs of the group and should be judged relative to its effects upon social organization and continued group cooperation.

Another difference between behavior characterized as representing moral realism and action subject to autonomous morality is the child's comprehension of duty and obligation. In moral realism, responsibility is defined in terms of obedience to authority. In autonomous morality, in contrast, the child's actions are judged relative to his consideration of its effect upon the group, particularly his concern for the group's welfare and his recognition of the needs of others. Finally, punishment is viewed on a somewhat more sophisticated level than it was previously. The simple philosophy of an eye for an eye is replaced by the child's acceptance of the principle of restitution in kind.

Moral judgment, as suggested earlier, is assumed to be mediated through two facets of development, namely, maturation and experience. Maturation, as indicated through the concepts of egocentrism and realism, allows the child to overcome his limited perspective of his environment and his role within the environment. Through maturation, cognitive growth, leading to an acceptance of the views of others and the recognition of objective relations, occurs. The second sphere of influence facilitating moral growth is experience. However, this experience is of a special sort. Specifically, it is Piaget's belief that as the child shifts his primary interactions from the family, particularly adults, to the realm of peer relations, he is placed in a different social role. As suggested earlier in this chapter, this allows the mutual exchange of ideas, the experimentation of varied behavior forms, and the establishment of group rules and social structure. Through increasing cognitive maturity and social relations based on reciprocity and mutual interest, the child will hopefully develop an autonomous frame of reference within which he will exercise moral judgments.

A number of researchers have attempted to expand or modify Piaget's views on moral development. The most significant changes in this area stem from the work of Kohlberg (1969). Kohlberg has succeeded in extending the stage concept to include many more facets of moral judgment than was initially envisioned by Piaget and has developed a system of inquiry based upon clinical type interviews similar to those employed initially by Piaget in his studies of other facets of cognitive growth. Kohlberg's studies of moral judgment led to his isolation of three major levels of moral orientation, each consisting of two stages. These levels of development consist of a premoral phase of morality, a morality based on conventional role conformity, and a morality formed through self-accepted moral principles. Premoral morality is characterized by the control of behavior by external factors. In terms of the child's behavior, standards are completely defined by others and motivation stems from the desire to avoid punishment or to receive favors. Morality based on conventional role conformity consists of the performance of good acts and maintenance of standards according to conventions established by the social order. The control of conduct is still external insofar as authority dictates order. However, motivation is rested within the person. The final level of moral development is morality of self-accepted moral principles. Morality, here, is defined through the sharing of standards as well as rights and duties among all members of the social order. Both laws and the desire to adhere to rules are a function of individual choice; conduct and motivation are both internal. A schematic presentation of these stages of moral development is offered in Table 17–3.

TABLE 17–3
STAGES OF CHILDREN'S MORAL DEVELOPMENT

Level	Stage
Premoral Morality	1. Obedience and punishment orientation.
	Acceptance of superior power; fear of punishment as aversive stimulation.
	2. Naïve hedonistic and instrumental orientation.
	Acts are defined as right because they lead to pleasurable consequences.
Convention Role Conformity	3. Good-boy morality.
	Orientation to approval and pleasing others. A good person is defined as one who possesses virtues.
	4. Authority and social-order maintaining morality.
	Orientation is directed toward duty and demonstrating respect to authority.
Self-Accepted Moral Principles	5. Morality of contract, individual rights, and democratically accepted law.
	Norms of behavior defined in terms of group rights and obligations.
	6. Morality of individual principles of conscience.
	Expansion of stage 5 to jointly include principles of self-consciousness as a directing force in moral choice.

Adapted from Kohlberg (1969).

Aggression

The last form of social adaptation discussed in this section is aggression. This mode of human activity has been of interest to a variety of social scientists since the initiation of formal scholarship. All societies have been plagued with both internal and external forms of aggression. Of late, however, this topic has received new and dramatic interest. We turn our attention now to the question of how aggression occurs in children and is maintained over time.

Several questions have been raised concerning the scope and importance of varied factors, of intrapersonal and interpersonal origin, as these factors influence the development of aggression. These questions may be stated in the following manner: (1) what are the motivational conditions associated with aggression; (2) how does the child come to possess aggressive responses to be used in his relations with others; and (3) what factors contribute to support the child's continued employment of aggressive responses in interpersonal affairs. In other terms, these issues reflect concern for the motivation, learning, and support contingencies that have come to be associated with aggression, as well as other forms of behavior.

The Motive to be Aggressive. In a sense, there is no one motive or instigating force responsible for aggression. Biological factors appear to influence the development of various behaviors including aggression. However, there is little doubt that these variables, whether of genetic or constitutional variation, do not operate alone. That is, biological forces interact, or come to fruition, within a sphere of interpersonal and social influences. For example, it has been observed that boys are more aggressive than girls. Although there is some evidence that boys may be inherently more strongly disposed to behave aggressively, it has also been recognized that aggression is a highly sex-typed attribute. Not only are boys encouraged to behave aggressively (whereas the reverse is true of girls) but assertive behavior is considered a valued attribute among male adults. Several factors, such as frustration, have been associated with aggression.

The major impetus to the recent study of aggression may be traced to the frustration-aggression hypothesis. This position, which has guided a substantial number of research inquiries, states that aggression is the principal response to the frustration of an ongoing response sequence. That is, the child, frustrated in his attempt to pursue initiated behavior, will upon encountering frustration respond aggressively to the agent or object of interference. Of course, several factors will inhibit the response on occasion, including the strength of the initial drive as well as the nature of the frustration. In situations where interference is not related to important goal states, frustration is less likely to lead to aggression. Or where the frustrating agent is of greater strength and is capable of punishing the child's aggression (e.g., the mother), the child learns to inhibit the direct expression of his anger.

Subsequent research among children and adults has not supported the frustration-aggression hypothesis. To some extent this has been a function of a widening use of terminology and testing of conditions that are not directly comparable to situations envisioned within the framework of the original hypothesis. However, in some careful tests of the hypothesis, as well as observational studies, there has been little direct evidence in support of this view. One clue to the inadequacy of this model may be drawn from its lack of social referent. Specifically, the model says nothing about how responses are initially acquired or how motivation develops relative to social agents who both frustrate and gratify children's needs. Furthermore, in some societies aggression is a well-monitored response. For example, in Western middle-class homes the child is expected not to engage in aggression toward his parents or siblings. However, he is taught to exhibit such

Later
Childhood

477

behavior if he is attacked or provoked by members of the external community, particularly peers.

Although the frustration-aggression hypothesis proved too broad for predicting behavior, the abstraction of some of its features, including the redefinition of frustration in interpersonal terms, has generated some interesting studies. Among young children, punitiveness, rejection, and restrictiveness have been related to aggression. These relations have been dramatically depicted in particularly brutal homes, as reported in the clinical literature. However, in more well-formed family settings, the depiction of punitiveness, rejection, and restrictiveness as child-rearing variables has not been as closely associated with children's aggression. To some extent, available relations hold only for aggression toward parents and among younger children. In studies of older children such variables, although initially stimuli to aggression, seem to play an inhibitory role as the child grows older. That is, the role of punitiveness, rejection, and restrictiveness may be of less consequence in accounting for aggression over time. In any event, a more detailed inspection of child-rearing practices and their immediate behavioral effects, and the developmental consequences of the long-range effects of particular styles of socialization is warranted.

Modeling and Aggression. A second source of influence upon the development of aggression is the availability of salient models. Through modeling, the child learns how to behave aggressively in social situations. As such, the role of parental and other models has received considerable inquiry. Sears et al. (1957) report that the influence of a parent's punishment upon the development of aggression may be twofold. As indicated earlier, the parent may create frustration through punishment, which leads to the child's behaving in an angry aggressive tone. However, the parent's use of punishment also serves as a model for the learning of aggression, perhaps at a time when the parent wishes to persuade the child to inhibit such behavior. Sears and his colleagues suggest that parental aggression provides a "living example of the use of aggression at the very moment they are trying to teach the child not to be aggressive" (p. 266).

Additional and more extensive investigations of aggressive modeling have been reported by Bandura and Walters (1963). They note that exposure to aggressive models may produce a number of effects. For example, they suggest that the child, through observation of aggressive models, will acquire imitative response paterns. That is, the child will learn new responses. Second, they find that observation may result in the disinhibition of similar responses observed by the child initially in some other context, but which he suppressed as being inappropriate or forbidden in social situations. Third, Bandura and Walters note that by viewing aggression the child is more inclined to exhibit similar behavior that may exist even though it has not been subject to censure. For example, through the mechanism of behavioral contagion, the young child often imitates similarly observed behavior without apparent cause or provocation. For example, young children observing a favorite television program will adopt some of the mannerisms of the performers even though similar behavior was previously acquired but was neither censured nor performed. Under these circumstances the child may be encouraged to practice responses, such as aggression, that he would not normally exhibit.

A number of other observations have been made regarding the child's learning and performing of aggressive responses. It has been noted that a special distinction may be offered between what the child learns and what he is willing to perform. The acquisition of particular response types appears to be governed by principles of associationism. On the other hand, the major influence of the model on the performance of observed actions seems to be exerted through the administration of reinforcements. Specifically, the child learns the act in question by observing the behavior of the model and the situational context in which that behavior occurs. In contrast, the child performs the act as a function of rewards that he sees accruing to the model or that he sees transfering to him through the exhibition of similar responses. In developmental terms, these findings suggest that a base level or potentiality to behave aggressively may be established in the child that will later be enacted behaviorally as a function of reinforcements or sanctions encountered in the environment. To be sure, the child may in fact learn how to behave aggressively, but through force of circumstances or controls placed upon his behavior he may be less willing to exhibit such learning immediately. Accordingly, the long-range consequences of such learning may not be directly known.

One question that has not been addressed concerning the role of modeling is whether models exert similar influences at varying ages. We know, for example, that the young child readily imitates models exposed to him in his relations with his environment. However, imitation among older children is more discrete and discriminatory, possibly reflecting a greater awareness of the consequences of such behavior as well as an expanded repertoire of alternate behaviors. Under these conditions, we would assume that exposure to aggressive models should have different effects at varying ages.

In addition to age, modeling must be viewed in relationship to the range of experiences with people that may surround the child. Furthermore, insofar as exposure to aggressive modeling may come from a variety of sources in the child's environment, it must be determined which sources are most critical to such learning. Finally, because of the social implications of aggression, it must be determined whether those principles of observational learning that appear to lead to the acquisition of aggressive responses can also be employed in the development, under alternative modeling conditions, of more prosocial response patterns.

Norms, Reinforcement, and Aggression. As indicated in the last section, principles of reinforcement appear to be highly instrumental in the child's practice and demonstration of acquired response patterns. As found in a number of experiments, children exposed to negatively sanctioned aggressive models learn the aggressive response but are less likely to display such behavior. Furthermore, in operant learning research, it has been found that the frequency of children's aggressive behavior may be successfully reduced when teachers or significant adults (e.g., the parents) systematically ignore aggression and reward cooperative and nonaggressive actions.

Although reinforcement following a specific behavior appears to be highly instrumental in enhancing subsequent behavior, this principle seems more appropriate to the young child than his older counterpart. In the older child, identification and incorporation of social norms, which leads to the control of behavior previous to its occurrence, appears to be an equally significant outcome. That is, as the child matures aggression is less likely to be viewed or employed as an isolated behavioral characteristic. Rather, as with other components of personality, aggression will come under the yoke of broader avenues of socialization.

The direct impact of socialization and culture upon aggression has yet to be demonstrated. Two problems appear to surround research in this area. First, in order to better evaluate the role of socialization in the development of norms concerning aggression, there is a strong need to differentiate between the impact of various sources of normative learning. Although norms are primarily transmitted to the child by his parents during the first five or six years, the impact of a wider social setting emerges when the child enters school. Both school and peers form independent conditions for learning one's culture. Correspondingly, a child responding to a single parental or adult referent should behave differently than one relying on peer-derived norms.

A second problem in this area is the need to define whether normative learning concerning aggression is a unitary or diverse process. That is, we need to discover whether socialization leads to the generalization of experiences from one situation to another. Furthermore, it may be asked whether uniformity in rule transmission occurs over time. Finally, it may be inquired how socialization agents, as representatives of social order, exhibit behavioral norms in their relations with the child. That is, we should determine the extent to which socialization agents provide viable models for the incorporation of norms governing behavior.

IMPLICATIONS

UNDERSTANDING YOURSELF AND OTHERS

A unique result of human development is the creation of personal identity that stems from seeing one's self as a competent and thriving individual who can meet most situations successfully. Such personal identity serves as an anchorage point from which one can venture out into the dark corners of the world. Knowing and trusting one's self permits close identification with other people, because one remains constantly aware of his or her individuality. Only as a person approaches this kind of personal identity does continuing growth toward self-actualization remain possible.

It is important for us, as adults, to realize that the door to greater personal identity is never closed. All of us can still grow tremendously in self-awareness and, in so doing, establish renewed and meaningful personal identities. Certainly the exciting views of Piaget and others that mental life is continuously being constructed through new and varied experiences open the possibility for a fuller and deeper understanding of all human existence. As adults in the formal operational stage, we can deliberate on the more abstract and valuable human characteristics, such as wisdom, honesty, love, and altruism. As adults we are still in the developmental process of the life cycle, with the possible exception of biological growth. We add the word "possible" because there is increasing evidence that intelligence continues to grow throughout life. Such intellectual growth in adulthood argues for the existence of continued biochemical improvements within the nervous system. With this in mind, we should not hesitate to explore new dimensions in the biological, cognitive, affective, and social domains.

The stage of middle childhood is probably the one we remember the most. The age span from six to twelve marked our transition from a world of

The Life
Cycle

480

vague memories to a period when we came to grips with ourselves, others, and the physical environment. If these transition years were successful, the chances are that the following ones were equally fruitful. On the other hand, if our early years were not all that they could have been, there is still room for optimism, as argued for in the preceding paragraphs. For example, many adults who did poorly in school as youngsters are now known to be capable of doing far better. This is why many colleges are not only accepting such adults as students but giving them advanced placement when they score appropriately high on college equivalency examinations. Furthermore, there are adults who did not succeed in school as a result of undetected learning blocks. Today, with improved diagnostic and remedial procedures, many of these blocks can be removed so that ability to learn is greatly improved.

LIVING AND WORKING WITH CHILDREN DURING MIDDLE CHILDHOOD

Middle childhood is a relatively healthy period, with the exception of accidents. Nevertheless, children of this age are in need of psychosocial supports during times of illness or hospitalization. Particularly, they need to be allowed to release emotional tensions by talking about their feelings. At times they need to cry, even though such behavior is no longer as readily acceptable as it used to be during early childhood. All of us, but especially children, need to undergo catharsis during and after traumatic experiences.

Because young school children are more concerned with mental than physical appearances, this could be an ideal time to correct physical defects and to enhance physical competencies. The advantages of providing such help are threefold: (1) the beneficial results will immediately help the child in the psychological, social, and affective domains; (2) the advantages of such improvements will become more and more obvious during the forthcoming adolescent stage when youngsters become keenly aware of the structure and function of their bodies; and (3) the increased motor agility may facilitate the development of schemas or intelligence, if we accept the theories of Piaget, Hebb, Kephart, and others.

It seems that the middle-aged child is in the process of trying to "put it all together." Upon entering school, the child moves from the sanctuary of the home and neighborhood, where he was more or less the center of individualized attention, into the sphere of group activity, in which he is one of many. In so doing, the child needs a structured and somewhat protective atmosphere so that he can continue to develop trust, autonomy, and competencies. This extension of love and guidance becomes increasingly necessary as he is confronted with new demands from within himself as well as from the changing environment. He must direct his energies toward creating new ways of thinking and feeling as his previously successful strategies are stubbornly challenged by new and unbending physical, social, and psychological realities. During this period of transition and adaptation, the child needs a social and physical environment that is uniquely suited to his individual tempo of learning and relearning if he is not to be overwhelmed by new demands, and if he is to be sufficiently challenged to create new mental schemas within the framework of concrete operations. The creation of such continuous matches between the environment and the child's mental and physical growth is the great challenge for adults who live and work with school-aged children.

Later
Childhood

481

In the areas of social and moral development, the strongest influence is still the family, at least for the first few years of school. It is within the family setting that most children continue to learn the values and competencies that they will soon "field-test" with peer groups. If children have been permitted to learn and to experiment with values and ideas in the home in relaxed openness, and if they have trust in themselves and others, they are now likely to approach other social groups in a like manner. Such children can go out into the world with the experience of social and moral successes behind them. They can thus participate in social groups without a great deal of anxiety. Furthermore, with such democratically oriented, trusting, and rational families behind them, such children can still count on their parents to provide further advice and to serve as sounding boards as they experiment with new social and moral strategies.

DEVELOPING POSITIVE MODELS

Until the medical, social, and psychological professions accept integrated health as their model for human development, it will be very difficult to achieve optimal states of biological, cognitive, affective, and social health. In the interim, parents and caretakers, realizing the truth of the holistic principle, can supply their children with an abundance of psychosocial supports that are so necessary for achieving this integrated state of health.

Physical competencies can be improved by physical education programs that are individualized within a group setting. Such programs need to teach the skills deemed necessary or desirable by society, but they should also permit the individual to develop his own unique physical competencies.

In the cognitive domain, the best single promise seems to be learning based on the models of Piaget and Bruner and goals based on the characteristics of self-actualization. Such an approach would require constant experimentation in order to find the best combination and sequencing of external and internal variables for each child. We can set up varieties of educational models, but the implementation of any model is always a matter of individual experimentation with any particular child.

In the affective and social domains the best model seems to be parents who are trusting, loving, democratic, rational, and consistent. To be effective, such characteristics must be translated into actual behavior and demonstrable attitudes. There must be common participation in many activities and decisions; there must be a sincere sharing of ideas and feelings; there must be open discussion of differences of opinions; children must be given the opportunities to test in the outside world the conclusions reached in the family setting; love must be demonstrated both to family members and to people in general; fair play must be extended to everyone. You can add to this list, but remember that children do as we do, not as we say.

CHAPTER REFERENCES

Accident facts. Chicago: National Safety Council, 1967.

ACKERMAN, R. E. *Private communication,* master's thesis. U. S. International U., San Diego, Calif., 1973.

ANDERSON, T. The optimum age for beginning the study of modern languages. *International Review of Education,* 1960, **6**:298–306.

The Life
Cycle

AUSUBEL, DAVID P. and EDWARD V. SULLIVAN. *Theory and problems of child development.* (2nd ed). New York: Grune & Stratton, 1972.

AYRES, A. J. Perspectives on neurological bases of reading. In M. P. Douglas (ed.), *Claremont reading conference.* Claremont, Calif.: Claremont Graduate School Curriculum Laboratory, 1964.

BACKETT, E. M. and A. M. JOHNSTON. Social patterns of road accidents to children. Some characteristics of vulnerable families. *British Medical Journal,* 1969, 1:409.

BALDWIN, A. L. *Theories of child development.* New York: Wiley, 1967.

BANDURA, ALBERT and RICHARD H. WALTERS. *Social learning and personality development.* New York: Holt, 1963.

BARRETT, D. N. Demographic characteristics. In J. Samora (ed.), LaRaza: forgotten Americans. South Bend, Ind.: U. of Notre Dame, 1966.

BAYER, L. M. and M. M. SNYDER. Illness experiences of a group of normal children. *Child Development,* 1950, 21:93–120.

BELMONT, L. and H. G. BIRCH. Lateral dominance, lateral awareness and reading disability. *Child Development,* 1965, 36:57–71.

Bilingual education project, vol. (1) no. 2, March 1972. Chula Vista, Calif.

BIRNS, B. M. Individual differences in human neonates' responses to stimulation. *Child Development,* 1965, 30(1):249–256.

BOONE, D. and T. PRESCOTT. Development of left-right discrimination in normal children. *Perceptual Motor Skills,* 1968, 26:267–274.

BRITISH STUDY FINDS SOCIAL STRATA DETERMINES ACADEMIC SUCCESS. *Today's Child,* September 1972, 20(7): p. 7.

BRYAN, F. E. How large are children's vocabularies? *Elementary School Journal,* 1963, 54:210–216.

BRUNER, J. S. *The process of education.* New York: Vintage, 1960.

———. *The relevance of education.* New York: Norton, 1971.

———, R. R. OLIVER, P. M. GREENFIELD, et al. *Studies in cognitive growth.* New York: Wiley, 1966.

CAZDEN, C. B. The neglected situation in child language research and education. In F. Williams (ed.), *Language and poverty.* Chicago: Markham, 1970.

CHEAVENS, S. F. *Vernacular languages and education,* unpublished doctoral dissertation. University of Texas, 1957.

CLEMENTS, S. D. The child with minimal brain dysfunction—a profile. In *Children with minimal brain injury.* Chicago, National Society for Crippled Children and Adults, 1963.

COBB, H. V. Role-wishes and general wishes of children and adolescents. *Child Development,* 1954, 25:161–171.

COLEMAN, J. C. *Abnormal psychology.* Glenview, Ill.: Scott, Foresman, 1964.

CONNOLLY, K., K. BROWN and E. BASSETT. Developmental changes in some components of a motor skill. *British Journal of Psychology,* 1968, 59:305–314.

CRATTY, B. J. *Perceptual and motor development in infants and children.* New York: Macmillan, 1960.

——— and M. M. MARTIN. *Perceptual-motor efficiency in children.* Philadelphia: Lea and Febiger, 1969.

DAVIDSON, M. A., R. G. McINNES and R. W. PARNELL. The distribution of personality children: a combined psychological, psychiatric, and somatotype study. *British Journal of Educational Psychology,* 1957, 37:48–61.

DAVIS, F. B. *Philippine language-teaching experiment.* Quezon City, Philippine Islands: Allemar-Phoenix Publishing House, 1967.

DEUTSCH, M. The role of social class in language development and cognition. *American Journal of Orthopsychiatry,* 1965, 35:78–88.

——— and D. BROWN. Social differences in Negro-White intelligence differences. *Journal of Social Issues,* 1964, 20:24–33.

Later
Childhood

DOUGLAS, J. W. B. *The home and the school.* London: Macgibbon and Kee, 1964.

FEATHERSONE, J. The primary school revolution in Britain. *The New Republic,* 1968, 1–16.

FLAVELL, J. H. *The developmental psychology of Jean Piaget.* New York: Van Nostrand, 1963.

FREUD, S. *Civilization and its discontents.* London: Hogarth, 1930.

FRIES, C. C. *Linguistics and reading.* New York: Holt, 1962.

FROSTIG, M. *Developmental test of visual perception.* Palo Alto, Calif.: Consulting Psychologist P., 1964.

———, D. W. LETEVER and J. R. B. WHITTLESEY. A perceptual test for visual perception for evaluating normal and neurologically handicapped children. *Perceptual Motor Skills,* 1961, **12**:383–394.

FURTH, H. G. *Thinking without language: psychological implications of deafness.* London: Macmillan, 1966.

GAARDER, B. A. *Personal communication.* Washington, D. C.: U. S. Office of Ed., 1966.

———. Personal communication from paper presented at conference on development of bilingualism in children of varying linguistic and cultural heritages. Austin, Texas: Education Agency, 1967.

GLUECK, S. and E. GLUECK. *Family environment and delinquency.* Boston: Houghton, 1962.

GOLDBERG, E. M. *Family influences and psychosomatic illness.* London: Tavistock, 1959.

GOODENOUGH, F. L. The development of the reactive process from early childhood to maturity. *Journal of Experimental Psychology,* 1935, **18**:431–450.

GORDON, I. J. Stimulation via parent education. *Children,* March–April, 1969, **16**(2):57–59.

GOSS, A. M. Estimated versus actual physical strength in three ethnic groups. *Child Development,* 1968, **39**:283–291.

GRINKER, R. R. *Psychosomatic research.* New York: Norton, 1953.

GUILDFORD, J. P. A system of the psychomotor abilities. *American Journal of Psychology,* 1958, **71**:164–174.

HAIL, R. A. *Sound and spelling in English.* Philadelphia: Chilton, 1961.

HARLOW, H. F. and M. K. HARLOW. Social deprivation in monkeys. *Scientific American,* 1962(b), **207**(5):136–146.

HARPER, P. A. *Preventive pediatrics.* New York: Appleton, 1962.

HINKLE, L. E., JR. et al. Studies in human ecology. *American Psychiatry,* 1957, **114**:212–220.

HOFFMAN, L. Early childhood experiences and women's achievement motives. *Journal of Social Issues,* 1972, **28**:129–155.

HORN, T. D. *Reading readiness in grade one.* United States Cooperative Research Project no. 2648. Austin: U. of Texas, 1966.

HUNT, J. McV. Has compensatory education failed? Has it been attempted? *Harvard Educational Review,* 1969, **39**:278–300.

ILG, F. L. and L. B. BATES. *School readiness: behavior tests used at the Gesell Institute.* New York: Harper, 1965.

INHELDER, B. and J. PIAGET. *The early growth of logic in the child.* New York: Norton, 1964.

IRONSIDE, R. and A. P. JORGENSEN. The ocular manifestation of hysteria in relation to flying. *British Journal of Ophthalmology,* 1945, **29**:88–98.

JACOBSON, L. F. *Explorations of variations in education achievement among Mexican children, grades one to six,* unpublished doctoral dissertation. University of Calif., Berkeley, 1966.

KAGAN, J. The concept of identification. *Psychological Review,* 1958, **65**:296–305.

KAGAN, J. The deprived child: not doomed to be retarded. *Los Angeles Times,* part 4, February 25, 1973, 1, 7.

KEPHART, N. C. *The brain-injured child in the classroom.* National Society for Crippled Children and Adults, 1963.

KOHLBERG, L. Moral development and identification. In H. W. Stevenson (ed.), *Child psychology.* Chicago: U. of Chicago, 1963.

————. The cognitive-developmental approach to socialization. In D. A. Goslin (ed.), *Handbook of Socialization Theory and Research.* Chicago: Rand McNally, 1969.

KOHN, M. and B. L. ROSMAN. Relationship of preschool social-emotional functioning to later intellectual achievement. *Developmental Psychology,* 1973, 6:3.

KRALL, V. Personality characteristics of accident-repeating children. *Journal of Abnormal and Social Psychology,* 1953, 48:99–107.

KRAUS, H. and R. P. HIRSCHLAND. Minimum muscular fitness tests in school children. *Research Quarterly,* 1954, 25:178–185.

LADO, R. *Linguistics across cultures.* Ann Arbor: U. of Michigan, 1957.

LASTRA, Y. *El habla y la educacion de los ninos de origen Mejicano en Los Angeles.* Paper presented at the Fifth Symposium of the Inter-American Program of Linguistics and Language Teaching. Sao Paulo, Brazil, January 1969.

LAVATELLI, C. S. *Piaget's theory applied to an early childhood curriculum.* Cambridge, Mass.: Center for Media Development, 1970.

LEVINE, S. Stimulation in infancy. *Scientific American,* 1960, 202:80–86.

LIBAW, F., J. O. LUGO and W. L. KIMBALL. *The lingua plan.* Los Angeles, Calif.: The Galton Institute, 1968. (ED 020504, Leasco Information Products Inc., 1968, Bethesda, Md.)

LIEBERT, R. M., R. D. ODOM, J. H. HILL and R. L. HUFF. Effects of age and rule familiarity on the production of modeled language constructions. *Developmental Psychology,* 1969, 1:109–112.

LOBAN, W. D. *The language of elementary school children,* research report no. 1. National Council of Teachers of English, Champaign, Ill., 1963.

LUGO, J. O. *A comparison of degrees of bilingualism and measures of school achievement among Mexican-American pupils,* doctoral dissertation, U.S.C. Ann Arbor, Mich.: U. Microfilms, 1971, no 71–7724.

LURIA, A. R. *The role of speech in the regulation of normal and abnormal behavior.* New York: Pergamon, 1961.

LYNN, D. B. Sex-role and parental identification. *Child Development,* 1962, 33:555–564.

————. *Parental and sex-role identification.* Berkeley: McCutchan, 1969.

McCARTHY, D. *Language development.* In L. Carmichael (ed.), *Manual of child psychology,* 2nd ed. New York: Wiley, 1954.

McFARLAND, R. A. and R. C. MOORE. Childhood accidents and injuries. In N. B. Talbot, J. Kagan and L. Eisenberg (eds.), *Behavioral science in pediatric medicine.* Philadelphia: Saunders, 1971.

MENYUK, P. *The acquisition and development of language.* Englewood Cliffs, N. J.: Prentice-Hall, 1971.

METFESSEL, N. S. and M. W. SENG. Correlates with the school success and failures of economically disadvantaged children. In T. D. Horn (ed.), *Reading for the disadvantaged.* N. Y.: Harcourt, 1970.

MILLER, G. A. *Language and communication.* New York: McGraw-Hill, 1951.

MISCHEL, W. Sex-typing and socialization. In P. H. Mussen (ed.), *Carmichael's Manual of Child Psychology.* New York: Wiley, 1970.

MODIANO, N. *A comparative study of two approaches to the teaching of reading in the national language,* unpublished doctoral dissertation. New York University, 1966.

MUSSEN, P. H., J. J. CONGER and J. KAGAN. *Child development and personality*. New York: Harper, 1969.

NATIONAL EDUCATION ASSOCIATION. *The N.E.A. Tucson survey on the teaching of Spanish to Spanish-speaking children*. Washington, D.C.: National Education Association, 1966.

NICOLSON, A. B. and C. HANLEY. Indices of physiological maturation: deprivations and interrelationships. *Child Psychology*, 1953, **34**(1):3–38.

ONTARIO ASSOCIATION FOR CHILDREN WITH LEARNING DISABILITIES, mimeographed paper. Toronto, Canada.

OTT, E. H. English in bilingual education. *In Reports: bilingual education in three cultures*. Southwest Council for Bilingual Education, El Paso, Texas, Nov., 1968.

PARNELL, R. W. Physique and mental breakdown in young adults. *British Medical Journal*, 1957, **1**:1485–1490.

PARSONS, TALCOTT and ROBERT F. BALES. *Family, socialization and interaction process*. New York: Free Press, 1955.

PEAL, E. and W. LAMBERT. The relation of bilingualism to intelligence. *Psychological Monographs: General and Applied*, no. 546, **76**(27), 1962.

PECK, R. F., R. J. HAVIGHURST et al. *The psychology of character development*. New York: Science Editions, 1967.

PENFIELD, E. and L. ROBERTS. *Speech and brain mechanism*. Princeton: Princeton U. P., 1956.

PIAGET, J. *The language and thought of the child*. London: Routledge and Kegan Paul, 1959.

————. *The moral judgment of the child*. New York: Free Press, 1932.

————. *Play, dreams, and imitation in childhood*. New York: Norton, 1962.

————. *Science of education and the psychology of the child*. New York: Orion, 1970.

———— and B. INHELDER. Diagnosis of mental operations and theory of intelligence. *American Journal of Deficiencies*, 1947, **51**(3):401–406.

PULASKI, M. A. S. *Understanding Piaget*. New York: Harper, 1971.

RIPPLE, R. E. and V. O. ROCKCASTLE (eds.). *Piaget rediscovered: a report of the conference on cognitive studies and curriculum development*. Ithaca, N. Y.: School of Ed., Cornell U., March 1964.

SCHIFFER, G. G. and E. S. HUNT. *Illness among children*. Washington, D. C.: Children's Bureau, no. 405, 1968.

SEARS, R. R. Identification as a form of behavioral development. In D. B. Harris (ed.), *The concept of development*. Minneapolis: U. of Minnesota, 1957.

————, ELEANOR E. MACCOBY and HARRY LEVIN. *Patterns of child rearing*. New York: Harper, 1957.

SEASHORE, H. G. The development of a beam walking test and its use in measuring development of balance in children. *Research Quarterly*, 1949, **18**: 246–259.

SELYE, H. *The stress of life*. New York: McGraw, 1956.

SHANE, H. *Linguistics and the classroom teacher*. Washington, D. C.: Association for Supervision and Curriculum Development, National Education Association, 1967.

SHELDON, W. H. Constitutional factors in personality. In J. McV. Hunt (ed.), *Personality and the behavior disorders*, vol. 1. New York: Ronald, 1944.

SHUY, R. (ed.). *Social dialects and language learning*. Champaign, Ill.: Proceedings of the Bloomington, Indiana Conference. National Council of Teachers of English, 1965.

SLOAN, W. The Lincoln-Oseretsky motor development scale. *Genetic Psychology Monographs*, 1955, **51**:183–251.

STARR, P. H. Psychosomatic considerations of diabetes in childhood. *Journal of Nervous and Mental Disorders,* 1955, **121**:493–504.

STOKE, S. M. An inquiry into the concept of identification, 1950, **76**:163–189.

Survey of the public educational system of Puerto Rico. New York: Teachers College Bureau of Publications, Columbia U., 1926.

TEMPLIN, M. C. The study of articulation and language development during the early school years. In F. Smith and G. A. Miller (eds.), *The genesis of language.* Cambridge, Mass.: M.I.T., 1966.

―――. *Longitudinal study of English morphology in children with varying articulation in kindergarten.* Paper presented at the meeting of the Society for Research in Child Development, Santa Monica, Calif., 1969.

THOMAS, O. *Transformational grammar and the teacher of English.* New York: Holt, 1965.

THOMPSON, H. et al. Teaching English to Indian students. In *Education for cross-cultural enrichment.* Lawrence, Kan.: Haskell, 1964.

TORRANCE, E. P. *Assessing the creative thinking abilities of children.* Minneapolis: Bureau of Educational Research, 1960.

VYGOTSKY, L. S. *Thought and language.* New York: Wiley, 1962.

WALKER, R. N. Body build and behavior in young children: 1: body build and nursery school teachers ratings. *Monograph of the Society for Research in Child Development,* 1962, **27**(3).

WAPNER, S. and L. CIRILLO. Imitation of a model's hand movements: age changes in transposition of left-right relations. *Child Development,* 1968, **39**:887–894.

WATSON, E. J. and A. M. JOHNSON. The emotional significance of acquired physical disfigurement in children. *American Journal of Orthopsychiatry,* 1958, **28**:85–97.

WHIPPLE, D. V. *Dynamics of development: euthenic pediatrics.* New York: McGraw-Hill, 1966.

WHITE, B. W. The control of child-environmental interaction: a conceptual approach to accident occurrence. *Pediatrics,* 1969, **44**:799.

WOLF, R. M. *The identification and measurement of environmental process variables related to intelligence,* unpublished doctoral dissertation. U. of Chicago, 1963.

RECOMMENDED FURTHER READING

BERMAN, L. M. *New priorities in the curriculum.* Columbus, Oh.: Merrill, 1968.

BLACKMAN, G. J. *The deviant child in the classroom.* Belmont, Calif.: Wadsworth, 1968.

BREARLY, M. (ed.). *The teaching of young children: some applications of Piaget's learning theory.* New York: Schocken, 1970.

CHESS, S. *An introduction to child psychiatry.* New York: Grune, 1959.

COLE, M., J. GAY, J. A. GLICK and D. W. SHARP. The cultural context of learning and thinking. New York: Basic, 1971.

CRITCHLEY, M. *The dyslexic child.* London: Heinemann Medical Books, 1970.

GINOTT, H. *Teacher and child.* New York: Macmillan, 1972.

HURLEY, R. *Poverty and mental retardation.* New York: Vintage, 1969.

NEIL, A. S. *Summerhill: a radical approach to child rearing.* New York: Hart, 1960.

PECK, M. J. and M. J. SCHULTZ. *Teaching ideas that make learning fun.* West Nyack, N. Y.: Parker, 1971.

SCHURR, E. L. *Movement experiences for children.* New York: Appleton, 1967.

VYGOTSKY, L. S. *Thought and language.* Cambridge, Mass.: M.I.T., 1971.

WALLIS, E. L. and G. LOGAN. *Exercise for children.* Englewood Cliffs, N. J.: Prentice-Hall, 1966.

WOLFF, S. *Children under stress.* Baltimore: Penguin, 1969.

Later
Childhood

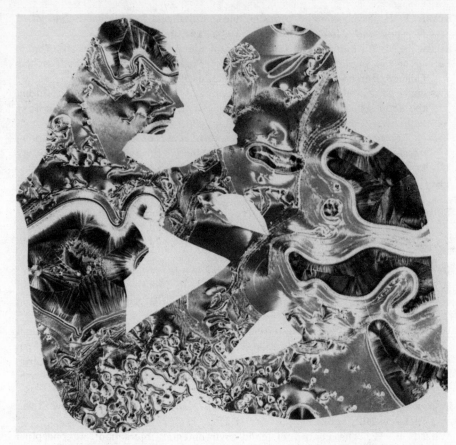

Adolescence

DOUGLAS KIMMEL, Ph.D.
City College of the City University of New York

Prelude
Basic Theory and Research
  Biological Domain
    Physical Development
    Sexual Maturation
    Individual Assets and
      Liabilities
    Biological Aspects of the
      Self-Concept
  Cognitive Domain
    Formal Operations Stage of
      Intellectual Development
    Creativity

Affective Domain
  Autonomy
  Relations with the Family
  Relations with Friends and
    Society
  Developments in Feelings
Social Domain
  Socialization of the Adolescent
  Identity Formation in
    Adolescence
  Growth Trends in
    Late Adolescence

Implications
Understanding Yourself and
  Others

Living and Working with Children, Adolescents, and Adults
Developing Positive Models

PRELUDE

As we shift our focus to later stages of the life cycle, the number of years involved in the stage increases. In this chapter on adolescence, we cover almost as many years as the child has lived up to adolescence; and in the next chapter on adulthood, the length of time jumps to sixty or more years from the beginning of adulthood until death. This increasing span of time within these two "stages" of the life span reflects two important differences between these later years of life and childhood: first, the rate of progression through significant events slows down after the early years of childhood; and second, social factors become more important in setting the mileposts that mark off important stages or turning points. For example, the first two years of life are filled with major events; the speed of development during this period is very fast and these events are based to a large extent on biological maturation.

In contrast, adolescence is begun by a major biological event, puberty, but the meaning and content of adolescence is primarily determined by social factors. The major events that occur during the period of adolescence —Bar or Bas Mitzvah, Confirmation, being legally able to drive, drink, vote, and marry—are all social mileposts of adolescence. Thus, in an important way, the spotlight shifts from the individual's developmental sequence in a small family group to the individual interacting with an ever-widening social network. This social network is more important for understanding adolescent development than it is for understanding child development. In fact, the stage of adolescence itself may be seen as a result of our culture. In other cultures, adolescence either does not exist in any way as it does in the United States, or it exists in a different form from ours. Of course, most Western societies allow a period of adolescence, but even in countries such as the United States and Denmark, there are differences in the issues that are important to adolescents such as the quality of their relations with their parents and the values and attitudes that are emphasized by society (Kandel and Lesser, 1972). In other societies, such as the historic American Indian tribes, the period of adolescence lasted only a few days or weeks. The boy would be put through an initiation rite that might involve his going out into the forest with only a knife and being required to survive alone for a week or two; when he returned to the village there would be a ceremony and the boy was then a *man;* he was in between a boy and a man for only a short time. Girls also went through an initiation rite in some tribes (and other societies) as well. For example, Grinnell (1923) describes this initiation rite of the Cheyenne Indians:

> The passage of a girl from childhood to young womanhood was considered as hardly less important to the tribe than to her own family. She was now to become the mother of children and thus to contribute her part toward adding to the number of the tribe and so to its power and importance.

Adolescence

When a young girl reached the age of puberty and had her first menstrual period, she, of course, told her mother, who in turn informed the father. Such an important family event was not kept secret. It was the custom among well-to-do people for the father of the girl publically to announce from the lodge door what had happened and as an evidence of his satisfaction to give away a horse.

The girl unbraided her hair and bathed, and afterward older women painted her whole body with red. Then, with a robe about her naked body, she sat near the fire, a coal was drawn from it and put before her, and sweet grass, juniper needles, and white sage were sprinkled on it. The girl bent forward over the coal and held her robe about it, so that the smoke rising from the incense was confined and passed about her and over her whole body. Then she and her grandmother left the home lodge, and went into another small one near by, where she remained for four days. (p. 129)

This chapter has three goals. First, since there are clear changes in the biological, cognitive, affective, and social domains during adolescence, we need to consider these important changes; and, as we have noted, the social domain begins to become the more prominent domain during adolescence. Second, since the adolescent is obviously a whole person, these four domains are all interrelated and interact together to produce growth and development during adolescence. For example, sexual maturation (which is a biological event) has clear effects on the affective and social domains, whereas the intellectual domain is trying to make sense out of all of these changes. Thus, these domains interact upon one another and need to be seen as interdependent if we are to really understand adolescence in general and specific adolescents in particular. And third, as we probably all remember from our own adolescence, this time of life is not the easiest and smoothest; yet it is a time when many important questions are raised and resolved in some way. As a result, some adolescents may need help to develop optimally. Since we have the benefit of our own experience with adolescence and will have, by the end of this chapter, gained some understanding of adolescence, we may be better able to be active participants in helping adolescents develop to their fullest potential. Since an important part of learning is to experience the material firsthand, we would encourage you to talk with some adolescents to see what they have to teach you. One need only look around to see areas or places where adolescents are in need of help; volunteer work in such places can be an extremely useful learning experience and can help you to put this chapter in a personally meaningful perspective.

BASIC THEORY AND RESEARCH

In our society, adolescence lasts from puberty (around the age of eleven or twelve on the average) until the taking on of relatively full adult responsibilities—such as marriage, parenthood, full-time work, and independent living. Clearly, the end point of the adolescent stage is not well defined in terms of years—one adolescent may spend only five or six years in this period; another may extend the period of adolescence through college and graduate school; and still another may be socially an adult but still trying to

The Life
Cycle

resolve some of the basic adolescent issues such as "Who am I?" However, it is clear that young adolescents (puberty to fifteen or sixteen) are quite different from late adolescents (fifteen to sixteen on to twenty-one or twenty-five); it is thus generally useful to talk about early and late adolescents separately. Those adolescents who extend their period of transition from childhood to adulthood through a long period of college and graduate school may be seen as living in a kind of distinct substage that Keniston (1968) calls *youth*.

Essentially, adolescence refers to the period of transition from childhood to adulthood. In our society, this period has been lengthened for many adolescents by the social necessity of graduating from high school and attending college in order to get a good job. According to Erikson (1968) this special kind of extension has taken on the character of a *moratorium*— that is, a period of relative freedom from adult responsibilities and relative freedom from rapid physical change. At best, this moratorium allows the adolescent to resolve some of the basic questions about who he is, where he is going, and how he fits in with the rest of society. At worst, this moratorium extends the period of confusion and of searching, and makes the period of adolescence a long, difficult, and painful period of life. Probably, these best and worst elements are both combined in differing degrees for most adolescents in our society.

At the same time that the length of the adolescent period has increased, the complexity of the adolescent issues has also increased. In simpler societies, where the son follows in his father's footsteps and may serve as an apprentice in early adolescence and move up to a full working adult in what would otherwise be late adolescence, and where the daughter learns the role of women from her mother and gets married in what would otherwise be late adolescence, the period of transition is shorter, simpler, and less confusing. In our complex society, adolescents have often exceeded their parents' education (if not in years, then in content), and often they plan to have different jobs from their parents. They not only have to decide what kind of work they want to do and what kind of values they want to hold in this changing society, but they also have to decide what it means to be a man or a woman and what it means to be a responsible adult. Thus, adolescents today not only are faced with making the transition from what they were like as children to what they will be like as adults, but are also frequently faced with reevaluating what it means to be an adult. The various liberation movements—black, chicano, women, gay—are all presenting new conceptions of adulthood. These kinds of questions become particularly important during late adolescence and during the period of youth (for those who extend this moratorium past adolescence itself).

In sum, adolescence has been extended in our society, largely because of the increasing complexity and alternatives of adult life. This extension has provided more time to deal with complex issues, but also has increased the possibility of a long period of "storm and stress" that has been the key description of adolescence in our society ever since it was first studied (Hall, 1904). Storm and stress does not necessarily describe adolescence in all societies, however; for example, Margaret Mead (1928) reported on several South Sea Island societies where adolescence was a time of natural transition with little emotional stress. Nonetheless, at present, adolescence has three distinct subperiods: early adolescence, late adolescence, and for

Adolescence

some individuals (especially those who "drop out" from society or become "activists" or continue on to college and graduate school) there is a period of youth. The central issues in these three periods are, in order: Who am I as a person? How do I connect who I have decided I am with society's expectations? And for youth: How can I really be myself in a society that doesn't meet my needs? For the most part, our discussion of the four domains focuses on early and late adolescence; nonetheless, the substage of youth is an interesting, although not necessarily typical stage, and the recent works of Keniston (1968) are worth reading.

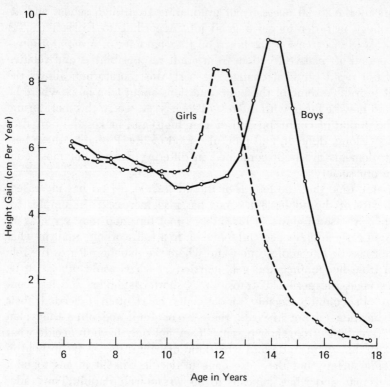

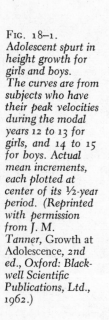

Fig. 18–1.
Adolescent spurt in height growth for girls and boys. The curves are from subjects who have their peak velocities during the modal years 12 to 13 for girls, and 14 to 15 for boys. Actual mean increments, each plotted at center of its ½-year period. (Reprinted with permission from J. M. Tanner, Growth at Adolescence, 2nd ed., Oxford: Blackwell Scientific Publications, Ltd., 1962.)

BIOLOGICAL DOMAIN

Adolescence begins with the biological event of puberty along with the physical changes (in height, strength, and bodily proportions) as well as the sexual changes that are the crucial biological aspects of early adolescence. Not only do these biological changes affect the adolescent's internal physiology but also his social and affective domains as well as his image of the self.

Physical Development

The adolescent growth spurt is the most obvious and recognizable mark of puberty. It occurs in all adolescents, although its intensity and duration varies from individual to individual. As with all biological events, it occurs earlier in girls (between ten and a half and thirteen on the average) than in boys (between twelve and a half and fifteen). Since boys mature about two years later than girls, girls are taller than boys at the beginning of the growth spurt; the greater increase in height for boys results in part from the later onset of puberty in boys. Nearly all of the parts of the body increase

The Life
Cycle

492

in size at a generally similar rate; the few exceptions are the brain, skull, and reproductive organs. The order of increased growth is fairly regular—leg length is first, body breadth begins a few months later, and trunk length increases about a year later; most of the increase in height results from the increase in trunk length (Tanner, 1971).

Physical strength also increases at this time, especially for boys. Before puberty there is little difference in strength between boys and girls, but boys rapidly exceed girls in athletic ability after puberty. Boys gain more muscle bulk, have a greater increase in the number of red blood cells (which carry oxygen to the muscles), and experience more of an increase in the alkali reserve in the blood (which allows greater quantities of lactic acid produced by muscles to be absorbed by the blood). Lung capacity also increases markedly in boys. In both boys and girls, the heart grows rapidly. However, girls are more mature than boys at all ages and also have lower mortality rates than boys at all ages.

What are some of the social and psychological effects of these changes? Since there is considerable individual variation in the age at which these changes begin, one adolescent may have completed the growth spurt before another has begun. Some fifteen-year-old boys may be quite athletic, strong, and big, whereas others are not. Some early maturing girls may tower over their friends, and especially over their male classmates, and may also be awkward, self-conscious, and generally unaccustomed to the rapid changes that have occurred in their bodies. Clearly, one's self-concept and one's social interaction (popularity, acceptance, skill in getting along with others) are likely to be affected by these physical changes. Fortunately, they are transient—the slow developers will catch up and may be taller, increasing their feelings of well-being and decreasing the anxiety of those who grew up faster.

Sexual Maturation

The growth of pubic hair, the breasts, the penis, and testes are probably of at least equal importance to the adolescent as is the increase in their height and strength. Typically, these sexual developments occur at about the same time as the other physical developments of adolescents. In boys, growth of the testes usually begins the changes at puberty; the penis begins growing at about the time of the beginning of the height spurt and ends its growth about a year before the time of the greatest increase in physical strength. Pubic hair begins at about the same time (ten to fifteen) and spreads across the body to the underarms, legs, face, and chest (depending, of course, on parental and racial heredity). In girls—whose development again precedes boys by about two years—growth of pubic hair and breasts and the height spurt all occur at about the same time (age eight or nine to thirteen or fourteen). Menarche, or the first menstruation, occurs near the middle of the physical changes—at about age ten to sixteen and a half. (Fig. 18–2.)

As with the physical changes, there is great individual variation in sexual maturation. Thus, a boy may have completed all of the changes before another boy of the same age has experienced the first enlargement of his testes. And this difference may have important psychological and social effects on the adolescent. In a locker room, the differences in genital maturity are as obvious as are the physical differences on the football field. One girl may be menstruating and experiencing surprising shifts in moods

Adolescence

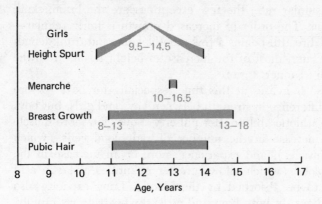

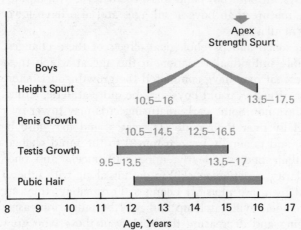

FIG. 18–2. *Sequence of important events during adolescence. The average boy and girl are represented. The range of ages within which each event charted may begin and end is given by the figures placed directly below its start and finish. (Adapted from Tanner, 1971, p. 915. Reprinted with permission from Daedalus, copyright © 1971 by the American Academy of Arts and Sciences.)*

while her classmates are still wondering what it will be like to menstruate.

One important aspect of these changes is the differences in the way boys and girls view their maturing sexuality. Bardwick (1971) suggests that boys see their developing masculinity as purely positive, pleasurable, and satisfying. It is a good thing, a mark of becoming a man; masturbation and anticipation about sexual acts are pleasant. Bardwick believes that this stage is different for girls, however, for their sexual maturity combines anticipations of pleasure with anticipations of pain. For girls, menstruation is both a satisfying mark of becoming a woman and, for some, an event that is characterized as "unclean" or "the curse," and that presents distinct hygienic problems. And whereas sexual intercourse may seem potentially pleasurable to a girl, there is also some fear of being penetrated by the male's penis—this anticipated event is thus both pleasant and potentially painful or threatening. Bardwick believes that girls are ambivalent about their sexuality, and that they tend to discover their sexuality later than boys, since they do not have as easily accessible a source of sexual pleasure and masturbation as boys do.

Sexual maturation also brings a marked change in the adolescent's social interactions and leisure time pursuits. There is an increase in sex hormones and in androgen (a hormone similar to the male sex hormone) in both male and female adolescents, and androgen has also been implicated in sexual arousability in both men and women (Bardwick, 1971). Perhaps it is this increase in androgen, but whatever the cause, boys and girls become more

The Life Cycle

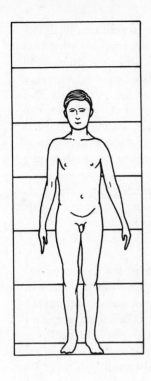
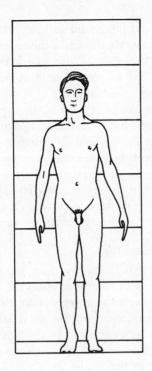
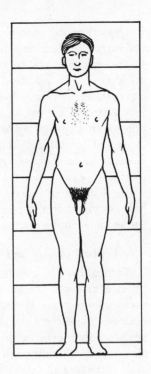
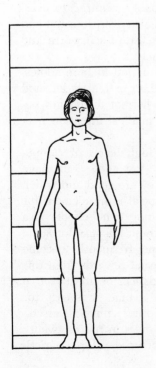
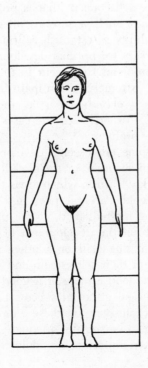
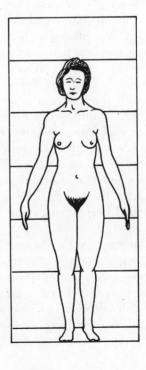

FIG. 18–3.
*Differing degrees
of pubertal develop-
ment at the same
chronological
age. Upper row
shows three boys
all age 14.75 years.
Lower row shows
three girls all age
12.75 years.
(Adapted from
Tanner, 1971,
p. 916. Reprinted
with permission
from Daedalus,
copyright © 1971
by the American
Academy of Arts
and Sciences.)*

495

interested in one another and interested in each other in profoundly different ways than before puberty. Much of this increased interest and attraction to the opposite sex is at the core of the social and affective changes in adolescence. In addition, this increased interest in the opposite sex may again differ markedly between adolescents of the same age. Certainly, the fact that girls are two years ahead of boys is one aspect of the problem; the other is that two girls (or two boys) of the same age may be very interested or not at all interested in dating and interacting with the opposite sex. Because there is often a great deal of social pressure within the adolescent's groups to date, what often happens is that early maturing boys and girls will get together and do their thing, whereas late maturing boys and girls will get together and secretly wonder what it is all about. We return to this subject later in the discussion of affective changes during adolescence.

Individual Assets and Liabilities

Physical health is an obvious factor that may transcend the more general physical changes in adolescence. Improved child health care has had marked dividends in many Western countries (especially Britain and Scandinavia) because adolescents in these countries are markedly taller, stronger, and healthier than ever before. In most areas in this country, physical health is also rather high, although child care in urban ghetto areas and in some rural areas is among the poorest in the world. Poor physical health also takes its toll at adolescence. One aspect of the improved child health care is that weaker children are now surviving to adolescence so that some frail or handicapped adolescents, who might not have survived previously, now have to cope with the challenges and possibilities of adolescence. The difficulties that might occur for an adolescent with severe asthma, or a heart murmur, or a physical handicap (such as blindness, deafness, or lack of a limb) may be serious and require some special help to ensure that he will develop a strongly positive self-concept that is probably required to overcome these physical obstacles. Such persons are often also overprotected and are thus limited in their ability to establish a firm sense of self-worth and competence that are necessary for optimal development.

Less extreme physical problems that occur in this period include adolescents who are overweight, extremely late in maturing, or extremely affected with the affliction of acne (related in part to the hormonal changes occurring during this period). In such extreme cases, medical attention may be useful to help correct the problem.

At the other extreme, some adolescents develop high levels of competencies at some physical, intellectual, or social skill. Most adolescents have a range of talents and quickly learn in which areas they are good and which areas they might as well avoid. Parental, peer, and social reinforcement for good performances (on the football field, at the piano, or in school) also helps to encourage or prohibit the development of these talents. But some adolescents clearly excel at one skill or another and frequently become tempted to gain almost all of their self-esteem and social rewards from this one area. Although being a good athlete or a good dancer or an attractive person may bring a great deal of social success for a time, it is easy for such adolescents to focus exclusively on these (and other) physical assets; this may not prepare them to be socially adequate adults in ten or twenty or thirty years. It is thus often important for adolescents to develop a variety of strengths and to try their hand at things in which they might not be fully successful at first, so that they can fully explore their potentials and develop a range of skills that will carry them through adolescence into adulthood.

Biological Aspects of the Self-Concept

The *self-concept* may be defined as the way we see ourselves and the list of attributes we think others would see in us if they knew us totally. This is the *actual* (or real) *self-concept*. There is also the *ideal self-concept,* which is the way we would like to be if we were perfect. And there is the *perceived self-concept,* which others see in us and that very good (and honest) friends would tell us about ourselves, or that persons in a sensitivity group might provide as "feedback" about how they see us. Most of this self-concept consists of things we consciously recognize about ourselves; but part of it is also made up of unrecognized aspects of ourselves (Jersild, 1963) that

FIG. 18–4.
Self-image:
as idealized:
as deprecated.

497

influence how we think of ourselves; but we are not fully aware of these unrecognized aspects or how they influence the way we see ourselves. For example, we might dislike ourselves because our parents or friends might act as if there is something wrong with us—but we may not be aware of this; instead we may only be aware that we see ourselves (our actual self-concept) as very different from what we would like to be (our ideal self-concept).

An important part of this self-concept is associated with our body—the way we see our physical self and the way we think others see our body. Thus, especially during adolescence when the body is changing very rapidly, the bodily aspect of the self-concept is quite important. If one feels too tall or too fat or too sexually mature, or that his penis is too short or her breasts are too small, these self-perceptions will influence the individual's self-concept away from what one feels one would "ideally" like to be. Conversely, if one feels that one's body is great, that the changes that have occurred during adolescence are wonderful, and that the body is a great asset in all regards, this perception will obviously increase one's self-esteem and will be an important part of a positive self-concept. Few adolescents probably feel so positively about their bodies—at least during early adolescence; and this may be part of the reason for their concentration on clothes, following the latest style trends, and occasional careful attention to grooming (especially before dates). Most men can probably remember how important the growth of the beard, body hair, and penis seemed to be during adolescence; and most women probably remember how important the growth of their breasts and their physical appearance seemed to be at this time. Indeed, these physical—bodily—characteristics are important aspects of the self-concept; this is especially true in adolescence, but continues to be true during adulthood as well. Physical deformity or the loss of a limb at any time during one's life may have serious effects on one's self-concept.

COGNITIVE DOMAIN

Only a part of the vast changes that occur during early adolescence are obvious physical changes. An equally important and far-reaching set of changes occurs in the individual's intellectual processes. These changes have a wide range of effects because intellectual processes are essentially at the core of human functioning. If we think differently—or in more complex ways—this affects the way we interpret the social environment and the kinds of solutions we find to personal problems; it influences the way we interpret and respond to our feelings; it changes the way in which we perceive and interpret our political, religious, and economic institutions; and it changes the way in which we ask questions about the meaning of life and the basic questions of "who am I?" or "what kind of an adult will I become?"

Formal Operations Stage of Intellectual Development

Piaget's conception of intellectual development, which has been discussed in earlier chapters as it characterizes the thinking of children, continues to develop at least through adolescence. The important turning point from concrete operations (where the child can solve problems that are concretely present and that he can manipulate) to *formal operations* (characterized by abstract thought) occurs around the time of puberty and is a major shift in intellectual capacity.

Formal operations is a very complex kind of thinking ability, which is useful for solving abstract logical, mathematical, or physical problems. But most of us probably do not use it very much in daily problem solving. Typically, we turn on the light switch, and if the light does not go on, we try the switch again, then replace the bulb, and then call for help. This is essentially concrete operations thinking. But if we were to sit down and draw a wiring diagram and analyze the problem abstractly, we could devise a series of experiments to determine how far the current is traveling and by carrying out these experiments we could locate the cause of the problem. Similarly, when the car does not start, we typically rely on such concrete operations as turning the key repeatedly and perhaps engage in some pre-operational (magical) solutions as putting the gearshift in "neutral" instead of "park," or kicking the tire or opening the hood and looking. When we finally call a mechanic, he analyzes the problem logically, tries an experiment or two, and then tows the car to the garage for a series of expensive experiments before he discovers that the battery is dead, the carburetor is clogged, or that the pistons have disintegrated.

In general, formal operations involves the ability to think abstractly—about the meaning of life, the effect of nuclear particles on the nucleus of an atom, the square root of —1, or what life will be like in fifty years. It implies that complex mathematics, physics, and logic are not fully comprehensible by younger children, but can be understood by adolescents; it suggests that religious, philosophical, and ethical questions can be asked and considered in a new light; and it suggests that the questions of "Who am I?" take on a new meaning during adolescence.

Practical Implications. Such an important change in intellectual processes obviously opens up a new realm of educational possibilities for adolescents. Complex mathematics and advanced physics that could not previously be understood may suddenly become comprehensible and very interesting. Others may react by raising new and higher order questions in classes or in personal investigations. In many ways, questions of "how do I do it?" are replaced by questions of "what does it mean?" or "what would happen if this experiment were carried out on the moon?" Educators working with adolescents may be familiar with these changes in thinking and may also be aware that some students have not yet attained this ability although they are the same chronological age as their formal operations classmates. Such differences between individuals and the challenges presented by this highly powerful mode of thinking are challenging educational issues. For example, how can classes be organized so that students may make the most of this new intellectual skill and fully utilize the possibilities it presents?

It may also have practical implications for language development, since abstract words and thoughts become comprehensible for the first time at this stage of life; and this may provide a powerful tool for exploring the abstract qualities of life and the universe. Philosophical and religious words and concepts may also take on a new meaning. "He ascended into Heaven," which at a concrete level implies physical ascent, in formal operations implies a more spiritual understanding; such abstract interpretations of doctrine may lead to serious debates between adolescents and clergymen. In addition, feelings (that are abstract especially when someone else is having the feeling) can begin to be talked about more readily, and by late adolescence there may be a great deal of energy invested in understanding one's own feelings and those of others—as in sensitivity groups. After all, what is love or joy or anger or guilt? Why do I feel them? Do they feel the same for you as they do for me? These are abstract questions, different from the child's concrete labeling of feelings and important for the adolescent to explore.

Consider the effects of this advance in thinking ability for occupational choice. How does one choose an occupation? Does it not involve, in part, an abstract analysis of one's qualifications and the occupation's demands, and one's abstract imagining of oneself in that occupation at some point in the future? The number of occupations is immense, and the choice is difficult. If one had to rely on the role playing or modeling of childhood alone in choosing an occupation, the task would be very difficult. After all, what is a psychologist or a physicist or a steam fitter or a nurse?

One of the most important effects of this increase in cognitive development is its influence on moral thinking. Kohlberg (1964) has found that young children make moral decisions on a different basis than older children or adolescents do, and that this difference reflects their level of cognitive development. For example, young children think in terms of avoiding punishment or receiving rewards; older children think in terms of being "good"; but the highest levels (corresponding to formal operations) involve abstract moral principles such as "the greatest good for the greatest number." Perhaps some of this abstract moral thinking is illustrated by the criticism expressed by many college students about war and poverty. But, as with formal operations in general, not all adults use these higher levels of moral thought in their daily lives—and even if they did, the interpretation or the action resulting from them may differ.

Effects on Adolescent Issues. The basic questions that Erikson (1968) finds central to this period of adolescence are "who am I?" and "what is the continuity between who I was as a child, who I am now, and who I will be in the future?" These questions evoke an abstract answer from those adolescents who have achieved formal operations. And perhaps because of the advance of formal operations, these issues take on the importance that Erikson has noted during adolescence. For a younger child, the question "who am I?" is a concrete question; for adolescents, it is a shattering question striking them to their core and raising significant questions about the meaning of life, the nature of society, the nature of mankind, and such ultimate concerns as the meaning and reality of God.

Adolescents often find these questions fascinating and delve deeply into religion or philosophy. Others focus on the evils of society and join protest marches. Some adolescents ignore these questions completely, perhaps in part because they are too threatening, and instead they hang on firmly to such concrete forms of identity as "top student" or "athlete" or "delinquent." In general, the period of adolescence is characterized by at least some inquisitive exploration of basic questions and a reexamination of values, attitudes, and beliefs. In part, these explorations are made possible by the intellectual development at this stage; in part, they result from the sexual maturation that brings up many new questions about one's identity and values.

This is not to say, however, that these explorations are purely intellectual ones. Indeed, trying to sort out one's *feelings* about who I am, where I'm going, and what's right and wrong are at the core of this process. What am I feeling? Why am I feeling this way? What will it be like when I get older?

These emotional questions combine with a kind of arrogance and lead to such expressions of feeling as—"no one has felt this way before," "no one really understands me," "I know what I want and where I'm going," "just leave me alone, I'm all right!" Not only do the questions take on new abstract dimensions but also the answers seem to be absolute and there is often little room for compromise; it is as if after applying the abstract moral principle the adolescent is capable of understanding he seems to assume that everyone can see it clearly his way and there should be no question about his rightness. Sometimes adolescents can be difficult to put up with—or to communicate with.

Creativity

The opening up of new abstract possibilities also opens the door for a marked advance in creativity during the adolescent stage. The complexity of defining just what creativity is was discussed at length in earlier chapters. But most of us can think of adolescents who suddenly begin writing rather good poetry or short stories or who compose music or write plays—often dealing with very important adolescent issues—such as love, tenderness, sexuality, the meaning of life, or the relations with parents. Other adolescents apply their abstract thinking ability to solving scientific problems, building "inventions," or just daydreaming (fantasizing) about what the future will be like for them. Other adolescents use their creativity to invent new ways to get into trouble, to make money, to "rip off" others, or to become leaders. In many ways, this period of adolescence is one of the most creative of the life span, but the creativity is often very fresh or raw and not yet refined into a socially recognized creative product; thus, this creativity may not be encouraged (which is unfortunate) or it may be channeled into ways that are negative for the individual adolescent (even the most creative delinquents eventually are caught, and jail seldom produces optimally functioning adults).

Thus much of the task of working with adolescents in this regard is to encourage creativity as well as to aid in leading the adolescent to discipline his creativity so that it can rise to its fullest expression of his individuality as well as communicate effectively with others. Even when the creativity is tending toward negative manifestations (such as finding new ways to peddle drugs to kids), the creativity itself may be encouraged and hopefully channeled into ways that lead toward more optimal growth for the adolescent. Tasks such as these require a great deal of creativity on the part of those working with the adolescents as well.

AFFECTIVE DOMAIN

The adolescent has lived with two very important persons—namely, his parents—for a dozen years and will probably live with them for a few more years. But adolescents are also shifting their emotional ties to a broader social network of friends and teachers, and other adults; this network extends to all of society as the adolescent has increasing experience with different kinds of people he previously never imagined existed. There is thus typically a gradual shift on the part of the adolescent from emotional dependence on the parents and the family to greater independence and autonomy. This shift is one of the most difficult issues during this period, for both adolescents and their parents. On the one hand, adolescents want

Adolescence

greater freedom and independence (but also need a secure place to return when that independence becomes a bit frightening); on the other hand, parents want their children to grow up but also hate to see them making mistakes and becoming less dependent on their guidance and support. Both parents and adolescents tend to be ambivalent about this growing independence: they both want it, yet don't want it. Parents often tend to hold on to the adolescent more than the adolescent wishes; and the adolescent wants freedom and autonomy before he is quite capable of handling those responsibilities.

Autonomy

Goethals and Klos (1970) have suggested three types of parental attitudes toward their adolescent's search for autonomy: the "overadequate parent," the "not-quite-adequate parent," and the "ideally adequate parent." The overadequate parent thwarts the adolescent's search for independence and self-reliance by trying to do too much to protect and shelter him. This type of parent may appear to be concerned and affectionate, but is often intrusive into the adolescent's life and overly concerned with social prescriptions, family traditions, and respect from the children. Sometimes the adolescent's independence makes this parent feel unneeded. When the parents are markedly overadequate, the adolescent may be forced to rebel and to reject parental standards. Since the adolescent still needs a source of emotional support (especially to sever ties with the parents), he often turns to his peers for support and may overly conform to the behavior and attitudes of his friends. Also because the adolescent is rejecting his parents, he may prolong his adolescence in order to prevent becoming an adult like his parents, or he may date or marry persons who are unacceptable to the parents.

Not-quite-adequate parents, at the other extreme, are not sure of themselves and thus try to keep the adolescent from adding to their problems. They may hold adult standards for the adolescent or may try to impose their own unfulfilled expectations on him. They tend to be unresponsive and not very affectionate, and the child typically feels deprived. The adolescent then winds up in a bind, because he cannot meet the parents' expectations, and yet hungers for their recognition; the more he seeks to please the parents, the less responsive they become because they cannot give what their adolescent really wants—a strong, supportive relationship that will encourage the adolescent's autonomous growth and self-fulfilling independence.

Some of the characteristics of the "ideally adequate parent" that Goethals and Klos (1970) believe tend to produce a more autonomous adolescent are:

(1) That the parent recognizes the adolescent as a separate person in his own right, which implies the independent or competent behavior by the adolescent is gratifying rather than threatening to the parent; (2) that the parent can show genuine care or concern but not over-involvement, and can give or offer but not impose; and (3) that the parent is able to terminate old ways of relating when they no longer are adequate or appropriate, which implies an openness to change that is so necessary for any ongoing relationship. (pp. 22–23)

Relations with the Family

Adolescents typically have two parents, both of whom are then important for the individual; if one or both parents is missing, the adolescent may need to find some parent-substitute figures to provide the support, advice, and affection that is needed to progress readily through the various changes and crises that confront adolescents. However, children and adolescents are amazingly resourceful. We are continually amazed at how well adolescents manage to cope with family situations that would seemingly destroy any possibility for optimal development; probably such family "messes" have important effects, but generally, adolescents somehow manage to get through them—and indeed, if parents had to be perfect, none of us would have made it this far and we would certainly approach our own parenthood with great fear and trembling!

It is likely that for boys and girls alike, both mothers and fathers are important. It has long been thought that fathers are especially important for the proper development of boys; but recent evidence suggests that fathers are quite important for the development of their daughters as well (Hetherington, 1972). And mothers have often received too much of the "blame" for the inadequate development of their children (especially sons). Indeed it seems that a more useful approach is to view the family as a unit and to pay more attention to the way in which the adolescent responds to that family unit rather than to the characteristics of the family—or of the individual family members (Novak and van der Veen, 1970).

Also important for the adolescent are the relationships with other siblings (brothers and sisters) and with other family members (grandparents and other relatives). Some adolescents may be traumatized by the outstanding success of older brothers or sisters and have to find a way to succeed or to realize their unique potentials in some field other than the one chosen by their successful older sibling. Also older siblings really grow up in a different family situation from their younger siblings, and this difference may make the adolescent issues more difficult in some areas, but easier in others, depending on the issue involved—some younger siblings are granted more freedom to be different from parental expectations, whereas some older siblings have more freedom to choose their area of excellence without having to worry about competition from other siblings. Grandparents are important family members who may provide an important emotional support, buffering the adolescent from their parents; and they also provide a valuable historical perspective to the family and to the culture. Adolescents and grandparents typically share a great deal in common and may be more similar in some ways than the adolescent and his parents. Since we tend to live in an age-segregated society, we believe that it is important for adolescents to have intimate contact with persons of their grandparents' age.

Relations with Friends and Society

One of the most common observations of adolescents is that they tend to be highly conforming to the styles, behaviors, and attitudes of their peers, or persons of the same age. Probably much of this conformity results from an important need of the adolescent to be accepted and to belong to a social group resulting from his decreasing reliance on the family. That is,

Adolescence

503

as the emotional tie with the family becomes less of a support, and as the adolescent rebels (in little or big ways) against his parents, it is important to have another source of emotional support and self-esteem. This support is often provided by the peer group. In Denmark, where adolescents feel greater independence and thus do not need to break away from their parents to the degree they do in this country, the peer group is less important; also instead of having many friends, the Danish adolescents tend to have a few very close friends; still, in both countries adolescents turn to their parents for help in solving problems and turn to their peers for companionship (Kandel and Lesser, 1972).

The peer group represents a microcosm of society in many ways: it is a small group of people who interact with one another in ways that are similar to the ways in which adults in society interact—there are leaders and followers; there are "in-groups" and "out-groups"; and there are power struggles, emotional supports, affection, and tasks to be accomplished. In Sullivan's (1953) conception, the peer group is a very important aspect of adolescent development. Before adolescence, boys (Sullivan does not discuss girls) form what he calls "chumships" in which they learn to value the integrity and to respect the desires of others; they also learn some basic lessons about affection and intimate caring for another person. After puberty, when interest shifts to girls, these boys retain their old group for emotional support as they reach out to explore heterosexual relationships. Eventually, girls may be brought into these peer groups, and this kind of casual social interaction is important in learning how to relate to the opposite sex. Even in college, coed dorms serve this important function of learning how to relate casually to the opposite sex so that when there is a truly intimate relationship, such as marriage, there is less of an abrupt change from the premarital relationship (of scheduled perfumed, well-groomed dates) to the marital relationship of daily routine (hair curlers and whiskers in the basin) with a beloved partner.

Developments in Feelings

Goethals and Klos (1970) describe two important aspects of adolescent development as learning to manage anxiety and working through initial attempts at sexual intimacy. An important part of being an autonomous person (which ideally is progressing well during late adolescence) is dealing with the anxiety involved in being one's own person—independent and autonomous—and being open to new experiences that may be somewhat threatening to the individual. Somehow the adolescent has to outgrow his childish views of himself, his mother, and his father. He must come to recognize his own potentials, strengths, weaknesses, and begin to formulate the goals for his life—and these can bring some realistic anxiety, since one can never predict what the future will hold. Eventually the adolescent, who believes for several years that his parents do not understand him, comes to relate with them as friends who do, in fact, understand him and who are leading lives that are actually understandable to him. It takes time and considerable emotional strength and support for the adolescent to come to see other people and himself as they really are; but this development is an important one for optimal development into mature adulthood.

The Life Cycle
The beginnings of these later developments take place in early adolescence. Feelings tend to become more complex (related, in part, to the

increased abstractness and complexity of intellectual thinking) and many adolescents spend considerable time and effort seeking to understand their feelings; others try to shut their feelings off, hoping they will go away; but of course they do not, and if they are shut off completely, professional help may be needed to open up these anxiety-producing feelings to awareness. Feelings of love and affection take on new meanings; they grow beyond the child's simplistic love of his parents to love of his chums in preadolescence and to romantic loves of his early "crushes" in adolescence; love may even extend to a love of mankind during late adolescence. Other feelings also come to be experienced in more complexity such as anger, hostility, joy, happiness, and sexual attraction. "Negative" feelings such as fear, anger, hostility, and anxiety—which all humans feel—are often more threatening than the "positive" feelings of love, joy, happiness, and sexual attraction. Somehow it seems "wrong" to feel fear or hate, but "right" to feel love or happiness. Isn't that strange, if it is true? For we all feel these feelings, and they are important internal aspects of our human interaction with other persons. Not allowing ourselves to experience a real feeling (such as hate or love) can block the whole feeling process and rob us of a whole range of important cues to what is going on inside us. The interesting thing, often seen in psychotherapy, is that feelings which are blocked inside seem very frightening indeed; but when they finally are felt and expressed verbally, they do not seem so scary after all—it is the blocking inside that makes them so upsetting. Somehow adolescents need to allow themselves the freedom to feel their feelings in all of their complexity and richness. Statements such as "you shouldn't feel that way" are nonsense; they *are* feeling that way. If the feelings don't get felt, the adolescent cannot work through what these feelings mean and how he can express them without hurting himself or others. In our view, there is nothing wrong with feeling *any* feeling that is really inside; the only point where right and wrong are at all relevant is at the point where the feeling is translated into behavior that damages the individual or another person. Feelings that are not felt can lead to as much damaging behavior as any feeling that is felt. Feeling and talking over a feeling that is very negative (such as "I hate you and want to kill you when you do that") can lead to growth for the individual and maybe even for the relationship; but if that feeling is locked up inside, it can corrupt the whole feeling process.

Sexual feelings are particularly important and difficult for adolescents to deal with, for they are new to them and there is so much cultural pressure about sexual feelings ("Don't feel that!" "Men shouldn't feel that" "Good girls don't think about those things" and the like). But, of course, sexual feelings are very human feelings; and sexual feelings are probably much more complex than social pressures would have us believe. Sometimes adolescents still feel very guilty about sexual feelings, masturbation, sexual relations, or sexual fantasies—despite some relaxation of social pressures about sex that has come about in recent years. But, after all, the only thing wrong with masturbation is that it is lonely. Sexual relations are more complex because another human being is involved and their complex needs must be considered as well as the possibility of pregnancy and venereal disease. Moral values are also clearly important for both persons involved in a sexual relationship. Equally important for adolescents is adequate information about sex and venereal disease. Some adolescents have sexual

Adolescence

desires or fantasies which they feel they "should not have." Some of these fantasies may be perfectly normal, but the person has not yet experienced enough different people to know that. And some adolescents may have homosexual desires or fantasies and be traumatized about these because of the great social pressures against such relationships. Nonetheless, many adults find homosexual relationships to be a meaningful style of life and argue that the only "pathological" thing about them is society's attitude of repression. In general, adolescents require some time and experience to deal with their sexual feelings and to find the comfort and intimacy to engage in sexual relations that are meaningful for them. Sometimes they may need some help or counsel about these issues—but unless the parent or other adult to whom they turn for advice is comfortable about their own sexuality, this advice may not be very helpful; adolescents thus often learn about sex as best they can from their peers.

Initial sexual relationships may be painful because of the guilt, anxiety, social pressures, and lack of feelings of comfort on the part of both participants. Usually there are several romantic relationships that are essentially "transitional relationships" (Goethals and Klos, 1970) between the pre-adolescent friendships with chums of the same sex and fully intimate relationships such as marriage where the uniqueness of both persons is recognized and both persons are allowed to continue growing and changing with the loving support and encouragement of the partner.

SOCIAL DOMAIN

Many of the developments in the important social domain have already been suggested because they interact so clearly with the other domains. For example, the relations with the family slowly evolve from one of dependence to one of autonomy in which the young adult ideally responds to his parents as friends who are important persons who have had greater and different experiences. Relations with peers tend to replace the family as a source of emotional support and self-esteem, but as the adolescent develops a firm sense of independence and autonomy, the peers recede somewhat in importance; deeper friendships that are now more selectively chosen further his growth, and supply companionship during adulthood. Relations with the community expand in early adolescence and continue to expand during adulthood, as the person becomes more involved, committed, and an increasing participant in community affairs. Relations with religion often intensify during adolescence as important philosophical questions about the meaning of life are raised and a more abstract, spiritual understanding of religious beliefs becomes possible as a result of the intellectual development of formal operations. In later adolescence these religious commitments may lose some of their importance when more "earthly" matters of dating, occupational choice, and earning a living become important; but religious involvement often increases again when the adult has children and wants to provide them with a religious education. Of course, some adolescents question their faith and decide to reject it—this may be temporary (until they have children of their own) or a lifelong philosophy.

One important social area we have not discussed is the adolescent's relationship with education. Indeed, much of the adolescent's time is spent in school, which, together with the teachers, has an important effect on the adolescent. It is in school that one learns the kinds of intellectual and occupational skills at which one is proficient, and which areas of study should be avoided. Grades, as objectionable as they may be, do provide some useful feedback on this important matter. High schools also provide another important function, the value of which may be debated. That is, schools often "track" students into "college-bound paths" or into "vocational paths." These decisions are sometimes made on the basis of IQ test scores and grades, with little involvement of the person who is being "tracked." These decisions can become irreversible so that a "vocational" student who later decides to go to college may not have the necessary courses and skills. Thus in an important way, high schools tend to determine the career paths of the students (Cicourel and Kitsuse, 1968). These authors also point out that high schools often function as "clearing houses" for students, providing links between parents, police, and colleges or vocational schools without the direct involvement of the student. Thus, some students may become typed as "delinquents" or "college material"; this social typing can effectively limit the adolescent's freedom by limiting the alternatives that are available to him. Unfortunately, it may be easier to fit the "type" and to conform to the school's (and teacher's) expectations than it is to discover one's individual uniqueness and to grow optimally into a fully functioning adult.

Socialization of the Adolescent

The socialization process, that is, the process by which social values, attitudes, and expectations are communicated from one person to another, begins at birth and continues throughout the life span. In adolescence, the principal persons involved in socializing the adolescent are the peers, the teachers, and the parents (in about that order). In many ways there is a "youth culture" in our society where young people share many common values, attitudes, and beliefs. These are the result of socialization by peers and by the media (such as newspapers, magazines, and television), which tell an adolescent what he "should" think, feel, and buy. Of course, no one fully conforms to these socialization pressures; but they are real and do affect our behavior in important ways. Certainly, teachers, parents, and friends influence our attitudes and values and play an important role in socializing adolescents into the roles that they will be expected to play in. adulthood—as workers, spouses, and parents. Much of this socialization is vital to help us play our roles in ways that fit in with the way other people play their roles. But it can be limiting as well; and adolescents might be helped if they had just one person who said that it is all right to write poetry even if everyone else thinks that makes you a "sissy"—or it's all right to study gymnastics even if people call you a "tomboy"—if we were simple robots fully controlled by socialization, this would be a dull world indeed!

Identity Formation in Adolescence

According to Erikson (1968), the central turning point that characterizes adolescence (especially in our society) is the resolution of the *identity crisis*. As we have stated earlier, the central issues during adolescence are often: "Who am I?" "How can I be the same person now that I was as a child and will be as an adult?" and "How can I connect my self-explorations with the opportunities and demands of society?" These issues involve the basic question of identity—the sense of knowing who it is that is me—as a man or a woman; as an intelligent or athletic or creative or popular person;

as a person with my body and my parents and my experience (and so on). This basic identity question is typically faced in early adolescence (with the aid of formal operations). But in addition to "Who am I as a unique person?" this question also involves the continuity of who I was as a child, who I am now, and who I shall be in the future. A person with a firm sense of identity also has a firm sense of continuity and sameness with the past that is also projected into the future. These important tasks are at the core of much of adolescence, and we have discussed them at several points in this chapter.

In later adolescence, these identity issues, if resolved fairly well up to that point, take on a new tone. The issue then becomes one of hooking up my sense of continuous identity with society. This may take the form of vocational choice or marriage or political activism. The question is how do I (as I know myself) fit in with society—where is the place that I can make mine? For most adolescents, there is a place where they feel relatively comfortable, and as they refurnish it with their own unique impression, it comes to serve as a firm launching point into marriage, parenthood, occupational advancement, and adulthood. For some persons, however, the problems of society are too clearly present to allow them to simply find their niche; instead, society or some aspect of it must be changed. These persons are the ones Keniston (1968) described as being in the stage of "youth"— caught between adolescence and adulthood.

Growth Trends in Late Adolescence

Robert White (1966) outlined five growth trends in young adulthood on the basis of his studies of normal lives in progress. The first is "the stabilizing of ego identity"—essentially the point we just discussed that identity not only becomes more sharp and clear but also more consistent and free from transient influences. In late adolescence, individuals have tended to select their social roles they will continue into adulthood; they tend to select and limit the experience they seek out; they have made decisions about their personal styles; they are tending toward increasing self-consistency across their various sexual, social, family, occupational, and marital roles. Thus, their identity, once rather fluid and changeable, takes on a more stable character—not unchangeable or rigid, ideally, but relatively stable and trustable.

White's second growth trend is "the freeing of personal relationships." In general, during late adolescence, relationships with other persons (including parents) become more responsive to the other person's real nature —they are deeper and involve more time so that the other person's uniqueness can be explored and appreciated—and relationships become more selective and concentrated so that they are also deeper than the relatively superficial and exploratory relationships in early adolescence. There is an important sense in which one must have a fairly firm sense of identity before one can really explore another's uniqueness in a deep personal relationship. If one is still trying to "find oneself," then often others are used to test out oneself and as a "sounding board" for one's growing identity. This may be very useful for establishing an identity; but it usually doesn't lead to very deep and meaningful relationships.

The Life Cycle

The third growth trend is a "deepening of interests" defined as some activity that "engages a person in a whole-hearted fashion." The young adult ideally comes to feel a growing command over some sphere of interest and increasing competence in that field. The reward is then from doing something that is interesting for its own sake. The ideal process is that something is undertaken (acting, music, studying, wood carving, writing, or learning about black history) and it is satisfying; this leads to feelings of competence that, in turn, lead to increased interest.

The fourth growth trend is toward a "humanizing of values"—this involves recognizing the human meaning of values and the development of a value system that is becoming the person's own system. It also involves an increasing empathy for all kinds of persons and the development of a unifying philosophy of values. In many ways this trend—for it is an ideal that not everyone reaches—is reminiscent of Kohlberg's (1964) higher stages of moral development discussed earlier.

The fifth trend is toward an "expansion of caring"—a real increased caring for persons who are suffering and a caring for the welfare of others. It ideally involves a true love for mankind and compassion for those who are suffering. It involves feeling pain when others hurt; for suffering when others are in need, and feeling the despair and loneliness of those who are neglected. Perhaps not many adolescents (or adults) progress very far on this trend, but we suspect that we all recognize the possibility for this kind of caring within us, and if this is to become a better world, we might have to listen more carefully to these caring tendencies within us.

IMPLICATIONS

UNDERSTANDING YOURSELF AND OTHERS

Nearly all of us have been or still are adolescents; we see adolescents all around us. Hopefully this chapter has provided some insight into what this difficult, exciting, and challenging time of life involves. Perhaps it has brought back vivid memories of painful and joyful moments that didn't really seem to make sense then—possibly if they are thought about and felt through now they might make more sense. In our psychology courses we ask the students to write an anonymous autobiography of their adolescence; we are amazed at how they made it through their assorted difficulties so well and they are relieved at how different these adolescent struggles seem from the perspective of a few years. Most of these autobiographies conclude with some statement such as: "I haven't worked through all of this yet, and some of these things still hang me up, but I feel like I'm making progress." This is the way it is with all of us—and should be if we are to be fully functioning persons open to new experiences and to new interpretations of old experiences.

LIVING AND WORKING WITH CHILDREN, ADOLESCENTS, AND ADULTS

Perhaps the most important consideration here is that adolescents are human persons who are doing the best they can to become fully functioning individuals. We might be able to help listen to the obstacles they are "up against" and help them to talk about their feelings and concerns and to gain a better understanding of how they are feeling and experiencing this period of their lives. Hopefully this chapter has sensitized us to some of the impor-

Adolescence

tant issues they may be facing; hopefully this book will provide a useful humanistic perspective for caring about and facilitating the growth of all people with whom we may interact.

DEVELOPING POSITIVE MODELS

Typically adolescents affect their parents in ways that are as important as the ways in which parents bring up their adolescents. Ideally, parents should have rich and rewarding lives of their own so that they can allow their adolescents to grow up and to achieve independence and autonomy at their own rate, with the emotional support they may need for this difficult process when they need it—but without being overadequate or pushing the adolescent out from the necessary family security too fast. Sometimes adolescents need help in getting this message across to their parents; sometimes parents need help to realize that their lives will not be empty and meaningless once they let their children grow into their own independent adulthood. Both parents and adolescents should be aware that they are very likely to feel ambivalent about the increasing autonomy, sexuality, and independent exploration of adolescents—they will both want it, yet not want it. Ideally, an open, supportive, and yet caring family atmosphere can be combined with the maturing, increasingly responsible adolescent leading to optimal growth and development of both the adolescent and his parents.

CHAPTER REFERENCES

BARDWICK, J. *Psychology of women*. New York: Harper, 1971.

CICOUREL, A. V. and J. I. KITSUSE. The social organization of the high school and deviant adolescent careers. In E. Rubington and M. S. Weinberg (eds.), *Deviance: the interactionist perspective*. New York: Macmillan, 1968.

ERIKSON, E. H. *Identity: youth and crisis*. New York: W. W. Norton, 1968.

GOETHALS, G. W. and D. S. KLOS. *Experiencing youth*. Boston: Little, Brown, 1970.

GRINNELL, G. B. *The Cheyenne Indians, their history and ways of life*, vol. 1. New Haven: Yale U. P., 1923.

HALL, G. S. *Adolescence: its psychology and its relations to physiology, anthropology, sociology, sex, crime, religion and education*, 2 vols. New York: Appleton, 1904.

HETHERINGTON, E. M. Effects of father absence on personality development in adolescent daughters. *Developmental psychology*, 1972, 7:313–326.

JERSILD, A. T. *The psychology of adolescence*, 2nd ed. New York: Macmillan, 1963.

KANDEL, D. B. and G. S. LESSER. *Youth in two worlds*. San Francisco: Jossey-Bass, 1972.

KENISTON, K. *Young radicals: notes on committed youth*. New York: Harcourt, 1968.

KOHLBERG, L. Development of moral character and moral ideology. In M. L. Hoffman and L. W. Hoffman (eds.), *Review of child development research*, vol. 1. New York: Russell Sage, 1964.

MEAD, M. *Coming of age in Samoa*. New York: Morrow, 1928.

NOVAK, A. L. and F. VAN DER VEEN. Family concepts and emotional disturbance in the families of disturbed adolescents with normal siblings. *Family Process*, 1970, 9:157–171.

SULLIVAN, H. S. *The interpersonal theory of psychiatry*. H. S. Perry and M. L. Gawel (eds.), New York: Norton, 1953.

The Life
Cycle

TANNER, J. M. Sequence, tempo, and individual variation in the growth and development of boys and girls aged twelve to sixteen. *Daedalus*, 1971, 100:907–930.

WHITE, R. *Lives in progress.* New York: Holt, 1966.

RECOMMENDED FURTHER READING

COLE, L. and I. N. HALL. *Psychology of adolescence,* 7th ed. New York: Holt, 1969.

MITCHELL, J. J. *Adolescence: some critical issues.* New York: Holt, 1972.

POWELL, M. *Psychology of adolescence,* 2nd ed. Indianapolis, Ind.: Bobbs-Merrill, 1971.

ROGERS, D. *Adolescence: a psychological perspective.* Monterey, Calif.: Brooks-Cole, 1972.

WINDER, A. E. and D. L. ANGUS. *Adolescence: contemporary studies.* New York: Van Nostrand, 1968.

Adolescence

Early and Middle Adulthood

DOUGLAS KIMMEL, Ph.D.
City College of the City University of New York

Prelude
Basic Theory and Research
  Biological Domain
    Physiological Changes During
      Adulthood
    Sexuality
    Maturing Biological
      Self-Concept
  Cognitive Domain
    Intelligence
    Creativity
  Affective Domain
    Personality Issues and
      Changes

Emotional Problems and
  Challenges During
  Adulthood
Social Domain
  Occupation: Work, Careers,
    and Jobs
  Family: Marriage, Parenthood,
    and Grandparenthood
  Leisure: Hobbies, Education,
    and Growth
  Effects of Social Factors
Implications
  Understanding Yourself and
  Others

WHEN does adulthood begin? What marks that fine line between adolescence and the beginnings of adulthood? To be sure, the period of adulthood is a long one that encompasses many of the most productive, creative, and potentially fulfilling years of a person's life. But the beginning and ending points of this period of life are not at all precise. One person might look and act like an adult at age sixteen or eighteen—he might be married, working, self-supporting, and living miles away from his parents; another person might be forty-five but still living at home, unmarried, and still trying to deal with some of the "adolescent" issues discussed in the last chapter. So it is not altogether clear when one becomes an adult—and it may vary considerably from one person to another. Perhaps it makes the most sense to view the beginning of adulthood as being marked by a series of *milestones*. One milestone might be leaving the parents' home; another might be working full time; another might be marriage; and another might be parenthood. These are social events that mark the beginning of adulthood in our society; in another society, becoming an adult might be very different—it might mean killing a buffalo or moving from your village to your wife's village or learning how to cook the ceremonial food.

These socially defined milestones indicate a kind of *social* age for an individual. *Chronological age* is also used to mark the beginning of adulthood; for example, in most states the age of eighteen or twenty-one marks one's legal status as an adult. There may also be a kind of *psychological age*, which reflects the psychological maturity of the individual. There is also a *biological age* that indicates the biological maturity of the person. These various ages (Birren, 1959) may be combined to produce a more complex description of when one becomes an adult—or what being an adult means. That is, one person might be socially and chronologically an adult, biologically an adult, but psychologically immature. Another person might be socially, biologically, and psychologically an adult, but chronologically "too young." One adult might be chronologically forty-five, socially twenty-five (just married, no children), psychologically forty-five (mature, competent, productive, and feeling successful), but biologically seventy (because of too little exercise, too much smoking, and too much cholesterol and fat that shorten life expectancy). To make this picture even more complete, we might also include an "existential age" (how old a person feels he is) and a "perceived age" (how old other people think a person is). Thus, *age* is a very complicated index and can mean many different things. The beginning of adulthood—or the end of the middle years of adulthood and the beginning of old age—are not easy to define. Neugarten et al. (1965) found that middle-aged people generally feel that "middle age" begins at forty and lasts until fifty, that a young adult is between eighteen and twenty-two or twenty-four, and that an old person is sixty or sixty-five to seventy-five (see Table 19–1). It might be interesting to see what ages a class of young people thinks defines the beginning of young adulthood, middle adulthood, and old age.

If we assume that adulthood begins when an individual feels he is an adult, when society treats him as an adult, and when he has begun to deal with adult problems and concerns (such as responsibility, intimacy with another person, productivity, and parenthood) with a reasonable degree of

Early and
Middle
Adulthood

513

TABLE 19-1
OPINIONS OF MIDDLE-CLASS, MIDDLE-AGED PEOPLE REGARDING VARIOUS AGE-RELATED CHARACTERISTICS

Characteristic	Age at Which it Is Considered Most Appropriate	Percent Who Agree Men N=50	Women N=43
Best age for a man to marry	20–25	80	90
Best age for a woman to marry	19–24	85	90
When most people should become grandparents	45–50	84	79
Best age for most people to finish school and go to work	20–22	86	82
When most men should be settled on a career	24–26	74	64
When most men hold their top jobs	45–50	71	58
When most people should be ready to retire	60–65	83	86
A young man	18–22	84	83
A middle-aged man	40–50	86	75
An old man	65–75	75	57
A young woman	18–24	89	88
A middle-aged woman	40–50	87	77
An old woman	60–75	83	87
When a man has the most responsibilities	35–50	79	75
When a man accomplishes most	40–50	82	71
The prime of life for a man	35–50	86	80
When a woman has the most responsibilities	25–40	93	91
When a woman accomplishes most	30–45	94	92
A good looking woman	20–35	92	82

Adapted by permission from B. L. Neugarten, J. W. Moore, and J. C. Lowe. Age norms, age constraints, and adult socialization. *American Journal of Sociology,* 1965, **70**(6), 710–717. Copyright © 1965 by the University of Chicago.

independence and maturity, then—in our society at least—he would seem to be an adult, and we want to understand what he is like and how an adult can become a more fully human person during these forty (or so) years between becoming an adult and entering old age.

One fundamental question during these adult years is: how much does the past (childhood and adolescence experiences) influence the person during adulthood? Some psychologists (such as Freud) imply that most of the basic personality is established in childhood and the adult does not change much for the remainder of his life. However, we know that we have changed and hope that we might continue to change as we grow older. And some sociologists suggest that when a person is put in a new situation, or when he becomes a parent or a grandparent, or when he changes from a worker to a foreman (for example), he changes because of the new demands of his new situation. Some psychologists have suggested that when a woman becomes pregnant, or goes through menopause, or when a man has a heart attack that the woman or man changes in important ways.

The task of this chapter, then, is to discuss some of the ways adults change as they grow older, gain experience, and pass through social and biological milestones. But at the same time, adults remain fairly consistent as they age —you remember your Aunt Martha as she was five or ten years ago and she is still pretty much the same today; your friends will recognize you in ten

The Life
Cycle

or twenty or thirty years as being the same person, even though you will also have changed.

Thus, we describe some of the changes that occur during adulthood in each of the four domains. We also point out the continuity of life and the way in which much of what happens in adulthood builds upon what happened earlier. We suggest ways to attain, continue to develop, and revise the original goals that an individual has so that he continues to progress toward a more fully human person during these important young and middle adult years.

BASIC THEORY AND RESEARCH

The spotlight of careful scientific investigation of the biological, social, cognitive, and affective changes during the life span has only recently been focused on these early and middle adult years. Thus, there is somewhat less information available about them than is true for childhood and adolescence or for the aged years. Yet, in many ways, these years represent the building toward and often the fulfillment of one's hopes, dreams, and major accomplishments. These are the years of marriage, parenthood, occupational advancement, and major economic productivity. Often these years see the growth of one's children from infancy into their own homes and marriages and the beginning of one's own grandparenthood. They may see the death of one's parents, possibly the death of one's spouse, and perhaps a serious illness. They may lead to one becoming rich and famous, productive and stable, or stagnated and unhappy. They may see a divorce and remarriage, a traumatic economic or physical loss, or the failure of one's children. Typically, they are challenging, exciting, risky, and rewarding years that involve a great deal of physical effort, emotional energy, and provide considerable opportunities for personal growth and fulfillment.

BIOLOGICAL DOMAIN

Essentially all of one's physical growth and maturation is completed at the beginning of adulthood. An adult is capable of reproducing children and is at the peak of his physical strength and vigor. Although some see a "downhill slide" beginning at about the age of thirty, this is primarily a result of our society's emphasis on youth (smooth skin, full heads of hair, slim bodies, and physical endurance) and of the lack of exercise for many adults in our society. There is little decline in physical ability to function adequately between youth and even age sixty-five (or older) if the body is not affected by disease or allowed to deteriorate. And if we recognize that unwrinkled skin might be taken as an indication of a lack of experience, whereas a wrinkled face and gray hair may reflect a sign of valuable experience and possible wisdom, and tells a vivid story of triumph over life's varied crises— that is, if our society were to value history, experience, and wisdom instead of freshness, innocence, and youth—then the meaning of growing old in our society would be very different. Our advertising themes would also be very different.

Physiological Changes During Adulthood

In the absence of disease and the accumulated effects of overeating, lack of exercise, injury, and various kinds of pollution, the physiological changes up to at least age sixty-five are rather trivial. There is some decline in physical strength and endurance, although athletes who continue their sport (or dancers who continue practicing and performing) are able to perform up to age forty or fifty although they may perform in somewhat less demanding roles at the later ages. But most of us lose the high degree of physical vigor that was characteristic of youth fairly early in adulthood. We eat too much and exercise too little; this forces the heart to work harder and some foods (or fats) that we eat contain cholesterol that gradually builds up in the blood vessels and blocks the efficient circulation of blood, again forcing the heart to work harder. Thus, the physical body develops the so-called "middle age paunch" and the muscles become soft and flabby. Those who smoke or live in polluted cities or work with asbestos or in coal industries (for example) may be exposed to highly injurious chemicals or particles in the air that contaminate the lungs. The link between lung cancer (or heart disease) and cigarette smoking is now an accepted fact; "black lung disease" is a frequent ailment of coal miners; and breathing asbestos particles is thought by some physicians to be highly injurious. There are probably many other hazards (in addition to polluted air) to which we are exposed daily that affect adults simply because they have been exposed to them longer than young people.

Disease is the most important physiological factor during adulthood. Birren et al. (1963) found that very healthy old men (sixty-five to ninety) were within the same range as younger men (age twenty-one to forty) on a variety of medical tests—such as the amount of hemoglobin in the blood, blood pressure, and flow of blood to the brain—for those aged subjects who were in excellent health, however, some physiological tests did show the effects of age—such as a decline in breathing capacity of the lungs and a slowing down of the time required to react to a stimulus (such as light that causes the pupils to contract). However, when there was even a small amount of disease present, such as arteriosclerosis (hardening of the arteries), there was much impact. Disease was found to affect not only physiological measures but also psychological and social variables. For example, arteriosclerosis could reduce the blood flow to the brain and also reduce the physical ability of the person to move about in the community and participate in community events. Thus, although there are some changes in physiological functions with age, the presence of disease is a far more important factor. If one is able to pass through the years of adulthood without disease —especially chronic disease such as diabetes, high blood pressure, or arteriosclerosis—then the physiological changes are relatively minor. Medical advances, which so far have had their most dramatic effect on curing childhood diseases, are now beginning to focus on these chronic diseases, such as heart disease and cancer, that are not only major causes of death but also take a heavy toll on an affected adult's ability to function as a fully human person during adulthood.

Some of the typical changes that occur with age in the absence of disease include decreased ability to see close objects distinctly (hence, many adults require reading glasses or bifocals), a gradual "yellowing" of the lens of the eye that affects color vision, and a decreased ability to see clearly when light is low. Most of these changes, however, are either correctable with glasses or have little important effect until old age. Periodontal (or gum) disease also becomes more common in middle age, sometimes forcing the removal of teeth or other dental surgery; but this is also a disease that many dentists believe can be prevented. There is also a gradual loss of hearing—especially for the higher frequencies—during adulthood, but this change typically does not affect a person's ability to hear well enough for all practical purposes until old age and may not be very severe even then in the absence of disease. There is some loss of athletic ability (probably related primarily to the decline in lung capacity), but this loss is probably more marked than necessary as a result of overeating and lack of exercise.

In general, there is a trend toward decreased efficiency of the body with age, which is most manifest in the body's ability to adjust to stress. Thus, older persons are more susceptible to disease and take longer to recover from exercise or physiological stresses than young people. Selye (1950) has described this as an important cause of aging—that with age persons become less able to adapt to stress, whether it be physical, emotional, or environmental. In principle, this seems to be true, but it is unknown how much of this change is the result of accumulated physiological defects that build up as persons spend more time alive, how much is the result of disease that builds up in some people but not in others, and how much is a result of the simple wear and tear of living. Actually, we do not yet know what causes people to age physiologically; indeed, it may be that the length of life will be expanded considerably further than medical science has been able to do so far by curing disease. It might be, as Comfort (1972) has suggested, that we are on the brink of developing a means to stretch out the life span so that, ideally, we might live, disease-free, another decade or two. However, unless life is added to years, there is little point in adding years to life!

Menopause. The single physiological change during adulthood that most resembles the changes at puberty or in early childhood is *menopause*. This event, the point when the menstrual cycle ceases, occurs in women typically at the age of about forty-five to fifty. Sometimes it is a gradual time of infrequent or irregular menses; sometimes it occurs more abruptly. We do not know exactly why it happens or what the exact cause of it is, but for some reason the ovaries stop responding to the hormones that previously had triggered them to produce an egg and to produce the female sex hormones, *estrogen* and *progesterone*. Thus, after menopause, a woman is no longer capable of producing a child, and she no longer produces nearly as much estrogen as she once did; also the monthly cycling of the hormone level in the body stops and in an important way the internal environment of her body changes. Neugarten et al. (1963) studied attitudes about the menopause of younger, menopausal, and older women and found that about one-half of each age group agrees that it is an unpleasant, depressing, and troublesome event (see Table 19–2); nearly as many disagreed, however.

Typical symptoms that have been associated with this "change of life" include hot flashes (feeling warm and perspiring for a few moments), irritability, changeable moods, and sometimes depression. It is estimated that somewhere between 50 and 85 per cent of the menopausal women experience some of these symptoms (Bardwick, 1971). However, whether these symptoms result from physiological changes (especially the drop in estrogen) or from other factors such as lack of knowledge about what will happen, fears about losing one's sexuality or femininity, and fears about "growing old" is not known. Nonetheless, it seems clear that replacement of the estrogen—either by injections or tablets of artificial estrogen—reduces

Early and Middle Adulthood

517

TABLE 19-2
WOMEN'S ATTITUDES TOWARD MENOPAUSE: BY AGE

Illustrative Items	Per Cent of Women Who Agree with Statement			
	Ages 21–30 (N=50)	Ages 31–44 (N=52)	Ages 45–55 (N=100)	Ages 56–65 (N=65)
Menopause is an unpleasant experience for a woman.	56	44	58	55
Women should expect some trouble during the menopause.	60	46	59	58
In truth, just about every woman is depressed about the change of life.	48	29	40	28
Women generally feel better after the menopause than they have for years.	32	20	68	67
A woman gets more confidence in herself after the change of life.	12	21	52	42
After the change of life, a woman feels freer to do things for herself.	16	24	74	65
Many women think menopause is the best thing that ever happened to them.	14	31	46	40
Going through the menopause really does not change a woman in any important way.	58	55	74	83
Women who have trouble with the menopause are usually those who have nothing to do with their time.	58	50	71	70
Women who have trouble in the menopause are those who are expecting it.	48	56	76	63
Women worry about losing their minds during the menopause.	28	35	51	24
A woman is concerned about how her husband will feel toward her after the menopause.	58	44	41	21
A woman in menopause is likely to do crazy things she herself does not understand.	40	56	53	40
Menopause is a mysterious thing that most women don't understand.	46	46	59	46
If the truth were really known, most women would like to have themselves a fling at this time in their lives.	8	33	32	24
After the menopause, a woman is more interested in sex than she was before.	14	27	35	21

Adapted by permission from B. L. Neugarten, V. Wood, R. J. Kraines and B. Loomis. Women's attitudes toward the menopause. *Vita Humana*, 1963, **6**:140–151.

these symptoms and also precludes other changes such as a decline in elasticity of the skin that appears to result from "estrogen starvation" (Masters and Johnson, 1970).

Since men do not menstruate, they cannot experience a menopause. Nor do men experience such a drastic drop in hormone production with age; rather, there is a gradual decline in the production of testosterone with age, and low levels are not reached until old age. Also, men do not lose the ability to produce fertile sperm until old age, and on occasion children are fathered by rather old men.

Sexuality

For both men and women advancing age sets no limit to sexuality. Women seem to become more responsive to sexuality during the middle years of adulthood. This may be related to both greater experience and to the effects of pregnancy that increases the flow of blood that seems to be related to orgasm (Sherfey, 1972). Men decline in some measures of sexual response (such as the capacity for repeated orgasms) very rapidly from adolescence to middle age, but there are few important physiological changes in the ability to experience satisfying sexual relations until very old age. Masters and Johnson (1970) report that a man's inability to achieve an erection or engage in intercourse is related to a range of nonphysiological factors such as overindulgence in food or drink, boredom, overwork, or anxiety about losing his ability to have sex. Even in old age, as long as a man has maintained effective sexual experiences, there is no age limit set for his sexuality, at least to the seventies or eighties. Older men, however, are more vulnerable to the lack of sexual stimulation than younger men; a long period of abstinence while one's wife is ill or hospitalized may result in his inability to achieve an erection. Women remain capable of satisfying sexual relations indefinitely; menopause, especially if there is estrogen replacement or frequent sexual experience, does not reduce a woman's ability to have intercourse or to achieve orgasm (Masters and Johnson, 1970). In fact, women sometimes see menopause as a freeing experience, for there is no longer any need to worry about the possibility of pregnancy.

The most prevalent causes of sexual abstinence in adulthood (and old age) is probably the loss of one's partner through death or divorce, social attitudes that strongly suggest that sex is for the young, and external factors such as pressure from the job or boredom with the spouse. One of the effects of the "double standard" for men and women is that women (who tend to live longer than men) marry older men and are thus even more likely to outlive their spouses; there is then little possibility for them to find another marital and sexual partner since old women outnumber old men by about three to two; and the old men are nearly always married.

Maturing Biological Self-Concept

As an adult looks in the mirror through the years he notices a number of gradual changes; he may see these changes reflected in the reactions of others around him. These changes in physical appearance, in strength, and in energy need to be integrated into the person's conception of himself. Sometimes these changes are hidden by cosmetics or hair dye in an effort to avoid looking old or to keep young (for that is such a "good" thing in our society today). The realization of being "middle aged" may be scarcely noticed until someone or something suddenly calls one's attention to it: "I went to a PTA meeting today and noticed how much older I looked than the mothers whose children are just starting school" or "I interviewed this new man today and noticed how bright and enthusiastic he looked and I thought how fast I am approaching retirement."

The events of pregnancy and childbirth probably bring major changes in the self-concept for those women who become mothers. For nine months there is a growing and changing shape to one's body and a whole set of new internal experiences. Then there is the event of giving birth, an event that is both feared and longed for and which calls attention to the importance and the vulnerability of the human body. And suddenly there is another human that is (or at least was) part of oneself and is now also separate. The child grows and is a pale reflection of yourself when you were that age and also contrasts with who you are now.

At the same time, your parents (now aged) are also indications of where your future is pointing, and in them you can see yourself. These two experiences—the child you once were and the old person you will become—probably both contrast with and also clarify the biological self you see in the mirror now.

How does one actualize that bodily self so that you—and now your children—can become more fully human beings? What is it that is precious and leads you to strive for the highest you can attain in humanness? Is it a searching for lost youth, for those adolescent infatuations, that strength and beauty and smooth skin—possibly, but not very likely. The challenge still lies ahead; the future is still the goal. Somehow, with this body, I want to continue to grow and change.

It may be that, for the first time, the body has become a reality that must be considered—it can no longer be simply taken for granted. It is not always willing to do whatever you might wish; it cannot be ignored, for it is making demands on you, whereas in youth you made demands on it. Neugarten (1968a) reports that middle-aged people—especially women (in terms of their husbands)—"monitor their bodies" to check for symptoms of disease and to try to prevent disease. Somewhere during these years—possibly because of a desire to remain healthy and vigorous, or because one wants to do something athletic or vocational or has a hobby, or because of a close call with illness (such as a heart attack or cancer), one begins to pay attention to his body. No longer are our bodies the machines that are designed for our use (and abuse) wherever we want to go or whatever we want to do; instead, they demand more consideration in our thinking and decisions and behaviors.

Indeed, this should occur in early adulthood—before the middle-age effects of overeating and underexercise set in. It should be a concern before pregnancy, for the mother's body directly supports and affects the child's; it should be realized that our bodies are as precious as the air we breathe, the work we do, and the risks we take. If we are to add life to our years, as fully human persons, then we need as fully human bodies as we can attain. Our society has provided us with countless ways to dehumanize ourselves—not the least of which are drugs, cigarettes, chemicals, pollution, and occupational hazards that directly limit our bodily ability to become fully human adults.

COGNITIVE DOMAIN

According to Piaget's theory, the stages of cognitive development that have thus far been discovered typically complete their unfolding during adolescence. It may be that there are additional stages that unfold or may unfold in future generations as mankind's knowledge increases beyond its present state; but the stage of formal operations becomes available to the person during adolescence.

In adulthood, ideally, the person continues to be able to think in formal operations or in concrete operations or even in preoperational ways depending on the demands of the situation. However, the studies of adult thinking do not necessarily support this ideal possibility. Rather, not all adults clearly show formal operations reasoning, and a large proportion of American adults seem to never develop the capacity for abstract thinking (Kohlberg and Gilligan, 1971). Perhaps, since it is not necessary to think abstractly to solve most daily problems, many persons do not use formal operations and the ability is simply lost through disuse. However, one study found an increasing percentage of adults up to age thirty were able to solve a formal operations problem: 45 per cent at age ten to fifteen, 53 per cent at age sixteen to twenty, and 65 per cent at age twenty-one to thirty, but there is a slight drop to 57 per cent at age forty-five to fifty (Kohlberg and Gilligan). A decrease in the ability to think in concrete operations has also been found for persons over age sixty-five (Papalia, 1972). Indeed, it has been suggested that there may be a kind of reversal of the developmental process in old age such that the ability to think in formal and even in concrete operations is progressively lost in the very old people (Piaget, 1972). Additional research will have to be done before we can be sure that this is a developmental change (and not simply the result of differences in education or health) and to identify the exact meaning of these changes. But it seems that considering cognitive development as something that increases until adolescence and then remains stable may be too simple.

Intelligence

More attention has been given to research on age changes in *intelligence* than in the area of changes in cognitive stages. For some time it was accepted that performance on IQ tests increased up to about age thirty and then declined, but more recent studies of individuals as they grew from childhood into middle age indicate that there is little decline in IQ test performance at least until age fifty (Botwinick, 1967). Much of the change thought to occur previously seems better explained by differences in the amount of education that persons of different ages had received (Kimmel, 1974). It now appears that more "gifted" adults may actually increase slightly in IQ test performance with age, for example, between ages thirty and forty-four (Kangas and Bradway, 1971). Certainly, during the periods of early and middle adulthood, there is no decline in ability to learn or to solve problems for typical adults; these changes, as well as a general slowing down of intellectual processes occur (if at all) primarily in the later years of life.

Creativity

Creativity has also received considerable attention during the adult years. One set of studies (Lehman, 1953) found that the number of the *most highly creative productions* of persons in various academic and scientific occupations peaked during the decade of the thirties or forties and declined after that age (see Figure 19–1). Thus, about 80 per cent of their superior work was completed by age fifty. The rate for worthy, but less superior work

FIG. 19–1.
The most highly creative works of people in various scientific and academic occupations tend to be produced between ages 30–40.
(Reprinted with permission from J. Botwinick, Cognitive processes in maturity and old age. New York: © 1967 Springer Publishing Company, Inc., 200 Park Ave. S.; data from Lehman, 1953, p. 242, table 34.)

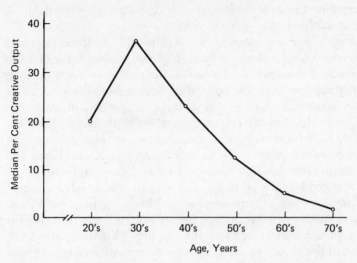

was found to peak somewhat later; the decline through the later years of life was more gradual than for high quality work. Lehman suggests that this decline with age is probably the result of a number of interacting factors, not necessarily directly related to age. These include a decline in physical vigor, more concern with practical matters, more mental disorders, and less motivation to try to achieve creativity once prestige and recognition have been achieved (Lehman, 1962).

Another set of studies (Dennis, 1966) defined creativity somewhat differently, and as might be expected, arrived at some different conclusions. Dennis studied the *total productivity* (not just the "high quality" works) of creative persons in the arts, sciences, and the humanities, and found that the period from forty to forty-nine was the most productive, or only slightly less than most productive, period of life. For historians and philosophers the decade of the seventies was as productive as the decade of the forties; scientists showed a significant decline in the decade of the seventies, whereas the decade from twenty to twenty-nine was the least productive. For artists, the decline was even sharper; and only for this group was the decade of the twenties more productive than the seventies (Figure 19–2).

FIG. 19–2.
The largest production of all creative work of people in the arts or sciences tends to occur between ages 40–49, but total creative production is spread throughout a lifetime.
(Reprinted with permission from J. Botwinick, Cognitive processes in maturity and old age. New York: © 1967 Springer Publishing Company, Inc., 200 Park Ave. S.; data from Dennis, 1966, p. 2, table 1.)

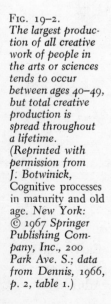
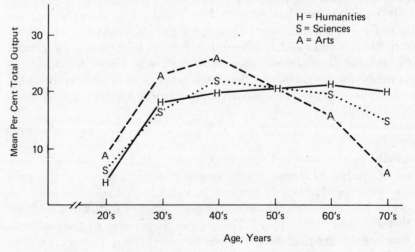

522

It would appear that a number of factors other than changes in intellectual ability with age are involved in these trends. For example, the amount of time required to produce a creative work is probably much longer in a scholarly field than it is in the arts; also the amount of study required for scholarly or scientific fields may be much longer than for the arts; and the help of assistants may be very useful for middle-aged scientists or scholars, but of little help for artists.

Thus, an individual's most creative works are likely to occur early, but creativity remains high throughout the creative person's lifetime. It seems that noncognitive factors—such as the amount of time free from pressing responsibilities that the person can devote to creativity—may be more important than age-related cognitive changes. Nonetheless, there may also be some tendency for younger persons to contribute more novel or unique solutions to problems, in part, because they may have a fresh perspective and have not yet learned to think about the field in conventional ways. At the same time, older persons might benefit from their accumulated knowledge and experience (as well as from research grants and assistants). Of course, sickness or premature death may cut off one's creativity during middle age; and failing health can reduce the time and energy, as well as the cognitive abilities, devoted to creativity.

Although most of us will probably not produce the kind of highly creative works that Lehman studied, we might be interested in finding creative ways of living and ways of being a creatively maturing person. An important part of this will involve continued learning, for as our society is changing rapidly as a result of technological changes, learning will continue to be necessary to understand and cope with the increasing complexity of daily life. The jobs we are preparing for today may change so that we will have to learn new skills as soon as we begin to work and continue learning new skills as the jobs continue changing and becoming more complex. More of the ordinary jobs of the future may become like the professions of today where continual learning and keeping up with the latest developments are mandatory. We might even look forward to some kind of "sabbatical leave" every few years where we would go back to school or to the library to learn new facets of the job. The technological revolution might also bring new learning experiences into the home by means of video tape cassettes or special television channels so that we could learn important new skills or broaden our knowledge of humanistic studies (including the arts and humanities) so that we will be able to make the complex kinds of decisions we will be faced with as adults in the future more responsibly.

Indeed, adulthood is an exciting and challenging period of life. It is the time when many things reach their culmination and when the past experiences become transformed into a kind of institutionalized and stable self that is competent, creative, and both self-reliant and interdependent with a web of significant other persons. Adulthood is a complex time of life that provides many potentials for human fulfillment, if we search out the creative human potentials within ourselves and eradicate the environmental pressures that block or hold back the realization of the full human potential (such as racism and poverty). Successful negotiation of this period of life and progress toward the ideal of human fulfillment does much to set the stage for the later years of the life span.

Early and
Middle
Adulthood

523

AFFECTIVE DOMAIN

The changes, challenges, and possibilities we have discussed in the biological and cognitive domains during adulthood bring with them important changes in the affective domain. For example, menopause (or pregnancy or a heart attack) can bring with it changes in the feelings one has about oneself; it can bring a reexamination of what it means to be a woman (or a man), of what it means to grow older, of what it means to be a human person. And the various crisis points in the occupational cycle or in the family cycle (see Social Domain) can bring with them a range of new feelings—competence, satisfaction, frustration, anxiety—that need to be dealt with and that affect one's conception of oneself. As one becomes a mother or father and rears one's children through the various pitfalls of childhood and adolescence, a great range of affective problems and responses come up and need to be resolved in some way. After a minor automobile accident involving your daughter and her boyfriend you may say to your husband: "I never did trust that boy Sue was going out with . . ." and then Sue tells you that she wants to marry him. Resolving such complex feelings that involve a number of other people—and their future—is a different task from coming to understand your own feelings during adolescence. But adults sometimes also have trouble understanding their own feelings and sometimes have difficulty in understanding the feelings of others who were brought up in a very different time (after World War II instead of during the Depression, for example). A range of feelings typically have to be faced only during adulthood—such as feelings about the death of one's parents, feelings about one's divorce, or feelings about the death of friends and contemporaries that bring on feelings about one's own death.

Consider, for example, the complex range of feelings adults have to face when their children are getting ready to leave home—a difficult period in many families. "Who will I be when I am no longer a mother?" "I am getting old." "Maybe I should consider going back to work." "I'm afraid Johnny isn't going to find what he wants to do." "I really wish Bill would go into business so he could take over for me when I retire." "Sue wants to move in with some boy, and I think she's pregnant." "If Jean would only stay home longer we could protect her (and I wouldn't be so lonely because Jim is so busy at the office that he's no husband to me at all)." "Jack is never going to get a job and support himself; maybe we should make him pay room and board and let him live here as long as he wants." Ambivalence; "please stay, but please go"; fear, anxiety, hope, trust, wanting to do "the right thing" are all involved at once. The fine line between being "overprotective" and providing enough support and independence is a difficult one for most parents (and adolescents are seldom consistently satisfied with either independence or constraint). But most adolescents find a way to get away, and most parents find a way to get their lives back together. Ideally, everyone grows a bit in the process.

Personality Issues and Changes

Erikson (1963) described the developmental issues during this period of early and middle adulthood as *Intimacy vs. Isolation* and *Generativity vs. Stagnation*. In his developmental scheme, these issues follow the adolescent issue of *Identity vs. Identity Confusion* and set the stage for the old age

The Life
Cycle

issue of *Integrity* (or meaningfulness) *vs. Despair.* Erikson suggests that once a person has a firm sense of who he is—as a sexual, working, social individual—he then turns toward others and seeks a mutually satisfying intimate relationship with another person. If he fails in this stage, he remains isolated from others. Most of us probably resolve this issue somewhere between these two extremes, ideally close to the intimacy end of the spectrum. Once this issue is resolved, for better or worse, the person turns to the issue of "generativity," that is, "what can I do that will outlive me, will leave my mark on the world?" It might be "generating" children and raising them to maturity; it might be producing or creating something that will outlive oneself. The danger in this stage is "stagnation"—not really doing anything productive, not amounting to anything. Again, most of us will probably end up somewhere between these extremes; perhaps the task is to discover what one might do to realize one's unique human potentials and then to find a way to do this—the author suspects that in Erikson's sense this would be generativity.

Among the other views of personality growth and development during these adult years is one that early adulthood consists of a period of preparatory expansion of social participation, responsibilities, and activities. This is followed by a culmination period during middle age in which productivity, social activities, and personal relations reach their highest point. The next period is marked by psychological and biological crises (such as the death of friends, sickness, and menopause) but results in a culmination of creative and philanthropic activities with some restriction of social activities. Sickness and/or retirement ushers in the fifth period, which is characterized by a kind of looking back and letting go of the plan one has built up for his life (Frenkel-Brunswik, 1963). A similar view sees *growth and expansion* motives prevailing during the early and middle years of adulthood, but *anxiety and threat* motives dominating the later years (Kuhlen, 1964).

Undoubtedly considerable change occurs in adults during these years as the perspective of life changes from planning for the future and being actively engaged in a wide range of activities to a gradual realization of the finiteness of life and the necessity for equipping the next generation to carry on after oneself. But there is also considerable continuity of personality during the life span. For example, one's well-established methods of coping with stress or with changes probably do not change very much, and the way in which one reacts to retirement (for instance) reflects personality factors very clearly (Reichard et al., 1962).

Several studies have sought to identify how much people change and how much they remain consistent as they grow older. The results indicate that people remain fairly consistent when they evaluate themselves at different times in their lives, but characteristics measured by various personality tests show more change with age (Mischel, 1969). Thus, people remain fairly consistent while they also change. Neugarten (1968b) has suggested that there is a personality shift toward "increased interiority" often beginning in the decade of the fifties; that is, the person of this age may begin to turn inward, become more reflective, and respond more to inner personality pressures and less to external social pressures. Many older persons thus become more "like themselves" with age and possibly pay less attention to conforming to external pressures. Although young people may seem to be fairly similar to one another because they tend to conform (but clearly

Early and
Middle
Adulthood

525

also have distinct individual personalities), older people may seem to be even more different from one another as their personalities stand out more clearly.

In addition, an individual's past experience and the personality patterns that were established earlier in life continue to play an important role in adulthood. We tend to respond to similar situations in similar ways and tend to cope with problems in much the same way as we did earlier. Also, unresolved personality conflicts may continue to affect an individual all through adulthood or may take on new importance as raising children or dealing with the responsibility and stress of adult life reawaken old problems or unresolved conflicts.

Emotional Problems and Challenges During Adulthood

Since becoming a fully functioning person during adulthood requires building upon the earlier experiences of childhood and adolescence as well as incorporating the challenges and possible failures of adult life, adults sometimes find themselves facing more than they can cope with. This may lead to the severe symptoms of psychosis (such as schizophrenia), where the person is unable to separate reality from what seems to outside observers as fantasy; or it may take the form of neurosis where the person feels a great deal of anxiety and may be unable to function effectively. Such emotional dysfunctions or family and marital problems or general problems in living may lead the person to seek professional help and, in some cases, may require hospitalization. A variety of new forms of psychotherapy as well as medical advances in discovering medications have been beneficial in helping adults to resolve or deal with their emotional problems. Although our understanding of the variety of emotional disturbances is far from perfect, it seems clear that if pressures are extreme enough, anyone can be driven to the "breaking point" and also that many people with serious emotional problems manage to overcome them and become fully productive members of society. For some persons it may be that a "nervous breakdown" is a necessary step toward becoming a more fully human person; a step that most of us, perhaps fortunately, do not have to take.

The entire range of psychopathology is represented during the adult years. However public attention has recently been drawn to one particularly prevalent type of emotional difficulty in adulthood—severe depression. All persons feel depressed from time to time, but some persons —especially during the adult years—may feel extremely depressed, unable to sleep, unable to work, and possibly suicidal. Sometimes this is set off by a crisis during the middle years of adulthood—such as a divorce, or being passed over for promotion, or the death of one's parents. Sometimes identifiable childhood factors can be found that seem to be associated with the symptoms. Sometimes environmental stress of day-to-day living and the pressures of modern urban life seem to be the primary causes of depression. Both young and old and successful and ordinary persons may have to fight this melancholia or depression. In most cases professional help allows an individual to regain his ability to strive for full human fulfillment. This example also points out that overwhelming challenges during adulthood may be as much a part of the goal of human fulfillment as simply sailing a smooth course through the years.

Perhaps the greatest challenge during adulthood is self-renewal—that is,

The Life
Cycle

continuing to develop and change and to allow one's potential to develop. Adulthood is not an uncomplicated unfolding of one's early goals and plans —that would be incredibly dull. Instead, it is a series of possibilities that require continuing self-exploration, education, resetting of goals, and progressive development of skills for relating to others and for understanding oneself. In a real sense, when one stops changing, learning, and striving for fulfillment, the point and challenge of life is gone. The task is to find ways to keep on living as fully as possible through all of one's days.

SOCIAL DOMAIN

Although few biological events (except menopause) distinctly influence adult development in the absence of disease, there is a wide range of social influences that are paramount in adulthood. Most of the time and effort of these years is devoted to the occupation, the family, and to leisure. Each is a social phenemonon and each provides us with a great deal of satisfaction and frustration, but also provides us with the possibility of growth and development of our human potential.

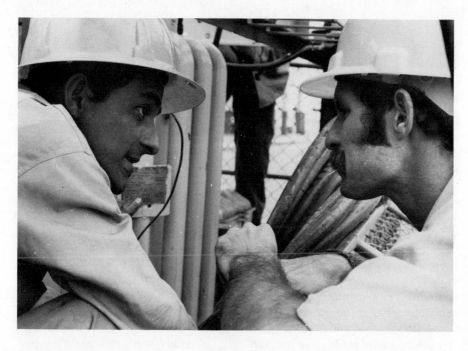

FIG. 19–3. *Peace Corps volunteer (right) at work in Ecuador. For most adults, their work is a most important factor in determining their self-concept.*

Occupation: Work, Careers, and Jobs

The job is an important source of one's identity. It provides an important source of self-esteem and is a major aspect of one's self-concept during adulthood. Beginning with the first full-time job and continuing until retirement, the occupation is one of the major sources of productivity and one of the major causes of frustration in adulthood. Vocational choice is an important task in adolescence and often leads into the first job or the first step in a career ladder. But the choice process seldom ends there, and many persons change jobs several times during their work life. We might even suggest that women typically begin in one (occupational) career or job,

Early and
Middle
Adulthood

527

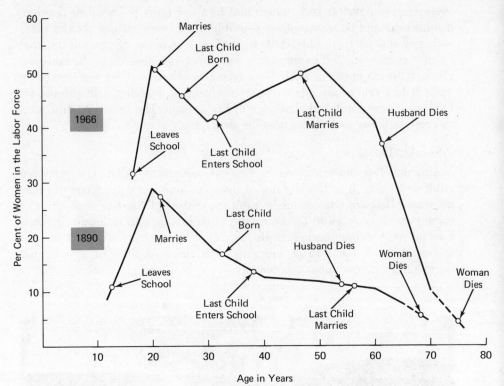

FIG. 19–4.
*Work patterns in
relation to sig-
nificant events in
women's lives.
(Adapted by per-
mission from B. L.
Neugarten and
J. W. Moore. The
changing age-status
system. In B. L.
Neugarten (ed.),
Middle age and
aging, p. 12. Chi-
cago: U. of Chicago.
Copyright © 1968
by the University
of Chicago.)*

then often shift to the career of "mother" and, after the children are in school or have left home, return to work (Figure 19–4).

There are at least three normative crisis points in the occupation: learning the job and the mutual fitting-together process that goes on between the new employee and his job, changing jobs, and leaving the occupation at retirement. Ideally, there is a fairly good "fit" between the person's needs, aspirations, and values and the satisfactions, demands, and challenges of the occupation. When one first begins work, there is a further refinement of this "fit" so that the person changes and modifies his job to fit himself. This is certainly the case in professions or other careers; it is less true in semi-skilled work, although even there some of this "fitting-together" process undoubtedly takes place. If one remains on the job, it is either out of economic necessity or because the job provides more satisfactions than frustrations. Because of our increasing technology combined with increasing education, some workers at routine (e.g. assembly-line) jobs seem to be finding a relatively low degree of satisfaction. What does one then do? One possibility is to ignore the job and find satisfaction in the family or in leisure that the income from the job may provide; or just keep working at the job because it is necessary for survival. Another possibility is to change jobs and find one that provides more satisfaction (or fewer frustrations). A third possibility, which is currently being tried at some assembly-line plants, is to rotate jobs so that one continues to learn new skills and may also feel that one is taking some responsibility for the finished product.

When the satisfaction-to-frustration ratio of the job becomes too low for an individual, he often changes jobs. This can be a crisis point, for it may involve a reexamination of his vocational choice decisions and may also

The Life
Cycle

528

bring about a reevaluation of one's identity and goals in life if the shift is a major one. Or a change in jobs may result from a progressive unfolding of one's goals, as in the shift from lawyer to congressman or from nurse to hospital administrator. Occupational goals are seldom fixed and rigid; ideally, fully human persons should continue learning and evaluating where they are and what they can do so that the job will be meaningful—either personally or in terms of providing economic resources to the family.

However, there is probably a kind of "midlife" crisis somewhere in the forties or early fifties for most persons (or at least those involved in careers). By that time it is usually apparent whether one will reach the goals toward which one was working—"If another person is brought in to be president although I was next in line then maybe I'd better consider moving to another company or resign myself to not becoming president. . . ." Or, "now that it is clear I will never do those things I wanted to do as a young man, maybe I'd better accept the fact that I won't be a famous biologist. . . ." Also by that time, in our society, which has set retirement at about age sixty-five, if one doesn't change jobs by age forty-five or fifty, it is not likely that another company will hire him; or if one gets "laid off" on the fiftieth birthday, then finding another job is likely to be very difficult because younger men will work for a lower salary and are more willing to be trained. Also, pensions are expensive for the company (or union), and they are not likely to hire someone with only a dozen more years to pay into the pension fund before retirement.

Retirement, which in some ways resembles the rite of passage between childhood and adulthood in other societies, is also a major transition point for adults in our society. For some, it is a welcome relief from a difficult, low-paying job; for others, it is a chance to do something else (perceived as more meaningful); and for some, it is an unwelcome event forced on them, which to them is an indication of their meaninglessness and marks the beginning of old age. In any event, retirement typically brings a marked decline in income, often to one-half or one-third of preretirement earnings (Maddox, 1966). And it brings with it a major transition in life.

Family: Marriage, Parenthood, and Grandparenthood

There have been impressive changes in the family cycle since the turn of the century. Not only are young people marrying later, on the average, but children are leaving home when their parents are younger, and parents are living longer today than they did in 1900 (see Table 19-3). These changes are the results of a combination of trends toward greater education (before marriage), fewer children, and improved medical care. This means that if a couple has two children, both children are likely to grow to adulthood, whereas in the past a couple would have more children since it was common for one or two children to die in infancy or childhood; in addition, improved medical care has increased the life expectancy of adults.

The family cycle may be seen as a series of phases (Duvall, 1971): marriage, birth of the first child, family with schoolage children, family with adolescents, empty nest family, and retired family. Each phase has its unique characteristics, challenges, and difficulties. For example, after the couple has become accustomed to living with each other, they are confronted with a third family member whose needs are constant and imperative. Even if the couple is in the midst of sexual intercourse and the baby

TABLE 19-3
CHANGES IN THE AGE AT WHICH SIGNIFICANT FAMILY EVENTS OCCUR

Event	1890	1940	1950	1959	1980(?)
Wife:					
First married	22.0	21.5	20.1	20.2	19.5–20.4
Birth of last child	31.9	27.1	26.1	25.8	27–28
Marriage of last child	55.3	50.0	47.6	47.1	48–49
Death of husband	53.3	60.9	61.4	63.6	65–66
Husband:					
First married	26.1	24.3	22.8	22.3	22–23
Birth of last child	36.0	29.9	28.8	27.9	29–30
Marriage of last child	59.4	52.8	50.3	49.2	51–52
Death of wife	57.4	63.6	64.1	65.7	68–69

Adapted by permission from B. L. Neugarten and J. W. Moore. The changing age-status system. In B. L. Neugarten (ed.), *Middle age and aging*, p. 6. Copyright © 1968 by the University of Chicago.

cries, his needs are urgent. Suddenly, the parents have to learn how to rear a baby. This point may be a crisis in the family cycle, for it disrupts the couple relationship that existed before the baby was born. It may have caused the mother to give up her job to care for the child (or might the father have taken a "paternity leave"?), and a baby is a clear sign of adult responsibility that may be just a bit frightening even after all the other milestones on the road to adulthood have been passed. The challenge is to not only be a fully human person but also to become a fully human parent who somehow finds the courage, patience, tolerance, and openness to continue to grow and to help the child to grow. The breadwinner (father?) also has a significant new responsibility at this time, and the economic drain with this and later births may be heavy. He will feel considerable pressure to start investing in life insurance, encyclopedias, and savings for college, all the while still having to pay the monthly bills.

By the time the child is an adolescent, the parents have changed and have grown a great deal. But the parents' changes are only beginning; providing the support and encouragement for an adolescent to "find himself" while also providing realistic restrictions for the adolescent (for one's own sanity as well as the adolescent's) is like walking a tightrope. All those things you wrote down that you would never do to your adolescent when you got to be parents somehow no longer seem relevant now that your daughter wants to spend her summer vacation exploring the moon (just think ahead twenty-five years). And just when you have managed to (relatively) successfully steer your adolescents through the various pitfalls that may exist for them, you are faced with having them leave home and go out on their own. If current trends continue, you will then be about forty or forty-five and just about to become grandparents.

Suddenly your spouse is the only one left in the home—that big home (apartment or suburban home and summer cottage) you won't finish paying for until you are older. And most important of all, you and your spouse have to start talking to one another again and fighting with one another again —maybe for the first time in years. It is little surprise that reports of marital

The Life
Cycle

adjustment are lowest at this "empty nest" phase of the family cycle (see Table 19-4). For those couples who do not divorce at this time—or who say, as

TABLE 19-4
MARITAL SATISFACTION BY PRESENT STAGE OF THE FAMILY CYCLE

| | Husbands | | | Wives | | | |
| | Satisfaction | | | Satisfaction | | | Each Sample |
Stage of Family	Very	Quite	Less	Very	Quite	Less	N
Establishment	55%	39%	6%	74%	22%	4%	51
New parents	69	23	8	76	18	6	51
Preschool children	61	31	8	50	33	17	82
Schoolage children	39	45	16	35	44	21	244
Adolescent children	44	41	15	17	38	15	227
Empty nest	9	25	66	8	16	76	64
Postparental	24	13	63	17	13	70	30
Aging family	66	30	4	82	14	4	50
Total of all stages	44	37	19	45	33	22	799

Adapted by permission from B. C. Rollins and H. Feldman. Marital satisfaction over the family life cycle. *Journal of Marriage and the Family,* 1970, **32:**20–28.

the author's father recently did, "We've only been married thirty years; we need to give it a chance to work out!"—marital satisfaction typically increases (Rollins and Feldman, 1970). Indeed, this period may be one of the most happy periods for some couples, especially those in the upper middle class (Deutscher, 1964). The wife has made it through her crisis point of the "empty nest" and menopause; the husband's major crisis of retirement is still in the future; and although he may be striving too hard to reach his occupational goals, the family responsibilities are lighter and there is some recovery from the economic strain of raising children; and there are also new in-laws and grandchildren who, ideally, provide more satisfaction than frustration.

Sometimes families break up—with death or divorce; this can be a major crisis point for the entire family. Currently about one-quarter of all marriages end in divorce, and the chance of a first marriage ending in divorce is about one in five. As with a change in occupation, a divorce brings a reevaluation of one's identity, one's self-concept, and one's plans and goals for the future; however divorce also involves a great deal of emotion, so the intensity of the crisis is probably much greater than in changing jobs. It is difficult to tell whether men or women get the worst deal in a divorce— men usually lose their children, have to pay alimony and child-support, and have to learn basic household chores in order to survive, but they may have an easier time remarrying. Women may lose a larger part of their identity and have a more difficult time remarrying (especially if they have children), but it is a very difficult time for both partners, and for the children as well. However, divorce may become a necessity if the marriage fails and both partners as well as the children are to become more fully human persons. Ideal marriages allow both persons to continue to grow and to develop

Early and Middle Adulthood

their potential and to learn and change from experience. And that involves a risk. Sometimes the couple grows and changes together or in compatible ways and both persons are able to mature together over a period of forty or fifty or sixty years. Other couples, for a variety of reasons, grow apart or find that one partner is blocking the other's growth, or realize that the marriage was not suited to each partner's human potentials from the beginning. For example, if a wife or husband spends days at home watching television and caring for the children while the husband or wife is earning a professional degree or making rapid strides in a career, the couple may grow apart and, especially if one person is growing while the other is not, the marriage may be heading toward a divorce. The children of this couple may get sucked into the fights (which become increasingly "unfair"—unfair fights are those where each person hits at the other's weakest spots, in contrast to a fair fight where each person expresses the anger, but avoids really hurting the other person). Sometimes the parents fight through their children, using them as pawns in these unfair fights, which can be very damaging to the children. Divorce can thus sometimes be necessary to return the former spouses to the path of human fulfillment, as painful as the divorce may be. Of course, an ideal marriage (or reasonable approximation of one) can be a very useful pathway to human fulfillment.

Not every person is necessarily most fulfilled by marriage nor is every person necessarily cut out to be a parent. Despite the considerable social pressure (nearly everyone gets married eventually, at least for a while), marriage is not a golden path to human fulfillment. It is a challenge, a responsibility, and a socially supported opportunity for mutual growth and fulfillment. But there are several experimental family styles (such as communes or "open marriages" or "living together") that are possible meaningful alternatives for some persons. There is also a growing awareness of homosexual relationships as a meaningful alternative to heterosexual marriage for some persons.

Leisure: Hobbies, Education, and Growth

The possibility of spending more time in a variety of leisure pursuits is increasing in our society as the amount of time spent working decreases. Technological advances, such as automation, have increased the productivity of every worker, and the forty-hour week is now showing signs of shrinking to fewer hours or to a four-day ten-hour-a-day week. This allows a person to take a second job, for economic reasons, or to simply have more "free time." But if one elects more free time, what does one do with this leisure?

Ideally, this potential increase in leisure time allows great opportunities for human fulfillment since the time can be used in individually meaningful ways. It might be used for continuing education (some colleges are opening their doors to retired persons who want to work toward a degree). The time might be used for socially relevant projects such as aiding teachers in elementary school (some programs exist to train grandmothers and grandfathers to work as volunteer teacher's aides), or for working with emotionally disturbed or retarded children. This time might also be used for helping minority or poor persons to learn English, the skills of business, or the skills of rearing children. It might be used for participation in community or consumer or ecology projects. And such leisure-time involvements could lead the person back to school or the library to learn a new field or a second

The Life
Cycle

532

or third field of competence. Adults ideally continue to grow and to develop their human potentials, and the increase in leisure time would be an important avenue for this pursuit.

Effects of Social Factors

It is apparent that adults—and their life styles—differ considerably on the basis of social class, ethnic background, and rural or urban environ-

FIG. 19–5.

ments. For example, an upper middle-class professional is likely to have a different view of himself and the world than a poor person struggling for survival in an urban ghetto. For the person struggling for survival, fulfilling one's human potential may mean providing one's children with enough to eat, a pair of shoes, and a realistic education about survival in a hostile (racist) world. For a person of a different ethnic background it may involve coping with an English-speaking society that differs in values and expectations from one's homeland. And for the person living in rural America, it may involve a very different style of life—coping with an unpredictable environment, lacking readily available medical services, and possibly coping with a degree of poverty as severe as in any urban area.

One striking example of the effects of these factors, which has received little public attention, is the plight of the American Indian. The life expectancy among this group is a shocking forty-six years; 63 per cent of Indians live in homes with inadequate heating, and 21 per cent of Indian homes have no electric power. Their life is characterized by inadequate nutrition, insufficient medical services, and poor transportation (U.S. Senate, 1971). Clearly, the goals of becoming a fully human person for this disadvantaged group in our affluent society demands immediate changes in these very basic conditions of life; indeed, the plight of the Indians raises the question of why their life-maintaining conditions have been allowed to persist at such a low level for so long.

IMPLICATIONS

UNDERSTANDING YOURSELF AND OTHERS

Hopefully this chapter has provided a different kind of perspective on human development from the earlier chapters, which focused on where we

Early and
Middle
Adulthood

have been. This chapter has tried to provide a look into the future. This may be useful not only in terms of your own planning of what you would like to have happen in your future life, but may also have provided you with a glimpse of how life looks to adults like your parents. Somehow, if you have a sense of what it means to your parents when, for example, their children become independent and leave home, it may be easier to help them (and yourself) to negotiate this difficult period. Thus, it is the author's hope that this chapter has helped make you a bit more aware of what your parents— and other adults in our society—are "up against," so that you may understand them a bit better and so that you might be a bit more prepared for what will happen when you get there.

What are your parents "up against"? How can adults continue to develop and change and to realize their human potential? What difference does it make whether one is an adult in the upper middle class or in the working class? What difference does it make whether one is a man or a woman during these adult years? Is there a sense in which both men and women need to be "liberated" from sex roles that are too confining so that they may become more fully human as individuals? How can one rear children in a way that allows them to develop to the fullest of their human potential while their parents also continue to develop to their fullest potential? Hopefully this chapter has provided some clues to these important questions— and to a host of others that would stagger our minds if we were to list them all. But this chapter has provided only clues, for these questions are part of the excitement and challenge of adulthood. Each person must search out meaningful answers to these questions for themselves. It is in that process of searching that human growth may be located. It is that process of searching that education ideally prepares a person for—at any age: sixteen, thirty-six, sixty-six, or eighty-six.

Perhaps an interesting first step might be to sit down and really listen to some adults talk about their lives—young adults, middle aged adults, and old adults. Or, perhaps a class project might be to invite some parents and grandparents for a "rap session" in small groups. It might even be that developing one's full human potential begins with the ability to listen to oneself and to other people who are different from you in age and social class. After all, there's no expert on what it means to be a sixty-year-old grandfather that is quite like a sixty-year-old grandfather.

CHAPTER REFERENCES

BARDWICK, J. M. *Psychology of women.* New York: Harper, 1971.

BIRREN, J. E. Principles of research on aging. In J. E. Birren (ed.), *Handbook of aging and the individual.* Chicago: U. of Chicago, 1959.

———, R. N. BUTLER, S. W. GREENHOUSE, L. SOKOLOFF and M. R. YARROW (eds.) *Human aging: a biological and behavioral study.* Washington, D. C.: U. S. Govt. Printing Office (Pub. No. (HSM) 71–9051), 1963.

BOTWINICK, J. *Cognitive processes in maturity and old age.* New York: Springer, 1967.

COMFORT, A. *The prospects of longevity.* Paper presented at the Gerontological Society Meeting, December 1972.

DENNIS, W. Creative productivity between the ages of twenty and eighty years. *Journal of Gerontology,* 1966, **21**(1), 1–8.

DEUTSCHER, I. The quality of postparental life. *Journal of marriage and the family*, 1964, **26**(1), 263–268.

DUVALL, E. M. *Family development*, 4th ed. Philadelphia: Lippincott, 1971.

ERIKSON, E. H. *Childhood and society*, 2nd ed. New York: Norton, 1963.

FRENKEL-BRUNSWIK, E. Adjustments and reorientation in the course of the life span. In R. G. Kuhlen and G. C. Thompson (eds.), *Psychological studies of human development*, rev. ed. New York: Appleton, 1963.

KANGAS, J. and K. BRADWAY. Intelligence at middle age: a 39-year follow-up. *Developmental Psychology*, 1971, **5**:333–337.

KIMMEL, D. *Adulthood and aging*. New York: Wiley, 1974.

KOHLBERG, L. and C. GILLIGAN. The adolescent as a philosopher: the discovery of the self in a postconventional world. *Daedalus*, 1971, **100**:1051–1086.

KUHLEN, R. G. Developmental changes in motivation during the adult years. In J. E. Birren (ed.), *Relations of development and aging*. Springfield, Ill.: Thomas, 1964.

LEHMAN, H. C. *Age and achievement*. Princeton, N. J.: Princeton U. P., 1953.

———. The creative production rates of present versus past generations of scientists. *Journal of Gerontology*, 1962, **17**(4), 409–417.

MADDOX, G. L. Persistence of life style among the elderly. *Proceedings of the Seventh International Congress of Gerontology*, 1966, **6**:309–311.

MASTERS, W. H. and V. E. JOHNSON. *Human sexual inadequacy*. Boston: Little, Brown, 1970.

MISCHEL, W. Continuity and change in personality. *American Psychologist*, 1969, **24**:1012–1018.

NEUGARTEN, B. L. The awareness of middle age. In B. L. Neugarten (ed.), *Middle age and aging*. Chicago: U. of Chicago, 1968a.

———. Adult personality: toward a psychology of the life cycle. In B. L. Neugarten (ed.), *Middle age and aging*. Chicago: U. of Chicago, 1968b.

——— and J. W. MOORE. The changing age-status system. In B. L. Neugarten (ed.), *Middle age and aging*. Chicago: U. of Chicago, 1968.

———, J. W. MOORE and J. C. LOWE. Age norms, age constraints, and adult socialization. *American Journal of Sociology*, 1965, **70**(6), 710–717.

———, V. WOOD, R. J. KRAINES and B. LOOMIS. Women's attitudes toward the menopause. *Vita Humana*, 1963, **6**:140–151.

PAPALIA, D. E. The status of several conservation abilities across the life span. *Human Development*, 1972, **15**:229–243.

PIAGET, J. Discussion with the faculty of the City University of New York, October 1972.

REICHARD, S., F. LIVSON and P. G. PETERSON. *Aging and personality*. New York: Wiley, 1962.

ROLLINS, B. C. and H. FELDMAN. Marital satisfaction over the family life cycle. *Journal of Marriage and the Family*, 1970, **32**:20–28.

SELYE, H. *The physiology and pathology of exposure to stress*. Montreal: Acta, Inc., Medical Publishers, 1950.

SHERFEY, M. J. *The nature and evolution of female sexuality*. New York: Random, 1972.

U. S. SENATE, SPECIAL COMMITTEE ON AGING. *A pre-White House conference on aging: summary of development and data*. Washington, D. C.: U. S. Govt. Printing Office, 1971.

RECOMMENDED FURTHER READING

DUVALL, E. M. *Family development*, 4th ed. Philadelphia: Lippincott, 1971.

KIMMEL, D. *Adulthood and aging*. New York: Wiley, 1974.

NEUGARTEN, B. L. (ed.). *Middle age and aging*. Chicago: U. of Chicago, 1968.

Early and
Middle
Adulthood

Old Age and Death

MARGARET L. FRANKS, R.N., M.A.
JOY DAN GRAVES, R.N., M.S.
Department of Nursing
Cypress College, California

Prelude
Basic Theory and Research
  Biological Domain
    Physical Changes in Aging
  Cognitive Domain
    Information Input and Storage
  Affective Domain
    Need Fulfillment
  Social Domain
    Characteristics of the Aged
      Population
    Disengagement and Social
      Aging
    Death: The Final
      Developmental Stage

Implications
  Understanding Yourself and
    Others
  Living and Working with Chil-
    dren, Adolescents, and Adults
  Developing Positive Models

536

PRELUDE

THE PROPORTION of aged individuals in our society has increased during this century. Federal government figures indicate that aged individuals, people who are sixty-five years of age or older, number over 19 million. This means that almost one in every ten persons is aged. By 1985, the aged population is expected to increase to 25 million, with New York and California each expected to have in excess of 2 million aged in their total populations (Health, Education, and Welfare, 1970).

In the traditional Chinese culture, the aged were highly respected and cared for by the family, whereas in the Eskimo culture, grandmother was pushed out on an iceflow to die when she became useless. The culture of the United States, in many instances, appears to resemble the Eskimo culture and the iceflow is often called the Golden Age Home. The attitude and services prevailing in this country are designed to remove the old from their homes and place them in custodial care facilities (Blenkner, 1968). From this trend, one can generalize that the younger generation no longer assigns status and respect to the aged generation, and the abandonment of our aged is a societal norm. By comparison, Shelton (1969) found that the Igbo tribesman of eastern Nigeria value dependency in their aged and involve them in productive care of the children and the administration of tribal affairs. In Canada today (as well as in some parts of the United States) old people are being utilized as foster grandparents at child-care agencies and in this activity are kept in the mainstream of life. Board and care facilities for the aged could be built near child-care agencies in the United States, and both generations could benefit from this arrangement as they do in Canada.

Terminology. Aging is a natural phenomenon that refers to changes that occur during the life span and result in differences in structure and function between the youthful generation and the elder generation. *Gerontology* is the study of aging and includes elements of biology, psychology, and sociology. *Geriatrics,* a newly developed field of medicine, is the field of medical specialty dealing with the health problems of the aged.

It is useful to distinguish the various aspects of the aging process in humans. *Social aging* refers to the social habits and roles of an individual with respect to his culture and society. As social aging progresses, the individual usually experiences a decrease in meaningful social interactions. The *biological aging* of a person refers to the physical changes in the body systems during the latter decades of the life span. Biological aging may begin long before the individual reaches the chronological age of sixty-five. *Cognitive aging* refers to a decreasing ability to assimilate new information and a difficulty in learning new behaviors. *Affective aging* refers to the reduced adaptive capacities of the individual in relation to an altered environment. For example, the aged frequently have difficulty in orientation when they are moved to a new home or hospital. These processes do not occur at a given age or set time in all individuals. One person may appear to have aged considerably in all aspects at age sixty, whereas another person may be actively learning a new job or functioning in a newly acquired role at the same age.

General Problems of Aging. The problems of the aged become more acute as the aging process continues. Four major categories of needs or

Old Age and Death

537

problems emerge: health, housing or living arrangements, income maintenance and employment, and interpersonal relations. Health problems increase with advancing age. The degenerative diseases, such as heart disease, stroke, and diabetes, appear in the latter decades of life as a result of a wearing out of the body organs. The mental processes also deteriorate. Multiple diseases are common in one person in old age. An increased amount of the older person's income, which is usually limited, must be spent for medical care and medicine. Living arrangements may need to be changed as one grows older. Many older people are not able to maintain their homes and find it necessary to move in with relatives, rooming houses, or homes for the aged. Employment is a serious problem for the older worker. With changing technology, his skills become obsolete and he has difficulty finding work for which he is prepared. Employers are reluctant to retrain old workers because of their limited work lives. Changes take place in a person's interpersonal relations as he grows older. His parents die and his children mature and leave home. Grandchildren are born, and he has a new role of grandfather. His spouse and friends die. Retirement from work severs his ties with a peer group of other workers. New interests and roles are needed to fill the life of the individual. The drastic decrease in income at the time of retirement may make it difficult for the individual to develop new interests and find satisfying social activity and roles.

BASIC THEORY AND RESEARCH

BIOLOGICAL DOMAIN

Physical Changes in Aging

Physical aging is thought to begin when *catabolism* overpowers *anabolism* in the human body. Catabolism is the breakdown of cells and their protoplasm into simpler compounds, whereas anabolism involves the building of protoplasm from simpler compounds. Protoplasm is the living substance of the body and forms the body cells. Fibrous tissue often replaces the normal tissue that is lost as a result of catabolism in the different body parts or organs. Chronological age and the physical aging process do not follow the same schedule. Therefore, physical changes take place at different rates in different individuals. All of the body systems are affected by the aging process. Organ reserves are used, and the repair process is much slower than it was when the individual was younger.

Cardiovascular Changes. The cardiovascular system, in particular, is subjected to great stresses during life and probably suffers the greatest degenerative effects in old age. The output of the heart is decreased, and the volume of oxygen-carrying blood to all parts of the body is subsequently reduced. The linings of the blood vessels are also subject to degenerative changes, and fatty plaques (called *atheroma*) are often deposited in the innermost lining of the blood vessels. This process coupled with the growth of fibrous tissue in the middle lining of the blood vessels is thought to give rise to the increased rigidity of *arteriosclerosis* ("hardening of the arteries").

Physical Appearance Changes. The appearance of the skin changes markedly. The secretory and excretory glands of the skin function less and the skin becomes less elastic, wrinkled, dry, and withered. The layer of fatty tissue just beneath the skin tends to disappear, and the smooth roundness of the trunk and extremities is lost. The tissues of the joints and bones stiffen, and the range of movement of the joints becomes markedly decreased. The older person frequently complains of pain and stiffness in his joints. Demineralization of the bones occurs with the result that the bones become brittle and the aged person may easily suffer fractures of the bones. The general mobility of the aged person is lessened and he is forced to move about more slowly. These skeletal and muscular changes often give rise to the stereotype of an old person who is small and lean, with thin, wrinkled skin, standing bent-over with partially flexed knees and hips and an arched back and neck.

Respiratory Changes. Respiratory movements of the chest decrease as a result of the increase in fibrous tissue in the chest walls and lungs. Less oxygen is consumed, and lower respiratory tract (lung) infections appear more frequently in older people. By comparison, younger individuals tend mostly to have infections of the upper respiratory tract (throat and sinuses).

Nutritive Changes. Tooth decay, loss of the teeth, and degeneration of the jaw bone make the highly enjoyable function of eating more difficult for the older person. Chewing is more difficult and may necessitate a modification in the diet. Decreased production of digestive juices coupled with poor muscle tone and activity in the intestines often lead to complaints of indigestion and constipation by the older person. (A large portion of their often meager income is often spent for antacids and laxatives.)

Atrophy of the taste buds and of the sense of smell further diminish the pleasure of eating. Food has little taste to the old person, and one should bear this fact in mind when cooking for the elderly. Since protein foods and fresh fruit and vegetables are more expensive than carbohydrate foods, the elderly tend to eat more crackers, breads, and cereals. From this eating pattern, they may develop anemia and deficiencies of important vitamins, and become more prone to infections.

Adaptation to Stress. Stress is an ever-present factor in an individual's life. Adaptation to stress requires energy. Hans Selye (1956) categorized the responses to stress into a three-stage general adaption syndrome (G.A.S.): (1) the initial alarm reaction; (2) the stage of resistance; and (3) the stage of exhaustion with repeated stress causing tissue injury or aging.

The older person has had more stress placed on his body during his lifetime. After prolonged exposure to stress, his resistance breaks down and exhaustion sets in. Because the reserve of energy has been used over a prolonged period of time, the older person has less energy available for adaption and exhaustion sets in sooner than in the younger person.

Rest cannot restore lost energy for people after prolonged exposure to a stressful situation. Reserves of energy for adaption cannot be completely replaced, and each stress leaves scars.

The aged person under stress is biologically more vulnerable than the younger person with a larger reserve of energy. The adaption processes of aging are not suddenly present. How well an individual has adapted to stress throughout his life will affect how well he adapts to stress during old age. However, because of the relatively limited energy available to

Old Age and Death

539

the older person for adaption, the individual and those who work with the aged need to consider ways to prevent stress and to conserve energy.

Neurological and Sensory Changes. The nervous system suffers generalized impairment mainly as a result of its decreased blood supply. The neurons or nerve cells of the brain are replaced by nonfunctional connective tissues that results in forgetfulness, irritability, and lack of adaptive cognitive processes in the old person. There are corresponding changes in the other sensory organs. Vision is less acute as the lens of the eye builds up the layers of dead cells within itself, color perception is decreased, and the ciliary muscle loses its elasticity and functions less well in accommodating to changes in light level. These visual changes make driving a car more hazardous for the older individual. Hearing losses often begun in the thirties become much more pronounced in old age. Vestibular functioning decreases, and the elderly person is more prone to falls and accidents. One can easily understand that because of their sensory losses, older people are highly accident prone when they walk about on the streets of a city, particularly during hours of peak traffic.

COGNITIVE DOMAIN

It is often said that older people have a difficult time learning new material. Freud stated that past the age of fifty, the elasticity of the mental process on which treatment (psychoanalysis) is based is lacking and that the rigidity of older people tends to result in fixed opinions and reactions that are difficult to change.

Overlearned Behavior. Behavior that is effectively learned and repeated over the course of many years often becomes overlearned, that is, it is done automatically. Overlearned activities are difficult to change. If you have lived for a long time, you have well-developed habits and fixed opinions. Research has shown that rats trained to jump over a gap in order to get to food will fail to take a diet when it is provided without this impediment. Behavior acquired under excessive frustration (jumping a gap, or sixty years of coping with life's problems) may become abnormally fixated and thus resistant to change.

Compulsive behavior, such as cigarette smoking, incessant humming, or nail biting acts to reduce tension and is, therefore, very resistant to change. For example, if someone has smoked cigarettes for seventy years to relieve his tension, it would be difficult (if not impossible) to change that behavior through substitution. In other words, "old habits are hard to break." If young people find it hard to break old habits, then consider the implications for the older person who is forced to learn a new way of living when he is moved from his own home to that of his son or daughter, where he must adjust his old habits to a new environment.

Information Input and Storage

Perception refers to the process of interpreting or attaching meaning to the sensory input. Older people have a continual background of neural noise that makes it more difficult for them to sort out and perceive complex sensory input. In working with older people, it is best to present fewer stimuli at one time. For instance, if you are talking to an older person, turn off the television set and try to eliminate as many outside noises as possible. Talk slowly and relate only one message at a time. The sorting out process takes longer in the older person.

Memories from the past are more vivid to the older person than are more recent memories. Older memories have had more time to consolidate and are stronger. Newer memories are the first to fade and the last to return. Older people may also experience an inability to recall time patterns. They may mix up the old and the new.

Intelligence. Research seems to indicate that general intelligence reaches a peak and remains at that level even into old age if there is no extensive physical deterioration or neurological damage (Cowdry, 1968).

Education and continued stimulation seem to play an important role in maintaining intellectual capacity in old age. With the increased tendency for adult education programs, we may expect that the average intelligence level of the older population will increase. This change should be anticipated and planned for in our society.

Mental Deterioration. Damage to the brain caused by extensive physical deterioration or neurological disease often results in an inability to think effectively. Two degenerative disorders that occur as a result of the aging process are Pick's syndrome and Alzheimer's syndrome. Alzheimer's syndrome results in an impairment of memory for recent events and a loss of orientation for time and place. There may also be an inability to speak (aphasia). An older person suffering from Pick's syndrome experiences difficulty in concentration and learning, and an inability to react on an emotional level that is appropriate to the stimuli. An example would be the man who is told that his wife has just died, who responds with, "That's nice, what are we having for dinner?"

AFFECTIVE DOMAIN

Old age is the phase of life in which a person's self-image undergoes its final revision. The individual makes his final assessment of the worth of his life and evaluates his successes and failures.

How well a person adapts to old age is in part predicated on how well he has adapted to the other cycles of his life. If the individual experienced a crisis in his emotional life each time a new adjustment was needed, he will probably experience difficulty in old age. Obviously, such factors as geographic location, economic situation, and physical health can also affect this adaptive process.

Need Fulfillment

Effective adjustment, for all individuals, is largely the result of being able to satisfy one's needs. In Maslow's conceptualization, once the basic biological needs of the individual have been met, the person is free to seek gratification of his security needs, his social needs, and his ego needs, and finally attain a state of self-actualization. Within this framework, consider the relative level of needs for the individual approaching old age. Many older people are living in a state of poverty, unable to meet the very basic physiological needs for food and shelter and without hope or motivation for the achievement of a higher level of goals. Some, however, are capable of meeting these basic needs and are motivated to tackle the tasks at the next level.

Old Age and Death

541

Pensions, old age assistance, and Social Security programs provide some of our aged with financial assistance, granting them some measure of security. If these are adequate, the older individual may be ready to move to the next level.

The aged individual has the same need to love and to be loved as does the younger person; however, he doesn't have the same opportunity to meet these needs. He is often separated from his family, friends, and associates; work groups are no longer accessible; it becomes more difficult to be admitted into a group. Adaption is more difficult.

The ego needs of the older person remain intact. He too needs to have self-esteem and respect from his fellow man. It is also essential for an older person to have a purpose in life.

An older individual who overcomes these obstacles may be motivated to work on tasks at the highest level in the needs hierarchy. The need to be creative and to be altruistic is particularly important in old age in order to enable one to gain attention and approval from others, and to compensate for a lessening of physical attraction and the loss of loved ones.

Many official and voluntary agencies have been organized to provide services for the older individual. The level of motivation of their individual clients should be considered in planning agency activities. The agency's efforts to provide socialization may result in frustration if the individual is still struggling to meet his physiological needs. The individual is frustrated because his need is for food for this week and all that the agency is offering him is "an opportunity to socialize and play cards."

SOCIAL DOMAIN

Characteristics of the Aged Population

In this country women outlive men by about seven years, on the average. After age sixty-five, the ratio of women to men is approximately 1.35 to 1, giving rise to a socially disadvantaged group, the unpaired females. For many older women, the death of the husband also means the loss of her chief social role as wife and homemaker, and no doubt accounts for a portion of the high rate of depression and suicide found among this age group. In addition, widows very often are excluded from social gatherings and therefore forced into isolation.

Older men also have a point at which a crisis is faced as a result of role loss. This occurs at retirement. Faced with this change in status from provider, wage earner, and worker, the older man often experiences severe depression and in many cases, suicide results (Health, Education, and Welfare, 1970).

Approximately 5 per cent of the aged population live in institutions, and among these groups, women outnumber men by more than 20 per cent. There are two reasons for this: (1) it is more socially acceptable for a single man to live alone or with nonrelatives than it is for an elderly woman; and (2) many older widowers remarry a younger woman.

With regard to income, the older person is seriously disadvantaged. Of the older families 30 per cent had incomes of less than $3,000 in 1968, whereas 40 per cent of the elderly living alone or with nonrelatives had annual incomes of less than $1,500. In most cases, this income is "fixed,"

The Life
Cycle

that is, it does not increase with the rise in the cost of living (Health, Education, and Welfare, 1970).

Whites make up 92 per cent of the aged population, although they comprise only 89 per cent of the total population. This is a result of the generally shorter life expectancy of nonwhites; a result of chronic malnutrition and health care deficiencies.

Of those in the older population group, 50 per cent have completed elementary school, 22 per cent have attended high school, and 12 per cent have attended college. The remaining 16 per cent are functionally illiterate.

One must obviously conclude from these figures that the aged segment of our population is in a disadvantaged position physically, emotionally, economically, and educationally.

Almost 90 per cent of the aged receive Social Security benefits. Social Security (Old Age, Survivors, and Disability Insurance) is compulsory; it is sponsored by the federal government and covers the majority of American workers. Payments during retirement are based on the amount that has been paid by the individual during working years, and his age at retirement. Of the aged 20 per cent have wages from self-employment. Most of the larger companies have retirement or pension plans for their employees, and payments are usually proportional to the number of years spent as an employee with the company. Other retired persons may be covered by the Civil Service Retirement system or the Veterans Administration. Despite the numerous retirement plans, the income of most aged persons fell below federal poverty level standards in 1968.

Federally sponsored health insurance programs (Medicare) and various state-sponsored programs are now available for the care of older people. The Health Insurance of the Aged Act, Title XVIII of the Social Security Act, helps persons over sixty-five pay their medical, hospital, and other costs. The Medicare program consists of two parts: (1) hospital insurance and (2) supplementary medical insurance, which is voluntary. The individual pays half of the premium for the supplementary insurance and the federal government pays the other half. Title XIX of the Social Security Amendments of 1965 provides grants to states to provide medical services to low-income aged and other needy individuals. This program is known as Medi-Cal in California and as Medicaid in New York.

Disengagement and Social Aging

In 1961, Cumming and Henry suggested that the process of social aging follows a well-defined pattern of disengagement. Briefly stated, the stages in the disengagement theory are as follows:

1. *Change in role function*—For men this could be decreased occupational productivity accompanied by changes in attitude about work.
2. *Loss of role*—For women, this usually accompanies the death of the husband. For men, it is produced by retirement.
3. *Reduction in social interactions*—With loss of role, social contacts are reduced, self-concept is diminished, and morale is lowered. Very often eccentric adjustment results in further reduction in social interaction with corresponding depression and self-concept damage.
4. *Awareness of the scarcity of time remaining*—This produces a further

FIG. 20-1.

curtailing of activities in the interest of time. The inevitability of death is recognized.

When disengagement reaches an advanced state, most of the individual's life-sustaining bonds have been broken, and the person is ready for total disengagement: death.

Havighurst (1968) and others have indicated that disengagement is not an inevitable process, and have suggested, as an alternative, an activity theory for reversing the disengagement process. According to Havighurst, the older person has the same basic needs as the middle-aged individual, and the optimal pattern of aging should consist of extending the activities of middle age as long as possible. Havighurst also points out that the decrease in social interaction so often found in older people is partly the result of the withdrawal of society from the individual rather than the individual from society. To counteract this phenomenon, the individual must vigorously resist the limitation of his social world.

The Life
Cycle

Death: The Final Developmental Stage

Among primitive peoples, the fear of the dead and the mourners was well established. Among the Maoris, anyone who had handled a dead body was cut off from interaction with others. He could not enter any house or touch food with his hands, which were tabooed or unclean. Food was thrown on the ground for him, which he ate without using his hands. Clad in rags, his body rubbed with red ochre stain and vile-smelling shark oil, solitary seclusion for a specific period of time was his lot. Such was the reward for having ministered to the dead. Restrictions on the mourners' hands, in relation to food, was universal throughout Polynesia. In Tonga, the tabooed period of time was from three to ten months, depending on the status of the mourner himself (Frazer, 1935).

Among the Shuswap of British Columbia, mourners had to seclude themselves and build a sweathouse by a creek, where they sweated and bathed alternately for the required length of time. The seclusion was necessary because the ghost of the deceased was hovering over them. In British New Guinea a widower was not allowed to show himself in public, plant a garden, or join a party of hunters because the ghost of the deceased wife would ruin the garden or frighten away the game. These primitive people firmly believed that the ghosts of the departed were evil and took great delight in harming the living (Frazer, 1935).

In primitive societies, there was also a widespread universal prohibition against pronouncing the name of the deceased. This custom sometimes held during the period of mourning only, but in some areas (South America), the prohibition was of a more permanent nature. The primitive people looked upon the mention of the deceased's name as a conjuration that would result in the immediate appearance of the dead person. Their goal was to prevent any conjuration and resulting appearances of the deceased (Freud, 1938).

The oldest evidence of our predecessors' attitudes toward death has been found in their ways of disposing of the dead bodies. Archeological evidence seems to show that funeral rites were practiced by Neanderthal man. Funeral rites change from one society to another, but all seem to signify that a human being has dignity by virtue of his body. Cannibalism and mutilation of the dead, as well as human sacrifice, were practiced largely because of the special significance attached to the human being (Toynbee, 1968).

Death Attitude in the Young. Nagy (1959) studied the child's attitude toward death. From three to five years of age, the child does not recognize death as a regular and final process; it is a further existence under changed circumstances. From five to nine years, the child personifies death as a ghost or deathman who carries people away. From nine to ten years of age, the child finally recognizes death as a terminal event in life. However, Wahl (1959) has noted that the fear of death (thanatophobia) occurs as early as the third year of life. Wahl (1959) suggested that to understand the child's attitude toward death, one must understand the struggle of the child to come to terms with this realization. When a child has lost a grandparent or a favorate pet through death and asks his parent for an explanation, his real fears reside in the unspoken questions. First, "Did I cause it?" Second, "Will it happen to you soon?" and third, "Will this happen to me?" The task of the parent is to persuade the child that he is not personally responsible, that the deceased did not leave him for reasons of disapproval or hostility, and to reassure the child that the parent is not likely to depart soon. Thus, the child expresses the emotions of love, grief, guilt, anger, and fear when he has a personal experience with the loss of a loved one through death. Again, this is the same ambivalence of emotions that was common in primitive people.

Contemporary Attitudes Toward Death. Our culture places high value on youth, beauty, high-level occupations, and social class, and our orientation is toward future activity. Aging and dying are avoided and/or denied in this value system. In the death of each person, we are reminded of our own mortality. In this identification process we see ourself surrendering life.

The death of the elderly appears to be much less disturbing to members of Western society than does the dying of the young, because the aged are not especially valued. Surveys have often found that nurses, for example, feel that more importance should be attached to saving the young person's life than an older person's life.

Thus, the recent research supports somewhat the notion that Western society has practiced and is practicing the avoidance pattern in dealing with the aged and/or the dying aged patient.

Stages of Dying. Elisabeth Kubler Ross (1969) spent several years working with dying patients and has summarized her observations into five stages of dying.

The first stage of dying is *denial and isolation.* It is during this stage that the initial defense mechanism is used, "no, not me." The use of this defense mechanism gives the person a chance to "put it all together" and become accustomed to what is going to happen, that is, he is going to die (Ross, 1969).

The second stage of dying is *anger.* "I'm going to die, but why me? I've lived a good life; why me?" This stage is a difficult one for family members and for workers who must often carry the brunt of the individual's anger. As the person is helped to resolve his anger at being the one chosen to die, he is ready to move on to the next stage (Ross, 1969).

The *bargaining* stage is the third stage of dying. It is at this time that he begins to look around for a way to prolong life. Literature has instances of a person selling his soul to the devil to gain a little more time to live. "Bargains are usually made with God and are kept a secret" (Ross, 1969). An example might be, if only I could live to see my grandchild, I would devote the rest of my time to God's work.

The fourth stage of dying is *depression.* The causes for depression are loss, either real loss or threatened loss. Both of these losses are present when an individual faces impending death. The real losses are associated with hospitalization, loss of health, separation from loved ones, and the anticipated loss of life itself (Ross, 1969). Older people's greatest problem psychologically is depression. This should not be a surprising fact because they are in effect preparing themselves for death.

The final and fifth stage of dying is *acceptance.* If a person has reached this stage through help and guidance, he is ready to accept the loss of life and loved ones. This is not a happy type of acceptance; just an acceptance of the inevitable fact that he is going to die.

The Life Cycle

An example of the courage found during this fifth stage of acceptance appears in a "Tribute to Our Mother" written by Phil Snyder, who gave his permission for us to share this with you. We wish to thank him for sharing this compassionate statement about not only his mother's death but about her life, which was a model of love for life and for her fellow man.

Mother's final illness has caused us to think that life seems to demand most of us when we are least able to give it. In any event, this was true in our Mother's case. She was half paralyzed with a stroke, hardly able to swallow, barely able to speak, and with her body deprived of almost all of its physical force. Yet in this crippled condition, Mother lived as she had always lived. She may have been afraid, but she did not manifest it. She knew that she was probably dying because, at the beginning of her first wakeful moment following a long and a deep sleep, she requested that her brother Joseph administer to her. She thought not so much of her own pains and problems as of others. She wanted to know of an aunt how an uncle was; she was pleased with her own children when they told her that they had visited this uncle, her husband's brother, in a convalescent home. She was concerned that her responsibilities to the hospital and to her doctors be discharged. She tried to introduce her visitors to each other. And she actually asked if her children, crying at her side, needed anything which she could provide for them. In short, Mother, during her final mortal act, when terribly crippled, still managed to give life what it asked of her. Her gentleness and her strength dominated her life even in her extremity.

Mother's mortal life, as she herself would phrase it, is over. We, her children, take pride and comfort in the fact that it was a full life, one lived in dignity and one dominated by humane values. Mother kept her mind united with her heart. Mother's influence with those who knew her will certainly continue. As for her brothers and sister, as for her sons- and daughters-in-laws, as for her grandchildren, and as for her children, they will remember her with tears and smiles all the days of their lives. And for the children of Mary Janette Case Snyder especially, her life will remain in memory what it always was in fact: a compass and a rock by which they guided and on which they built their own lives, with love and with respect for their parents.

So good-by, Mother. May peace be with you, dear gentle spirit.

IMPLICATIONS

UNDERSTANDING YOURSELF AND OTHERS

Because of increasing longevity of life the number of families that consist of three or even four generations can be expected to rise in the years to come. How well families adapt to this arrangement will depend on their understanding and acceptance of each other's abilities and limitations.

We have indicated some of the general characteristics of the aged individual and suggested ways of overcoming some of these limitations. You should consider your own activities, needs, and learning patterns in relation to these factors, in order to determine if some of these could have beneficial implications for the young as well as the elderly.

Old Age and Death

Living and Working with Children, Adolescents, and Adults

It is important for all persons who interact with the aged to realize that they have the same needs as younger people, and less resources are available to help them meet their needs. Their need for social interaction is often ignored by family members and workers. Family members should find the time to visit their aged relatives, invite the aged to their homes on occasions, or remember their birthdays and holidays with cards or small gifts. Usually, the aged like to visit with children and are able to relate to young children in games and stories. A truly meaningful relationship can be developed for the elderly in the foster-grandparent program.

Some of the aged living in the community are not aware of the health or income plans to which they are entitled. Many older people are proud and do not want to accept charity. Neighbors, friends, and acquaintances can help them by explaining the benefits that may be available to them. If possible, it is better to allow the older person some choice in the selection of his living arrangements, life style, and social interactions. Our society has not accepted disengagement as an optimum adjustment pattern for the aged. However, it may be that life in a health care facility demands a certain amount of disengagement on the part of the individual, either voluntarily or involuntarily.

When one considers the mechanism of physical aging and the attendant losses of normal body functions, he can readily perceive the necessity for modifying the expectations of performance from the elderly. The aged person must be allowed to move at his own pace and not be pushed or hurried by a younger person. Since the older person has lost some of his sensory protective mechanisms, he may need a more sheltered environment in which he can move about safely. This has been considered in the communities for senior citizens. Curbs are lower, the streets have cul-de-sacs, and ramps are replacing steps. More innovations of this nature are needed in communities serving all age groups.

Developing Positive Models

A person should explore his feelings concerning his old age and death, when living with or working with an old person who is facing death. Denial of the old person's death may be a coping mechanism used by the worker or family member. The aged learn to interpret the cues and messages from their caretakers and to respond in the manner desired by the caretaker. The aged person may be forced to remain silent about his fears, his anger, or his frustrations in the dying process. Health workers should practice the techniques of therapeutic interaction and allow the dying patient to release some of his negative feelings concerning his impending death. Societal values and norms need to be modified to include dying and death as an integral part of the life cycle. The aged, then, would not suffer abandonment, isolation, and bitter loneliness at the close of their lives.

The authors of this book would like to end this chapter by sharing with you what we believe to be two positive models of more fully human persons as they write about their feelings of getting older. The first was written by Edith Gable, a woman who, along with her husband, spends much of her free time visiting the sick and dying in hospitals and

The Life
Cycle

convalescent homes: a woman who gives hope and love to both young and old. The second was written by Lillian Johnson, one of our typists, who also reflects compassion for understanding the young as well as life in general. The authors wish to thank them for granting us permission to share their feelings with you.

> When I grow old
> God grant every child will feel the
> texture of my soul
> And will not turn away from me
> As a thorn on a blighted vine
> When I grow old
>
> When I grow old
> God grant that I might have some task
> that must be done
> Or some-one fare the worse
> That in some corner of this earth
> Some-one will need my hand
> When I grow old

> *Edith Gable*

THE RETIREMENT YEARS
Lillian Johnson

Now that I have retired after working thirty years in an office, I find that I have the time for all the things I had wanted to do, and had put off when the clock was my master. I have more time to think, to take walks with the dogs and enjoy the changing seasons. I notice the old buildings with their ornate trim and wonder who built these houses, who lived there, what pleasures and tragedies life brought to them, and if they were able to accept and survive.

Accepting is not always easy. Not to be going to work every day, not to be a part of the business community, not to feel that you are contributing, and especially not to have that semimonthly paycheck coming in—all require major adjustments in one's thinking.

The clock now simply tells me the time—not that I am running late. It took a long time to unwind, and accept, but I made it and am content. Books I bought and wanted to read now get read and, more important, I have the time to think about what the author is saying.

I had always believed that I could not possibly stay home for any period of time without literally climbing the walls. Well, nature in her wisdom took care of that and my health precludes any wall-climbing activity on my part.

TV news and the daily newspaper bring the events of the world to my doorstep. I now have the time to keep track of pending legislation, and of the voting records of the various elected representatives at both the state and federal levels (and they are well aware of this fact).

Living near two colleges, I have had the opportunity to do typing for a number of students, and I have been fascinated by both the students

Old Age and Death

549

and the papers. Their fresh approach—the quality of their learning—their outlook on life. Over the holidays while at a house party I sat and listened to the flow of conversation. I listened to young people, some of whom had dropped out of school and were now paying the awful price of an inadequate education; some were college graduates with good jobs, some teaching, some in research, all making contributions to fuller lives for themselves and others; some of the other guests were people in the forty-five–fifty-five-year range, still working, some of them gradually coming to the realization that one day in the not-too-distant future they would be retiring, and vaguely worried and unhappy at the prospect. Telling them to accept—that it is not so bad, in fact, it can be quite enjoyable, is not the answer. They have to find that for themselves.

But living has taught me one thing. Everyone has problems. The way the problems are handled can mean the success or failure, the happiness or misery of any lifetime. I read long ago that when a problem is troubling you, think of the very worst outcome of that problem. Face this outcome squarely, and if you can live with this, then the problem shrinks into dimensions that can be handled. This worked remarkably well for me over the half century that I have been problem solving. And I know one thing—in spite of the sorrows and disappointments, and remembering the triumphs and moments of indescribable joy—I'd do it again!

CHAPTER REFERENCES

BLENKNER, M. The place of the nursing home among community resources. *Journal of Geriatric Psychiatry,* January, 1968.

BRILL, A. (ed.). *The basic writings of Sigmund Freud.* New York: Random, 1938. Random, 1938.

COWDRY, E. V. *The care of the geriatric patient.* St. Louis: C. V. Mosby, 1968.

CUMMING, E. and W. HENRY. *Growing old: the aging process of disengagement.* New York: Basic, 1961.

FRAZER, J. G. *Aftermath, a supplement to the golden bough.* New York: Macmillan, 1935.

———. *The golden bough: a study in magic and religion.* New York: Macmillan, 1922.

HAVIGHURST, R., B. NEUGARTEN and S. TOBIN. Personality and patterns of aging. In B. Neugarten (ed.), *Middle age and aging.* Chicago: U. of Chicago, 1968.

HEALTH, EDUCATION AND WELFARE, 1970. Older Americans speak to the nation, prologue to the 1971 White House conference on aging.

NAGY, M. The child's view of death. In H. Feifel (ed.), *The meaning of death.* New York: McGraw-Hill, 1959.

Ross, E. *On death and dying.* New York: Macmillan, 1969.

SELYE, H. *The stress of life.* New York: McGraw-Hill, 1956.

SHELTON, A. Igbo child-rearing, eldership, and dependence: a comparison of two cultures. In R. Kalish (ed.), *The dependencies of old people.* Institute of Gerontology, Ann Arbor, U. of Michigan, 1969.

TOYNBEE, A. *Man's concern with death.* London: Hadder & Stoughton, 1968.

WAHL, C. *The fear of death.* In H. Feifel (ed.), *The meaning of death.* New York: McGraw-Hill, 1959.

BIRREN, J. and J. SZAFRAN. *Contemporary gerontology concepts and issues,* Summer Institute for Advanced Study in Gerontology, U.S.C., 1969.

GLASER, B. and A. STRAUSS. *Awareness of dying.* Chicago: Aldine, 1965.

KALISH, R. The effects of death upon the family. In L. Pearson (ed.), *Death and dying: current issues in the treatment of the dying person.* Cleveland: The Press of Case Western Reserve U., 1969.

MASLOW, A. H. A theory of human motivation. *Psychological Review,* 1943, **50:** 370–396.

REICHARD, S., F. LIVSON and P. PETERSON. Adjustment to retirement. In B. Neugarten (ed.), *Middle age and aging.* Chicago: U. of Chicago, 1968.

ROBINSON, L. *Psychological aspects of the care of hospitalized patients.* Philadelphia: A. Davis, 1968.

ROSE, A. A current theoretical issue in social gerontology. In B. Neugarten (ed.), *Middle age and aging.* Chicago: U. of Chicago P., 1968.

Old Age and Death

Reducing Barriers to Becoming
a More Fully Human Person

HENRY J. PARIS, M.S.W.
Fullerton, California

Prelude
Basic Theory and Research
  Mental Retardation
  Neurological Handicaps
    Dynamics of Behavior
Implications for Reducing Barriers

PRELUDE

REDUCING the barriers to full human development is an ever-present, universally encountered, individual experience. It is the purpose of this chapter to examine some of those barriers and to share ways in which they may be overcome. Strong emphasis is made on the relationship between the biological, affective, cognitive, and social domains. It is believed that human fulfillment or failure is not the result of one determinant alone but rather that of a complex series of interrelated factors. It is our goal to demonstrate the relationship of one to the other to reduce barriers to becoming a more fully human person.

This chapter is also written to add to the reader's personal experience and understanding of some of the intricacies and impediments to human development. Emphasis is placed on enlarging the reader's subjective experience rather than conveying theory and research. Both the narrative and the abundant use of anecdotal material are intended to arouse your interest and curiosity about the subject and, hopefully, lead to your individual quest for more information on the matter.

In an attempt to narrow the potential scope of this very broad subject, our discussion is limited to children suffering from mental retardation and neurological handicaps.

BASIC THEORY AND RESEARCH

MENTAL RETARDATION

Paradoxically, physiological barriers to human fulfillment have been viewed as being both the most amenable and the most intractible to treatment. Historically, their very diagnosis rang a psychological death knell for the patient, his family, and the society in which he lived. Today, a far more realistic and hopeful response to biological limitations may be made because of the increased awareness of the interrelated nature of the physical, emotional, and social components of the total person.

Take, for example, the diagnosis of mental retardation. No longer does it necessarily mean a lifetime of institutionalization and an inability to perform in the most rudimentary manner, perpetual dependency on the family, or the barren life of the social isolate. Diagnostic and treatment centers are discovering a rich panorama of alternatives for the retardate, his family, and his society. Of critical importance to overcoming the potential barriers inherent in the diagnosis of mental retardation is a clear understanding of the particular mentally retarded person's specific problems and needs, gained through careful examination, testing, and observation.

The fulfillment of the individual's human potential is intrinsic to the treatment plan whether it is carried out in an inpatient or outpatient setting. Each individual, from the minimally to the most profoundly retarded, is given a goal to attain that is within his grasp. For one person that might mean feeding himself; for another it might mean learning to read; and, for still another, learning a job skill.

Setting Goals. Careful diagnostic work-ups furnish the basis and suggest the means of overcoming some of the retarded child's barriers. Some of the potential areas of focus are as follows: (1) with the parents—talking through the family's feelings in terms of what the child actually is and can be, rather than what the parents wish or are afraid he is or may become; (2) counseling the parents about child-parent relations and directing them toward self-help groups and associations for retarded children so that they may obtain support and help from other parents faced with similar problems; (3) with the child—assessment of the emotional as well as the intellectual level of functioning to determine problems that might further depress functioning and inhibit growth; (4) recommendation as to what educational setting is best suited to help the child grow; (5) exploration as to short, interim, and longer term goals and potentials for the child with recommendation as to the techniques (e.g., structuring, behavior modification, environmental manipulation, work with parental attitudes, and expectation) that might enhance achievement of those goals.

Treatments. Some specific ways in which mentally retarded children can be helped to fulfill their potentials are through the use of special techniques such as the following:

1. *Structuring*—carefully controlling the child's environment to allow only those activities and experiences that the child is ready to attempt.

2. *Reinforcement*—consistent and immediate rewarding for positive behavior on the part of the child.

3. *Social interaction*—selectively providing opportunity for the child to be with family, friends, and other exceptional children.

4. *Education*—formal programs such as those offered for the Trainable Mentally Retarded (TMR) and the Educable Mentally Retarded (EMR).

The following anecdotal material may help illustrate some of these ideas and, specifically point out the interrelatedness of the social, emotional, and physical factors in mental retardation:

Cindy, age six, was diagnosed as having Down's syndrome (mongoloidism) and had had extensive thoracic surgery to repair a congenital heart defect. Cindy looked forward and enjoyed participation in her Educable Mentally Retarded (EMR) class. She played with neighborhood children. She delighted in helping her mother with simple, light household chores. She looked for opportunities to run errands for the family and glowed in their appreciative response and recognition of her efforts. She enjoyed going to her brother's football practice with her father where she engaged herself in talking with him or playing with other small children. Her self-sufficiency, ability to verbalize, and acceptance of self all belied her obvious physical characteristics and diagnosis of Down's syndrome. Cindy was the youngest of four children. She was born when her parents were in their forties. Her parents enjoyed a warm and sustaining relationship with one another in spite of a number of financial reverses that had befallen the family. Their reaction to Cindy's birth and diagnosis had been one of shock and apprehension for the future. Counseling and association with other parents of children who were also retarded helped them separate the reality of Cindy's problems and needs from their own fears. It made them aware that a nurturing, supportive family would be as important for this child's growth and development as with any of their other children. Reinforced by this awareness, they felt they had something to give Cindy who, in turn, beautifully reflected their emotional investment.

The Life Cycle

Another approach is the use of operant conditioning to bring about growth in a child. This is dramatically illustrated in a film made by Meyerson and

Kerr * where an eight-year-old profoundly retarded girl is taught to walk for the first time.

> The child was propped up between two chairs and given a small spoonful of ice cream each time she turned her head from one to the other therapist sitting in each chair. Initially, the ice cream was used as a reinforcer to reward her successive moving of her head left and right and back again. Gradually, the chairs were moved apart requiring some body movement in order for her to reach one or another therapist (more specifically get another spoonful of ice cream). When the chairs were moved sufficiently apart that she could not hold on to one of them to reach the other, a third therapist rigged a rope through a pully in the ceiling above the two chairs. He held one end of the rope and the other (with a handle attached) was given to the child that she might balance herself as she took her otherwise unsupported steps from one to the other chair. Again the distance was increased. When she seemed more steady, the third therapist let go of his end of the rope entirely. She continued walking holding onto her end of the rope as if she still needed it to balance herself. Later, all but one foot of the rope was removed leaving her walking back and forth carefully hanging on to the unattached rope and handle. Successively the handle was removed at which time she began holding the rope with one hand only; the rope was shortened down to two inches; and, finally, the remaining piece of rope was removed from her altogether and, she was given back one thread of the remaining two inches. She now traversed fifteen to twenty feet between each chair. Soon she dropped the one remaining thread and she was walking totally unassisted.

Mental retardation, in some ways, is a social disease in that its level of impairment reflects, to a degree, the attitudes and responses of society toward it. Since retardation cannot be measured directly, but only by inference from the degree of impairment, the attitude of those around the mentally retarded individual is critical to his level of functioning (impairment) (Freedman and Kaplan, 1967). In the cases described, the diagnosis alone did not fully indicate either the qualitative or quantitative potentials of functioning. Both children appear to have developed significantly from their respective levels as a result of a sustaining, structured environment for the one, and operant conditioning for the other. One child appears to have moved from a moderate to a mild level of retardation; the other from a profound to a severe level. It is not uncommon for a child in an EMR or TMR class, for instance, to show significant increases in social skills and IQ. Although these changes may never progress to the point where the child need no longer be considered retarded, they may permit a degree of self-actualization that was previously not thought possible for that particular child.

NEUROLOGICAL HANDICAPS

The label neurological handicap is one of many that describes a physiological/emotional syndrome known by a variety of names, including: learn-

---

* Film produced by Lee Meyerson and Nancy Kerr under auspices of U.S. Ed. Research Project grant to Valley of Sun School for Mentally Retarded.

ing disorder (Koppitz, 1971), minimal brain damage, maturational lag, hyperactive or hyperkinetic child syndrome, and minimal brain dysfunction, to name a few.

Dynamics of Behavior

Regardless of the particular label, these children reflect dysfunction in a number of areas: impulse control, attention and cognitive functions, motor activity and coordination, and interpersonal relations (Wender, 1971).

The decreased experience of both pleasure and pain that these children experience has multiple ramifications both in terms of presenting barriers to growth and in terms of overcoming those barriers. It facilitates understanding why this group, which has the same basic needs as anyone else, so often impress us as being demanding, insatiable, and pleasure-seeking. It is not that they need so much more; it is that they subjectively experience so much less. It is as if they partially screened out, or subjectively failed to fully register pleasurable and painful inputs. Subtle expressions of pleasure or approval and disapproval might then be entirely lost (Wender, 1971).

In one situation several hyperkinetic children were given an exercise consisting of nonverbally transmitting the emotions of happiness, sadness, and anger by using facial expressions only. Some of the children had difficulty doing so; almost all had significant difficulty recognizing one or more of the feelings transmitted. The implication for a parent or teacher who relies on subtleties such as an approving or disapproving look is quite clear. That kind of message is totally lost on some hyperkinetic children. For any emotion to be understood by that child, it must be explicitly stated; otherwise, it may never even register.

This factor sets up the foundations for an interminable cycle of insatiable desire for material gratification, love, and attention on the one hand, and a repeated feeling of lack of complete satisfaction on the other. Such children are less responsive to either reward and punishment, or to social influence. For example, a hyperkinetic child may function well on a one-to-one basis, but be out of control in a group. Interestingly, hyperkinetic children often exhibit a poor response to punishment rather than resistance to reward. The implication is that the judicious use of explicit positive reinforcers in a structured situation may be a more effective way of reaching these children rather than the combination of punishment given within the frame of more generalized expressions of love and acceptance (Wender, 1971).

A high level of poorly controlled activity is another primary characteristic of hyperkinetic children. It shows itself in ongoing hyperactive, restless motor activity (difficulty in staying put) and is associated with inattention and distractability.

A third primary characteristic of hyperkinetic children is their outgoing, social aggressiveness, which is usually ineptly or inappropriately carried out. For example, these children are often described as striking up conversations with total strangers. They are likely to ask socially inappropriate questions and "run out" of things to say after an overcompensated greeting.

A short attention span combined with an excessive attraction to stimuli leads to numerous internal and external problems for the hyperkinetic child. Parents of these children complain that they never complete what they started to do, that they jump from one thing to another, that nothing holds their attention, and that they can't ignore what is going on around them. From an educational standpoint these children are more likely to have problems, simply because learning demands a long attention span, a high frustration tolerance, and an eagerness to please.

From a personality viewpoint, hyperkinetic children appear to have no controls and seem to be extremely impulsive. They also demonstrate parental or cultural values to a lesser degree than other children.[*] The decreased experience of pleasure-pain may possibly lead to an increased independence of parental and cultural supports, which in turn might mediate a decrease in identification with them. This lack of identification is sometimes expressed by the child in negative, obstructive, or oppositional behavior and attitudes. To a degree, this behavior may be viewed as an inadequate way of trying to maintain control.

Feelings of low self-esteem are commonplace among the neurologically handicapped. Such feelings are not necessarily neurotic in that, for many, there is an overwhelming awareness of their very real interpersonal, scholastic, and athletic shortcomings. The greater than average drive and the poorer controls that these children exhibit often lead to recurring episodes of "acting up." To the extent these children may have incorporated parental and social standards, this behavior sometimes leaves them with varying degrees of feeling "wrong" on the one hand, and inadequate on the other. Their unabashed self-centeredness, insatiable demand for gratification, and poor controls frequently lead to confrontation between them and other children that evoke disappointment, disapproval, and, at times, even disaffection. Low self-esteem, then, may come for the hyperkinetic child from his repeated failure to achieve accompanied by the repeated experience of the displeasure of others.

The hyperkinetic child's reaction to his basic characteristics and to the external responses to these characteristics are worthy of note: provocative attention-seeking behavior such as teasing, bullying, domineering, and passive-aggressive behavior; self-destructive attention-seeking behavior, such as daredevil acts and playing the class clown; cover-up behavior, such as cheating, lying, rationalizing; and neurotic mechanisms, such as depression and anxiety.

In the light of the negative characteristics that the hyperkinetic child presents, it is not difficult to appreciate his impact on his environment and, conversely, the reaction of the environment to him. As an infant, he is likely to be colicky, insatiable, irritable, and unpredictable. His mother's best efforts may still leave him unsatisfied, producing within her a growing feeling of frustration and inadequacy, leading to intensified nurturing efforts, more frustration, and, very often, feelings of hopelessness and rejection (Wender, 1971).

This mutual frustration frequently extends to parental disputes (mutual feelings and accusations that the spouse is being too demanding or too lenient; not loving enough, being overprotective, and the like), or to alliances

---

[*] Interestingly, this appears to be more a question of their not acting according to parental or cultural standards rather than not having assimilated them. This impression is supported by the observation that proper medication will frequently bring about many of the desired behaviors to which the child had previously seemed totally oblivious (Adler, 1972, Wender, 1971).

Reducing Barriers to Becoming a More Fully Human Person

557

between the child and one parent to the exclusion of the other parent. It can also set up and foster ongoing targets on which the family may then focus all of its other differences and problems.

We have described hyperkinesis to this degree because we feel that understanding the wide variety of its manifestations is a step toward overcoming the many barriers that neurological dysfunction presents. Most of us accept the relationship of gross aberrations to their physiological antecedents. We are prepared, for instance, to accept epileptic seizures as being related to dysfunctions of the brain (as opposed to emotions, evidence of weakness, or possession by a spirit). However, we are not as prepared to accept as physiological the manifestations of such emotionally tinged entities as boisterous or bullying behavior. It is still easier to believe that all behavioral problems are the result of conscious or unconscious parental or societal abuses or ineptitude, or weakness on the part of the child, rather than a sign of possible physiological dysfunctioning or variation.

Neurological evaluation, electroencephalographs, psychological testing, perceptual evaluation, and case history are some of the methods used to help establish the presence of the syndrome. Some researchers feel that the child's response to specific medication is the most definitive means of making the proper diagnosis. In practice, a child is given one medication that is known to produce results in children with the syndrome. If the child's symptoms subside, then it is assumed that he is hyperkinetic. If the symptoms return upon withdrawal of the medication, then the diagnostic impression is reinforced. The diagnosis is thus based partially on clinical observations, tests, history, and trial use of medication (Wender, 1971).

Treatments. Because of the imprecision of the available instruments, it is difficult to completely differentiate behaviors that are the product of the hyperkinetic syndrome as opposed to those that are purely emotionally mediated. If a child is to be helped, an approach must be used that will encompass the emotional as well as the biological factors. Wender (1971) indicates:

> Medication can facilitate learning, but it cannot provide compensation for the several years in which a child may have been severely handicapped in learning. It can help a child learn to read, but it cannot teach him. Drugs can make the child more amenable to discipline and more lovable, but they cannot provide the experience of having been loved, trusted, admired and accepted in the past.

Medication alone is not the answer for other reasons. The barriers that the hyperkinetic condition presents are barriers not only for the child but also for his parents and any institution that deals with him. Overcoming those barriers will include many factors: education of the child and parent as to the nature of the problem; clarification of the role of drugs in its management; clarification of the interpersonal and behavioral manifestations of the condition; and developing means by which both the patient and his family can mobilize and deal with the condition.

Whether hyperkinesis is described as a problem of congenital variation or biochemical difference, or similar phrase, the goal remains that of helping parents recognize and deal with its manifestations as being other than willful or "bad" behavior. Such an understanding can often decrease parental hostility and guilt and allow them to avoid the alternatives of overpermissiveness and overcontrol toward the child by the establishment of uneven, inconsistent rules. By decreasing the hyperkinetic child's responsibility for his unacceptable behavior, parental hostility and its accompanying guilt can also be lessened.

Environmental structuring (a time to eat, to go to bed, and to do homework); a system of explicit, immediate, consistent rewards and punishments (along the lines of operant conditioning); and a collaborative effort between parents to present a caring, united front are some of the essential ingredients in dealing with a hyperkinetic child.

Participation in informational and self-help groups such as the Association for the Neurologically Handicapped and behavior modification training groups for parents can provide information on how to deal with day to day problems and renew courage to face the demands and difficulties that the child's syndrome continually poses.

Other avenues of approach are those of *educational* and *psychological* intervention.

Special Education. Special education programs such as learning disability classes, educationally handicapped classes, contained classrooms, and opportunity programs are other potential resources within the school system. These special programs are intended to give a time-limited, specifically focused corrective experience. Most of these programs are characterized by small classes, specially trained teachers and aides, and the use of multiple media teaching techniques to elicit desired responses in the child. Careful structuring in these classrooms permits a broad latitude of activities and behaviors and facilitates the use of operant conditioning techniques.

Psychological interventions include those performed by the attending physician; the support, clarification, and information received from self-help groups; parent education groups and seminars; direct intervention with the patient in individual and group situations with the purpose of developing internal structure and controls; and, finally, work with the individual and family in dealing with the emotional aspects of the problem. Examples of the latter two processes might serve to clarify these approaches.

A treatment group was formed for a group of hyperkinetic children in the age range of ten through twelve. Each child had difficulty in controlling his impulses, in not responding to stimuli, and in controlling his anger when frustrated. All showed varying degrees of poorly controlled activity and inability to stop once started. Some of the children had been referred to the treatment program because of ongoing discipline problems including fighting, outbursts of rage, lying, stealing, and setting fires. Others were there because of exasperating insatiability and low self-esteem. All of the children had some degree of poor peer and/or family relationships.

The group was structured to meet for one hour twice a week. The treatment approach was eclectic but initially emphasized behavior modification techniques with progressive movement to more "talking" therapeutic approaches as the group became able to better respond to them. The group met in a ten foot by fourteen foot room that was empty except for large, padded mats on the floor and one chair. The initial sessions were designed to establish guidelines for each child's interfering behaviors to determine which of a series of stimuli presented and withdrawn evoked positive, negative, or neutral responses from each child, and, finally, to explore the efficacy of a variety of reinforcers on each child's behavior.

When they first joined the group, the children's responses included: withdrawal and indifference; anger; active participation; testing and teasing; aggressive behavior; and a very high level of poorly controlled motor activity. The therapist remained essentially nonverbal, showing facial signs that indicated neither approval nor disapproval. He introduced stimuli one at a time, noting individual responses to each one before removing it from the room. He noted the response of an individual to his looking at a child, being next to him, placing a hand on his shoulder, not looking at him, and having the child sit on a chair. The child's interfering behaviors were peremptorily dealt with by telling the child to "sit on the chair," "stand up," or "sit down." If the child complied with each command, he was allowed to return to his former acceptable activity or to participate in a new one. If the child continued his unacceptable behavior, the procedure was repeated in rapid-fire succession until the child ceased his unacceptable behavior.

The chair was used as a means of withdrawing reinforcement from the child by separating him momentarily, a few feet away from the group.

In addition to physical proximity, the leader used brief words of praise, such as "that's good," "keep it up," "I like that." Later, without explanation, the therapist wrote his initials on a piece of paper and gave the paper to a child whenever he wished to reinforce that child's behavior. At first, the children were puzzled by what must have appeared as curious behavior to them. As each child figured out what the scrawl was, talked to another child about it, or even became more involved with the group (in the case of one particular child), he was given an initial on his piece of paper. The use of the initials turned out to be a highly potent reinforcer for all the children. Later, they learned that a column of ten initials on their paper could be exchanged for an activity of their choice such as a game, playing with a particular toy, painting, or receiving a cookie at the end of the session.

As might be expected, each child's struggle for control of his environment continued in familiar ways (albeit sometimes unacceptable or inappropriate) within the group. It manifested itself in countless ways, sometimes blatantly, but more often subtly. For example, a child would ask the therapist to hand him something. Rather than reach to the therapist's hand to take it, the child would hold his hand next to himself nonverbally suggesting that the therapist come to him. Some children tried repeatedly to have the therapist reach over to them, or they might drop whatever they wanted to give the therapist on the floor close to him, but not immediately within his reach. In each instance, the therapist would merely look without expression at the child while holding his hand next to himself ready to receive the object. Nothing was said disapproving of the behavior, but a "thank you," a smile, or a pat on the shoulder might be given the moment the object was handed over properly.

One means of helping the group develop controls over their incessant motor activity was having them immobilize themselves for a few seconds at a time. This was accomplished by letting each child assume whatever position might be most comfortable for him and, having him hold perfectly still in that position for thirty seconds. The increments were later extended to sixty and ninety seconds. Each increment successfully completed was reinforced.

Another method used to develop control was to instruct the group that at the word *freeze* they were to stop their activity in whatever position they might be and hold it while the therapist counted to ten.

Social skills were encouraged by having one child pick a partner for an activity. Activities that required mutual cooperation from two or more individuals were given greater opportunity for reinforcement. Social ineptness and abrasiveness were discouraged by reinforcing competing behaviors such as storytelling, joke telling, and game playing.

Social skills were also approached by having each child convey and/or experience feelings such as anger, sadness, and happiness. For example, two children were asked to face one another. One was instructed to facially transmit without words the feeling written on a piece of paper (that only he saw) to his partner. If the latter could correctly identify the feeling conveyed, both children would receive a reinforcer. Later, each child was shown a card on which a situation was briefly described and was again asked to nonverbally express his feeling about the situation described on the card. Both exercises produced interesting discoveries as previously noted; some children could not convey even the most basic human emotions. Even more children could not correctly discriminate feelings of happiness from those of sadness and anger. Repeated exercises gradually helped them associate particular facial expressions with specific feelings.

Asking each child to relate to the group the significant things that were happening in his life was yet another device used to increase the child's ability to verbalize and interface with his peers. The group's response to these narratives was initially that of inattention and indifference. With reinforcement, each child became better able to tolerate being a listener (rather than being listened to), paying attention (rather than receiving it), and responding to another's needs (rather than having their own needs met).

The group approach to the treatment of hyperkinetic children has a strong focus on retraining and reshaping their behavior. The idea is that if a child can be trained to act and react in a certain situation, he may generalize his learning to other situations as well (Skinner, 1961). The use of operant conditioning techniques with the behavioral components of the child's problems are rewarding.

Don, age twelve, was a large, heavy child who resisted and avoided any and all forms of physical activity. He loathed athletics of any kind and detested calisthenics particularly. It was fascinating to observe this young-

Reducing
Barriers to
Becoming a
More Fully
Human Person

561

ster's response to the offer of reinforcement for doing thirty seconds of calisthenics. Not only did he complete the first thirty he was willing to do sixty for the same reinforcer. His satisfaction with himself for his activity increased to the point that he was voluntarily running back and forth for one minute at a time.

The example is reflective of the power of a well-selected reinforcer and of the emotional gratifications that are sometimes obtained through such mechanistic devices as behavior modification. Don was not only pleased with the "points" he was making but just as much with himself for what he was doing.

The structuring of the group and the judicious application and withdrawal of reinforcers permits a degree of behavioral retraining that mediates personal and interpersonal satisfactions that were previously not obtainable in some children. In short, the consistency of rules, predictability of reactions, immediacy of response, and emphasis on positive behavior not only combine to reshape behavior but also open avenues to the realm of individual and interpersonal feelings.

Psychotherapy. Although therapy may begin with the immediate goal of helping the individual develop means of controlling his behavior and responses (in addition to his use of medication), it ultimately involves dealing with the emotional consequences that sometimes have far greater impact than the basic condition that precipitates them. Poor self-image, inadequate interpersonal relations, and neurotic symptoms are frequently the by-product of unrecognized and untreated neurological dysfunction. Although it was emphasized earlier that it would be a mistake to ignore possible neurological components in behavioral or affective disorders in children, it would be equally wrong to ignore the high probability of there being emotional aspects as well. Separating the emotional from the neurological is important from the standpoint of what labels (if any) should be attached to the child, what treatment approach will be used, and what realistic goals can be achieved.

Peter, age eight, was suspended from school after increasing episodes of classroom disruption culminating in an episode of jumping from desk top to desk top, swinging from the classroom lighting fixtures, emitting animal-like sounds, and verbal and physical abuse toward his teachers and peers.

Examination revealed that Peter's symptoms had been observable in varying degrees for as long as he had been in school. These symptoms included not only those of hyperkinesis but also those suggestive of borderline-to-frank childhood psychosis.

Arrangements were immediately made for appropriate medication for his psychotic-like symptoms as well as those suggestive of hyperkinesis. Home teaching was begun and individual and family group therapy started. During the next several months, Peter became sufficiently reintegrated to accompany his home teacher to the school for his lesson, entered the Educable Handicapped program on a limited day basis, and, later on a full day basis. Treatment continued for the next two years during which time extensive work was done with both parents (one of whom was diagnosed as paranoid schizophrenic, and the other as chronically anxious) in resolving their individual, marital, and parental problems. Because of the nature of the total individual and family needs, it was decided to work with them in a family group approach as well as individually and conjointly. An art therapy approach proved to be verbally facilitating and integrative, as well as nonthreatening for the family. The father became less anxious, the mother became better able to function at home and in the neighborhood, and Peter was eventually placed in a regular class for specific subjects and, later, on a full-time basis.

Peter presents both a very unusual and a very typical case study. On the one hand, few children who are referred to the program present such severe emotional pathology either within themselves or within their family. On the other hand, the blurring of neurological and psychological symptoms is not at all atypical. In some ways, it can be readily understood why the situation reached such a state before being referred. Peter's restlessness, lack of control, impulsivity, social ineptness, temper outbursts, and peculiar verbalizations had been known to everyone who came in contact with him over a long period of time. All of his acquaintances had been conditioned to accept increasingly pathological behavior from him, for no reason other than the fact that that particular behavior was associated with Peter. It was not until his behavior took a sudden dramatic turn that someone decided that something should be done. All too frequently, children with personality disorders are not diagnosed until after a crisis occurs. This may be related to the fact that parents and other interested adults either fail to recognize early signs and symptoms of emotional or neurological dysfunctioning or incorrectly interpret these symptoms to be "bad" behavior. This misperception accompanied with its negative anticipation postpones, and sometimes precludes, intervention at a point when it would be most effective to help the child.

Repeated reference has been made to the interrelatedness of the physiological and the emotional. That the physiological can produce emotional stress and distress is well recognized. Take, for example, the flat, listless feelings that so frequently accompany a cold, or the irritability that accompanies pain in some individuals. On the other hand, emotions themselves are known to produce physiological changes. A growing body of knowledge points to the fact that emotions are subject to a variety of influences including social and environmental factors.

The conclusion can be drawn that the emotional environment, the psychological atmosphere so to speak, can also produce physiological reactions. This was previously stated in terms of the potential impact of emotional stresses on the retardate's low test scores, and again later with regard to the hyperkinetic child.

Jan, age four months, was referred for psychological consultation during her second admission to the pediatric ward for severe dehydration as a result of explosive vomiting. Both admissions had been characterized by a prompt remission of the symptoms and a relatively rapid return to normal fluid levels and body weight. She responded well to personal ministrations and seemed generally alert to the activities in the ward around her. The case history revealed that Jan was the only child of very young, anxious parents who were having problems associated with their very limited finances. The father's job took him away from home quite frequently and it was not uncommon for the couple to have heated verbal exchanges immediately prior to his leaving the house for work. Under these circumstances, the mother would pick up Jan and rock her while holding her very tightly in her arms. Shortly thereafter Jan would start vomiting.

The relationship of emotional stress with symptom formation is not always as clear as in this example. Without ever intending to do so, the mother was using the infant to console herself, and in the process transmitted her own anxiety to the child. The child's vomiting was reactive. Intervention took the form of helping the couple face the reality of their mutually unmet needs and in finding ways of helping each to help the other. The mother was instructed not to pick up the child under the circumstances described and was helped to find other ways of dealing with her upset. The child responded to the more relaxed family atmosphere and there were no recurrences of her vomiting.

IMPLICATIONS FOR REDUCING BARRIERS

The potential for barriers is everpresent throughout the child's development from its prenatal existence on through its adolescence. Each stage in life is accompanied by its vicissitudes and rewards, and its opportunities for growth and for regression. Alexander (1948) states:

> The progression from birth to maturity can be viewed as a series of steps toward the mastery of functions which make the human being independent of its parents. Man first learns to masticate food and focus his eyes; then to coordinate movements which make grabbing possible. He then learns to walk, speak, and take a reasoned view of the world, and finally achieves maturity in his sexual development. The child, however, clearly resists his own progress toward maturity and clings to acquired adjustments in accordance with the principle of inertia. Whenever he is tired of the arduous task of constant readaptation or is confronted with new and difficult situations, he tends to fall back on earlier modes of behavior. Particularly successful previous adjustments serve as fixation points to which he regresses in times of emotional stress.

All of us have observed this phenomenon in one form or another. The young child who is under conditions of fatigue or in an unusual situation may put his thumb in his mouth although he would never do so otherwise. The independent child who generally is gregarious and spontaneous may be seen retiring behind his mother's skirts when placed in an entirely new situation.

From this standpoint, two generalizations regarding development may be made: (1) the individual does not move from one position (behavior, attitude, feeling) to another unless the second position seems more attractive than, and just as possible as, the first; and (2) that when placed under stress, the individual will revert to whatever developmental position afforded him the greatest sense of security in dealing with stress.

Each developmental stage has its own obstacles to full human development, as noted elsewhere in this book. Spitz (1951) and Bowlby (1952) among others have described the significant relationship between mothering experiences, infant survival, and optimum growth. In repeated instances, children failed to thrive and develop adequately in the absence of touching, holding, and communicating experiences with their mothers (or mother surrogates).

Ginott (1965) eloquently described the ongoing cycles of hopeful (if at times unrealistic) anticipation and disappointment that go on between parent and child. Erikson (1963) delineated the very special demands that the adolescent places on himself and his environment in order to feel at peace with both. Menninger (1963) described growth and life as a continuum between integration and disintegration. INTEGRATION, in this case, is broadly defined as the *harmonious merging of internal needs with external demands at minimal psychological costs and maximum sense of well-being.* Conversely, DISINTEGRATION is perceived as a *feeling of falling apart as a result of a subjectively perceived inability to meet either one's own or reality's needs.* Optimally, the child grows in an environment in which his internal and external demands (stresses) are commensurate with his internal and external psychological resources. As those resources develop, so does his capacity to successfully cope with either set of needs.

By combining Menninger's concept that symptoms serve as a balance to maintain an equilibrium with Alexander's remarks concerning the organism's tendency to revert to an earlier form of response in the face of pressure, it is easier to understand the impact of life's stresses on the individual child's system of dealing with stress.

Ron B., age thirteen, was referred by his mother for treatment because of poor academic performance, school avoidance, repeated involvement in minor neighborhood mischief, and alternating feelings of overdependence and exaggerated strivings for independence. Mrs. B. was puzzled by the suddenness and severity of Ron's symptoms which she felt had appeared approximately six months before. Ron's parents had divorced nine months earlier. Although his relationship with his father had never been close, Ron enjoyed his father's interests of hunting and motorcycling. Ron had long ago associated his participation in these outings with his father as a reflection of his father's good mood and feelings toward him, the latter being firmly associated in his mind (perhaps unrealistically) with his own "good" behavior.

Mrs. B. seemed to be in conflict over the divorce, which she believed was a wise decision, but was increasingly concerned regarding its impact on Ron. She wanted to tell Ron "exactly" why she had taken the action (and thereby relieve her own guilt feelings), but she recognized the inappropriateness of sharing this with a thirteen-year-old. She resolved her dilemma by saying nothing and by trying to make up to Ron for the fact that he had no father in the house. In the process, she grew to feel increasingly frustrated and irritable. She felt guilty, made up for it, felt further overextended and more angry, and on and on. From his standpoint, Ron was convinced that his behavior must have caused the divorce. He became increasingly angry at himself, disappointed in the few opportunities to see his father, and annoyed with his mother's alternating moods of being oversolicitious and overly strict. At first, he tried being good, but that didn't work. He found it hard to concentrate on what he was doing;

his marks went down. Soon he told himself he didn't care. In fact, he didn't care if he went to school or not and began staying home whenever he could talk his mother into allowing him to do so.

We see in Ron some symptoms that developed as a means of maintaining a tenuous sense of well-being between his internal and external environments. We also witness his reverting to an earlier, previously psychologically accommodating dependency state of being home with mother.

Ron responded well to psychotherapeutic intervention. Both his anxiety and his depression dissipated as he was able to recognize the possibility that his parents could have serious problems without his being the cause of them. This awareness was mediated in part by the parents being encouraged to tell Ron that he had nothing to do with their divorce. The mother was further helped to recognize that she could not be both father and mother to Ron; that Ron would ultimately be best off wherever his parents were best off; and that Ron needed firm, consistent, external controls until such times as his own could take over. The father was approached in terms that he need not set up an entertainment spectacular for his son, and that Ron would very much like to be with him on a regular visiting basis, with or without special activities.

Leo R., age ten, was referred at a time of extended crisis secondary to his increasing poor peer relationships, feelings of persecution, baiting and testing behavior at home, and a multiplicity of neurotic traits (including facial tics, grimacing, ear blocking, nose pulling, and head grabbing). Examination revealed remarkably pressurized speech and multiple neurotic traits in a bright, highly anxious, restless youngster whose behavior alternated between obsequious pleasing and manipulative baiting. He indicated hatred toward others, particularly his sister, whom he felt was the chief cause of his problems. He progressed through the sessions by "gorging" himself on activities, constantly checking both how much time he had left and the therapist's reactions to him. His verbalizations, gestures, and mannerisms revolved around the themes of being destroyed, diminished, rejected, and the like, and seemed to an extent to be projections of his own hostile feelings. His patterns of behavior also seemed to be in response to those that he sensed in his parents. The relationship between Mr. and Mrs. R. was generally that of hostile dependency. The cycles of hatred and guilt and provocation and atonement were never-ending. Mr. R. attacked by accusing Mrs. R. of not loving him, by baiting her constantly with impossible and unrealistic demands, and by demeaning her when she disintegrated because she couldn't keep up. For her part, she completely castrated him, and then pointed out his ineffectiveness to him. Apart from one another, however, they functioned effectively. The relationship between Leo and his mother was also characteristically a hostile and dependent one. Here again, cycles of hatred and guilt, provocation and atonement were never-ending. Leo, too, attacked his mother by accusing her of not loving him, by baiting her constantly with insatiable demands, and by teasing his sister, with whom Mrs. R. was very much identified. Concomitantly, he would not let his mother out of his sight.

The case of Leo and his family further illustrates the theory of homeostatic balances. It is introduced, however, more from the point of view of illustrating the remarkable impact of the emotional environment upon the formation and diminution of symptoms. It may also be viewed as an example of mutually supported neuroses, in that no neurosis could have thrived as well as each did without collusion (unconscious as it may have been) from each of the principals.

Leo's symptoms existed as a psychologically expensive means of preventing disintegration. Leo attached himself to the therapist, alternating between clinging, demanding and manipulating. Nevertheless, the opportunity to verbalize and understand his heretofore feelings of hatred and abandonment greatly helped him restructure himself. His problems, however, continued to manifest themselves in varying degrees, until the marital situation was resolved through divorce, after several agonizing episodes of separation and reconciliation, severe psychosomatic reactions, and several courses of interrupted therapy. Significantly, Leo's symptoms progressively improved with the dissolution of his parents' marriage.

In conclusion, this chapter has focused on examining physiological and emotional barriers to human fulfillment. It has explored facets and problems of mental retardation, hyperkinesis, and emotional manifestations by examining the total person and emphasizing the interrelatedness of the many parts of his emotional and social environment. Self-awareness and education, particularly parent education, seems to be the keystone of any program aimed at overall reduction of barriers to becoming a more fully human person.

Hopefully, this material will have stimulated sufficient interest and curiosity within the reader to make him want to pursue individually the issues that are raised but not fully answered here.

CHAPTER REFERENCES

ADLER, S. and K. TERRY. *Your overactive child: normal or not?* New York: Medcom P., 1972.

ALEXANDER, F. *Fundamentals of psychoanalysis.* New York: W. W. Norton, 1948.

BOWLBY, J. *Maternal care and mental health.* Geneva, Switzerland: WHO, 1952.

ERIKSON, E. H. *Childhood and society.* New York: Norton, 1964.

FREEDMAN, A. M. and H. I. KAPLAN (eds.). *Comprehensive textbook of psychiatry.* Baltimore: Williams & Wilkins, 1967.

GINOTT, H. G. *Between parent and child.* New York: Macmillan, 1965.

KOPPITZ, E. M. *Children with learning disabilities.* New York: Grune & Stratton, 1971.

MENNINGER, K., M. MAYMAN and P. PRUYSER. *The vital balance.* New York: Viking Press, 1963.

SKINNER, B. F. *Cumulative record,* enlarged ed. New York: Appleton, 1961.

SPITZ, R. A. Hospitalism. In *Psychoanalytic study of the child.* New York: International U. P., 1951.

WENDER, P. H. *Minimal brain dysfunction in children.* New York: Wiley, 1971.

RECOMMENDED FURTHER READING

ADLER, A. *Social interest: a challenge to mankind.* New York: Capricorn, 1964.

BRADFIELD, R. D. (ed.). *Behavior modification: the human effort.* San Rafael, Calif.: Dimensions, 1970.

COLEMAN, J. C. *Abnormal psychology and modern life*. Chicago: Scott, Foresman, 1964.

EATON, J. W. and R. J. WEIL. *Culture and mental disorders*. New York: Free Press, 1955.

MACMILLAN, D. L. *Behavior modification in education*. New York: Macmillan, 1973.

ROBINSON, R., D. E. DEMARCHE and M. K. WAGLE. *Community resources in mental health*. New York: Basic Books, 1960.

WATSON, D. L. and R. G. THARP. *Self-directed behavior: self-modification for personal adjustment*. Belmont, Calif.: Brooks-Cole, 1972.

Epilogue

THE LIFE cycle is over—our task is over—and now your task begins: the evaluation, the implementation, the carrying out, and the integration of some of the basic goals as stated in our preface. To summarize briefly and to serve as a "check list" for this evaluation process of our "systems-analysis" approach to the text, we hope:

1. You have developed additional insights and understanding of your own developmental stages. This in turn may have helped you to know yourself better, care for yourself more, respect your uniqueness as a person, and assume additional responsibility for your own growth into a more fully human person. In short, if we have been successful here, you now love yourself more.

2. As a result of moving more toward self-acceptance and self-love, we hope you now have grown further in some dimensions of caring for, respecting, and being more responsible toward not only your parents but your fellow men (at whatever stage of development). In short, we hope that you have developed additional compassion or "brotherly love" for those around you.

3. You have built some additional "windows of perception" through which you may now better understand the developmental "vistas" of the human as he plays out his life drama during the various stages of life.

4. You recognize the tentativeness and incompleteness of many of these ways of viewing man's evolving drama.

5. As parents, and potential parents, that you will interact with your children with not only more information and understanding but with more empathy and compassion.

6. Also, as parents and potential parents, that you will think of developing your own models of a more fully human person and integrate these into your own family interactions.

7. As potential professionals who will be working with children in whatever capacity, that you have additional knowledge and theories upon which to integrate and build with your own observations and experiences.

8. You now appreciate more the importance of the contributions of the various disciplines for understanding and developing more fully human persons.

9. You became excited and stimulated by some of the research and theory as well as limits of our knowledge so that you may consider entering the emerging field of human development and/or you will do further reading or in-depth study of some of these areas.

A final phase of the systems approach in the design of this text is the feedback process necessary for us to determine if we, in fact, came close to achieving the goals we set. Our form of feedback will come from the faculty members who use our text over the next few years. Their letters with suggestions and criticisms will help immeasurably in this evaluation phase and in our future revisions. However, we often feel that the actual reactions from you, the reader, are as important a part of this feedback process as those of the teacher. Thus, the authors welcome your reactions and comments at any time.

Author Index

Abercrombie, M. L. J., 366
Abravanel, E., 364
Ackerman, R. E., 449
Adelson, J., 218
Ader, R., 256
Adler, Alfred, 170, 188
Adler, S., 557
Adorno, T. W., 172
Ainsworth, 310, 313, 316, 330–33, 336
Aitken, F. C., 289
Aldrich, C. A., 289
Alexander, F., 564
Allport, G. W., 104, 156
Allport, Gordon, 173
Alpert, A. P., 327
Ambrose, J. A., 309, 311
Ames, L. B., 369
Anderson, J. E., 96, 97
Anderson, T., 56, 448
Anokhin, P. K., 273, 294
Anttonen, R. G., 226n.
Aries, P., 20, 24
Aristotle, 37, 42, 95
Arsenian, S., 228
Ausubel, David P., 461
Ayres, A. J., 435

Backett, E. M., 429
Bagby, J. W., 157
Baker, J. B. E., 254
Bales, Robert F., 465, 467
Bandura, A., 375, 478
Bannister, Roger, 114
Bardwick, J., 494, 517
Barrett, D. N., 446
Barron, F., 141
Bates, L. B., 435
Bayer, L. M., 427
Bayley, N., 122, 365, 386
Bell, R. B., 236
Bell, S. M., 316, 330, 331, 333, 336
Belmont, L., 439
Bender, M. B., 364
Berger, P. L., 71
Bergman, P., 327
Bettelheim, B., 236
Beyrl, F., 360, 361
Binet, Alfred, 96, 136, 226
Birch, H., 314, 327, 439
Birns, B. M., 86, 297, 429
Birren, J. E., 513, 516
Blenkner, M., 537
Bloom, B. S., 14, 370, 386, 387, 389, 450
Bonner, Hubert, 183, 191
Boone, D., 439

Borman, Frank, 52
Botwinick, J., 521
Bowlby, J., 310, 312, 313, 316, 317, 328, 330, 564
Boyd, W., 43
Boyer, M., 56
Brackbill, Y., 98
Bradway, K., 521
Brenda, C. E., 218
Bridger, W. H., 297, 314
Brim, O. G., 236
Bronfenbrenner, Urie, 7, 58–60, 62, 63
Bronson, G. W., 310
Brown, J. L., 314
Brown, W. J., 218
Bruner, Jerome, 15, 101, 295, 385, 416, 442, 443, 455
Bryan, F. E., 373, 445
Buber, M., 42, 188
Bugental, J. F. T., 42, 159
Burgess, E. W., 235, 236
Burke, B. S., 252
Burt, C., 135

Calhoun, A. W., 22–24
Canon, R., 20
Carmichael, L., 254, 278, 279, 305
Casler, L., 150
Castker, B. M., 368
Catalano, F. L., 374
Cavan, Ruth, 236
Cazden, C., 376, 446
Centerwall, S. A., 224
Centerwall, W. R., 224
Chapin, H. D., 150
Chess, S., 314, 327
Chomsky, N., 374
Christie, R., 173
Cicourel, A. V., 507
Cirillo, L., 439
Clausen, J. A., 76, 174, 175
Clements, S. D., 428
Cobb, H. V., 425
Cohen, A. K., 78
Cohen, Stewart, 348, 422
Coleman, James C., 89, 142
Coleman, J. S., 175, 218, 227, 371
Combs, Arthur W., 175, 181–83
Comenius, Jan Amos, 43, 95
Comfort, A., 517
Comte, Auguste, 154
Connolly, K., 295, 433
Corner, G. W., 242
Corrigan, R. E., 10
Cottle, Thomas, 77

Cottrell, L. S., 157, 236
Cowdry, E. V., 541
Cratty, B. J., 123, 275, 366, 433, 434
Crowell, D. H., 278
Cruikshank, R. M., 282
Cumming, E., 543

Daley, L. C., 39, 43
Darcy, F. B., 227
Darwin, Charles, 43, 95
Dave, R. H., 371
Davidson, M. A., 425
Davis, F. B., 447
De Cecco, J. P., 10
Dechant, E. V., 133
De Fleur, M. L., 79n.
Delacato, C., 284, 336, 368, 369
Denenberg, V. H., 296
Dennis, W., 87n., 96, 122, 522
DeSmidt, L. S., 258
Deutsch, M., 443, 453
Deutscher, I., 531
Devereux, E. C., Jr., 58, 59
Dewey, John, 38, 39, 42, 95
deWolfe, Evelyn, 73, 74
Dickens, Charles, 95
Doman, G., 336, 368, 369
Douglas, J. W. B., 453
Dressler, D., 79n.
DuBos, R., 119
Duhl, L. J., 79
Dunn, Halbert L., 118
Duval, E. M., 529
Dymond, R., 157

Earle, A., 25
Ebbs, J. H., 252
Eichorn, D. H., 352
Einstein, Albert, 144
Eisenberg, R. B., 305
Elkin, F., 169
Engles, R. E., 327
Entwisle, D. R., 374, 375
Erikson, E. H., 101, 172, 317–19, 398–99, 401, 407–11, 491, 500, 507, 524–25, 565
Escalona, S., 314, 327
Ewing, A. C., 42
Eysenck, H. J., 429

Fabun, D., 124
Falkner, F., 249, 250, 252, 256, 257, 353, 365
Fantz, R. L., 258, 281, 295
Faust, O. A., 326

Index

571

Featherstone, J., 442
Feind, C., 279
Feldman, H., 531
Ferguson, A., 365
Fernald, G., 364
Fernleib, M., 289
Ferreira, A. J., 255
Fink, M., 364
Finney, J. C., 79
Fisher, A., 136
Fisher, J. L., 136
Flavell, J. H., 366, 441
Fleming, E. S., 226n.
Flesher, I., 368
Foote, N., 157
Forbes, J., 57
Formby, D., 313
Frank, Lawrence K., 98
Franklin, Benjamin, 28
Franks, Margaret L., 536
Frazer, G., 545
Freedman, A. M., 555
Freedman, D. G., 310, 311, 313
Frenkel-Brunswik, E., 127, 525
Freud, S., 134, 150, 191–92,
    201–203, 397–98, 404–407,
    410–11, 424, 432, 450, 463,
    464, 466, 545
Frieden, B., 235
Fries, C. C., 445
Fries, M. E., 291
Fromm, Erich, 81, 149–53, 160,
    188, 231
Frost, J. L., 225
Frostig, G., 433, 435
Furth, H. G., 381, 443

Gaarder, A. Bruce, 447, 448
Gable, Edith, 549
Gage, N. L., 156
Gaver, J. R., 223, 224
Gerwitz, J. L., 311
Gesell, A., 97, 122, 276, 280,
    282, 283, 435
Getzels, J. W., 139, 142
Gibson, E. J., 358, 362
Gibson, J. J., 362
Gilligan, C., 521
Ginott, H. G., 565
Glassow, R. N., 122
Glueck, E., 425
Glueck, S., 425
Goethals, G. W., 502, 504
Golann, S. E., 142
Goldberg, E. M., 431
Goldfarb, W., 327
Goldman, J. R., 296
Goldstein, A. G., 363
Gollin, E. S., 363
Good, H. G., 43
Goodenough, F. L., 433
Goodwin, M. S., 326
Gordon, I. J., 451
Gordon, T., 313
Goss, A. M., 434
Gough, H. G., 350

Graves, Joy Dan, 536
Green, W., 235
Greulich, W. W., 355
Grimm, E. R., 255
Grinker, R. R., 432
Guilford, J. P., 137–38, 140,
    143, 434
Gullickson, G. R., 278
Guttmacher, A. F., 263

Hail, R. A., 445
Haire, M., 157
Hall, C. S., 150, 170
Hall, Granville S., 96, 491
Haller, M., 280
Hammer, J. H., 251
Hampton, M. C., 217
Hanley, C., 424
Harlow, H., 328, 329
Harper, P. A., 427
Harris, J. A., 351
Havighurst, R. J., 77, 154, 155,
    387, 388, 438, 544
Heard, C., 287
Hebb, D. O., 300, 366
Heinicke, C., 316
Held, Richard, 296, 297
Hellman, H., 120
Henry, W., 543
Hersch, J., 22
Hershey, G. L., 133
Hetherington, E. M., 503
Hewitt, E. S., 287
Hildreth, G. H., 369
Hinkle, L. E., Jr., 430, 431
Hirschland, R. P., 433, 434
Hodges, H. M., Jr., 79n. 173
Hoffman, L., 471
Hoffman, M. L., 156
Hohle, R. H., 280
Holmberg, A. R., 258
Holt, L. E., Jr., 278
Hooker, D., 254
Horn, T. D., 446
Horowitz, W. A., 137
Howell, M. C., 357
Hunt, E. P., 356
Hunt, E. S., 425
Hunt, H. F., 296
Hunt, J. M., 300
Hunt, J. McV., 451
Hurlock, E. B., 354
Hytten, F. E., 289

Ilg, F. L., 276, 435
Illingworth, R. S., 115, 117,
    275, 283, 285, 366
Illsley, R., 218
Inhelder, B., 364, 440
Ironside, R., 432

Jackson, P. W., 139, 142
Jackson, R. L., 352
Jacobson, L., 226

Jacobson, L. F., 449
Jacoby, A. P., 230
James, William, 38, 40–42
Jaspers, Karl, 42
Jensen, A. R., 386n.
Jensen, K., 278
Jersild, Arthur T., 4, 8, 384, 497
Johnson, A. M., 425
Johnson, Lillian, 549
Johnson, Lyndon, 388
Johnson, V. E., 518, 519
Johnston, A. M., 429
Jones, E., 389
Jones, K. L., 219
Jones, M. C., 281
Jorgensen, A. P., 432
Jost, H., 255
Jourard, S. M., 151, 159, 161,
    172

Kadushin, A., 236
Kagan, Jerome, 225, 281, 300,
    451, 452, 465
Kandel, D. B., 489, 504
Kangas, J., 521
Kaplan, M. I., 555
Karas, G. G., 296
Kaufman, R. A., 10
Kelley, E. C., 172
Kelly, H. G., 352
Keniston, K., 491, 492, 508
Kennedy, W., 227
Keogh, J. F., 122
Kephart, N. C., 366, 428
Kerr, N., 555
Kessen, W., 281, 394
Kidd, A. H., 364
Kiefer, M., 21
Kierkegaard, S., 40, 42, 104
Kimball, W. L., 449n.
Kimmel, Douglas, 488, 512, 521
Kitsuse, J. I., 507
Klineberg, O., 227
Klos, D. S., 502, 504
Knobloch, H., 217, 227, 250
Kogan, N., 140
Kohlberg, L., 411, 438, 468,
    474–76, 500, 509, 521
Kohn, M., 450
Komarovsky, M., 235
Koppitz, E. M., 556
Kraimes, J., 518
Kraus, H., 433, 434
Kris, E., 142
Kroll, V., 429
Kruse, P., 122
Kuhlen, R. G., 525

LaCrosse, E. Robert, 320
Lado, R., 445
Lambert, W. E., 65, 228, 448
Langer, J., 386
Lastra, Yolanda, 449
Lavatelli, C. S., 442

Lawrence, M. M., 279
Lee, E. S., 227
Lehman, H. C., 521–23
LeMasters, E. E., 229–30, 235, 264
Lenneberg, E. H., 305, 306, 308, 372
Lerner, M., 236
Lesser, G. S., 489, 504
Leventhal, A. S., 280
Levin, H., 291
Levine, S., 296, 432
Lewis, E. C., 235
Lewis, H. M., 306, 307
Lewis, M., 295
Lewis, S. J., 290
Libaw, F., 449n.
Lichtenberg, P., 254, 308
Liebert, R. M., 445
Light, R. J., 226
Lindzey, G., 170
Ling, B. C., 281
Lipps, T., 256
Lipsett, Lewis P., 258, 300
Livingston, S. K., 217
Loban, W. D., 445, 446, 450
Locke, John, 43
Loomis, B., 518
Lowe, J. C., 514
Lowrey, G. H., 352
Lowrey, R., 287
Lugo, James O., 20, 133, 348, 368, 422, 449
Luria, A. R., 443
Lynn, D. B., 469, 470

Maas, H., 327
McCall, R. B., 281
McCarthy, D., 307, 308, 373, 374, 445
McClelland, D. C., 59
Maccoby, E. E., 291, 367
McFarland, R. A., 428
McGraw, M. B., 122, 275, 291
MacKenberg, E., 363
McNeil, D., 374
Maddox, G. L., 529
Malakhovskaia, D. B., 294
Marshall, D. S., 258
Martin, M. M., 433
Maslow, Abraham, 104, 128, 139, 141, 142, 160, 171, 184–89, 192, 232, 541
Masters, W. H., 518, 519
May, Rollo, 40, 42
Mead, M., 326, 491
Meals, D. W., 10
Meili-Dworetski, G., 359
Menninger, K., 565
Menyuk, P., 305, 307, 445
Metfessel, N. S., 387, 452
Meyer, A., 28
Meyer, E., 361
Meyerson, L., 554
Miegs, C., 23
Miller, G. A., 445

Mills, C. W., 80
Mischel, W., 466, 525
Misiak, H., 96
Modiano, N., 447
Montagu, A., 150, 235
Montagu, M. F. A., 92, 217, 218, 242, 248, 252–56
Moore, J. W., 514, 530
Moore, R. C., 428
Morgan, G. A., 310
Morrisett, L. N., 99
Moss, H. A., 313
Murphy, G., 156
Murphy, L. B., 308
Mussen, P. H., 97, 280, 452

Nagy, M., 545
Nakazima, S., 305
Nakosteen, N., 42
Nelson, W. E., 284
Neugarten, B. L., 77, 513, 514, 517, 518, 520, 525, 528, 530
Newcomb, T. M., 173
Newson, E., 313
Newson, J., 313
Newton, N., 258, 259
Nicolson, A. B., 424
Nietzsche, F., 104
Nixon, Richard, 389
Norton, D. G., 308
Novak, A. L., 503
Nuckolls, K. B., 256

Orton, S. T., 369
Otis, L. S., 296
Ott, E. H., 448
Otto, H. A., 136

Papalia, D. E., 521
Paris, Henry J., 552
Parnell, R. W., 425
Parsons, Talcott, 465, 467
Parten, M. B., 401
Pasamanich, B., 217, 227, 250
Patai, R., 235
Pavlov, Ivan, 116, 191, 291, 375
Peal, E., 228, 448
Pearson, Karl, 226
Peck, R. F., 154, 155, 438
Peer, L. A., 255
Peiper, A., 281
Penfield, E., 448
Pennock, J. L., 263
Penrose, L. S., 218
Perin, C., 388
Peterson, D. R., 350
Peterson, J., 137
Piaget, Jean, 101, 281, 300–304, 363, 364, 376–81, 384–86, 389, 390, 399–400, 416, 423, 438, 440–43, 451, 455–57, 474, 475, 498, 521
Pick, A. D., 362

Pikler, E., 339
Pines, Maya, 319, 321
Plato, 36–37, 42, 95
Power, E., 27, 42
Prader, A., 353
Pratt, K. C., 278, 280, 295
Prehoda, R. W., 120–22
Prescott, E., 389
Prescott, T., 439
Provence, Sally, 335
Prugh, D. G., 326, 328, 329
Pulaski, M. A. S., 382, 441

Radhakrishnan, S., 42
Rank, O., 188
Rapp, D. W., 59
Reese, H. W., 300
Reichard, S., 525
Reisman, D., 172
Remy, R. M., 151
Rheingold, H. L., 309, 312, 394
Ricciuti, H. A., 310
Richardson, S. A., 263
Richmond, J. B., 88
Ripple, R. E., 442
Rivoire, J. L., 364
Roberts, K. E., 290
Roberts, L., 448
Robertson, J., 316
Robinson, R. J., 273, 294
Rockcastle, V. O., 442
Rodgers, R. R., 59
Roe, A., 139
Rogers, C. R., 104, 141, 156, 185
Rollins, B. C., 531
Roosevelt, Theodore, 97
Rosenthal, R., 226
Rosenzweig, N. R., 358
Rosman, B. L., 450
Ross, Elisabeth Kubler, 546
Rossi, A. S., 230, 262
Rousseau, Jean Jacques, 43, 95
Rudel, R. G., 364
Russell, Keith P., 266

Sahakian, W. S., 42
Salapatek, P., 281
Salber, E. J., 289
Sale, June, 388
Salk, L., 280
Salzen, E. A., 309
Sanford, F. H., 278
Sartre, J. P., 42
Schachtel, E. G., 156
Schachter, S., 459
Schaffer, H. R., 310, 313
Schiffer, C. G., 355, 356, 425
Schoelkopf, J. A., 290
Scott, Walter, 95
Sears, R. R., 291, 464, 478
Seashore, H. G., 434
Sebald, H., 219

Selye, H., 430, 517, 539
Senn, M. J., 262
Sexton, V., 96
Shane, H., 444
Shapiro, H., 285
Shaw, K. N. F., 224
Sheldon, W. H., 424, 425
Shelton, A., 537
Sherfey, M. J., 519
Sherman, I. C., 281, 282
Sherman, M., 281, 282
Shirley, M. M., 122
Shulman, D., 141
Simmons, M. A., 273
Simon, T., 96, 136, 137
Simpson, W. J., 253
Simsarian, R. L., 289
Skinner, B. F., 192, 292, 375, 561
Sloan, W., 433
Smart, M. S., 218
Smart, R. C., 218
Smith, H. P., 133
Smith, M. B., 174
Smythe, D. W., 287
Snyder, M. M., 351, 352, 426
Snyder, Phil, 547
Sontag, L. W., 246, 253, 255
Spears, W., 280
Spiker, C. C., 359
Spitz, R. A., 322–27, 564
Spitzer, R. L., 368
Staats, A., 375
Starr, P. H., 431
Steiner, I. D., 157
Stephens, W. E., 368
Stevenson, H. W., 385
Stewart, A. H., 297
Stoch, M., 287
Stoke, S. M., 466
Stott, L. H., 43
Stout, D. B., 258
Stratton, P., 295
Strean, L. P., 255

Strom, R. D., 144
Suci, G. J., 58, 59
Sullivan, Edward V., 461
Sullivan, H. S., 188, 504

Talbot, N. B., 357
Tanner, J. M., 353, 492, 494, 495
Taylor, C. W., 139, 140, 142
Teller, J. D., 43
Templin, M., 376, 445
Tennes, K. H., 310
Terman, Lewis M., 96
Teuber, H. L., 364
Thackeray, William, 95
Thomas, A., 314, 315, 327
Thomas, O., 445
Thompson, C., 188
Thompson, G. G., 280, 283
Thompson, H., 446
Thorndike, E. L., 96, 191
Thrum, M. A., 282
Thurstones, L. L., 137
Tichauer, R., 258
Tillich, P., 188
Titchener, E. B., 156
Titus, H. H., 34, 37, 42
Toch, H. H., 157
Toffler, Alvin, 166
Tomlin, E. W. F., 34, 42, 43
Torrance, E. P., 142, 144, 452
Tournier, P., 188
Toynbee, A., 545
Trasler, G., 327
Tuddenham, P. D., 351, 352
Turner, E. K., 255

Uzgiris, I. C., 287

van der Veen, F., 503
Vurpillot, E., 363
Vygostsky, L. S., 443

Wahl, C., 545
Waik, R. D., 358
Walker, R. N., 425
Wallace, R. F., 253
Wallach, M. A., 140
Wallin, P., 235, 236
Walters, Richard H., 478
Wapner, S., 439
Watson, E. H., 352
Watson, E. J., 425
Watson, J. B., 191, 309
Watson, R. I., 42
Watts, J. C., 320
Wender, P. H., 556–58
Wenger, M. A., 272
Werner, H., 359
Westheimer, I., 316
Whetnall, E., 280
Whipple, D. V., 426
White, B. L., 10, 296, 297, 319–21, 436
White, B. W., 429
White, Robert, 508
White, S. H., 359
Whiting, B. B., 264
Whitsell, L. J., 368
Widdowson, E. M., 354
Wiener, M., 364
Wohlwill, J. F., 364
Wolf, K. M., 326, 327
Wolf, R. M., 387, 453
Wolff, P. H., 273, 309, 313
Wood, V., 518
Woodruff, C. W., 355
Wylie, R. C., 151

Yarrow, L. J., 259–61, 326, 327
Yarrow, M. R., 9
Young, J. Z., 119

Zangwill, O. L., 368
Zintz, M., 66

Index

574

Subject Index

Abnormalities, *see* Birth defects
Accidents in childhood, 428–29
Accommodation in learning, 302
Achievement, *see* Success
Activity, mass to specific, 276
Adaptation in learning, 302
Adolescence, 488–510
  developmental tasks of, 77–78
  nutrition in, 217
  philosophy of, 43
  socialization during, 77
Adoption, 74
Adulthood, early and middle, 513–34
  sociology of, 78
  (*See also* Man; Parents; Old age)
Affection and tactile stimulation, 66
Affective domain, 103, 148–62
  altruism, 153–56
  empathy, 156–57
  love, 148–53
  of motor development, 367
Africa, immigration from, 53
Age, characteristics related to, 514
  chronological, biological, and psychological, 513
  family events and, 530
Aggression, 476–80
Aging, 120
  problems of, 537–38
  social, biological, cognitive, and affective, 537
  sociological aspects of, 542–44
  (*See also* Old age)
Alcoholic addiction, 253–54
Alienation, 110
Altruism, 153–56
Alzheimer's syndrome, 541
Ambiguity, toleration of, 141–42
American Indians, 64, 66–67, 446, 489–90, 533
American Psychological Association, 4, 97, 100
Anaclitic depression, 324–25
Anal stage, 405–406
Animism, 382–84
Anthropology, science of, 52
Arteriosclerosis, 516, 538
Asia, immigrants from, 53
Assimilation in learning, 302
Association, process of, 441
Association for Humanistic Psychology, 193
Attachment in infancy, 316–17

Audition, 280–81
Authenticity of being, 158–59
Authoritarian personality, 172–73
Autonomy, 171–72
  in adolescence, 502
  of creative person, 141
  Erikson on, 407
  Maslow on, 187
Aversive behavior and learning, 388
Axiology, 35–40

Babies, unwanted, 225
  (*See also* Infants; Preconception stage)
Babinski reflex, 294
Balance, body, 434
Behavior, adaptability of, 89–90
  aversive, and learning, 388
  childlike and creativity, 142
  cooperative, 154–56
  in neurological handicaps, 556–64
  overlearned, 540
  variability of, in infancy, 86–88
Behavioral processes in becoming a more fully human person, 189
Behavioral value systems, comparison of, 66–67
  (*See also* Child rearing)
Behaviorist, on more fully human person, 191–92, 194–99
  talks to parents, 204–206
Bicultural education, 449–50
Bilingualism, 227–28, 446–50
Biological domain, 103, 112–28
Biological perspectives, 84
Biology model, humanistic, 128
Birth defects, 218–25, 255–59
Birth process, 246–49
Birth rate, 234
Black Americans, 64, 223–24, 227, 357, 374–75, 434, 446
Blood disorders and newborn, 222–23
Body, self-concept of, 125, 497–98
  (*See also* Motor development; Physical development; Self-concept)
Bones, growth of, 351–52
Boys, 58–60, 469–70, 493–96, 504
  (*See also* Sex role)

Brain, 119, 136, 271–73
Brain dysfunction, minimal, 427, 428, 556
  (*See also* Neurological handicaps)
Breast feeding, 249, 289

Cardiovascular changes in aging, 516, 538
Careers, 527–29
Case history method, 102
Catholics, 226
Central nervous system and behavior, 119
Cephalocaudal sequence, 276
Cerebral dominance, 368–69
Change, *see* Social change
Child(ren), as adults, 20–22, 30
  birth defects and, 220–25
    (*See also* Birth defects)
  competence of, influenced by mother, 321
  death of, in early 1900s, 150
    (*See also* Infant mortality)
  death attitude in, 545–46
  deprived of mothers, 322–28
  disadvantaged, 388–89
  early memories of, 4–5
  folk beliefs about raising, 235–36
  handicapped, *see* Handicaps
  history of, 20–24
    of education of, 25–29
  Jourard on people who work with, 161
  learning development of young, *see* Learning
  letters of, 6
  modern concept of, 23–25
  physical maturity of, 30 (*See also* Motor development; Physical development)
  preschool, 415–16
  reasons for having, 264
  six-year-old, 436
  stages of development of, 103
  study of whole, 8–9
  twentieth-century, 25
  welfare of, improving, 99
  world population of, 253 (*See also* Infants)
Child labor, 22–23
Child psychology, *see* Psychology
Child rearing, cross-national, 58–64
  of future, 9–10
  philosophy and goals of, 47
  social class and, 230–31

Childbearing, age of parents and, 217
Childbirth, process of, 246–49
    (See also Pregnancy)
Childhood,
    early, 349–417
        gross motor attributes in, 123
        socialization in family, 76
    later, 423–82
        socialization in, 77
    philosophy of, 43
    (See also Child)
Childlike behavior and creativity, 142
Chromosomes, 84–86, 216, 219
Circular reactions in learning, 303–304
Classification skills, 440–41
Cleft palates, 255
Cognitive-development theory, 411–13
    moral development and, 474–76
    Piaget on, 300–304
Cognitive domain, 103, 131–44
    (See also Intelligence; Learning)
Combination, process of, 441
Communication disorders in early childhood, 373–74
Compassion, 169–71
Compensatory education, 451–52
Conception, 242–43
Conceptual thought, 440–42
Concrete stage, 437–38, 442
Conditioned responses, 116, 118
Conditioning, 291–95
    classical, 291–92
        language development and, 375
    instrumental, 292
    operant, 375
    in mental retardation, 554
Conservation, growth of, 439–40
    lack of, in early childhood, 381–83
Constancy, size, object, and perceptional, 360–62
Control, locus of, 397
Cooley's anemia, 224
Cooperative behavior, 154–56
Crawling, 283–84
Creativity, 139–42, 307–308
    in adolescence, 501
    in adulthood, 521–23
    Bonner on, 184–85
    characteristics of, 140–42
    in early childhood, 389–90
    in later childhood, 454–57
    research in, 452
Creeping, 284–85
Cross cultural methods, 102
    (See also Bilingualism)
Cross-national child-rearing, 58–64

Cross-national studies, on learning, 385
    of physical competencies, 122
    (See also Bicultural education; Cultures)
Cross-sectional studies, 102
Crying in infancy, 305, 312–14, 332
Cultures, death in various, 545
    membership competencies, 123–24
    (See also Bicultural education; Cross-national studies; Immigrants)
Cuna Indians, 258–59
Cutaneous senses, 277–78

Death, contemporary attitudes toward, 546
    in old age, 545–47
    stages of, 546–47
    in various cultures, 545
    (See also Infant mortality)
Decentration, 382, 439
Defects, birth, 218–25, 256–59
    genetic, 92
Democratic personality, 172–73, 187
Dental care, 356
Depression in adulthood, 526
Developing potentialities, 9
Development, basic principles of early, 276–77
    biological, 114
    of infant, 271–87
    physical, 122–23 (See also Physical development)
    rates of, 351
    stages of, 101–103, 153
    (See also Cognitive development; Moral development; Motor development)
Developmental domains and child psychologist, 102, 103
Developmental psychology, basic theory and research, 8–14
Diet, see Nutrition
Differentiation, cellular, 243
Differentiation-integration, 276
Disabilities, in communication, 374
    learning, 427, 555–56
Disadvantaged children, 388–89, 451–53
Discipline, history of, 22
Disease(s), in adulthood, 516
    ethnic-related, 223–24
    infectious, in pregnancy, 254
    (See also Illness)
Disintegration, emotional, 565, 567
Disorders, brain, 427
    (See also Disabilities; Minimal brain dysfunction)
Divorce, 531–32
    rate of, 234

DNA (deoxyribonucleic acid), 85
Dominance, cerebral, and hand, foot, and eye, 368–69
Down's syndrome, 218, 554
Drug addict, 114
    as parent, 219–20
Drugs, and newborn, 219
    prenatal period, 253–54
Dyslexia, 427n.

Economic aspects of child rearing, 263
    (See also Poverty; Socioeconomic aspects)
Ectomorph, 424–25
Education, adult, 532
    bilingual-bicultural, 446–50
    in child care, 261–63
    compensatory, 451–52
    Dewey on, 39
    goals of, and philosophy, 47
    home, 386–88, 450–52
    for hyperkinetic child, 559–64
    of mentally retarded, 554–55
    preschool, 388–89
    trends in, in United States, 25–29
    (See also Learning; School)
Egocentric thought, 378–80
Egocentrism to other-centeredness, 438–39
Electra Complex, 406
Embryonic period, 243–44
    (See also Fetal stage)
Emotional maturity and self-concept, 158–60
Emotional projection, 157
Emotional stress, see Stress
Emotions, 148
    in adulthood, 526–27
    in aging, 541–42
    in infancy, 309–334
        variability and continuity in, 314–15
    maternal, in pregnancy, 254–56
    (See also Affective domain; Feelings; Neurological handicaps)
English child-rearing practices, 59–60
Environment and heredity, 227
Epistemology, 35–38, 40
Equilibrium in learning development, 301–302
Ethnic groups and intelligence testing, 226–27
    (See also Cultures; Immigrants; Names of ethnic groups)
Eugenics, 91
Europe, child rearing in, 64
    immigrants from, 53
Existentialism, 40–42, 46, 47

Experiences, openness to, 141
  peak, Maslow on, 188
Experimental methods, 102
Exteroceptors, 279
Eyedness, 368–69

Family, adolescent's relations
    with, 503
  in adulthood, 529–32
  affective domain and, 231–32
  changing American, 234
  child's place in, 24–25
  home environment and school
    success and, 453 (See also
    Education, home)
  modern, compared with "good
    old days," 70–71
  philosophies on style of, 45–
    49
  physical growth and, 353
  role of, in development, 458–
    59
  as socializing institution, 76
Family planning, 233–36
Fathers, 6, 150, 467
  (See also Parents)
Fear response, 309–10
Federal government, see Gov-
    ernment programs
Feeding, mother-infant interac-
    tion during, 330–33
  (See also Breast feeding; Nu-
    trition)
Feel, sense of, 116, 118
Feelings, 148, 158, 159, 409
  in adolescence, 504–506
  in early childhood, 390–94
  (See also Emotions; Self-con-
    cept)
Fellow feeling, 170–71
Fernald School, UCLA, 427
Fertilization, 243
Fetal stage, 244–47
Filipino children, 447
Form perception, 359
Formal operations, stage of,
    442–43
  intellectual development and,
    in adolescence, 498–501
French in America, 55
French-Canadian college stu-
    dents, 65
Friends in adolescence, 503–504
  (See also Peers)
Frostig's Developmental Test of
    Visual Perception, 435
Frustration-aggression hypothe-
    sis, 477–78

General adaption syndrome
    (G.A.S.), 539
Generalization in learning, 292
Genetic adequacy, 113–18
Genetic counseling, 91–92, 224

Genetic defects, 92
  (See also Birth defects)
Genetic intervention, 91
Genetics, 84–86
  birth defects and, 223–24
  intellectual potential and, 134
  sex determination and, 216
Genital stage, 407
Genotype, 89
Geriatrics, 537
German measles (rubella), 254
Germans in America, 56–57
Germany, child rearing in, 58–
    59
Gerontology, 537
Girls, 26, 58–60, 469–71, 493–
    96
  (See also Sex role)
Goals, life, 110–28
Gonorrhea, 218
Government programs, for aged,
    543
  bilingual education and, 446
  in family planning, 234
  laws and, affecting family,
    262–63
  in preschool education, 388–
    89
  of research in child psychol-
    ogy, 99
Grandparenthood, 529–32
Grasping reflex, 275
Growth, in adulthood, 532
  different rates of, 276–77
  height, in adolescence, 492
  optimal, 114–15
  physical, cross-national study
    of, 122, 124
  health and, 350–58, 424–25
  (See also Development;
    Physical development)
Guilt, Erikson on, 408–409

Habitation, 297
Handedness, 368–69, 439
Handicaps, language and, 446
  in later childhood, 426–27
  neurological, 427–28, 555–64
  (See also Birth defects)
Health, integrated, 429
  in later childhood, 424–25
  love and, 432
  mental, goal of, 112, 148
  physical, 118–21
  physical growth and, 350–58
  preconception and, 216–20
  psychological, and creativity,
    139
  learning and, 134
Health care in adolescence, 496
Hearing, 116, 118, 279–81
Height, in adolescence, 492
  average, for children, 352
  cross-national study of, 124
Hemophilia, 223
Heredity, 84–87

Heredity [cont.]
  birth defects and, 222–24
  environment and, in intelli-
    gence, 227
History, of childhood, 20–24
  of education, 25–29
Hobbies in adulthood, 532–33
Holistic principle of develop-
    ment, infant, 276
Homolateral creeping, 283–84
Human person, see Person
Humanist talks to parents, 206–
    207
Humanistic biology model of
    Maslow, 128
Humanistic philosophy in fam-
    ily style, 48
Humanistic psychology, 41
Humanistic view of more fully
    human person, 192–93
  table on, 194–99
Humanitarianism in education,
    27
Humor, and creativity, 142
  sense of, 159
Hyperactive child, 429n., 556
Hyperkinetic child, 556–64

Idealism, philosophical, 36–37,
    42, 46
Identification, in empathy, 157
  in learning, 293
  with parents, 172, 462–66
Identity, 172
  in adolescence, 507–508
  cultural heritage and, 65
  process of, in conceptual
    thought, 441
  (See also Alienation; Self-
    concept)
Identity crisis, 35
Igbo tribesmen, 537
Illness, in later childhood, 425–
    26
  physical growth and, 353–55
  (See also Disease)
Imaginative play, 381, 389
Imitation in learning, 293
  (See also Identification)
Immigrants to United States,
    by nationality, 54–58
  table on, 53
Income level and infant mor-
    tality, 252
  (See also Socioeconomic as-
    pects)
Independence, 171
  (See also Autonomy)
Indians, American, 64, 66–67,
    446, 489–90, 533
  of Guatemala, 451
Individual and philosophical
    realism, 37
  (See also Self-concept)
Industry, Erikson on, 409
Infant(s), 73–77, 271–340

Index

Infant(s) [*cont.*]
babbling of, 305–306
behavior of, publications on, 98
variability of, 86–88
crying of, 305, 312–14, 332
death of, *see* Infant mortality
deprived of mothers, 322–28
health of, and preconception, 217–21
interaction of, with mother, 259–61, 330–33
health and, 328–30
learning by, 116–18, 258
need for love of, 150
newborn, drug-addicted, 114
motor behaviors of, 86–88
variability in behavior of, 87, 88
social goals of, 316–34
stimulation model for, 337–40
in strange situation, 333
temperament of, 314–15
unwanted, 225
White on, 10
(*See also* Feeding; Mother; Newborn; Prenatal stage)
Infant mortality, 150, 249–57, 323, 324
Infectious diseases in pregnancy, 254
Inferiority, Erikson on feelings of, 409
(*See also* Self-concept)
Information processing by individual, 132–34
Initiative, Erikson on, 408–409
Integration, emotional, 565
in infancy, 276
perceptual, in early childhood, 364–65
of separate functions, 286
Intellectual competency, 134–39
Intellectual development, in adolescence, formal operations stage, 498–501
in early childhood, 370–89
Intellectual growth in early childhood, 358–59
Intelligence, in adulthood, 521
in aging, 541
creating, 455–57
creativity and, 139–40
in early childhood, 366–67, 377, 385
past, present, and future view of, 134–36
perception and, in later childhood, 435
school success and, 450–51
success and, 225
Intelligence tests, 96, 136–40, 143, 144, 226–28, 322, 370–71, 386, 387, 434–35, 521
International studies on language, 447–49

International studies on language [*cont.*]
(*See also* Cross-national studies)
Interoceptors, 278
Interpersonal relations and identification, 462–66
(*See also* Identification; Peer group)
Interview methods, 102
Intuitive stage of thought, 381, 383
Iowa Child Welfare Research Station, 97
IQ tests, 136–40, 143, 144, 226–28, 322, 521
(*See also* Intelligence tests)
Irreversibility in early childhood, 382
Italians in America, 55–56

Jews, 64, 224, 226, 228
Jobs, 527–29

Kinesthesis, 278
Kraus-Weber Test, 433, 434

Labes dorsalis, 278–79
Labyrinthine righting reflex, 275
Language development, 304–308, 359, 371–76, 443–46
(*See also* Bilingual education)
Latency stage, 407
Learning, basic processes of, 291–94
cognitive: insights, reasoning, and creative imagination, 294
cognitive model for, 456
communication disorders and, 373–74
as creativity, 455
development of, 294–300
(*See also* Cognitive development)
discriminative, 292
in early childhood, improving, 115–18
Piaget and, 385–86
thinking and, 377–89
in infancy, 116–18, 258
language and, 445–46
in later childhood, 437–43
Piaget's theory of, 300–304
(*See also* Piaget)
preschool, at home, 386–88
stimulus-response, 293
(*See also* Education; School)
Learning disability, 427, 555–56
Learning theory, 96
social-, 413–14
Left-to-right orientation, 364
Leisure, 532–33
Life expectancy, 119–22, 357

Life goals, 110–28
Lincoln-Oseretsky Motor Development Scale, 433
Linguistic description, 443–45
(*See also* Language development)
Locomotion, 282–83
Longevity, 119–22, 357
Longitudinal studies, 102
Love, 148–53
in family, 231–32
health and, 432
in identification, 465
self, 150–51 (*See also* Self-concept)
table on types of, 153
Lysergic acid (LSD), 219

Malformations, *see* Birth defects
Man, Erikson's eight stages of, 318
lifetimes of, 166
nature of, Maslow on, 186
(*See also* Men; Person, more fully human)
Manipulation as motor skill, 286
Marasmus, 150
Marriage, in adulthood, 529–32
parenthood and, 229–31
Massachusetts, laws on education in, 26, 28
Maternal-care variables, 332–33
(*See also* Mother)
Math, "new," 441
Maturing, of emotional self-concept, 158–60
of social self-concept, 173–75
Maturity and love, 152
Meaning, word, 306–307
Medicare, 543
Memory, in aging, 541
childhood, 4–7
Men, age-related characteristics of, 514
(*See also* Fathers; Parents)
Menopause, 517–19
Mental deterioration in aging, 541
Mental health, 112, 148
(*See also* Health)
Mental retardation, 451, 553–55
(*See also* Minimal brain dysfunction)
Mesomorph, 424–25
Mexican-Americans, 57, 446, 449
Minimal brain dysfunction, 427, 428, 556
(*See also* Neurological handicaps)
Minority groups, 64, 226–28
(*See also* Bilingual education; Socio-economic aspects; name of group)
Modeling, 375
aggression and, 478–79

Modified System Approach, 10–12

Mongolism, 218, 554

Moral development, 10, 26, 438, 471–76

Moro reflex, 273–75

Morphology, 89

Mother, age of, and health in childbearing, 217–19, 222 (*See also* Preconception)
deprivation of, 322–28
disturbed, 327–28
healthy interaction of, with infant, 328–30 (*See also* Parent-child relationship)
identification and, 463–65
influence of, on children and infants, 319–34
love of, 149–50
relations of, with infant, 328–30, 394
response of, to newborn, 259–61
role of, 467
types of, 321
unwed, 218
variables in care of, 332–33 (*See also* Parents)

Motivation, intrinsic, 302–303

Motor attributes, gross, of early childhood, 123

Motor behaviors of newborn infants, 86–88

Motor development, 282–87
in early childhood, 365–67
perceptual, 365–66
in later childhood, 432–35
speech and, 308
visual-, 296–97 (*See also* Physical competencies)

Motor skills, developing, 338–39

Multiplication, cellular, 243

Neonatal stage, 247–49 (*See also* Infants; Newborn)

Nervous system, and behavior, 119
healthy, 133

Neurological changes in aging, 540

Neurological organization in early childhood, 368–69

Neurologically handicapped child, 427–28, 555–64

Neurosis, creativity, and intelligence, 139 (*See also* Psychotherapy)

Newborn, behavior of, and maternal stress, 255
drugs and, 219 (*See also* Infant)

Norms and aggression, 479–80

North America, immigrants from, 53

Nutrition, by income, 252

Nutrition [*cont.*]
of infants and children, 287–90
maternal, 250–52
in preconception and pregnancy, 216–17

Nutritive changes in aging, 539

Object constancy, 361–63

Observation methods, 102

Occupation in adulthood, 527–29

Oedipal Complex, 406, 464

Old age, sociology of, 78 (*See also* Aging)

Ontology, 35–40

Openness, to experiences, 141
of fully human person, 172–73

Oral reflexes, 273

Oral stage, 405

Organic sense, 279

Ovum, 242–43

Pain, sense of, 278

Parent(s), age of, 217–19
becoming, 529–32
drug addict as, 219–20
emotional aspects of becoming, 229–33
folk beliefs about becoming, 235–36
memories of their children, 5
philosophy of, 45, 46

Parent-child relationships, faulty, 431
psychological problems and, 563–67
school succes and, 453–54
sex-role development and, 467–69 (*See also* Father; Mother)

Peace Corps, 174, 527

Peer group, 460–62, 503–504

Perception, in aging, 540
of others, 157

Perceptional constancy, 362

Perceptual deficits, 435

Perceptual development, 277–82

Perceptual integration, 364

Perceptual-motor development, 358–68
in later childhood, 434–35

Person, adequate, 181–83
fully functioning, 185
more fully human, 112, 181–83, 552–67
proactive, Bonner on, 183–85
self-actualizing, 182, 183, 185–89, 232

Personality, in adulthood, 524–26
democratic, 187
open, democratic, and authoritarian, 172–73

Personality [*cont.*]
(*See also* Temperament)

Phallic stage, 406

Phenomenalism, 384

Phenotypes, 89–90

Phenylketonuria (PKU), 224

Philosophy, 33–49
areas of study within, 34–37
of childhood and adolescence, 43
definition of, 34
of family style, 45–49
outline of five basic, 42

Physical aspects, of adulthood, 515–19
of aging, 538–40

Physical characteristics, 89

Physical competencies, 121–25
in later childhood, 423–24

Physical development, 122–23
in adolescence, 492–96 (*See also* Development)

Physical fitness, 434

Physical health, 118–21 (*See also* Health)

Physical self-concept, integrated, 127
positive, 125–26
realistic, 126–27

Physiology, changes in, in adulthood, 515–19
influences on, 85
phenotype and, 89
stress and, 429–30

Physique, three basic components of, 424–25

Pick's syndrome, 541

Placenta, 244

Play, imaginative, 381, 389, 394–402

Poland, child rearing in, 64
immigrants to America from, 54–55

Population, issues in, 233–34
world child, 253

Positive supporting reflexes, 275

Potential, developing, 9

Poverty, achievement in school and, 387
education and, 388–89
infant mortality and, 252 (*See also* Socioeconomic aspects)

Practice, distributive and massed, 388

Praise, 453

Pragmatism, 38–39, 42
in family style, 46–48

Preconception stage, 217–38

Preconceptual stage of thought, 377–78, 380–81

Preformationism, 216

Pregnancy, 242–57
drugs in, 253–54
diseases in, 254
influence of emotions in, 254–56

Pregnancy [*cont.*]
  nutrition in, 250–52
  (*See also* Prenatal stage)
Prenatal stage, 72, 85, 242–47, 250–57
  (*See also* Genetic counseling; Preconception stage)
Preoperational stage of thought, 377
Preschool education, 388–89, 415–16
  at home, 386–88, 450
President's Commission on Population Growth and the American Future, 218
Pressure, sense of, 278
Proactive person, 183–85
Proprioceptors, 277
Proximal-distal sequence, 276
Psychoanalysis and moral development, 473–74
Psychoanalyst talks to parents, 201–204
Psychoanalytic orientations, Freud and Erikson, 410
Psychoanalytic view of more fully human person, 190–91, 194–99
Psychological aspects of neurological problems, 563
Psychological care for hyperkinetic child, 559–60
Psychological health, *see* Health
Psychological perspectives, 95
Psychological problems, 565–67
Psychological testing, 96–97
Psychologist, child, 95–104
  on more fully human person 190–91, 194–99
Psychology, existential, 40–41
  humanistic, 41
  Jersild on child, 4, 8
  philosophy and, 35
Psychomotor components, 85
Psychosexual theory of development, 404–405
Psychosocial somatic disorders, 430–32
Psychotherapy for hyperkinetic child, 562–63
Pueblo Indians, 66–67
Puerto Rican children, 57, 447

Radiation during pregnancy, 256, 257
Reactions of infants and temperament, 314–15
  (*See also* Responses)
Reading, 359–60, 364
  cerebral dominance and, 368–69
Reading readiness, 452–53
Realism, in children, 384
  philosophical, 37, 42, 46
Reality, ability to face, 175
  Maslow on, 187

Redundancy, decreasing need for, 363–64
Reflexes, of infant, 273–75, 294, 303
  integration of, 286
  smiling, 311
Reinforcement, 375
  aggression and, 479–80
  in learning, 386, 388
Reinforcement schedules, 292
Religion, childbearing and, 263
  family style and, 46–47
  philosophy and, 38, 42, 46
Resacralizing, 188
Research, 7–14, 104
Respiratory changes in aging, 539
Responses, basic infant, 309–14
  (*See also* Conditioning; Reflexes)
Retardation, *see* Mental retardation
Retirement years, 549–50
Reversibility, 382, 439, 441
Rewards in reinforcement, 292–93
Rh factor, 222–23
Role theory, 403–404
  (*See also* Sex role)
Rubella, 254
Russia, *see* Soviet Union

Schema, 302
Schizophrenia, 148
School, progress in, knowledge about, 453–54
  role of, in development, 459–61
  success in, *see* Success, school
  (*See also* Education; Learning)
Self, of infant, 340
Self-actualization, 182, 183, 185
  family supports and, 232
  Maslow on, 185–89
Self-concept, 151
  biological aspects of, in adolescence, 497–98
  biologically maturing, 125–27
  of body, 125, 497–98
  Combs on, 182–83
  in early childhood, 366–67
  Erikson on, 407–410
  Maslow on, 186–87
  maturing, 142–43
    biological, 125–27, 519–20
    emotional, 158–60
    social, 173–75
  more fully human person and, 199–200
  occupation and, 427
  physical, 85
    positive, realistic, and integrated, 125–27
  positive, 171, 172
  school success and, 453, 454

Self-concept [*cont.*]
  (*See also* Identity)
Self-confidence of creative person, 141
Self-esteem, of hyperkinetic child, 557
  of parents, 232
  vicious versus benign, 174
Self-fulfilling prophecies, 226
Self-love, 150–51, 157
Sensori-motor stage in learning, 303
Sensory awareness, 115, 116
Sensory changes in aging, 540
Sensory development, 277–82
Separation, maternal, 324–27
Sex determination, 216
Sex differences, in child rearing, 60
  in growth, 352–53
  (*See also* Boys; Girls)
Sex roles, 149*n*., 463–64, 466–71
Sexual intimacy in adolescence, 504–506
Sexual maturation in adolescence, 493–96
Sexuality in adulthood, 519
  (*See also* Psychosexual development)
Shame and doubt, Erikson on, 407–408
Sickle cell anemia, 223
Siriono Indians, 258–59
Size constancy, 360–61
Skeletal age, 351–53
Skin, 277–78
Sleep, 295
Smell, sense of, 116, 118, 277
Smiling responses, 310–13
Smoking in pregnancy, 253
Social aspects, of adulthood, 533
  of aging, 542–44
  of development, 457–62 (*See also* Social development)
  of language development, 374–75
  of motor development, 367, 434
  nonsocial and, of six-year-old, 436
Social behavior, crying as, 313–14
Social change, 166–67, 234
Social class, in childbearing, 263
  parenthood and, 230–31
  (*See also* Socioeconomic aspects)
Social development in early childhood, 403–407
  (*See also* Socialization)
Social domain, 103, 166–78
  in family planning, 233–36
Social goals in infancy, 316–34
Social growth trends in late adolescence, 508–509
Social interest, 170

Social-learning theory, 413–14, 472–73
Social Security, 543
Socialization, of adolescence, 503–504, 507
  definition of, 169
  in early childhood, 75–76, 402–403
  humanly, 169–70
Sociological aspects, of achievement in school, 387
  of infant mortality, 252, 256
  of intelligence tests, 228
  of language, 446
  of reading readiness and school success, 452–53
Sociologists, activities of, 78–79
  interests of, 72, 77
  perspective of, in children and adolescents, 70–72, 80
Somatic disorders, psychosocial, 430–32
South America, immigrants from, 53
Soviet Union, 60–64, 446–47
Spanish language, 57–58, 446–49
Species-wide physical competencies, 121–23
Speech and motor development, 308
  (See also Language)
Spermatozoa, 242
Spontaneity, 159
Sports, success in, 434
Standing, 285
Stanford-Binet test, 136
Stimulation in infancy, 295–97
  (See also Conditioning)
Stimulation model for infants, 337–40
Stimulus-response in learning, 293
Stress, ability to handle, 159–60
  in aging, 539–40
  on child, 564–66
  in early childhood, 429–32
  in later childhood, 429–30

Structure-of-intellect model, Guilford's, 137–38
Success, school, bicultural education and, 449
  home environment and, 453
  intelligence and, 225
  pathways to, 450–54
  social aspects of, 387, 452–53
  striving for, 425, 434–35
Sucking, 290
  reflex, 273
Survey methods, 102
Swimming reflex, 275
Syphilis, 218–19
Systems analysis, 10–11

Talents, multi-intellectual, 136–39
Taste, sense of, 116, 277
Tay-Sachs disease, 224
Teacher, importance of, 460–61
Teaching machines, 133
Teen-agers, see Adolescents
Teeth, 352, 356
Temperament of infants, 314–15
Tests, bicultural education and, 449–50
  intelligence, see Intelligence tests
  methods of, 102
  for perceptual deficits, 435
  psychological, 96–97
Theory in child psychology, 104
Thermal sensitivity, 278
Thinking, cognitive model for, 456
  conceptual, 440–42
  creative, 140–42 (See also Intelligence)
  in early childhood, 376
  egocentric, 378–80
  language and, 443
  in later childhood, 437–43
  learning and, 377–89
Toilet training, 290–91
Tonic-neck-reflex, 275
Touch, sense of, 278

Transduction, 380
Trust, 151–52, 157, 172
  in infancy, 317–19

Umbilical cord, 244
United States, child-rearing practices in, 58–63
  cross-national child-rearing practices in, 58–63
  education of children in, 25–29
  foreign-born in, by states, 54–58
  immigrants to, by nationality, 54–58
  table on, 53
  pluralistic nature of, 54–58
  (See also Government programs)

Values and parenthood, 232
Variability, 87–88
Venereal disease, 218–19
Vestibular reflex, 279
Vision, 116, 118, 281–82
  development of, in infancy, 295–97
VISTA, 353
Visual perception development, 359, 363–64, 435

Walking, 284–85
  cross-pattern, 369, 370
  homolateral, 369, 370
Wechsler test, 136
Weights, average, of children, 352
White House Conferences, 97, 162, 265
Women, age-related characteristics of, 514
  menopause of, 517–19
  (See also Mother)
Work, in adulthood, 527–29
  children and, 22